From the reviews of *Life Class*

'Why is Athill such a compel   e
always seems to be on a quest, and   It
is only when you are caught up in the act of reading   ou
realise how rarely in literature one encounters such a purity of
intention, and this, coupled with her purity of expression, is what
makes her memoirs so unputdownable . . . *Life Class* is a good
name for this bumper collection of four of her memoirs, because
as you read it, you feel you are being taught not only how to live
but, as importantly, how to die . . . This is a wonderful collection
of memoirs, a hopeful letter from the front line of life' Craig Brown,
Mail on Sunday

'Athill's volumes of recollection, now brought together . . . [in] *Life
Class*, are a sturdy breakwater against the tides of ghosted sleb
kiss'n'tell . . . *Life Class* demonstrates that real life is not the
privilege of the great and the good, the famous and adored: it lies
within all our reach' *The Times*

'For a vital account of being a woman in the 20th century, one can
turn to Diana Athill. Aged 92, she has released *Life Class*, a
selection of her memoirs that chronicle the growth of a woman
from a privileged childhood of horses and country estates to a
middle-class existence in André Deutsch's publishing house and
love affairs, to a late contemplation on old age. The prose is
breathtaking, and the honesty exhilarating' *Independent on Sunday*

'As well as being a portrait of a life in letters, Athill's writing is a
careful unpicking of the emotional strictures of a particular class at
a particular time' *Observer*

'Diana Athill is one of our most captivating and truth-seeking
memoir writers' *Good Housekeeping*

'A collection of four candid and brilliantly observed memoirs
covering everything from Diana's childhood, her life during the
Second World War and her publishing career to her reflections on
sex and death. A real must-read' *Woman & Home*

LIFE CLASS

The Selected Memoirs
of Diana Athill

GRANTA

Granta Publications, 12 Addison Avenue, London W11 4QR

First published in Great Britain by Granta Books 2009
This paperback edition published by Granta Books 2010

This book consists of four previously published volumes: *Yesterday Morning*,
first published by Granta Books 2002, paperback edition published 2003;
Instead of a Letter, first published by Chatto & Windus 1963, published by
Robin Clark 1981, published by Granta Books 2001; *Stet*, first published by
Granta Books 2000, paperback edition published 2001; *Somewhere Towards the
End*, first published by Granta Books 2008, paperback edition published 2009.

A CIP catalogue record for this book
is available from the British Library.

1 3 5 7 9 10 8 6 4 2

ISBN 978 1 84708 146 9

Printed and bound in Great Britain by
CPI Bookmarque, Croydon

Contents

INTRODUCTION

In the early 1980s, the publisher André Deutsch had an idea for a book I could write about the partition of India. I didn't take it up, which I regret now because it was a good suggestion and I was wrong to imagine, as I told him, that 'everything' had already been written about the subject. Instead, I proposed a thought of my own: a book about Indian railways, part travel account, part technical history and part family memoir. Too *many* parts, clearly, but André liked the idea and a few weeks later I went to his office, where he took out a fountain pen and ceremonially wrote a cheque, saying words to the effect that this was his happiest moment since the day he thought he'd signed up George Orwell (as I guess he told many writers of first books) and then stealing a cigarette from my packet to smoke in celebration.

I went to India for a year and did too much research. There was certainly a lot to find out, but the finding out eventually became a way of postponing the writing. Soon after I came home to London, Mrs Gandhi was assassinated in Delhi, which meant there was further postponement as I turned back to journalism. Then one day the phone rang and it was André, wondering how the book was 'coming along'. The truth was that it wasn't coming along, but I wrote two short chapters in a panic and sent them in as evidence that his money hadn't gone completely to waste. André's response was to invite me to his office for lunch. It was there that I met a brisk woman in glasses, who told me that what I had written was very good and then read a page or two of it aloud to us: to André, perhaps because he had never bothered to read it himself (the thought occurred to me only later), and to me perhaps to persuade me that what I'd written was as good as she said, and the book worth persevering with.

She had a fine voice, precise and low, of the kind many more people had then than now, though even in 1984 her kind of accent had lost its claim to be the English that the nicest and best people spoke. 'Patrician', 'RP' and 'Oxbridge' would be the easy adjectives, though what it reminded me of was listening to the BBC's Home Service as a boy and watching British films of the same period where pretty well everyone spoke like this other than junior policemen and Cockney chars in pinafores. No matter. She read aloud – a few hundred words about an old-fashioned grocer's shop in an Indian railway town – and the fact was that her voice's elegance and intelligence seemed to elevate what I'd written, just as words scribbled in ballpoint seem profoundly transformed when set in twelve-point Baskerville. There may have been an almost maternal element to her encouragement. She certainly had something of the kindly schoolmistress or university tutor about her: her thick-framed glasses, her enthusiasm, her opinion that I simply *had* to go on with it otherwise I'd be letting myself down. As life turned out, I didn't go on with it; I went back to newspapers and returned André's advance, and therefore as an illustration of Diana Athill's persuasive editorial technique my story is unsatisfactory, showing nothing more than how my torpor, fear and the need to make money could defeat one of the finest minds in British publishing. All I know is that if anyone could have drawn that book out of me it would have been her.

Diana would have been sixty-six then. She had been André's right-hand woman for nearly forty years and went on serving the company that bore his name, even after André had left it, for another eight. André was the entrepreneurial spirit behind the enterprise but it was mainly Diana who developed its reputation for good books by finding and fostering writers such as Jean Rhys and V.S. Naipaul. The story of her long professional life as an editor is brilliantly told in *Stet*, the second book in this anthology, and there's no need to add to it here. What I didn't know when I met her was that she was also a writer; or rather *had been* a writer, because her most recent book had been published nearly twenty years before. Few people remembered her novel (*Don't Look at Me Like That*, 1967) or her story collection (*An Unavoidable Delay*, 1962), which found a publisher in the USA but none in Britain. It was the middle book of her small 1960s oeuvre that knowledgeable readers, particularly women, mentioned when I said that I'd met her. 'Oh, but you must read *Instead of a Letter*,' they said. The book wasn't easy to find. It had been republished a few times since it first appeared in 1962 and probably was more often in print than out of it, but by the early 1980s *Instead of a Letter* was more of a cult than the popular classic it deserved to be. The times weren't right. Literary taste was still largely dictated by male sensibilities, and, while feminist publishing in Britain had begun to thrive, Athill didn't quite fit its political agenda. As to the book's form, 'memoir' had yet to be established as a successful category in bookshops. Writers wrote them, of course, but rarely did they become known for the memoir alone (J.R. Ackerley and Laurie Lee may be two exceptions). Publishers and readers thought instead of 'autobiographies', in which intimate personal disclosure took a back seat to records of achievement. The boundary between the two forms is blurred and bridgeable: V.S. Pritchett's wonderful account of his early life, *A Cab at the Door*, was described as 'autobiography' when it first appeared in 1968, whereas now it would have 'memoir' written all over it. Gore Vidal explained the difference in this way: 'A memoir is how one remembers one's own life, while an autobiography is history, requiring research, dates, facts double-checked'. His statement is arguable, but it has the virtue of simplicity. More important, by stressing subjective, unverified memory it permits the memoirist to misremember and, unconsciously or otherwise, to embroider and invent – an indulgence, it has to be said, that Diana Athill has never been interested to take.

At any rate, I got *Instead of a Letter* from the library. It told

Diana's story from birth to the age of forty-two, a life begun idyllically in the English countryside, a life rich with privilege and promise – horses, sailing, books, an Oxford education – until, aged twenty-two, she is jilted by her fiancé and her dreams of a future as an RAF pilot's wife turn to dust. Happiness vanishes for the next twenty years. Rejection destroys her confidence, especially in her relationships with men, and she regains it fully only in early middle age, not through the once hoped-for avenues of marriage and children but when she begins to write and has a story published in a newspaper. Put like that it seems an ordinary enough progression – happy, then unhappy, then happy enough – and perhaps an advertisement for a creative-writing school (*'Miserable? Jilted? Then learn to write the Miss Lonelyhearts way!'*). But at that time I had never read a book like it, and to my mind only a few memoirs have equalled it since.

The most memorable and pleasing aspect of memoirs often comes from the picture they offer of a character or a period. We remember V.S. Pritchett's rackety father besotted by Christian Science and mistresses, or John McGahern's loving mother walking her son through the lanes of County Leitrim, or Blake Morrison's father bluffing his Yorkshire way out of and into trouble. The writer attends as a witness, but his own selfhood – what he was like – is present at most as an interlocutor of the character of others. Direct self-description is one of the hardest tasks a writer can undertake, because self-knowledge is so difficult and because the risks of self-indulgence, self-dramatization and falsity of all kinds are so great (and easily spotted and mocked). Diana's book was certainly about herself, and the core of it about the severe disappointment that altered, and for a long time deadened, the course of her life. In other hands, it could have been a long wallow with an unconvincingly bright little salvation at the end. Many books are now constructed on this principle: look, I was an addict; behold, my suffering when I was abused. Often the authors say their motive is to give consolation and hope to others in the same position. *Instead of a Letter* certainly had this effect. About a hundred readers (ninety-nine of them women) wrote to her after the book was first published to share their experience and say how much comfort the book had provided – a large response to an unknown writer when authorship was much less publicized than it is now, and when communication involved the trouble of taking out pen and paper and buying a stamp. To be jilted, to have one's engagement broken off, left a public as well as a private scar (I remember the hush around the subject when in the 1950s it happened to an older cousin of mine). The distress caused by rejection may well be a historical constant in human beings, but at least since 1962 our more open and casual attitudes towards sex and marriage mean that the humiliation is no longer so deep. 'Guilt never caused me any serious distress, but humiliation did,' Diana writes in this anthology's third book, *Yesterday Morning*. 'Humiliation . . . was the sharpest misery I knew.'

An instructive story of self-help wasn't, however, what she intended by *Instead of a Letter*, nor is it by any means the book's most important attraction. Like thousands of other readers before and since, what held me about the writing was its candour. The quality has since become an Athill trademark, though in itself candour is no guarantee of literary pleasure or interest: frank books aren't always good books and can often be tedious by boasting of their frankness. Athill's way of being candid is more subtle and its effect more persuasive. The reader feels that what he is reading is as true a portrait of the writer and her experience as any words on paper can achieve. Part of this comes from her considerable gift as a maker of sentences, which are so lucid and direct; some of it is owed to the breaking of taboos that then surrounded female sexual behaviour; most of it, though, stems from her triumphant struggle to 'get it right', a lesson she learned from two of the writers she edited. Jean Rhys told her that the trick of good writing was 'to get it as it was, as it really was'. Vidia Naipaul said that 'provided you really get it right, the reader will understand'.

All feeling and experience occur inside specific contexts – a room, a field, a conversation, a country house, a crowded pub – and by getting these things 'right', as a good novelist might, Diana opened up what could have been a narrow story of injury and self-absorption into a book that takes pleasure in the world. Also, the harder thing, she got herself right by letting us see how she appeared to others. A chilling moment comes in *Instead of a Letter* when, soon after her engagement has been broken off, she reads a passage in her younger sister's diary. Her sister had a boyfriend who would hold her hand but refused to kiss her, though she was 'dizzy with expectation' that he might. This, remember, was early 1940. Diana read her diary entry: 'He told me that he was not going to kiss me though he wanted to. He said that I was going to be a fascinating woman but that I mustn't begin that sort of thing too soon or it would spoil me. *Look at Di, he said, you don't want to be like her. And of course I don't.*' More than twenty years later, Diana wrote that 'the shrivelling sensation of reading those words is something I still flinch from recalling'. She saw with a 'shameful, accepting humility . . . that I *was* diseased in other people's eyes: that unhappiness was not a misfortune but a taint. In the depths of my being I must have wanted to kill my sister for it, but all I recognised was a shuddering acknowledgment that out of the mouths of babes . . .' She then decided that she would be a model sister to her sibling, rejoicing at her triumphs and fretting over her sorrows. 'But there was a streak of falsity in it: I was over-compensating for my resentment at the scar she had left with her innocent, idle thrust.'

In a first-person narrative, someone else's diary can offer a useful change in the point of view. Another diary crops up in Diana's second memoir, *After a Funeral*, which was published in 1986. The book – Diana preferred to call it a 'documentary' – recounts the tragic story of 'Didi', a promising writer from Egypt who went to stay with Diana as her lodger after she befriended him as his publisher ('Didi' was in fact Waguih Ghali, whose novel *Beer in the Snooker Club* was published by Deutsch in 1964.) Their relationship becomes difficult and, on his part, bitter. Sex isn't the issue. Diana has a partner, called Luke in the book, and though she begins by wanting Didi she has sex with him only once, when both of them are drunk. One evening she goes into Didi's room and finds that he has left his diary open on his desk. She reads:

I have started to detest her. I find her unbearable . . . my reactions
to Diana are sparked by my physical antipathy to Diana. I find
it impossible to live in the same flat as someone whose physical
body seems to provoke mine to cringe. This has led me to detest
everything she does, says or writes . . . I'd be sitting in my
room watching a stupid thing on telly and annoyed with myself
for not switching it off and working . . . In her sitting-room her
typewriter would go tick tick tick tick tick. 'Christ,' I'd tell myself,
'there she is, hammering away at that bloody mediocre muck –
dishing out one tedious stupid sentence after another, and thinking –
no, *pretending* it is writing.

To quote such a passage about oneself in a book by oneself
takes . . . what? Courage certainly, but also an unusually strong
sense of duty towards the truth and the usefulness of truth to
literature. In *Yesterday Morning* she writes that the damage lies do –
the context is the anti-Catholic prejudices of her grandfather – may
be 'the central reason for trying to write the truth, even if indecent,
about oneself.' That may be the moral reason, but there is also a
literary one: Rhys's 'to get it as it was, as it really was'. She exposes
for all to see her pragmatic code of personal behaviour. Private
diaries left lying around invite themselves to be read; married
men can be fucked so long as nobody finds out (or worse, confesses)
and the harmony of the marital home is kept intact. This is the
way she was – as probably many of us are and will go on being.
The consequence is that Diana in her books doesn't always come
across as the most likeable of women. When Didi in his diary
notes that she pronounces 'spritzer' as 'SpritzA!' – Colonel Blimp
speaking – the reader may feel a certain sympathy with his
antagonism, even though accents are harmless accidents of birth.
But if she were more likeable, would she be more sympathetic – or
as believable?

The qualities that come with being a writer of Diana's sort aren't
always attractive. After she and Didi have their drunken sex, Didi
comes into the kitchen the next day and pleads with her not to tell
her lover.

'Promise me one thing. Promise that this is one thing you'll never tell Luke about.'

'Of course I won't, I promise.' (I was already mulling in my head the written account, as exact as possible, which I was going to show Luke one day.)

Graham Greene's famous dictum about the 'chip of ice' that lurks in every writer's heart has never had a better illustration. It would be hopelessly wrong, however, to think of Diana as all ice: a cold-eyed writing machine. The reason that we can read Didi's diaries and letters is that he left them to her in a letter in which he described her as the person he loved most. Then he killed himself, despite her enormous kindness to him, in his rent-free room in the flat where more than forty years later, as I write this, she still lives.

Recently I went to see her there. The flat is on the top floor of the last house in a Victorian cul-de-sac that ends in the green open spaces of Primrose Hill and has a fine view south across central London. Her cousin, the journalist Barbara Smith, owns the house and keeps an apartment on the ground floor; they have had this arrangement for half Diana's life, but when I visited her, in March 2009, Diana was making plans to move into a residential home for old people while she still had all her wits about her and could save friends and relations the trouble of making decisions on her behalf. Three months before, she had turned ninety-one. When a person is that age the present tense is safest deployed with fingers crossed, though there are very few signs of serious failing. She has a hearing aid and walks with the aid of a handsome silver-topped stick and uses a stair-lift to take her up (but not down) the four flights to her flat, but she still drives her little car and her conversation is as witty and direct as ever. She looks majestic.

As Diana's former publisher, I edited three of the four books that make up this collection. Very little needs to be said about that. The typescript arrived, a few suggestions for changes were made, Diana absorbed them with her quick editorial brain, and a slightly amended typescript was soon in the post. Editing her was pure pleasure because I loved reading her; it was like having someone speak into your ear, someone humane and self-amused and wise that you wanted to hear. 'Good writing' is difficult to define, and definitions differ according to taste, but you know it when you see it, which is rarer than publishing companies would have you suppose. I remember my excitement when I read the first few pages of the typescript that became *Somewhere Towards the End* (Diana's choice of title and a good one, as her titles always are). The book arose out of a brief conversation and the exchange of a postcard or two: it seemed to me that while the memoir genre abounded in accounts of youth – the 'coming-of-age narrative' is a literary cliché of our times – very few books have let us know about life at the other end of the road. In fact, other than self-help guides (take a cod-liver oil capsule every day) and the late novels of Philip Roth, I could think of none. There are, of course, books about the process of dying by victims of cruel and slow terminal disease, but writers have been shy of the subject of *just being old*, as if shame and indignity had replaced wisdom and experience as the best-known qualities of great age. Our conversation hardly amounted to an editorial briefing and I had no word of progress for a couple of years. Then a few early pages arrived and with them the first vivid sense of what it is like to become old, like reports from another country that we shall all, if spared earlier elimination, shortly be moving to. In different hands, the book could have been filled with a sentimental longing for the past, brittle cheer towards the present, or the religious consolation of the future. None of those things could ever have appealed to Diana. Instead, *Somewhere Towards the End* is a beautifully turned series of episodes, none of them sermonic, in which the author reveals how she has come to terms (or not) with what she calls 'falling away' and the unavoidable fact of death. It was, wrote the late Simon Gray – no stranger himself to intimations of mortality – both 'exhilarating and comforting' in its good sense, candour and lively spirit. Every passage is rooted in specifics. On the second page, she describes her new tree fern (£18 from the Thompson & Morgan plant catalogue) and her doubts that she will live long enough to see it reach mature height: a small thought, but it immediately takes us inside the mind of someone going on for ninety. She has 'got it right', and continues to get it right throughout the book, in the sense that we utterly believe that this is how life is and was for her. She describes her final lover, Sam:

> We rarely did anything together except make ourselves a pleasant little supper and go to bed, because we had very little in common apart from liking sex . . . We also shared painful feet, which was almost as important as liking sex, because when you start feeling your age it is comforting to be with someone in the same condition. You recognize it in each other, but there is no need to go on about it. We never mentioned our feet, just kicked our shoes off as soon as we could.

Stet, Yesterday Morning, Somewhere Towards the End: they may not be her last books – fingers crossed again – but they represent the late flowering of a writing career previously conducted in sporadic bursts. All were written when she was in her eighties and all are memoirs. Sometimes they overlap; they weren't planned as a sequence. A few places and people in them wear a light disguise; when Diana began to write, it wasn't done to name names in intimate personal histories. Now it seems reasonable to name two of them, because of the important part they played in shaping her life.

The first is a place. 'Beckton', the country house and estate where Diana spent so much of her childhood, is in fact Ditchingham Hall in Norfolk, just across the river Waveney from Suffolk. Her mother's grandfather, a Yorkshire doctor enriched by railway shares and a good marriage, bought it in the 1890s. A cousin of hers still lives there. (Diana herself is far from well off. Publishing never paid her much, partly owing to her indifference about asking for more, which she came to see 'as foolish, if not reprehensible', and she had no inheritance. Having no money, Diana finds it easy to talk about. The royalties from her greatest success, *Somewhere Towards the End* will pay for her stay in the old people's home, somewhere closer towards the end.)

The second is a person. 'Paul', the young pilot who broke her heart, was Tony Irvine. As squadron leader A.T. Irvine he died in the late afternoon of April 13, Easter Sunday, 1941, when his Blenheim bomber crashed into a mountain near the village of Vigla in northern Greece. Germany had just begun its invasion of Greece and a squadron of seven Blenheims set out to bomb troop formations before they poured south through the Monastir Gap. German fighters attacked the Blenheims ('dreadful, clumsy planes' in Diana's recollection) and six were shot down in the space of four minutes. Irvine's plane was last seen climbing into the mist that surrounded the mountainside, possibly trying to escape. The following day its wreckage was found eighty-four feet below the peak. Irvine had married by that time and his wife was pregnant with a son. When Irvine's father died, long after, this son found a letter from Diana among his possessions and got in touch with her. They met one or twice. He must now be a man in his late sixties.

'Just say,' I said to Diana, 'that Paul hadn't jilted you, that you'd married him. Would you have written a book?'

Her reply was quick but thoughtful. 'If I'd been an air force wife, I probably wouldn't have written a book. If I'd been an air force widow, I might have done.'

In any event, a long time passed before she started on the book that became *Instead of a Letter*. She said she had no intention of writing it, no premeditation, no structure, no model presented by the books of other writers. 'That book *happened to me*,' she said, meaning that it had somehow taken charge of her and couldn't be stopped. She had written nine stories for her collection and begun a tenth. 'It was going to be about my grandmother but it fizzled out and I put it away. Then I took it out again and it simply *went on*. I couldn't stop. I wrote it even in the office in any spare moment. There was no plan and it's remained for me a very baffling book, but it worked as a piece of therapy to a quite extraordinary extent.'

She realized she could write, and that she was best at it when not covering reality with the polite wallpaper of fiction but by recounting experience as it really had been, as honestly as she could evoke it to her own satisfaction: 'I've never actually planned a book,' she said. 'I've never thought of readers.' In the forty-seven years since, only six books have followed, which brings her total to eight. She said, 'I've never written anything unless I've wanted to. I really am an amateur.'

I thought of her self-description – 'amateur' – as I went down the stairs and began to walk across Primrose Hill. Really, we should have more of them. More people who write only when they feel they have something to tell us; more writers driven by the scrupulous need to make us see clearly and exactly what they have witnessed and felt.

I walked on over the rise. London was now spread all across the horizon in its familiar jumble of offices and monuments. I thought of how Diana was born somewhere off to the right in Kensington during a Zeppelin raid (December 21, 1917) and of how she had seen this city in so many different ages and moods. In *Instead of a Letter*, she and Paul take a ride in London's last hansom cab – before the war and before her humiliating rejection. Before The Fall, you might say sadly, until you remember how Diana rose from it to find her singular voice. If anyone in future wants to know how an intelligent Englishwoman led her life in the twentieth century, her inner and outer life, from birth to a very old age, hers are books that will need to be read. As for now, they can simply be enjoyed.

Ian Jack
May 2009

YESTERDAY
MORNING

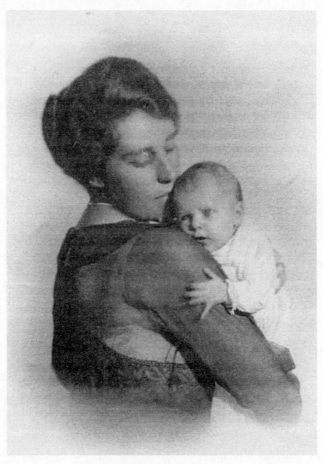

Diana Athill with her mother, 1918

NOW

'OH MY GOD,' said my mother. 'Can I really have a daughter who is seventy?' and we both burst out laughing.

She was ninety-two. It was eight years since she had driven a car, six since social services had supplied her with a seat to help her bathe without getting stuck in the tub. She needed two sticks when she made her daily inspection of her garden, and had given up the needlepoint embroidery she loved because her sight was no longer good enough. She was well aware of being a very old woman, but she still felt like the Kitty Athill she had always been, so it was *absurd* to have another old woman as a daughter.

Another person, however, might have forgotten her own name before reaching that age, so it is impossible to generalize about growing old. Why, I was once asked, do so few people send back reports about life out on that frontier; and the answer is that some no longer have the ability because they have lost their wits, some no longer have the energy because they are beset by aches and pains and ailments, and those lucky enough to have hung on to their health feel just like they felt before they were old except for not being able to do an increasing number of things, and for an awareness of their bodies as sources of a slight malaise, often forgettable but always there if they think about it.

I belong to the last group, touch wood (once you have made it into your eighties you don't say something like that without glancing nervously over your shoulder). The main things I can no

longer do are drink alcohol, walk fast or far, enjoy music, and make
love. Hideous deprivations, you might think – indeed, if someone
had listed them twenty years ago I would have been too appalled to
go on reading, so I must quickly add that they are less hideous than
they sound.

Drink, for instance: I did not have to say to myself 'Drink is no
longer good for me *so I must give it up*'. What happened was that I
began to wake up in the night quite often with a horrid pain which
got worse and worse until I threw up, and eventually concluded
that what caused this unpleasantness was alcohol. I took a long time
to get there because often I had drunk no more than one or two
glasses of wine with dinner, and who would suppose that one or
two glasses of wine could make one ill? But they did, and by the
time I understood as much, I was so tired of all that miserable
sickness that I said goodbye to alcohol quite happily and began
positively to enjoy water.

Being bad at walking is tiresome, but not so tiresome for me as
it would be for some. In my youth I never walked where I could
ride a horse, and later never where I could drive a car, which I can
still do. My happiest times have been spent in chairs or beds:
possibly I would actually like it if I became wheelchair-bound.

The loss of pleasure in music because of increasing deafness is
sadder. The sounds can still be heard, but are distorted into
ugliness. The piano comes through almost unaltered, but strings
and birdsong are scratchy and painful, while most high voices are
squawks. But against that, silence, like pure cold water, has become
lovely.

As for sex – some very old women say that it still gives them
pleasure, so clearly it varies from person to person. With me its
ebbing was the first of the physical indications of old age: my body
began slowly to lose responsiveness in my sixties, long before my
mind did. For a while it could be restored by novelty, which allowed
me an enjoyable little Indian summer, but when it became a real
effort, and then a mockery, it made me sad: being forced to fake
something which had been such an important pleasure was far
more depressing than doing without it.

It seems to me that once one has got over the shock of realizing that a loss is a symptom of old age, the loss itself is easy to bear because you no longer want the thing that has gone. Music is the only thing I would really like to have back (whisky would be nice, but not nice enough to fret about). If a hearing-aid is developed which truly does restore their real nature to those nasty little scratchy sounds which make silence seem lovely, then I will welcome it.

The big event of old age – the thing which replaces love and creativity as a source of drama – is death. Probably the knowledge that it can't fail to come fairly soon is seriously frightening. I say 'probably' because to be as frightened as I suspect I might be would be so disagreeable that I have to dodge it – as everyone must, no doubt. There are many ways of dodging. The one I favour is being rational: saying 'Everyone who ever was, is and shall be, comes to the end of life. So does every *thing*. It is one of the absolute certainties, as *ordinary* as anything can be, so it can't be all that bad.' Having said that, you then allow your mind to occupy itself with other matters – you do not need to force it, it is only too pleased to do so.

And I have also been granted another specific against unseemly fear, which is remembering the death of my mother. She died in June, 1990, the day before her ninety-sixth birthday. That week she had bought a eucalyptus tree, and Sid Pooley, who with his wife had been working in her garden for years, came to plant it for her. She went out to show him where, and when he looked up from digging the hole he saw that she was not quite herself. 'Are you all right?' he asked, and she said she was feeling a bit odd and had better go back to the house. When Sid had helped her back and put her into her chair in the sitting room, he telephoned Eileen Barry, her home help and friend, who came quickly. Having had much experience of old people, Eileen suspected heart failure, so before telephoning me and my brother she got my mother into the little cottage hospital which we are lucky enough still to have. It used to be run by Anglican nuns who have a convent in the village, and my

grandfather was one of its founders. At that time it had only two
private rooms and two wards, one for old women, the other for old
men (most of its patients are very old: younger people are treated
at the county hospital. An elderly cousin of mine, on hearing a
rumour that our little hospital might be closed, exclaimed: 'Oh no!
Where shall we die?'). Both the rooms were occupied, and the
women's ward was full, so they found my mother a bed in the
men's ward and put screens round it.

I got there, after a misleadingly reassuring telephone call, early
next morning, and found my brother Andrew and my cousin Joyce
beside my mother's bed. My sister could not be there because she
lived in Zimbabwe. It was frightening: my mother's face was almost
purple, she was gasping for breath, and they told me she had just
vomited black stuff. It seemed that she must die at any moment.
When I put my hand on hers and leant over her, she opened her
eyes, which wandered for a moment and then met mine – and a
wonderful thing happened: a smile seemed to come flaming up
from deep inside her, illuminating her whole face. Andrew was to
say later 'That was an *amazing* smile she gave you,' and so it was:
the complete expression of a lifetime's almost always unspoken but
never doubted love, coming to me like a precious gift.

Eventually a doctor came and gave her a shot – morphine, I
suppose – and one of the little rooms was made ready for her. She
fell into a deep, drugged sleep and the sister in charge said firmly
that nothing was going to happen that night (the day had seemed
endless – it was astounding to realize that it was over), so we had
better go away until next morning. Andrew drove off to his home
sixty miles away in north Norfolk, and Joyce and I went to my
mother's house, fed her dog, scrambled some eggs and went to
bed – I in my mother's bed, which felt odd but comforting.

And next morning she was better, sitting up against a bank of
pillows in her quiet little room, pale but like herself. Her voice
seemed almost strong when she said 'Oh darling – could you brush
my hair? It feels so horrible.' When I had done that I went to find
Sister, exclaiming when I did so 'She's much better!' That kind
woman put her hand on my arm and said: 'She's *feeling* much

better, but she is still very very poorly' – and I understood that she was warning me not to expect recovery.

All that day my mother was sleepy, but herself. From time to time she murmured that she would like a sip of water, or the bedpan, and she told me that although her desk looked untidy I would find her will and other necessary papers in one of its drawers. 'But Aunt Kit,' said Joyce – my mother's eldest niece, and the one dearest to her – 'you'll be back there yourself in a few days,' to which she answered sharply 'Don't be absurd, I could go any minute.' Twice she emerged from a doze into a state of slight confusion, once thinking her dog had been in the room, then reminding me to pay for the wreath of poppies she put on my father's grave every November, which was five months away. The next time she woke, after quite a long sleep, she said: 'Did I tell you that Jack drove me over to Raveningham last week to buy that eucalyptus?'

'You told me he was going to,' I said. 'Was it fun?'

And she answered in a dreamy voice: 'It was absolutely divine.'

Then she turned her head away and went back to sleep.

Jack, who drove her that afternoon, told me later that it *had* been an exceptionally lovely day – June at its most beautiful – and that she had asked him to go by a lane she specially loved because she often rode that way as a girl. 'She did enjoy every minute of it,' he said.

A few minutes after she had fallen asleep Joyce and I decided that we had better go to feed her dog, and before we had been in her house fifteen minutes, Sister telephoned to tell me that she was dead.

The nurse who let me into her room when I went back to say goodbye to her was embarrassed because, although they had closed her eyes, they had not propped up her chin. She looked just as she sometimes looked when she went to sleep in her chair with her head leaning back, so that her jaw dropped: not a dignified deathbed image, but too familiar to be distressing. And anyway, I was far from distress. I was full of gratitude because she had come to the end of her days with an image in her mind of an afternoon that had

My mother in her garden

been 'absolutely divine'. One dreadful day, one of sleepiness, then that. She had bequeathed me, as well as that wonderful smile, the knowledge that an old person's death is not necessarily terrible.

That a woman of ninety-six was lucky enough to die an easy death without losing her wits or the ability to enjoy her chosen way of life in her own house: there was nothing much to mourn in that. Naturally I was to miss my mother – would often catch myself thinking that I must tell her something amusing or ask her something important – but I would also come to feel that mothers are never quite lost. Increasingly I see how much of her is still with me, literally in that I carry her genes within me, and also because of how much my attitudes and outlook were shaped by the upbringing she gave me. And when she died I avoided – though narrowly – what is sometimes the worst part of mourning: the burden of guilt about the dead person's last years which can threaten people after a parent's death.

My mother would never have dreamt of saying that she was

lonely and sometimes afraid, but of course she was; and it became worse when, a few years before her death, she began to have attacks of vertigo. She knew they were not dangerous (unless one of them caused her to fall dangerously), but they were very unpleasant and enduring them alone called for considerable courage. My brother and I bullied her into accepting one of those lockets which send out an alarm call, but we couldn't make her wear it. I knew she ought to have someone living with her – and I also knew how relieved and happy she would be if that someone was me.

Because I was one of the founding directors of the publishing house André Deutsch Limited, I was still working there, and I still needed to work. Publishing had been rewarding in many ways, but not financially (partly owing to my own indifference, which I now see as foolish, if not reprehensible). I had almost no savings, nor did my mother have any money to spare. She was the extravagant one in a set of sensibly frugal siblings, and although her extravagance was touchingly modest (buying a hundred daffodil bulbs instead of twenty, for example) it had left her in an awkward position. My father had retired from the Army as a lieutenant-colonel, so the pension paid to his widow was small, and although my maternal grandfather had set up a trust for his four daughters which no doubt seemed generous when he did it, by the time my mother reached her nineties it brought her in less than a thousand a year. Like her sisters, when widowed she gravitated home, which meant to the estate then owned by my uncle, where their mother still lived. My uncle sold her very cheaply a tumbledown cottage, and she somehow scraped together the money – helped, I think, by a sister – to convert it into a charming little house . . . and then found herself without enough money to live in it. Her brother came to the rescue. He bought back the now much more valuable cottage and let her go on living in it on condition that it would return to the estate after her death, so she was able to buy herself an annuity. It was a relief to her children that she could continue living in the house which suited her so well, but it did mean that if I were to give up my job she could offer me no security in return.

The truth was that I would not have much in the way of security whatever happened, so this was not really so much of a problem as I tried to think it was. I fear that I dwelt on it in the hope of convincing myself that I had a good reason for not moving in with her. It was hard to admit how appalled I was by the prospect of giving up my job – or more exactly, of giving up the life I had made for myself in London. My brother, who had a family to support, offered to have her to live with him if it became necessary, and it was not his fault that nothing would have made her accept life in someone else's household. My sister in Zimbabwe also had a family. I have no children, and the man with whom I live has always been as little possessive as I am myself, so theoretically I had the mobility to move in with her, and no doubt if we had absolutely had to we *could* have managed financially. But I, too, was an old woman, only twenty-one years younger than she was. I, too, had built myself a life which suited me, and the prospect of giving it up seemed to me dreadful. All the more so in that although I loved her, we had little in common beyond kinship, so when I was with her I always had to put my own nature on hold and exist in terms of hers. When younger, she had entered into her children's interests rather well, but by about her mid-eighties she stopped bothering to make the effort to do so. It was on her ground that we had to meet, and although I liked her ground, it was astonishingly exhausting to be cut off so completely from my own, even for the few days of a weekend. To bear it all the time, I felt, would be beyond me.

But during one of the many weekends I was now spending with her she had an exceptionally severe attack of vertigo. I was sitting up late over some work, so I heard the thump as she fell down in her bedroom. I rushed upstairs and was able to heave her into a chair, wrap a blanket round her (she went ice-cold during these attacks), and supply her with a basin before the retching began – the way the dizziness affected her like sea-sickness was the worst part of it. Usually the attacks lasted about half an hour, but this one went on and on. There was nothing for me to do but hold her head and add to her wrappings, and as the night went by I became frightened. Every now and then she gasped 'It will pass, it will pass,' but it didn't, and surely the strain of all that dreadful retching must be more than her poor old heart could stand? So I decided to call out the doctor. He came quickly, gave her an injection, and stayed with us to make sure that it would work, which it soon did. As I helped her into bed at about three in the morning, I realized that the time had come when I *must* take action.

I decided on a compromise: from then on I would divide each week between London and Norfolk, three days in the office, four with my mother. When I was not there I would gamble on her being kept safe by Eileen Barry early every morning, Sid and Ruby Pooley looking in every afternoon, and the generous alertness of kind neighbours (oh, the luck of Sid, in fact, being there when the time came).

Even that limited sacrifice of my own time seemed painful at first. The day I arranged it with the office and announced it to my mother, I collapsed with what I thought was flu, but understood two days later, with shame, to be nothing but strangled protest. It is extremely humbling to remember that my cousin Joyce, who like me was only twenty-one years younger than her mother and who adored her own house, moved in with my aunt full-time for months and months and never gave the slightest hint of boredom or regret. But once the first resistance was over, the arrangement worked well. My mother was happy – knowing there would be no more than three days alone seemed to make it feel less like loneliness and more like waiting for something agreeable to happen – and her happiness made me glad. And when she died, if I had believed in God I would have gone down on my knees and thanked him for the extra time I spent with her during her last two years.

What caused the kind of grief that twists the guts was not losing my mother, but losing the place where she lived which, wherever I myself happened to be living, had always been 'home'. My maternal grandparents' estate in Norfolk, just across the border from Suffolk, was where my mother, her siblings, her children and most of their cousins were rooted. This was because my grandmother was so much loved by her four daughters and her son that they all came back to her whenever they could, bringing their children with them and leaving them with her when they had to live abroad. Her son was a cavalry officer and her three married daughters chose military husbands, two in the Army, one who moved from the Army to the RAF after being one of the founder members of the Royal Flying Corps, so a good deal of living abroad went on. My brother and sister and I spent a large part of our early childhood and all our teenage years in the Hall Farm, just across the park from my grandparents' house – which we thought of as 'Gran's house' because my grandfather died when I was six. When it passed to my uncle and then from him to his daughter, the house ceased being the magnet it had been previously, but its land, the two little villages within its sphere of influence, the local market town – all that went on being 'home' while my mother lived there. Driving from London, when I reached the market town and turned into the road which I had traversed hundreds of times more often than any other road, I used to get – still get – an extraordinary feeling of entering my own body, as though I had become something like the giant human figure that was on display in the Dome and was at the same time a person moving through it.

It took us a month or so to sort out my mother's possessions and prepare her house for its return to the estate, which promptly sold it – luckily to great friends of ours. Then, one day, I suddenly realized that I was driving that road for the last time. I would of course be returning to Norfolk to stay with my brother, or with Joyce, but I would no longer have a reason to drive this way – and the thought of doing the trip not because I was coming home, but just to see what was going on there, seemed so horrible that I almost wept. Realizing it was ridiculous to mind so much, I made a great effort to reason myself out of this grief, but was successful only on the surface. It did not occur to me that the grief might soon be dispelled.

This happened thanks to my cousin Barbara, to whom I already owed my home in London. Although she is eight years younger than I am we have been friends since the mid-fifties when, soon after coming to London for her first job, she was looking for somewhere to live and I had half a flat to offer. It was very much a young person's first flat, with nothing on its floors but dingy underfelt, and a sparse collection of furniture cast off by other people; but it was large enough to take a lodger, which helped us to pay the rent. When Barbara, after finding her way into political journalism, married the lodger, I moved off to a happy spell in Chelsea, sharing a house with a friend; but some years later the ground shifted simultaneously under both Barbara's life and mine, she bought a large house and I moved into it with her, renting its top floor. And when eventually my ineptitude with money made me unable to afford even the modest rent I had been paying, Barbara let me go on living there anyway, so that I have continued to enjoy a life civilized far beyond my means. Without her generosity I and my old companion would, by now, be living in a pair of bedsitters in Stoke Newington . . . in other words, our gratitude is inexpressible.

Barbara's mother, like mine, had been drawn home after her husband's death and had bought and converted a cottage on the estate – just one field separated the sisters, who had tea with each other every day. My aunt was the older of the two, but she outlived my mother by eighteen months; and she, whose husband had retired as a general and whose scrupulous frugality ought to have been a lesson to us all, was able to leave her house to her son and daughter. They agreed that Barbara should buy her brother out, and Barbara then suggested that I should add a room to it (André Deutsch added enough to my savings to make this possible), thus making it just large enough for us to share it as a country retreat. So here I am, still driving that old road almost every weekend, which has made the difference between a bearable old age and a happy one, and has given birth to this book.

Something I like about old age is that you can so easily let your mind drift. The present no longer contains much that demands concentrated thought: no more love affairs, no more work excitements or problems, no more (or very little) planning of entertainment or travel. Day-to-day life is so much simpler and

more repetitive than it used to be that you can allow your mind to
wander. The best times for it are in the morning, snug in bed
putting off getting up, and in the evening, idling one's way towards
sleep. Sometimes I find myself telling a story which has grown out
of some small incident – perhaps a man in the park that morning
was humiliated by his lack of control over his dog, and a mini-
drama weaves itself round him. Or I have heard that a friend is ill,
and spend a long time recalling her and her ways, imagining her
feelings, foreseeing her future. Often I choose a time or place and
let myself loose in it: Venice on a September morning, perhaps, or
Santa Fe full of flowering lilacs as it was when I once spent a week
there. One scene will lead to another, one event connect
mysteriously with another of a different kind, and people I haven't
thought about for years will materialize. And since the place where
I spent my childhood has been restored to me . . . well, everyone
knows that what comes back to the old most often is their distant
past, and that is confirmed again and again in my own experience.
In the last two or three years I have learnt what a vast amount of my
childhood is stuffed away below the level of consciousness, much
of it probably never to emerge but a surprising amount of it ready
to become available, and all of it *there*. It has become obvious that
what an old person is – provided he or she has not gone gaga – is
not just the deteriorating body going through its necessarily
simplified and sometimes boring occupations, but a mobile
reservoir of experience.

Being this reservoir expands one's sense of importance, but
because people are usually unable to benefit from experience which
is not their own, it is better not to talk about it too much. Perhaps
it is otherwise in societies which traditionally revere their elders
(lucky old them!), but not with us. Generally what one has to
expect is that the accumulation so essential to oneself is destined to
vanish quite soon in a puff of smoke out of a crematorium chimney.
(In fact it won't have even that amount of visibility: how a modern
crematorium deals with the smoke problem I do not know, but
certainly it is not allowed to upset the neighbours.)

The knowledge that this is so must, I suppose, be one of the chief triggers of autobiography. 'But if I turn it into a book,' one feels, '*there it will still be.*' Whether anyone will want to read it is up to them: at least it will be there for whoever does. I have acted on this impulse twice before, once in relation to my experience of love (*Instead of a Letter*), once in relation to my life in publishing (*Stet*), and both times there was a fair number of people who wanted to read the resulting book; so now, when what has bubbled up asking for the same kind of expression is the material at the bottom of the reservoir – the stuff which, on the whole, causes a person to be what he or she is – I dare to do it again.

Aged seven, with my brother Andrew and little sister Patience

THEN

LESSONS

I LONG TO BE a fish, water flowing as easily through lungs as over skin and allowing supple movement or lazy suspension. I lean over the rail of the bridge which spans the weir, and stare into the pool below it. Brown yet transparent, with golden gleams, like clear dark jelly. It makes me lick my lips with thirst.

The summer of my ninth year was hot, so the lake was low and only a little water spilt over the weir into the pool. After heavy rain it roared over and to prevent a flood the gate in the weir's bowels was cranked open so that, in addition to the overspill, a flying buttress of water escaped lower down, out of the lake's depths. Today's trickle was less exciting, but it allowed the pool to lie at peace. It was hard to decide between violent beauties and tranquil ones because things ought to have an order – good, better, best – and when they didn't it made me uneasy. But if it was impossible to decide between the tumultuous weir and the still pool, at least it was obvious that each was best when it was 'most' – and the pool today could not have been more what a pool on a hot summer day ought to be.

There were yellow water-lilies – wild ones, which I believed to be rare. The ones up in the garden, big and white with golden centres, were specially planted and originated in the Orient (was I told that, or was it just that they looked like it?), and that was surely usually the truth about water-lilies. We might be the only people in England who had wild ones growing in their pools as though living in India or Persia . . . one of those places from which precious things came. And my uncle saw a kingfisher here. All I could see now were dragon-flies zigzagging swiftly between hover and hover, and a moorhen stepping through the grass near the bridge, probably a parent of the eggs my brother and I ate that spring. The nest was anchored beyond arm's reach, so we took the eggs with a spoon tied to a long cane. Luckily they were new-laid – cracking a moorhen's egg was always an anxious business.

The contents of an egg which was too far gone echoed other horrors: there was sometimes, for instance, a dead animal hidden in long grass. The gamekeeper's 'larders' in the woods – wire strung with the rotting corpses of weasels, stoats, rats, jays, carrion crows and other threats to his pheasants and partridges – these were bad enough, but I knew where they were and could avoid them, or if I had to pass one because I was with someone who might think me silly, I could steel myself in advance, and look away. But sliding into a ditch to get at a clump of primroses: then, if there was suddenly a dead animal, my very blood recoiled. The worst was last summer, wading through a field of wheat (though trying not to trample it down, which was forbidden) for the pleasure of being in all that gold and smelling its warmth. My foot came down on a dead rabbit. Swerving, I almost landed on another, and realized that all round among the wheatstalks, partly hidden by the undergrowth of weeds, were collapsed skeletons with their loathsome tatters of fur – a sort of rabbit graveyard: how to escape without treading on another? Then panic sent me plunging out of the wheat. I could remember it only in quickly blinked-away glimpses, it was so dreadful. It did not stop me walking again through tall growth, or climbing into ditches, or exploring woods, but I was much more careful which diminished the pleasure.

It was a puzzle, the way things were rarely exactly what they ought to be. If I had run myself into a sweat, and the grass was so soft and green that it should have been caressing when I flopped down in it, there was usually a thistle or a hidden stone, or after a few seconds my legs would start to itch because of ants crawling over them. And if music started to climb higher and higher, instead of going up into absolute height it always turned and came down again. Height, depth, softness, sweetness – there was never quite enough of them. 'Why can't all food be sweet?' I had asked not long ago, and the answer was 'You couldn't have sweet if you didn't have sour'. What a senseless rule!

It wasn't like that in the serial story I told Andrew every evening, when we were in bed. The story was called 'Hal's Adventures'. 'Why Hal?' my mother asked – we knew no one of that name – and I explained that it was short for 'Halbert'. 'But there's no such name. There's Albert or there's Henry – Hal is short for Henry.' I could not accept that because the abbreviation of Henry must so obviously be Hen; so Hal went on being short for Halbert, my hero who could command magic at a pinch and was absolute ruler of his people.

Hal's closest friend and lieutenant was Thomas, who was trusty and also dull: all I bothered to know about him was that he had brown hair (Hal's was auburn) and blue eyes. Thomas had a pretty princess with curly golden hair, but Hal's princess was dark and tragic-looking, with hair that fell to her knees in smooth waves. If I could have had my way the story would have consisted almost entirely of what the princesses were wearing, what kind of horses they were all riding, what jewels adorned their chariots and thrones, what silks were heaped on their beds. Everything in their palaces was what it should be – all the food as delicious as strawberries and peaches, all the colours luminous. Once Hal and his entourage discovered a river of perfect beauty. Its water was as clear as diamonds and it ran over a broad smooth bed of spring-green grass.

My brother wanted events, not descriptions. I was bad at these, although I knew that marvellous things must happen in Hal's world if only I could hit on them. Since I couldn't, it always ended by being another battle between Hal's forces and the Pubbies.

We had set out to invent a whole secret language, but it had stopped at a special grunt for 'goodnight', 'jolyon' for 'penis', 'jellybolees' for 'buttocks' and 'pubby'. I felt ashamed of our lack of seriousness when we gave up. A pubby person was a person we despised: fat, soft, silly, scared. The Pubbies in the story were an obscene and treacherous army, always defeated, and tortured when taken prisoner. Once Hal and Thomas made them sit naked astride a wall with jagged glass on top of it, and bounce up and down – a stroke of genius which went down so well with Andrew that it often had to be repeated.

The worst thing we ever did to a pubby in real life was to push him into a bed of nettles as though by accident. Usually we went no further than acting aloof and showing off. The pubby would be handed over by its parents and our own – 'Why don't you take Michael to see the calves?'– and after a greeting which adults would think no worse than shy, we would start running along the tops of walls, jumping up to catch a branch over which to somersault, throwing stones at things (risky, because to miss made you look silly). If after a while the pubby joined in and proved as able as we were, he would be promoted – often with enthusiasm – to friend. If he was nervous, or didn't like to get dirty, or was simply not interested, he was condemned.

I would never forget the day when I stood by myself on the bridge because it had so much in it: it was summer; it was in this place – our grandparents' home – which all of us children felt in our bones to be our own; and it was near water. And perhaps also because I was alone, although I wasn't really. Andrew and two of our cousins were quite near, climbing trees. I was separate because I was sulking. Their enthusiasm for tree-climbing had outweighed mine for something else, and 'She's sulking, she's sulking,' they had jeered. The way to lift sulks above absurdity was to enlarge and prolong them. If I didn't speak another word all morning – no, all day – that would show them. At first they wouldn't notice, then they'd be puzzled, then alarmed. By the evening everyone from our grandmother down to Patience, our little sister, would be pleading with me to speak, or tiptoeing about, consulting in whispers as to what should be done . . . But while we were running down the slope of the park to the edge of the lake, and making our way along it towards the weir and the bridge, I felt resolution failing: words and laughter were almost escaping. I stayed by the bridge to save what dignity I could. By the time I heard shrieks of 'A hornet – look, a hornet!' my immersion in the things I was watching had purged me of resentment so that I could run to see the hornet (there was a nest of them in one of the trees) without noticing that I had capitulated. I remembered it briefly that evening: a whole day – how it would have impressed them all! But what could I do about my own frailty?

Childhood is so often remembered as summery presumably because summer is the season allowing children in northern climates the most freedom: the longest holidays come then and they can be out of doors, away from the adult-organized house – most themselves. That water is so central is harder to explain. A classic Freudian interpretation is that water and sand represent urine and faeces, essential playthings because with them the child can act out infant fantasies . . . Can that be true? With us the fascination of water coincided through early childhood with an acknowledged interest in urine and faeces, so there was no need for the latter to appear under a disguise. When we were seven and five years old my brother (who was the younger) asked me: 'Which do you like best, bigs or littles?' I knew just what he meant: these things existed in our minds as a subject, in the same way that interior decoration might exist in the minds of adults. When he said 'I like bigs best' his preference left me incredulous, as though he'd said 'I like garden gnomes'. To me littles was far more attractive – when I fell in love with the gardener's 'boy' I imagined him urinating, and I went through a phase of doing it myself in odd places – under a corner of the carpet in the bedroom for example – leaving a few drops here and there like a dog establishing its territory. It did not occur to me that urine smelt: I was stunned when this habit was discovered, and so frightened and ashamed that I must have known all along that I was committing a bad breach of the rules, even though I hadn't thought about it. I was caught while staying in an aunt's house, and my flustered nanny shut me in my bedroom, where I waited for some unimaginable punishment contained in the thought 'They will tell Mummy and Daddy'. I had never been smacked, never deprived of anything I wanted, never even sent to bed or stood in a corner – well, yes, stood in a corner once, but it seemed silly rather than mortifying. Adult disapproval was the only weapon used against me, so it was fully potent: the unimaginable punishment might, perhaps, be that my parents' disgust would make them unable to love me.

My aunt came into the room. The only thing I was aware of was a longing to vanish. 'You *are* a disgusting little guttersnipe, aren't you?' said the aunt, disdainful rather than angry. When I understood that I need expect nothing worse than that, my relief was so great that I could hardly comprehend it. My parents would never know! (When I was home again a doctor came although I wasn't ill, and pronounced my bladder sound, but I didn't connect the two events.) The incident soon faded – but I never again experienced the impulse to pee in corners.

No, the disturbances caused in us by water were not the same as the titillations caused by urine. Water inspired sensations of longing or impulses towards creativity (many dams were built). Water running shallow over pebbles, humped to the shapes of the stones; or over sand, trilling in minute puckers of ripple; water still and shadowy over mud, disorderly and silvered where it broke against an obstacle; water in muscular swirls and eddies: each of its moods had its own quality and evoked its particular response. It frightened only when in flood, yellow with soil, carrying clumps of scum, moving too fast. There was a terrifying book on the nursery shelves about the Mississippi in flood and a family of children swept away, clinging to the roof of their house . . . A stream in spate, even the disciplined stream which bisected the kitchen garden, was suddenly related to the Mississippi and became a threat – but a fascinating threat. Water linked with poetry rather than with sex.

Dabbling in streams was not the only way in which we expressed the urge to make things. When it came over us it was always the same – a strong, almost tormenting need to do something – but what? Often it short-circuited into bad temper: 'What shall we

Fishing for newts in the kitchen garden

do? – Mummy, we don't know what to *do*.' – 'Why don't you go and dress-up?' – '*No!*' . . . everything anyone suggested seemed futile. But usually the urge had its own solution within it, needing only to be recognized. Was this the house-building itch? No. Was it the dam-building feeling? No, not quite. Was it the signal for going over to the farm and finishing the cave we were digging into the side of a straw-stack? No-o-o . . . not today. What about making a pig-mush? Of course, that was it!

Making a pig-mush had to be done by Andrew and me alone, because no one else had quite the right feeling for it. We had been given an enormous old iron saucepan, now chocolate-coloured with rust, which we left lying about in the bottom orchard (the one for cooking-apples and quinces) for months between each pig-mush fit, and sometimes had trouble finding. The pig-sty was near the orchard, and first we would go and look at the pigs because it was necessary to work up a feeling of love and pity. Poor things. *Poor* things, in that stinking yard where the muck came halfway up the fence (pigs were not kept scientifically in those days). Nothing to do but lie about in that muck all day waiting for their food, and when the food came it was always the same: meal made into a sloppy porridge with water. Never mind, pigs, you're going to have a treat now. We're going to make a pig-mush for you, we won't be long.

The basis of it, to give it body, was a few handfuls of the pigs' own meal mixed with water in the usual way. The mush's beauty lay in its other ingredients. Some were obvious, such as apples, carrots and wholesome-looking fresh green grass, but as the work progressed the creative fever would mount, and we would scurry about the garden and even up to the house, to beg from the cook. Six pink, six white, six red rose petals; a handful of mint; pinches of salt and pepper; some icing-sugar; two senna-pods (the taste would be disguised and they'd do the pigs a lot of good); a little duckweed? Why not. Then some crumbled Madeira cake and some asparagus tops, and two bruised peaches which had fallen off one of the trees espaliered on the kitchen-garden wall. We might even dare to pick a perfect one – a crime, but what an undreamt of delicacy for the pigs! It could take most of an afternoon before the saucepan was brimming and the feeling came over us that there wasn't much more to be done to it now. Then a thorough last stirring, and it was carried to the pig-sty and balanced on the fence above the trough. The pigs would come surging and squealing, and there was an anxious moment before the pan was tipped: it would be disaster if the mush splashed uselessly over a pig's thrusting shoulders instead of into the trough. An opening – quick! . . . and the mush would be poured. One panful between five or six pigs was gone in a flash, of course, but we were sure that quality made up for lack of quantity, and would stand gazing tenderly at the pigs, deeply satisfied at having gratified such an urgent need.

Once a year one of the pigs was slaughtered in the lower yard. It was a good thing to be a girl then, feeling no challenge in this. Andrew, at the age of six, was moved by a mixture of curiosity and bravado to feel that he must watch, but it never occurred to me to do anything but stay as far from the yard as possible. Our cousin John was unable to admit that he felt as I did, so the two little boys went down to the yard together. Johnnie gave way before it was through, which was lucky for my brother, who could bolster his pride by sneering. 'Johnnie was sick – he ran away and was sick into the beech-hedge – but I didn't mind it at all.' His face was still greenish as he spoke, and his eyes were furious and scared. I thought him a fool as well as disgusting.

And in spite of all that bravado over the pig-killing, it was I who had to kill the hedgehog.

Much of what we were taught by our elders we resented or at best endured; a great deal of it we were later to reject; but some things we accepted without question. These things went into our minds as the kind of lore to which additions can be made if experience warrants it, but which is essentially true. Into this category came anything to do with animals, whether tame or wild. This was accepted so readily because our elders' attitude towards animals resembled our own, and also because it was obvious that on this subject the grown-ups knew what they were talking about. One article of the lore concerned sick or maimed animals: they must be cured if possible, but if it wasn't they must be killed quickly and efficiently 'to put them out of their agony'. We had not only been told this, but had seen it in operation. Out with a gentle-hearted aunt, we had come across a rabbit in a trap. We had seen her tempted to believe that it was less badly hurt than it was, but conclude that it could only die a slow death; we had seen her find a heavy stick and, making an obvious effort to overcome pity and revulsion, kill it with a blow to the skull. Hindsight suggests that there was sometimes confusion as to whose agony was being ended, the victim's or the spectator's, but there was no sadism in it: we knew that a hated deed had been performed because it had the moral weight of a duty.

My brother and I found the dying hedgehog in the Cedar Walk – the ornamental plantation which girdled the kitchen garden. It could still move feebly, but something terrible had happened to it and there was a ragged wound in its side. Andrew stooped over it, and recoiled. 'It's got maggots.' I overcame my horror to peer. The hedgehog was rotting alive.

We knew we should kill it. We looked at each other, I hoping he would say 'I'll find a stick.' Instead Andrew backed away and said 'I can't.' This collapse put him in my hands. I could have tormented him with it, but instead I felt suddenly aware of my seniority, and protective. I didn't blame him for dropping his front – he was closer to me for it – and I knew that I must assume responsibility.

A hedgehog has a very small head and a body which, because of its spines, can't be gripped. I couldn't touch it, anyway – my revulsion was such that I could look at it only out of the corners of my eyes. Part of the duty is that death should be instantaneous, so it was out of the question to rain random blows on the hedgehog with a stick: I needed to find a weapon large and heavy enough to be sure of crushing its head even if my aim was not exact. We were near the boiler-house built against the outside of the kitchen-garden wall to heat the vinery on the wall's other side. 'We could put it in the stove,' said Andrew sickly. We knew that we couldn't, but it drew my attention to the building which had recently been repaired. There was a pile of bricks beside it. 'A brick,' I said. 'Suppose you don't hit hard enough?', and I imagined striking the blow only to see the hedgehog worse maimed than before but still alive. But if I put the brick on top of the hedgehog and jumped on it with all my weight . . .

Andrew backed further away. Telling myself, 'Don't think, just do, it's got to be done, don't think,' I ran for the brick, put it in place and jumped, all as fast as I could. There was a sensation rather than a sound of crunching, but I was hardly aware of it; it was as though I were running away from horror so fast that it couldn't catch up. But before I could in fact run I still had to kick the brick away to make sure the hedgehog was finished. I kicked it, and we bolted. Relief that it was over swept away the horror, and pride filled me at having been able to do the impossible. I felt strong, and Andrew was subdued by admiration, but there was no question of triumphing over him because we had shared the experience too closely. Soon we started laughing and pushing each other about. Many years later I was to hear someone arguing that the elation of soldiers coming out of battle after having killed proved the existence of mankind's murderous impulses. 'Fool!' I thought. 'The murderous impulses exist, no doubt, but *that*'s no proof of them. They're elated because they've *survived* killing.' I myself, although I didn't know it then, had used up my whole reservoir of courage for killing. Never again would I be able to put an animal 'out of its agony', however extreme that agony was.

In spite of this concern for animals ours was a hunting, shooting family: many pheasants, partridges, ducks and hares were killed every winter for its pleasure. No foxes – but only because it was not fox country; the hounds were harriers. The children and women often sprang traps set to catch the 'vermin' which might interfere with sport, but the women also walked out with the guns and most of them rode to hounds as soon as they were old enough to handle a pony. We were proud of the good shots and good horsemen among us, and aspired to a similar expertise. We and our cousins would have thought anyone arguing against blood sports thoroughly pubby.

I didn't want to shoot or watch shooting, though I didn't question that shooting was part of adult life; my brother was impatient for his first gun. He had no wish to hunt; I daydreamed about it from the day I was first taken out on a leading-rein. My preference for riding to hounds was determined partly by the fact that the rider does not himself inflict death and needn't even see it, and partly by the inexactness of my eye which meant that I would never be able to shoot well, whereas I was good at riding. Andrew had a good eye but lacked confidence on a horse. Both of us would have adored a tame fox or hare or pheasant, and liked stories of hunted game being saved from pursuers – we could imagine ourselves tricking hounds onto a false scent and sheltering a panting animal in our arms until it could run safely away. We had no inkling of the inconsistency of our attitudes.

The reason why enjoying blood sports and loving animals didn't seem contradictory to us was because the two things occupied different areas of experience. The sports were a matter of acquiring skills which were difficult and exciting to practise, of proving yourself able and brave, and of graduating to the status of adult. And not only did they seem as inevitable as the seasons, but they were felt to be particularly *ours*: class came into it, even for the very young. On the whole 'poor people' didn't hunt or shoot. Those who did, and were good at it, had special merit because their ability was surprising; those who did, and were bad at it, were comic. We felt that these activities and the rituals which surrounded them were somehow part of the superiority with which our families were blessed: an attitude so intrinsic to higher-class rural life at the time that you needed to be distanced from that life in some way in order to escape it.

Against this, loving animals was much like loving people: we didn't think of ourselves as 'loving dogs' or 'loving horses', but as loving Lola and Kim, Acoushla and Cinders. No one was personally acquainted with the animals which were pursued and killed – they were not unlike those distant Chinese children who, it was said, would be glad to eat up cold rice pudding. It was a pity that Chinese children were hungry, and it was a pity that game animals were frightened and killed, but what could you do about it? Whereas your dog and the pony you rode were your *close friends*, and what was more: they shared your pleasures. It was obvious that gun-dogs loved to play their part in a shoot, and that there was nothing a pony enjoyed more than being ridden to hounds.

Take Cinders, for example. He was not my first pony – that had been Molly, a dear old ambulant bean-bag whose role, played to perfection, had been to inspire trust. Cinders was my first pony for proper riding, with whom I continued until I outgrew him at about twelve; and he was a wicked bully. The theory was that because he had not been gelded until he was three, he still believed himself to be a stallion – and he did, indeed, chivvy the mares into groups and threaten approaching rivals although they were all twice his size. He also, when out to grass, used to bully children, so that trying to catch him was always a drama. He would flatten his ears, roll his eyes and chase us back over the fence, then swivel round and launch a kick in our direction as though mocking us. Often we would have to call our mother, who had mastered him long ago by swearing at him in a loud voice and beating him with a walking-stick. He never tried his tricks on her. It took me a long time to summon up the same authority over him, but I finally succeeded. And the lovable thing about Cinders was that once his opponent managed to get a bridle on him he called it quits not only with a good grace but with generosity: no pony displayed more evident enjoyment in our rides, or was more eager to take on a formidable obstacle when out hunting. Once we came to a place where the way out of a field had been blocked by a sheep-pen – a rectangle of hurdles – so that the jump was an in-and-out. I was on the verge of hesitation, but Cinders would have none of that, and bounced me over this double jump so stylishly that when, a few days later, the Master of Hounds met my father he described it as 'a splendid sight'. It must in fact have been nearer comic than splendid – pure Thelwell – because Cinders was a tubby little pony and I, at that time, wore round glasses and two short pigtails which assorted oddly with the bowler hat *de rigueur* when out hunting. But luckily for me, I was aware only of the glory of it. Discovering that you were braver than you thought, and the

On Cinders, when he was very young: 'pure Thelwell'

delightful collaboration with your beloved mount: those were the joys of riding to hounds as far as I was concerned, and firmly though I turned against blood sports once I had grown up, I was never able to regret having once known those joys.

'You 'ont never do it *that* way, bor,' said our best friend, Wilfred, who was the cowman's son, when my brother was trying to knock a tin of paint off a beam in the loft by lashing at it with a piece of cord. He said 'bor' (boy) not because he was much older – he was the same age as I was – but because in Norfolk everyone was 'bor', just as everything was 'little' and 'old' ('That's a funny li'l old car', we might say, hoping to sound like our friend). 'You 'ont never do it that way, bor, that ain't the way to go about it.'

Piqued, my brother said snootily: 'Why do you always say *ain't*? The proper way to say it is *isn't*.'

'You're wrong there,' said Wilfred placidly. 'The proper way to say it is *is not*.'

And snubs to us, I thought, with surprise and pleasure. It was not Wilfred's scoring over my brother that pleased me, but his scoring over both of us, because for a moment I had identified with the jibe and had simultaneously been made to feel uncomfortable by it. For a flash, we had both belonged to a world superior to Wilfred's, which had felt wrong. His answer had demolished that superiority and had given him a dignity which I wanted him to possess. I was, after all, in love with him, though not so passionately as I was with the gardener's boy who was romantically distanced by being in his teens.

If blood sports were as inevitable as the seasons, class differences were as natural as weather; and thus, like the sports, embraced contradictions which we failed to perceive. *Of course* Wilfred was our best friend – we itched every day for the moment when we could scoot across the park to the farm and join him – and a friend not only congenial, but admirable. He went to bed later than we did, for one thing, and ate tinned salmon which we were not allowed, and knew more than we did about farming matters. He was also more sober and responsible than we were, so if he condemned something as silly we expected him to be right. And he was handsome: I often put him in peril in my daydreams so that I could rescue him and perhaps even kiss him before he recovered consciousness. Yet in spite of all this he never came into our house and we never went into his. We might call for him, or he for us, but then the caller would wait shyly by the door while an adult summoned the one called on. And neither side even noticed this.

In spite of taking class too much for granted to question it, we were not unaware of it. We knew it because this whole place belonged to us (to our grandparents, but we made no distinction). The house, the park, the lake, the farm and other farms as far as we ever had occasion to walk or ride: all ours. No other house known to us was so big or appeared on yellowing postcards sold in the village post office. We knew it because when our mother overheard us boasting to a visiting child that the house had twenty bedrooms, she told us afterwards that we must never talk like that: it was ill-bred to boast of what you had to anyone who had less. We knew it because when I had been impertinent to a housemaid I had been sharply scolded: 'You must *never* be rude to servants because, you see, they can't answer back' (they could, and did – but it was true that they couldn't punish me: I saw that, and granted justice to the dictum). We knew it, too, because we had heard grown-ups ask 'Is he not a gentleman?' or describe someone as 'not quite', and the tone of voice was rich in meaning. There was nothing wrong in being a gamekeeper or a ploughman, a butler or a cook, a saddler or a tailor, but these people existed on another plane; and if someone who belonged on that plane tried to behave as though he didn't, he became both deplorable and comic. There was likely to be a strong taint of pubbiness about such a person, and our natural appetite for victims made this idea acceptable. Indeed, we found this little-considered but pervasive sense of class sustaining: one can hardly fail to feel the better for being sure one is the best.

It was rare, however, for us to be offensive – perhaps the *ain't – is not* incident was the only one of its kind between us and Wilfred. We had few occasions for the open exercise of snobbery: most of the people we knew were of our own class or else of the rural working class which was shaped by economics and custom to fit in with ours. Other people were more likely to be seen at a distance than known. There was, for instance, a girl who came out hunting in a top hat and patent-leather boots – a sort of music-hall parody of the clothes worn for hunting in the shires, which even in its purest form would have been 'wrong' in our county, where the pack was an unpretentious one. We were careful not to look at her too pointedly – it was embarrassing that she didn't know that she was a figure of fun – and were civil if we had to speak to her. But when we were among ourselves she was laughed at and despised, and none of us questioned our own attitude.

There was, however, a counter-weight to class snobbery which was felt particularly by children: humility about abilities evidently superior to their own, and about things outside their own experience. A lot of Londoners were said to be very 'common' – but they lived in London! Even when very young these people could find their way about in complex, noisy streets, knew which buses went where, went often to the cinema, ate fish and chips, ice-cream and tinned peaches . . . However unthinkingly our own class-superiority was accepted in theory, in practice it was possible for some 'inferior' person's gifts or sophistication to be seen as impressive and enviable. The smugness was formidable, but it was not quite leak-proof.

Being country children, we were inclined to despise toys: doing something with real objects was more satisfying than playing with sham ones. Beloved White Rabbit, back almost in my babyhood, was a person not a toy. Andrew's comforter was a ragged bit of shawl called Shollah Baa; Patience's was a blanket called Blanket; mine was White Rabbit. He didn't have much hair, sat up on his hind legs, and held a carrot between his paws: and I wouldn't know that I'd thought of him as a person if I didn't remember so clearly what I felt when they took him away.

He had lost one eye and his carrot, his ears had twice come off and been sewn on again by Nanny, he was no longer white. But what decided them – my mother and Nanny – that he must go was that he'd started to leak sawdust into my cot every night. They must have had a discussion about how he could be removed without distressing me too much, and my mother must have been delighted when she hit on a solution: she went back to the shop where she had bought him and found that they still had his twin. So one evening when I went to bed I found, to my horror, a stranger lying on my pillow.

I howled. And the more they kept saying 'But look – he's just the same' the worse it was. How could they not understand that someone looking like someone else didn't mean that he *was* that person? They had taken White Rabbit away, and what had they done to him? Where was he now? He was all alone, he was lost – it was dreadful to think what he must be feeling . . . and Mummy couldn't understand that this silly white stranger couldn't possibly make it better. Indeed White Rabbit was not a toy: he gave me my first experience of grief for another's pain, and my first awareness that grown-ups could be fallible.

Later, I had just two toys worth playing with, the first of which was my farm. The lead animals arrived in flocks at birthdays and Christmases, until they covered a good part of the drawing room floor when properly set out. There were buildings, tractors, wagons and people, too – and fencing, though never enough of that. 'What do you want for your farm this Christmas?' – 'More fencing.' – 'Are you sure, darling? Isn't it rather dull?' They didn't see that I needed to enclose more land because it was absurd to have cows, sheep, horses and pigs all in one field, as they never were in real life. What I envisaged was a *proper* farm, with a realistic number of enclosures, even some fields empty of animals because they were down to wheat or sugar-beet . . .

The Meccano set, too, reproduced real things: cranes which lifted loads, bridges which could be winched up to let ships through. Because I was lazy, and was believed to have little practical sense, everyone was surprised when I commandeered this set which belonged to Johnnie who was away at school. I was clever with it, working patiently on elaborate constructions, and (as I'd been with the farm) anxious to possess more parts so that I could achieve greater verisimilitude. But this addiction was so uncharacteristic that no one trusted it to last, and Meccano was expensive – so 'my' set was reclaimed by its owner, and I accepted that my interest in it had been no more than a whim . . . accepted, but with regret. I had an inkling that unrecognized capabilities were being written off. And I was right. Many years later, first needlepoint, then dress-making, then gardening were to prove that I am indeed much better at doing things with my hands than my elders, followed by myself, had supposed.

Laziness: it was laziness that made one drift in the direction towards which they pushed one. In spite of the energy children put into their activities, it is inertia which most threatens their development into rational beings ('Why can't you behave like a rational being?' an early governess, much despised, used to say to me – so often that the expression became a joke, meaning nothing but this woman's silliness). Our greatest pleasures were those which were most accessible. Like almost all children we thought jelly the most delicious of foods, and jelly is the food which offers least resistance. Do what is fun, don't do what is difficult: that was the principle we followed. And the grown-ups, recognizing that this principle is innate in everyone, believed that our upbringing should combat it. They thought it would be hard on us to grow up unaware that people often have to do things they don't immediately want to do – not only to fit in with other people but also, sometimes, to reach ends desired by themselves.

So you must wash your hands before coming to the table; you must shut – not bang – doors behind you; you must remember to say 'please' and 'thank-you'; given chocolates, you must offer them round before eating one yourself; you mustn't shove or grab or shout; you must go to bed without fuss when the time comes: 'manners', though considered important in themselves, were also insisted on as being character-forming. The rules, laid down clearly, reached back to a time before we could remember, so that following them wasn't painful. We would not have observed them if we had not been made to, but we didn't resent them more than any other tiresome but inevitable thing such as thistles in grass or pebbles on beaches. It seemed natural to me that I should be made to conform to certain patterns of social behaviour, just as it seemed natural that I had to sit down to lessons, like it or not (though I should not have believed it if someone had told me that I would end up deeply grateful for having been taught how to parse a sentence).

In theory grown-ups, particularly our mother, would have liked to go further in character-forming. She saw the social viability conferred by these mild disciplines as minimal, and would have liked us to become individuals of exceptional ability and virtue. What we would need for this was 'will-power'.

She had a decisive, even slightly high-handed manner and bright blue eyes, so she used to appear formidable when she spoke of will-power. We understood it to be something by which the old Adam could be controlled, the lazy could become energetic, the stupid clever. Together with 'self-control' it propped an austere ideal: a way of life in which you were indifferent to comfort, ate only for the energy food provides, never thought about yourself, and accomplished great achievements.

It was an attractive idea. When I was about eleven it seemed to me that I only had to get the knack of it and I would be able to move mountains – or at least an oak tree (I was riding through the park as I thought this). I decided then and there that every day I would do one thing I didn't want to do, limbering up gradually to mountain-moving strength. As I advanced in the discipline I would become able to do long division, then my painful progress through Latin would become swift and smooth, and then greater rewards would appear – power not only over myself (might I become able to levitate?) but over other people and things. The kind of achievement will-power would make possible blurred in my mind with the rewards of faith, which were also sometimes canvassed, though in church and scripture lessons rather than by my mother. To silence a thunderstorm, for instance, by saying 'Peace, be still', as Jesus had done: I had failed when I tried to do that because the muscles of my will were still too feeble: I would have to believe *much* more strongly if I was going to bring it off. Surely getting out of bed the minute I woke up in the morning, or saying 'no' to a peach at dessert would be a small daily price to pay for being able to do that?

Not, however, one single step in this programme did I take: by the next day my mind was occupied with other things. And this was also exactly what happened to my mother who, in spite of her positive manner, was as far as any child from putting her principles into practice. However authoritatively she spoke about will-power, her only conspicuous exercise of it was in getting what she wanted; and although I didn't consciously compare the image of my mother as austere and puritanical with that of my mother in action, or draw any recognized conclusion from these obviously contradictory images, both images were nevertheless there: it was an evident fact of life that stern resolutions were more often broken than kept.

Luckily this was also true about pocket money. Just as Mum would have liked to have had will-power, so she would have liked to have been sensible about money. If her own upbringing had equipped her badly for this there was all the more reason to see to it that her children's equipped them well. Her usual slapdash way of handing out pennies or sixpences whenever we wanted to buy sweets or an ice-cream would obviously lead us to suppose money appeared from the blue whenever we wanted: it would be unfair to us and likely to lead to tiresomeness, as she knew from her own experience. So: 'From today you are each going to get sixpence a week pocket money, and you'll have to think very carefully how you spend it because you won't get a penny more.' Each time she said this we felt alarmed. Her manner was so firm that we couldn't doubt the reality of the tedious responsibility with which we were now going to have to live. How depressing, simply *not being able* to buy a pennyworth of acid drops on a Thursday because of Tuesday's fudge: trotting across the park to make delicious choices in the little post-office-cum-village-shop was one of life's pleasures. But it would be weak and babyish not to accept the challenge, so we would take our first sixpences and soberly resolve to do our best.

The first sixpences of a pocket money drive were always the last. What with one thing and another she would forget about it.

Once she had an idea about our upbringing which was supposed to be liberating rather than disciplinary. She had met a high-minded and progressive couple, and she must at that time have been in a mood of defiance against her own background. No doubt she thought it odd, at first, that their children called them by their first names, and even odder that none of their doors was ever locked, so that a child could enter the bathroom while its father or mother was naked in the bath, but after the first surprise she took to these ideas, suddenly seeing that the time had come to prove herself a modern mother. She came home from that visit bright-eyed, though a little less decisive than usual: she didn't say we *must* call her and Dad by their Christian names, only that we could if we wanted to; and that because it was silly and unhealthy to be embarrassed by nakedness, she *wouldn't mind* if we happened to see her without clothes. Clearly she was half-hoping for these innovations rather than ordaining them. 'Good heavens!' was what we thought, staring at her with a mixture of admiration and embarrassment at her daring. We saw at once that she was doing the sort of thing we did ourselves, defying the established order in a fit of 'over-excitement'. It was generous of her, but it was also foolish. We did try out their Christian names once or twice, for the fun of it, but 'Mummy' and 'Daddy' meant what they meant, whereas the names were empty, so there was no point in going on with it. And as for seeing my mother and father naked – that was a most uncomfortable idea. Child to child, nakedness was nothing; child to adult, it was outside our experience and ought to stay there. So progressive informality went the way of pocket money. Lines of conduct or systems of any sort, apart from those hallowed by custom, were too much trouble to keep up. Our laziness, although it was often chided by the grown-ups, was sheltered by theirs.

My own lack of will-power worried me in only one way, which fortunately cropped up only when lessons included doing sums. At these I was so bad that I felt it must be blameworthy. The others understood 'fractions' and 'decimals' quite easily, so surely I too ought to be able to understand them – surely if I tried hard enough

I could? I never did, so that must mean that although I felt that I was trying hard enough, I wasn't. I was never bullied about it – indeed, much kindness and patience went into attempts to help me – but I still felt twinges of guilt from time to time. It wasn't until many years into adulthood that I learnt something that suggested the incapacity was not my fault.

Five counters of different colours lined up on a table; the three-year-old child, already so good at the alphabet, being taught to count: one, two, three, four, five. I get it right at once and Mummy is delighted: 'Look, she can count up to five already!' But by the time an audience has collected the counters have been shuffled, and this time I say 'Five, two, four, three, one'. 'No, darling . . .' but I insist 'Yes'. They try again and again, until suddenly someone understands that I had never been counting, I had been naming. The yellow counter at the end of the row is called 'five', and it is still called 'five' when it comes at the beginning. They have to give up or I would be in tears at their misunderstanding. It was many days before I grasped what they meant by 'counting', and I was to remain a namer, not a numberer, for the rest of my life: a trait as innate as colour blindness, for which I could justifiably feel regret, but not guilt.

Guilt never caused me any serious distress, but humiliation did: humiliation, even if caused by something trivial, hit directly on surface nerves and was the sharpest misery I knew. To look silly. As soon as I took it into my head that something made me look silly, it became impossible to bear.

'Oh, do stop grizzling. Look, if you're really cold get down and run – that'll warm you up in no time.' Seven years old, I was perched on the front seat of the dog-cart between Mum and Revel, the groom. It was a bitter afternoon in January and we were bouncing over the frozen tussocks of Longmeadow, having taken a bale of hay up to some ponies out to grass. Much of the family's time was spent in such occupations, pleasures disguised as jobs and pursued as earnestly as any job. Revel could have taken the hay out by himself, but the dog-cart existed, yellow and black, elegant on its high wheels in a wasp-like way, and there was a young mare who would look good in it if she could be broken to harness. Mum was working at this, making use of opportunities to drive her out over the fields, getting her accustomed to being between shafts before taking her out to meet traffic on the roads. We had a car, so it was not necessary to have a horse and cart. It was simply fun that could be taken seriously.

Fun in theory, at least. To me, that day, it was extremely disagreeable. I had on my gum-boots, my fleecy gloves, and a huge scarf over my coat, crossed over my chest and fastened in the small of my back with a safety-pin. I was also wearing two jerseys, a liberty-bodice and a woolly vest, and my black velour hat with its domed crown and saucer brim – a sure indication of exceptional coldness, because we hardly ever wore hats. I was so bundled up that movement was difficult, and within the bundling I was becoming colder and colder, fingers going white and numb within the thick gloves, feet in agony within the socks lining the boots. Naturally I had been pleased to go out for this drive, because I took it for granted that the dog-cart was 'fun'; but now that we had turned towards home so that the wind was in our faces, pinching our noses to blue and making our eyes stream, I started to whimper and complain.

'Get down and run,' said Mum impatiently, pulling the mare to a halt. 'No, I don't want to.' – 'Oh, for heaven's sake – go on, hop down quickly.' – '*No . . .*' and the whimpering became a howl. Couldn't Mum see what I could see: the dog-cart rattling off over the field, while behind – falling ever further behind – stumbled an absurd little figure, its gum-boots tripping over frozen molehills, its arms sticking out because of the thickness of its wrappings, its silly hat like a black mushroom bobbing against the white background of hoarfrost? *Think how absurd that figure would look to Revel!* So what if running would make me warm – I would rather die of cold than become that figure in this admired man's eyes.

'*Why* won't you get down?' asked my exasperated mother. 'Because it would be so silly,' I sobbed. 'But it's much sillier to sit here snivelling and freezing.' Howl – howl – howl, because that was true, and Revel, who was keeping out of the scene, staring ahead in an abstracted way, must already have thought me very stupid. But now getting down seemed worse than ever, because the ridiculous figure would be sobbing, its nose would be running, it would be a disgraceful spectacle as well as a comic one – not only my mind, but every muscle in my body locked in refusal of this humiliation.

Another humiliation, even worse, came at about the same time from a sudden reversal of my role in a public place. My mother had taken Andrew and me up to London on one of our rare excursions to buy shoes or visit the dentist. These trips were exciting because moving staircases, the underground, buses, taxis, lifts, crowds – all the commonplaces of London life – were unfamiliar enough to be glamorous. Mum, more beautiful than ever in her best clothes, became extraordinarily impressive because of her assurance: her certainty as to which bus to take, her ability to swoop through the dazzle and glitter of a huge shop straight from the door to the department we needed. To us London was high life, and its highest points were reached in restaurants.

Because the object of these trips was usually Daniel Neal's, the children's clothing specialists, or a dentist or doctor in the Harley Street area, we would lunch in one of Oxford Street's big stores: Marshall & Snelgrove, Debenham & Freebody, or John Lewis. That a restaurant covered a vast floor space and contained a great many tables made it all the grander to us – Lyons' Corner House would have thrilled us. We would be hushed with pleasurable expectation as the lift carried us up, watching the lift-man's skilful manipulation of his machine with admiration. Sometimes he had to adjust the level before the doors would slide open smoothly – an inch or two up or down, so that we could step out gracefully onto the silencing carpet of the restaurant floor. Then a black-gowned lady would cast a general's eye over the confusing vista of tables, single one out and usher us towards it. All would be bustle and tinkle, but muted, and the tablecloths and cutlery, being unlike our own at home, must surely be more elegant.

We knew in advance what we would choose from the menu:

fried fish, in its crisply golden coat of breadcrumbs, and fruit salad. We never had fried food at home because it was considered unhealthy, and all the fruit we ate, whether cooked or not, was fresh, so the jewel colours, bland texture and syrupy sweetness of tinned fruit salad was to us unspeakably delicious. We were sure that restaurant food was food at its rarest and best.

My romanticism made me relish these occasions even more than Andrew did. He, although he enjoyed the food and the excitement, never wavered in his certainty that the country was best, whereas I could easily be seduced by notions of sophistication and the *mondaine*. So when at the end of one such lunch he wanted to pee and I didn't, I was pleased to be left alone at the table while Mum took him to the cloakroom. I pushed my chair a little way from the table, hooked an elbow over the back of it, and began to examine the lunching ladies, seeing their hats, furs, gloves and handbags as very smart.

Suddenly it occurred to me that now I was on my own at the table, anyone noticing me might think me *alone in London*. They might suppose that I had been doing my shopping all by myself, was in the restaurant and had ordered my meal all by myself, and was going to pay for it all by myself with money out of my own pocket. How deeply impressed they would be if they thought this! Some of the ladies might be whispering to each other even now, 'Look at that little girl over there, lunching all by herself in a restaurant and so *young*!' This idea enchanted me, and I began carefully to adjust my pose to one of greater nonchalance and assurance. I let one hand dangle over the back of the chair while with the other I 'toyed' with a fork; I tilted my head at what I was sure was a graceful angle, and willed my face into an expression of blasé hauteur. My eyebrows arched, my lips drooped; with perfect conviction I felt my face become that of one of the beautiful mannequins I had admired in Mum's copies of *Vogue*. (They were 'mannequins', not 'models' in those days: 'models' took clothes off, rather than showed them off, being the people who posed for artists.)

I was so deep in this role that I didn't notice Mum and Andrew weaving their way back towards me through the tables. The first I knew of their return was Mum's furious whisper: 'For God's sake sit up straight and stop gaping – everyone will think you're half-witted!' I was too stunned by the humiliation of it to cry.

Incidents – and there were many – in which something wished on us by my elders seemed an affront to my dignity, or in which my own image of myself betrayed me into absurdity, were the cause of the most acute mortification I experienced, but it cannot be said that they harmed me. They resulted in dignity's becoming less touchy and more discriminating, and behaviour better judged. Perhaps a more delicate understanding of my susceptibilities might have hindered more than it helped: the quickest way to learn to avoid or humour wasps is to be stung by one.

The restaurant of a big store was not in our eyes what it was in our mother's, nor was the flavour of its food on our tongues what it was on hers. We saw grandeur in size and quantity, deliciousness in sweetness and softness. We were easily moved to admire beauty, but had no idea of 'taste'.

Satin was beautiful because it was sleek; pink was beautiful because it was the colour of roses. So pink satin was very beautiful. So if you could have an enormous room decorated in pink with satin curtains and upholstery, it would be breathtaking, and it would be even better if all the furniture were made of gold and silver, because gold and silver were beautiful for their shininess.

It was the same with pictures. Brightness and richness were what moved us – and also the picture's subject. In an illustration to a story about children lost in a forest, the children must look like real children and the forest must be elaborately leafy and thorny and dark: we were bored and disappointed if the shapes were simplified and the colours flat. However clever the use of a few flat colours, however enticing those colours in themselves, they were not showing us what we wanted to see. And if an illustration which grown-ups saw as deplorably vulgar *did* show us what we wanted, and showed it with an ebullience of detail and colour, then we loved it.

Luckily no one bothered much about educating our taste. Every now and then someone who didn't know us very well would give us for Christmas an artily illustrated book and we would ignore it; and every now and then some grown-up would make it clear that he or she thought comics dreadfully ugly, and we would think 'Oh well, grown-ups!' On the whole we were allowed to go on seeing the redness of red and the blueness of blue, even if that red and blue together were boringly 'obvious', and experiencing the sadness of sad and the happiness of happy, even if the story which embodied them was painfully sentimental. And there was plenty of more grown-up reading about if we felt like turning to it, which of course we would do sooner or later.

My favourite picture when I was about eleven, more evocative in my eyes even than illustrations by Edmund Dulac or Arthur Rackham, both of whom I loved, was a particularly insipid drawing of a princess in a fairy story by A. A. Milne. This princess, whose anatomy was quite lost in the swirls of her floating hair and raiment (indeed from the disposition of the swirls she could not have *had* any anatomy), happened to have features which I coveted: a swan-like neck and clouds of black hair. And her dress, supposing any body could have been found ethereal enough to wear it, was wonderfully becoming. The artist had studied Beardsley, so that feeble though the drawing was, it contained echoes of a dreamy decadence. Time and again I would turn back to it, unable to see why my mother and my governess could see nothing in it. To me it was the essence of unattainable elegance – and it was witty, too: there was something about the way the jewelled slipper peeped out, the fingers tapered and the necklace was implied by playful dots which suggested wit. A real Beardsley might have alarmed me. From this bad drawing I was getting as much pleasure and stimulation as I would get from a real Beardsley when I was older, without any reference to the artist's skill, simply because this, I was sure, was how the princess in the story looked and dressed. And when I discovered Beardsley I did not appreciate him the less for having been seduced by his feeble imitator: instead I enjoyed him the more because he reminded me of my princess.

'Art' was the engraving of *Dignity and Impudence* above the nursery fireplace, and the three watercolours by my great-grandfather on the wall opposite the nursery windows, only one of which was interesting because it was a little bit like the view of the gamekeeper's cottage near the weir although, disappointingly, it was actually a picture of some unknown place in Yorkshire. Later 'art' stretched to include two pleasant silvery-blue East Anglian landscapes by Arnesbury Brown, bought by my grandfather and much more attractive than the other downstairs pictures, most of which were all but invisible behind brown varnish. But – oddly – 'art' did not include the five best pictures in the house.

These were portraits of people I knew, so I didn't think of them in terms of artistry. They would have been bad if the likeness had been at fault, but since in all of them it was excellent I saw the drawings of my aunts Peggy, Joyce and Doro and of my uncle Bill simply as *them*, as a photograph would have been; and would have seen the oil painting of my mother in the same way if she had not loathed it so much that I had to suppose that there was something wrong with it.

They were all by William Strang, a painter chosen by my grandfather because – I guess – Strang's portraits made him think of Holbein. One of the most precious books in Gramps's library was a huge volume, to be looked at only with the utmost carefulness, of Holbein portraits. Because the faces revealed when you turned back the tissues between the pages were often quite old and plain, they did not interest me, but I respected them because we all knew that they were greatly admired by Gramps. There must have been something special about the reproductions to make the book so precious – and indeed, when I think of the book now what I see with my mind's eye resembles the real thing so convincingly that they must have been exceptionally good.

William Strang drew beautifully and was a gravely honest observer: his portraits do have much of Holbein's entranced delicacy of line and calm closeness of attention: Gramps had chosen well.

My mother detested her portrait because it was such a good painting of a self-conscious seventeen-year-old resenting the ordeal

My mother, by William Strang, 1912

of sitting for it. She had not wanted to be 'done'; and when told that she must put up with it had thought that she would be asked to change into a becoming frock, but Mr Strang said no, her beastly old blue serge would do. Then, when he sent her out to pick a few of the wallflowers which were struggling against the frost – it was a bitter day – and she jammed them into a glass just anyhow, expecting him to arrange them attractively, he simply left them like that. And then he wanted her raised up a bit so he made her sit on two cushions, only to go ahead and *paint* the cushions instead of making it look as though the chair were the right height, *and* he painted her hands all red and hideous, which they were of course, but only because it was such a cold day. And on top of all that she couldn't think of a thing to say to the horrid man, so he obviously considered her a bore, and because he was so bored by her he hadn't bothered to make her look nice. Given her own way, she would have burnt that portrait.

Almost ninety years later her nephew Philip, who now owns it, lent it to Norwich museum for an exhibition of Norfolk portraits. When I reached the room devoted to the twentieth century, there was Kitty Carr, dominating it. What an eye-opener! Not till that moment had I been able to see through my mother's prejudice to the painting itself, and fully recognize its quality. It was easily the best painting in that gallery.

If art was a small and random collection of objects, music was an even smaller thing: scales and 'The Merry Peasant' thumped out laboriously under the tuition of Miss Doe, who visited once a week from our local market town, and was kind but not inspiring. Luckily this dispiriting introduction was counter-balanced by three Gilbert and Sullivan records and one of Paul Robeson singing 'Water Boy' and 'Swing Low, Sweet Chariot', all of which we loved and often played, which had been bought by an aunt and lived in a dark corner of the morning room with a small dusty gramophone. And another, even more thrilling glimpse of what music might be like was granted to Andrew and me when we were taken to Norwich to see our first (and for a long time only) movie: *Ben Hur*. Among the incidental music to it (played, I suppose, on a piano in front of the screen) was Schumann's 'Träumerei', by which we were ravished, and which someone unearthed when we got home in a pile of old sheet-music on the morning-room upright piano. I was able to pick out a little of the right hand, and did so over and over again to our delight; though I think we were enjoying the screened images it evoked more than the music itself. This little sprinkling of musical seed would have to lie dormant for a long time.

My parents bought their first wireless (as we called radios then) when I was eleven and we were living for two years in Hertfordshire. We were allowed to listen at tea-time when Henry Hall's dance band was playing, and soon became addicted to our favourite tunes, but we never imagined seeing the music-makers in the flesh or even buying records. We had no gramophone in that house, and I cannot remember anyone having a wireless in my grandmother's. Even in my late teens, when I was besotted by tunes I had danced to such as 'Smoke Gets in Your Eyes' and 'I've Got You Under My Skin', my only way of submerging myself in them between the times when I heard them at dances was by picking them out on the piano or singing them in the bath.

What you have never had you don't miss: we did not feel deprived of entertainment, and thought it natural that going to London to see *Peter Pan* should be a unique event. We got our kicks from what was at hand: reading, riding, picnics, swimming in the icy North Sea, dances, acting in our own plays, Bonfire Night, Christmas, Easter, Harvest Festival. Unlike most modern children we knew who Guy Fawkes was and why we burnt him on Bonfire Night (though I am glad to say we were taught that he was a baddie simply because he had tried to blow up parliament, not because he was a Catholic – slightly surprising in a household so prejudiced against Roman Catholicism). Of all the feasts, Christmas was of course the best . . . but no public entertainment has ever thrilled me more than my first Harvest Festival.

The excitement started the day before, when we went with cousins armed with walking-sticks and thick gloves to a neglected field (I suppose its clay soil was too heavy to be worth cultivating) where the tussocky grass was full of thistles and the surrounding hedges, dense with brambles, were almost tree-high. It was the best place for picking long sprays of bramble loaded with blackberries, some already ripe, some still red or green – and that was what the walking-sticks with their hooked handles and the thick gloves were for. With these sprays, next morning, a leather-gauntleted aunt was going to wreathe the font in the church – and we also had to find bunches of scarlet hips and haws with which she could punctuate her wreath.

Every autumn has one or two days which are perfect, and this was such a day: still, sunlit, the sky's blue very soft, almost silvery, because of the faintest possible hint of mist in the air. A long vista on such a day resembles a Chinese scroll-painting, the lower parts of trees and hills delicately veiled, their tops clear against the sky; and even a close-up of a hedge is simultaneously softened and enriched by the atmosphere. And there is the smell of autumn, as faint and pervasive as the mist – leaves beginning to decay? The smoke of bonfires? Stillness, light, colour, scent – all combine into a perfection made poignant because soon – so soon! – it will be over.

The sweet sorrow of parting, sadness as luxury – it is odd that young children should be susceptible to such a feeling, but Andrew and I certainly were. We loved having tears brought to our eyes by the cuckoo's call, which seemed to us in certain moods like the voice of innumerable vanished summers; and the evanescence of autumn's perfection made our hearts ache in the same delicious way.

And the next day after this lovely one was going to be even better, because we were going to be allowed to stay up for the Harvest Festival service. Our usual bedtime was six-thirty (we were six and four years old, put to bed at the same time for Nanny's convenience). The service began just when we were normally being tucked in, but we would be there! We were going to be out in the darkness of night, under the huge red harvest moon, and then in the brilliant church, and then, when we got home, we were going to have not ordinary bedtime milk and biscuits, but *real supper*!

And the church truly *was* brilliant. As soon as we were through the door, there was the font under its rich wild wreath, surrounded by pyramids of fruit and vegetables with a vast and glorious golden pumpkin as the centre-piece. All the ends of the pews, the whole way up the aisle, had sheaves of wheat and oats and barley tied to them. The screen and the pulpit were lavishly decorated with dahlias, michaelmas daisies and chrysanthemums mixed with more wheat, oats and barley, and in each window's wide recess a different still-life had been composed, some of them including loaves of bread and baskets of eggs (custom dictated who decorated which window, and they vied with each other to splendid effect). It would have been gorgeous enough in daylight, and in the glow of lamp and candlelight it was magical. *And* – for us this was an enchanting finishing touch – there were bats flittering about up near the roof; *and* the hymns were the best we had ever heard. We were so much taken with one of them that we went on chanting it for days afterwards:

> We plough the fields and sca-a-tter
> The good seed on the land
> But it is fed and wa-a-tered
> By God's almighty hand . . .

I still sometimes sing that hymn when I'm driving, safely out of the hearing of anyone with a good ear.

Lessons, though accepted with docility, were not interesting and were always much the same whoever was being our governess because our parents subscribed to a system of home education called P.N.E.U. It supplied the textbooks and even, I think, the timetables, and it set us exams from time to time which it marked – not that anyone, parents, governesses or pupils, ever paid any attention to this ritual. The best thing about P.N.E.U. was that it disapproved of tiring minds, which meant that all the lessons were very short. Perhaps we sometimes did lessons in the afternoon, but if so it was not often: I can't remember any, and the importance of being out of doors was an article of faith with the whole family, so that the grown-ups would have been against it.

The first two of the seven governesses we had came into the category 'Nursery Governess' which meant that they taught Andrew as well as me. When he was sent off to his preparatory school at the age of eight, my schoolroom companions were my cousin Pen, and various daughters of neighbours who shared the cost of the governess with my parents. The nursery governesses were unlucky, because they superseded Nanny, whom we loved – and the first of them was the unluckiest because she was French as well. Her accent, her clothes, the way she used knives and forks, her nervousness of animals, her smell of eau de Cologne and her unhappiness all made her unacceptable. She suffered severely from the cold, hated the food, and must have felt miserably lonely, stuck away so deep in this foreign country in a household where the adults found her presence a bore and were no more than civil to her, and her charges were resentful. This forlornness was a guarantee of failure because, like animals, we responded to assurance in our handlers: lack of it made us uneasy and hostile, quick to take advantage of feeble gestures of propitiation and rebellious against inept attempts to be firm. What we learnt from her was two words of French – *tais-toi* – and the simultaneously exciting and shocking fact, hitherto unsuspected, that children can be cruel to adults.

The first of the real governesses frightened us and the single term that she was with us has become a little capsule of oblivion: I no longer have any idea of what she did or how our mother realized that she must get rid of her at once, only a vague memory of the relief I felt when she had gone. Surely if she had done anything dramatically cruel to us it would have stuck in my mind, so I suspect it was nothing worse than irritability and lack of kindness – which, considering that no one had ever been even the least bit nasty to us, would have been enough to dismay us.

After her came the regular governesses. They left quickly, if they were boring because we saw them off, if they were charming because they got married, until we came to dear Ursula who was absorbed into the family and remained with us until I was sent to boarding school at the age of fourteen. She ought to have been a failure because she was plain, but it took her only a few days to win me over, and my mother too. She was kind, sensible, funny, easy-going. She loved animals and she found the P.N.E.U. syllabus as boring as I did, so she varied it with agreeable inventions of her own. Everybody liked having Ursula in the house, and I was to feel deeply indignant on her behalf when I got to school and the headmistress described me as the least well-grounded girl who had ever come her way.

One of Ursula's strengths was that she fully understood the importance of horses: she was almost as good as Mum at mastering Cinders. She was the daughter of a country parson, and I suppose her family background must have been similar to our own.

By the time she arrived I had long stopped *being* a horse – grazing on green patches of carpet, drinking from blue ones, stamping and pawing the ground, shying when alarmed. That had ended not long after the wedding at which I, a five-year-old bridesmaid, had become a family joke by standing in the aisle whisking my fringed sash behind me and nibbling my posy of flowers. By age ten or so I had reached the stage of daydreaming the perfect horse, an exquisite grey, half Arab for the fine head and fiery eye, half Irish hunter for its ability to soar over huge obstacles. I would settle down to this dream with relish, first establishing the horse's appearance, then grooming it and harnessing it faultlessly, and the dream would trail off into frustration because the relationship didn't offer enough complexity. It felt much the same as those I would have a little later about dressing for a dance where I would meet someone to fall in love with, but it didn't provide enough material for the feelings to feed on.

Our real horses – or rather ponies – were not dreamt about any more than members of the family. There was never a time when I longed for a real pony, because I always had one. To begin with, one was put into a little wicker chair-saddle, sitting sideways on a donkey or the ancient pony who – wearing leather boots strapped over her hooves – pulled the lawnmower. Then, when legs had become long enough to straddle though not yet long enough to reach stirrups, there would be a soft felt saddle on dear old Molly. We never went on walks along roads anyway, and it was easier for a mother, grandmother or nanny to lead an animal across fields than it was to push a pram. 'Sit up straight', 'keep your heels down', 'don't jab at her mouth', were instructions given not in the form of 'riding lessons' but in the same way as 'don't talk with your mouth full' or 'shut the door after you'. By the time a child was enough in control to be let off the leading-rein she would be at home on a pony, and by the age of about ten she needed no encouragement to become enthusiastic about horse management.

For some six to eight years the books Pen and I most wanted to receive at Christmas and birthdays were horse books. I accumulated a big collection of them: not only stories about girls (it was always girls) and their ponies, but also technical books on horse care and training. After Andrew had gone to school, Pen and I spent hours in the harness-room cleaning bits, soaping saddles and rubbing neat's-foot oil into reins and stirrup-leathers to keep them supple. At twelve we knew all there is to know about looking after and schooling a pony, and could put our knowledge into practice. The only reason why we were good riders rather than excellent ones, and our ponies adequately schooled rather than faultlessly so, was laziness. Schooling a horse to perfection requires almost as much dedication and self-discipline as training to be a ballet dancer – tedious exercises must be carried out every day and never skimped – and we would go about it only spasmodically because the temptation of riding simply for fun was too strong. Therefore, although I could go well out hunting, I was not exceptional when the finer points of horsemanship were called for. In the show-ring, if I did well in a jumping competition I always knew it was the result of luck: my pony had *happened* to take off the right distance before each fence, whereas the serious horseman is able to contrive that it will do so. I felt guilty about this.

But not guilty enough to spoil pleasure. The extension of power offered by a pony, the ease and speed of movement, the tapping of unsuspected courage, the satisfaction of collaboration with another creature and of controlling it in order to improve that collaboration, the joy of fussing over it – of loving it – these, from the age of about eight to about sixteen were the most completely realized delights of my life. The smell of a pony was good to me. I would kiss its velvety muzzle with sensuous pleasure, and every shape and texture it offered was familiar and congenial to my hands. There was hardly a movement a horse could make which I could not interpret. A horse will rest a back hoof just to rest it, or again, in a slightly different way, because it needs to urinate. It is uncomfortable for it to urinate if the full weight of its rider is resting on the hollow of its back: the rider should pitch his weight forward onto its withers to allow it the necessary freedom. To see another rider failing to interpret this signal would anger me: how could anyone who rode be so insensitive and inconsiderate? And how could anyone fail to know that his horse was thirsty, or was about to roll, or was being chafed by its girth? The ignorance and stupidity – the *pubbiness* – of anyone who didn't understand horses was beyond question.

Each animal being different, it was naturally impossible for my relationships with all of them to be equally harmonious. With one it was straightforward friendship, with another a concerned and slightly anxious love because it was too highly strung for its own good. And with Cinders, of course, it was a mock-battle of wills. Even when he was very old, almost as broad as he was long, his blue-roan coat gone frosty grey, he was up to his tricks. I would go out to pass the time of day with him as he dozed under a tree, and he would make a lunge at me; I would slap his nose, laughing, and he would lower his head to present his little furry ears for a rub, apparently knowing it was all a joke as well as I did.

We all anthropomorphized our animals to some extent, but were usually prevented by the attentiveness of our observation from doing it to the point of sentimentality. Indeed, it might be more accurate to say that we came nearer to seeing humans as animals. The study of animal behaviour was not generally recognized as a science at the time – certainly the public was still unaware of its

bearing on the study of human behaviour – but when popular
books began to be published on its findings I felt that it was all very
familiar: it was no news to me that the habits of a vole, a goose or
a chimpanzee could be linked with my own.

Me on Acoushla; Patience on Patsy; Pen on Zingaro; Anne on Nora, 1928

THE HOUSE

THE HOUSE AND estate which conditioned our lives and bred our smugness was not, in fact, what we and our cousins felt it to be: a place that had belonged to us 'for ever'. It had been bought by our great-grandfather, a Yorkshire doctor who had married money, and then was left even more by a grateful patient, a Miss Greenwood. The legacy must have been quite substantial because my grandfather, his only son, was given her name: William Greenwood Carr. And the 'county' pleasures of hunting and shooting were not, as they seemed to be, bred into our bones. That same great-grandfather's parents, whose generation had moved from the yeomanry to the professions (medicine and law), were serious-minded Yorkshire people who believed that the most valuable thing money could buy was education, and had sent their son to Oxford. There, being a lover of horses, he took to riding to hounds. His mother, unpacking for him when he came home at the end of a winter term, found top boots and a pink coat, and was deeply shocked. The young man was told that he had not been sent south to scamper across the countryside with a lot of idle spendthrifts – and was told it so severely that he never rode again, but channelled his love of horses into breeding handsome pairs of them to draw his carriage. Nor did his son, our grandfather, ride, except to jog about his farms. It was our parent's generation – some of them – who had taken to 'county' ways.

My grandfather in his turn would dismay his father while at

Gran's house, 1920s

Oxford, on his part of their climb away from their roots: an incident preserved not by family legend, like the top boots and pink coat, but in four letters in the mass of correspondence kept by my grandmother: four letters which happened to be among those that I read after her death.

They were written in Yorkshire in the late 1870s – my great-grandparents had not yet moved south – and were addressed to their son William at University College. The first was only a few lines – a shot across the bows that must have given Willy a nasty turn – announcing that Papa is so dismayed that he cannot at the moment say anything more: he will be writing at length as soon as he has been able to regain his composure. The second letter explains his shock. Willy had written to say that he had asked for the hand in marriage of Margaret Bright, one of the four daughters of the Master of his college.

On first reading I assumed from the opening lines of this letter that Doctor Carr was outraged because he supposed his son to have fallen for a girl below his station – 'What a pompous old horror,' I thought. The tone was too agitated to be just a matter of 'Don't be absurd, boy, you are much too young to think of marrying', which would not have been unreasonable. But I soon saw that I was wrong. Papa was in a panic, and the panic was at the boy's presumption: he was aghast at what Dr Bright – 'that distinguished scholar and gentleman' – must be thinking of the impertinent advantage taken of his hospitality by the boy he had so graciously invited into his house. It had clearly not occurred to Papa that Dr Bright, a widower with four daughters, perhaps made a point of inviting carefully vetted young men to tea as an obvious way to getting his girls married. Instead, Doctor Carr had suddenly and disconcertingly seen his own handsome, intelligent and soon to be well-off son in a new light: as a cheeky clodhopper from the sticks.

The intensity of his panic is made clear by a letter to Willy from his mama, written on the same day, and beginning 'Oh Willy, Willy, how can you have done this to me': 'this' meaning 'send Papa into such a dreadful state' rather than 'get engaged'. Her letter is one of mind-boggling self-centredness. She is apparently indifferent to the rights or wrongs of Willy's love affair, and concentrates entirely on what she is having to suffer from Papa's frantic reaction. She has taken to her bed; she is unable to eat the least morsel of food; her headache is blinding. There is a distinct suggestion of an habitual connivance between mother and son against the father, and what the mother seems to be attempting is a revival of this connivance, regardless of what has caused the trouble.

The fourth letter is also from her, written about a month later. In the interval Dr Bright must have let them know that he is happy about the match, and proposed bringing Margaret to Yorkshire to meet them; and Willy has written to Mama, asking her to be kind to Margaret, who will naturally be feeling nervous. Mama's answer begins: 'Dearest Willy, you ask me to be kind to Margaret because she will be feeling nervous. She cannot be nearly so nervous as I will be . . .'; and goes on for two sides about the suffering that she is bound to undergo.

Her letters persuaded me that there must be a gene for querulous self-absorption. One of her granddaughters was always puzzlingly unlike her siblings in being weepy and self-absorbed. It was a joke in our part of the family that you could safely bet on her bringing any subject whatever round to herself within half a minute. 'You've bought a pair of leather gloves? Oh, how I wish I'd bought leather ones instead of those silly woolly things I got last month . . .' As soon as I had read my great-grandmother's first letter I said to my mother: 'Good God – this is Aunt D.'

Possibly the plaintive Mrs Carr saw her husband's agitation as something inflicted on her, rather than as something to share, chiefly because she did not share it. Coming, as she did, from a family richer and higher on the social scale than his, she was unlikely to see the Master's daughter as beyond her son's reach. It was she who caused them to move south for her health's sake, and they would not have been able to buy such a fine house and so much land without her money, so for all her apparent feebleness she carried weight.

The Carrs made the move to Norfolk before my mother was born to Willy and Margaret, but it was not until she was five that the house was inherited by her father, who enlarged it. It was a substantial rectangular house built in the 1730s, overlooking a beautifully landscaped park and lake. My grandfather extended it into a U-shape and added a graceful terrace from which to enjoy the view. He reactivated a nearby kiln which had provided the bricks for the original building, so the new bricks matched perfectly; and because his taste ran to eighteenth-century reading and artefacts, so did the architectural style of his extension. Other newly rich men in East Anglia created mediaeval extravaganzas, but in him there was still much Yorkshire puritanism and common sense, which combined with my grandmother's academic background to give the family sobriety.

Having read history at Oxford, my grandfather had then turned to law, but he practised as a barrister for only a very short time before coming into his father's money, which must have been astutely invested – largely, according to my mother, in railways. She told me that he carried on his watch chain a little key, which meant that when the family travelled up to Yorkshire to visit relations they could have the train stopped wherever they wanted. She thought, too, that there was Carr money 'in that railway across Canada to the Pacific'. My grandfather was a good and businesslike farmer, and for years I assumed that the land was what the family lived on: but there must have been a considerable amount of money in the background, profitably invested, to allow him to enlarge the house so handsomely.

He also enlarged the estate, buying a wood here, a farm there, and when my mother was a little girl she and the sister next to her in age used to be given the job of taking the estate map down from the wall and colouring the new additions pink, 'like the British Empire'. This was gratifying, but was also seen as a bit of a joke. No fuss was made about it, but in my grandfather's house it was always in the air that being well-off was no excuse for getting too big for your boots: unseemly or irresponsible behaviour would be condemned as vulgar or (perhaps the family's most chastening word) silly. I think my grandmother's love for her William lent a pleasing glow to his background: it was from her I gained the impression that 'Yorkshireness' meant sturdiness and honesty. She was proud of the trace of Yorkshire in her husband's pronunciation of certain words, such as 'cassle' for 'castle' and 'larndry' for 'laundry', and her favourite Charlotte Brontë novel was *Shirley*, partly because Shirley was such a spirited young woman, but also because it gave such a good picture of Yorkshire's industrial development. Her affection for the aspect of the family which was furthest from being 'county' probably served as a useful pinch of seasoning in the spell cast over her grandchildren by her house and its surroundings.

Everything important in my life seemed to be a property of that place: the house and the gardens, the fields, woods and waters belonging to it. Beauty belonged to it, and the underlying fierceness which must be accepted with beauty; animals belonged to it, and so did books and all my other pleasures; safety belonged to it, and so did my knowledge of good and evil and my wobbly preference for good. Of course my mother was really more important, but hers was an importance so vital that it belonged inside me, like the essential but unconsidered importance of breathing; and at a pinch the place could stand in even for her, and had once done so.

When I was about a year old my father, then an army officer, was seconded to a frontier commission which was attempting to confirm the boundary between Abyssinia (as Ethiopia then was) and Eritrea. My mother could join him there if she wished to, and to miss such an adventure would clearly have been absurd, particularly since the most baby-loving of my aunts, still unmarried, was living in her parents' house and would dearly love to take charge of me there for the three or four months my mother would be away.

I cannot remember those months, but I recognize two traces of them. The first is that although the aunt was in some ways an annoying woman, I would always love her with a special warmth; and the second is that until I was about seven I used to have irrational fits of panic: *Mummy has gone away and isn't going to come back*. This would happen if she left me in the car and went into a shop to pick something up, or if I woke up soon after going to bed and the house was silent. I think that something inside me was always capable of saying 'Don't be ridiculous, people don't disappear without warning', but that did not prevent a violently physical certainty of abandonment. In the car (these must have been the panic's earliest manifestations) I would be crying by the time my mother returned – and oh, the magic in her crossness at this silly fuss I was making at being left for three minutes! In the silent house I would make more determined efforts to reason with myself, but still it would end in my having to get out of bed, creep to the top of the stairs, and listen. Soon a door would open or shut, and I would hear footsteps or a voice . . . Life downstairs was going on as usual, after all, and I could return to bed in an ecstasy of relief.

And now I think that possibly the way in which places, particularly that one, would always matter to me – at some level, more than people – was a third trace left by those months.

★

We did not live in our grandmother's house all the time, nor did the families of our two sets of cousins on our mother's side: our homes were where our fathers happened to be serving. But we were always there for holidays and always stayed there when our parents were unable to take us with them to foreign parts; and Andrew, Patience and I were there far more than any of the others. Our father retired from the Royal Artillery in the late 1920s – reluctantly, because he would have been posted to India if he had not done so, but my mother had refused to go there with him – and got a job in a company that mined mica which meant that he was either working in London or travelling abroad. From then on, except for a couple of years when we had a house in Hertfordshire, we lived at the Hall Farm on the estate and saw my father only at weekends. Hardly a day passed when we were not in and out of the big house.

Before that, for one whole perfect summer, I lived there without the rest of my family.

As a child, I was somewhat given to sore throats, swollen glands, and stomach upsets which were diagnosed as colitis – never enough seriously to interfere with my pleasures for any length of time, but

The Hall Farm

enough to make visits to doctors less rare than they were for others. This time the doctor was a bald one, with very soft hands and half-moon glasses. Like other doctors I had been taken to in London he lived in a dark and magnificent house which conferred importance on me and Mum when we entered it, and like all doctors anywhere, in my experience, he was kind and courteous and tried to amuse me with jokes which, although they were not funny, were pleasing: that such a dignified man should take this trouble was flattering. So was having a young woman in a white coat to help me undress, and the gravity of the ritual was impressive. I never thought of being anything but docile on such occasions, even when I had to swallow a barium meal: it was as though I had been given a part in a play, with Mum (my manager) in the wings to encourage me. It was important that I should not let us down.

After this examination the white-coated lady took me back to the waiting-room and gave me a solitaire board to play with, while the doctor talked to Mum. I sensed that my part must have been a bigger one than usual, and indeed Mum's face when she came to collect me was serious. 'Did he say what I've got?' I asked: and she replied: 'Yes, darling. He thinks you must stop lessons for a time. It's not anything to worry about, really – you haven't actually *got* consumption, but you see some people have a tendency to consumption – that means it's sort of asleep in your glands and if you were very run down or anything it might start up, so he thinks you ought to have a very long rest.' – 'Long? How long?' – 'A few months, I think.' – *'In bed?'* – 'Oh, no, darling, I don't think that's necessary. I expect you'll go to stay with Gran.'

In stories girls who had consumption died. They became frailer and frailer and more and more interesting – by the time Beth died in *Good Wives* she had become so weak that she said her sewing-needle was heavy, which had impressed me as much as it had astonished me. It was alarming to think of myself as one of this sisterhood, and I was subdued as I got into the taxi. Could I really have something that might make me die? I had not taken in the bit about 'asleep in my glands', only the word 'consumption'. For some minutes it was as though I were preparing myself to be very frightened, but before I reached that stage the impossibility of it had asserted itself – and besides, hadn't Mum said no lessons, and that I'd go to Gran's . . . Was I really going to spend a whole summer there, with no lessons: my idea of perfect bliss?

The taxi took us to Mum's club, where we were staying, to meet Dad for tea. He was waiting in the library, where several ladies were already grouped round little tables. 'Hullo,' he said, as we came through the door, 'What's the news?' – and I, fear dismissed, was suddenly aware of the drama of my situation. In a loud and boastful voice I announced: 'I've got consumption.'

'Sshh!' said my mother, blushing scarlet. 'You must *never* say that. Go upstairs at once and take off your hat and coat.' I was so dismayed that I was unable to notice how the ladies in the room had reacted, but I feared from my parents' expressions that they had been disgusted rather than awestruck. If consumption was no more to be talked about than constipation there seemed little point in having it, and from that moment I stopped thinking about it.

So did everyone else. Because the doctor had advised it, I was sent to Gran's, the windows of my bedroom were nailed open – a symbolic precaution considering that she allowed no shut bedroom windows in her house anyway – and I was given a goat to milk and look after myself, which was unmixed pleasure. Cows' milk, in those days, was not pasteurized, so did hold a real risk of tuberculosis. In fact TB was still a serious threat: not so long before, all the daughters of a nearby big house had died of it. But in this case it must soon have become apparent to everyone that the specialist's diagnosis was fantasy. My health that summer was excellent and the special attention soon faded away. My three favourite cousins, Joyce, Anne (the redhead) and Pen (the one nearest me in age) were also there, presumably because their father was in some particularly inhospitable part of the world. They had to do lessons every morning with a lugubrious tutor who came pedalling down the drive on a bicycle so old-fashioned that it made one think of penny-farthings (to his dismay I used to wreathe it in enormous scarlet poppies to express my glee at being exempt). It was a summer of riding, reading, play-writing, dressing-up, and of not even noticing that Andrew, now at his prep-school, was no longer my chief playmate and closest friend.

I had been allotted the bedroom I loved best, the Corner Room, where I slept in a canopied bed and spent minutes on end studying the huge Pre-Raphaelite engraving above the chimney-piece which showed Christian maidens about to be martyred by Roman centurions. One of the centurions was in love with the most beautiful of the maidens and had taken her aside in order to plead with her to deny her faith. He held her hand, almost in tears, but she had her eyes raised to Heaven, stricken (because she loved him in return) but too noble to give way. The question was: did I want to look, when I grew up, like this maiden, or like one of her companions who, although her robe was less becoming, had longer hair. (Though a fair-skinned, mouse-coloured child, I was determined to have, when I grew up, immensely long and seriously black hair.) The maidens were there in the morning, and at night the smell of the honeysuckle on the terrace came in through the wide-open windows, with the occasional squawk of a moorhen down on the lake, or a volley of quacking from the wild ducks, or the harsh cry of the herons which colonized the nearest island.

These noises seemed to be heard by something inside me rather than by my ears. Like the screeching of the owls, some of them could have been frightening. They were eerie noises, *night* noises: if you hadn't known what made them they would have caused your heart to jump and your scalp to prickle. But I knew them. I had always known them, back through the immemorial length of all my life. They, like the cockling of pheasants before a thunderstorm and the cooing of wood-pigeons and the note of the cuckoo, were the voices of this place. Heard elsewhere, they were only simulacra of themselves; here they were restored to their true nature, as I was to mine.

Once, when I was young enough to share the Corner Room with Andrew, there was an earthquake. That afternoon the sky had gone livid and the grown-ups had said 'There's going to be a thunderstorm – and a good thing too, it'll clear the air.' But there was no thunderstorm. The yellow sky darkened to brown so that the lights had to be switched on, and everyone said 'Extraordinary!' Then bedtime came, I in the canopied bed, he in a little one across its foot. I woke with a jerk because of a roaring noise, and he woke too, saying 'What is it? What is it?!' I said, trying to sound calm, 'It's the thunderstorm.' He was still frightened of thunder but I didn't mind it so much, so I knew I ought to reassure him. 'It isn't thunder,' he said – and I thought 'A very big wind?' Then I realized that the bed and everything else was shuddering – it was the shuddering house that was roaring. Almost at once there were running footsteps in the passage and our mother came in wearing her dressing-gown – it must be the middle of the night. 'You must get up, darlings, it's a little earthquake, we may have to go out in the garden.' But as she spoke, the shuddering stopped. And then there was a silence so huge that it was more frightening than the roaring.

And sure enough, the newspaper said next day that there had been an earthquake, though it was described, annoyingly, as being felt more strongly in Wales.

Once I suffered terrible earache in the Corner Room ('mastoid', they said, and told me afterwards that I had been lucky not to have had an operation; but to my mind an operation would have made it more dignified). That was the first time in my life that I experienced atrocious pain, pain so bad that I rolled myself into a ball in the middle of the bed with the sheet over me like a tent, and one of the grown-ups cried. And once, in that room, when I was so small that Andrew was not yet born, I was in a cot, Mum and Dad in the big bed, and Mum said in a low voice 'Use the slop-pail,' and there was a trickling noise so that I understood that Dad was doing littles – it was amazing that a grown-up should do that. And once Andrew and I invented a game of getting round the same room without touching foot to floor, which involved climbing across the chimney-piece and could only be played secretly because grown-ups would expect us to break things. And over and over again I finished a book which had been interrupted by bedtime, snug under the sheet with a flashlight which had to be hidden quickly if I heard approaching footsteps. Good things were at their best in that room, and bad things were made better by it. Every room I slept in in Gran's house had some special charm about it (except the night nursery, which had a ghost) but the Corner Room was the most interesting of them all.

I called the thing in the night nursery a ghost for want of a better word: it was not like ghosts were supposed to be – more like a monster. I saw it twice, while still young enough to be sat on a pot after breakfast. Because I always took a long time Nanny would leave me there and go back to the day nursery, saying 'Call when you're finished', and I would sit there, bored, feeling the pot's rim engraving a circle round my buttocks. The night nursery looked out over what was called the shrubbery but was nearer to being a little wood – yew trees mostly, and one huge beech which almost curtained the windows, making this room the only gloomily dark one in the house. Sitting on my pot, I would stare out at the leaves of the beech tree, and I was doing this when the 'ghost' appeared.

It was a grey thing like the tip of an elephant's trunk, and it seemed to be groping down towards the outside of the window as though the creature it belonged to were squatting on the roof, reaching down over the gutter. Only a little bit of it appeared at first, withdrawing quickly but riveting my eyes to the place where it had been. Then it came again, more of it, and I screamed. The scream had terror in it, so Nanny came running, but she couldn't understand me when I tried to explain what I'd seen, and ended by telling me that I must have been imagining something; and when I had calmed down I supposed that this was so. Back on my pot next day, I repeated this reassuring explanation to myself: 'I imagined something'. And then I went on to bolster my courage by telling myself that even if I hadn't, the thing was not going to hurt me. It was a *kind* thing, and probably all it ever ate was beech leaves. I so much wanted it not to come – not to be able to come – that I imagined it eating so many beech leaves that it had made itself sick – I even said: '*Poor* thing, it's so sick today that it can't come.' But it did come. It was a much darker grey this time, but it was obviously the same thing and it was *not* kind. I was frantic with fear, and after that I was no longer left alone on my pot in this room. And other people began to say how they had never really liked the night nursery, and that it had a spooky sort of feeling to it.

Some seventy years later I woke one morning in a bed beside a window, and without putting on the glasses which I had worn since I was twelve to remedy my short sight, I looked upwards out of the window to see whether the sky was blue or grey – and there was my 'ghost'. With a tiny tweak of panic, I was back in the night nursery, but only for a split second. This time, though still as short-sighted as ever, I could interpret the grey object: the tail of a pigeon which was perching on the gutter.

The house provided only two other mysterious experiences – minor ones, but at least they remain unexplained. A long time before I was born, my grandfather was sitting one evening in the library and heard a shattering of glass in the dining room next door. He jumped up and ran to the dining room, supposing either that the footman (who ought to have been in bed by that time anyway) had dropped a tray of glasses, or that a burglar, trying to open a window, had slipped and fallen through it. There was nothing amiss, and no explanation of the sound was ever discovered. Not long afterwards my mother was in the Cedar Walk with her dog when she saw the gamekeeper at a distance, through the trees. She started towards him, wanting to give him a message, when her dog suddenly stopped and began to growl and tremble, his hackles rising, staring at where the man was standing. She looked in surprise at the dog, then towards the gamekeeper for an explanation – and there was no one there. My cousin Pen and I liked this story, and sometimes went out after dark hoping to see the Cedar Walk ghost; we used to put on the hooded loden-cloth cloaks which hung in the back passage for everyone's use, as they seemed appropriate wear for such an expedition. But once we were out there in the dark, among the looming cedar trees, it would become only too likely that the ghost really would appear, so we would skedaddle back to the house, singing hymns to ward him off.

The place's other bogeys were purely imaginary, and thus our fear of them something to be ashamed of: the wolves, for example. One Christmas holiday Andrew and I were sleeping on the attic floor, in the Tank Room, so-called because one of its two large built-in cupboards gave access to the water tanks. It was a pleasant room with a sloping ceiling and a relaxed atmosphere, in spite of a spice of danger coming from the tanks' gurglings and the presence in the other cupboard of a lion's head sewn into a dustsheet, which had been left there by some visiting relation and never reclaimed. We liked being up there, but Nanny found it a nuisance, because the room was as far from the nursery as the layout of the house permitted. After nursery tea, when she was getting us washed, brushed and dressed in our prettiest clothes for our hour with the grown-ups in Gran's drawing room, almost always she would find that she had forgotten to bring down a hairbrush or a pair of shoes, whereupon she would say the words I dreaded: 'Run up to the Tank Room and fetch it for me, there's a good girl.' And I would be ashamed to say that I was frightened of the wolves, so off I had to go.

Out through the little 'play-room', a bare ante-chamber to the nursery containing nothing but the toy-cupboard and a canary in a cage on the windowsill, and along the 'green passage': that was all right, because the warmth and sounds of the nursery could still be sensed. Then turn right – tap tap, two steps on bare boards between the humble green carpet and the rich patterned one of the passage which ran like a gallery across the well of the front stairs, onto which the doors of the best bedrooms opened. Here I could have lingered happily, because it was lit by the chandelier hanging over the stairwell and the life of the house rose up like a perfume: a sense of someone writing letters in the library where the fire was dying down (it was allowed to go out when the drawing room fire was lit for the evening); of Gran already in her bright drawing room; of the butler putting away the silver tea things in the pantry;

of Mrs Wiseman, the cook, beginning to prepare dinner in the kitchen. And there were precious things to look at: a chest of carved ivory, a cabinet containing small objects of silver and tortoiseshell, a bowl with huntsmen on stiff-legged horses galloping round it, a cut-glass comport on a little table – very beautiful, but you must be careful not to knock against the table. But if I spent too long dawdling by these things Nanny would wonder what I was doing. I had to go on and turn another corner to the right into the corridor.

The corridor had a high arched ceiling (I thought that all passages with arched ceilings were called corridors), and it was dark. Perhaps I couldn't yet reach the light switch, and even if I could it would only have mitigated the gloom, not dispelled it, because the house's electricity came from a pump down by the stables, and was always dim and fluctuating except in the most important rooms. As soon as I was round the corner into the darkness all the house's sounds were shut off, and the wolves were ahead of me. They lurked in the big best spare-room at the end of the corridor, beyond the point where the stairs sprang up: the 'golden stairs' which we loved in daylight because they *were* golden, of unstained polished oak without a carpet, and spiralled round inside the wall of a tower-like protuberance within an inner angle of the house's U-shape, bisecting two very tall windows as they did so. Anything in the house that was a little odd seemed to us special, but now the slipperiness of these stairs was a worry, because I had to get up them very fast, before I could hear the rattle of claws behind me. It was a desperate scramble, made more desperate by breathlessness, because as soon as I'd turned into the corridor I'd had to start singing as loudly as I could – hymns, of course, like we did in the Cedar Walk – and I mustn't stop for a moment. The ones I knew best were 'While Shepherds Watched' and 'Once in Royal David's City'. I went without pause from the verses I knew of one to those I knew of the other, and back again, and I couldn't stop even when I reached the top of the stairs and got into the Tank Room. It was a little better up there because I could turn on the light, but there was a possibility that one or two of the wolves had slipped ahead of me into the lion cupboard, and anyway the ones that hadn't followed me up the stairs were still waiting at the bottom . . . Not until I had skidded round the corner out of the corridor could I stop singing, draw a long breath, and hear a grown-up's voice saying inside me: '*There* you are – there aren't any wolves at all, you were only imagining them.'

But all this might never have happened, once we were in the drawing room. It was by no means the only time of day when we saw our parents and grandmother. We were in and out of the household's adult life all day, only those of us too young to be able to eat tidily being removed to the nursery for meals (it hung over us for a while as a mild and never executed threat: 'If you can't eat properly you'll have to go back to having lunch in the nursery'). Nurses were there to keep us clean – to mop up babies and chivvy the older ones through their baths and into appropriate clothes – and to air and exercise those of us too young to join in adult walks and rides, not to segregate us. But although 'downstairs' was never forbidden territory, it was only during the hour or so after tea that it was *dedicated to us*.

Then the grown-ups gathered in the drawing room especially for the children's pleasure, and the children became pretty, neat and good-tempered especially for that of the grown-ups. All that shadowed the occasion was its ending. When the drawing room door half-opened and a discreet head poked round it to summon those of us who still had to be put to bed before dinner, then howls would break out: ritual howls, not unpleasant. The grown-ups would indulge them, saying 'Just five more minutes, Nanny, I'll send them up as soon as we've finished this chapter – only three more pages', and there would be mollifying promises of goodnight kisses once we were bathed and in bed. 'After tea' was rarely marred by disharmony.

The drawing room had white walls, pale chintzes, shining furniture of rosewood, walnut and ormolu, ornaments of silver and porcelain, and flowers. Its smell was of freesias, violets, lilies of the valley, chrysanthemums, daphne. Only when we were older did it smell of roses – roses were summer, and in summer we would be out of doors after tea, no one settling in the drawing room until after the younger children were in bed. Roses in the drawing room were to belong to growing-up.

The daphne was the most delicious of the drawing room smells. There were seasons when we might or might not be in the house, but we were always there at Christmas, when the daphne was brought in from the greenhouse – there had never been a Christmas that didn't smell of daphne. It was a special kind which flourished only for our grandmother: a miniature tree, its leaves pointed, smooth and yellow-green, its inconspicuous flowers a faded pink. The scent filled the whole large room, delicate, sweet, belonging with exquisite intensity to this place and no other.

When I came into the drawing room I would usually go first to the flowers. Most of them stood massed on a table with ornate legs and a sheet of glass on its top, while others in smaller vases were on the little ormolu-decorated tables on either side of the

Margaret Carr: 'Gran'

chimney-piece – a special silver bowl on the table next to Gran's chair was almost always full of Parma violets. I would dawdle round the flower table comparing velvety petals with satiny ones, tangy scents with sweet ones, watching the way in which even the stillest flowers seem minutely to vibrate, dipping nose and lips here and there, and saving the daphne till last. When I breathed it I seemed to be breathing the whole room, the whole house, and my grandmother's love.

We were not allowed to romp in the drawing room – anyone wanting to play rough games could go into the morning room where the furniture was less frail. But we could bring our own toys in if we had become tired of those which lived in the toy-cupboard – those dear, small, battered toys which had served child after child. We could play with those, or at I Spy, or Hunt the Thimble, or spillikins, or dominoes, or cards, or mah-jong, according to age or inclination. But the chief occupation was being read to.

Our ages spanned about twelve years, so if all the cousins were in the house together, as we often were, suitable reading ranged widely. Sometimes *Johnny Crow's Garden* or *Squirrel Nutkin* would be going on, low-voiced, at one side of the fireplace, and *The Thirty-Nine Steps* or *Little Women* on the other; but more often we all listened to the same thing without thought of its being 'too young' or 'too old' for us. We could drift away from or back to the group as we wished, or do something else and listen with half an ear. Old favourites would be relived as they were newly enjoyed by someone younger, the gist of books above one's head absorbed as they were discovered by someone older. *Ivanhoe*, *The Jungle Book*, the *Alice* books, *The Wind in the Willows*, *Struwwelpeter*, *Winnie-the-Pooh*, *What Katy Did*, *Jackanapes*, *Treasure Island*, *The Prisoner of Zenda*, *Peter Rabbit*, *The Princess and the Goblin* – all of them and many others were read to every child, our grandmother's voice weaving its spells back and forth from our babyhood to our adolescence, binding us, without our being aware of it, into a shared experience which extended back from her grandchildren to her children, and sometimes even to her own childhood. Nothing we enjoyed in that house was dearer to us than those evenings, and to this day I can summon up the silky feel of the drawing room carpet as I sat on it contentedly beside Gran's chair.

Carpets were a reliable guide to the standing of the house's inhabitants: precious in the drawing room; handsome in the morning room, library and dining room, and on the front stairs; good in the best bedrooms; becoming plainer and more serviceable as the bedrooms became smaller; changing to linoleum in the nursery, and disappearing altogether on the back stairs and the attic passage onto which the maids' bedrooms opened. There were two back stairs, one from the kitchen to the landing on the first floor which led to the nurseries and the menservants' bedrooms (that wing of the house was only two floors high), and one in the main body of the house rising from the ground floor right to the top. Both were unpolished and uncarpeted, with steep, narrow treads, grey and a bit splintery. Maids could use the golden stairs as well, because they offered the only convenient way between the first and attic floors at that end of the house, but none of them ever set foot on the front stairs except to clean them. In the maids' bedrooms there were squares of old carpet as rugs beside the beds. Getting up on a winter's morning in those rooms was even colder than in the family's rooms – no bedroom was ever heated unless its occupant was ill – because the maids' rooms had only an uninsulated roof above them and draughts whistling up between the floor boards. And the maids had to get up at half-past six, or earlier if there were guests in the house.

There had been a bathroom on their floor since I could remember, but it had not been installed until after I was born. Before that the maids had washed in basins of cold water, as the menservants continued to do – unless, perhaps, the footman went down and fetched hot water for himself and the butler from the kitchen. The men did have a bathroom, but it must have been considered a mistaken extravagance as soon as it was installed, because the tub had never been connected and the room had become a box-room. There was not even a WC for the men, who had to use an outdoor privy in the shrubbery behind the kitchen, which the night nursery overlooked. (This may not have been seen as a great hardship, because my grandfather himself chose to use it after breakfast every morning: if you caught sight of him on his way there, with *The Times* under his arm, you had to pretend you hadn't.) On the other hand, the kitchen, scullery and servants' hall were all warmer than any of the other rooms in the house. No doubt Gran insisted in theory on open windows there, as she did everywhere else, but she rarely went into the kitchen except for the short time each morning when she discussed the meals for the day with Mrs Wiseman, and never into the servants' hall (unless she snooped at night as some of the maids believed, but I don't). We were taught that at least this room and their bedrooms must be private to the servants, and that it was bad manners to intrude; if one of us was sent with a message to the servants' hall we approached it shyly and hesitated before knocking on its door. The sounds coming from behind the door were often cheerful, and the silence which fell when it had been opened, while not quite hostile, suggested a secret life being suspended. We often invaded the kitchen, where Mrs Wiseman would give us a kind welcome and offer titbits, but we were never invited into the hall.

To begin with the servants were the butler and his footman; the cook, her kitchen-maid and her scullery-maid; the head housemaid with her two or three under-housemaids; and Gran's personal attendant – her 'lady's maid'. The coachman (still called that because he dated from before cars, but his successor was called the groom), the chauffeur, the head-gardener and his two under-gardeners all lived outside in their own houses, and so did the old woman with hair-sprouting warts who came to do the washing in the steamy laundry, and spread it to dry in the bleach – a grassy space sheltered by yew hedges.

The work of the junior maids was overseen by their seniors, but they were chosen by my grandmother. Dorothy Morris remembers Gran coming to her family's cottage in 1936 to assess her potential as a kitchen-maid, and taking her on at fifteen shillings a month. Dorothy thought that she had never seen anyone so beautiful, but she also observed that Gran kept a white-gloved hand between her bottom and their horsehair sofa. 'She thinks it may not be clean was my supposition, and I felt some indignation on behalf of my mother, who slaved fiercely to keep the tumbledown place spotless.'

The first butler I can remember was a casting-director's dream for the role: he was called Mr Rowberry, and was tall, bow-fronted and immensely sedate – though he did once make a joke: looking down his nose at an errant puppy, he said: 'They say it's a French poodle, but *I* call it a French puddle,' which struck me as witty beyond words. When his successor retired, the then footman was promoted but was given no footman under him and no livery. He wore a plain dark suit and the children didn't think him a proper butler. That was as far as retrenchment went before the beginning of the Second World War; and it was far enough, in our eyes. Other and much simpler ways of living seemed natural to all of us in other houses, but in this house the way things had always been was the way things ought to be.

When we went up to the attic it was on our way to the roof, or to the dressing-up chest, or to visit Ethel, Gran's lady's maid. She worked up there as well as slept: her pleasant room was a bed-sitting room with a sewing-table, a pigeon-bosomed dressmaker's dummy, and much interesting bric-a-brac. Her photographs and ornaments had stories attached to them, which she liked to tell, and she would give us snippets of material and ribbon. A gentle, sentimental woman, she was affectionate to the little ones and admiring to the older ones, whose dresses she often made; and we were fond of her, partly for her genuine kindness and partly because no one else accepted – or seemed to accept – our superiority so unthinkingly and whole-heartedly. She appeared to *love* 'the gentry' for being what it was.

The dressing-up chest belonged with bad weather – preferably a thunderstorm. There would be the restlessness and uneasiness caused by the heavy feeling of the approaching storm and the unnatural darkening of the air, then the excitement of the crashing thunder, the sudden drumming of rain, gutters filling and spilling, and a scurry in the house as maids ran from room to room shutting the tall sash windows which squealed as they were slammed up or down. Voices would be raised: 'Have you shut the Corner Room? Oh Lord! The garden chairs are out on the terrace.' The house would become a fortress of security and because outdoor activities were so decisively cut off, indoor ones would take on their full significance.

The chest was such a tangle that although we knew everything in it, we always felt that some unfamiliar treasure might emerge. Old evening dresses, satin shoes with cut-steel buckles, lengths of gauze, peasant blouses bought in fits of mistaken enthusiasm on holidays, ribbons, feathers, sequin trimmings, velvet jackets . . . Everything was crushed and smelt slightly musty, and the grown-ups used to laugh and exclaim in dismay at it – 'that *dreadful* old kimono!' – but to us it was all beautiful. We rarely quarrelled over who would wear what. If we were dressing in order to act in a play, choice was dictated by the character one was playing, and if we were dressing for dressing's sake – as we often were – it was almost as strictly dictated by our personalities. One cousin would be aiming for a comic effect, another for something swashbuckling, another for the regal; and the older ones, taking it less seriously than their juniors, would be prepared to sacrifice a cloak or a muslin rose for the sake of peace.

I early and ruthlessly established a claim on what was most romantic, dressing up in order to become a princess or a bride. The trailing, the gauzy, the feathery, the white were what I ferreted out of the heap, with a special preference for veils. My only rival for the romantic was Pen – the others thought me so funny as I teetered about in my princess's raiment that they indulged me. And I could usually defeat poor Pen by the strength of my passion. She would have liked to wear the white velvet bodice and the gauze veil secured by the tinsel crown, but I, once in the mood for dressing-up, *had* to wear them. I thirsted to become what I felt I became in these garments, so much so that even being laughed at failed to weaken their spell. Once, when I was seven, I hit on a headdress which seemed to me inspired. I wanted to be a princess in a twin-horned coif with a veil suspended from the horns – I had seen such a princess in an illustrated history book. There was no such head-dress in the chest, but it came to me that I could take off my knickers and wear them on my head. I was skinny, so the waist-elastic fitted snugly, and the legs stuffed with tissue paper stood up firmly enough as the horns to hold the veil. Although my elders' laughter was fond, I knew perfectly well that it arose from their thinking me absurd, but this had no effect on my own belief in what I had become. I went into a bedroom to look at myself in a long mirror, and I saw myself graceful and beautiful, my face grave under the bloomers, slightly tragic – utterly remote from whatever *they* were seeing. (One day I would be driving along a road in Holland and would catch sight of a grotesque little figure wandering dreamily through an orchard: a child of about seven wearing a pair of her mother's evening shoes, a tattered chiffon dress which trailed in the grass, and a length of white butter-muslin over her head. The whiff I caught of what that child was being almost took my breath away.)

The boys did not dress up, except for plays. Nothing was ever bought for the chest, and women cast off far more clothes than men, so there was little in it with which a boy could express what he wanted to be: no cowboy hats, no bandoleers, no Indian feathers, no weapons. Before being sent to their preparatory schools at the age of eight the boys were subjected to no propaganda about manliness beyond the often disregarded rule that they must be gentle and considerate towards girls, but in two ways, however different the temperaments within the sexes, there was a clear divergence from the start: the girls responded to dress and the boys thought it a bore, and the girls loved horses while the boys were indifferent to them. Being brave was admired regardless of gender, and when we went up on the roof there was nothing to choose between us for daring.

Daring came into it because the point of going up onto the roof was walking round the gutters. The two wings of the house were topped with pitched roofs sloping down to ordinary gutters, but the original part of the house – its main rectangular body – was different. When you climbed up the little stairs next to Ethel's room and unbolted the door at the top of them, you emerged onto a flat field of lead islanded with stout brick chimneys and surrounded by a tiled ridge too high to see over. If you clambered up the inner slope of this ridge and peered over its top, you saw that its steep outer slope, from which dormer windows jutted at intervals, ran down to a flat-bottomed lead gutter almost a foot wide. The idea of sliding down the tiled slope into this gutter at any point between the windows was a little frightening because one would be unable to control the speed of the slide; but if you went down beside one of the windows you had a sort of narrow channel into which to wedge your feet and could find hand-holds on the window, so it became child's play. There would obviously be no problem about walking along that nice wide gutter once you had reached it.

Now that I am old I have a bad head for heights, and it was not too good even in middle age: I remember very disagreeable sensations taking me by surprise when, at the top of a tower somewhere in Italy, I looked down and found that I could see the faraway ground through the open-work iron structure on which I was standing. So ghostly pangs of vertigo now afflict me when I think that once I stood in that gutter, wondering what on earth my mother was fussing about as she stood far below me, clutching her throat in evident anguish while calling up to us to stay quite still – quite *quite* still – until someone had rushed upstairs and opened the window just ahead of us so that we could climb in. So strictly speaking, I suppose, it was not daring that the boys and girls shared in that particular bit of child's play, so much as unawareness of the need for it.

The most important thing about the place, for us children, was its feeling of permanence. It was possible to imagine going away from it, but not possible to imagine its not being there, unchanged, to come back to. This may have been less strongly felt by the grown-ups – only our uncle was young enough to have almost no memory of the time before they lived there – but for us it was what we had *always* known. And if anyone had told us, as we perched on the roof-ridge and looked out over the park, 'This view will cease to exist long before you die', we would have thought him mad. Indeed, much later when I was twenty-two and facing the fact that war had come, I leant my forehead against the trunk of one of the beeches which were such an important part of that view, and comforted myself by saying: 'Well, thank God that whatever happens to us, *you* will still be here when it's over.'

By the end of the war that beech tree had gone. So, very soon afterwards, had the long stand of beeches which rimmed the back park, the noble island of beeches round which the front drive curved, and – most incredible of the lot – the grandest of them all, the huge beech guarding the entrance to the shrubbery behind the rose garden under which I once stood willing my future ghost to inhabit its shade. No person was responsible for their vanishing. Beeches have a lifespan of about two hundred and fifty years, and these, having all been planted at the same time, all died more or less together. Later, Dutch elm disease laid low several other of the park's great beauties, then the most splendid of the cedars was cut down because its roots were threatening the house's foundations, and fierce winds blew down other important trees. Quite gone, now, is the eighteenth-century landscaping of park and garden which used to give the place its charm.

I was once told by a man whose job was looking after the estates of rich people, that one of his dreams was that he would be allowed to sweep away the decaying remains of some great piece of eighteenth-century landscaping, and replant it to a new design. Patching, he said, was useless. Such parks were works of art, and when time destroys them, as it inevitably must, the only right answer is to replace them with another, different, work of art. But who, nowadays, has the money or the vision to plant for the future on a grand scale? He knew that his dream was a crazy one. And certainly in 'our' park the band of quick-growing trees that has now been planted along its edge, between it and the road, although it must have cost a great deal, makes no claim to be landscaping. All it does is shelter the house from view.

How glad I am that it was impossible to imagine the future, and that I had the luck to take – or to mistake – for granted an eighteenth-century landscape just before it fell to pieces, as my natural habitat.

GOD AND GRAMPS

E VEN IF WALKING the gutters was fun, not brave, courage was considered an important virtue – perhaps not more important than honesty, but more attractive. We knew we ought to be honest, but we wanted to be brave.

Much of this feeling about courage was derived from Geoffrey Salmond, husband of my mother's eldest sister Peggy and father of Joyce, Anne, Pen and John. He was the uncle who ended in the RAF – indeed as head of it. When he was a dashing and amusing young army officer he, with his brother Jack and a small group of friends, became enamoured of that fascinating invention the flying machine, which at that stage appeared to be put together of cardboard and string. They were among the first Englishmen to fly, first as amateurs, soon afterwards as members of the Royal Flying Corps, which they got going. Early in the First World War Geoff played an important part in persuading the War Office that airborne men would be invaluable at finding out what was going on behind the enemy's lines – he was one of the Flying Corps thinkers, as well as a daring pilot. After the war he made the first ever flight across the Himalayas, when navigation was a matter of peering earthwards and following rivers and (when there were any) roads. He also became the commander of the RAF in India, and contributed a good deal to the development of civil aviation.

His adoring wife understood from the beginning that on no account must she betray how much she feared for him when he was flying: if you were married to a hero it was your duty to be heroic too, and never to burden him with an image of yourself being unhappy for fear of losing him. She played her part to perfection: all their lives her daughters would remember how proudly their father told them that she was 'as brave as a lion'.

She was to need this courage, poor Aunt Peggy. First Geoff died of bone cancer when he was only middle-aged, then their son John, who had followed his father into the RAF, was killed in the Second World War. I did not see her under the immediate impact of these two terrible blows, but I know what got her through them: the conviction that to give way would be unworthy of Geoffrey Salmond's wife. She and her daughters, although they never spoke of it, were always thereafter to have about them a faint aura of dedication to an inspiring memory. They were examples of the valuable aspect of that Good Behaviour so well understood by the novelist Molly Keane.

It is an ideal that can, of course, be damaging. Once, when my mother was eighty, the husband of a good friend of hers died suddenly, and when I arrived for a weekend two days later she told me about it with feeling, knowing how deeply her friend would feel her loss. I said 'Oh God, I must call her'; and when I had done so my mother muttered in a shamefaced way 'How brave you are.' – 'Brave?' – 'She might have cried.' It turned out that she had not yet dared to get in touch with her friend: a fear of raw emotion that can cripple human responses, as well as support endurance.

When we were children there were, of course, no undercurrents to being brave. It was just a stylish way to behave, at which the Salmonds were a good deal better than I was. I was well aware that if we were faced with a really hairy jump in cold blood, Pen would be much readier than I to put her pony at it; anyone could be brave out hunting because of the excitement, but she was always brave. From time to time it worried me: in a situation which required real heroism – if someone was drowning in a turbulent river, perhaps, or trapped in a burning house – would I be able to rise to the occasion? It didn't feel likely, but on the other hand it was possible that nobody felt it likely – that given such a situation you responded in the right way either automatically, or because you were so frightened of what people would think if you didn't that doing it was the lesser evil. I could only hope . . .

We knew the Bible well – or rather, those parts of it read to us by Gran, starting when we were very young: Joseph and his brethren, Samson and Delilah, David and Jonathan, Samuel and Eli, Christ walking on the water, the miracle of the loaves and fishes, and of course the story of Jesus's birth. Gran read or told those stories as though they were about real events which were parts of everyone's knowledge and life. She loved most of the books she read to us, but she loved the Bible best: the Old Testament stories, particularly, she told with contained relish. She introduced us to poetry only through narrative verse, chiefly Macaulay's and Scott's, but it was to poetry more broadly speaking that she led us through the Bible, by the vibration of her response to it. To poetry, rather than to morality, in that it made little impression as a source of a sense of right and wrong.

My grandparents were sensible and modest people, so I doubt that either of them would have presumed to claim that he or she was a *good* Christian, but equally I am sure neither of them doubted that Christians they were. They were regular churchgoers; they respected the Sacraments; they obeyed the Ten Commandments; they felt strongly – even passionately – that faith should be drawn as directly as possible from the Bible without the intervention of a priesthood (hence their detestation of Roman Catholics). But if they actually *believed* in the Incarnation, which I take to be Christianity's central tenet, their conduct concealed the fact. It seemed much more like the conduct of people moved by common sense combined with an ideal of gentlemanly behaviour than it did like the conduct of people seeking communion with God.

What people like them would have said in response to such a thought was that a person's beliefs – his really important, inner beliefs – were a matter between himself and God, too important to be lightly exposed. About which I feel doubtful. It seems to me more likely that what could not be lightly exposed was a person's really important inner disbelief.

As far as I was concerned, they gave me an extraordinarily undemanding God. It was His love and His understanding that were emphasized, so much so that I found it cheering, not alarming, to remember that He knew everything about me: every thought, every motive, every illegitimate desire. Because He knew every single thing, and understood it, then He knew the strength of temptations and how, considering my frailty, I didn't do too badly against them. People might misunderstand, He wouldn't. Whatever tensions there were (and there were some), the bedrock of trust had not been cracked: what I expected from life and from God was love, forgiveness and protection. I was threatened only if naughty or silly, and then, however resentful I might feel at the moment, I knew well enough that it was my own fault, and I needed to call on no great moral energy to accept that fact. This was because most of the sins committed by me and the other children didn't matter very much to anyone and certainly not to God. The only sin taken really seriously was the one which, if you brought it off successfully, would make nonsense of adult control: lying.

The dreadfulness of lying was brought home to me when I was four years old. All the family's children were at a tea party in a neighbour's garden, where there was a cherry tree trained against a wall: overwhelmingly tempting because cherries were rare in our county and their smooth redness was so perfect. They were, in fact, the bitter kind grown for jam-making, but I was unaware of that as I gazed longingly, feeling in anticipation the protective net's fine thread as I pushed fingers through it, the slight harshness of the leaves, the plumpness of the fruit. I didn't dare, though. This was Cousin Minnie's garden, not ours, and she was proud of her cherries. But I was hand in hand with my cousin Anne, four years my senior, who was showing me how to play hide-and-seek properly, and who was touched by my expression. 'We oughtn't to,' she said – and then, generously: 'Look, *I* mustn't because I know that it's wrong, but *you* can have just one.' So I took the cherry she picked for me, bit into it, let it drop because of its unexpected sharpness, clutched at it – and squashed it against the front of my frock. There in the middle of my stomach was a large red stain, advertising my theft for all the world to see.

My consternation was so great that I didn't howl, only stared appalled at my cousin. Hers was even greater. She was a redhead of remarkable untidiness, her socks always wrinkled round her ankles, her bloomers always showing under her skirt, always longing to do right and ending by doing wrong. A clown and a tragedienne, she laughed and cried with abandon, loved to act and to tell stories, rejoiced in ideas of nobility, self-sacrifice and daring. The person she would most have liked to have been was the Boy who Stood on the Burning Deck – a poem which she often declaimed. She was adored by us, the younger ones, because of her loving kindness and her entertainment value; and now I knew at once that she would shoulder the responsibility for my sin.

And sure enough, 'Don't cry,' she said. 'It's all my fault and I know what we'll do. We'll run home very quickly and I'll wash your dress, and by the time they all get back they won't be able to see any stain and no one will know.'

It was easy to leave the garden by a back way without anyone seeing, and then we only had to cross a lane to be in the park of my grandparents' house. 'Faster, faster!' cried Anne, becoming the Red Queen, and I was whirled along like Alice in the picture. Anne had an inkling that the disappearance of two members of the tea party, one of them only four, would cause alarm. I didn't think of this or anything else, having simply become part of a situation compounded of urgency and secrecy out of which I was about to be miraculously delivered. We covered half a mile of park and garden at high speed, pausing sometimes to gasp and clutch at the stitches in our sides, crept up to and into the house, and bolted into a bathroom. 'Quick, quick, undress – look, I'll run the bath – if they come I'll say I'm giving you your bath and it won't be a lie because you'll be in it.'

No sooner was I in the bath and the stained frock in the hand-basin than there came a rattling at the door. 'Are you in there?' 'What are you doing? Open the door at once – what are you *doing*?' My mother's voice was agitated – the adults had had time to suppose that the older child had fled in panic at some disaster overtaking the younger one. The bedraggled frock came out of the basin with the stain still there – it was no good saying 'I'm giving her her bath' with the evidence glaring. Anne had one last inspiration: 'Sh!' she whispered, 'I'll pretend I'm going to the lav,' and she whipped down her knickers, sat on the pan and began to grunt with conscientious realism. I sat in the chilly water (there had been no time to adjust the temperature), as quiet as a mouse, overcome by the daring of this last device, and still trusting my protector's ingenuity.

'I *know* you aren't just going to the lavatory,' cried my mother (how? What hope against these guilt-detecting eyes which would see through doors?); 'Let me in AT ONCE!' And when the door was opened at last and the tearful confession had been made, it turned out – and this was amazing – that stealing the cherry hadn't been a sin at all, nor even had staining the dress. It was, explained my mother, *the lie* that had been so very wrong. But I had never *said* I hadn't stolen the cherry – surely lies were *words*? But no: it appeared that a lie could be something as complex and exhausting as running all the way across the park and sneaking into the house and pretending to have a bath. It was a cheering thought, once absorbed, because it proved that hiding sins was much more trouble than admitting them; and I have never since then been much of a liar. Excepting on those very rare occasions when the absolute necessity for it has been so overwhelming that it didn't feel like lying at all.

Which must, I suppose, have been the case with my grandfather – the apparently impeccable source of his household's wholesome atmosphere – when his only son, while still an undergraduate at Oxford, announced that he wished to become engaged to a young woman who was a Roman Catholic. This comic recurrence of crisis at Oxford, which seems to have become almost a tradition, was something that none of us knew about until recently, when it turned up in another old suitcase crammed with letters kept by my grandmother.

My grandparents had never met the young woman, who lived in the north of England with her aunt – perhaps she was an orphan. How my uncle met her is not revealed, but they had known each

William Greenwood Carr: 'Gramps'

other well for two years: this is stated in the first of the letters, from the young woman's aunt to my grandfather, which protests in courteous and reasonable terms at his forbidding the engagement without ever having met her niece. She says that the two young people know each other well, that the attachment between them is sincere, and that her niece is a good and sensible girl as well as a charming one, and does not deserve a dismissal so sudden and cruel. She goes on to say that while she agrees with him in theory that it is best if husband and wife are of the same faith, she must point out that she herself is a Protestant who has been married to a Roman Catholic for thirty years without any problems, so she can assure him from her own experience, as well as that of other couples of her acquaintance, that a 'mixed marriage' is not by any means necessarily disastrous. She is not asking – she says – that he reverse his decision at once, but she does feel that it would be only fair for him and his wife to meet her niece before finally forbidding the engagement.

The second letter is my grandfather's answer, in the form of a copy made in my grandmother's hand. It is brusque. Even, he says, if the young woman is foolish enough to wish to become engaged to an idle and frivolous young man who has so far shown no inclination whatever to earn a living, her aunt must surely see that it is her duty to forbid it, given that his estate happens to be entailed in such a way that his son, if he marries a Roman Catholic, will never inherit a penny. End of letter. And end, obviously, of engagement. *And my grandfather was lying*: no such entail existed.

It gives me great satisfaction to report that as soon as my grandfather was dead – he died in his sixties, while his son was still quite young – my uncle, who could always get whatever he wanted from a doting mother, married not only a Roman Catholic, but an Italian Roman Catholic – a veritable emissary from the Scarlet Woman of Rome. For that was what low-church Protestants of my grandparents' generation felt 'papists' to be.

At first that lie of my grandfather's made me laugh. On consideration it is not funny. Many an Ulsterman has become a murderer because he did not feel that ridding the world of a Catholic – or a Protestant, as the case might be – counted as murder. To him the act of murder feels righteous: the end has justified the means, as preventing his son from marrying a Catholic seemed to my grandfather to justify his lie. In both cases the humanity of the victim has been obscured by what the murderer and the liar feel to be an overwhelming necessity.

It is often said of monstrous evils such as genocide that we must not let ourselves forget them because the potential for such crimes lurks in all of us. I have said it myself, thinking that it must be true – but secretly I have never been able to *feel* that it is true of me. Now, however, having seen the obvious link between my grandfather's attitude to Catholics and that of Protestants in Northern Ireland, I have to acknowledge that I was led to it by seeing the link between my own few felt-to-be necessary lies and my grandfather's . . . There is a connecting thread there, between the almost harmless use of a psychological mechanism which can be brought into play when a need for self-justification is felt, and an evil use of it. Hugely different though the ends may be, the mechanism is the same. This kind of discovery must, I suppose, be the central reason for trying to write the truth, even if indecent, about oneself.

If you no longer lied, you were left with all those nice little sins than which lying was so much worse. It was wrong to steal grapes from the vinery, peaches from the kitchen-garden wall, lump sugar from the fat white jars in Gran's store cupboard. It was wrong to slide down haystacks in such a way that the stack was damaged and rain could get into the hay. It was wrong to scatter the grain heaped in the granary by wading through it. It was wrong to leave gates open so that cattle could stray. It was wrong to neglect an animal for whom one was responsible. Some of these rules, like the ones about animals and (later) the one about never pointing a gun at anyone even if it wasn't loaded, we never thought of breaking because that would be improper behaviour in our own eyes. Others we broke constantly because the forbidden pleasures were irresistible. Our awareness of the 'sinfulness' of these wrongdoings came from our own need for excitement, rather than from outside.

There were also, of course, aspects of one's own behaviour that one knew grown-ups would disapprove of such as our early interest in excretion and (from the age of ten or eleven, in my case) an eagerness to discover everything possible about sex. But those were so private that they didn't feel like sins – though whether this was because even God couldn't know about them, or because of His understanding, I can't now remember.

Sometimes a sin was discovered unexpectedly: who would have guessed it was sinful to organize a church service in an unoccupied spare bedroom on a Sunday when colds had prevented us from going to church? This was during a short period of religious fervour when I was about ten. It was Anne and her elder sister who thought of it, and who insisted on secrecy in case our service might amount to the mysterious sin of taking God's name in vain. 'It will only be all right' I was told severely, 'if *all* of us are absolutely sincere.' That was fine: I felt tremendously sincere. A glow of virtue flooded me, and I was smugly aware of God's surprised pleasure at our piety.

Unfortunately Anne decided to write the numbers of the hymns we would sing on cards and stick them up as though in a real church, and while doing so upset a bottle of Indian ink on a white counterpane . . . clear proof that we didn't have God's approval, even before the frightful moment when Hannah, the head housemaid, came in to see what all the whispering and giggling was about, and discovered the blotch.

Piety was often connected with our grandfather, because he had died. One morning, when I was six, we had all been made to sit quietly in the morning room while my mother read to us – an unusual event at that time of the day, but agreeable. Suddenly, from upstairs, there came a scream. It was a sound so foreign to our experience that we didn't quite believe we had heard it. Mum put down the book, stared into space for a few seconds, then got up and went out of the room without saying a word. Later that day Nanny took us out for a walk, and as we passed the front of the house I noticed that all three windows of the room in which Gramps had been lying ill were wide open. I asked why, and Nanny hushed me. Coming back from the walk we met Gran, who was going down to the stable-yard to feed her doves, as she always did. She looked tired. Before Nanny could stop me I ran up to her and asked 'Why are all Gramps's windows open?' – 'He's not there any more, my darling,' Gran said, her face full of sorrow and tenderness. 'He's gone away to Heaven to be with God.' The windows must have been open so that his soul could fly out of them. Later, it was a disappointment to learn I was too young for funerals. I longed to see the team of Suffolk Punches taking him to the church on one of the farm wagons, specially decked out for the occasion, and even more, to see Susan being led along behind. She was the little black hackney he always drove when he went to Norwich, who whizzed him along so fast that they covered the twelve miles in less than an hour.

Being with God made Gramps – in life a distant figure, presumably benign but never cosy – more approachable. He blended with God, and there was a time during the pious period when I felt that my prayers would be more effective if I said them in the room where he died. It took courage to go into that room (the one where the wolves used to lurk, now reverted to being the very best spare-room, too grand for children to sleep in), and even more courage to kneel down at the foot of the stately four-poster. I said the Our Father, and waited. The holiness in the room and the holiness in my heart seemed to swell, and to be about to merge – the sensation was almost physical – and Gramps's (or God's) presence, so earnestly hoped for to begin with, began to loom . . . Both times I did this my nerve failed, and I crept out of the room knowing I was a coward in giving up before what might have been going to happen actually did so.

The only time Gramps's spirit did intervene, it was in a manner both practical and kind. On a summer Sunday, when for some reason Pen and I had not been taken to church, we were left in charge of the dogs. If they were not shut up (which no one could bear to inflict on them) these dogs, not the gun-dogs but the family's pets, would disappear on hunting expeditions whenever they got a chance. It was a really bad sin to let the dogs go hunting, because they disturbed the game which enraged keepers, fathers and uncles, and they also risked getting stuck down rabbit-holes or caught in traps, which appalled everyone. The worst offender was Lola, Gran's poodle, a sober little dog of impeccable behaviour except that she was a devil for hunting, took with her any other dog who happened to be there, and would sometimes stay out for several days and nights during which everyone fretted and mourned.

On this Sunday we took several volumes of old *Punches* and climbed into the 'spreading-tree', an ancient larch trained into the shape of a table and propped on wooden supports. Easy to climb into, fragrant and feathery, it offered places where its twigs interlaced to form hammocks. Much time was spent in it, and much time was spent studying old *Punches*.

These – many volumes of them – lived behind the sofa in the morning room. Sometimes I sat on the floor in the cosy narrows between bookshelf and back of sofa, and looked at them there; but they were not the precious kind of book which had to be handled delicately, so could be lugged off wherever you wished. They were not for reading – the narrow columns of tiny type, so small that instead of looking like blackness on whiteness it gave the impression of foggy greyness, were too off-putting. It was the pictures with their rambling captions which fascinated me. I liked best the ones with horses in them – and most nineteenth-century outdoor scenes included horses – and the ones of handsome Edwardian ladies drawn by du Maurier, whose dresses I admired. The earlier ladies, in crinolines sometimes so huge that they got stuck in doorways, were funny but not so appealing (Gran said that she and her sisters used to despise girls who wore huge crinolines and laced their corsets so tightly that they fainted; and indeed, the only crinoline in the dressing-up chest was a modest one). It didn't occur to me that *Punch* was better than history books, but it was: it didn't seem to be about anything as abstract as 'the Past', just about how things used to be.

That day, up in the spreading-tree, the *Punches* were as absorbing as ever. When the family came back from church . . . no dogs.

Lunch would be served in a few minutes, but still neither of us felt it unjust when they rounded on us and said: 'Go out and find them, and don't come back until you have.' In tears, but unresentful, we set off through the park towards the bridge and weir simply because we had been shooed in that direction, our bare legs swished by the long grasses of summer. The dogs wouldn't still be in the park – Lola was too serious for the mild sport offered there – and it was only too possible that they had crossed the bridge into the woods stretching on either hand on the far side of the lake. When we reached the bridge the proliferation of potential directions overwhelmed us. We stood there, calling feebly 'Lola! Jeanie! Tarry!' knowing they were probably out of earshot by now, and wouldn't answer to being called anyway. Guilt and hopelessness combined, and we wept again.

'We'd better try the sand-field,' said Pen, two years my senior and, like her sister Anne, more given to virtue and self-sacrifice than I was. The sand-field, so-called for its light soil, adjoined the park and had a large rabbit population. When we scrambled through the hedge we saw that none of the rabbits were about: a hopeful sign – they might have gone to earth because the dogs had passed this way. We agreed that it was worth going on, and started towards the gap in the far hedge where once a gate had hung.

This gap was now full of a tall green growth, and we could soon see what it was: stinging-nettles. The hedge was impenetrable and the nettles merged at each side with its undergrowth of brambles. There was no path through, and the nettles stood as tall as us. Any adult would have walked up to the top of the field and round into the next one by another way, but we had become hypnotized by our impossible task and were capable of seeing no solution but going back home or going straight on. It was hot, we were hungry, the nettles smelt rank and were full of midges. 'We *can't* get through,' I sobbed; but Pen, on whom the situation was working differently, said: 'We must. We must pray.'

'To God, or to Gramps?' I asked.

'To both – and you must *really mean it*.'

'Shall we kneel down?'

No, said Pen, to kneel down out of doors would be showing-off. It would be enough if we shut our eyes and put our hands together. Even so, I felt uncomfortably exposed in the tense silence of our praying. 'Please, please God, and please Gramps, don't let the nettles sting me – us – and let the dogs be on the other side.'

Pen went first, silent but steady, her hands still together. I had a track to follow, but still the hairy leaves brushed my legs and arms, and sometimes even my neck. They might have been buttercups. So astounded were we when we reached the other side, both unstung, that we were unable to speak, and we were not surprised, only awestruck when we looked out over the field to see two of the dogs circling a clump of brambles, and earth dug by Lola showering out of its centre.

We took the dogs back by a different route, didn't talk about our miracle, and never tempted God or Gramps by asking for another. Partly this was because the pious fit was evaporating anyway, partly it was because we were scared. Whatever powers we had touched in Heaven or ourselves, we felt that nettles ought to sting.

What brought us to heel morally far more effectively than talk of Right and Wrong was the word that had such remarkable potency in our family: silly. It was the word most often used by grown-ups when they were scolding, and it worked so well because while 'naughty' or 'bad' added drama to a situation, and even hinted at forces which might be beyond your control, 'silly' was something you could easily be (very likely had been, in whatever was the case in point); and silliness was, or you felt it ought to be, within your control. It was a maddening, snubbing little word, and you often raged against it, but in the end it contributed a great deal to giving us the idea that people are responsible for their own actions, and ought to be prepared to accept their consequences. Far more than God, up there in His marvellous world of all-embracing love, and of magic, it belonged to the world we understood.

PAIN

THERE WAS, of course, pain, and pain of a kind more serious than that caused by the puzzles and humiliations of being young. Ours came from unhappiness between our parents.

Mothers were more important than fathers because fathers were often away, even when not posted overseas: and ours, though kind, was squeamish. He had a phobia about vomiting, so the ease with which babies spill their contents made him wary of us in our infancy. I know how powerful this revulsion can be because I have shared it, and for many years, if I had the misfortune to see or hear someone throwing up I would feel ill all day and for months afterwards whenever I chanced to recall it. I was eventually cured (more or less) by having from time to time to look after someone ill: in those circumstances, I could, by making a tremendous effort, overcome the phobia. But Dad never had to nurse anyone, so he was always afflicted by it, and it is possible that subconsciously he continued to see us, until we were safely grown-up, as creatures who *might* give him a horrible experience. He gave only the most dutiful of goodnight pecks and never hugged or stroked us.

We enjoyed him when he was funny, as he often was – indeed, on the only occasion he read to us he made it so tremendously funny that it was a new kind of experience, and I was disappointed that he never read to us again. We were happy to share jokes with him: for instance the *Who-is-Captain-of-this-ship-I-AM* that had to be shouted to stop a dithering argument about what we were going to do – the first person to get it out won, and it was usually but not always him. And he was brilliant at remembering comic songs. We – or at least I – knew that he was a very nice man. Nevertheless, we mirrored his lack of physical warmth. And, what is more, I have never in my life been attracted to a man of his physical type: fair-haired, blue-eyed, pink-skinned. And my brother once told me that when he was a boy he found Dad repulsive.

How could a trim man with pleasant features, an unusually agreeable nature and a lively sense of humour have become repulsive? It was a fate laid down for him long before he met her by his wife's mother, my beloved Gran.

Gran believed that no lady could want to be kissed by a man unless she truly loved him enough to marry him; and that no gentleman would dream of trying to kiss a lady unless he truly loved her enough to propose marriage. And this belief she handed down to her daughters. In most families there are both accepters and rejecters of parental beliefs, but in this one all the daughters turned out to be accepters (one of them found it impossible quite to fit in, but she blamed herself for it and did her gallant best to make up for it). Certainly my mother, the youngest, although spirited and full of *joie de vivre*, cheerfully accepted what her adored mother had taught her.

When she was nineteen, early in the second year of the First World War, she went to a dance and met a young army officer who had been invalided home from the front. Her friends all liked him, he was easy to talk to, and he loved country things as much as she did. He fell in love with her on sight, and before the evening was out had kissed her in the conservatory – and she had thoroughly enjoyed being kissed. It was the most exciting thing that had ever happened to her. My father was one of those gentlemen who would not have kissed a lady unless he had truly fallen in love with her, so very soon afterwards he asked her to marry him. Naturally she said yes. She knew she liked him, but more than that: she was sure she couldn't possibly enjoy being kissed so much if she didn't love him. It did not occur to her that lively girls enjoy being kissed because being kissed is fun.

Whether my father was a virgin, as my mother certainly was, I

Mum and Dad's wedding day, 1916

do not know, but I am sure that if he was not, it was by only a very narrow margin. He was a clergyman's son who had gone from his public school straight to the Royal Military Academy at Woolwich, and who – four years before meeting my mother – had received the following letter from the man about to be his commanding officer in the regiment he was joining straight from the Academy. And – more to the point – he was going to keep that letter all his life as an inspiration.

. . . I make section commanders very independent and make them entirely responsible for their men, horses, barrackrooms and discipline, as far as possible. I expect them to know their men and horses intimately, and see to their clothing, kits and all details of the equipment in the gun park, and to be good instructors in gunnery and musketry, riding and driving drills, and a friendly adviser to them in all other matters.

In the same way I expect my officers to come to me whenever in difficulty, official or private affairs, as I make myself responsible for them. A smart, keen officer makes, by example, smart, keen NCOs and men. In matters of duty one cannot be too particular, and I hold that supervision over an officer, to see whether he performs his duty or not, should never be required. An officer holding the King's Commission should never require supervision in the routine of his duty. He does his work whether seen or unseen as a gentleman, and 'plays the game' in spirit as well as letter in accordance with his C.O.'s desires. Play up for those under you whom you serve, and the result spells success in the Army for a man of ability.

Bad language and an overbearing manner does not get good work out of anyone. The Briton can be easily led but is a tough man to drive. Leading not driving is the system.

On parade I am your C.O. and expect soldierlike smartness in every action and address. Off parade I hope to be your instructor and adviser and companion in all field sports and pastimes. This letter I fear is rather of the nature of a 'jaw' but I thought it better to let you know what to expect.

I know you are a keen sportsman, and will stretch points to give you leave for hunting, shooting, fishing, football, cricket etc, but I do not care about 'racing men' and the class of people who go off to loaf about in Town. There is plenty of sport here to fill up all your time. We have a regimental pack of harriers – the subscription to it is five shillings a month in winter and two and sixpence in summer. Two afternoons a week we meet and you can gallop to your heart's content – but you must look after your horses on return! The Tidworth Foxhounds are also handy. There is football and hockey galore.

A keen sportsman usually makes the best soldier. He learns to acquire an 'eye for a country' and to keep himself fit, deny himself luxuries to take part in sport, and obtains a knowledge of men and manners which cannot be learnt elsewhere. He keeps himself morally and physically fit and those are the conditions requisite to enable him to learn instruction in soldiering.

To turn to other matters – you can have a good horse from Government for £10 a year, and this will probably be enough to commence with. If another is within your means (and I should like to hear from your people on the subject) no doubt we can pick up a cheap one for £30 or £40. The additional horse would cost you about £3 a month. As regards kit – a good hunting saddle and bridle (Sowters for choice) and a secondhand saddle from Parkers in St Martin's Lane (or elsewhere) and an exercising snaffle bridle. Bandages and a fawn rug with your initials on it (from the Stores) will set you up in horse kit except for a few odds and ends you can get from Battery stores.

As regards kit – a dark grey hunting frock coat which can be worn with a pot hat and butcher boots, and tan-coloured breeches, make a good harrier hunting kit. Daniells has our regimental hunt button, but if you want to do things cheaply go to Moss, 21 King Street, Covent Garden for the grey frock coat – he also has our hunt button which of course should be *black* ones, not brass. Later on, as you come along, we can think about white breeches and top boots and a top hat for foxhunting.

When fellows can mount themselves decently and go decently they are allowed to blossom out into a 'pink' coat, but there is plenty of time for that! Hunting kit is an economy as people cannot hunt in walking clothes. It ruins them and they look horrible and serve no purpose afterwards.

Butcher boots with soft legs and black tops look well, but plain butcher boots are good enough. Bartley makes the best boots, but old Craig and Davis are cheaper and can make a decent boot for many people.

A short hunting crop and brown leather thong. I get mine from near Weedon – Sharpe, Whipmaker, Flore, Weedon – and have them made 22 inches long. He is a cheap man.

In other matters write to me, and I will tell you what to do.
You can send this letter on to your people in case they want
any further information about your future surroundings.
. . .Yours sincerely.

D. G. Geddes

It is clear that any young man to whom D. G. Geddes stood *in
loco parentis* would need to be determinedly dissident if he wanted
to 'loaf about in Town' – which meant, of course, pursue the
company of women, to say nothing of gaining sexual experience of
them; and my gentle and honourable father was not even slightly
dissident by nature.

My mother had been told nothing about sex, except that she
might not at first like the thing men wanted to do, but would
get used to it. The only criticism of her mother I ever heard her
utter, almost a lifetime later, was that it had been wrong of her
not to overcome her embarrassment and say more. My mother's
honeymoon came – as it did to many brides of her generation – as
a shock.

Just before the war she had been sent abroad to a 'finishing
school', as was the custom in her sort of family: it was a way of
keeping girls at 'the awkward age' (we would say teenagers)
occupied. Smart people chose Paris, but Switzerland or Germany
seemed less risky to most parents, so my mother's lot was Dresden
and included exposure to a certain amount of Wagner which she
described in a letter home as 'lovely of course, but very long and
very noisy'. Another letter, addressed to a sister, is headed NOT
TO BE SHOWN TO ANYBODY NOT EVEN MOTHER, and
starts 'I say not even Mother because I am going to be vulgar and
I don't want darling little Mother to know how vulgar I can be.'

She then tells how, when she was out with other girls for an
evening stroll chaperoned by Mademoiselle, she saw approaching
under the lime trees a group of hussars, and soon realized that one
of them was gazing at her with alarming intensity. His gaze held her
throughout his approach, and as they passed each other his head
swivelled as though her face had magnetized his eyes. She blushed

scarlet 'from head to foot', and as she walked on she prayed that when the hussars reached the end of the promenade they would leave it, not turn round as Mademoiselle and her charges would do, to walk back. But no sooner had the girls started their return than she saw the hussars coming towards her again, and again he was gazing at her. And this time, when they passed each other, she (though still blushing furiously) lifted her eyes to meet his – and smiled! End of vulgarity.

Not much happened to increase her sophistication between then and her marriage. The discovery of what she was expected to do in bed with her husband threw her. She was a healthily passionate girl, but passion collided with ignorance so disastrously that the connection between the deliciousness of being kissed and the sexual act was broken. Full sex was not just disappointing, it was embarrassing and horrid. And my father – inexperienced, shy about physical demonstrations of affection, and probably ashamed of his own sexual impulses – was far from being able to prove her wrong. He was particularly at a disadvantage because it had not been *him* to whom she had responded so eagerly when he kissed her, only the fun of being kissed: he was not, physically, the type of man to whom she was drawn.

She did get used to it, and the first years of their marriage went reasonably well, helped by his being away a good deal, then by her being pregnant with me, and then, immediately after the war's end, by their sharing the adventure in Abyssinia – though that was rather spoilt by the beginning of her second pregnancy. But soon after my brother's birth she met a man – one of my father's fellow-officers – with whom she discovered what being in love and making love were really like, and that was the end of any attempt on her part at married happiness.

It was not, however, the end of the marriage. Her parents found out that she was having an affair: found out through the agency of the same sister to whom she had reported smiling at the hussar. That sister, though asked not to show the letter to anyone, NOT EVEN MOTHER, had promptly done just that, as was proved by my finding it in Gran's collection of all the letters she had ever received from her daughters. 'She always was a sneak,' said my mother, aged eighty-five – and so indeed she was. On a visit to London in about 1922 this sister was waiting for a friend in the hall of the University Women's Club, of which Mum was a member, when my mother swept in accompanied by an unknown man, looking so radiantly beautiful that for a moment she was not recognizable. What was said I do not know, but when my aunt got home next day she reported to their father: 'Kitty is having an affair.'

My aunt told me this herself, when I was driving her back from London to Norfolk one day, and why she told me I have never been able to work out. She was always slightly given to little paroxysms of confession, but this was not little, and nothing led up to it: we had just been laughing at some extravagance of my mother's when she suddenly said: 'Oh, poor Kit – I once did such a terrible thing to her, I could never tell you what it was.' Naturally I protested that to say so much without saying more was unforgivable, and – not very unwillingly – she gave way. What happened then, she said, was that Gramps wrote to my mother saying that unless she broke with this man at once the family would never see her again, my father found this letter in my mother's handbag, and my mother had a nervous breakdown and had to go into a nursing-home for a 'sleep-cure'.

Poking about in her handbag is so unlike my father that at first I found it hard to believe. But if the letter arrived by the first post, at breakfast time, and she opened it in front of him – 'Oh, look, a letter from Dad' . . . The shock would have been undisguisable, she would almost have fainted, would certainly have had to leave the room with it as fast as possible. And even if it didn't happen like that, there were other ways in which he could have known that the letter had come, then seen her dismay. And although he was not a particularly observant man, it seems likely that someone whose wife was so lit-up by an affair that her own sister had almost failed to recognize her, would already have had an inkling that something was up. My father may well have been in a tormented state for weeks, struggling to believe that his suspicions were unfounded, so that her reaction to her father's letter was the last straw.

'Sleep-cures' were popular during the twenties: the patient was sedated so heavily for several days that she was oblivious of whatever was done to her in the way of nourishment and evacuation (it sounds delicious).

I don't know whether my parents discussed divorce, but I doubt it. If my mother had got divorced she would have been cast out by her parents (perhaps, in the end, not; but she would have been convinced that this would happen at the time) and would have lost her children: it is improbable that my father, who truly loved her, could have borne inflicting all that on her, and certain that she would not have demanded it. Even if her lover was in a position to marry her – and I have no idea whether he was – I think she was too much a daughter to face the prospect of losing her parents in any circumstances, and probably too much a mother (though less so than she would later become) to face losing us.

From then on she *knew* that she loathed being touched by my father, although her guilt prevented her from entirely denying him his 'rights'. To continue having sex, even if only occasionally, with someone whose touch has become hateful, is nerve-racking; while on his side, poor man, to be unable to resist making love to someone you adore, even though you know she can hardly bear it, is misery. So the quarrels began – not, or not publicly, about what was really wrong, but about an endless series of little things: his unpunctuality, her extravagance, whether to do this or that, whether to go here or there . . . It became impossible for them to be together for more than two days running without there being a row, almost always started by her. There was never any physical violence worse than flouncing out of rooms and banging doors, but the emotional disturbance was acute.

It was only after my father's death that I learnt (again from letters) how sad and patient he had been. As soon as the Second World War began he had returned to the Army, and had the good fortune to be sent to Ethiopia to run an officers' training corps for Haile Selassie (he could speak Amharic – in fact he was probably the only officer in the British Army who could). This was a quirky kind of occupation that suited him – he became known for communicating with his headquarters by means of homing pigeons, which he trained. But the process of demobilization took a long time to reach him at his exotic outpost – a pink palace at Harar – and he was feeling pretty homesick by the time he wrote to my mother to tell her he would soon be back. It is distressing to know that he then, so many years after their trouble began, felt that he must *apologize* for his imminent reappearance, as something which she was unable to enjoy. 'I am so dreadfully sorry, my darling, that I have never been able to make you feel about me like Peggy feels about Geoff.'

Andrew and I, although no one we knew had been divorced, were aware of it as a possibility. From time to time we said to each other: 'Why don't they get divorced? It would be better than all this quarrelling.' It was years before it dawned on me that, given the law as it was then, if they had, we would have lost her. An aunt would presumably have been recruited to look after us: one of my father's two unmarried sisters, both of whom we liked well enough as aunts but who were unthinkable as mother-substitutes. Once I was grown-up, the thought of how much had been preserved for us by their decision to stay together made me profoundly grateful, though it was always painful to know of their pain.

It was institutionalized romanticism that did the damage: the fatal glorification of sexual excitement into Falling In Love, the dangerous concept of marriage as being In Love For Life. My mother had accepted those notions wholeheartedly, so when she found herself offending against them she thought herself nothing less than wicked. I am sure that she believed no one else among 'our sort of people' (people in books and so on didn't count) had ever done what she had done: a fearful burden to carry, but at that time unquestioned.

And even now I hesitate to say plainly what I myself believe about marital infidelity, because I know how cold-blooded it will seem to many people, among them some whom I love.

I believe that when the first flush of delight at being together has passed, infidelity is certainly not inevitable, but is and always has been very likely to take place if occasion offers. In most people's lives occasion offers only rarely unless pursued, and some people choose not to pursue, but not many will reject it if it turns up, as became perfectly clear during the war. I also believe that if infidelity does not cause heartbreak in a spouse or deprive children of a parent, and if it cheers up the two rule-breakers, thereby adding to the pleasure abroad in the world, it does no harm. I have never, therefore, seen any reason for all the mopping and mowing which goes on about it.

I do think, however, that even in the best-managed cases a couple ought to be very sure indeed that they understand each other before they indulge in mutual confession. For those who dislike dishonesty this is quite hard to accept – but think of what Tolstoy put poor Sonia through by his gross self-indulgence in honesty! It is up to the unfaithful to recognize the damage that might result from their conduct, and to avoid it if possible. Though of course they may, in their turn, start romanticizing what they are doing; and that, only too often, will cause mayhem. Falling In Love! I can still remember the ravishing sensation, the surge of vitality which gave brightness to the eyes and shine to the hair, the intoxication of it, as against the warm nourishing glow of plain *loving*. But 'intoxication' is what it is: it is as seductive and dangerous as alcohol, and should be handled as cautiously. How generations of romanticizing Romance can be counter-balanced is hard to see, but it ought to be done.

It is sad to think of my parents condemned to go through all their adult lives without any loving sex, harnessed together as mutual sources of unhappiness and guilt. It does, however, become less sad if I look at their marriage as a whole, because that reveals that they did somehow manage to develop the muscle to bear their burden. After he came home from Ethiopia it appears that both became less vulnerable, and when his job gave him the chance to live for six years in Southern Rhodesia (as Zimbabwe was then called), not only did she agree to accompany him, but she also enjoyed the experience. They had first to travel across Africa, sharing the driving of a truck, then build a house, living in a pair of *rondavels* until it was finished, and once he started managing the factory he had been sent to set up, she found much interest and entertainment in running their establishment and made many friends. They came back to England with a working companionship in place, and when he died in 1968, twenty years before she did, it was his generosity and gentleness that lived on in her mind. And she, in her long widowhood, was far from showing any sign of being embittered by past sadness. Instead she became calmer, kinder, wiser and more practically creative than most old women: someone who, rather than nurturing her sorrows, had preserved and worked on all the elements in her life – and there were many – that were worth having. Neither of them, in fact, allowed their less than happy marriage to become, in the end, as tragic as it might have been.

As children we, of course, had no idea of any reason why it might be tragic. All we knew was that there were rows, which we hated. I think Andrew knew more clearly than I did how much he hated them – he was younger than I was, and more vulnerable. I often managed to make myself think that I was irritated rather than frightened: 'How can they be *so silly*?' I used to say to myself; or, more often, 'How can *he* be so silly, always doing just the thing to make her lose her temper?' Because although it was clear to me that it was usually my mother who started the row, it was always my father I blamed for it. I 'sided' – we all three did, strongly – with her. Somehow – God knows how, because she certainly never *said* anything to indicate it – the fact that he had become repulsive to her conveyed itself to us, and as her nerves twanged, so did ours. What we desperately wanted when they were rowing was not that she would pull herself together and stop it, but that *he would go away*.

My grandmother was to say to me one day, when I was grown-up, 'Poor little girl, those quarrels used to make you so ill,' and I was astonished. Later still, when I had observed my own reactions to the stress of living in London during the bombing raids, I understood that she was right. I used to be surprised by the extent to which I was *not* frightened by the raids – but for the first time since I was a little girl I began to suffer again from colitis. So *that* was why I used to get those tummy-aches and sick-attacks when I was a child! I had been able to feel that I didn't so very much mind the rows because I *wasn't* minding them, I was stomaching them. And on consideration, I think I was lucky. It was a less painful way of getting through something bad than being fully aware of how bad it was, as my brother was.

But for us, quarrelling parents were not nearly – not anything like – so bad as they would have been if we had been less lucky in our circumstances. For one thing, there was always a buffer state of relations, nannies, governesses, housemaids, grooms, gardeners, farm friends around us, going on in its usual way, *continuing to be the same*, whatever was happening between our parents. It was one of those people who provided us with a useful formula: 'Your mummy and your daddy are both very nice people: it's just that perhaps they oughtn't to have got married to each other.' Andrew and I often used to repeat this formula and found it efficacious: it was the sort of thing grown-ups said, so it gave a feeling of detachment and superiority. And in addition to all these helpful people we had something even more valuable. We had space.

We came nearest to not having it when we lived for a couple of years in a five-bedroomed house in Hertfordshire with no land of its own except an orchard and a paddock. By then we had graduated from nursery to schoolroom, so we were eating all our meals with the grown-ups. Neither parent wished to shut us away (we were never shut away at any time, it was only that the layout of the larger house allowed much more spreading-out). So in 'the cottage' our family mingled closely all day except during lesson-time, and tensions had to be experienced by us all. Ursula's benign presence prevented it from being hell, but it was certainly a great deal worse than it ever was in Gran's house or the Farm, where we could simply disappear into our own world, forget the grown-ups, and enjoy life as much as ever. It chills my blood to think what it must be like for the children – the many, many children – of quarrelling parents who have to live without the space in which to create a world of their own.

The other source of pain was our own behaviour, and the pain was inflicted on the two cousins younger than ourselves.

Although we were the recipients of affectionate attention from older cousins, we did not transmit it onwards. Even Patience, before she became old enough to be a friend, received little from Andrew and me but teasing and irritable tolerance. I have sometimes watched with surprise and admiration the unselfconscious way a group of working-class children will accept responsibility for a baby, if their mother has sent it out in their care. If anyone had suggested such a task to us we would have gone on strike. One reason for this was, I think, the nursery/schoolroom split: when you moved out of the nursery you began to live a life quite different from that of the children still in it – even to see a good deal less of them. But Joyce and Anne had continued to be kind to us across that divide, so I fear that Andrew and I simply had less generous natures. And he, after having felt the stress of our parents' misery more acutely than I did, had then been forced to endure intense unhappiness by being sent away, at the age of eight, to boarding school: an unhappiness which naturally affected his behaviour.

To be sent away from home was the most frightful thing either of us could possibly imagine. I didn't have to imagine it until much later, when I was old enough to understand the reasons for it. Andrew knew that it was going to happen because it happened to all boys, but at the age of eight there is a big gap between the theoretical knowledge of something and the thing itself. When they actually put him in a car, drove him off and handed him over he had no alternative to bearing what felt unbearable.

He has never said that he was bullied at school, and he was quite a tough little boy so probably he wasn't. He was just exiled from all that he most passionately loved, in a place where nothing spoke to him. For a long time I kept two poems he sent me, one from his preparatory school, the other from Wellington, his public school: pathetic, clumsy little poems, one headed BURN THIS AT ONCE and the other NOT TO BE SHOWN TO ANYONE, 'anyone' underlined three times. Both were about being in a cold, dark place, dreaming of spring and birdsong and a dewy morning, then waking up and there, still, was the coldness and darkness.

Andrew (with catapult) and John on the terrace

So I knew he was unhappy. But I cannot remember thinking much about it – or feeling much about it, for that matter. Certainly I never questioned his fate: boys had to go to boarding schools, it was what always happened to them, poor things, and there was nothing anyone could do about it. Meanwhile I had my friendships with Pen and with other girls who did lessons with me, I had my ponies, I had my books, I had falling in love . . . I had moved out of the world I used to share with Andrew, when we busied ourselves together like squirrels or moles in the branches or the roots of adult life. The world I was now inhabiting was quite different. Only years later, when I was in my thirties, did I have a dream which told me how much I had known.

I dreamt that he and I, in high spirits, were running across grass together – and suddenly he was gone. I turned to see what had become of him and there were two men in uniform crouched over something stretched on the ground. Curious, and still happy, I ran back towards them, calling out 'What have you got there?' – and it was Andrew. One of the men half-rose and turned towards me, his eyes glaring; the other crouched lower over Andrew, one hand on his throat, the other clamped over his mouth. A scream of horror jolted out of me, waking me, and I lay there hearing my own voice moaning: 'Poor little boy – oh poor, poor little boy.'

It is easy to see how it worked on him. Having been exiled by the people he had thought to be his infallible protectors, when he was allowed back for limited periods he slid into rejecting them: an exile they had made him so an exile he would be. What had *not* rejected him was the place. He had been sent away from it, but it was still there, waiting for him. So what he did when he came back was burrow as deeply into the place, and stay as far from the family, as he could. It was not an instant or complete process, but gradually it became apparent that his preferred friends were boys from the village, his preferred dress was a smelly old many-pocketed gamekeeper's waistcoat, his preferred speech was broad Norfolk. At school he did as badly as he could (he would have to spend a year at a crammer before he could get into an agricultural college), and at home he behaved as badly as he dared. Which was sometimes so shamefully badly that it included tormenting a little boy eight years younger than himself.

Our two youngest cousins, Barbara and Colin, never felt as the rest of us did that they belonged to our beloved place. Barbara, with her brother Jimmy, had come for short visits when she was very young indeed, and had then been carried away to India by her parents; and in India the family was tragically stricken: Jimmy fell ill, and died. While we as little children had been wrapped snugly in the fabric of country life in Norfolk, she as a little child had been exposed to a blast of pain beyond our imagining. Her father's posting as Commander-in-Chief of a district centring on Bangalore still had two years to run, so her parents could not return at once to England. Feeling that they must not risk keeping Barbara and her little brother Colin in India, they first sent Colin and his nanny home to Gran's house, and about a year later her mother brought Barbara back too, and left her there. It would be for only a year, and where could the children be better cared for?

To a child of seven, 'only a year' might as well have been five or ten years; and my grandmother and her resident daughter, an aunt very dear to me, must have suffered some kind of blackout to their imaginations. They were not, of course, positively unkind, but to Barbara they did not seem loving. Perhaps no one could have seemed adequately loving, now that she was so far away from her very loving parents; but I do faintly remember comments about 'a rather sulky little girl' which suggest that they failed to understand how deeply unhappy she was – how traumatic Jimmy's death had been, and how it was possible for 'home' to be utterly unlike home to someone very young, lonely and unhappy, to whom it had never been anything of the sort.

When her parents came back they found a house in Dorset which worked a happy spell on Barbara and which she would later remember rather as we remembered Gran's house. But the latter had acquired unhappy associations. While she and Colin had been parentless there she had known not only loneliness, but anxiety: she had had to protect Colin – or so she felt – from Andrew. No doubt my brother would have protested 'I was only teasing him'; but teasing is always ambiguous and often masks cruelty (to which that protest can add a nasty little twist), and my sister confirms that at that time Andrew was often 'really horrid' to his juniors. I think that 'tormenting' was what the 'teasing' felt like to the victim and looked like to Barbara.

It was a shock to me when she told me about it, because I never had the least inkling of it. There were eight years between Barbara and me, and only two between me and Andrew, yet I had somehow contrived to ignore his unhappiness, and had been oblivious to the resulting 'horridness'. The picture it brings to my mind is of chickens pottering contentedly about their run as though nothing were wrong, while in a corner a group of them is pecking all the feathers out of one of their number.

My own theory about the boarding school phenomenon is that it was a reaction by the leisured classes to infantile sexuality. When a young Victorian mother (and my own mother was still Victorian in this respect) gazed fondly at her sweet, innocent baby boy in his nakedness, and suddenly his tiny penis stood up, I think she was horrified. Surely this little being, right at the start of life, couldn't have anything to do with what men liked to do in bed . . . but look at it! It clearly had. There, in the male creature, was the old Adam, even now.

So with boys you had to be very careful: however adorable they were, it was not wise to hug or kiss them too much. Some mothers even tried to turn them into girls, but that was obviously wrong – you wanted your little boy to grow up into a manly man, of course you did. But God forbid that the manliness should start before it had to, or that it should get out of hand. So the best thing to do was to isolate boys from the feminine, the sensuous, even before they could fully perceive it – to give them to trainers who would teach them to consume all their energy by *running about* a great deal . . .

It was not a problem that exercised the working classes, because their sons had to get out there and work as soon as they were out of short pants (or sooner – an old man in our village had been hired out to a farmer by his dad to pick stones off fields when he was eight years old). It arose from having time, as well as space. Of course boarding schools soon became muffled in blah about forming character and training boys to be leaders of men; and of course some families simply found it boring to have unfinished young people underfoot. But ours liked having us there, they wept genuine tears as they sent their little boys away. The imperative at work was a primitive one.

It is extraordinary that the men assented to it even more eagerly than the women. One can only assume that most men, being able to recognize their own sexiness, could easily, if caught young enough, be made to see it as bad; and then found it hard to understand the various kinds of damage done to them by this crude way of suppressing it. Or rather, of trying to suppress it, because naturally it did not succeed. My brother, for one, was to spend a good deal of his youth being far from seemly in his sexual behaviour.

But he did grow up to be a likeable man. He was to become the fond and understanding father of four sons, none of whom he sent to boarding school; and at Christmas lunch in his eightieth year he could look round the table at which sat all those sons, their wives and their children, and make the following pronouncement: 'At the risk of embarrassing you all horribly, and making my wife very cross, I want to say something. I want to say that *I have never been happier in all my life than I am today* when I look round this table and see you all here, still wanting to come back to us.' And when I said to him after lunch: 'And not only do they all still want to come back, but they're such an interesting lot, as well as being so nice,' he looked very sheepish and mumbled: 'I suppose you could say that Mary and I must have done *something* right' – which had, indeed, been evident for many years.

The truth is that although there are people who are permanently twisted out of shape as a result of painful childhood experiences, a great many more are not. And my brother is one of them.

FALLING IN LOVE

FALLING IN LOVE resembled riding, in that it was always there, even before I was aware of it. I can remember being told that I had wanted to marry a boy called John Sherbroke, but not the wanting: all that remains of that boy is a moment of embarrassment when he had come to tea, and Nanny, about to lift him out of his high chair, asked him 'Do you want to sit down?' That was her euphemism for using the chamber-pot, and I knew at once from his puzzled expression that in the Sherbroke nursery it must be called something else. Sure enough, he said 'I *am* sitting down,' and Nanny was slightly flustered. She had been silly, I thought. She should just have offered him the pot. The first infatuation that I can remember is the one with Denis, the gardener's boy, which happened when I was about four – or so I believe for reasons given when I described the experience in *Stet*. It took the form of romantic daydreams.

The only daydream material provided by the world came from fairy stories: no newspapers or magazines crossed the threshold of the nursery (Mum's *Vogue* came later), there was no television, grown-ups didn't talk to us about love. It was from fairy stories that I formed my notion of what glamour was: a princess. The Sleeping Beauty, Cinderella, the many princesses who had to be competed for by princes and who were won by the sons of humble men, that tiresome princess who was kept awake by a pea under a huge pile of mattresses (it was not possible quite to believe in that one): all of them ensured that the companions of Hal and Thomas were princesses, and that it was a princess I was trying to turn into when I called on the magic of dressing-up. But when I fell in love I didn't dream of myself as a princess being courted: that was too far from reality. Instead I used a different scenario, and where I got it from I do not know . . . Or didn't, until I reached this very point, when suddenly a name was spoken in my head: Grace Darling.

Of course it was Grace Darling, the gallant daughter of the lighthouse keeper, rowing her boat through the raging waves to rescue the shipwrecked sailors. *She* came into the nursery: nannies and nursery-maids loved to tell her story, and in some nurseries (not ours, alas) to sing her song. Jessica Mitford wrote a book about Grace and her myth, and could still sing her song with great spirit when I last met her, not long before her death; but I had forgotten her for years and years, until I first heard Jessica mention her. And now I remember her again, because she it must have been who sent me up cliffs, down pits, into burning houses, across flooding rivers, to rescue imperilled Denis, or Wilfred the cowman's son.

Those were deeply satisfying daydreams, because after the excitement of the rescue came the finale, in which my beloved, recovering from his swoon, opened his eyes and saw me bending over him. At that point Grace Darling retired and a princess took over: *my* princess, the essential me, the one Pen was not allowed to play. The princess with the cloud of night-black hair.

By the time David, recognized by me as my first real love and even acknowledged as such by other people, came on the scene, both Grace and the princess were beginning to fade out. I was eight when his parents rented the Hall Farm for a year: *our* house, because we had lived in it for a while when Dad was abroad (and would return to it when he was working in London). We were staying with Gran when this family of strangers moved in, and Andrew and I, all set for hostilities, crossed the back park and the water meadow on a scouting expedition, to size the invaders up.

David was away at school. It was his younger brother Robin

whom we met in the orchard, a small stout figure in a blue coat who turned his back on us to stomp away through the apple trees – shy rather than inimical, as it turned out. We followed him at a distance. When he climbed into one of the very old, half-fallen-down trees, we climbed after him. Whereupon something about him decided us almost at once that he was not a pubby, so we stopped resenting him and he became a friend.

Robin often referred to his big brother in a way which suggested that when David came home for the holidays we should respect him. He could do things we couldn't do, knew things we didn't know. Sometimes it was implied that if we got uppish David would put us in our place, which might have made us wary of him, but didn't. Robin was so much our kind of person that we were happy to fall in with his attitude, and looked forward eagerly to his brother's homecoming.

I don't remember *falling*, only *having fallen*: the hollow shape of love was in existence before we met, and was then gradually filled with this new reality. What I am sure of is that of all the loves in my life this was the most soundly based. I loved him because he was kind, brave, honest and reliable: a boy gentle to those younger than himself, who never seemed tempted to show off and who could check a dangerous game, such as climbing the hay-elevator with its rows of sharp up-curving prongs, without fearing that anyone would think him sissy.

When we were together, as we often were, in a group of my cousins and his, we were friends. Loving him made me happy if he picked me when choosing a team for a game, and even happier if he danced with me at a party, though he didn't dance very well; but it did not clutter me with self-consciousness. I did not expect him to know that I loved him, nor did I mind his not knowing. We wrote to each other when he was away at school and I kept his letters tied up with a blue ribbon, going to bed delighted if one of them began 'My dear Di' instead of plain 'Dear Di', or ended 'Much love' instead of 'Love'. I daydreamed about him as I had about the others, but the dreams were less far-fetched.

The princess vanished for ever when I was eleven, meeting her end in the bathroom of the Hertfordshire house – an apt setting. There was, of course, only one bathroom in that house, and it was of the utmost austerity. I would be approaching my thirties before I knew anyone who made their bathroom pretty, and was older still before the words 'en suite' began to appear in the vocabulary of house agents. In that same dreary little bathroom my mother had recently told me about menstruation, saying that it was a terrible bore but that one got used to it and it didn't hurt – for which sensible approach I became grateful when a friend told me that *her* mother tried to make her call it 'my little friend'. I had started to let my hair grow, hoping for plaits long enough to sit on, and was disappointed because they refused to do more than touch my shoulders. Having wiped the steam from the mirror, I was leaning on the washbasin to study their progress when a chilling thought swam into my mind: however much my appearance changed when I grew up – and surely it would change quite a lot? – it *must*! . . . but however much it did, I was never going to have huge dark eyes and a cloud of black hair.

Never.

It was not possible.

Blue eyes and mouse-coloured hair that refused to be more than shoulder-length: that was me, so I had better lump it.

It was a hard thought to take. And from that day on, if I tried to push a daydream too far into fantasy it stopped working.

Sometimes I managed to persuade a daydream to climax in a kiss, but in real life the only time David and I made physical contact, beyond hauling each other up a wall or dancing, was when we were at an agricultural show with our parents and had wandered off together. We were enjoying the smell of trodden grass, the music of the brass band, the splendour of the Shire horses with their manes and tails so elaborately braided and cockaded with colour, the brooding serenity of the beef cattle, the gleaming vermilion and sky-blue paint on the wagons and tractors. We were having a good time together . . . and suddenly I realized with a jolt that we were arm in arm.

It was the most wonderfully disturbing thing that had ever

happened: too much to bear. As though the jolt had been an electric shock, we started apart. I blushed too violently to be able to look at him and see if he was blushing too. I raged at myself inwardly for my lack of control: why, oh why hadn't I hidden my noticing so that my arm could have stayed in his, and me aware of it? How long had we been walking like that? Perhaps for a long time, and *I had missed it*! And which of us had first reached for the other? I wanted desperately for it to have been he, but it was no good: nothing could be fetched up but that we had been close and at ease. And now we were behaving like grown-ups, sparing each other embarrassment by pretending nothing had happened. I loved him the more for the way he did this . . . but oh God, suppose it was I who had taken his arm and he had thought 'How silly' but had been too kind to make a sign . . . But if that had been so, surely he would not have been walking and talking so naturally at the moment when I noticed: even if I *did* make the first move he couldn't have minded. I was to treasure that afternoon for a long time.

But there were temptations to infidelity even during that first love. He was not a very articulate boy, and what he laughed at most readily was farce. He would thoroughly enjoy it if someone sat down where there wasn't a chair – indeed, amusing events of a banana-skin type made landmarks for him: 'the time the wasp got into Uncle Harry's shirt', 'the time Mummy put salt instead of sugar into the fruit salad': he would refer to such occasions with almost pious regularity. There came a time when boys who found humour in ideas rather than predicaments began to have charm for me.

The first of these tempted me badly. Tim. He gave an impression of recklessness as well as of wit, he had a gift for words, and grown-up ways which seemed almost awe-inspiringly sophisticated, and he lent much sparkle to our activities. It was he who dubbed dam-building 'dearie-me building' after we had been scolded for swearing. I repeated his witticisms constantly; I only had to say 'We built a dearie-me' to myself in order to giggle. I thought about him often, and saw the possibility of changing allegiance.

By then I must have been twelve, the boys in their early teens. A group of parents – ours, some of our cousins', and those of both boys – had decided to spend part of the summer holidays together in Devonshire, some of them camping, some in a nearby hotel. We were among the campers, organized with military precision by my father in a group of tents clustered round a marquee, two rough fields away from the top of high cliffs. It was a lovely place, across the estuary from Salcombe, to which we were rowed by a ferryman when we went shopping for supplies. Golden, shell-strewn sand in little cliff-bound coves, rock-pools full of limpets and sea anemones, and sparkling blue water – all this was astonishing to us, accustomed as we were to the austere seaside places of East Anglia where the most majestic sight would be – if you were lucky – a stretch of sand-dunes, and the sea washing the shingle was usually nearer to gravy-coloured than blue. The holiday must have been hard work for parents, but for us it was the best we had ever had, and for me it was extra-good because of love. Which boat would I go out in today, David's, or Tim's? Had either of them noticed my successful dive from the high rock? Which of them would come with me to the spring to fill the drinking-water bucket? It didn't really matter which, because the presence of either was enough to fill an occasion with pleasure; but although neither boy was aware of me as anything but one among several playmates, I felt that I ought to make a choice. It would be a private matter, entailing no change in conduct, but to me it seemed necessary.

But it did not seem simple. I had been loving David for what seemed to me as good as ever, and now that I saw the possibility of loving someone else I was shocked as well as thrilled. I had not known that I was capable of such fickleness.

One evening when the flaps of my tent had been hitched back because of the heat, I lay in my sleeping bag doing two things at once: watching night fall, and reaching a decision. How could I be comfortable in my skin if I didn't know who I loved? Nightfall was beautiful and decision-making was important. Again and again my eyes followed the line of a distant, heathery hill, which swept down and then slightly up again to end in a promontory jutting out to sea. I wanted to fix its profile in my mind (I was always storing up nostalgia), and the way its colours slowly blurred into the darkness of a silhouette, and the sky's cool green deepened to night-colour. And I wanted to catch a star at the moment of its becoming visible, which seemed to be impossible. I stared at an empty piece of sky, glanced away for a moment, looked back – and there was a star as though it had always been present. The air was moist on the exposed part of my face, so I knew the grass was already thick with dew, and a cricket was chirruping, though not under my groundsheet as sometimes happened. Going to sleep out of doors in this wild place was so beautiful that it gave me an ache in my heart. And which of the two boys did I love?

David, of course. Alas. I felt cool inside, and solid, as though I had dug down to a base of some sort. 'What a pity', I thought, because I would so much have enjoyed loving Tim. But it wasn't David's fault that he was less amusing. It would be disloyal to abandon him because of that, when he had been a part of my life for so long. And he was so kind, so generous, so good – how could I turn against someone who had done nothing but continue to be himself? When I thought of him, his rival's very charm seemed a source of unfair advantage of which I could not approve. David was to remain my love for another two years, until I met the man, in my eyes grown-up, to whom I would eventually become engaged.

There was no – or no conscious – physicality in these early loves, yet while they were going on I was spending a great deal of time thinking about sex. Indeed, from the age of eleven, when revelation occurred, except when my mind was being positively invaded in one way or another, I thought of little else.

Revelation took the form of a small black book with nothing written on its cover. Why I pulled it out of a bookcase's bottom shelf where it was tucked away in a corner, I cannot imagine, but when I had read on its title-page the words 'Wise Parenthood' I started to turn the pages, supposing I was about to discover some method of raising children properly that my mother had once hoped to follow. As a result, I was never to suffer what she suffered on her honeymoon. From that early age I knew – not approximately but exactly – what men and women do in bed; and I also knew that it was one of life's best pleasures, and that I was going to start enjoying it *the minute I was old enough*.

The revelatrix was Marie Stopes, that absurd – even monstrous – woman who yet did more for her fellow-women than almost anyone else in the twentieth century. She made contraception acceptable, and on the way there she taught everyone who read her what she taught me. And in my case her lessons were supplemented by a posse of bawdy balladeers who had been collected into six volumes bound in white leather which dwelt in my grandfather's smoking room. Those, too, I fell on by chance.

Every year, either just before or just after the great Spring Cleaning to which her house was always subjected under Hannah's generalship, Gran 'did' Gramps's books. His library was extensive and valuable, in her eyes almost sacred, so that no one else was allowed to clean the books, not even Hannah. Gran would put on a cotton overall and one of her sunbonnets to keep the dust out of her beautiful white hair, and every single book she would take out, clap-clap to blow away any dirt settling between the pages, wipe with a soft clean duster, and (if the binding was leather) polish with a special unguent which she kept in a stone jar. She did the library, the morning room and the smoking room, and it took her weeks.

She was halfway through the smoking room when I went in to loll on the sofa and keep her company. The handsome white volumes, which she had piled on the floor near the desk, caught my eye, and I saw the word 'Ballads' on their spines. 'What are those?' I asked, with what I thought was virtuous curiosity – ballads were supposed to appeal to children because they were usually hearty, but they bored me. 'You wouldn't be interested in those,' said Gran, much too quickly – and in a flash my secret prowler was on to it. That evening, as soon as the house's silence assured me that the grown-ups were safely in the drawing room or the servants' hall, I nipped down and abducted one of the volumes to read under my bedclothes. In those days we didn't use the expression 'Wow' – but 'WOW' it was.

So I was unusually well-informed for my age, and I found the information wildly exciting – and yet, being in love was one of the things that served to take my mind off sex. I find it surprising now, but *then* it didn't enter my head that it should be otherwise. Children – because the word 'teenagers' was not yet in use, 'children' included people a good deal older than it includes now – children did not *do* sex. If a child of thirteen or fourteen dressed or behaved in contradiction of this 'fact', I saw them much as I saw someone who dressed or behaved in the wrong way when riding to hounds: absurd, and lacking in taste. When, in my mid-teens, I learnt that someone I actually knew had in fact 'done it', I was appalled – so much so that for a day or two I believed I would never recover from the shock; which was an odd reaction considering that what had been done was something I myself had been dreaming of eagerly for – by then – at least five years. (Fortunately my recovery from this shock was very much more rapid than I expected it to be.)

Women much younger than I am, belonging to generations in which lovemaking between teenagers is taken for granted, sometimes say that they embarked on sex when they did chiefly because it was expected of them: they would have looked silly to their contemporaries if they had been unwilling. Which makes me suppose that my own lack of resentment at having to wait so long to be 'old enough' was largely due to there being no peer pressure. If everybody you know, young as well as old, is thinking in the same way, you need to be a strongly dissident person to think differently. And it is possible – even probable – that some part of me was glad to be given so much time.

The acceptance of a constraint which may seem strange to many people nowadays, gained me, in the years between fourteen and eighteen, an intense experience of erotic pleasure, getting nearer and nearer to that of full lovemaking, which was thoroughly enjoyable. The first time a man's hand closed on mine and I turned mine so that our palms met was so exquisitely exciting that it still stirs me to remember it. Then came the first time someone sitting beside me in the back of a car put an arm round me and pulled me towards him so that my head rested on his shoulder; the first time a man, having done that, brushed my forehead with his lips (urgent question: would it be cheating to count that as *being kissed*?); the first real kiss, followed by the first open-mouthed kiss; the first hand on a breast, followed by the first unbuttoning leading to hand and lips on a bare breast (a tremendously exciting leap forward, that was) . . . And so it went on, incident by incident, each one pondered, savoured, dreamt about: the haze of sexy daydreaming through which I floated in those days must have been almost tangible.

It didn't matter much who was doing the touching or kissing, because I had fallen in love when I was fifteen (goodbye, dear David, goodbye!) and was quite sure that it was Paul's bed into which I would eventually sink; but he was five years older than I was and I had to catch up with him before I could expect him to fall in love with me. I was practising . . . and loving every moment of it.

Dances were where it mostly happened, ranging from modest 'hops' in small houses to full-scale balls in big ones, and including going with a group of friends to places such as the Assembly Rooms in Norwich where public dances were held, usually on a Saturday night. Mine was the first generation of country-house girls allowed to go to dances unchaperoned. To begin with we were driven in my grandmother's sedate car (complete with fur rug, footwarmer and speaking-tube) by Mr Youngman, her chauffeur, who collected us at midnight. The earliest moves in love's game were therefore given an extra thrill by taking place secretly, under that rug. But soon young men with wheels were invited to dinner and drove us to the dances . . . The true beginning of the sexual revolution for us came long before the sixties, with the car. Once a man and girl who had been dancing together all evening were able to drive home alone together in that little capsule of safe privacy, the deliciously slow progress towards loss of virginity accelerated to a rush.

Being sent to boarding school helped to check this rush, as far as I was concerned, and probably for other girls, too (though I gained the impression that I was looking forward to its conclusion more eagerly than most of my friends). School happened to me when I was fourteen, and made freedom part-time. A result of no one's recognizing the teens as a separate condition was impatience to be grown-up: although I no longer felt like a child, I was having to bide my time before bursting forth as what I did feel like, which was more or less adult. Boarding school was a good way of getting through this not-quite-yet time; it controlled restlessness within a discipline that I could accept because it was part of the set-up as a whole, not directed at me as an individual.

There was one moment, some time in my seventeenth year, when I broke ranks. A particularly good dance was being given by some grand neighbours of ours, not long before the end of my school's winter term. It seemed a pity that I should miss it, so much so that my mother hit on a solution: my teeth did in fact need attention, so she asked my headmistress if she could take me for a day's visit to a London dentist, which would mean keeping me out for a night – and the date of the dentist's appointment (this, of course, was not revealed) was that of the dance, for which we could get back from London just in time. It was a delightfully daring plan: no present-day schoolgirl can have any idea of the convent-like seclusion imposed by headmistresses in my day. Letters were censored, outings apart from those at half-term were forbidden, no girl was ever allowed to leave the school grounds alone, and it didn't occur to anyone that parent and child might communicate by telephone. Permission to visit a London dentist was a favour so great that even by its agonizing self (no injections in those days except for extractions) it would have been a treat.

Early on the morning after the dance my father drove me back to school, and left a note for the headmistress, with whom he got on well, confessing that I had been to a dance. His almost obsessive honesty compelled him to it, but he certainly didn't feel that he was purging a serious sin: he expected her to find it funny.

Instead, I was summoned to her study and threatened with expulsion. So violently did she berate me that what began as a schoolgirl's dismay at being found out suddenly switched to an adult's astonishment at absurd over-reaction, so that when at last she thundered: 'Have you no sense of honour at all?' I answered coldly: '*Not* if that is what you mean by a sense of honour.' I can no longer remember how the interview ended, except for having a gratifying sense that she was disconcerted; and she must, when she recovered from her rage, have seen that she was making a mountain out of a molehill. She did, to my father's amusement, write him a pompous little note telling him that he had not behaved like a gentleman, but she did not expel me – indeed, I ended as the school's head girl. The incident remained in my mind as a pleasing one – the tip of a toe in the sea of being grown-up.

At no time was school as painful for me as it had been for Andrew. A person of fourteen has a better sense of time than one of eight, so although the thirteen weeks of my first term looked hideously long, they did not look endless, and even during that term I could see the point of being educated. Later, although my recognition of the school's quality was always grudging and I never stopped wanting to be free of it, I did see that as schools went it was a good one. I enjoyed the friends I made there, it taught me a lot and got me into Oxford, and it also turned me round and shoved me gently but firmly away from what was behind me, towards real life.

Diana Athill, 2000

NOW

L OOKING BACK, I see that I moved away from childhood expecting the answer 'Yes!' And to begin with it *was* a return to Eden – to the house, the horses, the dances, the freedom to read what I liked – and an Eden with wider horizons than formerly. There was a year between school and university which I spent at home as a grown-up, which might have become claustrophobic if I had thought it would last longer than that, but Oxford was coming and after Oxford real life, so I felt free to luxuriate in that year rather than to chafe at its restrictions.

It is extraordinary that in 1935–36 anyone could have felt so sure that the future was going to be happy. At school we had access to all the serious newspapers and weeklies, and were encouraged to think about what we read. Considering myself a serious-minded girl, I had also read a certain amount of left-wing and pacifist literature: I knew that Britain was a scandalous mess and that the Versailles Treaty had sown the seeds of a second world war, and I had responded by glibly declaring myself a socialist and a pacifist. But my guts were not listening to my head.

I was not alone in this. The Sunday *Observer*, more than any other newspaper, was alert to what was going on in Germany and prescient as to where it was heading: every weekend its Cassandra-like leaders wailed their warning. And my father cancelled his subscription. This was not because he disbelieved the message, but because he found it all too easy to believe. He knew what he was going to do when the worst happened: he was on the reserve, so he

would be back in the Army straight away without a moment's
hesitation; but he was damned if he was going to waste good time
brooding on it in advance. And I suppose I, in a less reasoned way,
felt the same. But how I managed to make this work – to go on
actually *feeling* as though my future was a happy one – I can't
explain.

Perhaps it was being in love, and knowing at last that the man
I called Paul in *Instead of a Letter*, for whose response I had been
waiting trustfully since I was fifteen, was now in love with me.
We were going to be married (he was in the RAF, flying
bombers: why was I not terrified for him?). So perhaps the gut-
expectation of the answer 'Yes!' came from my certainty of that,
as much as it did from conditioning. I ought to have been able to
feel the reality of the 'No!' which was soon to come to the world's
peace, but I had no way of foreseeing the 'No!' ahead of me
within my own life.

Both came. The gates of Eden clanged shut. I have told the story
of unhappy love and my recovery from it in *Instead of a Letter*, so
I will say no more here than that first his letters stopped coming,
then one came asking me to release him from our engagement
because he was about to marry someone else, and soon after that
he was killed. I have also, in *Stet*, told the story of the good life I had
in publishing in spite of this unhappiness – some of it even while
the unhappiness was still there. And now I can see more clearly
than I used to, how the roots of this life-saving career can be traced
back to the childhood I have been describing in this book.

Someone from a family in which everyone obviously found books
one of life's main sources of pleasure could hardly fail to grab at
a chance to work in publishing if offered. I had been brought up
in the knowledge that books were fun, as well as important. My
father's passion for P. G. Wodehouse, which I shared, almost
amounted to an addiction, so that when he came home with the
latest Wodehouse which he, naturally, had to finish before anyone
else could so much as touch it, I was so frantic at having to wait
for it that I would have darted in and snatched it if he had given

me the smallest chance. And at the same time the greatness of great writers was seen as greatness of the most solemn kind. Books were up there with nature and love as the things which mattered most.

And so, in my old age, they still are. To me the radio always meant music, so when my hearing began to go I listened less and less, and now not at all; and television, which never seemed as enjoyable as I hoped it would be, has become something for which I can rarely be bothered to walk into the next room (I wouldn't dream of having it in my own). So books are impossible to do without.

Some of this dependence is a matter of habit: lacking a book which I actually want to read, I will munch away on one which means little to me, though never on one which annoys me – I would rather clean the silver or patch a sheet than do that. And when this happens, I will forget the book within a week. Most often it will be a novel because fiction, these days, has to be more than just well-written (as most of it is) to hold me. Like most of the old people I know, what I am looking for is material for my own imagination to work on, rather than experience predigested by someone else into a story.

The fiction-writers I am still able fully to enjoy are those like Alice Munro, Raymond Carver, Pat Barker or Hilary Mantel who pay such close attention to their subject that one almost forgets their intervention between oneself and whatever it is. 'Look-at-me!' writing of the Martin Amis kind, much as it attracts many people, has always left me cold, as do fanciful capers however inventive. To me they seem to intrude between the reader and the raw material of life, rather than to illuminate it, and never having had much patience with them, now I have none. Although eccentricity does not necessarily put me off. A recent discovery, David Foster Wallace, who seems to be obsessional almost to the point of madness so that too often he threatens to smother the reader, has nevertheless done some of the best writing I have ever read, for which I am very grateful.

As well as turning more often to non-fiction, I indulge in

another habit common among old people: rereading old favourites, some of them so old as to come from my earliest days. In the little Norfolk house where I spend many weekends there are shelves still full of books from my cousin's childhood, many of which also figured in mine, and it is amusing to pull out, say, *The Count of Monte Cristo* and find that it is, indeed, an excellent story; or one of Daphne du Maurier's lesser works and think 'Oh my God, how could I *ever* . . . !' A few books which I read greedily, not in childhood but as a very young woman, I avoid reading again because I suspect they would fill me with shame: the novels of Charles Morgan, for instance, best sellers in their day, well reviewed and eagerly consumed by many, including me – and now I'm pretty sure they were pretentious garbage. And some of my most beloved books – those of Tolstoy and Jane Austen, for example – I have deliberately left aside for a long time because I want to come back to them once more before I die with a fresh eye.

Two other occupations which I love, and which came to me late in life as though they were discoveries, grew in fact from long-buried roots: gardening and needlework.

My mother and my aunts were enthusiastic and knowledgeable gardeners and I always enjoyed what their enthusiasm produced, but I never felt the smallest tingle of interest in the actual occupation of gardening – never pulled a weed or sowed a seed, or imagined myself doing so in the future, until I was in my sixties, when Barbara, leaving London to do a six-year stint for her paper in Washington, said to me rather apologetically: 'Do you think you could just sort of keep an eye on the garden so that it doesn't go *quite* wild?' The garden was a neglected London lawn with a rose-bed at one side of it, full of valiant roses which had been old when we moved into the house. It had one crab-apple tree planted when Barbara's son was born, a vast laurel and even vaster and fiendishly thorny pyracantha which combined to shade most of the space, and very little charm. It had served a happy purpose as a playground for children and habitat for guinea-pigs, but had never been much loved for itself. The day after Barbara left I leant out of my bedroom window, gave the garden a long look, and found myself thinking 'There's nothing for it: I'll have to re-seed the lawn and do the whole thing over from scratch'. Which I did, at considerable expense of money and work, and as soon as one plant put into the earth by my own inexpert hands performed the miracle of actually *growing*, I was hooked.

Now, alas, I can no longer do more than a very little gardening with my own hands, and have had greatly to simplify the London garden; but in the much larger and more complicated Norfolk garden I have luckily been able to call on the help of a neighbour who is as full of ideas as she is of energy, and – as we tell each other constantly – 'we are getting there'. And pottering about in it, doing the small things that I am still able to do, is a deep and peaceful pleasure.

That I also followed my mother into doing needlepoint embroidery is even odder, because I used to watch her at it with amazement – almost with horror – at the slowness of it, at the patience it required. If she decided that something had gone wrong, so that she must unpick what she had done and start again . . . no, I couldn't see how anyone could *bear* such a task, and as for finding it enjoyable . . . ! What tempted me into it was a book we published – *A Pageant of Pattern for Needlepoint Canvas* by a brilliant American amateur called Sherlee Lantz – which showed me that I could work to my own designs instead of following patterns painted on the canvas, as my mother had always done. Stitching your own design is far more exciting, because you are never quite sure how it's going to turn out. I had always wanted to paint and had even gone through a spell as a Sunday painter, abandoned when I realized that I was not going to be able to give enough time to it to become any good. Now I discovered that if I didn't think of myself as 'drawing', but simply as marking out what I wanted to put on the canvas – then I could in fact draw! And away I went, having a lovely time and not hesitating for a minute if it became apparent that something needed to be unpicked and done over again. It is true that there comes a time when one can't think of anyone else for whom to make a cushion or a chair-seat or a fire-screen or a hanging . . . but all the same, I expect I shall go back to it when I have finished writing. There is something astonishingly satisfying about holding in your hands a physical object that didn't exist until you made it.

If you took a group of octogenarians – let's say a hundred old reservoirs of experience – my guess is that about a quarter of them would *look* as though their contents were mostly disagreeable: as though, if they were turned inside out, you would see disappointment, disapproval, pain. None of my family has looked like that, and neither do I. And my reluctant conclusion is that this is because of the privileges we all enjoyed as a result of being born into the upper reaches of the middle class, and in the country.

To take the simplest things first: we were fed on ample amounts of healthy food, all of it fresh, and we had access to up-to-date medical care and sanitation and were taught the basic rules of hygiene such as enough sleep, plenty of fresh air and exercise, and don't drink too much. On top of that we were given good educations so that we could keep our minds occupied and find interest in a wide range of subjects, and enough leisure to indulge in enjoyable hobbies. And the standards of behaviour set by our forebears were reasonable, because they had not been *over*-privileged to the point of becoming arrogant or self-indulgent (that balance, I believe, has been important). In my generation, anyway, our childhood was directed with common sense as well as with love, and our surroundings were so secure and pleasant that we could be free of constant surveillance. And above all we lived in a place which we felt was ours and which we loved: we were rooted.

Of course I don't mean that people with other backgrounds cannot flourish. It is self-evident that they do – and remarkably, so do some people with backgrounds insalubrious enough to cripple, proof that innate qualities can withstand lack of nurture in a marvellous way. Those are the people who most deserve celebration: the ones who challenge easy pessimism about humanity, and who have warmed me, when I have met them, with currents of hope. Two of them, Morris Stock and Daphne Anderson, I remembered in *Stet*; and a third, to my great good fortune has become a friend in my old age: Andrea Ashworth, whose *Once in a House on Fire* never fails to leave a sort of amazed happiness in those who read it. The opposite can also be true: people born in fortunate circumstances can prove to have natures which warp in spite of it. So it would be absurd to claim too much on the grounds of any individual's experience, and all I mean to say is that it seems likely to be *easier* to reach a contented and sturdy old age if you have had my kind of luck, and I can't imagine myself having done so without it. Apart from anything else, there is that ingrained self-confidence which comes from the indecent sense of superiority which we were allowed to have as children. My own surface self-confidence was smashed when Paul jilted me, and I am not sure that I would have survived without the support of the secret – the inadmissible – self-confidence which underlay it.

But chiefly it is the place for which I am grateful, not as it now is, but as it was. It is that which constantly makes its way to the top of the rag-bag of memories that I have become. Suddenly I will see the chaffinch's nest which Pen and I found on a winter's morning when, under a hard blue sky, every single twig and thread was coated with sparkling hoarfrost. Chaffinches make the neatest, prettiest nest of all, and that one had been turned into an exquisite miracle of silver and diamonds. Or the stream above the weir which marks the lake's beginning, where it runs shallow under alders and we had decided to bathe naked – it seemed like a wild thing to do. We rode out to it bareback in nothing but cotton frocks, turned the ponies loose to graze, scrambled down the bank, stripped off our frocks – and found that the water didn't even reach our knees. Having got so far we felt we had to lie down in it, which was cold and uncomfortable because the bottom was gravel, not mud, which was why the water running limpid over gold had looked so tempting. And no sooner had we pulled on our frocks and vaulted onto our ponies (bare pony under wet bare bottoms felt very odd) than Aunt Joyce appeared, walking her dog. Why, she asked, were we wet? So we had to tell her – would she think our nakedness wicked? But when she said it would have made more sense to choose a deeper place and wear swimsuits she was laughing, so that was all right. Or the huge old hollow oak at the bottom of the farm orchard, with flames roaring out of it as though it was a giant's torch, when Andrew, then seven, had thought he could smoke out a wasps' nest (or was it a hornets'?) by lighting a fire inside it – the tree went on burning all night. Or the two trees in the orchard which bore little yellow apples, delicious if eaten off the branch but useless otherwise, on the day when my mother and I took our watercolour boxes and sat down to paint them in blossom – oh, the smell of apple-blossom on a sunny day! . . .

Here I am almost at my end, and my beginning rises up to meet me – or rather, even when I thought I was far away from it, it was always there, and now I have come back to it. And because in my eyes it was always so beautiful, it delights me yet again. It is too much to ask – I ought not to allow myself even to think of it – but perhaps it is not entirely impossible that I might, like my mother, come to the end of my days murmuring about some random memory: 'It was absolutely divine'.

In the kitchen garden with Andrew, circa 1925

INSTEAD OF
A LETTER

Introduction

I FIRST MET Diana Athill when we shared a stage at a book festival in the summer of 2000. We had come to Hay-on-Wye to talk about the memoirs we had written: *Once in a House on Fire*, about my growing up under tough circumstances in Manchester; and *Stet*, about Athill's fifty years in London book publishing. At eighty-two, this solidly confident and brisk lady was more than half a century older than me. The audience might have imagined that, other than our both having written about our lives, we had very little in common. But we hit it off immediately. Surprisingly youthful, Diana was formidable yet full of fun – and unafraid to talk about things that others might shy away from. On that first occasion, my pleasure in meeting her was heightened by an odd sort of déjà vu, for in her voice and her eyes I recognized all the humour and wisdom that I knew from her writing.

Athill's language combines immediacy, ease and precision of expression. A lifetime of reading and editing makes itself felt in the fine structure and pace of each of her books. Above all, she is a virtuoso at what she calls 'seeing things'. Sitting down to write her first story, she told herself, 'I'm going to get it *just as it was*.'

'My aunt and my own temperament equipped me with eyes,' Athill says in *Instead of a Letter*, as she describes an enlightening moment. 'I was drawing horses, as I constantly did, when [my aunt] leant over my shoulder and said, "Draw a naked man – a man or a woman."' The young Diana drew 'a shapeless forked radish'. Seeing the look on her aunt's face, she knew 'that I had failed in some way: that there was something of significance I should have been able to do with the human body instead of being embarrassed by it.'

That childhood epiphany occurred in the early 1920s; eighty years on, Diana Athill is recognized as a remarkably honest anatomist of human psychology. Her books bristle with intimacy. She looks at life, and herself, with peeling lucidity. Her writing is vivacious and unsentimental; often funny and painful in the same wince; piercing yet charming. These qualities shine through both her fiction and her non-fiction. Yet for most of her working life – spent as chief editor at the publishing house of André Deutsch, which she helped to found – Diana Athill did not regard herself primarily as a writer. She was forty-four years old when her first book, *Instead of a Letter*, was published in 1962. The autobiography of an ordinary person, someone of no great public eminence, *Instead of a Letter* was a curious work of non-fiction – what its author referred to as a 'documentary', and what we would today call a 'memoir'. Athill went on to publish several other books: a collection of short stories (*An Unavoidable Delay*, 1962), a novel (*Don't Look at Me Like That*, 1967) and two more 'documentaries' (*After a Funeral*, 1986 and *Make Believe*, 1993). But she never relinquished her day job, which offered her security and standing (she was known to be one of the best book editors in London) as well as satisfaction. As her work saved her from having to write for a living, she wrote only when she felt confident that she had something to say.

Athill's fifty years in publishing are the subject of her sixth book, *Stet*, which received enthusiastic and widespread acclaim in Britain (where it was published by Granta Books in 2000) and in North America. She had not published a book for almost a decade, and many readers were new to her lively and intelligent voice. *Stet* told the story of her relationship with André Deutsch (who died the year the book came out), the man who had been her boss, close friend and (briefly) lover, and narrated the history of the books she helped shape, giving sharp and entertaining cameos of authors such as V. S. Naipaul, Jean Rhys and Brian Moore. Memoirs set in the world of publishing make up a small and not particularly popular genre, but *Stet* broke out of the boundaries of its obvious audience (not a large one) and became, as many reviewers noted, that thing called a 'classic' – a book to be enjoyed by people who had never crossed a publisher's doorstep, had never wanted to, and never would. This was a victory for her skill as a writer, and for the personality in her writing. For all its candour and nuance, however, *Stet* is only obliquely self-revealing. Having introduced us to an individual already formed, it leaves us wondering how Athill came to be the person she is, how she came to see the way she sees.

Instead of a Letter, Athill's most personal book, allows us to watch the formation of that character. At its heart lies the tragic story of how she fell in love for the first time, eventually to suffer severe disappointment and attacks of grief and loneliness that eroded her self-esteem. In this memoir, we witness a soul first being drained of vitality, then slowly, painstakingly returning to life. We see Athill emerge, not only alive, but full of vivacity, blessed with a way of seeing that is lyrically sensitive yet grounded in a thumpingly pragmatic, sensibly-proportioned approach to herself and to life.

Athill's vision is especially remarkable given the insularity of her privileged background. 'There I used to be,' she writes of her idyllic beginnings in the Norfolk countryside, 'as snug and as smug as anyone, believing with the best that we were the best.' Born in 1917, the daughter of an army colonel, she spent much of her childhood at her grandparents' house where, in spite of her family's ailing finances,

necessities included a head gardener with two men under him, two grooms, a chauffeur, a butler and a footman, a cook and a kitchenmaid with a scullery maid to help them, a head housemaid with two under-housemaids, and my grandmother's lady's maid. They included, too, animals for our pleasure and governesses and schools for our instruction. They included books and a great deal of wholesome food, linen sheets rather than cotton, and three separate rooms for being in at different times of the day, not counting the dining-room, the smoking-room, the front hall, in which, for some reason, my grandmother always had tea, and the nursery.

Swathed in comfort, boasting an armigerous ancestry rich with 'rustic Athill knights', she seemed poised to grow up and go out into the world with her 'sense of superiority' unruffled. Yet, even at the age of ten, Diana had shocked her grandmother with a flight of fancy that suggested she understood there was a more turbulent world beyond the shelter of nursery teas:

I thought that it was as though people were confined in a bowl which was floating on a sea. While snug at the bottom of the bowl they lived their lives complacently, but the bowl spun and tossed on the sea and its spinning sometimes sent one of them up its side until he could see over its rim. All round would be the endless chaos of dangerous, cold grey water, unsuspected till then, and anyone who had seen it and had understood that what he had thought was safety was only a little bowl, would not be able to bear it.

Through reading books and with the encouragement of the aunt who had nudged her to try her hand at drawing nudes, Diana began to sense that 'the family's way of thinking' was narrowly trammelled. Still, she galloped – largely unquestioning – through an adolescence that revolved around 'horses and sex', in which 'hours – weeks, months, years' were spent thinking about clothes. By the time she left school, she had grown to be an 'exuberant, slightly gauche girl', 'affected and a little arrogant', her attitudes in danger of hardening into blinkered self-satisfaction.

Meanwhile, 'Paul began'. A high-spirited man who 'went like steel to magnet for the essence of any person, place, activity or situation, working from no preconception or preferred framework,' Paul was an Oxford undergraduate who came to the family house to tutor Athill's younger brother. At fifteen, Diana fell fervently in love – with the man, and with his embrace of life – and, in that moment, 'the lines of my life were laid down'. She learned, through her irrepressibly open-minded lover, to regard difference without prejudice, to move between worlds, even bring them together. It was Paul, Athill tells us, who 'broke down my conditioning and made me anxious to meet people as people, regardless of class or race: a freedom from shackles which did not then chafe me, but which would probably have become locked on me, for which I shall always thank him.'

The social breadth of this new vision was matched by an intense sensuality that intoxicated Diana.

> When [Paul] went with me to pick primroses one Easter . . . he was astonished at my matter-of-fact attitude to the thick cushions of flowers in a certain part of the wood. I took it for granted that primroses grew thickly there – they always did. He, who lived either in London or on the coast, where they did not flourish, *saw* them.

Paul buried his face in a clump of primroses, laughing. After that, Diana *saw:*

> At once the frail, reddish, slightly hairy stalks of the primroses, their delicate petals, the neat funnels of their centres, the young leaves, folded and lettuce-green among the darker, broader old ones, the grouping of each constellation of flowers, their delicious, rain-fresh scent – everything about them became alive.

In the mid-1930s, Athill went up to Oxford to study English Literature. During her three years there, she became engaged to Paul, at the same time enjoying sundry 'subsidiary relationships' with other men: 'little explosions of meeting' that 'were constantly blasting new shafts into the mine of experience.' She and her friends lived in the shadow of impending war, but managed to be happy, to avoid feeling blighted by 'this horror about life'. 'I was frivolous, and I was lazy,' she says of her undergraduate self, 'and it seems to me now that I was lucky to be those things, because by being able almost all the time to slide sideways, not to think, I could store three years away like jewels before it came.'

The horror, when 'it' hit, came not only in the form of the Second World War and its bombs. In a cruelly protracted way, Diana lost Paul. The shock of this rejection tore a hole in her life, marking the start of what she refers to as 'twenty years of unhappiness'. Her contented childhood and her happy years at Oxford had given her a stability and resilience that ultimately helped her to retain her 'bias towards being *well-disposed* to life.' But for a long time, 'the most intense emotion [she] could conceive of was one of pain.'

Athill's account of the 'revolting humiliations' of grief and of the spartan emotional existence into which she sank during the war is pungent with sadness and haunted by a creeping threat of sourness. 'A long, flat unhappiness of that sort drains one, substitutes for blood some thin, acid fluid with a disagreeable smell,' she observes. 'Years of emptiness. Years leprous with boredom, drained by the war of meaning.' Having found a modest job working for the BBC's Overseas Service, she 'retreated into a curious hermit existence' while her 'soul shrank to the size of a pea.'

Athill analyses her misery – and her attempts to dodge or defeat it – with exquisite acuity. *Instead of a Letter* glitters with chiaruscuro effects, evincing the author's life-saving skill at seeing in the dark. 'After the late shift the tiny sequins of the traffic lights, reduced by masks during the blackout, changed from red to amber to green down the whole length of empty, silent Oxford Street. They looked as though they were signalling a whispered conversation, and they were the kind of thing with which I filled my days.'

To fill her nights as well as her days, Athill began to 'grab at emotion' in a series of 'foolish' and brief sexual encounters. In these harsher, sadder passages, *Instead of a Letter* is suffused with an unusual kind of intimacy. The narrative not only explores the recesses of Athill's psyche and 'the body's truth', revealing her most private thoughts, feelings and actions, but also invites the reader to watch the writer watching herself. 'I would split in two,' she says of her trance-like phase of casual affairs, 'one half going obediently and easily through the routine, the other watching with an ironic amusement.' The sharpness of what she elsewhere refers to as her 'beady eye' (trained, to such comic and discomfiting effect, upon others in her later memoirs) is here very often turned upon herself.

This 'watching half' of Athill keeps her work refreshingly free of self-absorption. Escaping the characteristic dangers of memoir, she reveals herself without sliding into narcissism, and lights up the smallest, most ordinary details of her life in a way that conveys their significance and appeal without distorting them through exaggeration or sentimentality. Hers is a rare kind of candour: she addresses her readers with a strikingly modern lack of squeamishness and secrecy about personal experience, but is never gratuitously shocking or cloyingly confessional. It is, as she acknowledges, 'difficult to consider with detachment' such experiences as promiscuity, abortion, and the life-threatening miscarriage she describes in *After a Funeral*. But Athill writes with a detachment that is carefully calibrated. Her memoirs have a distinctive introspective quality – free of claustrophobia, yet never less than fully engaged. Rendering her ordeals and delights, she pulls us into her story, her consciousness, without pushing us into the sticky position of voyeurs. She makes us privy to sometimes shocking intimacies but spares us the imposition of any self-pity. The depth of her psychological probing is matched and relieved by a tonic buoyancy in the telling.

Despite its frequent sadness, *Instead of a Letter* is a radiant and inspiring book. Its final episodes surge with a sense of revival as Athill describes how 'one by one, nerves which I thought to be dead have come to life.' It also reveals how she became a writer: the very moment, as so often in her work, brought to life.

One January morning in 1958: 'I was crossing the Outer Circle in Regent's Park, bringing my dog in from her walk, when a passing car slowed, accelerated again, slowed and stopped.' A comic moment of misrecognized identity and mistaken assumptions followed, leaving Athill feeling 'extraordinarily alive and cheerful'. As soon as she got home, she began to jot down memories inspired by her brief encounter with the man in the car. 'At that point it happened': propelled by 'the energy, the feeling of something bubbling inside me,' her first story 'came straight out, with no pause.'

Beyond her commitment 'to get it *just as it was*', and a determination to write a story that she 'meant people to read', Athill had no clearly defined sense of her literary enterprise. She distinguished between 'invented' stories and those that corresponded more closely to her own experience, but made no sharper distinction between fiction and non-fiction, except to observe that, although she felt prouder of the 'invented' stories, the others were usually better.

Instead of a Letter began as an impromptu experiment. Looking back (forty years later) on the genesis of her first book, Athill remembered:

> I put a piece of paper in my typewriter and began to write – about my grandmother! And from there it went on – this is literally true – without my ever knowing when I sat down to write what I was going to say. I would be dying to say it, whatever it was – really itching to get back to the typewriter the moment I got home from the office (and sometimes scribbling away under my desk when I was in the office) – but I never knew what it was going to be.

The editor-turned-author was, without realizing it, contributing to the birth of a new kind of literature. Memoir has grown to be a popular genre, unveiling lives whose richness lurks in private moments rather than public achievement. But in the late 1950s, when Athill began to write, there was no obvious and welcoming category to contain what she was saying and how she was saying it. She expressed herself with a literary and emotional openness that was remarkable for its time – and helps to account for the enduring freshness of her writing.

In this uncannily still-vivid book, Athill offers – lightly, generously – a kaleidoscope of meditations on love, sex and rejection, on pain, humiliation and loss, on aloneness and friendship and faith,

Englishness, class and race. Her thoughts are often ebullient with wit, always marked by a passionate push towards personal and social honesty, a commitment 'to understand, to be aware, to touch the truth'. *Instead of a Letter* shows us how a person can save herself by 'seeing things', keeping her eyes open and on the world.

Andrea Ashworth

1

M Y MATERNAL GRANDMOTHER died of old age, a long and painful process. Heart and arteries began to show signs of wearing out when she was ninety-two years old, but it was not until two years later that they failed her and precipitated her – still lucid, still herself – into death. By the end, pain and exhaustion had loosened her grip on life so that when she 'recovered' yet again from a heart attack she would whisper, 'Why doesn't God let me die?' but for a long time she was afraid of what was happening to her. She was afraid of death, and she was sorrowful – which was worse – because she had much time in which to ask herself what her life had been for, and often she could not answer.

I was not much with her at that time. Her son and her daughters, who lived near or with her, laboured through it at her side, but her grandchildren were scattered and saw her only when they visited their parents. But once I happened to be there when she was very ill and everyone was more than usually worn out, so I took a night watch. I sat in her cold room (if the windows were shut she felt suffocated), watching the dark hollows of her eyes and the shocking dark hole of her mouth – it was unbearable that Gran, always so completely in control of appearances, should lie with her mouth agape. I listened to the rhythm of her breathing. Sometimes it would stop for a whole minute and the winter night would be absolutely still. In the long silences I prayed to her God, 'Please, please don't let her start breathing again,' and knew that if she died it would not be frightening, that I should feel peace. But each time the harsh, snoring breaths would begin again, hauling her back to another awakening and to more pain and physical humiliation. It was some weeks after that, when she had rallied to the extent of writing an angry letter to the local paper about a new road of which she disapproved, and of ordering a dentist to her bedside to make her a new set of false teeth, that she turned her beautiful speckled eyes towards me one afternoon and said in so many words: 'What have I lived for?'

It was she who should have been able to tell me that. All her life she had been a churchgoing Christian of apparently unshaken faith. But she was on her own then: not suffering, like Doctor Johnson, from fear of the consequences of her sinfulness according to the teachings of that faith, but simply unsupported by it. I said to her what I believed: that she had lived, at the very least, for what her life had been. The long, hard months of dying could eclipse her life, but they did not expunge it. What she had created for us, her family, by loving and being loved, still existed, would continue to exist, and could not have existed without her. 'Do you really think that it has been worth something?' she asked, and I held her hands and told her that I believed it with all my heart. Then I went away, and wondered. For her it might well be the truth. She had created a world for us. Even if I had been the only one of her descendants to have been rooted in that world (and perhaps I was one of the least deeply rooted of them all), something that her love had made would still be alive. But what of a woman who had never had the chance, or had missed the chance, to create something like that? What of myself? That was a question to whistle up an icy wind, and I was out in it. I waited for the shivering to start.

Well, it has not started yet, and I would like to know why. Which is my reason for sitting down to write this.

2

IT IS STRANGE to have loved someone like my grandmother, with whom I came to disagree on almost everything of importance. In anyone but her the values she held seem to me absurd or shocking, yet there she is: the dominant figure in my curiously matriarchal family, her memory warm with love, pleasure, and gratitude.

When she was a girl, one of four handsome daughters of a Master of an Oxford college, she swore that she would never be kissed by any man but the one she would marry, and she never was. She met her husband when he was an undergraduate: a man with frosty blue eyes and a trace of Yorkshire accent ('cassel' for castle, 'larndry' for laundry), who read for the bar but did not practise for long because he inherited his father's estate, which I shall call Beckton. It was not in Yorkshire but in East Anglia, to which his family had moved because his mother was supposed to be delicate and to need a softer climate. She must in fact have been a hardy woman in spite of delicate looks, for she lived to a good age, and if the climate of East Anglia is softer than that of Yorkshire, heaven forbid that I should ever have to winter in the latter.

My grandmother bore her husband four daughters, of whom my mother was the youngest; and at last, when I suspect that a sense of failure was beginning to prey on her, one son. She despised women, or thought that she did. Intelligent herself, happy to send two of her girls to Oxford when it was still uncommon, and proud of any success her female grandchildren might achieve in unwomanly careers, she yet insisted that women's minds were inferior to men's. There was some kind of ambiguity at work here, for although masculine superiority was never questioned, the climate of my grandmother's house was markedly feminine and her daughters' husbands always seemed to be slightly on the fringe of it. On a subject suitable to men – war, politics, a question of local government, the appointment of a clergyman to a living – she would turn to a son-in-law with a formal deference: 'I have been wanting to ask you – ought I to write to the bishop . . .?' but if she intended to write to the bishop, that was what she would do, whatever the son-in-law said. It was not that the deference was false, but perhaps it was paid to a figure too masculine, too infallible to exist: a pattern of manhood to which the real men in the family failed wholly to conform.

Whether my grandfather conformed to it or not I do not know, for he died when I was six. If he did not, it was through no fault of his wife's. All I know of their relationship is that their two writing-desks in the library at Beckton Manor were so placed that his was near the fire and hers far from it, and that when, after his death, she referred to him it was always as though he were unquestionable in whatever he said or did. The references were infrequent, but they followed a pattern: 'Grandpapa always said . . .' and so it was; 'Grandpapa would never let the children . . .' and so they never did; 'Grandpapa was very fond of . . .' and so it was good. That she had adored him was an article of faith in the family, but during her last illness she disconcerted one of her daughters. They were talking of her fear of death. 'I don't understand why you are so afraid,' said her daughter. 'You have always been religious – surely you believe in an afterlife and that you will meet Dad again?' My grandmother, it seems, said nothing. 'But,' I was told, 'she gave me such a *very odd* look, it quite shocked me.' The look may have referred to the afterlife in general, but her daughter had an uncomfortable feeling that it referred to Grandpapa.

What do I know about him? That he had blunt, North Country good looks; that he had discriminating taste in silver and wine and built up a large and excellent library with its emphasis on history; that when he enlarged Beckton Manor, making it U-shaped instead of L-shaped, he set up a kiln to make small bricks matching those of the house, which was built in about 1760, and employed skilled workmen to carve stone to a Georgian design round his new front door and to mould plaster swags to crown the Adams chimney-piece he put in his new drawing room. A man of taste, but backward-looking. He would give sixpences to his children for learning *Lycidas* before they were eight, wrote in well managed Johnsonian cadences a thesis on the Serbs (whom he called Servs), and travelled modestly in Italy and Greece, bringing back stone urns for the terrace wall and insisting that his accompanying children put permanganate in the foreign water with which they had to brush their teeth. He was a good farmer. The estate at Beckton is of a thousand acres, some of the land rented out to tenants but much of it attached to the Manor Farm. My grandfather employed a bailiff from Yorkshire, but he took most of the management on himself and did it well.

I cannot recall any word spoken to me by my grandfather. His children's talk of him has always been as unquestioning as his widow's, and sometimes affectionate. He was not quite a tyrant, perhaps, but they convey that he ruled his roost as though by divine right, and I do not think that I would have liked him. Death lent him a sort of holiness for a time. His soul flew out of open sash windows and 'went to Heaven to be with God', which gave him a share of God's benevolence. After that he did a miracle for me, permitting me to walk unstung through a bed of nettles. Each spring, when we made cowslip balls for my grandmother's birthday, we put the best of them on his grave, an austere grey slab with the words 'Tomorrow to fresh woods and pastures new' carved on it, but the feeling of piety and love which attended this tribute was engendered by the act rather than directed towards the memory of a real man. And the things I owe him – Beckton as a place in which to grow up, books as an indispensable part of life – soon came to seem Gran's dispensation, not his.

She went on being there. After breakfast she would put on an

overall and brush the dogs out on the terrace by the steps which led
into the library. Wearing thick leather gloves she would garden in
her greenhouse, or the rose beds, would cut flowers for the house
and would arrange them in the 'flower room', where the vases were
kept and where the dogs slept. She wrote many letters on small
sheets of black-edged paper, in writing so like shorthand that only
her daughters knew the secret of reading it. She went for a long
walk every day and took a strong dose of senna pods every night:
fresh air and open bowels were, she considered, all that was
necessary for health. Her housekeeping, to which she paid vigilant
attention, was simplified by custom. Vegetables, milk, eggs, and
butter all came from the estate; hams were cured, honey was
harvested, or jam was made at fixed times, and the groceries were
ordered by post every month, from the Civil Service Stores in
London. It was a simple, rhythmical life in which she was only
concerned with the management, not the execution, but when
much later she moved to a smaller house and staff problems
combined with the dwindling of a fixed income forced her to do
things herself, she knew how to clean, dust, polish silver, and so on
much better than the rest of us, who had been doing it for years as
a matter of course.

The pleasures of her life were the place itself, which she adored,
her family, and reading: her existence should have been a tranquil
one. What was it that made anxiety such a distinct thread in it?
Never could anyone go away from Beckton without my
grandmother's eyes expressing real unhappiness. The journey
might be a short one, made for pleasure, but she still felt a clutch
of fear. We were not going to eat enough, and what we ate would
be unwholesome; we were going to sleep with our windows shut;
we were going to catch some infectious disease; a car was going to
skid or a train run off the rails. Bad things were likely to happen to
people if they went away. I have noticed this attitude in other people
whose lives are secure, comfortable, and sheltered by privilege so
that one would expect disaster to be far from their minds. I
suppose, whether they recognize it or not, it is an acknowledgment
of the forces besieging their position. My grandmother had a good

knowledge of history and read *The Times* daily: she knew what was happening in the world. Wars and rumours of war; communists abroad and socialists at home; rising taxes and falling respect for tradition. She, a conservative, a gentlewoman, a devout Protestant Christian and an owner of property, was automatically on the defensive against powers outside her control. She did not trust 'outside' and converted her distrust into fear of accident and careless eating. Over and over again I have heard her, or someone like her, say in a voice of real dismay, 'But you can't go on that train, you'll miss lunch!' as though they had become obsessed by the value of food because of some experience of hardship or starvation. In their time measured out not by coffee spoons but by dishes of roast beef, steak-and-kidney puddings, apple pie and cream, they have never once felt or expected to feel a pang of true hunger, so from where does this irrational panic come if it is not a symbol of something else?

My grandmother's anxiety increased as she grew older, because she felt that the right, the natural order of things would be for her to be able to provide for us all on her death, and it was clear that she could not do so; but when I was a child it was less explicit. It was simply darling Gran fussing, and if you teased her about it she smiled back ruefully, half amused by herself, half expressing 'It is all very well for you to laugh, if only you knew.'

My father had a family, but it did not own Beckton. It owned no land at all. My paternal grandfather, a clergyman in comfortable circumstances, shot himself for no good reason while I was still a baby (the coal had not been delivered on time, I believe: he had high blood pressure and would therefore fly into violent rages over small matters). It was as 'good' a family as my mother's and although it had left East Anglia long ago, it had a better claim than hers on our own beloved county, having several tombs and brasses there to prove the existence of rustic Athill knights and one fishmonger at a respectable distance in time. In spite of this my mother felt it to be a family inferior to hers, and somehow, I can no longer remember exactly in what way, conveyed this idea to her children. She always felt that possession by her was nine-tenths of anything's value, even a dog's. A woman who loved animals to the point of absurdity, she rarely admitted charm or breeding in a dog belonging to someone else. 'It's not a bad-looking puppy, I suppose,' she would say, 'but it's going to be leggy' – or, 'One of those hysterical dogs, always ready to make a fuss of strangers.' In the same way, her husband's family bored and irritated her. It was as though when they were first married and conflicting loyalties emerged – with whom, for instance, should they spend Christmas? – she had said like a child 'Bags I my family,' and had got away with it ever since.

Because of Beckton, this was easy to do. A house with twenty bedrooms, standing in a large garden and park with a thousand acres of land round it, can absorb children far more easily than can a neat six-bedroomed house with a two-acre garden, like that of my paternal grandmother, who lived in Devonshire. It was more *sensible* to go to Beckton for the holidays. And if we or any of our cousins had been ill, or our parents were abroad, Beckton Gran could house us with much pleasure and little inconvenience, while Devonshire Grannie, fond though she was of us, would have had to turn her house upside down. Besides, my father was an Army offcer with, during all my childhood, the rank of major, and with private means so small that they hardly counted. He lived above his income, modestly and anxiously, from the day he was married, but even by doing that he could not afford to give his wife and children so good a time as they had at Beckton: he would have felt churlish had he prevented their visits. I doubt, indeed, whether he could have done so if he had tried. My mother was strong-willed and he had the disadvantage of being the one *qui aimait*. So although I and my younger brother and sister knew that our official home was where he happened to be working – Woolwich, or when he retired from the Army and took a job in the city, Hertfordshire – our 'real' home, the place to which we 'came home' from other places, was Beckton.

Having bought a small glass bottle made in about 1785, club-shaped, with a delicate spiral rib from neck to base, I was looking at it with affection, enjoying the colour of the glass and the hint of irregularity in the shape. Why, I began to wonder, are objects made in England during that period so much my home territory when it comes to aesthetic pleasure? The products of other centuries and of other countries I have learnt to appreciate, but I cannot remember having to *learn* to delight in those of the English eighteenth century. Probably, I concluded, it is because so much of my upbringing took place in an eighteenth-century house. It was a thought with gratifying implications. I am glad that I have not inherited money or possessions, and I *would* be glad if I could be sure that I had not inherited any prejudices or attitudes of mind towards other people, but I liked the idea of a child's mind and eye unconsciously trained by graceful shapes, just proportions, and the details of good craftsmanship. It suggested that whatever faults the middling English gentry might have, they would be likely to possess a certain feeling for grace and style: good for us!

Then, unfortunately, I began to remember various objects bought by my relatives, prized by them and admired by myself before I left home and began to sniff round museums and listen to the opinions of people better educated in such matters than myself. I remembered certain lamps and pieces of china and materials for curtains or chair covers . . . It was true that we were all familiar with one kind of beauty so that if any of us became interested in aesthetics, that kind, being familiar, would be easy to start with; but it was clearly not true that we had gained from it any ingrained, generally applicable sense of quality or style. If the inhabitants of Beckton had to buy something new and were unable to afford to go to the right place for it (the family's fortunes have been coasting downhill all my life), choice would be conditioned not by knowledge, but by familiarity. The new object would be a pitiful, decadent bastard of the old and we would be cheerfully blind to the difference between patina and French polish, cut glass and moulded, a graceful curve and a clumsy one. Only a few members of my family had, if left to themselves, more natural taste than the people they most pitied and despised: the dwellers in suburbia. (The working classes were allowed a few distinct and even endearing merits: suburbanites – no!)

New purchases were not often made, partly because everything in Beckton Manor was certainly 'good' in the sense of being solid and enduring, partly because, even early in my lifetime, extravagance was condemned. It was still a rich man's house compared to those of the vast majority, but the family did not feel itself a rich family. There was a strict line drawn between necessities and luxuries, and luxuries were suspect.

During my early childhood, necessities included a head gardener with two men under him, two grooms, a chauffeur, a butler and a footman, a cook and a kitchenmaid with a scullery maid to help them, a head housemaid with two under-housemaids, and my grandmother's lady's maid. They included, too, animals for our pleasure and governesses and schools for our instruction. They included books, and a great deal of wholesome food, linen sheets rather than cotton, and three separate rooms for being in at different times ofthe day, not counting the dining-room, the smoking-room, the front hall, in which, for some reason, my grandmother always had tea, and the nursery. Capital being inviolate, there can, indeed, have been little income left over after the maintenance of all this at what was felt to be its proper level.

Clothes for my mother's generation and then for us were almost all made at home or in the village, except for the obligatory coat and skirt, and riding clothes, for which we went to a good tailor. My mother, happily for me, was the extravagant one of the family. She used to make gleeful and guilty forays to London for clothes, but it was an adventure, not routine. My grandfather had travelled a little (since it was before I can remember, I see it as Making the Grand Tour), but after his death it was unusual for anyone to take a holiday abroad, while to buy curtains for your bedroom simply because you were tired of the old ones was unheard of. If the old ones fell to pieces so that you *had* to replace them, you only considered the cheaper ranges of material (even my mother never considered the *most* expensive), and then – alas for that instinctive taste which, for a moment, I attributed to us. If you liked pink roses you chose pink roses, regardless of how the rest of the room was furnished. Sometimes you would recognize aesthetics to the point of saying 'The blue in the pattern picks up the blue in the carpet,' indicating a tiny blue motif in the design which, if examined closely, could be seen almost to match an equally inconspicuous blue twirl in the carpet's pattern; or sometimes you would speak the words which have sealed the fate of so many British interiors, and of the appearances of so many Englishwomen: 'It is a good colour because *it goes with anything*.'

Yet Beckton Manor was a charming house to be in, and so are almost all the English houses of its kind that I have known. Like its fellows, it had plenty of lovely things in it by chances of inheritance or the good taste of individuals, and it had something else as well. Its inhabitants might not be interested in decoration, but they were interested in nature: to flowers, trees, skies, landscapes and weather they responded with a strong sense of beauty, and without thinking of it they brought into the house as much of nature as they could. The tables loaded with cut flowers, the flowery chintzes, the indifferent watercolours of beloved places expressed the life lived from the house, and they pleased.

As a child, of course, I thought it not only lovely but inevitable: that was what a house should be. Any house which did not have those things in it, and which did not look out over terrace and park to a lake beyond which rose the Lake Covert (landscaped by Capability Brown, we all mistakenly believed), was only a poor attempt at a house. When my mother scolded me for bragging to a friend of the number of bedrooms at Beckton and the two islands in the lake, telling me that one should never show off about good fortune to those with less, she may have improved my manners but she did not diminish my sense of superiority. Even the cold was a matter of pride. Warmth did not rate as a necessity, since it was held to be the opposite of fresh air and therefore unhealthy, so everyone was crippled by chilblains from November to February. 'My sponge is *often* frozen solid in the morning,' I remember boasting to some less hardy, less fortunate child.

How guilty do I feel at having come in on the tail end of such a life and having loved so passionately a place founded on privilege the earning of which had become remote? I do not often refer to it, and when I think about it a figure appears opposite me: that of some faceless friend brought up in a Manchester back street, with a childhood very different from my own stored in his head. At his most charitable, I feel, he would be giving me a quizzical look; and if I were to repeat to him the kind of thing my grandmother, my parents, my other relatives of their generation and even some of my own would say about his accent, his clothes, his attitudes . . . Well, how could I repeat that kind of thing? And if he were a Jew or a Negro, or some other kind of foreigner not of noble birth (for a foreigner can only be guaranteed a gentleman by a title), then what could he feel towards my background less than disgust?

That smug, matter-of-fact assumption of superiority! Many landed families were richer and better bred than mine; nuances which mine recognized but which made no difference to their certainty. Except when it came to lords, whose acquaintance gave them a pleasure verging on the undignified, they were convinced that they were the best kind of people to be (indeed there was something a little fishy about anyone not a lord who was richer or grander than they were). When my grandparents dismissed someone as 'not a gentleman', their unthinking certainty had the force of a *moral judgment*; while the tinge of apology or defiance that crept into the same judgment when pronounced by my parents' generation was only faint.

This attitude was at the best comic, at the worst repulsive, for with what could that particular family support its certainty of being 'the best'? The abilities of most of its members were respectable but ordinary, their achievements no more than commonplace. None of them was unusually intelligent or energetic and most of them lacked imagination to a remarkable degree. Generous and affectionate they could be, but they hardly ever extended these qualities outside the family circle. Like anyone else they had their charms, their interesting quirks, their endearing or impressive aspects, and their standard of behaviour was, within certain limits, civilized and reliable, but it was not just in matters of taste that they were no better than anyone else: physically, intellectually, and morally they were no more than middling. Yet they despised almost all the rest of the world, excepting people as nearly as possible replicas of themselves, as though their status as English country gentlefolk made them exceptional beings; something of which they fell short even by their own standards, for they were not well enough connected, and Beckton was not a large enough estate, for them to come anywhere near the top of the ladder of snobbery.

What made my family so profoundly self-satisfied? That question has puzzled me more with every year of my life. The satisfaction in itself was not objectionable, since people can only function comfortably if they have it; but its obverse – the disdain or distrust of anyone not of their kind – that was stupid, ugly, and pitiful, and it is a curious sensation to be bound by enduring ties of love and habit to a set of people who so stubbornly displayed it. All that money spent on education, and so little thinking done as a result of it! Reactions still triggered by the sound of a vowel, the cut of a coat, the turn of a phrase . . . 'He was wearing what I think he would have called a *sports jacket*,' said one of them, only the other day (he would have called it a tweed coat), and that, as far as the wearer of the sports jacket was concerned, was that. Once imbued with such reactions, it is impossible entirely to escape them: I know that until the day I die I shall be unable to avoid *noticing* 'raound' for 'round', 'involave' for 'involve' (on that one an Army officer of my acquaintance used to turn down candidates for a commission), because a built-in mechanism will always click, however much I dislike it, 'placing' everyone I meet as though for a second it was my parents eyes and ears at work, not mine. But once it has clicked it can very easily be disregarded. The puzzle lies in the choice not to disregard it.

An old man near death once gave my uncle great pleasure by telling him that a treasured memory – something which had remained for years in his mind as a vignette of the England he loved – had been a glimpse, once caught as he was driving by, of my uncle riding in the park at Beckton. It is a pretty park, well planted with groups of beech and oak trees, sloping gracefully down to the lake beyond which the wood known as the Lake

Covert rises, and mildly dominated by the house (to the left of the picture as the old man approached it), standing on its balustraded terrace with a great cedar tree at one corner of it to break its slightly austere Georgian lines. 'It was a perfect October afternoon,' said the old man. 'There was the Lake Covert, all golden in its autumn leaves, reflected in the water, and there were you, cantering along beside the lake on that black of yours – what a beautiful horse he was – with a couple of dogs running behind you. I watched you and I thought, Now that's a lovely scene, that's England, and I've never forgotten it.'

Describing the conversation, and the old man's emotion my uncle gave a slight deprecating laugh, but he was not only touched, he was satisfied. That man had recognized in him and his setting what he himself felt deeply to be their true nature, and as he savoured it he was likable rather than absurd. He was moved by a vision of something which he dearly loved and which had comforted him when, during the war, he was badly wounded: he felt genuinely that it was worth dying for. To have said to him, 'But you are not England. You and what you represent are only a tiny fraction of England and an archaic one at that, preserved not by deeds or virtue but by money most of which you yourself do not earn' – to have said that would have been to have attacked not a fancy but a rooted belief. He might have answered, 'All right, so it is preserved by money: money in the hands of the right people, of people like us. What further argument do you need for the existence of such people and such money?' He and his like have been snug all their lives, and snugness breeds smugness – but smugness is too small a word for what it feels like *from inside*. From inside, it feels like moral and aesthetic *rightness*; from inside, it is people like me, who question it, who look stupid, ugly, and pitiful – and ungrateful, too. Why admit that the grammar-school boy, the self-made businessman, the artist, the foreigner or whatever are just as likely to be 'the best' as we are, when such an admission must attack certainty, the cosiest of all the gifts bestowed by privilege? It is not only ingratitude, it is treachery.

Treacherous I may be, but ungrateful I am not. I consider it good fortune to have been born of Beckton's youngest daughter, not of its son, at a point in time and a position in the family where diminishing resources had brought unthinking certainty up against the facts of life and worn it comparatively thin. Never to have broken through its smothering folds would have been, I have always thought, extremely depressing. But on the other hand, not to have enjoyed a childhood wrapped warmly in those folds – that would be a sad loss. There I used to be, as snug and as smug as anyone, believing with the best that we were the best – and if security is the thing for children, which it surely is, then how lucky I was.

Beckton and Gran: they blur together. When I think of her I may see a handsome woman with crisp, pure-white hair (it turned when she was thirty), wearing a black, black-and-white, or grey dress with a crossover bodice and a lace collar (she was in her eighties before she forgot her widow's status to the point of wearing a dress made of soft, pinky-red wool). Her eyes, with lids that droop slightly in an odd way at the outer corners, are speckled green and grey, capable of an ironic expression but usually full of affection, and she will be looking at me attentively, ready to be amused or interested by what I am saying (for one did not say to Gran the things which would have shocked or displeased her). I may see this woman, or I may think of getting out of the car to open the white gate between park and lawn, breathing that first, almost drinkable, smell of grass, flowers, and cedar tree which was the assurance that we were home. Then images come crowding in: the stream in the kitchen garden in which the newts and tadpoles lived; the marble children under a tree on the library chimneypiece; the scalloped black-green leather which would pull off from the edges of the nursery bookshelves; the goat-shed in the lower stable yard made into a bower of beech branches by a cousin and myself, because tender young beech leaves on the branch were what our goats liked best (we gave them senna pods, too, when we thought they needed them, and sometimes an aspirin or a spoonful of cough linctus). Very clear is the chasm between the back of the sofa and the bookshelves in the morning room, where I would squat for hours to read bound volumes of *Punch*, and the smell of the plush curtains over the double door between morning room and front hall, in which I had only to muffle myself, at one time, in order to begin writing a play in which a cousin was to take the part of a good, blond and slightly insipid princess while I was to be the dark, wicked one, like Sir Rider Haggard's She-Who-Must-Be-Obeyed. 'Go and play in the morning room, darlings,' people would say. It was the room to which children graduated from the nursery, where one could bounce on the furniture or litter the floor with Meccano or cutting-out.

There was only one unpleasant thing in that house: the ghost in the night nursery, where at our smallest we usually had to sleep. It was not an ordinary ghost but a disgusting presence, a slimy grey thing like a stubby elephant's trunk which reached down over the gutter and groped at the window one morning while I was sitting alone on my pot. No one liked that room, which was at the back of the house, looking out on to a gloomy thicket of yew trees, on the old principle, not otherwise observed, of pushing children out of the way with the servants. But no one thought of telling my grandmother about that, so it was nothing to do with her. Every other sound, smell, and texture in the place I loved quite consciously from the earliest time I can remember, and I loved it so much not only because I felt it to be beautiful, but because its presiding genius, my grandmother, loved me.

In relationships outside her family she was not a loving woman, nor a tolerant one. Her servants she distrusted, not (the older, long-established ones anyway) in terms of honesty so much as of sense. She expected them to be ninnies, and to be dirty, and how they managed not to be the latter is hard to see, considering that it was years before anyone thought of putting in a bathroom on the attic floor where they lived, while they were not allowed to use ours. Of people who differed from her on politics or religion she was fiercely scornful, particularly of anyone who believed that the Pope spoke God's word, or who was a socialist. Of foreigners she was not only scornful, but distrustful as well. If they thought that they could govern their own countries better than we could she considered them both fools and traitors. Outside the ramifications of what might be called the greater family as opposed to the central family –

the second cousins and so on, about whose fortunes she was always completely and mysteriously informed and whom she wished well – she had no intimate friends.

Described like this, she sounds a disagreeable woman, yet no one ever met her without being charmed. The charm came from the warmth of her personality, and the warmth came from the dynamo of love at work in her for the benefit of her children and her children's children. She was not soft with them. She mocked them if their politics veered to the left, scolded them if they did not eat properly, and criticized any folly they might get up to unless it was something really grave, like marrying a foreigner or having an extra-marital love affair. About that kind of thing she would either keep silent, or would choose not to know. But although her family could cause her impatience or grief, they could not diminish her love – and the only grief they could have caused her when still young would have been by illness or death. In her house we could be excited by our own misdemeanours, but we could never feel that they put us in peril, so for us this autocratic woman, whose sharp intelligence was deliberately confined to so narrow a range, created a benign air which we could always breathe again, even in middle age, simply by going back to the place where she lived.

I shocked her once. I was about ten years old and had thought of an image for life. I thought that it was as though people were confined in a bowl which was floating on a sea. While snug at the bottom of the bowl they lived their lives complacently, but the bowl spun and tossed on the sea and its spinning sometimes sent one of them up its side until he could see over the rim. All round would be the endless chaos of dangerous, cold grey water, unsuspected till then, and anyone who had seen it and had understood that what he had thought was safety was only a little bowl, would not be able to bear it. That, I decided, was the origin of madness. I was proud of this idea, described it to my grandmother, and was disconcerted to see her so upset. It was not at all clever, she said sharply, to think that life was aimless, and she told me to remember the then Prince of Wales, who had recently made some statement of high purpose and idealism to a gathering of Boy Scouts.

I was disappointed by this response, which did not seem to me to recognize the implications of my idea, but I remember it because in spite of my disappointment, its inadequacy did not matter. I noted that in some ways I would have to differ from Gran but I did not feel betrayed, because there she was as she spoke, wearing the kind of dress she always wore, with her beautiful hair and her dear, kind eyes watching me with the anxiety I thought was a joke and the love which I would never think of questioning. I myself might incline more to the bowl theory than the Prince of Wales theory, but clearly whatever Gran believed was *good*, because it was believed by Gran.

3

I FELT OUTRAGED when someone first pointed out to me that my grandmother's house was not 'mine'. When she died, or decided to make way for my uncle, it would be his, and then his son's, or, if he had no son, his daughter's. Supposing he had no children, I asked hopefully (he was still unmarried at the time). Working on the assumption that succession to the estate would follow the pattern established by the monarchy, it appeared that at least twelve people, seven of them my contemporaries, would have to die before I would have a claim, and I hardly felt I ought to pray for this however much I would have liked to.

Perhaps this realization came near the time when I lay sprawled on short grass in the back park one spring morning – there were lambs about, and daisies – facing the knowledge that in three years' time I would be thirteen. What made the passage of so long a stretch of time real to me I cannot remember, but it was appalling, giving me a horrible sensation as though my insides had gone cold and empty. To be in my teens, I saw suddenly, would be to leave childhood behind, to be in a world where impossible things could happen. I would become able to believe that the place would go to my uncle; I would become able to foresee a time when, perhaps, I could no longer return to it as though it were my home. Where would my home be? Some place like those in which I had already lived with my parents and brother and sister; a house and garden just big enough for us, with none of our past worked into it and no territory round it to call our own. Already, when we rode across country from the house my parents rented in Hertfordshire, we had to *ask permission* from the owners of the land, which had seemed to me humiliating. And the business of earning my living – it would not be something my father talked about when he was feeling pompous ('You will have to earn your living one day'), but something I should have *to do*. I do not think that I was shocked by the prospect; only frightened. It would surely be difficult and disagreeable, and, because the norm of existence was life at Beckton, it would be unnatural.

In fact, my grandmother went on living in the house until the beginning of the war, when I was twenty-two; it was fully there to go back to. But whoever had given me that early, painful glimpse of the truth had done me a good turn. From that time my love of Beckton began, slowly, to take a wistful, nostalgic turn: I felt that I must treasure every detail of it against the future, and I remember standing under the great beech tree by the lawn, trying to will some essence of myself into the still green air so that after I was dead my ghost would materialize there. But at the same time my fear of what would follow began, with acceptance of mutability, to rub away and other things entering my life increased in value. That particular bowl, it seemed, spun on no grey sea. It would be sad to be pushed over the rim, but what surrounded it was a landscape, and the landscape, as it became increasingly real, began to look interesting.

My fear of 'thirteen' had been prophetic, all the same, for I believe I had reached that age when my mother told me that we had 'lost our money'. What really happened was that, having lived above their income for too long, my parents were at last rapped over the knuckles by their bank. We were in the Hertfordshire house at the time, my father having retired from the Army to avoid transporting his reluctant family to India, and taken a job in the City with a firm connected with the mining of mica. Our house was called The Cottage, but it had six bedrooms and was staffed with Margaret, the cook; Violet, her sister, who was not exactly a nanny but looked after the children; Ursula, the governess; Doris, the housemaid;

Mrs Knight, who 'came in', and deaf Gatwood, full-time gardener. My parents felt that they were living austerely because we ourselves looked after our ponies and they had not kept on their own hunters, nor did they indulge in any luxuries. My mother had no fur coat and no jewels except a couple of mediocre diamond rings and the string of small pearls given her as a wedding present by her father. There was rarely any drink in the house beyond a bottle of sherry, and the furniture was a job lot of stuff, none of it valuable or beautiful and some of it as utilitarian as the hospital beds inherited from a convalescent home for officers run by a great-aunt during the 1914–18 war. According to their lights, my father and mother were not extravagant people, but still the bank said that unless they followed a certain clearly defined plan they might not cash any more cheques.

My mother did not take this with any enduring seriousness, being a practical and energetic woman with no objection to doing things for herself, and having the comfortable feeling that Beckton was still there in the background. She broke the news to me, however, with an almost dramatic gravity – she always had an appetite for 'the worst' – so that I was impressed.

'Are we really *poor*?' I asked.

'Yes, darling, I'm afraid so.'

'Will Violet have to go? And Ursie?'

'Yes, I expect you will go to school.'

Doris, Margaret, and Mrs Knight went too, and we had to make our own beds and dust the bedrooms. As my mother said soon afterwards, 'the really *bloody* thing about being poor is that if you leave something on the floor when you go out, you know that it *will still be there* when you get back'. At that time I was exchanging two letters a term with a boy I had been in love with since I was nine years old, and I must have described our plight because I remember a letter of his beginning, 'Dear Diana, I am sorry to hear that you are now poor.' I was touched by his delicacy in saying no more about it than that.

It was not long before Beckton came to the rescue. We were going to leave Hertfordshire and live at the Manor Farm, we were told, and to the children the whole thing instantly became a delight. My mother probably had other reasons for making the move, but to us it seemed merely the happy solution of the family's financial problems, and we were so pleased by it that it did not occur to us to worry about my father, who would continue to work in London and could not, therefore, live so far from it except at weekends. He took lodgings with the family of a man who had once been his own father's coachman, and bicycled to the station every day because my mother had to have the car. I suppose that we felt, vaguely, that it was horrid for him, but it was a relief not to have him in the house. My brother and I had worked out a formula by then: 'Mummy and Daddy are both very nice people, but they don't suit each other, they should never have got married' – this, perhaps, was borrowed from Ursula or Violet. They were quarrelling fiercely at the time, and it was a relief not to have to watch for signs of trouble and to know that if, at weekends, it came (as it usually did) it could only last for two days.

I always *liked* my father – he was a likeable man – but if I ever felt anything warmer than liking it was when I was so young that I cannot remember it. I did not consciously take my mother's side when they quarrelled (indeed, I often felt something like hatred for her irrational flares of temper, and considered that my father, not she, was in the right) – but in our nerves all three of us children were more sympathetic to her than we were to him. It was not until much later that I understood the trouble to come from the simple but deadly poison of physical incompatibility which my father did not feel and my mother had been too inexperienced to recognize during their courtship, but even as small children we could sense the nature of her irritability.

To be constantly loved and desired by someone whose touch is repulsive to you is a profound outrage. You may be in such a situation by your own fault or folly, but whatever the surface facts, you remain the situation's victim because the offence you are receiving goes beyond reason, into such deep recesses of your being. Feeling wicked for her reactions, my mother stubbornly and bravely, though with occasional half-rebellions, went on being my father's wife, but her offended nature got its own back in many ways, and her children's instincts chimed with her instincts more readily than they did with my father's reason.

The scenes were always over trivialities. My mother was an impatient person, hating to wait about, hating slow meals, hating almost to hysteria being late for anything. My father was slow, deliberate, unpunctual. Taking his time over anything gave him a positive pleasure – as it does me. If, on a shopping expedition, he went into the post office to post a registered letter, he would certainly find someone with whom to gossip. Waiting with us in the car, my mother would know that he would do this: she would begin to simmer before two minutes were up. I would resent the way she was working up for a scene, since time mattered to me as little as it did to my father, but still I would begin to feel irritated by his slowness, even to despise it. My brother and I, in the back of the car, would exchange warning looks, and later one of us might say, 'Why is Daddy so *silly* – he always does just the thing to make her lose her temper.' Another thing in which, by nature, I was on my father's side but which came to irritate me, was his scrupulous honesty. He was the sort of man who will seek out the guard on a train to pay the excess fare if a crowd has caused him to travel in a first-class compartment with a second-class ticket. My mother had a streak of bandit in her, was usually prepared to get away with what she could, and used deliberately to enrage him by describing some minor delinquency of her own. With one side of me I admired my honourable father, but with another I saw him as absurd. Because my mother's irritation with him on such matters was a symptom, a release of nervous tension through permissible outlets, it had an infectious force beyond its apparent triviality.

Apart from this, my father did not much care for children. He was always pleasant to us, but he did not find childishness in itself seductive. When he sang, 'Bat, bat, come under my hat, and I'll give you a slice of *ba-a-a-con*', or 'Bony was a warrior', he was funny and we enjoyed it. We thought him clever when he made up nonsense verses for us, and later wrote plays for us to act, but the things he enjoyed doing with us were things which he enjoyed doing anyway because they exercised his talents or his sense of humour. Just to be with children, to watch them, to enter into their imaginations, was no pleasure to him, and he had no physical rapport with them. Nowadays I sometimes watch my brother handling three small sons, and I see exactly what it was that my father could not feel. My brother will throw his boys about, fondle them, sniff them, stand by a window to watch them as they play in the garden with an unconscious smile of pure pleasure on his face. He loves them with a comfortable, animal warmth, and they respond to it like crocuses in the sun. That is something that was outside my father's nature.

Much of myself comes from my father – my equable temperament, my powers of detachment, my enjoyment of poetry and of the absurd – and the better I knew him as an adult, the more clearly I saw that he was an agreeable, intelligent, upright and witty man. But I never felt closely bound to him; never felt, as I did about my mother, that for good or ill, this person and myself were made of the same substance.

So being separated from my father for so much of the time seemed, when I was thirteen, more of an advantage than otherwise, while living at the Farm – *that* was delight. It was a house to which we could go only to be happy. We knew it intimately, having already stayed there when we were younger and my father was abroad, and spending much of our time there when we were at the Manor. My mother's generation had passed legendary holidays there, to be near my great-grandparents. It was part of Beckton and for children the best part: a pleasure ground richer and more absorbing than garden or park, with the real business of the country going on in it. The first time we had stayed there, my brother and I had become distressed in our loyalties, because surely it was impossible for us to love any place better than Gran's house, and yet . . . It was my brother, then six years old, who had discovered the pleasures of nostalgia for us. We shared a large bedroom looking out over the farmyard, at the end of a passage and remote from the rest of the family so that we could talk and play with impunity for what seemed like hours after we had gone to bed. One evening, when we were leaning out of the window watching the horses drinking after late haymaking, a cuckoo began to call in the distance. 'Listen,' said my brother. 'It makes me feel funny – it makes me think terribly of being at the Manor.' I listened, and soon each hollow note seemed to be struck on my own heartstrings: tears began to come into my eyes. Past summers – not just the eight I had lived, but innumerable past summers, long and golden, and all experienced at Beckton Manor, seemed to be saying goodbye.

A few days later we discovered that when we heard a cuckoo while at the Manor, we could summon up exactly the same feeling for the Farm. After that we decided that the two houses were part of the same place, so that it did not matter which we loved best.

They were less than half a mile apart. You went out of the back door of the Manor, into the gravelled space between its two wings which in summer was decorated with tubs of fuchsias, down past the stables, through the bottom orchard and a corner of the plantation girdling the kitchen garden, and past three beech trees on which everyone had, at one time or another, carved their initials. The highest initials had grown blistered and blurred; the lowest – mine and my brother's – were clear and still the colour of sawdust. From there a footpath ran along the bottom of the back park beside a line of bat willows planted by my great-grandfather (they were never made into cricket bats, reaching and passing their prime during the last war, when no cricket bats were being made). This led to the stream, at the point where it slid over a little weir to become the beginnings of the lake. You crossed it on a broad footbridge, pausing to drop sticks into the water or just to stare into it, and came to the water meadow – a boggy meadow criss-crossed with little ditches choked with marsh marigolds and ragged robin. The path here was slightly raised, with planks, usually collapsed, over the drains which traversed it. We knew it so well that even in darkness we could tell where we had to take a long stride, or step to the left, or balance carefully because a plank was extra narrow. At the far side of the water meadow the path rose steeply to the small wooden gate into the Farm orchard, and at the top of that was the benevolent Dutch end-gable of the house, curving comfortably above white walls and partly screened by the row of beeches which bordered the back yard. The working buildings sprawled to the left, not at that time the responsibility of those who lived in the house, but definitely part of their territory. This house was to be the background of my growing up (we continued to live there, all but rent-free, for about twelve years); but the love we all felt for it was already established and was rooted in the knowledge we had of it from our earliest childhood.

Mouse droppings, husks of oats quivering in spiders' webs, piles of old sacks – the musty smell of a loft would make me hesitate now. I would stoop to avoid the wispy grey shreds hanging from rafters which cling to one's hair, step carefully to avoid the fangs of disused machinery. But when we were children we shinned along beams over which old pieces of stiff, cracked harness had been looped, and jumped off them into the hay at the end of the loft, near the chute down which it slid to the stable, raising a cloud of dust as we landed, so that motes swam for minutes on end. ('Never jump down into hay: there might be a chopper or a pitchfork buried in it. A little boy once jumped into a pile of hay and was cut *right in half.*') The picture of the farm buildings I carry in my mind is framed by the loft window – the opening into space with a pulley above it up to which sacks were hauled. When we were small my brother and I would squat there as silent as cats, unobserved, watching the cowman cross the yard with buckets of skimmed milk for the calves, or a horseman bringing in a pair of butterball-smooth Suffolk Punches, unharnessing them, then sending them with a slap on the rump to drink endlessly from the tank, burying their nostrils in the scummy water, after which they liked to hang about in the yard taking their ease for a while, until the man shouted at them and they plodded into the stable, each to his own place. They had names like Tory, Prince, Captain, Bess. When Tory died a new Tory took his place, but he had a different character, he should have had another name.

The granary had a dusty smell, too, but not like the loft's. Wheat, oats, barley, and sometimes beans – they were heaped like sand dunes and each made a different sound when you thrust your hands into the heap, or waded in it – which was forbidden because it scattered the grain. The stables, the cowsheds, the various yards in which animals were kept at different stages of their lives, all of them had their own smells, and none of the smells, however dungy, seemed to us displeasing. An adult watching children scurrying about a farm must see their movements as mysterious, like those of animals. What makes them decide to sit on a certain wall, stare solemnly for perhaps ten minutes at a certain pig, then jump down and run into a barn, clamber to the top of a pile of sugar beet? It is like the flitting of birds from tree to hedge. But I can remember that each building, each activity, each time of day had its own value and meaning – we went from one to another as an adult would decide to drop in at a picture gallery, or go into a shop to buy bread.

'Going to look at the bull,' for example, was not a random whim but an accepted pastime. A bull is a spectacle in himself. We hoisted ourselves up the stout timbers of his loose-box, and with our elbows on the top of the partition would stare at him while he stared back. Placid he might be (and our bulls usually were), but not to be trusted, they said: a bulk of violence rested behind that curly forehead and those small eyes, and when he shifted his feet in the straw or blew through his nostrils there was a shadow of threat in it. If, while we were watching him, the bull piddled or let his red penis protrude from its sheath, we counted it an event. He was sex as well as violence, and we were in awe of him.

The men who worked on the farm were patient and kind. The cowmen were too busy to be interesting companions, but the horsemen had time to talk as they took their teams out to the fields, and would let us ride with them either on a broad back or on a loaded wagon (how it would heave and rock, and sometimes the branches of a tree would sweep it so that you had to flatten yourself on the load). The man whose company we most enjoyed was the shepherd. He was alone a lot in outlying pastures, living out in a hut on wheels during the lambing season, and he was glad to talk. He presided over the most interesting ceremonies of the year: lambing, dipping, and shearing. His dogs were watchful and aloof to anything but their master and their job, so that if they wagged their tails when one spoke to them, one felt flattered. Like all shepherds, ours knew his sheep as individuals, and this seemed a magic power.

For a time, when I was about eight, the shepherd had a boy working with him called Jack Grey. Perhaps he was fifteen years old, but to my brother and me he seemed almost grown-up. His father, who was the woodman, came of gypsy stock and Jack had gypsy talents: he could make sounds which rabbits mistook for other rabbits, he poached, he could climb any tree and knew everything about birds and animals. We envied and admired him for living out of doors so much, and at the same time were impressed by his matter-of-fact attitude towards it, his remarks implying that we would not enjoy it as much as we supposed if it were part of a job. We collected birds' eggs then, under strict injunctions to take nothing unless there were at least four eggs in the nest and never to frighten the parent birds so that they would desert. Jack could climb higher trees than we could and was uninhibited by rules (which were awkward in the cases of birds which laid only two or three eggs). The treasures of our collection – our jay's, our heron's, and our sparrow hawk's eggs – came from him. We were with him whenever we could be, and he treated us as equals, not as children. Later he shot at and wounded his father, who had come home drunk and had threatened him. He pleaded self-defence but was sent to prison. Much later, when I was eighteen or nineteen, I was at a roller-skating rink (roller-skating had become a passion with me and my friends) and the attendant, a man at once sleek and seedy with heavily oiled hair and a flashy checked suit, knelt down in front of me to fasten my skates. He did not look up. I looked down at the hair plastered in straplike segments across the bent head, and I heard my voice – this is quite literal, I was unconscious of recognition or of forming words – I heard my voice saying 'Jack Grey'. He looked up and said 'Hullo, Miss Dinah', and then, after 'How are you' and 'It's a long time', we were at a loss. The exact nature of our earlier intimacy, what we had talked about besides birds and animals, I could not remember, but I was sharply aware of the ghost of friendship standing there between me and this shady-looking man. We smiled at each other shyly and I left the rink feeling shaky and unhappy. Perhaps as a boy Jack had welcomed the company of small children so kindly because already there were things in his life of which he needed to avoid thinking. I hope he knew how much we loved and admired him.

The friendships children make with their family's employees seem to the children friendships between equals. If a cowman, or my grandmother's head gardener, caught us at some mischief and said 'I'll tell your grandma on you', the words were, to us, no more than a formula: it was not the threat but the wrath of the speaker which had authority. It never occurred to us that even when the gardener caught us stealing his beloved grapes he would never actually clout us, nor did we notice that however intimate we were with Jack Grey, he never invited us to his house, nor we him to ours. A relationship which felt natural was possible because the lines laid down for it were so deeply engraved by time and custom that neither side thought of questioning them, but those lines defined a narrow area. When we went back to the Farm 'for good' I was in my early teens, no longer a child. I knew all the men on the farm, of course, but without realizing it I had moved out of the realm of friendship with them.

We were still at our poorest for our first year or so at the Farm, still without servants, though a woman used to come in to do the scrubbing and another to cook lunch. Soon after we settled in, I was sent to the back yard to bring in the cold meat we were going to eat for supper. It was kept in a perforated tin meat-safe hung on the wall in a cool place. I opened the safe, took out the dish – and the shelf was bare. For the first time since my mother had told me about our poverty I felt afraid: *there was nothing in our larder once that meat was eaten.* At the Manor the larder was an L-shaped room with a brick floor and wide shelves made of slate on which were crocks of preserved eggs, flat pans of milk waiting to have the cream skimmed on them, tins and tins of cakes, biscuits and buns, joints of meat, at least one ham, strings of sausages, pounds of butter, big cheeses, bowls of dripping, bottles of fruit, stone jars of currants – food on which the house could have lived for days if it had suddenly been cut off from the outside world. Whatever the breakfast dish in that house – kidneys on toast, or kedgeree, or bacon and mushrooms – there was always an egg boiled for every person there. A houseful of us could amount to sixteen or so, and sometimes no one ate a boiled egg (what *did* happen to them?). At our house in Hertfordshire the scale had not been so grand, but always beside what we were then eating there had been the remains of what we had eaten recently and something that we were soon going to eat: the larder had continuity. I stood in front of the empty meat-safe telling myself that it was silly to be scared, my mother would be buying more food tomorrow, but for a few moments poverty had become real. And because food did reappear on the shelf (and as soon as my mother had recovered her nerve, accumulated there as merrily as ever), I soon concluded that ours was not real poverty. I remained far away from the real thing, I hardly ever had the chance of glimpsing it, but that moment in the back yard had made me feel what a bare shelf was like, and understand that it could happen. It would be an exaggeration to say that it made me think, but it may have given me the beginnings of a sense of proportion.

My mother resembled my grandmother in her generosity towards her children. I never heard her say it, but she must have resolved that we, at least, should not suffer from the financial muddle into which the family had drifted, and it is only now that I see how much unfamiliar work she did about her house at that time. All she expected from me (my sister was five years younger) was that I should help her make beds and clean the bedrooms in the morning, wash up supper and sometimes cook it. It was almost always eggs, usually scrambled – she did not know any other cooking to teach me. Housekeeping generally became rough and ready – a pleasant state for children – and although even at that it must have weighed on her, it was never a bogy for anyone else. She did not mind things which ought to shine not shining, and she did not mind 'clean' dirt (earth, grass seeds, spilt dog biscuit). While there was a carelessly arranged vase of flowers on every surface flat enough to hold a vase, she felt her drawing-room pretty, and so it was. It smelt lovely, too, more like a garden than a room, and since most of its untidiness came from the litter of books on chair arms, footstools, and occasional tables, it was an agreeable room to be in.

That accumulation of books silting up the flower-free surfaces in the house: that, at bottom, I owe to my grandfathers. Both were men who took it for granted that a gentleman should have a good library, and my maternal grandfather's library was a very good one. In addition to this, my grandmother's father had been Master of an Oxford college, which meant that however unscholarly his descendants might be, they all esteemed scholarship: they might not read much (most of them, in fact, did), but they considered a house without books in it uncivilized. At the Manor, not only was the library walled with books, but the morning room and my grandfather's smoking-room as well, while the whole of one upstairs passage was given over to shelves containing more trivial volumes (delightful shelves, badly lit, from which you might fish a handbook on veterinary surgery or *The Scarlet Pimpernel*). There was an angle of bookshelves ceiling-high in the nursery, and although reading in the bath, in the WC, or in bed was forbidden to the younger children, everyone knew why one did it.

Reading ran in two currents. My grandfather's interest had been history, and most of the family, including my mother, inherited his tastes. Gibbon's *Decline and Fall of the Roman Empire* was my mother's bedside reading for a long time, and she knew Horace Walpole, Madame de Sévigné, and Mrs Delaney like old friends. On the other hand, one particularly beloved aunt, and my father, most enjoyed imaginative writing and poetry. My mother had no patience with books which were 'not true'. She always insisted that she actively detested poetry, finding it a lot of words about nothing, and she would not go to see a play by Shakespeare. My father revelled in Shakespeare and made frequent sorties into one poet or another. During the second world war, when, to his great content, he was back in the Army and serving abroad, he suddenly decided that he must read Dryden and wrote home for his complete works.

In a life where the adults took books so much for granted, it was natural that the children should do so too. About eighty per cent of our birthday and Christmas presents always consisted of books: it would have been impossible not to have become a compulsive reader. I developed the lust early and violently, following my father's tastes rather than my mother's, and would smuggle an electric torch to bed almost as early as I can remember so that I could continue to gobble my books under a tent of sheets. I was always puzzled by how *they* knew. Thump, thump, the steps would come along the passage, under the pillow would go book and torch and I would screw my eyes shut, but the minute the light went on and 'they' saw my body stretched so rigidly innocent under the blankets, they would say accusingly, 'You were reading!'

At other times they would say 'You must be skipping', or 'You can't remember books if you read so many at a time, so fast', but I never skipped, and any that I understood I did remember. Failing to understand did not prevent my reading. Before I was twelve I had been through most of Meredith in my grandfather's handsome, vellum-bound edition, undeterred by the fact that the involved prose was too much for me. Those submerged, and it was only years later, when I picked up *The Egotist* for what I thought to be the first time, that I rediscovered those sessions on the window seat in the morning-room. Pages of it seemed new to me, then I would come to a 'visual' passage – Clara wearing pink ribbons, finding her young man asleep under the cherry tree, for instance – and I would think, But I have been here before, I have *seen* this, and gradually the whole thing swam up: the slight warmth of the radiator boxed in under the window seat, the green damask on the flat cushion, the smooth binding and the thick, handmade paper with its ragged edges, and my grandmother coming in and saying 'Darling, are you really *enjoying* all those Merediths? He's rather grown-up for you.'

Boys, poor creatures, became part-exiles from our world when they were about eight years old and were sent to their preparatory schools. Girls stayed at home, with governesses. I had run through seven of them by the time we settled at the Farm, starting with 'nursery governesses' whom I shared with my brother (two years younger than myself), and going on, when he had been exiled, to better-qualified women shared with cousins or the daughters of neighbours. With ponies, goats, dogs, streams, tree houses, fruit stealing, and poetry writing to compete against, lessons could hardly be anything but a chore, and I suppose that it is this which has left me with an ineradicable feeling that work is the opposite of pleasure. I have tried to persuade myself out of this, but in vain. After twenty years of working in jobs usually congenial, I still leave my offce with the sensation of returning to life.

One of the governesses was sacked because she cowed us, to be forgotten quickly and thankfully. The rest were forgotten slowly and naturally, simply because they meant little to us. Fragments of them remain. A very early one had a kind horse face and was a sucker. Once, when I had irritated her beyond endurance and she had gone out of the room to recover her temper, I leant out of the window, picked a fat, creamy-pink rose from the wall, and laid it on her open book. My eyes must surely have been beady with calculation when she came back to the table, but she noticed nothing, she fell for it, her silly heart melted at the charming ways of children, and I felt a delicious sense of power.

More of Mademoiselle remains bccause we were cruel to her, and we had not until then realized that it was possible for children to be cruel to grown-ups. Her poor hands purple with chilblains, she would sit there weakly accepting our assurance that it was the custom in England to eat boiled eggs with honey, mustard, Ovaltine, and a pinch of birdseed stirred into them (we did it for several mornings to prove our point). Then she turned, and forced my sister, the baby of the family and not strictly under her jurisdiction, to eat all the fat on her cutlet. My brother and I did not think much of my sister at the time, but she rose to the occasion so well, being instantly sick on the table, that we rallied to her with cries of 'Poor little girl, you have been *cruel* to her,' and bolted into shrubberies and beyond, where we stayed all day, knowing that Mademoiselle would not venture further than lawns and flower gardens. We came in that evening knowing that we had been very naughty, but our mother used other words. 'You have been unkind,' she said. 'How could you have been so cruel to poor Mademoiselle?' The incident engraved a trace of uneasiness on my conscience which made me slightly less horrible than some to the duller, plainer mistresses once I was at school.

Only one governess remains solidly a person: Ursula, the last of them, who stayed with us for five years. Her broad red face and her thin, cottony hair augured ill for her, but her common sense and her affectionate heart soon prevailed. She loved dogs, she could corner a recalcitrant pony in a paddock almost as efficiently as my mother, she made jokes we thought funny, and she, too, in her heart, felt that real life was better than lessons. She taught me, one of my cousins, and two girls who lived near us, according to a pleasant system (still practised, I believe) by which we never worked for longer than twenty-five minutes at a time on any subject for fear of tiring young intelligences. Lessons often consisted of looking at smudgy reproductions of pictures by Pre-Raphaelites, then describing them. I was good at this and have loved irises and lilies ever since. When part of the syllabus proved dull – 'citizenship', for example, contained in a book with a dreary blue cover and crossheads printed in a clumsy bold type face – Ursula let it fade out and gave us essays on 'My Best Day's Hunting' to write instead. She was ruthless about good sense and good manners, though, and she did us good.

When the bank's lack of sympathy finally drove me to school (can it really have been cheaper than governesses, or had I become so uppish by then that they felt I needed it?), the headmistress told my mother that she had never before encountered a girl so badly grounded. I felt indignant on Ursula's behalf, but it was probably the truth. She enjoyed the things that we enjoyed too much, and skimped the rest. She must have reported me intelligent, because even in her day it was understood that I would be the one to go to

Oxford, but what, apart from my lust for reading and my facility for 'essays', led her to that conclusion, I now find it hard to see. I cannot remember employing my mind, at that time, on any subject other than horses and sex.

4

My parents' ideas on bringing up children (or rather my mother's, for my father was not much interested and left it to her), were slightly more progressive than those of the rest of the family. Sex was a distasteful subject to all of them, but I believe my mother would have given us honest answers if we had asked questions. She would have been embarrassed, though, and we knew it, so we did not ask. I cannot remember her telling me of any aspect of it except menstruation, which she did not describe as connected with the tricky subject of childbirth, but only as a boring thing which happened to women and, luckily, did not hurt. She got out of giving us 'little talks' or one of those hygienic handbooks for the young by letting us run loose with a lot of animals and forbidding us no book, however 'grown-up'. With this freedom, she believed, we would soon know all about it and, knowing all, would develop a healthy attitude towards it: which, in her terms, would have meant forgetting it. On the same principle, when I was older, she imposed no chaperonage on me but allowed me to come and go with my young men unchecked, hoping that trust would breed reliability. She was aware of the increasing freedom of the 'twenties, she had come to see her own upbringing as absurdly strait-laced, but she was at that stage of emancipation where it is believed that it can be applied to manners without affecting morals: a touching stage. 'You know that I trust you,' she would sometimes say, nervously. I was always grateful for this attitude, partly for its generosity, partly because its consequences were not what she expected.

Animals unaided did not do the trick. At eight or ten years old you can know all about bitches coming on heat, and how a bull mounts a cow, without connecting it with human beings. It was in a book that the odd, almost inconceivable fact that people do what animals do turned up under my hand, as solid as a stone. I think that my mother, in spite of her policy, had *hoped* that we would not chance on Marie Stopes's *Planned Parenthood* – small and black, it was pushed very far back on one of the lower shelves – but chance on it I did, at the age of eleven. Can I really have pulled it out with a slightly cynical amusement at the idea of our parents reading up on how to rear us methodically, which was what the title suggested to me? That is how I remember it.

The diagrams, and the clear descriptions of sexual intercourse, astonished and thrilled me: I had stumbled on the Answer. At first excitement was mixed with dismay – I had seen those awkward, panting, heaving animals: could human beings be so undignified? – but I got over that in a day or two and was soon borrowing Dr Stopes's reverent tone as I explained to Betty, then my closest friend, that it only seemed ugly to us because we did not have husbands: done with one's love it would be beautiful. Lord, but that was a full week! A summer week in the Hertfordshire house, because I remember hurrying through the fence between our paddock and the park round Betty's house, loaded almost to bursting point with information and impatient even of the moment it took to disengage my cotton frock from the brambles which caught at it. First the immense discovery, the reading and rereading, the digesting of the principle of the thing, and then of the fascinating details (it was a good idea to put a towel under your hips to keep the sheets clean – years later my first lover was much tickled when I got into bed for my deflowering equipped with a towel); then the complicated shift of focus, the act of faith almost, by which I converted what was dismaying into what was desirable.

According to the sort of theory half-held by my mother, that should have settled that: fully informed, Betty and I should have relapsed into thinking only of our animals, our games and our lessons, with sex pigeonholed until the time came for it. Instead, intoxicated by our discovery of what was clearly the most exciting thing in life, we rarely thought or spoke of anything else from the day I first read the book to the time, a couple of years later, when Betty's mother found one of my letters to her daughter and forbade the continuance of the friendship on the grounds that I was a dirty-minded little girl. This was unfair. I had access to more information than Betty had, but her interest in it was no less avid than mine. It was also humiliating, but one of the reasons that I believe my mother was prevented from helping us about sex more by shyness than by a fundamentally prudish attitude towards it is that she comforted me in my shame by taking the incident in a matter-of-fact way: it did not seem to surprise her that we had discussed such things – she did not consider me a monster, as I had half expected her to.

Marie Stopes taught me the facts; anonymous English ballad writers confirmed my belief that they were pleasures. The spring following my initiation we went, as usual, to stay at Beckton. My grandmother never allowed anyone else to spring-clean my grandfather's books: each year, with a scarf tied over her hair, she would spend weeks going through the shelves – clap-clap, a flick with a duster, then a quick polish to already gleaming bindings with some unguent prepared from an antiquary's recipe. She was doing the smoking-room one day, kneeling on the floor among stacks of books while I lolled on the sofa. 'What are those?' I asked idly, reaching for the top volume of a pile of six lovely ivory-coloured books with the one word 'Ballads' gleaming on their spines. I felt smug at asking. Ballads, I knew, were the kind of poem one ought to like best at my age, but I usually found them dull and preferred Elizabethan conceits or eighteenth-century elegancies ('Cupid and my Campaspe played/At cards for kisses' was one of my favourites). 'You wouldn't enjoy those,' said my grandmother too quickly, and added, half to herself, 'Horrible things, I can't think how they got here.' ('Men!' she must have been thinking.)

I was on to it at once, put back the volume I had picked up, and talked of something else. That evening I sneaked down, took one of the books at random, and carried it off to my bedroom.

The first poem I read was a long one, and dull, but it was about the gelding of the devil so it had its anatomical passages. Others were far more exciting. The collection was an orgy of rustic bawdy, full of farting and pissing and sex spelt out, embalmed in an atmosphere of guffawing, leering naughtiness. I went through four of the volumes in a fever, hiding them in my underclothes drawer, for in some ways children are as trusting as adults and it did not occur to me that they would be found there. They were, of course. The strange thing, considering how little we did for ourselves in the way of folding up or putting away, was that it did not happen sooner. No one said anything about it – they felt, I suppose, that the incident should be played down rather than up – but when I went to fetch the fifth volume, the whole set had gone. My sense of deprivation was violent; not far, I am sure, from what an alcoholic would feel if his secret stock of whisky was discovered and removed.

Those poems gave me physical sensations of excitement, which *Planned Parenthood* had not done. Flushed and wriggling, searching greedily back and forth for the sexiest passages, I must have been a displeasing sight as I read them. If, now, I found a little girl reading those books in that way, my impulse would be to stop her doing it. But I do not think it did me any harm. 'Dirty-minded' Betty's mother thought me, and dirty-minded I was, doing furtively what I felt to be wrong, but what is the dirty-mindedness of adolescents? Where does it come from, in families where the parents have made no attempt to force their children to think in such terms?

There are always the nuances of behaviour which betray adults' reactions to things whatever their rational policy may be; nuances picked up by children with infallible accuracy. There is always the sense of taboo which comes from silence. And there are always the effects of experiences connected with excretion – 'dirty little girl' over a wetted bed, or merely an adult's expression of distaste over a smelly chamberpot (or one's own distaste over it) – to attach an idea of dirtiness to anything belonging to the private parts of the body. But beyond these things there is something else which no attitude, however 'wholesome', can be sure of getting round: the fact that sex is an *activity*. To learn about it, then put it in cold storage – it is not so simple as that. Learn about sex, and you want, if it has not been deliberately smeared for you, to *act* it; and while, according to the mores of the society in which you live, you are too young for that, you must inevitably go through a period of tension and frustration. 'Dirty-mindedness' is the way – or one of the ways – in which this tension relieves itself, and what is so dreadful about that? 'Laughter of the wrong sort,' as a woman I knew called the titters released in classrooms by paintings of the nude, is not a charming sound, but it is a harmless substitute for illegitimate babies bred between teenage children. I dislike the picture of myself reading those ballads, but I do not wish that I had never done so.

Perhaps children who act it out by masturbating spend less time thinking about sex than I did. If I had known of the activity I should certainly have indulged in it, but I did not know of it, and not having a strong practical bent, I did not invent it. I doubt whether it would have made much difference. Physically precocious as I happened to be, I was bound to go through an obsessed stage; and having been spared neurotic extremes in my parents' attitude I was not likely to be damaged by it. I believe now that the way a person feels about sex, once he has struggled through adolescence, depends largely on other things than his 'sex education': on, for example, his imagination, his honesty, his capacity for tenderness, and his ability to comprehend the 'reality' of other people. Those are the things to fret about, rather than the little horror's passion for looking up rude words in the dictionary or peeping through keyholes.

Absorbing though my obsession with sex remained throughout my teens, it stayed in a watertight compartment: it did not leak out, or hardly leaked out, into my relationship with boys. From the age of nine to the age of fifteen, right through the hot early stages of the fever, I was protected by being in love with a boy of my own age, for the reason that he was kind, gentle, brave, honest, and reliable:

the most rational love of my life. In my daydreams he and I would rescue each other from appalling perils in order to melt together in an endless kiss; but in real life I should have been astounded if he had so much as pecked my cheek – something unthinkable: the nearest he came to expressing affection was to tell his mother that I was a good sport. Only once did a glimmer of true sexual feeling occur. At the end of a violent afternoon spent sliding down a haystack, he came panting up and flopped beside me. 'How red and sticky he looks,' I thought, with what I expected to be distaste – and suddenly, strongly, wanted to feel that hot cheek against mine. I recognized what was happening. 'So *that*,' I thought with surprise, 'is what it is really like!' and I felt adult for having experienced it – adult and secretive. It was not among the things on which I reported in my ill-fated correspondence with Betty.

5

'GOOD EVENING . . . Oh, my god, it's Paul's girl!'
'Maggie, you recognized me!'

'Recognized you? Of course I recognized you.'

Maggie held my arm for a moment after kissing me, looking as though she might cry, while I stood there feeling a curious internal vertigo. It was almost twenty years since I had last gone through the narrow door into the taproom of the Plough at Appleton, a small village about ten miles from Oxford; almost twenty years since Maggie and I had seen each other.

I had returned to it by chance. An Oxford friend not seen for years had come home to England with his family on leave. The village in which he had rented a house happened to be Appleton, and he had asked me to stay for a weekend. He had once known me very well, and remembered that it had been 'my' village although by the time I had met him I had become unwilling to visit it again because it was the place to which I had always gone with Paul. To my dismay, this friend was delighted that now, when everything was safely distant, he could be my escort along two hundred yards of country lane into such a significant patch of my past. It was the sort of thing which he himself enjoyed – he was a great man for pious pilgrimages, for gently melancholy evocations of youthful emotion. I had not thought of Maggie's for a long time and was horrified to feel such a violent revulsion from his sentimental kindness. It seemed to me a shocking intrusion on something which had nothing to do with him, and if a refusal would not have been even more sentimental than the visit, I would have been guilty of that rudeness.

And Maggie looked just the same; or perhaps as though she were having one of her 'bad days' after a thick Guinness evening, only now it was twenty years, not a hangover, that made her look like that. When I saw that she, too, did not know what to say, it was almost intolerable. It had taken a long time, but the whole thing had at last been put away as though behind a glass door – always there to be looked at, it need no longer be felt. But standing there in the taproom, with Maggie's hand on my arm . . . 'Oh, my god, it's Paul's girl!' Of course I was. And yet finally, conclusively, for ever, I was not. So vision skidded and squinted into dizziness.

Paul began long before the days when we went to Maggie's. When I was fifteen my parents decided to employ a tutor during the holidays, to cram my brother for the entrance examination to his public school. They offered the job to the son of a friend of theirs, who was at Oxford, and he, unable to take it, recommended a fellow undergraduate whom he knew to have run out of money and to be looking for a way of earning some. I was beginning to find my pure and unrequited love for the boy who thought me a good sport too quiet for my taste, so I fell in love in advance, first with the friend's son, then, when I heard that Paul was coming instead of him, with Paul. If he had been ugly or shy or snubbing I might have fallen out of love again when he appeared, but he was none of these things, so within two days the lines of my life were laid down.

I wrote to a friend of mine: 'The tutor's come, and he's a perfectly marvellous person. He's got brown eyes and fair hair and I suppose he ought to be taller really but he has got broad shoulders and a good figure, and he's country and London at the same time. He would be at home anywhere. He's very funny and he reads a lot, but he isn't a bit highbrow. We took a boat up the stream yesterday, through all that tangly bit beyond the wood, like going up the Amazon, and he made up a tremendous story about who we were and what we were doing. He knows more about birds than anyone I know, but he dances well too.'

Paul was very much as I described him. Fair-skinned myself, I am rarely attracted by fair people, but he, in spite of hair which in summer would bleach into golden streaks as though he had peroxided it, had an almost Latin pigmentation: sherry-coloured eyes and a matt skin which went with the compact, smooth cut of his features. He was common-sensical and quick-witted rather than clever, good-humoured and high-spirited rather than witty, but the distinctions were not at that time perceptible to me. He was confident, a charmer, and was considered by some of his elders and by more sober young men to be slightly delinquent because he was rarely out of money trouble and would make love to any willing woman, even though she might be the wife or daughter of a friend.

His chief quality – the thing I hit on with 'he would be at home anywhere', the thing for which I most loved him, the thing which influenced me, I now gratefully believe, more than any other quality in any other person – was that he went like steel to magnet for the essence of any person, place, activity, or situation, working from no preconception or preferred framework. He had his own touchstone for what he called 'genuineness', his own unformulated laws which determined whether people were 'real' or not. This eager acceptance of diversity of experience was immensely exciting to me, and of great value, coming as it did when I was ready to take any imprint which came my way. I had reached the stage of being vaguely and for the most part privately in opposition to the laws governing my family's outlook, but it was not a strong or reasoned opposition because there was not enought to oppose: I loved my family and my home, and I enjoyed all the things we did. It was Paul, with his simply expressed but passionately felt dicta – 'The great thing to remember is to *take people as they come*'; 'I hate people who aren't *natural* in any situation' – who broke down my conditioning and made me anxious to meet people as people, regardless of class or race: a freedom from shackles which did not then chafe me, but which would probably have become locked on me, for which I shall always thank him.

Paul used to boast of his 'sense of situation' and his 'way with people'. It was because he felt his way through life with such whiskers that he became at once a member of the household at the

Farm. He enjoyed the place and us as we felt we should be enjoyed; he steered clear of the divergencies that might have alienated my parents; and he plunged happily into the situation of moulding admiring youth as he felt it ought to be moulded. As far as I can remember he managed to hammer a certain amount of information into my brother's then resolutely closed mind, but chiefly he concentrated on opening our eyes to Life.

His family lived in London but spent most of each summer on the coast not far from us, where they had a cottage. His father was a businessman and, without being rich, had more money than mine. Paul had gone to Eton; my brother was going to Wellington. Paul, if his father had his way, would leave Oxford for a job in some organization like I.C.I. or Unilever; my brother, unless he developed some strong bent in another direction, would probably end up like my father, in the Army. Anyone who lived in London and who made money as Paul's father did (he sometimes lost it, too), by knowing what went on in the Stock Exchange, seemed to us so dashing as to be almost disreputable, while anyone who lived in the country and either just had money or, failing that, earned a salary seemed to them so salt-of-the-earth as to be almost dull. In spite of this the two families liked what they knew of each other and no one frowned on the intimacy which soon developed between Paul and me. After that first summer of employment as a tutor, he would come to stay for parties to be my escort, or I would go to stay at the cottage to sail with him and the youngest of his three sisters. She, two years older than he was, became for a time my substitute for Paul, the object on which I focussed my love and admiration, for I had found a letter in his bedroom from a girl with whom he had clearly slept, and this, with the four years between our ages (to fifteen, nineteen is grown-up.), had persuaded me that this love, too, must stay unrequited for a time. I was too sensible to hope to compete while still in pig-tails. So deliberately and fairly calmly, hanging about his sister as much as I was able, I settled down to wait.

The best days of that time were spent sailing. There is nothing to beat messing about in boats (well, yes: there is writing and making love and travelling and looking at pictures, but there is nothing *like* it, and it is good). Estuary sailing in a fourteen-foot half-decked cutter of doubtful class but sound performance was what Paul introduced me to, so estuary sailing is the kind I like best. To do more than poke my nose out to sea while inching along the coast from one river mouth to another, frightens me a little. Sailing on the open sea is surely even better, to those who are accustomed to it, but I remain uneasily aware of how extraordinary it is that so small and frail a man-made contraption as a sailing-boat can survive such gigantic and indifferent opposition. Water I have always loved, but the sea – there is too much of it. Only one thing is more frightening: cloud seen from above, on those hallucinating occasions when it takes the form of landscape. After a flight in such conditions I am haunted by those gullies, those escarpments, those cliff faces and peaks rising out of stretches of eroded desert. I cannot throw off the feeling that I have been watching a *real world*. The common-sense knowledge that if I were to float down on it by parachute I should go through it is bad enough; but worse is the nightmare image of landing on it, finding that it existed, but on unearthly terms – no water, no warmth, no growth – so that I would be the only living thing, with no prospect but to die slowly as I stumbled antlike through a world that was solid but belonged to an eternally foreign order of being. The sea, too, is a world with laws which do not accommodate human life. That human ingenuity has found ways of using it, even of playing with it, is foolhardiness.

But an estuary – from the first shift of shingle under rope soles, the first breath of river-mud smell, I was ready to be at home. The sound made by the planks of a jetty underfoot, the strands of seaweed drying on its piles above water level, unfolding beneath it; the glimpses of water between its planks and the feel of rough iron rings to which dinghies are made fast: I know no purer or simpler pleasure than sitting with legs dangling over the edge of a jetty while someone has gone to fetch the new tiller, or to fill water containers, or (more often) to see the man who is repairing the outboard motor.

The waiting about which attends any sort of boat's motor is the only thing I like about them. In use they are a torment. Chuf chuff chuff – silence. Chuff, a couple of smoke rings, a reek of petrol – silence. 'You'd better go up and take another sounding.' 'There's enough water but we're drifting to port.' 'God damn this bloody bastard.' The absence of a motor can be inconvenient, however, as I learnt when becalmed without one for a whole week on the Clyde, sailing with a man who allowed six inches of weed to flourish on the bottom of his already lumpish boat and who left wet sails huddled in a heap at the end of a day (Paul's ghost asking, 'What on earth are you doing with this frightful chap?').

That boat would hardly come about in anything less than a stiff breeze, and in the few light airs we had each morning it was no more handy than a dead whale. On those light airs, and on tide and current, we meandered slowly about the Clyde, getting stuck at last at an anchorage off a tiny island called the Little Cumbrae, in the middle of an hysterical ternery. The birds felt our presence an outrage the whole day long, their querulous screaming and wheeling turning our idle craft into some ravening sea monster, so that when on the second morning there was a breath of wind it was a relief to put off. A long reach took us to the edge of a sandbank running out from the mainland, and there the wind died. There was a mist. 'I'm going to row to the Great Cumbrae and ask for a tow home,' said the boat's owner – there was a village on the Great Cumbrae. 'You take soundings and anchor when you get between four and three fathoms.' He set off in a vile temper to row for more than a mile, vanishing into the mist after about fifty yards.

It was a thirty-foot boat, everything about it heavy and contrary. After I had got the anchor down I doubted whether it was holding in the sandy bottom, but I could not check whether we were drifting because I could see nothing to check by. Bits of flotsam on the oil-smooth water were certainly moving in relation to the boat, but was it because they were being carried on a slow current, or was it because the *boat* was being carried? I could sense the cat-backed sand lying in wait, expected every instant that deceptively gentle stroking sensation which heralds running quietly aground.

If we did? I saw myself going overboard into water up to my neck to prop her side against the tide's ebbing with oars and the table-top from the cabin. It would not be the first time I had done it, but I had never done it alone, without help. And supposing a squall struck? Squalls could come up in two minutes out of a dead calm on those mountain-surrounded waters, or so I had repeatedly been told: 'A very tricky estuary, you have to know it well.' I did not know it at all.

I tried to repeat poems to myself, and I tried to summarize the plot of *Emma* – not just what happened, but the exact order in which it happened – but every few minutes I would notice that a particular clot of weed was now floating to the right of the cleat for the jib sheet instead of to its left – that it had crept another six inches towards the stem. After half an hour my hands were sweating, and when something suddenly began to *snort* out of the mist I could feel the blood draining from my face. 'I am going mad!' I thought, until smooth shapes came rolling lazily out of the soft greyness: a couple of porpoises to distract me. They had never come so close before and made me happy for a few moments, but soon they went away again, and then there was nothing but a few invisible birds going over, lamenting like exiled ghosts. When I went below to get a whisky I could hear the rim of the glass clinking against my teeth. A book, I thought, and dug out an Agatha Christie from a mess of rotten cord and baked-bean tins, but could not concentrate. To be so scared is ridiculous, I thought. Even if we *do* run aground . . . But what if running aground and the squall *happen at the same moment*?

An hour later, back at my flotsam-watching, I heard a new sound: the tap-tap of a rope end against wood. A breeze was coming up. I licked my finger and stuck it in the air: it was coming offshore, off the sandbank. I'll give it five minutes, I thought, but in less than that time it was with me, a decent, steady breeze blowing in a direction which would sail me off that bank without any manoeuvring being necessary. I knew that I could do nothing single-handed with that horrible boat but sail her in open water with just the right amount of wind; I had rarely done more than crew for Paul and had always had his vigilant eye on me when I took the tiller, and anyway I was not strong enough to handle this awkward bitch. 'You will probably get in a mess,' I told myself, but I did not care. I would not have sat there another minute for a hundred pounds. I skinned my hands as I hauled the anchor in – her bows swung across the chain – and I fumbled and cursed and even cried as I struggled to get the sails up, but I managed it, felt them fill, heard the popple start under her bows, and off I went.

The breeze remained steady, so I could probably have succeeded in taking her into the harbour of the Great Cumbrae, where, no doubt, I should have fouled several people's moorings and brought shame upon myself, but I had in mind nothing so definite as that intention. Just to be under sail in open water was all I wanted. If I had not met the returning dinghy by pure chance, I might be sailing still. I brought the boat about and picked up her owner very neatly, but he, who had found no tow available, whose hands were raw and whose every muscle was aching, was in no state to appreciate it. It was not, in any way, a successful week, since even before that contretemps we had discovered that we had nothing to say to each other, but it was a week which proved the magic of boats. Displeasing though that one was, frustrating though the weather had been, and uncongenial as the boat's owner and I had found each other, what still lives in my memory (besides the sights and sounds, always a delight) is the sharpening tremor of fear in my nerves and the triumphant discovery that it blew away as soon as I was under sail.

The first time I had stayed with Paul's family in their seaside cottage I ate almost nothing for three days, chewing and chewing on mouthfuls which, I feared, would make me vomit if I swallowed them. Nor could I sleep – or not for one night, anyway. I lay listening to the sea on the shingle while feverish tiredness made the bed rock, and whatever I did to my hands clenched them, shook them, rubbed them, relaxed them – I could not rid them of a dull ache in the palms. This sensation is one that I have not experienced, now, for many years and will almost certainly never experience again, for what could be exciting enough to send my nerves into such a state? I must have spoken, I suppose, since everyone welcomed me kindly and they always seemed pleased to see me again, but I cannot remember doing anything but listen and watch. Paul at the Farm was familiar and unalarming – I even lectured him, sometimes, with fifteen-year-old solemnity – but Paul with a boat, Paul with his gay, wild, funny, grown-up sister: there was something piratical about them together, they had a careless way of flouting the law under which I still was, they were so sure that their own touchstones made nonsense of the conventions. My complete acceptance of everything they said, my rapt attentiveness to every nuance of their behaviour, flattered them both into adopting me. There was never a cabin boy more eager to stow away on a gallant pirate ship than I was to join those two in whatever they did.

Part of my tension came, of course, from love, but much of it was due to my ignorance of their chief occupation: sailing. Horses were my thing – and horses had taught me all the pitfalls of a sport. I knew well how *damned* was the rider who came to a meet in the wrong clothes, or worse, in clothes too right if his mount or riding was wrong; one shrewed glance at a newcomer and I could size him up, *in* or out. The man whose bridle had a coloured browband or who had shaped his horse's tail by clipping instead of pulling; the girl who showed curls on her forehead under her bowler, or who had plaited her horse's mane into more than seven plaits – they got short shrift from me. So thoroughly was I conditioned that I could no more have failed to react to such things than a dog could keep its hackles smooth if a strange dog came in at its front door.

So sailing, I knew, would also have its language, its ritual, its taboos. Like anyone of that age, I greatly minded making a fool of myself, and to do it on Paul's ground, under his eyes, would have been intolerable. I had to lie low, lurk in the undergrowth, all eyes and twitching whiskers, picking up clues. I had enough flair to avoid obvious mistakes. I knew, for instance, that I could not go far wrong in my clothes if I kept them warm, practical, and not showy. But all the rest I had to learn.

I never did learn enough to sail well myself. I was not there often enough, and when I was, my anxiety not to make mistakes kept me too docile so that I concentrated on doing what I was told rather than on working things out for myself. But I learnt that when a flight of dunlin zigzags against a thundery sky it is almost invisible until the birds turn so that for a moment all their bellies are exposed; then it is as though a faint streak of white lightning ran across the clouds. I learnt the gait of oyster catchers, the arrowy flight of terns, the ways in which water ruffles, goes sullen, or flashes with what were called locally 'tinkling cymbals' – those neat points of light reflected from every ripple. I learnt that when you wake up at night on a boat anchored far out from the shore, you sometimes hear people *walking* round it, and that when you tip a bucket of water overboard in the darkness, with luck a plunge of white flame will go showering into the depths. I learnt the creakings and patterings, the strainings and shudderings of boats, the gentle winging of sailing before the wind, the clatter of going about, the hissing and ripping of tacking. And I learnt the comfortable silences of two people sailing together, out of which, in the relaxed moments, you say whatever comes into your head. It was an intermittent apprenticeship in sharing profound pleasure.

Ashore, when I was a little older, we would drink beer and eat oysters or bread and cheese with pickled onions in small, dark pubs. I found that I could play darts fairly well – an agreeable surprise for someone with as little coordination between hand and eye as I have, to whom games were a mortification. There was a technique in getting in on a game of darts, or in getting accepted at all, for that matter. 'Foreigners', meaning people who have not been established locally for several years, are distrusted in East Anglia, and the comfortable gossip of watermen and farm labourers over their pints would stop when we came in. Usually when they saw that it was 'old paul' (everyone there is old, even a 'little old baby'), they would greet us with pleasure, for he had been about those parts for some years and was known to be 'all right', but even so it would have been a mistake to push in too eagerly, especially for a girl. Pub manners, on which Paul was an expert, demanded quietness, deference to whatever elder, male or female, was installed in 'his' or 'her' corner, familiarity (but not a *display* of familiarity) with water and country, and an appearance of being at ease without an impertinent assumption of being at home. After a while the presence of the well behaved 'foreigner' would be forgotten by the people who were always there, then remembered again, but in a different way: 'Anyone want a game of darts – what about the young lady?' – and we were off. If I were playing well – if, as on one triumphant occasion, I opened the game with plunk plunk, a double twenty – then we were off into celebration and festivity as well as acceptance. And nothing gave these times more flavour than the knowledge that I would have them to remember when I got back to school.

6

For I did have to go to school soon after we had 'lost our money' and retreated to the Farm. I had been there a term or two by the time Paul came to us. I had not wanted to go, but I had been too ignorant of school life to dread it as I ought. As most adults accept a disagreeable climate, or a dull job, or illness, so children accept the conditions of life wished on them by adults: not willingly, but with fatalism.

As schools go, it was a good school, and I knew as much even at the time. I was also prepared to believe that it would do me good, for at home I had begun to earn accusations of 'uppishness', 'sulks', and 'superiority' which I had not enjoyed. I had only been unable to see what I should do to stop earning them. If school would 'rub the corners off' me, as people said it would, if it would 'teach me to get on with other girls', then good luck to it. But I was not able, and did not see why I should be expected, to go beyond resigned endurance, and enjoy it.

It was a small school looking out over the North Sea. There must, somewhere, have been some kind of land mass between its playing fields and the North Pole, but it did not feel as though there was: in winter the sweat falling from your brow as you ran after a lacrosse ball (you never caught that ball if you were me) all but turned to icicles before it reached the ground. Irritatingly, the rigorous climate and our constant exposure to it, both outdoors and in, really were very healthy so that no one there ever had an infectious disease and only twice was I able to escape into the civilized privacy of the sickroom.

I was fourteen when I first set foot on the loose gravel made from small beach pebbles and went through the elaborate porch of white woodwork into that smell of polish, ink, and gym shoes; fourteen when I arrived, and almost eighteen when I left. A lifetime, it seemed. Good God, think only of one summer term! No stretch of time has ever looked so endless as those *thirteen weeks* before I had been able to black out one single day on my calendar. Three or four years ago I was walking down Oxford Street when I saw a shop-window display of school uniforms, trunks, and tuck boxes backed by a huge mockery of a schoolchild's calendar, the days blacked out up to the current date, crowned by the monstrous legend 'Only Five More Days to the *Beginning* of Term' . . . I stared at it in incredulous horror. Whoever designed that display can only have heard of boarding schools, never have been at one, for how could anyone who had experienced it forget the despair under the stolid endurance with which one crept forward, square by tiny square, towards that red-embellished date which meant freedom regained?

Apart from games, the things I had to do at school were not objectionable. Lessons I saw as necessary, often interesting, and sometimes enjoyable; I made friends whose companionship I appreciated. It was the *absence* of things which had to be endured: the absence of freedom, the absence of home, the absence of privacy, the absence of pleasures. When I understood that not for one minute of the day could I be alone, except in the lavatory, and that every minute had its ordained employment, my spirit shrivelled.

During my first term, when it was all strange as well as barbarous, I used to employ talismans. There was a thrush which sang outside my dormitory in the mornings, whose fountain of song, a voice from the outside world, I listened to so avidly that I learnt to recognize the bird's recurrent phrases. One of them, in particular, seemed like a promise, and I could get up more easily once I had heard it. Our cubicles in the dormitories were surrounded by white curtains hung on rails. At least, I thought, I can keep them pulled round my bed and *imagine* that I am alone. But on the first evening the monitor explained kindly that once we were undressed we must pull the curtains back. I did so, got into bed, and lay staring through tears at the band which held the curtains to a hook in the wall. One of the brass rings on the end of the band was squashed into an oval shape. I invested that ring with friendly powers, gave it a name – Theodore – and would touch it before going to sleep. Nobody else could know about it, nobody could guess at something so absurd, so the ring at least was something privately mine and could transmit little messages of reassurance. All through my schooldays, even when I was established and secure and had won an unusual number of freedoms by a mixture of luck, determination, and suppleness in accepting the role of 'a character', I maintained a private stable of symbols to keep me in touch with outside. Chrysanthemums were one. They smelt of the dance my grandmother gave for us every Christmas, always called 'Diana's dance' because my birthday fell at that time. There was a blue bowl in my headmistress's sitting room the beauty of which I chose to think was noticed by no one else; there were the frogs making slow and shameless love in the lily pond; there was Rufty, the matron's fat, cross smooth-haired fox terrier. These things would catch my eye as I went from class to class, or came in from the playing fields, and would say, 'Patience, outside hasn't stopped existing.' But no talisman was more comforting than the knowledge that I, anonymous as I might seem in my blue serge gym tunic and my black shoes with straps over the instep, was the girl who had played darts with Paul, Hooky Jimson, and old Gooseberry King in the back bar of the Swan. And after Paul had kissed me for the first time . . . 'I am ashamed of you,' said my headmistress. 'You are an intelligent girl, you can work when you want to. These marks are the result of feckless idleness.' I looked back at her serene and unmoved. Arrows of shame were in the air, all right, but all I had to do was to say to myself, 'Last holidays Paul kissed me,' and they melted away.

*

It was at school that my secret sin was first brought into the open: laziness. I was considered a clever girl, but lazy. It has been with me ever since, and the guilt I feel about it assures me that it is a sin, not an inability. It takes the form of an immense weight of inertia at the prospect of any activity that does not positively attract me: a weight that can literally paralyse my moral sense. That something *must* be done I know; that I *can* do it I know; but the force which prevents my doing it when it comes to the point, or makes me postpone it and postpone it until almost too late, is not a conscious defiance of the 'must' nor a deliberate denial of the 'can'. It is an atrophy of the part of my mind which can perceive the 'must' and 'can'. I slide off sideways, almost unconsciously, into doing something else, which I like doing. At school, with my algebra to prepare and a half-hour of good resolutions behind me, I would write a poem or would reach furtively behind me for a novel out of the communal study's bookshelf, by which they were foolish enough to give me a desk. It was a year before they understood that no amount of scolding or appealing to reason would cure me of this habit, and moved me to a desk from which I could not reach the shelf unobserved. I do the same sort of thing today, at the age of forty-two. I may have advertising copy to prepare. The copy date comes nearer – it is on me – it is *past* . . . and I find myself dictating a letter to an author telling him how much I enjoyed his newly submitted book. So often have I proved that this form of self-indulgence ends by making my life less agreeable rather than more so that my inability to control it almost frightens me; but that I should ever get the better of it now seems, alas, most unlikely.

Once my headmistress had sized me up, she used to deal with it by savaging me once a term, at a well-judged moment about two weeks before the end-of-term examinations. 'Diana – she wants you in her study.' With my heart in my boots and my record only too clear in my head I would trail along the dark corridor and tap at her door. She would be standing in front of her fireplace, wearing one of her brown or bottle-green knitted suits, hitching the skirt up a little, perhaps, to warm the backs of her legs. 'Miss Beggs tells me . . . Miss Huissendahl tells me . . .' and the shameful evidence would be put before me in a voice of such disgust, with such ponderous sarcasm, that I could have hit her. Almost in tears with resentment and humiliation, I would go back to the study and defiantly read a novel or write letters all through the next preparation period – but mysteriously, when the examinations came, my marks would be adequate. After a couple of years of this ritual I should have been dismayed if she had skipped it, for I liked to do well. I remember feeling indignant one term, when she left it until too late so that the only subject in which I came top was English. That I came top in anyway, because I liked it.

Even my headmistress, however, could not inject adequacy in mathematics. At the sight of figures I became, and still become, imbecile; and this is a block so immovable that I do not feel guilt at it – there is nothing I can do about it. What set it up I do not know. My first lessons in arithmetic, given by a beloved aunt, I remember with pleasure. We played with matchsticks and it made sense. But once I had mastered adding, subtracting, and dividing I reached a point beyond which nothing could make me go. So profound is my aversion to the symbols of number that I cannot even trust myself to number the pages of a typescript with any reliability: I will find on looking back over it that I have written '82, 83, 84, 76, 77'. Recognizing a hopeless case when they saw one, my teachers recommended that I should drop mathematics and take one of the permitted substitute subjects for the obligatory School Certificate examination of my day – botany, it was. I enjoyed dissecting blackberries and the heads of poppies and then making drawings of them, and was so thankful to be relieved of those nightmare numbers that I did quite well in it.

I do not regret knowing nothing about mathematics, but I am sorry that I had another, slightly less serious block about Latin, and I believe that it could have been undermined. If, after the barest minimum of grammar had been taught me, I had been let loose with a dictionary and, say, Ovid's *Ars Amatoria* . . . But oh, how badly Latin used to be taught! Those nameless girls, constantly making presents of goats to that boring queen! I used to hang on to the goats for all I was worth – I liked goats, goats interested me immensely – but they were never allowed to do anything in the least goatlike, so it was no good. I tried hard with Latin. If there was a choice of verbs to learn I would pick the ones which meant something to me, such as 'to dance', 'to ride', 'to drink' – and, of course, 'to love' – and I found that the future tense, which could be used as an incantation, stayed with me fairly well. 'I will dance, you will dance, he will dance' – pause to dream about 'he' – 'we will dance – I shall be wearing a dress with a huge skirt of shell-pink tulle – no, heavy gold lamé, perhaps – and he will . . .' Even more memorable was the form 'Let him love.' 'Let him love!' – my hair, for that scene, would have had to go raven black . . . I struggled through the school examinations; with stubborn holiday coaching from an elderly clergyman I survived the entrance examination for Oxford, and once there, with more extra coaching, I got through the first-year examination known as Pass Mods. And then, having spent all those years on it, having learnt what must have amounted to quite a *lot* of it, with one great 'Huff!' of relief I blew the whole language out of my mind. The only words of Latin I know today are a few future tenses and *veni, vidi, vici*.

In the Hall of my school, used as a chapel and for all communal occasions, there was, and I suppose still is, a board carrying the names of all the head girls. Mine (and this still seems to me very odd) is on it, which only goes to show how closely biographers should examine evidence. I had been there a long time by then, and had made myself comfortable. By having my appendix removed I had been excused games for all of one term, and the headmistress was tactful enough never to withdraw this blissful dispensation (perhaps the games mistress implored her not to) so that while others were thumping about after balls, I could go for walks. Once in the sixth form, I was free to sit in the little library instead of in the communal study, and attempts to stop me going to bed at eight-thirty, with the little ones, had long been abandoned. The point of that was that the little ones were too much in awe of me to bang on the bathroom door. I could lie alone in hot water for as much as ten minutes at a time (and Blanche Dubois was no more addicted to hot baths than I was while suffering school), and once in bed I might have, if I was lucky, a precious half-hour in an empty room. To begin with, a few girls had been mildly unkind to me for being bad at games and reading so much, but the two things had now become part of my public persona, funny and rather engaging. I was good-tempered and obliging, and had an easily won reputation as a wit: I could feel that people liked me. I expected my last year at school to be almost pleasant, particularly as School Certificate was behind me and I was specializing in English, my best subject, in preparation for Oxford.

It had not occurred to me that *everyone else had left*. Like flotsam stranded by a receding tide, there remained of the senior girls only myself and a large, kind, dull girl called Jennifer. The departing sixth form had to go through an almost parliamentary procedure for electing the new head girl, and after their session an anxious delegation came to me as I peacefully read *Sparkenbrooke* in the library, and said, 'We are awfully sorry, we know that you will hate it – but Jennifer *can't* be head girl – you can see that, can't you? So we *had* to elect you.'

'Nonsense,' I said. 'I won't do it. You can't make me if I don't want to.' They pleaded for a little while, then went away to ask the headmistress what they should do. While I waited, I examined my feelings. Horror had been my first reaction, but after that, had I been putting it on a little, was I not faintly pleased, underneath, at the prospect of such eminence? With immense smugness I decided that I was amused, yes, but *not* pleased: I really was a girl who so despised everything to do with school that nothing would persuade her to accept.

Then the old woman stumped in and said, 'Come into the garden.' She put her arm through mine and walked me briskly up and down among the roses, chuckling and saying flattering things like 'Look, you've got enough sense to see that all this is quite unimportant, but it would make life easier for me if you accepted.' I was fond of her by then. She had once nearly expelled me and had shouted, 'Have you no moral sense at all?' to which I had shouted back 'None, if that's what you call moral sense,' so we had battle scars to share. Soon I was arguing to myself 'Ah, why make so much fuss, it's not worth it,' but a secret feeling of importance was swelling in me. I made my own terms. I would have nothing to do, I said, with the head girl's traditional responsibility towards games (making up teams and so on); Jennifer must do that. All right, she said, and I accepted. And I did not feel ashamed. I still felt amused, and I did not feel very pleased, but I did, alas, feel a *little* pleased. I had shown that I did not want it, and now I had got it; I had made my little omelette, and it was not ungratifying to find the eggs still there.

I can truthfully say, however, that by the end of that short spell as queen of a tiny castle I came back to my first frame of mind. The very fact that I could from time to time feel myself becoming slightly corrupted by an apparent eminence – feeling self-satisfied, when no one knew better than I did how little reason there was for self-satisfaction – ended by confirming in me a native indifference to matters of status. It was all a lot of nonsense, I concluded, and whenever since then I have been in situations where official status was held to be important, I have continued to find that true.

On my last day of school, Packing Day, the day of joy, the day when we stayed up late after fruit salad for supper and sang, heaven knows why, the Eton Boating Song and Harrow's 'Forty-Years On', I looked down from my heights at the cheerfully bellowing crowd of girls and thought, 'Now perhaps – yes, surely – you will feel a moment of regret that it is ending?' But I did not. I knew that I had learnt a lot there, had made some good friends and had some amusing times. I remembered lying flat on my back on the big table in the middle of the study, so overcome by laughter that I thought they would have to carry me up to bed. I remembered drawing lessons in the summer garden, and playing the part of Mr Badger in *Toad of Toad Hall*. I remembered standing for Labour in the mock election we had run at the time of a real one (my grandmother sent my opponent a bundle of Conservative literature as ammunition). I had not, after my first two terms, been unhappy except when in trouble through my own fault – I had even enjoyed a lot of it. But never, for, a single day, had I been doing anything but wait for it to end and now it had ended. Thank God.

7

THAT I STOOD as Labour candidate in the school's mock election when all my family were unquestioning Conservatives was partly the result of Paul's influence, partly of my headmistress's. Paul was more or less apolitical, but he had jolted me out of conformity with my family's mores, He was anti-Them. Particularly he was, as an undergraduate disgusted by standards of material success which threatened to involve him in the kind of career he would detest. His father hoped that he would settle down as a Man in a Grey Flannel Suit, and of that, by temperament, he was the antithesis. He talked of most conservative conventions as tedious or funny and of some of them as immoral, and since, at that stage, whatever he said was Revealed Truth to me, rebellion rather than conformity inevitably became my line. It went with the modern poetry to which he had introduced me. His first present to me, some time in my fifteenth year, had been the complete works of Oscar Wilde and T. S. Eliot's collected poems, and while the Wilde had been just my cup of tea, the Eliot had been champagne. It was a brilliant present, coming from someone not himself a great reader of poetry ('I don't understand much of this,' he wrote in it, 'but I expect you will. Love, Paul'), but he had a flair for present-giving. Nonchalantly but neatly he pushed me into a kind of reading of which I knew nothing but for which I was ripe.

Whether my headmistress voted Liberal or Labour I do not know, but she and her sisters, one felt, had spent their distant youth in earnest concern for women's rights or the reform of education and the prison system: she came of a family with a good old-fashioned radical tradition, she was a pacifist, and she saw to it that the school library was salted with pacifist and Left Wing reading. She made no overt attempts to influence her pupils politically, seeing her task as that of teaching us to think for ourselves (not to mention that of retaining the confidence of our parents), but one of the reasons why she liked me in spite of my shortcomings was that in so far as I thought at all, my thinking went in what seemed to her the right direction. The national newspapers and the weeklies were always spread on a long table in the school's entrance hall; we were not forced to read them, but we were encouraged to. In the 'thirties anyone who had had her shell cracked for her and was not a moron could hardly read the papers without veering to the left. By the time I finished school I was an imperfectly informed but convinced socialist, pacifist, and agnostic.

My agnosticism did not have my headmistress's blessing, though, true to her principles of non-intervention in matters of conscience, she took no action when I stopped taking Communion. I had been brought up as a member of the Church of England, liking God. He knew everything about me but he was Love and he was Understanding, so it would be hard to do anything for which he would not forgive me. In the book of Bible stories from which my grandmother read to us on Sundays, he was a figure of benevolence manifesting himself in a landscape remarkable for its beautiful sunsets, and later, in the Bible itself and in Beckton Church (as familiar and beloved as the morning-room), he was a less material, more complex development of the same spirit. I have friends who turned their backs on the churches in which they were brought up because of the churches' irrational rigours; I was able to drift out of mine so easily because of its mildness.

The early vision of meaningless chaos beyond the rim of human experience with which I had confronted my dismayed grandmother had come to me, as far as I can recall, unprompted. It is echoed in the sensations given me by cloud landscapes, and was crystallized in an experience I had when going under an old-fashioned

anaesthetic at the age of sixteen, when I had my appendix out. As
a small child I had known the usual terror, no worse than anyone
else's, of *things* under my bed. I had readily accepted that these
monsters were imaginary and was not troubled by them for long,
but while I was going under the anaesthetic, one of them came out
and killed me. I had lost consciousness, then regained it, perhaps
because the anaesthetist had reduced the flow too soon. Opening
my eyes in a strange white room, I had not the least idea where I
was, why I was there – the strong white light seemed to be that of
terror at my helpless ignorance of my situation. Then something
came down over my face and I knew in a flare of horror that it was
a claw – the claw of the monster who *had* been under the bed all the
time, in spite of what they had said. Now it had come out and got
me, and in a moment I would be dead. I pitched over the edge of
a cliff and began to roll down into blackness, gasping to myself,
'They were lying, they were lying!' I got a fingerhold on the cliff
and clung to it frantically, knowing that once I could hold on no
longer I would be gone – gone into what I expected to be
nothingness. But as I peered into the blackness I saw that it was
worse than that, it was not nothingness. In cold, absolute horror I
saw that the endless night was full of moving shapes, galaxies of
dim light circling and interweaving *according to laws of their own*
which I, *by my very nature*, could never understand. I thought that
I was screaming aloud 'At least let me change!' but I could feel
conclusively that I was not going to change. I would have to let go
of that cliff and plunge into this new order of being, equipped with
nothing but my usual, totally inadequate self. It occurred to me that
I might start believing in God, and that if I did it might work – it
might give me whatever faculties were needed – but at the same
moment I felt it so shameful to clutch at belief simply because I was
in extremis that I could not bring myself to do it. So in desolation
and despair I let go, and down I went.

I did not draw any conclusions from these experiences, nor did
I consciously relate them to my religious belief, or lack of it, but I
suppose they were symptoms of an innate sense that God was not
so simple as man invented him; that if there was a God, he did not

necessarily exist to answer man's questions and smooth his way, as did the kindly God of whom I had been taught. The older I grew and the more I read of what was happening in the world, the less likely that seemed, but when I started to attend confirmation classes I was still assuming that in this matter 'they' were more likely to be right than I was, still expecting that with further instruction my doubts would vanish.

The clergyman who came to the school twice a week to prepare us was a gentle, ascetic-looking man of obvious goodness and subtle intelligence. He was better at talking to us about Plato than about Christ, which made me admire him, but at the same time his burnt-out face was that of a man moved more by the spirit than by intelligence: he clearly felt the real object of his classes to be more important than the interesting ideas with which he adorned them. I liked him and admired him, and was impressed by the picture he gave of the Protestant Christian faith. It was beautiful, I could see. It was something to which, if you believed in it, you would have to dedicate your whole life as this man had done – indeed, to believe in it and *not* to dedicate your whole life, *not* to give all you had to the poor, *not* to go out among the unenlightened as a guide, would surely be to make a nonsense of it. I was confirmed, and took Communion for the first time. 'You will find it such a *great* help and comfort in times of trouble,' wrote my godmother, but I was ready for more than that. It would not have surprised me if this mystery had tipped the balance of my doubt for good. It would not have surprised me, but it would most definitely have dismayed me: for if I did turn out to believe with all my heart, if as a logical consequence of belief I did have to give all I had to the poor and so on – just think what I would be giving up!

So how can I be sure what was the real cause of the complete lack of meaning which the sacrament had for me? I only know that I took it reverently, thought with concentration of Christ's crucifixion, and came out feeling just the same as I had felt when I went in. I was well enough instructed to know that to expect 'a sign' was absurd, but still I felt let down. Having gone through this I *ought* not, any longer, to be saying to myself things like 'But if it is not really the body and blood of Christ that I have tasted, why all this fuss about it? It is not – of that I am sure. It is a piece of symbolism to remind us, and how can a piece of symbolism be so *holy* as they make this out to be?' It looked as though God had not made up my mind for me, so I would have to make it up for myself.

Time telescopes, so whether it was for weeks or for months that I considered the matter I do not know. I came to the topsy-turvy conclusion that whether I believed or not depended on what I was prepared to do about it. The Ten Commandments, for example, of which confirmation classes had refreshed my memory: would I be prepared – would I be *able* – to keep them? I was having one of my happy interludes in the sickroom while I pondered them, lying there in comfortable solitude with a mild attack of tonsilitis and nothing to distract me. Most of them were easy, but when it came to 'Thou shalt not commit adultery' – I did not need to examine my heart, it was self-evident: the fact must be faced that I was absolutely sure to commit adultery just as soon as I got the chance. So, I thought, slightly awestruck but also relieved, I do not believe in God.

'Adultery' and 'God' were both, of course, shorthand terms. I knew the technical meaning of adultery, but I meant something different by it: I meant making love, whether married or not – but marriage would not come for years and love I was going to make *soon*. The obsession with sex in the abstract had faded out and been superseded by a wholehearted concentration on love, usually directed upon one man, but if Paul failed me it would be someone else, and too bad for Paul. We never discussed such things at my school, where the standard of purity was so high that we did not even understand the purpose of the rules which maintained it – the curtains drawn back at night, the ban on less than three girls being alone together. I felt that I knew more about sex and men than most of my companions, and thought about them more, but I would have felt it irresponsible and lacking in taste to spread my knowledge. On one thundery afternoon, during dancing class when we were practising stage falls, I lay sprawled on the parquet in my sage-green art-silk tunic and bloomers and my salmon-pink lisle stockings, thinking, 'If a stevedore' – why a stevedore? I am sure I had never met one – 'if a stevedore would come and rape me at this minute, I would let him.' It was an incongruous idea to have in that setting and I enjoyed it as such, feeling sorry for my companions, whom I supposed to be innocent of such emotions. As for me, I knew that I was made for love, and love meant lovemaking, and I was going to bring this two-things-in-one to a blazing consummation (no, not with a stevedore, that was a joke) as soon as possible. God forbade me to do so and I did not – I could not – feel that he was right.

For just as 'adultery' was shorthand, so was 'God'. I meant by the word that God I had been brought up on, the God of the Church of England as revealed to me by my family and teachers. It was his laws that I was going to break, and because of his convenient, English mildness, I was not afraid of breaking them. And because I was not afraid of breaking them, they were not laws. Anything which could be dismissed with such surprising easiness could not be the whole answer.

I have thought of more logical arguments for non-belief since then, and I have still felt no need to replace that God by another one, but I am not so sure that I ever really stopped 'believing'. I suppose I shall have to come back to this later, if I am to understand why I did not shiver after my dying grandmother asked me why she had lived.

8

FRENCH TAFFETA, THIN but crisp, striped with a pencil-point black line on the pure evening-sky blue which Mrs Siddons wore when Gainsborough painted her; grey silk velvet, dove-coloured in shadow, silver in light; another grey, corded silk veiled with chiffon, sashed with lemon yellow; more chiffon, pink over pink pearl embroidery on the breasts; more pearls, a trellis of them as a belt: dresses for dancing in! How many hours – weeks, months, years – did I spend thinking about clothes between the ages of fifteen and twenty? Day clothes too, of course, but evening-dresses were the ones which worked a change, making me feel like a mermaid, a swan, a willow tree, making me move differently, making me ready for love. Usually my mother made them for me; a shop dress was at the same time a luxury and (too often) a disappointment. My mother was clever and romantic about them, raiding shops and fashion magazines for ideas, spending far too much on materials, stitching into them, I see now, the gaiety she was not herself enjoying. She was only in her thirties. For what seemed like hours she would keep me standing in the middle of her drawing-room while she fitted me, both of us growing irritable and I never thinking that she might have been making dresses like that for herself. It was by her choice that we were living at the Farm, away from my father except at weekends, and her temperament was such that given her family, her garden, and her animals she could occupy, or appear to occupy, all of herself with energy and conviction. But there was another side to the coin. Not long ago she flipped it over for me, startling me by saying, 'Sometimes I used to wonder if I could bear it another day. No man, no fun, no travel – it was a dreary time.'

The gayest time of my life was a dreary time? I looked back and saw the frightening abyss between parents and their children: that young woman making the best of the situation into which she had stumbled, 'difficult' and contrary, leading her husband a dance but feeling ashamed of it so that she endured her wilful choice of an un-manned country life as a 'punishment', while I never questioned the front she put up: that was how she *was*. I accepted her thought and work for me, the generosity with which she turned me loose, as though it were her pleasure and my due. And when she lay awake fretting because I was being driven back from a dance by a young man, I held it against her: why, as I crept upstairs, must she always call apologetically, 'Darling, are you back? Was it a good party?' And when she betrayed anxiety as to how I was using my freedom – an anxiety usually suppressed and often justified from her point of view – anger flared in me.

Paul came and went and came again. Sometimes I would not see or hear from him for weeks, then there would be a long letter or a telephone call, he would rattle up the lane on a motor bicycle or in a second-hand car, and we would be off to a party together, or over to the coast for sailing.

He excelled as someone to do things with. When I remember him it is less for what we said to each other (although we always had plenty to say) than for what we did together. If Paul were playing with a dog, his pleasure in its silky ears, its movements and its expression would make the dog more real; if he were driving one of his old cars, his handling of it made the mere act of driving more interesting. Any place that he loved – the place he called Little Japan, for instance, where the flat land on either side of our sailing estuary curved up and fell again to the marshes in a sandy cliff on which grew a few wind-tortured Scotch firs – sprang its nature at me because of his relish. When he went with me to pick primroses one Easter – an annual ritual for the decoration of Beckton Church – he was astonished at my matter-of-fact attitude to the thick cushions of flowers in a certain part of the wood. I took it for granted that primroses grew thickly there – they always did. He, who lived either in London or on the coast, where they did not flourish, *saw* them. He squatted to bury his face in a clump, then laughed and said, 'My God, but they're marvellous. You're like that chap in the poem – a primrose by the river's brim a yellow primrose was to him!' At once the frail, reddish, slightly hairy stalks of the primroses, their delicate petals, the neat funnels of their centres, the young leaves, folded and lettuce-green among the darker, broader old ones, the grouping of each constellation of flowers, their delicious, rain-fresh scent – everything about them became alive.

He was a good illustration of that thing so difficult to explain to anyone who does not know it from experience: the point of participating in such sports as shooting. A good shot, he liked to exercise the skill, but to accompany Paul as he walked a rough shoot was to see that there was more in it than that. Any kind of hunting, whether with a gun or with hounds, brings the hunter into a close intimacy with the country over which he does it. He learns what kind of cover a partridge, for instance, will favour – learns it so intimately that he can almost feel himself crouching under the broad, wet leaves of a field of sugar beet. He knows what weather does to 'his' land, and to its animal inhabitants; he knows smells and textures, the sounds different sorts of fallen leaves make when he walks through them, the feel under his palm of the moss on the damp side of a tree trunk. Because of his pursuit his senses have to be more alert than those of even the most enthusiastic walker, so he takes more in. He has to contend with nature, not merely look at it, wading through heavy land, clambering through thorny hedges, allowing for wind, observing the light – and discovering, of course, as much as possible about the habits of the creatures he is after. People who have always been, as a matter of course against blood sports often gibe at the sportsman's professed affection for animals, but paradoxical though it may be, it is perfectly true that there is no surer way to identify with an animal than to hunt it. The man who shoots for pleasure only is doing, I myself now believe, something wantonly destructive – but I have no doubt that it is he who knows best *what it is like to be* a hare, a partridge, a pheasant, a pigeon . . . Paul knew this very well. He got from shooting the same kind of satisfaction that he got from sailing: that of playing with *real* things – water, wind, living creatures. Sailing was the better of the two, because there the game was more even: water and wind can kill you if you are not cleverer than they are. But shooting (and hunting, as I could have taught him) has the same power of engaging you more closely than anything but work with nature, with the elements.

His enjoyment and acceptance were as infectious at a theatre or an exhibition of pictures, dancing in a London nightclub (he took me to my first, finding the last remaining hansom cab in which to see me home) or gossiping in a village pub. I do not think that it was only because I loved him that I found it so, because I often saw other people responding to this quality in him, but no doubt the fact that I had fallen in love with him even before meeting him had made me specially ready to embrace it; and that, in its turn, had made him accept me as an ally from the beginning.

Our relationship developed slowly but steadily. Even after I had left school I would still react to any opinion of Paul's by going through the motions of accepting a Revealed Truth, but I began to find that afterwards I would sometimes blink and have second thoughts. I began to see that being five years older than I was did not prevent him from being young. He had a pontificating vein when he generalized and it was not *lèse-majesté* on my part if it sometimes struck me as funny, or even absurd. If Paul said 'It is *far* safer to drive fast than to drive slowly' I would not go so far as to say at once 'Don't be silly'; I would suppose that it must, in some mysterious way, be true, but later I would come back to the idea and think about it, and reach my own conclusions. Was he, for example, right when he expounded a theory of which he was fond for about a year: that all sexual relationships were basically the pursuit of an essential thrill which, in its purest essence, could only be found in rape? This, he warned me gravely, was why I should find making love with a man who loved me, and therefore could not rape me, a little disappointing. It seemed to me an impressive idea at first, but later I began to wonder if, possibly . . . I began to tease Paul more often, as well as to argue with him, and his elder-brotherly affection for me was a little modified each time we met.

There were plenty of other young men about – our county was well-endowed in that respect – and I never thought of holding them off for Paul's sake: the gaining of experience was too valuable and exciting in itself to be rejected. He was the man I loved, he was the man I was waiting for, but meanwhile if anyone else wanted to fall in love with me, or to kiss me, or to tell me I was attractive, I would welcome it greedily. It was pure chance that it was, in fact, Paul who kissed me first. By then I had been waiting for him for two years, which anyone over twenty-five should read as five, or eight, or ten, for it seemed an eternity. The vigil, I felt, had earned me recompenses which I was ready to grasp. But it so happened that going to a dance with my cousins, at just seventeen the youngest of the party and ready for anything, I met Paul unexpectedly after one of our gaps and he saw more sharply than he had seen before that I was growing up. He noticed it halfway through the evening, left his own party, and swooped me away from mine.

He took me out to sit in a parked car, put his arm round me and told me a fairy story – he liked to make up stories. I dared not move for fear that he would think I was uncomfortable, which I was, and take his arm away. When we were dancing again he said, 'Don't go home with them. I'll drive you if you think your mother will let me stay the night.' To an anxious elder cousin I announced that I was coming home separately, then disappeared; and she, when she got back to the Manor, telephoned my mother and asked, 'Is Diana home yet? Paul carried her off and I couldn't stop them.' Meanwhile, halted by shut gates at a level crossing, Paul had put his arm round me again and I, my heart thudding, had learnt how to relax and let my head fall against his shoulder. When he turned my face up and kissed me on the mouth, we were both surprised: I because his lips were cold and a little sticky whereas I had expected them to be warm and smooth; he because mine were hot and parted whereas he had expected them to be like a child's. He told me later that he had thought, 'The little devil, she has been at it already, this is not the first time,' but it was. I was thinking, 'Paul is kissing me!'; I was thinking, 'And high time, too'; I was thinking, 'Silly, of course his lips are cold, the night air has been blowing on his face'; I was thinking, 'It is natural for first kisses to be disappointing so it doesn't matter, it will be all right next time'. I was coming into my own at last, as I had always intended to, and the difference between anticipation and reality could only be to the advantage of reality, simply because it *was* reality.

When we arrived at the Farm my mother sat up in bed, furious with worry. 'How could you have behaved like that!' she said, 'Why did you take so long to get home, what did you do?' I meant to say nothing, but I was too full of it to keep it in. 'There was a train shunting at the level crossing,' I said. 'Paul kissed me.'

'Oh,' she said, and I could sense the clutch of fear in her stomach. 'Did he just kiss you, or did he – are you sure he didn't *mess you about*?'

I could not strike her because she was in bed and I was standing some paces away. I could only mutter savagely, 'How could you say that!' and slam out of her room thinking, 'Damn her, damn her, damn her!' I could still feel Paul's dinner jacket against my cheek, those surprising lips, and his hand lightly on my breast where my own hand held it; I was still wrapped about with *the most important moment of my life*, and she had said 'mess you about'.

'They are filthy!' I thought.

Poor parents, what are they to do?

From Christmas 1935 to October 1936 I stayed at home, losing the last shreds of my desire to conform to my family's plan for me by going up to Oxford. I had tried for a scholarship and failed; something of which I was ashamed but which was just becoming a relief when a great-aunt stepped in with an offer to help with my fees. 'Darling Aunt Mary,' they all said. 'How wonderful of her' – and I thought 'Interfering old crone.' Now this is a bad thing to remember: that never, other than formally, did I thank Aunt Mary for the three best years of my life.

I did not know that they were going to be so delightful because I saw them as a continuation of school. Here was I on my eighteenth birthday, and *still* they wanted to stuff education down my throat. But because the months ahead of me, before the first term began, looked so rich and free – a clovery green meadow to a pony who had stood in a stall all winter – I kicked up my heels and forgot about the future. New dresses, friends to stay, dances, reading what I liked, horses, hunting, tennis parties . . . If I had been asked 'Do you want to do this forever?' I should have answered with an emphatic no, critical as I had become of the structure on which it all rested, and depressing as I found even then the spectacle of girls older than myself who *were* doing it forever – taking the dogs for walks, arranging the flowers, helping their mothers at garden fêtes. No, I did not intend to be like that. But I did want to do it *now*.

Not all of it was pure pleasure. The tennis parties, for instance, almost amounted to misery. My eye sent messages to my hand no more quickly for a tennis ball than for a lacrosse ball; I was always the worst player there and I hated to show at a disadvantage. But they were a large part of our social life as soon as summer began, and that I would not miss. Besides, the white-clad figures against green lawns, the smell of new-mown grass, the taste of iced home-made lemonade, and the presence of men – once the playing was over the parties became enjoyable. Driving to them, I would practise a fierce self-discipline: 'It does not matter if you make a fool of yourself, it does not matter what they think. It is only vanity which makes you think that it matters and if you stop thinking it, it won't.' When this had only depressed me further I would switch to 'And anyway you dance better than they do, and you ride much better, and you read more, and you're a socialist.' It did not do much good, but even so the parties' pleasures were never wholly obscured by their pains.

Hunting had no pains – or rather, its pains were both private and shared, and sharpened its joys. That I was nervous almost to the point of throwing up at every meet, hearing the crack as my horse's forelegs hit the top bar of a gate, the crunch as one of its hooves came down on my skull, was at the same time an internal matter and something in which I was not alone. During the waiting about before the field moves off; many people are likely to be either unusually silent or unnaturally hearty. The more frightened you were, the more miraculous the vanishing of fear as soon as things started to happen; the more exciting the thud of hooves, the creak of leather, the more triumphant your thrusts ahead by risking a blind bit of fence while others were queuing for a straightforward bit. What instinct it is in a horse that gives it its passion for following hounds I do not understand. It is not only the obvious herd instinct, for I have often known horses who continued to quiver and dance, to be alert in every nerve, when we had lost the field and were riding alone, stretching our ears for the hounds' voices, and I once had a pony who was so mad about the sport that she would not eat when she got home after a long day but would lean against the door of her loose-box, straining to hear the intoxicating sounds from which I had had much trouble turning her away several hours before. Whatever it may be, it is shared by the rider, and it is not lust for blood. I used, whenever possible, to avoid being in at the kill, and of all the many people I have known who enjoyed hunting, not one took pleasure in the chase's logical conclusion.

A long hack home after a hard day could be physical torture: cold, stiff, often wet, you could reach a stage when your mount's every stride seemed a jolt, and every jolt drove your spine into the back of your head. That, and the nerves, were part of the game that made it more than a game, that extended you more than you thought you could be extended. At the Manor there would be a groom to take our ponies when we got in, but in Hertfordshire and at the Farm, where we looked after them ourselves, it went without saying that we rubbed them down, fed and watered them and put on their rugs before we plodded our own aching bodies up to their hot baths (oh, the agony of numb fingers coming alive in hot water) followed by tea-with-an-egg. Absurd though one may think the

English gentry's obsession with animals, a child gains something from their care. To be able to feel your own chills and fatigues in the body of another creature, to rub them away with a twist of straw and solace them with a bran-mash, is to identify with a being outside yourself.

My family's way of talking about its animals – horses, dogs, and goats – would have sounded absurd to anyone who had no experience of them or liking for them. We saw them not as docile or bad-tempered, ill- or well-trained, but as personalities with attributes similar to those of humans. 'Poor Cinders, he gets so bored in the lower shed,' we might say of a pony; or of a dog, 'Lola is in a very haughty mood.' This anthropomorphic approach to animals, despised by those who do not share it, can be taken to foolish extremes but does not seem to me to be an error. I think Freya Stark put her finger on it when she described the death of a lizard she had once owned. She was grieved to a degree she thought exaggerated until it occurred to her that the distance between the lizard and herself was far less than the distance between her and God, and in that way she expressed a truth which urbanized people forget: that *Homo sapiens* is not a creature apart, but one development of animal life. The more subtly developed animals *do* share with human beings certain muscular movements and actions which express similar states of consciousness; in them these actions are released more directly, by simpler stimuli, but at bottom they are not different and we flatter ourselves if we suppose too great a distance between our own behaviour and that of Pavlov's salivating dog.

I have always taken great pleasure in the company of animals, or even in their neutral presence – a rabbit hopping across a lawn or a bird teasing at some berries in a tree – and I am glad that I was brought up in such a way that this pushing out of feelers into a part of nature other than my own is possible to me. I am also glad that circumstances enabled me to go one step further in this than most of the people among whom I was raised, and ask myself the question 'If I feel like this about dogs and birds and horses – what about those poor foxes?'

It was hares and stags in my case, for ours was not a fox-hunting county and we had to make do with harriers and a pack of staghounds which hunted deer maintained for the purpose and captured alive after the day's sport, to be returned to their paddock. It was sometimes argued that the older, more experienced deer knew that this was going to happen and fled from the hounds for the fun of the thing, but they did not look as though they thought it fun. I hunted in order to ride. The subtleties of working hounds meant little to me, and throughout my youth the pleasure I got from riding was so great that I averted my eyes and shut my mind to thoughts of the creatures the hounds pursued, but the images registered, all the same. I cannot be certain whether I would have acknowledged them if those months between school and Oxford *had* 'gone on forever' and my country pleasures had continued unbroken, but I believe I might have done. My father did: he did not merely give up shooting, but came to loathe it.

As it happened I was living in London, and no longer killing anything, by the time I acknowledged that to kill for amusement was barbaric. Now I detest blood sports. I would never hunt again, nor would I go out to watch anyone shoot, nor even, I think, catch a fish unless I were without food. Living creatures have to prey on each other in order to exist, but not one of them can annihilate another *for its own amusement* without committing an outrage.

For the rest of that time I feel no guilt, though I often behaved badly. Badly in the conventional sense in that I flirted extravagantly with any man willing, considering a dance a failure unless I had been kissed at least once by someone, it did not much matter whom; and badly in another way, in that I became affected and a little arrogant, feeling myself more intelligent than most of my acquaintances, and sometimes (where were those Left Wing principles?) socially superior to some of them. I did not put it like that. At the smaller parties, the local parties, with the sons and daughters of parsons and estate agents and wine merchants and veterinary surgeons, I simply allowed myself to feel that I and my cousins were more dashing and stylish than they were, and showed off accordingly. We could be the stars of those parties (or felt we could be) and I can only hope that the good manners in which we had been trained prevented us from making such monkeys of ourselves as we might have done. If I went to a more sophisticated dance – a dance with people *from London* at it – it was another story. On such an occasion I would be hushed with admiration, and grateful for any attention I received: only if I went to such a dance with Paul could I be quite at ease.

But that exuberant, slightly gauche girl, wearing her hair in a curly fringe because a young man had said that she resembled Katharine Hepburn, does not weigh too much on my conscience. Even if I had never gone to Oxford, I would soon have stopped being eighteen years old.

9

I WENT UP TO Oxford in 1936 and I did not join the Communist Party while I was there. I cannot claim that this was because of intelligent criticism of Marxist principles, nor that I had an instinctive prescience greater than that of many of my more serious contemporaries: it was simply that I was lazy. Bad smells were as acrid in my nose as they were in the noses of any other Left Wing undergraduate at the time, and it seemed to me, as it did to others, that only an extreme, a revolutionary opposition to capitalist society would be effective. But to become an active Party member – that looked to me like hard work. As I had slid away from the Church of England, so I slid away from Communism, but with less excuse: for the first sliding I had felt valid reasons stirring behind the laziness, while for the second, at that time, I could feel none. I greatly admired anyone who committed himself and I did not believe that to be, in a desultory way, a member of the Oxford Labour Club and to cut sandwiches for hunger marchers was an appropriate response to the circumstances. 'I am,' I felt with regret, 'an essentially frivolous person.'

I felt like that not only when I considered the state of society, but whenever anything forced me to acknowledge that the war would soon be on us. 'We who live in the shadow of a war . . .' Stephen Spender's poetry I knew by heart several years before I went to Oxford – he had been one of my adolescent passions – and neither he, nor anyone else I read, nor the daily evidence of the news permitted ignorance. But 'Oh shut up, let's talk about something else,' I said. 'There's nothing we can do, anyway.' It was only at night that I would sometimes say to myself the words: 'It is really coming, you know. As things are, it can't fail to come.' One summer night at Oxford there were aeroplanes droning for an hour, circling or streaming over the town for what purpose I do not know. Bombing raids: Spain had given us plenty of book learning about them, but it is odd that I should have known so certainly that the steadily throbbing hum was that of bombers, not fighters. That's how they will sound, I thought, and almost, in the chill of dread, That's them. I cannot remember ever feeling colder or more hopeless when lying in later beds listening to real raids. It was no good pretending that it might not happen: it would. And I cried tears soon dried by their own inadequacy. All I could do about the coming war was to cry. Once I said to a friend, 'I shall kill myself when it starts,' and she replied, 'But that's silly – to kill yourself to avoid death.' It was not death I was thinking of avoiding, it was having to know this horror about life.

So yes: I was frivolous, and I was lazy, and it seems to me now that I was lucky to be those things, because by being able almost all the time to slide sideways, not to think, I could store three years away like jewels before it came.

All the way from home to Oxford I was in a near-coma of alarm, sleepy and detached as though I were watching events from far away and they did not really concern me. Nervousness still has this effect on me, which (though it had unfortunate results during University examinations, making me slapdash and flippant) is a fortunate quirk. Apart from going to school, the only journeys I had ever made alone had been for short visits to friends, for parties, when on arrival I would be met by expected faces and carried off to do expected and pleasurable things. Leaving home frightened me. The super-school for which I supposed myself bound chilled me. I had not believed that those lush green months were going to end so soon.

I had been to Oxford earlier for my interview, so I knew about the gasworks and the marmalade factory and the prison, those melancholy outriders to beauty when you arrive by rail. I knew, too, that my college was an undistinguished building, or sprawl of buildings. If my spirits had been high enough to be dashed, they would not have been dashed by these things. But I did not know quite how institutional my room would be, with its dark-blue curtains of cotton repp, its dark-blue screen round the washstand, its dark-blue cover on the bed and its mud-coloured carpet, limp with use. Oh dear. And then to have to venture out down those long corridors, peer at notice boards, find those other freshwomen ('freshers' I would have to call them, I supposed with distaste), all so confident and clever-looking. One had got out of a taxi just in front of me, tall, wearing a fur coat and carrying a bag of golf clubs. Another I had talked to at our interview and she had almond eyes, wore exquisite little shoes, and had dismissed some girl as 'the sort of girl who keeps count of the men who have kissed her' – which I did, too. It was strange that my two best friends should have been the first to catch my attention and to strike awe: Nan, terrified, paralysed with shyness, not knowing what to do with the horrible golf clubs her father had insisted on giving her; Margaret, more like the effect she made but as absorbed by love as I had ever been.

We trooped from interview to interview, being told what we were to do, what classes we were to attend, who was lecturing where, on what; and we were given copies of the Statutes to read. Good God, the restrictions! This would be worse than school. The Statutes have been revised since then, but at that time they appeared to date from my mothers' generation when a girl had to be accompanied by a woman don as chaperone if she went to tea with a man, and naturally no one explained that most of them were ignored.

The first day or two were much as I had feared they would be, though too fully occupied to allow homesickness. It was not until the weekend that the clouds lifted. On the Saturday there was a telegram waiting for me in my pigeonhole: 'FLYING DOWN TO COLLECT YOU TEN O'CLOCK TOMORROW WEAR RIDING CLOTHES PAUL.'

On Sunday I went in to breakfast in riding clothes. The haughty

Nan, her fur coat and golf clubs still casting their aura, had kindly kept me a place. Erroneous though my impression of her had been, it was nothing to hers of me when I casually mentioned that my young man was coming to see me *by aeroplane* and that we would spend the morning riding together – it was several days before these two dashing creatures faded away and the real girls met.

Paul had tried to please his father by working for Cadbury's but had not been able to endure it and had bolted into the Royal Air Force after a few months. He was stationed in Lincolnshire but could borrow a plane from time to time and land at Abingdon, where he could borrow a car. I did not much want to ride with him because I despised hired horses and it embarrassed me to see him doing anything at which he was not good – he hardly knew how to ride – but that he should have thought up this way of making me feel at home touched me so deeply that I would have ridden a donkey round Rotten Row all day. And after we had ridden he said, 'I'm going to take you to my favourite place.' We drove to Appleton and there I was, going into the taproom of the Plough for the first time, being introduced to Maggie, who, twenty years later, was to cry 'My God, it's Paul's girl.'

Maggie had a husband, known as Dad, but he was not a very efficient man. It was typical of him that when Paul was staying the night and had to get up at four in the morning to be back in Grantham in time for work, Dad would test the alarm clock to make sure that it was working and would forget to rewind it. He used to smile and nod and be gently shooed into the background by his wife, who ran the place. She looked a little cottage housewife rather than a pubkeeper (in spite of the occasional Guinness hangover), and she gave the impression that opening time was the beginning of a party. Gay, brisk, endlessly generous, she adored an invasion by any of the enterprising young men who had discovered her pub while they were at Oxford, calling them 'her boys' – and of all 'her boys', Paul seemed to be the favourite. She would always find a bed for him, lend him money, tell lies for him, scold him, pet him, give him good advice, and welcome his girls without giving any of them a hint that there had been others. She approved of me.

The taproom was narrow and dark, with a solid table down the middle of it and wooden settles along the wall. That was where evenings would begin, or where we would drink when we visited the place at lunchtime. But towards the end of an evening the sheep would divide from the goats – ordinary customers would stay in the taproom, while the more solid 'regulars' and honoured guests would move into the parlour. There was a piano with a pleated silk front in there, and a good deal of shabby furniture in a small space so that we could sit down. It was in the parlour that I spent the first of many Plough evenings, and that I heard the Poacher sing.

Maggie was all for a bit of music and would play herself when she could escape from the taproom. It started, that night, with songs like 'Shenandoah', or 'When Irish Eyes Are Smiling', which everyone knew, then went on to the soloists. In the corner sat the Poacher, his cap pulled down over his red face, shuffling his feet and grinning into his mug when people began to urge him. He was coy about it – heaven knows how many pints had to be poured down him before, suddenly, he lurched to his feet. There was a shout of pleasure and he was jostled into the cramped middle of the room. He took off his cap, looked into it for a moment, then slammed it back on to his head the wrong way round. Deliberately, dramatically, he got into his singing posture: one foot advanced, the knee bent, his right arm extended stiffly in front of him (the only other person I have seen in that position was a Maharajah posing for a photograph at the time of King George V's Jubilee). Everyone leant forward in their chairs, and a deep droning sound began, so that I thought 'But what was all the fuss about, the man can't sing at all!' and then I began to hear the words. The Poacher was singing songs composed by the people who had composed the 'Ballads' in my grandfather's wicked white volumes.

'Where did he get them from?' I whispered to Paul.

'From his father. And he got them from his father, and he got them from his. Nobody has ever written them down.'

Back they went into time, the pretty maidens going to market, falling into ditches and showing first their slim ankles, then their round knees, then their white thighs, then . . . A miller went down to his mill to see if his apprentice was filling sacks properly, and found him filling the miller's wife . . . A naive young shepherdess asked a young shepherd what it was that the rams were doing, and why . . . Some of them were not lewd but romantic, like the one about a girl lovelorn like a nightingale, leaning her bosom on a cruel thorn. Once the Poacher was launched, others joined in. They all knew the songs and loved them, sentimental or bawdy, and none of them thought of them as anything but 'the old songs' as opposed to 'modern jazz' – none of them thought it strange that they should still be singing them. But when I saw Maggie again after all those years, 'Oh, my dear,' she said to me, 'they never sing the old songs now, not ever. The young ones don't go for them any more and the Poacher's dead.'

I sat through that evening in spellbound silence, made shy by the family greeting Paul got, afraid that I should not be considered worthy. I drank my half-pint of beer to his pint, I watched, I listened, and happiness crept up like a rising tide. Later we drove off somewhere to see a man called Bernard – my first of many a confused exodus at closing time, the cool air of night so sweet on one's face, the handle on the car's door so strangely not quite where one expects it to be, the plans to go to such and such a place changing so mysteriously en route to arrival at another. Bernard was a homosexual, Paul told me as we went up the stairs, but a grand chap, great fun. Goodness, another first! I had never spoken to a homosexual in my life. And soon I was not just speaking to one but was in bed with him, snuggled between him and Paul and drinking whisky, because Bernard it turned out was in bed with a cold and his room was chilly. I was living! Thawed, happy, drunk, kissed, I was delivered back to my college two minutes before midnight – when the doors were shut – and I knew that I was going to love Oxford.

To me Oxford became a game at a time when play was life. The play of young animals, their pouncing and stalking and woolly wrestling, is serious. It is learning, without which they would not survive as adults, and that kind of play among human beings is too often restricted by economic necessity to childhood, in which a great deal is learnt, but not everything. Oxford struck me – I am not being wise after the event, it struck me like this at the time – as the perfect place for this kind of learning, or growing. Some of my friends became impatient of it, feeling it unreal, but I argued that if for three or four years you could have the advantages of being adult with none of the responsibilities, what more could you ask? And to have a whole city which, by custom, the young could treat as their own, to be able to walk down its High Street as confidently as though it were your garden path, to be free to be arrogant and absurd – to annoy other people by making loud, precious talk in restaurants, or to carry a grass snake with you when you went to parties – that was the kind of thing which you would never be able to do unselfconsciously anywhere else, and which you needed to do. Behind you were the prison walls of school and the deflating intimacy of family ('No one likes an *affected* girl,' when you had thought you were being witty), and in front of you were the necessary, not unwelcome, disciplines of a job or marriage. But here, now, in the present, was the chance to think and talk and behave in whatever way you wished, and this I could only see as a glorious good.

To say that I did no work while I was up would be to exaggerate only slightly. Certain things I could not avoid: writing an essay for my tutor once a week and attending classes, which were smaller and more intimate than lectures, consisting only of the people from one's own college, in one's own year, who were reading the same subject, visiting some don in his or her room as a group. It was only possible to be absent from a class with a watertight excuse, but no one knew whether one attended lectures or not, since they were a University, not a college, matter, given in the impersonal setting of the University Schools or in the hall of the lecturer's college. I soon thought up the argument that all lecturers wrote books on their subjects, and that one could benefit more from reading than from listening: an argument which would have had something in it if I *had* read, since no form of instruction is more soporific than words spoken to a large audience by someone who has often spoken them before. I must have attended about six lectures in the course of my three years. On those occasions I carried a pen and several sheets of paper, sincerely meaning to take the methodical notes on which, I had so often been told, everything depended. I would get to (3), or perhaps (3a), and then a drawing of a crocodile, a horse, a hat would appear, or a note to show at knee level to Margaret: 'Isn't that man with red hair the one who got drunk at Gerry's party?' 'No, he was fatter.'

I had chosen to read English because I reckoned that I would be reading it anyway, for pleasure. A good deal of it I did read, and wrote about with spirit though always at the last possible moment and too briefly, in essays which gave the impression of intelligence and enthusiasm. But native wit could not disguise for long so thorough a lack of application; indeed, when it came to the barbaric Anglo-Saxon language, an extensive knowledge of which was required, it could not disguise it at all. I was soon starting each term with a little talk from my Moral Tutor – the don responsible for one in a general way throughout one's career. Mine was a small, shy woman of great tact and delicacy of feeling, a scrupulous scholar and a scrupulous respecter of other people's liberties fastidiously disinclined, to bully. Gently, almost humbly, she would ask how I intended to work that term. 'You *ought* to get a First,' she would say during my first year. 'It would be such a pity if you did not.' In my second year it was 'You *ought* to get a Second.' In my third year we reached the point, painfully embarrassing to us both, when she had to steel herself to speak out. 'You cannot do enough work to catch up and avoid disaster if you continue to go out so much, and to act. Rehearsing takes up so much time. I am afraid I really must ask you to think seriously about cutting down your activities – giving up the acting, for instance – now that Schools are nearly on us.'

These interviews made me angry with the itchy, irritable anger which results from knowing yourself to be in the wrong, and after the anger had died down, they made me sorry that I should have inflicted such a disagreeable task on a woman who would so warmly have appreciated the pleasant one of praising me. They did not, however, influence my behaviour in the smallest degree. Even the acting I clung to, although I was no actress and did not think myself one. I only loved everything about it: being onstage, being backstage, making up, painting scenery, the smells, the lights, the sounds.

Intelligent in certain ways I may have been, but I was by nature entirely, hopelessly unscholarly. What I got from Oxford, on the level of formal education (apart from a Third Class degree, and if one were going to do badly the rare Fourth Class would at least have had the merit of dash), was no more than the reading of a few books which I might not otherwise have read and which I am glad to know, and a vague, general idea of what scholarship is. I can recognize it in others, I can wince at its imitations. But if that were all Oxford had given me – or rather, that I had been capable of taking from Oxford – I should have cost my parents and my great-aunt a lot of money for an appallingly small return.

I believe, however, that I owe to Oxford much of the stability and resilience which enabled me, later, to live through twenty years of unhappiness without coming to dislike life. I already had the advantages of a happy childhood and a naturally equable disposition, and three years of almost pure enjoyment added to those advantages confirmed in me a bias towards being *well-disposed* to life without which, lacking faith, lacking intellect, lacking energy, and, eventually, lacking confidence in myself, I might have foundered.

On the river at night, moving silently through the darkness under trees: suddenly the man punting whispers 'Look!' and I turn my head towards the bank. Three naked boys are dancing wildly but without a sound in the moonlight.

On the river at night again, moored in the cave of shadow made by a willow: music in the distance, coming slowly nearer. We stop kissing and another, solitary punter passes us without knowing we are there, with a gramophone in the stern of his punt on which 'The Swan of Tuonela' is playing into the night.

In someone's room on an October evening, the air outside the window turning deep blue: a long way away, someone begins to play the Last Post on a bugle and we stop talking while the whole of autumn, the whole of Oxford, the whole of time passing seems to be drawn up into an exquisite sadness. Even at my father's funeral, when the Last Post was played over his grave, it carried me back to that room.

People who have been happy in a first marriage are likely to be happy in a second: they are conditioned to companionship and affection. In the same way, I, having lived for so long in a place which I loved passionately, had a readiness to love another place: it was because of Beckton that Oxford, as a place, meant so much to me. I do not believe that I ever went out of my college, even if only to buy a tube of toothpaste, without taking conscious pleasure in something that I saw, some chime of bells, some smell. Coming back from a class I would deviate from the shortest way to go by the Turl, or by New College Lane or Magpie Lane, or some other street for which I had a particular affection, and I liked to walk by myself so that without distraction I could soak these streets and buildings up. The place seemed to me to give off a physical exhalation to which my very skin responded. If at Oxford anything had irritated, bored, or frustrated me, if I were unhappy or lonely or angry with myself, I could always be restored by the place. Towards the end of my time there I would go out with the deliberate intention of 'soaking up'.

The room which depressed me so much on my first arrival was not mine for long. Soon I was given the chance of moving into better accommodation, and got a room in the Old Building, looking over a lawn with apple trees growing out of neat rounds cut in the grass: 'the unicorn garden' Nan and I used to call it, because it had the look of a garden in a tapestry. My extravagant mother came to visit me and saw at once that all that dark blue, with the ugly washstand, was intolerable. With guilty excitement we hurried out shopping and I chose a shockingly expensive chintz for bed and curtains, and a neat cabinet to enclose the washing paraphernalia which, when shut, looked pretty with a bowl of roses on it. Once books, pictures, and china were arranged, that room became to my mind the most charming and adult-looking in the college, and from that day it was my habit to spend almost my whole allowance of a pound a week on flowers for its decoration. After the detestable promiscuity of school life and the pleasanter but no less unavoidable infringements of privacy in a family, a room of one's own was both an adventure and a reassurance. Thinking it pretty, I even kept it tidy: something which to this day I can only do to rooms I like.

I never used the common rooms except for the short periods during the mornings when I was winkled out of my own by a housemaid; and then, unless it was the morning before I had to produce an essay so that work was unavoidable, I would prefer to visit Nan or Margaret, or to meet friends for coffee in the town. Our social life sounds extraordinarily mild. Except for my escapades with Paul, it was meeting people for coffee, meeting people for a walk, going on the river, going to tea with people – those were by far the most frequent entertainments. There was a scattering of pub-crawls and sherry parties, but few of our young men had more money than we had ourselves, so that although a bottle of reasonably good sherry cost only seven and six, debauchery was usually beyond our means. Except for the summer term, which ended with the Commemoration balls, we were not likely to dance more than two or three times in the eight weeks, while dining at the George, at that time the dashing restaurant, had to be kept for special occasions. Paul took me there, of course, but my undergraduate friends would manage it only during the early, display-dance stage of a wooing.

Because mild though such occupations may sound, they were in fact nearer to being feverish. During nearly all of them love was being approached, made, or dissipated. Sprawling on beds in each other's rooms, Nan, Margaret, and I would certainly often discuss books, politics, religion, and the meaning of life, but more often we would discuss people, and most of the people we discussed were men.

When, and to whom, were we going to lose our virginity? That was our covert, and sometimes our overt, preoccupation. Both Margaret and I had come to Oxford officially in love, and Nan was soon to become engaged, though not for long. Since we all felt that this serious step was synonymous with the sealing of a great love, we should have had no problem – but we did. Not inevitably, but most often, to meet a new man, to be asked out by him, and to get to know him beyond a superficial point was to be embraced by him; and with the embrace he would become at once more than a casual aquaintance, he would become a new person to know. These little explosions of meeting were constantly blasting new shafts into the mine of experience, opening new galleries of relationship to be explored.

Sitting behind two girls in a bus not long ago, I heard one of them saying gravely, 'The trouble is, I'm beginning to think that it *is* possible to be in love with two people at once,' and her words gave me an instant feeling of exhaustion. Yes indeed, that *was* the trouble. How could it not be when the people one was meeting were all different, all real, none of them yet visibly crippled by the patterns their life would impose on them into distrust, or masochism, or boredom, or whatever deformity might overtake them later. I never believed that I would *marry* any of the men I came to know at Oxford – it was Paul whom I was going to marry – but this did not prevent them, sometimes, from being more immediately important to me than mere liking could account for. When Paul was out of sight he was not so much out of mind as tucked away into cold storage in the back of my mind, and during those times other relationships, intense, delightful, or harrowing, could flourish. We all, in the end, steered the course we believed to be right: Margaret married her love soon after leaving Oxford, Nan postponed decision until she was older, and I went to bed with Paul. But it was a serpentine wake that we left behind us before reaching those points, and regularly once a term, I for one would have to spend a day in bed for no other reason than nervous exhaustion.

In one of these subsidiary relationships I was all but trapped, reaching a stage in which I said to myself in so many words 'I love him so much that I would *even marry* him' and clinging to that stage even after I had laughed at my own momentary conception of marriage as a desperate resort. He was the first man I had met for whom I felt the tenderness which comes with physical accord in its purest form: that sympathy between skin and bone and nerves which on its own level is as rare as true temperamental affinity. Simply to look at his thin hands, the way his hair grew crisply above his ears, the slant of his eyelashes and the freckles on the bridge of his nose, gave me such intense pleasure that it *had* to involve the whole of me. I knew perfectly well that although he was a gentle and sweet-natured person, and had a kind of secret integrity of character which was deeply likeable, he was not someone with whom I could communicate. Ideas might flow between me and other people, and between him and other people, but they did not flow between me and him – we came up against a blank wall in each other and a marriage between us would have been a disaster. But we only had to kiss each other for this knowledge to vanish, and at the end of one summer term, when our long, shy lovemaking had reached a point of tension unbearable to him, we had a scene from which I emerged determined that the first thing I would do at the beginning of next term was to commit myself to him by sleeping with him.

I brewed this decision for the whole of the vacation, becoming more exalted as I became more nervous – and he, at his end, brewed it too, coming, though I did not know it, to an opposite conclusion. He was a level-headed young man with high principles, and he decided that to seduce a girl whom he liked but did not want to marry would be asking for trouble. We met again, I in my fine fever, he in his anxious lucidity – and no other meeting in my life, however much more grave in reality, has remained with me in its detail more painfully than that one. I have written a story about it so I will not describe it here. I will only say that the pain and humiliation and sense of loss seemed to be quite literally unbearable.

So unbearable were they that after two days I saw that I could not bear them. I wrote to Paul: 'Darling Paul,' I said, 'I am so miserable that I want to die. Robert does not love me. Do you think that you can come to Oxford *soon*?'

Back came a letter by return, telling me that even if Robert did not love me, Paul did; telling me that 'he will miss you more than he can bear and will throw care to the winds'; telling me that I must not stop loving or stop being unhappy 'because now you are living'; telling me to 'read Ralph Waldo Emerson in the Oxford Book of E. V.'; telling me that he was coming.

Before he arrived I did read Ralph Waldo Emerson, a poet whom I much despised but whose message now, coming through Paul, left me between crying and laughing:

> Give all to love;
> Obey thy heart;
> Friends, kindred, days,
> Estate, good fame,
> Plans, credit, and the Muse –
> Nothing refuse
>
> 'Tis a brave master;
> Let it have scope:
> Follow it utterly . . .

Oh, darling Paul! What a terrible poem to choose and what a splendid message to send! And when I reached the last three lines, miserable though I was, laughter won:

> Heartily know,
> When half-gods go
> The gods arrive.

Whatever Emerson may have intended by that, I had a pretty clear idea of what Paul meant. 'Oh my love,' I thought, 'what a conceited old thing you are.'

The comfort that letter gave, the gratitude and affection with which it filled me, were the most adult of all the love-feelings I had yet experienced for Paul. It was at the end of that term that I spent three nights with him in accommodating lodgings which he had discovered when he himself was up at Oxford, and it was during the next vacation that we became engaged.

10

REALITY, AS USUAL, was different from its anticipation. I discovered, for example, that the housework in hotels begins at extraordinary hours. When we spent the weekend of our engagement at Nottingham, which was not far from where Paul was stationed and could be disguised to my family as a weekend in his commanding officer's house, the vacuum cleaners began to hum almost as soon as the washing up of crockery after dinner ended. I had supposed that after making love one always fell into a deep and especially refreshing sleep, and now discovered that one could quite well lie awake all night, limbs twitching under the strain of immobility imposed by fear of disturbing the sleeper beside one. Nor did the earth move under me when we embraced, as Ernest Hemingway had said it would. I knew already that Paul, although an attractive man, was not to me especially attractive – not one of those men like Robert, in response to whose body my every nerve vibrated. Complete lovemaking confirmed this. It was comfortable and delightful with Paul, but not so totally exciting that my physical sensations became one with my emotional commitment.

I observed these differences from the anticipated, but they did not distress me; they interested me, rather. They interested me constantly and absorbingly in the way that details of life in a foreign country visited for the first time interest me, and I was perfectly confident that I should soon learn my way about them. After a few more weekends I should be able to turn over and stretch my legs

without worrying about Paul's sleep, and after a few more I would
find a way to be totally immersed in our lovemaking. In the short
time we were together this did, indeed, begin to happen. He was a
gentle and understanding initiator and we knew each other too well
for inhibitions or reserves. My confidence was soundly based.

Our families were neither surprised nor displeased when we told
them that we intended to marry; only a little anxious, mine because
they thought me young for it, his because they knew him to be wild.
They all pointed out that to live on four hundred pounds a year,
which was apparently what a pilot officer's pay came to in those
days, would not be easy, and they all kept telling us that there was
plenty of time. I did not see what time was needed for. We had
agreed that I should not cut short my three years at Oxford – Paul
had enjoyed his own time there too much to expect it of me – but
that we should be married once my precious last year was over was
as certain as the rising of the sun, so why wait before we said so?

I felt selfish in wanting that last year of freedom so much, but it
fitted in well. Soon after we had decided to get married, Paul heard
that he was to be posted to Egypt at the beginning of that year, and
we agreed that it would be a good thing for him to have time to
settle down to the kind of work he would be doing there, size up the
kind of life we would be living, and find us a house before I joined
him. So although I ought not, perhaps, to long so urgently for more
people, more emotions, more adventures before I married, I could
disguise the longing as common sense.

It is curious now to remember our relationship between my
growing up and Paul's departure for Egypt: I would hardly believe
in it if I did not still have letters to bear witness. For all that long-
short time in my teens I had been the lover waiting to be loved, and
for all the long – the really long – time that was to follow, I was to
revert to that role, but during this interval, when everything seemed
settled, I was confidently, even smugly, the beloved. Paul often told
me that he understood my wish to stay on at Oxford and that he
wanted me to have my fling, but after these generous gestures he
would report nightmares in which he saw me walking away down
a street with Robert, and would scribble a miserable note saying 'I

know I said I wouldn't mind, but I would, I can't help it.' We would have a wonderful afternoon over at Maggie's, spending hours lying together in the grass by the river, then idling back to the pub for drinks and gossip; and suddenly, rather drunk, I would snap at him with an accusation of possessiveness; or he would press me to decide on the time for a meeting and I would answer coldly that I could not be sure, and I had to see so-and-so, go to a dance with such-and-such. I was not deliberately playing the bitch. I felt that we had a lifetime together – and a lifetime in which Paul would certainly be unfaithful to me whereas I could not see myself being unfaithful to him – so that I still had and deserved time to play.

That he would be unfaithful was something that I could not doubt when I knew him so well. For a long time before our engagement he had reported to me on his affairs, filling me at first with awe and with pride that he should choose to confide in me, then with a feeling of security. One of them was 'a very gorgeous and exotic time, but it became indigestible, like an absolute orgy of rich, delicious fruit cake. I can't tell you how wonderful it was to get back to sanity and you.' This was when I was about seventeen, and although I felt a little wry at being considered plain, wholesome fare, I was flattered at being told about it. Later this kind of thing stopped, but even after we had begun to sleep together I had seen him answering a roving eye with an eye no less roving, and I did not believe as firmly as he did in his protestations of absolute fidelity for the rest of our lives. It would be a long time before Paul would be content to leave any situation unexplored.

Once, when we were already engaged, we went out to the Plough in a taxi and since we were both feeling liverish and hung-over, dismissed the cab before we got there so that we would walk the last mile. It was a winter day with a low grey sky above flat brown fields over which fieldfares were flitting. While Paul watched the birds, I watched him. It was soon after I had observed the exchange of roving glances; I was distressed that he should have been ready to click with a girl while I was actually present and he was penitent and extra tender, as he always was when he felt guilty. It will be all right for a long time, I thought. He won't love any of them, he will always come back to me. But I had better face the fact that it will be hell when I get old, when I am thirty – and I had a vision of a scraggy neck and pepper-and-salt hair reflected in my mirror. He will still be in his prime then, I thought. That's when I shall have to learn how to be clever, in case he finds love creeping up on him with one of them.

I knew that this problem existed, but it did not worry me deeply. I was sure that I was loved in spite of it, I could see for myself that when I, in my turn, had moments of considering Paul to be plain, wholesome fare, he was more distressed by the role than I was. Perhaps this contributed without my knowing it, to the slightly offhand manner I slipped into after we were engaged.

Whether that was so or not, the manner had brought him to heel so smartly before a few months were over that it led me into a new development of feeling. Seeing my carefree Paul so distressed, I began to understand that even someone who knew me as well as he did might be confused by my behaviour. If he were to take my love for granted as surely as I did, I must manifest it more clearly, and so I did. The prospect of a year's separation was becoming real; it was easier to sacrifice the small freedoms and the slight independence on which I had been insisting. 'Thank God,' he wrote from the ship, 'that before I left you managed to convince me that you love me as much as I love you. I shall never doubt it again.'

The end of Paul's embarkation leave coincided with the beginning of my term. We had spent a week sailing together at Burnham-on-Crouch, tarnishing my Woolworth's wedding ring in salt water and knowing a more relaxed and lovely intimacy than we had ever had before, and after it I went to London to stay with his family. Our last evening together was wretched. We drank too much and made love unsuccessfully, unhappiness making me cold and stiff, and Paul rough. He cried and I could think of nothing to say to comfort him, nor could I cry myself. The next morning, when he was seeing me off at Paddington, it was I who cried and he who was inarticulate. His parents, my parents, all our friends had been saying 'Never mind, a year is not *really* very long,' and now Paul fell back on this. 'Daddy told me that he waited four years for Mummy,' he said through tile train window, and I sobbed, 'I don't care. A year is *forever.*' When the train pulled out I thought of going into the lavatory to conceal my tears, but realised that if I indulged in this privacy I should never be able to check them. I stood in the corridor wrestling with them, facing the lavatory door so that the passengers who edged past me should not see my face.

It would have been a horrible farewell if that had been what it was, but in the few days he spent at Grantham before he sailed, Paul gave a typical twist to our parting. He did not warn me but wangled a day off, flew to Abingdon and turned up unexpectedly in Oxford. We clung to each other in the little den of a waiting room in which we had to receive visitors, and knew that everything had become smooth and natural again: the goodbyes were done with, we could be together. We went to Maggie's and were happy all that day, and when he left it was almost as though there were nothing special about our parting. A year had become just a year. In Egypt I was going to ride a white Arab stallion and keep a white saluki to run behind me. We were going to have four children – Paul had always wanted children on the grounds that creation, in whatever form, was the justification of living, so that for people like ourselves, who could not write or paint or compose, children were the thing. I had as yet no stirrings of maternal feeling, but was prepared to believe that I would like babies once they were there. 'I expect you will change your mind and come out to me sooner than you think,' said Paul, and I answered, 'I expect I shall.'

So Oxford became a good place to wait in. Flaking stone, blue mists over the river, laburnums showering over garden walls in the road leading to my college, the scent of stocks and roses from behind the walls, voices calling up to windows, and the charming frivolities of friendship now suddenly revealing a deeper value than I had suspected. Even love still went on, though now that I was committed to Paul it was different. Once the obsessing question of virginity had been solved, the clouds of sex rolled back a little and I became more familiar with affection, patience, tenderness, and understanding, all of which I accepted gratefully, even greedily, as something to keep me warm while I waited for Paul's letters. Perhaps, at that time, I enjoyed Oxford even more intensely, knowing that my 'real' life was already being lived for me – half of it, at any rate – in Egypt.

I was both nervous and arrogant at the prospect of becoming an 'RAF wife'. The other wives, I was sure, would talk of nothing but their servants and would play bridge every afternoon. I would have to be a rebellious and eccentric wife, I decided, and Paul's letters suggested that this could be achieved fairly easily. It was true that he reported that no one else on the station met Egyptians or ate Egyptian food – 'They might be Colonel Blimp in person, every one of them,' he said – but he himself had made the rounds of the Arab nightclubs in Cairo before he had been there a week, enjoyed the food and was guest of honour at an Arab village wedding within three weeks. He wrote about Egypt with a lively tourist's relish, easily tickled by the picturesque or the comic: not a particularly serious or understanding approach, but an open, welcoming one. He described the problems of sailing a dhow; the white Arab stallion was going to materialize – a man in the neighbouring village knew of a perfect one; we would ride far into the desert, we would sleep out, we would meet nomads. It seemed likely that by the time I arrived his 'Arab technique' would be almost as good as his 'pub technique'. The RAF wives, he said, were not so bad as I had expected and would be kind and helpful, but we would have more fun than they did: not for us the narrow circle of club, swimming pool, and bridge table.

He worked out a budget for us – something which neither of us had ever done – proving that we could live on £24 a month, with a furnished house, a servant, a car, and plenty to drink ('Mind you, we could live cheaper than £24 a month, but it would be more fun if we didn't'). 'Our gloomy pictures of marital boredom are quite impossible,' he wrote. 'My day and your day – an ordinary day, when we weren't doing anything special – would be like this: 5 a.m.: I get up and go to the camp in car to work. 7.30 a.m.: I return for breakfast, by which time you have got up and quite probably will have already been for a ride with the saluki on your white Arab. 8.30 a.m. to 12.30 p.m.: I work and fly. You drive into Cairo, do some shopping, bathe at the Ghezira sporting club and have some lovely looking Frenchman flattering you. 12.30 p.m.: Both home to lunch. 1.30 p.m. to 5.30 p.m.: The whole of Egypt sleeps in a temperature of about 105 in the shade, but a lovely, dry, energizing heat!!!! 5.30 p.m. to 6.30 p.m.: Tea and toast and baths and wanderings about in kimonos. 7.00 p.m.: Drinks and friends. 8.30 p.m.: Cairo for dinner, dancing, and cabaret. 2.00 a.m.: Bed.' Mentally turning half of the shopping time into reading time, I had to acknowledge that this deplorably idle life, provided it were lived with Paul, would be just the life for me.

I always knew when Paul's letters had come. Before I had opened my eyes in the morning, something in me would have sniffed the air and I would know. He wrote well, and at length, but not often, so that morning after morning lassitude would come over me again and I would have to struggle not to bury my face in the pillow and go back to sleep. Then a morning would come when I would be out of bed without thinking of it. I would try to dress slowly and calmly, and not to run downstairs, telling myself not to be excited in case I was wrong, but I was never wrong.

When Hitler invaded Czechoslovakia I knew that I had been a fool. We only had time to draw a deep breath before the war began, so I wrote to Paul telling him that I had indeed changed my mind and was ready to join him at once. He answered with delight, but hardly had his letter arrived than it was followed by a cable saying that he had been transferred to Transjordan, then in a state of emergency, and that we must revert to our plan of marrying at the end of the year. He was transferred. I had two more long, alive, loving letters from him, and then I never heard from him again until I received a formal note, two years later, asking me to release him from our engagement because he was about to marry someone else.

11

THE TIMES – WHEN the pain was nearest to the physical – to that of a finger crushed in a door, or a tooth under a drill – were not those in which I thought 'He no longer loves me' but those in which I thought 'He will not even write to tell me that he no longer loves me.' For weeks his silence seemed no more than his usual unreadiness as a letter writer; then, for months, the result of his absorption in his work and in the place where he was working, both of which he had described with vibrating enthusiasm. Such excuses I went on making for much longer than any detached observer could have accepted them, shutting my eyes in panic to the considerate silences and distressed expressions of my mother and my friends. I remembered what he had said in the third but last letter I had from him: 'Never write to me less often. I know that I don't deserve it, but it is terribly hard to write here and I'm bad at it anyway, so if you don't hear from me often enough you must never think it's because I am not thinking about you. I think about you *all the time* and I would die if you stopped writing to me.' So I went on writing, and I tried not to complain at getting no answers. But after a while my letters became involuntarily appealing, then humiliatingly pleading, then unconvincingly threatening. Before I myself became silent – after how long I cannot remember – I had thrown off all attempts at consideration, strategy, or pride: I had told him as nakedly as I could what his silence was doing to me – and still it continued.

If he had written to say, 'For such and such a reason I no longer want to marry you, I no longer love you,' I should have been stunned with grief and loss but it would have made some kind of sense and I could have come to terms with it. But that Paul, who had loved me, and who knew what I was now feeling, should have wiped out my existence so totally . . . I was often literally unable to believe it, it was something he *could not* do.

It was not until many years later that I learnt the reason for what had happened – a love affair, of course, although not with the girl he was to marry. Feelings of guilt snowball. When they have accumulated beyond a certain point, a sense that nothing can annul them makes any action seem inadequate, so that oblivion becomes the only easy answer. Paul, who was never good at doing anything which he disliked, must have felt at first that a time would come when he would be able to explain, then that the time had taken too long in coming. So he cheated; he shut his imagination.

If I had known him less well the whole thing might have been over comparatively quickly: I might have written him off as a monster, dropped all hope, and have been cured. Two things prevented this. One was the reaction common to almost everyone in such a situation: the terrible knowledge that if you accept the unworthiness of the object of your love, then your love itself is discredited and all the good in its past becomes poisoned retroactively. The other was the plain fact that Paul was not a monster. I had known him for so many of the longest years in a life-time, I had grown up with him, I had loved him, after the first spell of childish infatuation, with the sort of love which brings knowledge rather than illusion: I was unable to make a grotesque of him. He was a spoilt young man who lived intensely in the present, and I had always known that in whatever place he happened to be, his present would be there. It was not in his nature to live suspended between past and future, as I could do. So although there were many times when I was cornered by that worst of all manifestations of suffering – the certainty that what is happening, what is being done, is too painful to be borne, but that the logical consequence of this, which would be that therefore one would not have to bear it, is simply not going to come about – although this happened night after night, and although I laboured through long stretches of incredulity and anger, and great bogs of self-pity, I always came back to the knowledge that it was not Paul's fault that our relationship had become unreal to him.

Knowing this, I would not give him up. When he came back to England, I was sure, I would again become his present. At one point, about eighteen months after he had fallen silent, a cousin told me that a man she knew had met Paul at a drunken party, somewhere in Palestine, and that when Paul had learnt that this man knew Beckton, my family, and me, though only slightly, he had burst into tears (he always cried easily when thoroughly drunk). He had wept, he had said that he was a worthless brute, he had said that I was the only woman he really loved. My cousin, it seems to me, took a risk in passing on this report to me, because it might have led me to build some wild structure of hope, but in fact it did no harm because the structure was already there. I simply took it as confirmation of what I already believed: if Paul and I were to meet again – I could see that in all probability we would not, but if we did – it would be possible to overcome what had happened. More than any other image of him, I remembered a moment when, in a room full of people, he had come across to light my cigarette, our eyes had met, I had felt my own changing and I had seen his lighten from brown to gold as the flash of understanding passed between us. Whatever happened in the interval, I was convinced that if we saw each other again a moment would come when our eyes would do that; that while I remained myself and Paul was Paul, we could not be together without being as we had been.

Perhaps this might have happened if the war had not prevented his return to England. He was then cut off from us, and flying bombers, with the airman's usual cold knowledge of the chances against his ever coming home again. England and everything in it must soon have become incredibly remote to him, and who knows what chill stretches of loneliness he must have lived through, loving his lost home and his lost life as he did, before he met a girl who could give him warmth and certainty, and whom he married. He was killed before their son was born, but at least he knew that they were to have a child. It is now easy to be grateful to that girl for having existed (she married again, I am happy to say), but at the time . . .

His final letter, arriving after two years had passed, with its formal request 'to be released' from our engagement, seemed to me so cruel that I still cannot think of it as having been written by Paul. It seemed cruel not because of its contents but because of its wording. It was written in the kind of words men use in letters to women who, unless everything is 'cleared up', might sue them for breach of promise, and that Paul should write in that way to me seemed to annihilate the half of our years together that had existed in his mind. The manner was dictated, I can now see, by guilt and embarrassment. It would have been no more possible for Paul to remember me as such a woman than it would have been for me to remember him as mean or vindictive. But when the letter was brought up to me early one morning by my silent mother, my body went cold and limp on the bed at the image it suggested of what I had become in Paul's memory. Then I dropped the horrible piece of paper and thought, Well, anyway, it's over now. The final desolation was to see, even as I thought the words, that it was not. The picture which came into my mind was of a long bridge suspended between two towers. One of the towers was knocked away, so surely the bridge must fall – but it did not. Senselessly, absurdly, it went on extending into space.

The humiliations of grief are revolting. If only I had kept silent! But in the short letter I wrote back I permitted myself the whining, miserable words 'I hope you never make her as unhappy as you have made me' and I have never been more ashamed of anything I have done. That was the kind of thing about being unhappy which I loathed: the spectacle of oneself being turned into something despicable. That was what I struggled against, and for that reason I was pleased for many years by the knowledge that I had never for any length of time lost my hold on the truth of the situation: never, at bottom, held Paul 'guilty' for what had happened. But now I am not sure that this was so fortunate.

Paul was not any 'guiltier' than any other human being – all are capable of the unpardonable from time to time – but if I had let myself feel that he was, I believe the effects of his desertion might have been less far-reaching. By heaping blame on to him, I might have kept my confidence in myself intact. As it was, frightened by a vision of myself gone sour and self-pitying, I went further than allowing the situation not to be his fault – I took 'fault' on myself. 'Why should he have gone on loving me in absence?' I began asking myself bleakly. 'The fact that he was not able to do so proves that I am not the sort of person who has the right to expect such a thing.' During the nights which followed the blank, heavy days, when bitterness began to mount in me, I would hammer it down with this thought.

A long, flat unhappiness of that sort drains one, substitutes for blood some thin, acid fluid with a disagreeable smell. When in those days I stared at myself in the looking glass it seemed to me that I was the same as usual: my colour normal, enough flesh on my bones, my hair shiny. But I had proof that I was not the same. People had noticed me when I was happy, had chosen my company, and laughed with me and tried to make love to me. When I was no longer happy they did none of these things, they saw something about me which made them avoid me. I remember telling myself that this was subjective, that it was I who was not responding to other people – none of them had any quality other than being not-Paul – so the lack of contact came from me, not them: self-pity, I told myself, was working on my imagination. Before I went to a party I would try to persuade myself that if I expected to enjoy it I would do so, and then there would be no more of those eyes straying in search of other glances while flat talk was made. No one, I would assure myself, was thinking of me as diseased – why *should* anyone think of me in that way? But the most horrible moment of that horrible time was not imagined.

One of our family friends was an exceptionally attractive, slightly raffish man, nearer my parents' generation than my own, with whom I might well have fallen in love if I had not been otherwise occupied. He was just the man for it: tall, lean, very handsome in a fine-drawn way, he had bummed romantically about the world busting broncos, sailing on tramp steamers, ruining his health (who knew how?) in places full of parrots and mangrove swamps. My own acknowledgment of his charms remained detached, but not so that of my sister. She, five years younger than I was, felt his glamour to the point of hero worship, and he, tickled by this and observing that an attractive child was developing into a lovely girl, used to flirt with her. She was a busy diarist, filling fat notebooks by the dozen, writing 'Secret' on them and leaving them about in her bedroom so that her private life was not so private as she hoped. I am sure that my mother read those diaries from end to end, and I too would leaf through them from time to time, half amused, half sympathetic. My sister's passion for this man was faithfully recorded, and so was his mischievous but harmless response to it.

Once, driving her back from some party, he held her hand. When they got home they sat for some minutes in the car and she, dizzy with expectation, thought that he would kiss her. He did not. 'He told me that he was not going to kiss me although he wanted to. He said that I was going to be a fascinating woman but that I mustn't begin that sort of thing too soon or it would spoil me. *Look at Di, he said, you don't want to be like her. And of course I don't.*'

The shrivelling sensation of reading those words is something I still flinch from recalling. I could not even summon up indignation at their smugness and unfairness, or question the misconception that 'being like Di' resulted from being loved too soon instead of from misery at being loved no longer. With a shameful, accepting humility I saw that I was diseased in other people's eyes: that unhappiness was not a misfortune but a taint. In the depths of my being I must have wanted to kill my sister for it, but all I recognized was a shuddering acknowledgment that out of the mouths of babes . . . Pretty and vital as she was, for many years after that I saw her as prettier and more vital, and was prepared to take second place to her, to rejoice at her triumphs and fret over her sorrows like a model sister. This was not a bad thing, since she gave good reason for admiration and affection, but there was a streak of falsity

in it: I was over-compensating for my resentment at the scar she
had left with her innocent, idle thrust.

Some time after that, during the first May of the war, I was invited
for a week's sailing on the Broads. There would be six of us: Hugh,
the young doctor who had asked me, who would be paired with a
pretty cousin; an engaged couple, both of whom I liked; and a
friend of Hugh's to pair with me. The girls were to sleep on the
boat, the men ashore, in tents. Every week that the war continued
'phony' was, we knew, a week to grab. It had not yet closed the
Broads for defence purposes, but it had driven people off them, so
that we would see them as they are never ordinarily seen, free of
motor launches, houseboats, and picnickers. The weather was
miraculous, a springtime out of a pastoral poem, and I felt a lift of
heart at being invited. Sailing I loved, and Hugh must want me with
them or he would not have asked me. Perhaps I would be able to
enjoy something, at last, enough to break through the barrier and
get a foot back into life.

Two days before we were to start, Hugh telephoned to say that
the man invited for me had failed us, his leave had been cancelled.
It would make it less amusing for me, they feared, but please would
I come all the same, it was not the kind of party on which even
numbers mattered. I felt foreboding, but I went.

During most of each day it was true, even numbers did not
matter. We were busy sailing and sunning and preparing absurd
meals, all enjoying having those strange waterways to ourselves,
manoeuvring through the narrow cuts, coming quietly out on to the
wide expanses with nothing on them but coot, grebe, and duck. No
people. We seemed to have gone back in time to a wild, untouched
country. Both Hugh and the engaged ones knew of Paul's long
silence and were kind and welcoming, doing their best to include
me and to cheer me up. But the engaged ones *were* engaged – and
the little girl cousin was fiercely in love with Hugh. She had no
reason to be jealous of his amiability to me, but she was; and he,
although not deeply involved, was touched by her; he could not do
anything but treat her, gently, as his love. When the early evenings

fell, when we had wrestled with our primus stove and eaten, and the moon had sailed up above the rushes, it was inevitable that the two couples should link up.

The engaged ones would take the dinghy and paddle off, leaving an uneven wake of silvered ripples on the smooth, inky water. Hugh, the girl, and I would wash up, sit on the deck to talk in low voices, and the tension would mount. It was painfully beautiful. Reed warblers (Paul would have known if they were really reed warblers) would toss off little beads of song, almost like nightingales, and the uncanny booming of the bitterns – more like some ancient monster bellowing – sent shivers down my spine. After a while the couple's wish to be alone would force me to my feet. 'I know what I want to do,' I would say, my wretched humility brightening my voice. 'I'm going for a walk to see if I can get nearer to that bittern.' Hugh would go through the motions of asking the girl whether she wanted to go too, and she would go through the motions of deciding that no, on the whole she thought she was too sleepy.

I did not cry as I wandered by myself through the tufty marsh grass. I tried to be only my senses, soaking outwards into the beauty, savouring night-time, of which one always has too little – and I must have succeeded up to a point because when I remember that week the beauty is still sharply with me. But only a yogi could keep that up, and I had to face the truth. This was before I had heard of Paul's marriage, but far enough on for my belief in his return to have been reduced to its minimum: less a belief in his return, than a belief that *if* he returned, all might be well. On the night when the moon was full I had to put aside that belief. On that night there was no cloud in the sky, but there was a wind. It came rushing between the moon and the flat land, bending the forest of reeds where earth melted into water with such a steady, even thrust that it hardly made them rustle. With the same relentless flow it seemed to flood through my emptiness. Out on the Broad the engaged couple would be whispering and laughing; in the boat's cabin Hugh and the girl would be holding each other close and kissing. I stood under that moon, in that wind, and knew myself to be absolutely alone. It was so absolute that for a time I might have been my skeleton lying somewhere, as Paul's was soon to lie, to be picked clean by the elements.

It was a feeling far too powerful to be evaded; it had to be accepted. 'This is it,' I thought. 'This is how it is,' and with a sort of dull, weary recognition I saw that it could be endured, and that if *that* could be endured, then anything could be. After about an hour I went back to the boat to find that the others had reassembled as a party and were brewing tea. Hugh reached out and squeezed my hand in the cabin's almost-darkness, for which I am still grateful to him. And from that time I made better progress in my discipline against self-pity and it was less bad than it had been, or so I thought. But perhaps it was that experience of absolute acceptance which put the seal on my loneliness for so much of my life.

To be in love and engaged at nineteen, and disengaged at twenty-two, is not fatal: you have lost your love, you have lost your job (for that is what it amounts to for a woman, as surely as though she had been training to be a doctor, only to be prevented by circumstances from practising), but you are still very young. 'You are still very young,' I used to tell myself. 'It is absurd to consider your life ruined at this age. However improbable it may seem, someone else will take Paul's place.' And that, naturally, happened. What my self-admonishment did not take into account was the change brought about in my nature by my own loss of confidence.

Why should my sense of my own value in relationships with men have collapsed so completely? I have sometimes wondered whether the smallness of the part played by my father in my childhood may have been responsible. Did I once, long before I can remember, want to fall in love with him as little girls are supposed to do, and was I chilled by an indifference that left me with a tendency to expect rejection? It would make sense, it is the sort of explanation offered by convincing textbooks, but it seems a bit too simple to me.

Whatever the reason for it, there was a flaw of some sort in me which split under the impact of my abandonment by Paul and ran through all my subsequent relationships with men until I believed that I had come to the end of them. Love still took up most of my attention, but to describe in any detail my other affairs would be tedious, because they ran to a pattern. I could only be at ease in a relationship which I knew to be trivial. If I fell seriously in love it was with a fatalistic expectation of disaster, and disaster followed. By the time I had reached my thirties I was convinced that I lacked some vital quality necessary to inspire love, and it was not until my forties were approaching that I began to see the possibility that instead of lacking it, I might have been suppressing it; that my profound 'misfortune', of being unable to make the men I loved love me in return, might be the result of an attitude of my own which came from a subconscious equating of love with pain.

Twice I fell in love with happily married men – the first time quite soon after Paul's marriage. It felt like coming back to life with a vengeance, but I recognized from the beginning that it was 'hopeless', in that when he said 'love' he meant something less than I did, and the more I recognized this, the greater my secret abandon to the situation. It must have been chance that he repeated the pattern of Paul so exactly – going away, writing a few times, then silence – but although this second blow on the same spot was an agony, it was not unexpected: I had been waiting for it from the moment I realized that this was a 'real' man, not just a man who was not Paul. And both with that man and with my second married lover, I flattered myself that I was unselfish and fair-minded in not wanting to force them into leaving their wives: indeed, their affection for their wives, underlying their readiness to enjoy themselves with me, was something which I esteemed. I felt with both of them that they would not have been the kind of man I could have loved so much if they had been prepared to wreck long-standing marriages for my sake, and estimable though this attitude may be on the face of it, there now seems to me something fishy about it. I was hungry to be alive, so I was hungry to love – but was I hungry, in fact, for the companionship of those particular men, or of the third one, unmarried but not in love with me, whose reservations about me turned a lively attraction into infatuation so that I did not *fall* in love with him, but might have been *jumping* off a cliff? I have always shrunk from the idea of possessiveness, I have never tried to mould people into my own idea of them, and I have been satisfied with myself because of this; I have considered it a virtue. It may have been in part the virtue I took it to be, but I suspect now that it had other aspects as well: that if I did not grab at people, I grabbed at emotion, and that for many years the most intense emotion I could conceive of was one of pain.

12

'OF COURSE IT'S different for someone like you, a career woman . . .'

Good God! I thought, and was about to protest. But what is a woman with a job and no husband, once past thirty, if not a career woman? I remembered a book in a blue binding which, when I was twelve, I shared with my friend Betty: a book with questions in it, and spaces for the answers. Who is your favourite character in fiction? What is your favourite food? What is your ambition? Betty wrote that her ambition was to be a great actress. Mine was: 'To marry a man I love and who loves me.' I never went back on that and I do not go back on it now, but I have not made it; so a career woman is what I look like, and what do I think of *that*?

At Oxford and immediately after I left it, I was extremely naive about careers. So was the rest of my family. It is astonishing to remember how few working women we knew – none at all well, except for my mother's unmarried sister, who had been a hospital almoner until she was arbitrarily summoned home to live with my grandmother on my grandfather's death. Sometimes a report would come in that so-and-so's daughter – 'such a clever girl' – had got 'a wonderful job in the Foreign Office' or was 'doing so well on the *Manchester Guardian*'. We would admire this, but the mere fact that the girl was in such a job removed her from our sphere and made her seem a different kind of person from oneself. I never had any doubt that the kind of job I would like would be one connected with literature, painting, or the theatre, but that sort of thing seemed far outside my range. I had a humble idea of my own abilities. I lacked the proper arrogance of youth in that respect. Lazy and self-indulgent, I was a lively girl only in my capacity as a female, and once I was wounded in that capacity I became, to face the truth, dull. (Since I believe that any recognition of truth is salutary, this should be a bracing moment, but it does not feel like that: it feels sad.)

So instead of having some wild but inspiriting ambition I thought vaguely that I might like to be a journalist because I enjoyed writing letters and essays, or I might like to be a librarian because I enjoyed reading books. I did not have to read many newspapers before I saw that I was probably off-beam about the first, so the second was what, in a half-hearted way, I was planning to be when the war began.

The war began. I sat on the dining-room floor at the Farm with my sister, filling bags of hessian with fine, prickly chaff to make mattresses for refugees from London, while we listened to Chamberlain's announcement on the radio and swallowed our tears. (I do not remember that any of the refugees actually slept on those emergency mattresses, but most of them stampeded back to London quite as fast as if they had.)

I was no longer a pacifist in any formal sense. To make gestures against the war once it had come seemed as absurd as to make gestures against an earthquake or a hurricane. The horror had materialized and it must be endured, but to *participate* in it any further than I was compelled to do by *force majeure* did not occur to me. A mute, mulish loathing of the whole monstrous lunacy was what I felt; almost an indifference to how it ended, for no matter who won the war, it had happened; human beings – and I did not recognize much difference between German human beings and English ones – had proved capable of making it happen, and that fact could never be undone. Later, when 'unconditional surrender' was the watchword and furtive peace feelers from the Axis were being snubbed, the madness seemed to me to have become so great that my imagination could not even *try* to comprehend it.

To have become a nurse would have made sense to me, but I knew in my bones that I had no gift for nursing. To have joined one of the women's services was something that I could have done, becoming one of thousands of regimented women, learning to talk military jargon, growing ruddy under a uniform cap and broad-beamed in khaki bloomers. It seemed to me an intensely disagreeable prospect, but what particular right had I to avoid it? I cannot remember even attempting to think of a justification. I was determined that I would not do it unless 'they' came and got me, and that was that.

This refusal to take any part not forced on me seems to me now an unmistakable measure of smallness of spirit. To remain detached from the history of one's time, however insane its course, is fruitless even on the private level, since only by living what is happening (whether by joining it or by actively opposing it) can the individual apprehend its truth. Detestable as the 'white feather' mood of the First World War certainly must have been, an expression of all that was most ridiculous in 'patriotism' and most hysterical in suffering ('My man is going to be killed so why shouldn't you be killed too?'), it had in it a grain of truth: there can be no separateness from the guilt of belonging to the human species – not unless the individual withdraws into a complete vacuum and disclaims participation in the glories as well. There are two honest courses when war strikes: either to make some futile but positive gesture against it and suffer the consequences, or to live it – not in acceptance of its values, but in acceptance of the realities of the human condition. I did neither, and I have no doubt that I was wrong. 'Living' the war, for me, would have amounted to no more than putting on uniform and working, most probably, at some kind of clerical job for the purpose of 'releasing' a man so that he could kill and be killed. It would have been as stupid a thing to do as I felt it to be at the time, but by handing over my freedom in that way I would have tasted *what was happening*, which is the duty of anyone who wants to understand, to be aware, to touch the truth. It could be argued that the civilian jobs in which I ended up served the same purpose as a job in the services would have done, since I would not have been allowed to remain in those jobs if the officials responsible for directing my labours had not classified them as 'essential'. The difference was a subjective one. I chose civilian work because it represented the minimum loss of personal freedom possible in the circumstances, and loss of personal freedom was exactly the phenomenon most characteristic of the situation I should have been exploring. It was the people in concentration camps who were drinking most deeply the poison of what was happening; they, and men like the soldiers from West Africa and the Sudan, carried on the tide of madness into a war that could mean even less to them than it did to me. The actual consequences of any choice of mine were, of course, too infinitesimal to be perceptible outside my own skull; but within my skull, the choice I made was of a kind to build a wall between such people and myself.

It follows, naturally, that one should be to some extent 'engaged' at all times, not only in times of crisis: that I am no less wrong now than I was then, since I still take no part in any sort of political or social activity; I have never marched against the hydrogen bomb, I have never distributed leaflets urging the boycotting of South African goods. Whether, believing this, I shall some day turn to action, I do not know: given my record, it seems unlikely. Both by conditioning and by instinct I continue to cling to the wrappings of self-indulgence which keep safe my privacy and my female sense of another kind of truth running beside the social one: the body's truth of birth, coupling, death that can only be touched in personal relationships, and in contemplation.

Determined not to join the services, I answered an advertisement for women to build small boats in a factory at Southampton, supposing that because the boats were small the factory would be small too. I imagined it with a boatyard attached to it in which, though I might not be permitted to build a whole boat single-handed, I would work on recognizable features of boats – shape a tiller, perhaps, or screw cleats into place. The papers I received indicated that I was mistaken. Engagingly, one of them was a form on which I was to state whether I preferred my dungarees to be sky blue, apple green, or rose pink, but the rest of it gave a clear picture of monotonous hours doing something with metal at a factory bench. To anyone as spoilt as I was, the working day seemed atrociously long, and the wages made me sceptical forever of sweeping talk about big money earned by factory hands. Such talk was in the air – 'Those are the people who have the money, of course' – but the factory which might have been mine paid a disconcertingly small basic wage and only someone made of steel could have earned overtime. Because I could hardly back down at that stage, I said that I would wear sky blue overalls and waited for instructions, but my relief was great when I received an apologetic letter saying that they had no more vacancies after all.

Then I heard from a friend that the Admiralty, removed from London to Bath, was recruiting women busily. My enquiry was answered by a kind, discouraging letter asking why I wanted an ill-paid office girl's job when there were surely other things I could do, but I persisted. I did not want my refuge to be comfortable. To be bored, badly paid, but useful seemed to be what the situation required.

Bored I would have been, had it not been for Bath and the friends I made there; badly paid I was, pocketing fifteen shillings and ninepence a week after the money for my billet had been deducted; useful I was not. The permanent civil servants, uncomfortably overworked in requisitioned hotels and schools, had little time to teach undisciplined recruits, however willing. They were burdened not only by me, but by a large number of young men and women from the neighbourhood who saw working for them as a good way of filling in time before they were called up (if men) or could persuade their parents to let them go further afield (if women – labour was still undirected at that time). I was so conscious of my own inefficiency that I would have accepted brusque treatment as just, but the regulars were charmingly kind and patient. They gave me and my like documents marked 'SECRET' to carry from one room to another, they let us make tea (although we made it too weak), and they sat us down to use logarithm tables at which they supposed, mistakenly, no one could go wrong. In the end my harassed master used to give me a sheet of paper and say, 'Copy this on to that.' I would copy it carefully, he would say, 'Good, thank you very much' – but once I saw him slip my copy into the waste-paper basket.

I felt at first as though I were in an uneasy but not intolerable dream. The close ranks of inky desks in the dining-room of the Pulteney Hotel, the stacks of forms referred to by numbers and initials, the scratching nibs, the tin trays marked 'PENDING' – all this made sense to the others, obviously, but not to me. I knew that my sub-section of a sub-section of a department was concerned with transferring equipment for mine-sweepers from one naval base to another, but I could not envisage the equipment and no one seemed to know anything about it either before or after its transfer. Gravely and carefully, these rather tired middle-aged men laboured away at their ant-like task, and in the years they had spent on such things they had built up a small, snug office world with its own rites, necessities, taboos, and humours: not by any means a disagreeable world, not a world one could dislike or despise when one saw it at close quarters, but not a world to which I could imagine myself belonging. I would leave it each evening and return to a little box of a bedroom in a council house owned by a plate-layer. His wife would give me a sturdy supper, and then I would lie on my bed and read. After Beckton and Oxford, this was too *odd* to be depressing. I simply felt suspended, waiting dumbly to see if I would ever begin to find my bearings.

Soon my voice was noticed by a snobbish but helpful woman who had volunteered to drive for the Admiralty and ferried people to work from the remote suburb in which I was staying. Would I not like, she asked, to be transferred to more congenial billets? I had not supposed such a move to be possible, tried to suppress a start of hope (because the plate-layer's wife, though reserved, was a kind landlady), and mumbled that if it could be done . . . To my surprise she remembered to speak to the billeting office, and I was whisked into the town to be established with a family of Christian Scientists so astonishingly generous and welcoming that I have had a weakness for the sect ever since. In their benevolent, easygoing flat I could wake up.

Every day I walked to the office across the Royal Crescent, through the Circus, down Gay Street – oh, lovely Bath! There is no city in England more beautiful than that one, stepping down into its bowl of mist. There was always something to look at – a fanlight, a wrought-iron cage for a lantern, a magnolia growing out of a basement against the soot-dimmed golden grey of stone – but my chief daily joy was the great arc of the Crescent, with its broad, worn paving stones, its spacious view, and the curious silence it holds within its curve. A man who was walking me home one night said, 'It's like going into a church,' and I was speechless for several minutes in outrage at hearing my own feelings put into such clumsy words.

Before long I had become flippant about the job and had made one of the most charming of all my women friends. She emerged like a dragonfly from the dull envelope of a letter of introduction: 'Your dear Aunt tells me . . . We would be so pleased if you would come to tea on Sunday.' The youngest daughter of a spirited Irish family, polite but unenthusiastic, was sent to fetch me, and within an hour I had tapped a source of amusement and drama on which I can still, today, rely. Where Anne goes, disaster strikes: disaster too extreme for anything but laughter. If we borrowed her father's car without asking him, it was stolen; if we went to London for a night to meet young men, we lost either our tickets or the keys of our baggage, and our dresses split as we put them on; if we had no money but one penny and one half-crown, it was the half-crown we dropped into the slot on a lavatory door. 'Imagine what's happened *now*,' Anne would say (and still says), and out would come a vivid, exaggerated story of the bizarre, the macabre, or the absurd. I have always liked to watch pretty women and have enjoyed the company of gay ones: she, one of the prettiest and gayest I know, as well as one of the most generous, courageous, and, at times, infuriatingly perverse, became and remained a friend to be thankful for.

Living a new kind of life away from home, where I had been my unhappiest more recently than my happiest, I was often at that time able to dodge my misery over Paul. Laughter, frivolity, even silliness and affectation (and Anne and I must often have been silly and affected) are dependable salves in my experience, besides being strong threads in feminine friendships. I enjoyed much of my time at Bath and was sad when I decided that I had better resign before I was sacked, and go home to think about finding a 'real' job.

There was then a dreadful interlude when an aunt persuaded me that it was my duty to teach in the village school, understaffed and overcrowded with children from London to such a pitch that an untrained volunteer would be welcome. I did it for two terms, proving that teaching was not my *métier* but that I could call upon a certain amount of courage at a pinch. It was during that time that I met the first of my 'hopeless' loves, felt myself blaze into life again – it was so good while it lasted that even when I think I can see its unreality, I do not regret it – and sank back into even colder ashes. By the time chance had put me on to a 'real' job in the BBC, I was far from being alive.

It is strange to remember that when I was at Oxford, the BBC had glamour. When, before going down, we visited the Appointments Board which was supposed to help us find jobs, one after another of us said, 'Well, I rather thought the BBC . . .,' only to be laughed to scorn. (Does anyone ever get a job through a University Appointments Board, I wonder? I have never known anyone who did.) This made me see it as a stronghold of rare and brilliant people, so that to join it, although far down in the submerged seven-eighths which never sees a microphone, struck me as extraordinary. I did it because my Oxford friend Margaret had found a job in its recruitment office and tipped me off when a vacancy for which I might be suitable occurred.

For a time I was still prepared to grant glamour to the greater part of the Corporation, for I never saw it. My section, the part of an information service attached to the part of the BBC which broadcast to 'the Empire', had been evacuated to Evesham. 'The Empire' included, endearingly, I always thought, the USA, and it was some time before the Corporation got round to noticing this and changed the name of the Service. We worked in an ugly manor house overlooking Housman's Bredon Hill, and because we were a new development, without which the News Room and so on had managed successfully for many years, few people, to begin with, bothered to consult us. With this job I went into a curious hermit existence so drained of feeling that it seemed even more unreal than it was.

I became shy, a condition unfamiliar to me. We were scattered about Evesham in billets, with a couple of clubs at which we could meet each other. I went twice to one of the clubs and spoke to no one. Still assuming that they were all unusual and exceptionally intelligent people, and observing that they knew each other well, I felt that they would consider me drab and dull, and did not dare to make any claim on their attention. I went back to my billet and after that I never did anything in my spare time but read: not even when I had realized that most of these alarming people were middle-aged journalists of no particular distinction.

The only things that I enjoyed at Evesham were the beginnings of the early shift and the ends of the late one. We covered the hours from six in the morning until midnight, and the first and last person to be on duty worked alone. At half-past five in the dark of a winter morning, the BBC bus would put me down at the Manor's gates and I would make my way slowly up the drive, picking up firewood as I went. Having lit a fire in the grate of what had been one of the best bedrooms, I would fetch tea and sausages from the canteen and eat them sitting on the floor, watching my fire prosper. It was cold to begin with, and still, since only a skeleton staff was on at that hour, none of them in our part of the house. There was something secret and amusing about those picnic breakfasts, as though I were a tramp squatting in abandoned premises, and that slightly dotty pleasure is the only one I can remember from that time.

When we were transferred back to London and had become an accepted part of the BBC's machinery, it became an ordinary job and lasted for five years, until after the end of the war. It was never an exciting one but it kept us busy. We were supposed to be able to answer any question at any time, and usually we could: an information service is only a matter of knowing where to look. I liked most of the women with whom I worked, and if there was one I did not like she was usually disliked by all of us; it is not a bad thing in a group, I discovered, to have one unpopular member who will act as catalyst on the others. I came to be head of the section after a time, having first been 'passed over' in favour of a more efficient girl, which was supposed to be a drama. I was only slightly pleased when she turned out to be less efficient than had been expected and at last went away to have a baby, while the other women said, 'It should have been you in the first place.' I liked their liking me (it was lucky that they did, for it was, in fact, they who kept the section running), but my concern for the work was barely skin-deep. My concern for anything, at that time, was barely skin-deep.

My life became no more closely knit with the war. Paul was killed, but he had already gone away from me. A cousin was killed, but he was younger than I was and I had never been very close to him. Other people I knew were killed, but they did not belong to my daily life. These deaths were as though the poisonous atmosphere had condensed for a moment and a drop had fallen: horrible, but natural. The nearest violence came to my own person was when a room I was to sleep in that night was blown in, and when the curtains of another room suddenly, silently, bellied towards me, sweeping a china bowl off the window sill, and I had time to wonder whether I was having hallucinations before the sound of the explosion followed. I was not even affected by whatever feverish gaiety there may have been about (people speak of it in memoirs); it did not come my way. Years of emptiness. Years leprous with boredom, drained by the war of meaning. Other people's experience of them was far more painful, more dramatic, more tragic, more terrible than that; but that too, in its small, dim way, was hell.

During that time my soul shrank to the size of a pea. It had never been very large or succulent, or capable of sending out sprouts beyond the limits of self, but now it had almost shrivelled away. I became artful in avoiding pain and in living from one small sensation to another, because what else could one do when one had understood that, as far as one's personal life was concerned, one was a failure, doomed to be alone because one did not merit anything else, and when every day a part of one's job was to mark the wartime papers? I remember particularly a cutting about an elderly Pole who had killed himself, leaving a letter to say that he had tried everything to make people see what must be done for Poland but no one would listen. He was killing himself because it was the only gesture left him by which he might be able to draw people's attention to what was happening. He was a man who chose the other way, the opposite way to mine, and the poor old fanatic got about an inch and a half in a corner of the *Manchester Guardian*. If one were not to be a walking Francis Bacon picture, a gaping bloody mouth rent open in a perpetual scream, what could one do but go to the cinema and be grateful for an amusing film; go to bed and feel the smoothness of the sheets and the warmth of the blankets; go to the office and laugh because Helen's lover was at home on leave and she had asked Kathleen to say, if her mother telephoned, that she was staying with her. After the late shift the tiny sequins of the traffic lights, reduced by masks during the blackout, changed from red to amber to green down the whole length of empty, silent Oxford Street. They looked as though they were signalling a whispered conversation, and they were the kind of thing with which I filled my days.

Some people take refuge from emptiness in activity and excesses. They are the ones, I suppose, who cannot sleep for it. Mine was a dormouse escape, a hibernation. Instead of being unable to sleep I slept to excess, thinking lovingly of my bed during the day and getting into it with pleasure. Sleep for me has always been dreamless yet not negative, as though oblivion were a consciously welcomed good, so the only thing to dread about my nights was the slow, heavy emergence from them when an unthinking lack of enthusiasm for the days into which they pitched me made getting up an almost intolerable effort. Sleep at night, and a cautious huddling within limits during the day: walking to work along the same streets, eating the same meals, going back to the same room, then reading. In theory I longed to depart from this pattern and felt sorry for myself when I did not, but although I would have liked to have lived differently, the smallest alteration seemed to be beyond my energies.

I had to be feeling unusually *well* before I could go so far as to take a bus to the National Gallery on a day off, instead of sleeping all the morning and reading all the afternoon.

Within these absurd limitations imposed on me by inertia, there were palliatives to be found: the company of the few friends then accessible – and that I do not say more about my friends is because their lives are their own affair, not because they are not precious to me – and the books I read, and the little life spun within the walls of the office, which was often amusing. The intimacy between people working together is an agreeable thing and very real, in spite of the disconcerting way in which it vanishes as soon as the same people meet each other in different circumstances. And always, at any time, I could look at things, whether at leaves unfolding on a plane tree, or at people's faces in a bus, or at a pigeon strutting after its mate on a roof, or at pictures. Perhaps the nearest I came to being fully alive for months on end was when I was looking at pictures. This joy I owe partly to the natural acuteness of my response to visual images and partly to one of my aunts, the only one of my mother's sisters to remain unmarried and the only one of them to escape from the family's way of thinking.

An intelligent and sensitive girl, she was extremely short-sighted and had to wear glasses. It was this, I believe, that caused her, as well as the rest of the family, to think her plain in spite of looks which by present-day standards would be considered striking. As a child she had stammered, and quite early in her life she must have written herself off as a shy and unattractive girl. She went to Oxford and became the family bluestocking, much loved by everyone but little understood. Her greatest friend became an almoner in a hospital, and my aunt followed her example. They shared a flat in London, decorated with hand-woven materials and reproductions of Impressionist paintings, and they worked with dedication and enjoyment.

When my grandfather knew that he was about to die, he told his daughter that she must give up her work and come back to Beckton to look after her mother. No one questioned this. My grandmother must have been about sixty at the time, an extraordinarily healthy, able woman whose house was constantly filled by visiting children and grandchildren. With a little planning she need hardly ever have been alone, and she had a character strong enough to withstand loneliness if it had to. But according to her ideas of what was fitting, it was taken for granted that an unmarried daughter owed a duty to her parents compared to which her duty to her work was frivolous and her duty to herself did not exist. My mother, the other sisters, and their brother shared this belief. Their own children were still young and they had not yet foreseen their own acceptance (in my mother a splendidly generous one) of their daughters' rights to lives of their own. 'It horrifies me now,' my mother has said to me. 'How *could* we have let her be sacrificed like that? But at the time it just seemed natural.'

What my aunt felt about it she never said. She was not only a reserved woman, but the most genuinely unselfish person I have ever met. Silent, a little apart, she threw herself into work. She gardened, she served on committees, she taught Sunday school in the village, she became a Justice of the Peace. The books on her shelves were not quite like the books of the rest of the family, the pictures in her bedroom were not like their pictures, and she was the only one who would slip away for holidays abroad, walking in the Dolomites, or staying in rough inns in Italy or Yugoslavia. She loved small children and they loved her. Gently, diffidently, she dropped crumbs of poetry or romanticism or liberal opinion along their paths for them to pick up if they cared to. One of these crumbs was an occasion when she took me up to London to a great exhibition of French painting given in Burlington House in the early 'thirties.

I have never forgotten that exhibition. To be in London was exciting enough, and to be doing something so grown-up as visiting an exhibition was even better: I was ready to enjoy the pictures, and enjoy them I did. I loved the Watteaus and the Fragonards, which seemed to me glimpses of an exquisitely graceful life in which I longed to join, but the canvases which impressed me as the most beautiful of the lot were *La Source* and *La Belle Zélie* by Ingres. That marmoreal perfection, that polished, heightened realism of texture, conveyed to me Ideal Beauty. Why did my aunt stand for so much longer in front of a *baigneuse* by Renoir? Why did she say, undidactically as usual, that she thought it more lovely than the Ingres? I looked at it attentively and could only see a smudgy painting of a plain girl who was too fat and too red. But my darling aunt, who knew about pictures – she did like it better than *La Source*, I could see that without being told. So although I did not then *see* the Renoir, nor any of the other Impressionists except Manet's boy playing the fife, I understood that this was a limitation in myself, not in them: the first, the vital lesson for anyone who wants to enjoy painting. Looking at that Renoir was like meeting someone at a party and getting nowhere with him because one or both of you happen to be distrait. You do not discover until you meet again that he is going to be one of your best friends – but useless though the first meeting may have seemed, without it the second one would not have taken place.

There was another occasion, too, earlier than this, when my aunt dropped a hint about art and I picked it up. I was drawing horses, as I constantly did, when she leant over my shoulder and said, 'Draw a naked man – a man or a woman.' Disconcerted by a suggestion that seemed to me indecent, I hesitated. She, seeing what I was thinking, became embarrassed in her turn and said, 'Go on, you needn't put in his – er – his little arrangements if you don't want to.' So I drew a shapeless forked radish and she looked disappointed. I did not understand her fond hope that a child's eye would produce something original and alive, but I knew that I had failed in some way: that there was something of significance I should have been able to do with the human body instead of being embarrassed by it. When, after that, I looked at paintings of the nude, I was looking for beauty.

So my aunt and my own temperament equipped me with eyes, and seeing things remained, through the dreariest stretches of my life, a reason for living.

Another device for filling emptiness – a common one, difficult to consider with detachment – is promiscuity. Lack of energy prevented me from ranging about in pursuit of men, but if they turned up, I slept with them. I had started this soon after unhappiness set in, and if I am to be honest I must admit that I was less shrivelled when I was doing it than I was when I was not: when, for instance, during a long period at Evesham and in London, I was too cowed by the double blow I had received from love to do even that.

It always seemed to me that the factor of physical frustration on the simplest level, although it must have played its part, was much less important than the reassurance which came from the sense of being desired and the mitigation of boredom which came from having something to *do*. That I must iron my pretty dress and wash my best underclothes because on Friday the bell would ring and I would be going out to dinner with a man, however dull, was at least to appear to be living. It was going through the familiar motions, it was getting back into harness, even if the drive would not lead anywhere – and I was determined that it should not. Only in an encounter which contained no threat of serious emotion, no real relationship, could I, at that time, feel safe.

Sometimes these sorties were not to be regretted. If there was enough companionship and physical compatibility, a small expansion beyond the confines of my own predicament into another person's life was possible, some tenderness could be felt – and tenderness between bodies, though restricted, is real. At other times they were simply absurd, and I would be both amused and puzzled by them. I would meet a man with whom I had nothing in common, who was perhaps fat and garrulous, who told boring anecdotes and could not even dance well. He would make the first movements of a pass at me and I, a little warmed because he was behaving as though I were attractive, would make the first responses. Hands would be held under restaurant tables, or as we danced my body would yield to his pressure until our thighs were touching. At that point I would say to myself, 'Now steady! You do not want to go on with this, you know quite well that it will be deadly.' But whatever reason might be saying, once the first moves had been made there was no breaking the pattern. It was as though a familiar music had begun to play, I had stepped into a familiar measure, and to go against its rhythm was beyond me. A certain kind of look, certain words, gestures, and contacts, and all my faculties would go into a state of suspension: bed was the only conclusion. 'What is *obliging* me to do this?' I would wonder, going up in a hotel lift or watching someone who should have been a stranger as he put his keys and change on a dressing-table. I would split in two on those occasions, one half going obediently and easily through the routine, the other watching with an ironic amusement. When the dance had reached its inevitable conclusion and the night in bed with whoever it might be was over, the two halves would rejoin and I would wake up thinking, 'But I am mad! Never again!'

This was where complications could set in. Common courtesy would have seemed to me, during the night, to demand that if I was making love with this man I should appear to enjoy it, so how, without insulting him, could I avoid a repetition? He would be under the impression that he had met a girl of easy virtue and amorous temperament, and would look forward to other meetings. I used to be forced to spin elaborate tales of my own fickleness, neuroticness, bitchiness – 'You are well rid of me really, I promise.' Once, becoming hopelessly enmeshed in my own tangled web, I implied that it was only the man's ardour that had demolished my normally strong defences, whereupon he believed me and soon afterwards asked me to marry him: perhaps the most disconcerting thing that has ever happened to me.

These foolish and always short affairs were threadbare rags against a cold wind, but they were better than no rags at all. During the period when my spirits were too low for me to grasp at them, the shrivelling affected my body as well as my soul, my health deteriorated, my appetite dwindled, and sensations of faintness and nausea attacked me whenever I left my room or the office. I reached the stage of dreading the short walk between the two for fear that I should faint or vomit in the street. I went to a doctor, was told that I had become anaemic, and was sent home for a month's sick leave.

Beckton could always restore me. I used to imagine a 'scientific' reason for it: that the nature of its soil made its leaves and grasses give off a certain kind of exhalation which suited me above all others. But although as I sat in the train returning to London I felt better physically, I knew that at bottom I was the same: I would continue my dreary round unless I took some kind of action. 'It is not that life has deserted you,' I told myself. 'It is you who have deserted life.' I thought of the brisk injunctions in women's magazines – 'Take up an interest', 'Join a club'. At that sort of thing I could only laugh or shudder, it was too far outside my line of country. So I said to myself (it is not an inspiring thing to recall, but it is true) – I said to myself, 'Look, the next man you meet who. appears at all attracted to you, whatever he is like, however unreal he seems to you, you will revert to your bad old ways and will accept whatever happens.'

I went straight from the station to the office, for the late shift. After a little gossip the girls I was relieving collected their things and left me alone in the racket of typewriters and ticker-tape machines from the News Room next door which had come to seem like silence. I was about to go to the canteen for a coffee when the door opened and there stood a man whom I shall call Felix, a great womanizer and until recently the lover of a friend of mine who had left for a job abroad. 'Hullo, sweetie,' he said. 'Are you all alone?' A stocky little figure leaning against the door post, crinkling professional charmer's eyes. 'Yes,' I said, 'What can I do for you?' 'You can come out for a drink with me.' 'No, I can't, not until midnight, anyway.' 'All right, I'll come and collect you at midnight.'

Felix was anchored by marriage and was not a man whom I could admire enough to love. With him I could feel absolutely safe. At the same time he was a gay companion and we shared great pleasure in making love. Our relationship was pure *cinq-à-sept*, except that its venue was a restaurant where we would eat as good a dinner as could be found in wartime London, and drink a lot, before going to spend a night in an hotel or, if Felix's family was in the country, at his house. Neither of us ever set foot in each other's daily life. We would bring to our meetings incidents from it, if they were amusing or bizarre, but neither ever expected the other to take more than a passing interest in anything more grave; I would never, for example, have told Felix about money troubles except as a joke, and he would hardly have referred to any difficulties he might be having with his children. Our roles were clearly defined: to make each other laugh, and to give each other physical pleasure. At both of these he was very good. He was an excellent raconteur with a quick eye for character and an immense relish for the absurd, whose sympathies, though not profound, were wide. He had also the disarming honesty with which a rake will often feel that he can justify himself. He loved having money and making a vulgar show with it, because to make a show was more fun than being discreet. He loved success, even though he had got it by jettisoning his integrity as a writer. The relish with which he lived eclipsed any thought of how he might have lived.

I had become so emotionally impotent because of the tension between a conscious longing to love and a subconscious fear of it that my feelings for anyone, for a long time, had gone no further than a detached well-wishing. Towards Felix I could feel a positive affection, and it was not – most certainly it was not – to be despised. For two years I remained his mistress (or, more probably, one of his mistresses), and only put an end to it when restored vitality and confidence pushed me out again on to the perilous waters of deeper feeling. And although I was to capsize yet again, my years with Felix had made me more buoyant. With him I had been happy, though in an inglorious way, and I was by that much less likely to drown.

I wish I had never met Felix again after we had separated, but I did. Eight years later the telephone rang and I heard that familiar, husky voice, that contented chuckle, and cried, 'Felix! Come round at once!' As I opened the door to him I thought 'Heavens, he must have been having a hard day,' because he had something about him a little dishevelled and awry that I had never seen. Then I noticed a smell of alcohol – stale alcohol – that was almost sickening. 'He is drunk,' I thought with surprise, for in spite of all the whisky we had put away together I had never seen him drunk. We went out to dinner, and as the evening passed I realized slowly that this was no unfortunate chance. The bartender had greeted him with bored patience instead of with the old comradely twinkle, the head waiter had given us an obscure table, and no wonder, because Felix started making bawdy jokes, very loud. At one point, when he had eaten a little, he appeared to pull himself together and began to talk as he used to talk and to ask me questions about myself, but I soon realized that he was unable to listen to the answers. When he screwed up his eyes at me it was horrible – the scrag-end of charm, ossified with exploitation. Deliberately frivolous as he was, a hedonist, an opportunist, vulgar in some ways though with a flourish that seemed to me to redeem it, my dear Felix should have been able to bob his way merrily into old age in defiance of Nemesis, but he could not. When he died soon afterwards, people said it was from drink, and I could only suppose it to be so: a man who had actually said in my hearing, 'Don't be silly, you know that I can take it or leave it alone'; a man who would have detested himself in the role of object lesson for any end other than merriment or pleasure. I suppose he is an odd person towards whom to feel gratitude and tenderness, but those are the emotions his memory will always bring to life in me. Felix enjoyed women so much that he could not help making them feel valuable, indeed he would have considered it amateurish not to do so. It was he who began the slow process of my restoration.

13

THE SQUARE, SCRUBBED woman with cropped hair sat behind a desk on which was a vase of catkins. Her consulting room was decorated in cream and green, a combination I detest.

'Well, now,' she said in a voice intended to nip hysteria in the bud, 'it's not the end of the world.'

I had never thought it was. She saw, I supposed, a great many unmarried women who had become pregnant, so that she could hardly have avoided treating them according to formula, but I began at once to resent that she was applying her formula to me.

'In fact,' she went on, 'one might almost say that in wartime, when there is such a shortage of beds in the maternity wards and so on, it is simpler to have a baby when you are not married than when you are.'

'Oh?' I said.

'Yes, there is a lot of help available. I would strongly advise you to go on with it. It's your natural function and if you frustrate it you will find that a trauma results, a profound trauma. And it's quite simple when you have made up your mind to it – there are plenty of war widows about. You can change your job and wear a wedding ring and no one will suspect a thing.'

'But what about afterwards, when the baby is born?'

'That's the simplest part,' she said. 'I can put you in touch with organizations to look after that. There are three alternatives. One: you have the baby and its adoption is arranged beforehand. You

won't even see it. The committee is extremely careful in its vetting
of couples who want to adopt children – we make sure that they
really want them, as well as that they are able to support them, and
I can assure you that it is pure sentimentality to worry about the
child in that case. It will probably be a good deal better off with its
adopted parents than it would be with you.' She laughed as she
spoke: little shocks of briskness were the thing.

'I don't see much point,' I said, 'in going through nine months
of pregnancy and a birth, and not even *seeing* my child after all that.'
I had a vivid mental picture of waking in a hospital bed to an
emptiness through which I could never crawl.

'No. Well then, there's the second alternative: foster parents. We
find a foster mother for it and you are free to see it whenever you
like, and then, when you are in a better position to look after it,
when you are making more money or have got married, you can
take it back. You would be surprised at the number of men who can
be made to accept such a situation.'

What, I thought, if I never make any more money, or never get
married, or can't make a husband accept the situation? And what
of a child brought up by a woman who must seem to be its real
mother, only to be snatched away by someone who has been no
more than a visitor? It was less intolerable than the first prospect
but not something I would risk. I nodded and looked expectant.

'The third solution,' she said, 'is to my mind much the best. You
take your parents into your confidence straight away and get them
to help you keep the child. What have you got against that?'

'My parents,' I said. 'They would be horrified.'

'Do them good, silly old things,' said the woman.

I looked at her in astonishment. She was speaking of people of
whom she knew nothing – not their ages, nor their income, nor
their way of life, nor their feelings towards their daughter – so how
could she possibly presume to know whether it would do them
good or not? Her high-handed dismissal of my parents as 'silly old
things' was a piece of gross impertinence. I sat there thinking 'What
a frightful woman!' while she went on to explain that most families,
once an illegitimate child becomes a *fait accompli*, adapt themselves

to the situation after a time, however shocking they find it at first. 'You would probably find,' she said, 'that it would become your mother's favourite grandchild. I have seen that happen.'

My reason told me that she was right: that if I were to go on with this, it would have to be on those terms. I was earning only five pounds a week and could not save anything like enough money to make me independent. Someone would have to help me, and the child's father was not able to. It was probably true that my parents, after their first horror and distress, would come round to taking the responsibility – but if they did, it would only be at a great cost both emotionally and financially. Their lives as well as mine would be disrupted and complicated, and it seemed to me outrageous that I, because of my own folly, should force them into such a situation. This pregnancy was my business and no one else's.

'No,' I said.

'Well,' said the woman, 'you will regret it terribly if you have an abortion. You're in perfect shape physically – I would say that yours is an ideal pregnancy, so far. You will suffer in every way if you terminate it.' She looked down at her hands, then reached out to straighten a folder on her desk. When she looked up, her eyes were sharp with calculation. 'It is, of course,' she went on slowly, 'entirely your own business. It is entirely up to you if you want' – she paused a moment to throw the verb into relief – 'if you want *to murder* your first child' – and she watched me.

'Yes, it is,' I said, getting up. Her look, the choice of verb, had clarified my mind in a flash. I knew, now, that I must get on with the job of finding an abortionist.

Walking down the street, I began to laugh. 'The old blackmailer!' I thought. 'Murder, indeed!' Applied to an embryo two and a half months developed, the word, I was abruptly convinced, was nonsense. What was happening in my womb was still simply a physiological process concerning only me, a new departure of my body's. Later there would be a creature there to consider, but at this stage – no.

I had become pregnant by subconscious intention and had recognized the fact clearly as soon as it had happened. I had felt brilliantly well from the first day, and proud. I was already having fond dreams of babies in their prams, I knew that I wanted one, I knew that my body had plotted in order to achieve what it most needed – and not only my body but the subconscious layers of my mind. Until I had visited that woman I had seriously been considering bearing the child, but now I knew, without regret, that I would not. The birth of a child was not a matter of therapy for the mother. Would I have a trauma as a result of frustrating it? Too bad for me if I did. I was not going to become a mother unless I could do it properly.

As it turned out, the suffering of which the woman had warned me never materialized. Physically my health was distinctly improved by three months of pregnancy followed by a curettage, and any trauma that may have resulted has yet to manifest itself. I have often regretted my childlessness and I have caught myself up to my tricks again in attempts to remedy it, but neither of the two attitudes I thought likely have developed: I have never yearned over other people's children, nor have I recoiled from them. I like them, I enjoy their company, I find them interesting, and that seems to be that. I can only suppose that by nature I am a maternal woman but not passionately so.

How far did laziness and self-infulgence come into my decision? That they did so to some extent I am sure. One of the many strands of feeling running through me as I sat in that consulting room was certainly dismay at the prospect of having to find a new job and new lodgings, of having to uproot myself (although from a life which I knew to be empty and dull) and turn to solving practical difficulties outside my experience. My inertia was heavy on me, making me reluctant to face the inevitable complications of my situation. I was partly a coward, and a coward in the face of effort, rather than of anything else.

But although it is probable that my justification of my attitude was – and is – to some extent an attempt to rationalize this lack of spirit, the other elements in my argument did exist. It still seems to me that it is absurd for abortion to be illegal. I do not believe that something not conscious can be 'murdered' – the distinction between preventing life and putting an end to it is, to me, a clear one. Other women who bear the full consequences of their actions I admire and even, if they make a success of it, envy. Whether they have argued that life must be respected, or whether (which is, I imagine, more often the case) they have obeyed the dictates of their own hungers, they show a courage which I lacked. But in bestowing on a child the chancy fate of illegitimacy, they have shouldered a heavy responsibility. Only if I felt myself able to offer it security would I do it myself, and such security I could not offer at that time.

So I say, so I believe: but supposing the woman behind the desk had been one who, while putting forward the same arguments, had not alienated me by her manner, had spoken to *me* instead of to a pregnant girl of her own invention? . . . The points, perhaps, would have been switched, my life would have veered on to another course. Even though reason was mixed with my weakness to a point where they are hard to disentangle, it does not quite raise it above regret. I am glad that I did not risk giving a child a difficult life, but I am sorry that I was not the kind of girl who would have braved that risk.

14

THE WAR WAS in its third year or perhaps the beginning of its fourth. I was still working in the BBC, slightly better at living by then, since Felix was a part of my life and I had left bed-sitting rooms behind me for a flat which I shared with another girl – a commonplace event which must be remembered by millions of working women as a turning-point in their lives. Who could feel their circumstances anything but temporary, their condition anything but one of time-biding, while the daily mechanics of living consist of eating only what can be boiled on a gas-ring (frying is usually forbidden because of the smell and the spitting of fat on to the carpet), keeping half one's clothes in a suitcase under the divan or on top of the wardrobe, moving books and writing things from a table to a divan or chair before setting out a meal, and turning a divan from couch into bed every night before going to sleep in the froust of one's cigarette smoke? I had taken a modest pride in my ingenuity with small bedsitting rooms, the way in which I could make myself comfortable and control the ebullience of my too numerous possessions; so much so that when I first experienced the delicious freedom of a flat, I was astonished by the violence with which I cast off single-room living. I had not known that it had been horrible, but it was with horror that I decided 'Never again!'

In a flat we could give parties. To one of them a friend brought a small Hungarian said to be in publishing. He did not seem to be much amused by our company, although he did not whisper

audibly, as I have heard him do since then, 'Can we go now?' He
sat on the floor looking boyish and disdainful, then sang 'The
Foggy Foggy Dew' in a manner implying that he, personally, had
discovered this song. When he telephoned a few days later to invite
me to a play, I was surprised. I was also pleased because I believed
that anyone connected with publishing must be interesting.

It did not take us long to decide that our relationship would not
be an amorous one. Instead we slipped into a friendship of a
curiously intimate nature, nearer to the fraternal than anything I
had experienced within my family. My real brother, with whom I
had been close friends when we were small, had been taken out of
my life first by his schooling, then by what his schooling had done
to him. He had hated it and had spent much of his boyhood taking
refuge in stupidity and near-oafishness, happy only when disguised
as a gamekeeper or, better still, poacher, wearing an ancient, many-
pocketed waistcoat, talking dialect, and sloping about the woods at
Beckton either alone or with friends from the village. By the time
he began to emerge from this camouflage I was at Oxford, and after
that the war removed him. On the rare occasions when we met
there was always a comfortable freedom between us, an ability to
say or to listen to anything and a clear view of each other's
shortcomings which did not prevent affection, but we did not have
much in common beyond our temperaments and our memories.
With the Hungarian, André Deutsch, I shared a way of life,
political views, and interest in the arts, as well as an undemanding
kind of intimacy very similar to that I already knew with my
brother.

We began to see each other often and became, in a lopsided way,
each other's confidants: lopsided because while I had a tendency to
underestimate my own value, André had no doubt about his. He
was always ready to put himself out for friendship's sake in any
practical way – lend money, or bring round food if I were in bed
with influenza – but he did not find it easy to believe that I (or
anyone else) would be as interested in a discussion of my own life
as I would be in his.

He had come to England before the war broke out, ostensibly to complete his education but with a private determination to settle here. With liberal views and a Jewish father, he had decided while still a boy that Hungary under Horthy was not the country he would have chosen, whereas English literature, combined with everything he had heard about Great Britain, suggested to him that England was. So early and complete a transference of loyalties, made without any great pressure from events, seems to me unusual and strange. André had reacted to things which were in the air rather than to anything which had happened to him or his family. When I have questioned him about it he has answered no more than 'I just knew, always, that that was what I wanted to do.' Caught by the war, with no money but an occasional cheque from an uncle in Switzerland, he picked up jobs here and there and was working as floor manager in a big hotel when detectives came to remove him to the Isle of Man. To be an enemy alien was not, however, an unmixed evil. Internment did not last long, and once he was released he was free to take what civilian work he liked, provided he reported at the proper times to the Aliens' Office. He found his way by chance into the sales side of an old – indeed tottering – publishing house, and by the time I met him he had burrowed well into its structure, was saving a little money, and was already talking of starting a firm of his own.

André was my age – twenty-six. By that time he did not have a penny beyond what he earned, nor did he have a single relative, old friend, or useful connection in this country. I used to listen to his plans indulgently, contributing to them as one contributes to talk about what one will do when one wins the Irish Sweep. 'If you join me,' he said to me one day as we walked arm-in-arm through Soho, 'what would be the minimum money you would have to earn, to be comfortable?'

'I don't know,' I said. 'What am I earning now?' And he worked out for me, as he has so often done since, what my weekly salary came to by the year. It was three hundred and eighty-eight pounds, I believe – the BBC paid civil-service rates and Temporary Women Clerks, the category under which I worked, did not come high in those rates.

'What about five hundred pounds?' he asked, and I agreed to it, feeling that such a large sum could safely be considered since it existed only in his imagination. I had not yet understood that André is the kind of person in whom ideas and action are inseparable. It is true that when the time came, five hundred pounds proved at first to have been optimistic – but the time did come.

I have sometimes wondered whether, if chance had shouldered André into property, or manufacturing cars, or catering, his obsessive nature would have seized on that as it did on publishing. Perhaps it would have done, but it is hard to believe. Picture dealing, maybe, or concert promoting . . . The nature of his talent is practical, the demon which possesses him is a business demon rather than a literary one, yet it is impossible to imagine it functioning for an end unconcerned with artistic expression. The ultimate good for a business demon *ought* to be power through money, but André's demon drives for something else. He is immensely concerned with money, but as an idea rather than as something to possess: while he can have a car and good clothes he is indifferent to his own income. He will cry out in pain at the least mistake in the costing of a book or the most trivial slip in his opponent's favour during a deal, but the pain is aesthetic rather than pecuniary: he is offended in the way that a stylist is offended by a badly constructed sentence or an interior decorator by an ugly juxtaposition of objects. The only power without which he cannot live is that of being his own master – over other people he exercises it both reluctantly and clumsily. His business demon is one which, by some quirk, has become bound to the production of books so firmly that its energy would bleed away if it were cut off from them. Whatever he may say when he feels resentful at the demands of his own obsession, André is a man with a vocation.

No two people could be more different than he and I. He has the most exact and capacious memory I have ever encountered, while I can remember hardly anything but people and feelings; he is a fiend for detail, while I am sloppy; he has this instinctive understanding of money and what can be done with it – the structure of a company, the financing of a new enterprise, are things which he can grasp at once without any previous experience – while to me the simplest contract is sterile: words on paper which I can understand if I concentrate but which have no implications beyond the mere statement, none of which I can criticize in relation to a set of ideas. André has the sometimes blinkered driving force of the obsessive, to whom his own ends are both *necessary* and *right*. I have the detachment of the disassociated, always prepared to believe that the other side of the question may have something in it. Above all, André is active, he compels things to happen, while I am passive, I accept. It is easier for me to see what I have gained from our long partnership than it is to understand why he values it.

As soon as the war was over, André formed his company: Allan Wingate, it was called, we picked the name out of a hat in the belief that 'Deutsch' would still meet with prejudice. I had to round off my work at the BBC and then took a three-months holiday at Beckton, so I did not join him until 1946 and cannot exactly remember how the absurdly small capital was raised. It was little more than three thousand pounds. Part of it, I know, came from a man who made handbags, who liked books and who had sized up André as a young man who would go far. Printers, binders, and papermakers reached the same conclusion, allowing him generous credit and taking extraordinary trouble to be helpful. Partly they were charmed, for André is capable of exerting great charm, and partly they were convinced, because absolute conviction breeds conviction. It is fortunate that André is by inclination honest, for if he were a liar he would be one of those mesmeric pathological liars whose fabrications dupe everyone for years, simply because such liars believe in them themselves.

Our first office was two rooms, a passage, a WC and a box-room with a skylight next to the WC in which sat a sequence of morose little men who did our accounts. That they were morose was not surprising. The chief thing that I remember about those first few years was the agony of bills coming in: the agony of paying them when we had to, and the agony of not paying them when we could

get away with it. There is at all times a sum without which, the
pontiffs say, you cannot launch a publishing house. It stood in
those days at fifteen thousand pounds – five times what André had
been able to raise – and stands today at fifty thousand. At any
period I am sure that this sum can safely be halved by anyone
prepared to work hard, while by fanatics it can probably be
quartered. But in cutting it by five we had gone too near the
knuckle. What was to happen later could still have been avoided,
but the need to avoid it would not have arisen if we had begun with
more capital.

Meanwhile, in spite of money worries, we enjoyed ourselves. We
made a few mistakes, published one or two of those handsome
editions on handmade paper, illustrated with woodcuts by
expensive artists and bound in buckram, which few people can
resist producing when they first get their hands on the means of
bookmaking and which never earn their keep. But for the most part
we managed, thanks to Andre's vigilance over every halfpenny, to
produce our books at an economic price, and we succeeded, after
great difficulties, in organizing their distribution on the right lines.
That our overheads should have been unnecessarily high by as little
as a pound would have shocked us all: 'Have you switched off your
fire?' 'Why are you using a new envelope for this, don't you know
what stickers are *for*?' We kept our stock in the passage leading to
the WC where a narrow bench had been installed, and there, just
before a publication date, the whole firm would stand, working
away with sticky paper and string, under the benevolent eye of our
real packer, Mr Brown.

Mr Brown would always have to accompany whoever it was who
was making the London deliveries in Andre's small car, because
only a Union member could hand a parcel of books to another
Union member. I used to enjoy my turn on deliveries, listening to
a gentle burble of London lore, for Mr Brown, a compulsive talker,
prided himself that he knew every inch of the city, and so he did.
His interpretations of what he knew were sometimes eccentric,
museums becoming cathedrals, and monuments commemorating
events that had happened or people who had existed long after they

were erected. Strange things went on in Mr Brown's London, too: men in Islington bit off the heads of rats for a shilling, and there was a building near Westminster Cathedral full of holy images covered with blood – 'You know, all Christ and bloody Mary and that.' When I asked him how he knew, he told me that he had once spent a whole night there, packing singlehanded to oblige, and that all these images with the blood on them had got him down so much that he didn't half let out a yell when the bishop came in at three o'clock in the morning to offer him a glass of wine. 'Wine, that's what he called it, but if you ask me it wasn't nothing of the kind.' When I laughed and said, 'Do you mean that he was trying to poison you?' he answered, 'Well, I don't know that I'd go so far as to say *that*,' but in a doubtful voice. And then, he said, when morning came, a great many women arrived, all dressed in black from top to toe, and all of them crying as though heartbroken. Mr Brown often left his stories hanging at a point like that, but I was so disturbed by all these sad, black-clad women that I persuaded him to explain them. 'Well, they was all rank Catholics, you see,' he said, 'and some old cardinal had kicked the bucket. I tried to jolly them along, I did. You wouldn't see me taking on like that, I said, not for him anyway, he's just another man to me. Cor, they didn't half think me a *vile* man.'

Mr Brown called me by my first name, but I would have felt it impertinent to have addressed him by his – André was the only person who ever did. He was a fatherly man, and kind, although his kindness could be disconcerting. 'No,' he said, 'I don't hold with giving up my seat in a bus to a young girl, she's as fit to stand as I am, only when she's having her monthly I will.' 'But Mr Brown, how can you tell?' 'Tell? I can always tell. Tell at a glance with the lot of you, I can.' The intimacy of a small business is certainly no myth.

The firm prospered, in that the books coming its way became better and that we were selling the right number of them, but in publishing money goes out fast and comes in slowly, and we had no margin. Every now and then the bills would heap up beyond the danger point and something would have to be done. There would be a short period of blank despair when we faced the fact that none of us knew anyone with money, and then André would pick up a scent. Someone, it would turn out, did know someone who had heard of someone who had always wanted an interest in a publishing firm (once it was a manufacturer of lavatory seats). I have learnt by now that there is *always* someone about who wants such an interest, but in those days it used to seem a miracle. Meetings would be arranged, friendships would flare up, and a new director, more or less active as the case might be, would appear on the Board.

The trouble with directors recruited by André in this way – and at our peak we had six of them – was that they thought of themselves, not unreasonably, as directors, while we thought of them as stooges. I had no official finger in the pie at that time, being only an employee, not a partner, but because I knew André so well and had been working with him almost from the beginning, I was his close ally, no more willing than he was to see anyone else in control of a firm so essentially his own. Only the last man to join the Board had any practical experience of publishing, and none of them had anything like André's flair, eye for detail, or capacity for hard work.

André had been drawn to England by a romantic conception of it, and this he still retained. Confront him with an Hungarian goose and he would see it for what it was, but his English geese always began as swans. This led him into the folly of agreeing to 'a gentleman's agreement' instead of to a service agreement when we reached the ticklish point at which one of the infiltrating directors acquired fifty-one per cent of the shares in the company: the words 'a *gentleman's* agreement' sounded to André so much more British. That such an agreement should work when the other party, although having financial control, was expected to play the role of office boy (as he plaintively remarked) was a vain hope.

Tact was needed: tact, restraint, easygoing dispositions on both sides, and equal or complementary abilities all round. These conditions were lacking. The firm, while becoming outwardly more prosperous every day, deteriorated into a state of guerrilla warfare.

I blush for us now, when I remember the spirit with which we entered into it, but I still cannot see how either André or I could have continued to work with any pleasure or profit except on his terms.

After five years of hard work we had moved our office to a charming house in Knightsbridge; we had published some good and successful books; we were making a profit; we were at home in our trade: and there we sat in our office (all right, we would have acknowledged crossly, the money was not ours but without us there would have been no office at all) in what, by the last painful weeks of a painful year, amounted to a state of siege.

During that year tempers had worn quite away. One of our directors would draft a contract and André, always quick to scent danger, would pick it off his desk. 'Are you mad?' he would cry – and that the oversight he had spotted was a grave one did not make his intervention more acceptable. Another of them would write a blurb and I would take it upstairs and rewrite it without consulting him. That his version was embarrassing, and that he would not have agreed to alter it if I had asked him, did not prevent my action from being high-handed. And in the usual way, inexperience and ineptitude became clumsier for being jumped on, so that the jumping daily seemed more necessary. Soon we had reached the point of dissecting each other's characters with morbid relish behind each other's backs, then of rival factions taking each other out for a drink in attempts at conciliation, only to come back to the office with new foibles to dissect. One of our directors wept easily after his third drink. He did not seem to notice it, but tears would spill out of his round blue eyes and smear his broad face as he catalogued the insults he had received. I would feel sorry for him and for a moment would really believe that I was discussing ways of improving our relationship, but all the time I was watching this extraordinary spectacle with secret glee, ready to caricature it as soon as André and I were alone together. I doubt whether unhappy marriages bring out the worst in people any more surely than unhappy business partnerships.

The frightening thing about a situation such as this one is that when recriminations begin about recent events, two people, each absolutely convinced that he is speaking the truth, will advance two opposite versions of a conversation or a happening. When that point has been reached no intermediary – and several were called in – can bridge the gap. Once meetings start being held in lawyers' offices, you might as well give up.

We did not give up until everyone was shut in his separate room, communicating only through secretaries. At that point André had to allow himself to admit that he had no choice: the other man had financial control, André did not have a service agreement, 'gentleman' was a word that could hardly have been applied to any of us at that moment – we were beaten.

I cannot remember where it was that André and I sat down to digest the fact, but I have an impression that there was a table between us, with white cups on it. 'Well,' he said, 'what do we do now?' We looked at each other and it was hardly necessary to speak the words. There was nothing we could possibly do but start another publishing firm.

That André should have had no doubts about this was only natural, but that I should have felt as he did suggests that I had become, if not a career woman, at least a woman who had found a career. And so, I suppose, I had. I would have preferred, and I would still prefer, not to have to work for my living in an office, but if I must, then a publisher's office is the one to be in. The formation and progress of the new firm, in which our friend Nicolas Bentley and I became and remained the only working directors beside André, is a story to be kept in reserve in case André should one day want to write it, but if I am ever to say what I like about the game, I should be able to say it now.

Book X is not so good as Book Y. Books A, B, and C have good reasons for their existence but do not happen to interest me. Books D and E – God knows what we were thinking of when we took those on, they will both flop and they deserve to flop. Book F is embarrassing – I do not like it, I do not think it good, but it will make a lot of money and it is not actually pernicious. But books G,

H, I, J, and K: now there are books with which I am pleased to have been concerned, there are voices which deserve to be heard; and somewhere among them are my darlings, the books – not many of them, for in no generation are there many such writers – the books which, I believe, *had* to exist. This is why I like the work, and this is why other people in publishing like it, although some of them choose to affect a 'hard-headed-businessman' attitude and say at cocktail parties things like 'I never read books' or 'I can't stand writers'. If a publisher does not have a good head for business either on his own shoulders or on his partner's, he is a poor publisher, but if a good head for business were all he had, he would be making detergents or shoes or furnishing fabrics, not books.

Apart from that it is a job which suits me because it has a constant element of extemporization in it, if not lunacy. Its nature forbids the hardening of its arteries into routine. This often makes me bilious with rage, or sullen, or reckless: I long fiercely to know what it would be like to do work in which I could start something and be sure that I could carry it through to the end uninterrupted. But against that, I am not often bored.

I used to have a dream of a pretty office. When I became a director, I imagined, I would acknowledge the fact that the greater part of my waking life is spent at work and I would have a room which gave me pleasure, with a wide enough desk, a comfortable chair, decorative objects on the shelves, colours I enjoyed on the walls, pictures and plants. For several weeks I relished the thought of this room, but the day I moved into it was the last day it looked pretty. A meticulously neat person – our third partner, Nicolas Bentley, for instance – can keep paper at bay, but not someone as untidy and lacking in method as myself, and while most work involves paper, mine produces things made of it as well. How does one control paper? Letters and copies of letters not yet filed because I must be reminded to do something about them; a layout pad, and loose sheets from it with rough sketches on them; periodicals and cuttings from periodicals; memoranda on the backs of used envelopes; lists of publication dates, of contracts signed, of changes in the prices of books, of advertising space bought, of

people to invite to a party, of other people to whom
complimentary copies are to be sent; samples of paper for book
jackets or text; typescripts and synopses; reports on typescripts and
synopses; proofs, both in galley and in page; roughs submitted by
an artist for a jacket, or the finished artwork roosting with me so
that I remember to telephone the artist about a correction: a
perpetual autumn sheds its paper leaves, heaping them on to my
desk, drifting them into piles on my floor so that I cannot push my
chair back without tumbling them. My reference books can never
be dusted because of the paper lying on top of them and when I
want my ruler, my scissors, or my india-rubber, my hands grope
into the drifts on my desk and sheets of paper, unsettled, flutter to
join the paper on the floor. Only outsize matchboxes and bumper
tins of rubber solution are any good to me. The smaller sizes would
submerge with the bottles of coloured ink, the roll of Scotch tape,
and the pretty lustre shell which holds my paper clips. Only my
type-gauge usually remains above paper, because if I cannot see it
out of the corner of my eye I grow hysterical.

A type-gauge is a thin metal ruler marked with the units of
measurements for type: twelve points to a pica; a twelve-point em
is this long—; the type area of this page is twenty-two picas wide.
The type in which this page is set is a twelve-point type, and there
is one additional point of space between the lines. The type-gauge
is one of the tools of the typographer and has no business on an
editorial desk. But our firm, although it is growing too big to be
called a small firm, still feels like one; not so long ago any of us might
have had to turn our hand to anything, and we have got into the
habit of it. Because I can draw after a fashion and enjoy problems
of design, I was the one to whom it fell to lay out advertisements,
through which I came to know enough to lay out a book if I had to,
and to design odd jobs such as leaflets and showcards, and to
criticize other people's designs. Nowadays, if the production
department is overloaded, it will be to me that any overspill of
designing comes. It is in this part of the work that one comes nearest
to the actual making of a book as a physical object, that one learns
something of the printer's, binder's, and blockmaker's problems. It

is here that the element of craftsmanship comes in. Because this, like all making, is fascinating, my type-gauge has become a symbol of *being a bookmaker* as distinct from being a seller of books and an assessor of the merits of a writer's work, and of the three activities the making is the most comforting, the most sane in its procedures and dependable in its consequences.

So no sooner have I settled down to edit a typescript, or to read some unhappy writer's work which has been waiting for several weeks, than the internal telephone rings and the sales manager says, 'I promised Hatchards a showcard for such and such a book by the day after tomorrow. Is there any chance of it?' Pushing the typescript or book aside, I disinter the layout pad and begin to scrawl an idea to take to the sign-writer across the street (I shall have to take it across myself because I shall have to explain that the lettering is to be in such and such a style and that the girl is not supposed to have a squint although I have given her one). An idea is beginning to hatch when the telephone rings again: have I remembered that copy for our six-inch advertisement in the *Observer* has got to be sent in today, or have I made my notes yet on that draft letter to the lawyer about the possible libel action, or when will the blurb for the jacket of Book X be ready, or 'Mr Hackenpuffer is here with some drawings to show you, he says he has an appointment,' or 'There's a lady on the line who wants to submit a manuscript, only she says it's written in Polish so she must talk to an editor about it,' or 'Will you please speak to Mr Z, Mr Deutsch says he's out' (oh God, trouble!). On many days there comes a moment when a loud scream would be the only appropriate expression of feeling, and this is happening not only in my room but in André's room and in Nicolas Bentley's room (in spite of his neatness) and to some extent in all the other rooms. Even the specialists, snugly enclosed within their specialities – the sales manager, the production manager, the accountant, the chief invoicing clerk, the head packer – even they are dealing not with one process but with as many processes as there are books being produced and sold, for each book is a separate operation, with its own problems and timetable.

Many of the problems which beset a publishing firm do not come to me, but all of them are in the air. It is not a peaceful job.

In addition to the enjoyable liveliness which belongs to work unamenable to routine, there is another side of the job which I enjoy: meeting writers. An artist is not bound to be likeable and I have no doubt that many publishers could give examples of writers whose work they admired while they detested the authors as individuals. I have been lucky. Among the writers I have known, the better the artist, the more I have liked the man or woman. 'We are a neurotic lot, every last one of us,' one of them said to me, and certainly the good ones I have known have included the violently moody, the super-sensitive, the spiteful-about-other-people's-work, the hard drinker, the bad husband, the unable-to-communicate-in-speech, the cheerfully perverse, the conventionally amoral. Underneath whatever it may be, however, they have all had a private sanity which does not seem to me to be neurotic: they are the people to whom truth is important, and who can see things. The greatest pleasure I have found in publishing is in knowing such people.

The relationship is an easy one, because the publisher usually meets his writers only after having read something they have written, and if he has thought it good it does not much matter to him what the man will be like who is about to come through his door. He is feeling well-disposed for having liked the work; the writer is feeling well-disposed for his work having been liked; neither is under obligation to attempt a close personal relationship beyond that. It is a warm and at the same time undemanding beginning, in which, if genuine liking is going to flower, it can do so freely. My own feeling, if I have been truly excited by a book, is nearer to a curiously detached kind of love than to liking: I have looked at the head of the man or woman sitting opposite me and thought, 'It all came out of that head,' and I could have taken it between my hands and kissed it. There cannot be many other kinds of middlemen whose wares inspire feelings so satisfying as that.

It did not surprise me to discover in myself, when I first went into publishing, this profound respect for good writing. I had not thought much about it before because I had not had occasion to use it, but it was always there. How could it not have been? It was not only a matter of being reared in a reading family, it was a matter of having lived, quite literally, a great part of my life entirely in terms of the printed word, or of images on canvas or on the screen.

It is a startling realization. To have lived from 1917 to 1961 and to have known violence only through the printed word or through images; to have known social injustice and revolution only through the printed word or through images; to have seen Jews stumbling down concrete steps into the gas chamber only through the printed word or through images; to have experienced fear, hunger, loss of liberty, or courage, relief from want and the impulse to fight for freedom only through the written word or through images: this is astounding. I remember that when shadows on a screen formed the sticklike limbs of Belsen protruding at awkward angles from piles of bodies, the feet grotesquely big at the end of legs shrunk to bone, I was engulfed in a terrible silence of unreality – my own unreality, not that of the shadows. In the same way books have been my windows on to vast tracts of experience, both destructive and creative, in which I have not lived. To the poet, to the painter, to the writer of serious prose as distinct from the entertainer (much though I owe to the latter), I am so much in debt that if artists did not exist, I cannot imagine that I would. I shall be grateful all my life to André Deutsch for having come to my party and thus steered me into a job in which I have been able to get to know a few of what seem to me by far the most real human beings in the world.

15

So with the end of the war, work which I thought worth doing came my way. Had I been asked whether it made me happy, I would have answered 'Happy? No. But who is likely to have more than a few months of positive happiness during a lifetime?' That I was lucky I knew. My basic sense of failure was always present like a river bed, but the water running over the bed had become deeper than I had supposed it would ever be. My work brought enough incident and movement into my life for me to be content to exist with very little beyond that.

Of social life I had, and still have, almost none. I have never had a talent for acquaintance, only an enjoyment of intimacy. People who have more than three or four friends whom they wish to see often, who come and go to dinner parties and so on with a wide circle of acquaintances whose company they enjoy although they do not know them very well, fill me with envious admiration. When I was young I enjoyed parties so much that any was better than none – the murmur of voices and clink of glasses as I came up a staircase, the smell of the women's scent, the spurts of laughter, the sparkle of lights would delight me in themselves. Once during my twenties it occurred to me that a time would come when not only would I no longer dance but I would not mind not dancing, and I wept. But now, although I usually enjoy parties when I go to them (with the exception of large cocktail parties, which are the antithesis of social pleasure), I do not miss them, and I only missed them sharply in fits and starts during the years immediately after the war. Partly my seclusion came from lack of money and space, for I myself could not afford to entertain people other than casually, and partly it was the natural result of being a single woman moving into her thirties. Such new acquaintances as I made were usually married couples, most of whose friends were other married couples, and the occasions on which a spare woman can be comfortably fitted in are few. But chiefly, I suspect, it was my own unreadiness to offer more than a surface interest to strangers which left me so unusually isolated in this way, for other single women of my age often seem to lead more active social lives than I do.

I was not lonely because for many years I shared a flat with a cousin. My sister, who married during the war and went to live abroad soon after it, was less close to me than my cousin was and would not have been a more congenial companion, much as I liked her. Eight years younger than myself, my cousin was an exceptionally pretty girl with a haunting personality, so that her life was considerably fuller than mine, and I slid prematurely into an attitude common among good-natured middle-aged women: that of taking so strong an interest in other people's lives that it largely fills the emptiness of one's own. I was comfortable in the routine of those years, and when on rare occasions I felt a stab of misery my reaction to it was not revolt against my circumstances but a deliberate attempt to become resigned to them. But to say that satisfying work was something that had made me happy – that I could not have done. Something else, occupying only a fraction of each year and appearing to be marginal, made more difference to the colour of my days than did my work.

My holidays. I am not a traveller, only, once a year if I can manage it, a tourist. But those short journeys to France, Italy, Yugoslavia, or Greece have done more to alter my life than anything except love.

I owe them to the same aunt who taught me to enjoy painting. Before the war I had been taken abroad twice by my parents, driving fast round Europe on business trips, staying one night here, two nights there, never longer than the five or six nights we slept in Budapest. Most of each day was spent getting from place to place, and most of our meals were eaten with people to whom my father was selling mica, who were sometimes pleasant but rarely the companions we would have chosen. It was a useful bird's-eye view of Europe, but a frustrating one. We would be in Paris, Vienna, or Prague – places woven in my imagination from books, films, and hearsay into magical cities where anything might happen – and all that we would do was to go to bed early to be ready for an early start. I often had to share a room with my mother. I did not try to escape – my parents would not have allowed it, and I would have been scared – but I would long to lean out of the window into the foreign night, breathe the foreign smell of cigars, coffee, drains and unknown leaves, listen to the foreign dance music which always seemed to be coming so teasingly from lit doors and windows across the street. I wanted violently to be in these places, but with a man – with Paul, or with Robert, my Oxford love, or even with whatever man had been eyeing me across the room during dinner. Failing that, I wanted to sit by the window and write long letters to my friends describing my anguish. But I did not wish to hurt my parents by betraying how different I would have liked the journey to be, so I went to bed like a good girl, telling myself how lucky I was to be seeing these places (as indeed I was), and at breakfast the next morning I would be sulky.

Then, with the war, travel became impossible. I grew so accustomed to not thinking of it and to being short of money that I no longer saw it as something I could do. Given to inertia as I have always been, it is possible that if in 1947 my aunt had not unexpectedly sent me the money for a holiday abroad, I might never again have set foot on a Channel steamer.

It was a gift typical of her, offered shyly and suddenly, with no fuss. Can any other gift have bestowed so much pleasure? Without hesitation I plumped for Florence, and set off on that simple journey as tremulous with excitement as though I were crossing the Gobi desert. I expected to step out of the train into the gold, red, and blue of a painting by Fra Angelico, and shall never forget the shock of surprised recognition, the delicious anticipation-reality complex as I experienced it again on seeing that Florence was a crumbling biscuit baked pale by the sun, with a kind of beauty quite different from but much more disturbing than the beauty its name had held for me. I remembered Proust and his conjuring with names, this elaborate balancing of places not yet seen or no longer seen against places in their reality. 'That's not for me,' I thought. 'There's nothing to balance. This paving stone on which I am standing, that torn poster on that wall, that little dusty tree, that tomato skin in the gutter – any single object you like to name that I can see or touch is worth more to me than the whole of Petra or Angkor Vat in my imagination!'

Even more exciting than the discovery that Florence was real, was the discovery that the sudden distance between myself and my usual environment, the breaking of the daily habits by which I was conditioned, had released me from the creature produced by that conditioning. I felt as though I were my naked self, starting from scratch. A skin had been peeled off my eyes, my nerve-ends were exposed. I, who was usually able to sleep twelve or fourteen hours at a stretch if I were not woken, and would then get up reluctantly, found myself jumping out of bed at seven-thirty or eight in the morning, outraged by the idea that I should lie there one minute after my eyes had opened. There was no time to want anything but to be where I was and to see, see, see what I was seeing. That first turning loose after the war was the purest and most intense of all the holidays I have had, and it convinced me that from then on, whatever my circumstances, I must continue to travel abroad. It is not only seeing landscapes and works of art hitherto unseen, different kinds of building, faces of a different cast and complexion, behaviour formed in different moulds, which makes travelling important. It is the different eyes with which the traveller, startled out of habit by change, looks at these things.

To catalogue such ordinary journeys as mine would be tedious. I can put my finger on what I have gained from them by thinking of only one place from among those I have stayed in: the Greek island of Corfu, in the Ionian Sea.

I can recognize sandstone, chalk, and granite, but that is all. I cannot name the kind of rocks which lie under and jut through the thin skin of soil on Corfu, although the shapes of their abrupt and disorderly outcrops are printed on my brain. Hellenophiles sometimes refer to Corfu patronizingly as green and soft, because it is so much less nakedly rocky than the Cyclades or most of the mainland, but in spite of its richness of vegetation its skeleton is almost as near the surface as that of the rest of Greece. It is rock, not earth. Its bones are not the sort that make smooth, swelling lines; they heave, break, and tumble, and their debris, from which the supporting walls of olive terraces are built, is rough, layered, pocked. The terraces are not hard to climb at any point because of the foot and handholds offered by the crude masonry of the walls, but most of them have their 'paths': easy places made easier, where the rocks form steps or have been pressed by use into oblique, broken ledges where men climb regularly to the olive trees, and old women lead a goat or a donkey to be tethered on fresh grazing.

Each terrace has a different character. On some the stony earth, ochre or light terracotta, is almost bare, on others there are many thistles, among them a frail one of great beauty with steel-blue stems and leaves. On a recently grazed terrace the spiky grasses and small flowers will be flattened and scattered with dung, drying quickly into earthiness, while another will be green, with a higher percentage of what the English recognize as grass in its growth, and softer, more caressing plants. Each terrace has its tree or trees, with a slight depression round the roots to hold the rain when it comes.

I am a connoisseur of terraces. I look for one greener and therefore softer than the rest, with the best view possible and an old, well-grown tree to throw a wider and more opaque shade than a young tree can. Such a tree is easy to find on Corfu, where the method of cultivation (due, say other Greeks, to Corfiot laziness) is to leave olives alone and let them grow to a great age and size until they split and gnarl into extraordinary shapes. Their trunks become distorted, ropelike columns of bark-enclosed tendons which writhe apart, then join again, sometimes leaving windows of space so that you can look right through the tree. They give an impression of restless movement curiously at variance with their gentle, peaceful colouring. I have seen dull olive trees in France,

Italy, and some parts of Greece – little orchard trees, monotonous in shape and no more than pretty – but because of those on Corfu, the olive is the tree I would choose to keep if I could have only one: for the variety of shape, for the comforting roughness of its bark, for its minnow leaves, dark on top and silver underneath, which cast a shadow more delicately stippled than any other, and for its ancient usefulness, which makes it, like wheat, a symbolic thing.

There is one terrace at Paleokastritsa, on the west side of Corfu, which I first found six years ago and revisited last year. Its position favours the holding of moisture and it is almost meadowlike compared to its neighbours. It is possible, though – not particularly comfortable, to lie on it without spreading a rug or a towel against prickles. (One gets better at lying as the days pass. At first every pebble and spike and exploring ant is a discomfort; but after several days of sun and wine and oil one's body relaxes and becomes accommodating, so that one could almost sleep as Greek workmen sleep in the heat of the afternoon, lying loose and comfortable on roadside stones.)

Although this terrace would be a good place for sleeping, I have never slept on it because I found it impossible to stop looking. Below it, only a little masked by the silver tops of lower trees, is one of the bays of Paleokastritsa. This is a place where land and sea meet in an interlocking clover-leaf formation, three almost enclosed bays divided from each other by two steep promontories which may once have been islands, since they are joined to the steeper main island by a narrow strip of flat land. One of the promontories is crowned by a small monastery, but the one on which my terrace is has only rebarbative scrub and rock above its orchards. The best-known bay is under the monastery, round and dark blue, with a small hotel on its beach. The bay I overlooked is bigger, less regular in shape and more beautiful in colour. It is broken by a small promontory within it, and goes from navy blue near the open sea, through every shade of aquamarine, with depths of pure emerald under its cliffs and chunky emerald patches where a boat throws a shadow. Its depth and the nature of its sandy bottom combine in a ratio perfect for transparency, sparkle, and movement – I have never seen it when it was not netted with light, whereas some Mediterranean and Aegean bays, though lovely, can become almost too still, too smooth. Only to look at this bay is like drinking champagne would be if I enjoyed champagne, and to swim in it is something quite different from swimming in any other water that I know. From where I sat I looked back across it at the mainland. Just under the terrace is the strip of beach which edges the flat, linking neck, with a tiny, shacklike taverna, a few caiques and rowing-boats lying at anchor, where one or two fishermen, either old men or very young boys, move slowly about and sometimes call to each other. Beyond that, cliffs (at the bottom of one of them a little spring of fresh water bubbles up a few inches from the sea – one of the several places where Ulysses is supposed to have been found by Nausicaa, although there is no room for the bushes or reeds in which he hid his nakedness); above the cliffs steep, olive-fleeced, cypress-punctuated mountainside, rising to an abrupt escarpment with a sheer rock face which turns apricot-coloured in the evening sun and is rimmed by the rapid, stumbling line of the mountain's profile, plunging out and round to one's right to hit the sea on the far side of the bay.

All this is bathed in light and silence. It is silent in spite of the fishermen's voices or the occasional grinding of a truck or taxi creeping round the edge of the bay to visit the hotel or the monastery; silent in spite of a donkey on a lower terrace calling to another donkey on the further mountain. The braying of donkeys – that painfill, wheezing, lion-like sound – might be the voice of rock, as the creaking of cicadas might be the voice of sun. I once spent four hours alone on that terrace with an unread book and untouched writing-pad, turned by the spectacle into nothing but eyes, with no idea of the time that was passing until the sun went down.

Such pleasures can only be enjoyed alone and on foot. Earth, stone, water, trees must be touched and smelt in order to be fully realized. I have seen landscapes more magnificent from cars, buses, trains, and boats, and have been pleased to see them; but the ones I have *learnt*, the ones which have become part of the fabric of my memory, are those which have made the muscles of my legs ache, have scratched my ankles and caused sweat to drip off my forehead. Why I should still consider the conscientious hiker slightly absurd I cannot conceive. He is undoubtedly gaining a more intense and enduring experience than any other traveller.

A small, slow motor bicycle would be a good substitute for walking. I have been taken across Corfu from Paleokastritsa to the town of Corfu itself, a distance of just over twenty miles, riding pillion on such a machine, and a thousand nuances of a road which I thought I knew well became evident, its smells especially. The smells released in a Mediterranean climate by evening, when the baked herbs and aromatic leaves begin to breathe again, are almost as positive as clouds of colour, but only wisps of them can be caught from a car. I was riding behind the sedate manager of the hotel at Paleokastritsa, who liked a speed of about fifteen miles an hour: perfect in the circumstances. The friend who was with me was piloted by one of the waiters on a racier scooter, and would have been hurtled across the island like a thunderbolt had the manager and I not started out first and the waiter felt that it would be *lèse-majesté* to overtake his employer. So through the golden evening we trundled, weaving among the potholes to a dialogue of 'pip-pip', 'beep-beep', whenever we had to pass a donkey with a load of brushwood, or half a dozen thin sheep. It would, I thought, have been the ideal way to travel about Greece.

The hurtling came later, at one o'clock in the morning, when we were on our way back by taxi from the dinner to which we had been invited. In England a car or a restaurant with a radio in it depresses me. Had I been told of a taxi with not only a radio but a gramophone, I should have been appalled. How could one bear to drive through an arcadian landscape untouched by time, under a full moon at that, to the sound of rock and roll or even of bouzoukia? But given an evening drinking retsina with a soap manufacturer and a municipal electrician in Corfu, those great gales of sound became exhilarating. The taxi bounced, the moon reeled, scented breezes whipped our hair, the two men sang in passionate baritone voices and embraced us, and although the fierce, tomcat wailing of the Greek music was the better, even the Elvis Presley records played in our honour took on a throb and a swing which fitted them to the night. Only on Corfu have I seen taxis fitted with that device: a narrow, cushioned slot on gimbals under the dashboard, into which the driver shoves small records from the library which he keeps on the seat beside him. He only has to push them in and pull them out; the playing is automatic and undisturbed by even the most violent bouncing. Loud it has to be – loud and strident, with the hood of the car down and a road diversified by sharp bends and sudden stretches of unsurfaced stone. Then the music becomes not an offence but a celebration, one hears it as its addicts hear it, vulgarity is blown away, and its platitudes touch the nerves like truths.

Strenuous though the end of such an evening usually is, streaked with anxiety as to how to taper stormy declarations of premature and unreal passion into an agreeable acquaintanceship, I would not have missed the wild musical taxis of Corfu. Evenings like that – absurd, comic, undignified, even at times slightly alarming – following days like those I spent on the terrace: those are what I travel for. That I should see works of arts and monuments which I should not see otherwise, and that I should make the sudden but enduring friendships which sometimes blossom out of a time when inhibitions are melted by strangeness and renewed vitality, is certainly important; but the secret days and the comic evenings have been the best treasure I have brought back.

Anglo-Saxon and Scandinavian women are commonly supposed to go south in search of men, and so they often do. The neuroses of northern societies, in which men feel that they see too much of women, dovetail neatly with those of southern societies, where men feel that they see too little of them. Whether she shrinks or expands under it, no Englishwoman can remain unaware of having her sex openly recognized in street, train, or restaurant, after months at home during which the most startling recognition it has received has been the quick, sidelong twitch of a gooseberry eye here and there, which vanishes under a hat brim as soon as it has been observed. Whatever the weather, I feel cold when I return to London.

But societies which acknowledge the power of sex, and therefore shelter their respectable women (and thereby increase the power of sex – it is a spiral), are romanticized by societies with opposite tendencies. Much nonsense is talked by swaggering southerners and wistful northerners about the absence of puritanism and inhibition in the warmer parts of Europe. So much theorizing, so much emphasis on masculine *bella figura*, so much keeping of scores – it is not, perhaps, repressed sex that one encounters in countries like Italy and Greece, but it sometimes looks suspiciously like sex-in-the-head. And in spite of the millions of real and warm relationships that must exist, fat Yanni Hajikakkis, admittedly an extreme case, seems to me to have his significance.

He was a huge, thick-necked man with a bellow, who boasted that during his military service he had been the most spectacular sergeant in the Greek Army, able to make even colonels jump out of their boots when he let himself go. In ordinary conversation he would try to keep his voice down, but he never succeeded for more than a few sentences. Swimming with a friend of mine, at whom he was making a desultory pass, he could be heard across fifty yards of water and the beach, from the balconies of the small hotel which stood on its edge, as he argued, 'But you cannot like to make love with your husband or you would not be here without him.' In the Army he had been popular because he had never put his men in prison but had taken offenders outside and punched their heads, which, he told us, had made him much loved. Yanni was on holiday in Corfu when we met him, a prosperous store-owner from Salonika, rich, and contented with his lot except in one way. His mother was dead. His father was dead too, 'but for my father I am not suffering. For Mama . . . "Not Mama!" I say, "No, God, not my Mama, not my Mama!" But God did not hear . . . What is a man without his mother? In a man's life she is his angel, she is the only pure love. I make love to many women – I am a strong man as you see, I am always making love – but what are these whores to me? I love only my Mama and she loves only me, she would die for me – and now she is dead!'

Whenever Yanni spoke of his mama's death, and he spoke of it every time I met him, his big bold eyes would pop with tears, he would bow his head and drop his fists on the table so that the glasses rattled. Large, loud, and aggressively masculine though he was, through my head there would flash images of thousands of plump, soft, pale little boys – cherished, indulged little Greek boys of the middle and upper classes – growing up in a society which inspires western Europeans with nostalgia because its values are simpler and more ancient than our own, because its members believe that children love mothers, that brothers protect sisters, that insults should be revenged, and that something has been lost since they can no longer shoot their enemies without getting into trouble. No doubt there are some little Greek boys of that kind whose value as children and males in such a society does not mean that sweetmeats are stuffed between their lips even when they do not ask for them, or who are not allowed to stay up long past their bedtime because they cry and kick, but they are the minority. Mostly the baby, and particularly the boy baby, is god, and that this privileged status makes the best sort of man of him can appear doubtful.

'Now that you are so lonely,' I said to Yanni, 'why don't you get married?'

'Married? I will never marry! How can I find today such a girl as I would marry?'

What qualities would he require, I asked, and he catalogued them: she need not be rich because he was rich, and he held opinions too modern for him to insist on money as a matter of form; she need not be pretty, though it would be better if she were; she must come from a suitable family; she must be no more than seventeen so that he could be sure that she was a virgin (in England, he said, she would have to be under fifteen for that, from all he had heard). But above all 'she must be like my mother, she must be to me a mama'. It was distressing to think that this prosperous man, still only in his thirties, almost certainly would get married soon in spite of his protests: that some girl in her teens really *would* have to buckle down to being his mama because he felt in his bones that mamas were the only kind of women who were good. Englishmen are supposed to be split-minded about women, to divide them into 'good' and 'bad' according to whether they like men or not, but no Englishman I have ever met was more split-minded than poor fat Yanni, slumped over a cafe table and bellowing the loss of his mother like a calf bereft.

Some western Europeans go to Greece – I go to Greece – not only for its haunting beauty but to touch a life more straightforward and governed by simpler necessities than our own. After being spellbound by it we turn back to our own values and see them as over-complex, shoddy, and absurd – I have found myself envying Greek or Yugoslav women for their unquestioning acceptance of their status in a world more dominated by men than my own. But not when I was talking to Yanni; and not when, for example, I have ventured into a Greek restaurant at night in a provincial town – a restaurant kept as a preserve for men, by men, because men believe that it is right to keep their mothers, daughters, and sisters safely at home behind invisible bars. If there is a woman entertainer in the restaurant, singing bouzoukia, watch those hungry faces turned towards her, listen to the groan which greets her demure and lazy dancing – the pressure of frustration is explosive. The woman tourist who fondly believes herself to be succumbing to an uninhibited pagan is more likely to be serving as a crust thrown to a starving man – a deliberately starving man, who would only pick up a crust because a crust is worth nothing. If all she wants is to be free of her own inhibitions for a day or two, well and good, but I suspect that the freedom is often bestowed by someone no less cramped than herself.

Having too little money is an advantage in travelling which I regret losing. I am still far from being able to stay in really good hotels or to fly except on the cheaper night flights, but my standards are creeping up: cheap the flight may be, but it is a flight, and not a third-class train journey. It would be possible to travel more cheaply than necessity dictates, but fondly though I remember journeys made in less comfort, I feel myself reflecting a miniature image of the rich whose money forces them so inexorably into a certain manner of living. It seems an affectation not to take a room with a shower if I can afford it, although I know by experience that a hotel too small for showers will be less impersonal. I *know* that an excursion by local bus is more amusing and interesting than an excursion by taxi, in spite of the heat, the jolting, and the passenger who will vomit, but the money in my purse works a sinister distortion, emphasizing the bus's disadvantages, highlighting the taxi's luxury, so that against my will I find myself in the latter, and thus likely to meet other people of my own sort instead of the friendly, curious strangers in the bus. An insulating layer has been put between my naked self and the place I am visiting, and I have lost something by it. I can only be grateful that the layer is never likely to become thick.

From every journey I have made I have come home happier, and what I have gained from them has not vanished with time. It is not only that I have seen beautiful things with which to furnish my imagination, learnt interesting things, met interesting people, laughed a great deal. Something has happened as a result of all this: one by one, nerves which I thought to be dead have come to life.

16

B Y 1958, WHEN I was forty-one, I had come to feel that middle-age, provided I did not look more than a little way ahead, was a peaceful time rather than a depressing one. A deliberate myopia could give the impression that I was on a level plain rather than on a downhill slope. It was a long time since I had been in love, a long time since every unoccupied moment had been filled with thoughts of men, or of a man. Sometimes, when I went to bed, I would try to return to the memories, hopes, speculations, and dreams which had taken up so much of my time for so many years, but I would fall asleep before they had properly begun. I worked, and liked my job. I travelled, and loved it. I met my friends, and was as familiar with their troubles as though they were my own; and because trouble was the prevailing condition in the life of almost everyone I knew, my own calm, though negative, began to seem a good fortune. My grandmother had died, and soon afterwards my father, who had retired some years earlier and had been living with my mother in a house they had bought near Beckton during the war, when it had become necessary for the Farm to house a working bailiff. These deaths, and the ageing of my other relatives, who were shrinking a little and stiffening in their joints, while their loneliness and their fear of it showed through the chinks in their courage as they pushed their days so bravely from incident to incident, had put Beckton in a new light – or had made me notice the new light sharply for the first time. It was no longer a place to which I could go back for comfort; it had become a place to which I ought to bring comfort, and the meagreness with which I did this made me realize the degree to which I had become detached from my family. When I spent a weekend with my mother I could talk only of her affairs, or of the most superficial of my own, because on many of the subjects which touched me closely our opinions and emotions would be too different for easy communication.

Or so I felt, and continue to feel with people of her generation and background. I wish, now, that in my youth I had loved my family less. If I had not loved them I might have had the courage for revolt, instead of going quietly underground. If in my twenties I had been open about the sexual freedom I was practising, had pressed political arguments instead of sliding out of them into silence, had discussed my agnosticism instead of merely avoiding going to church, there might not have been the breach I expected and feared – or, if there had been, it might not have been permanent. With divergencies openly recognized it might have become possible for us to touch at more than a few well-defined points. Instead, I find myself apparently permanently inhibited in such relationships, even to keeping almost entirely silent on the most important thing that has ever happened to me.

For one January morning in 1958 I was crossing the Outer Circle in Regent's Park, bringing my dog in from her walk, when a passing car slowed, accelerated again, slowed and stopped. Supposing that the driver wanted to ask the way somewhere, I turned towards the car. The man peering back at me over his shoulder looked familiar. 'Why, it's Marcel!' I thought. Marcel was a diamond-polisher from Johannesburg whom I had once known well. I began to hurry towards him, smiling, but when I got nearer I saw that it was not Marcel. 'The name is Mustafa Ali from Istanbul,' said the stranger. 'I was wondering whether you would have a cup of coffee with me.'

I explained that I had mistaken him for someone else, told him I was busy, and crossed the road, laughing. 'What optimism,' I thought, 'at nine o'clock in the morning! And how odd that

someone looking so like Marcel should do such a Marcellish thing.'
I began to remember Marcel. For the rest of the day I felt
extraordinarily alive and cheerful, and that evening, as soon as I got
home, I began to write about Marcel.

It went smoothly for several pages – the little man was there in
front of me, I got him down – but when, next day, I reread what I
had done, it was clear that I could not persuade what I had written
into any shape. Marcel would have to belong to a story about
diamonds, and I did not know enough about the trade. 'Well, it was
rather fun remembering him,' I thought, putting it aside, but the
energy, the feeling of something bubbling inside me, was still there.
I went on thinking about him until he reminded me of another man
whom I had once known for a short time, and at that point it
happened. 'By God,' I thought with jubilation, 'I know what I'll do:
I'll write about *him*, and I'm going to get it *just as it was*.' That story
came straight out, with no pause, exactly as I meant it to, and I was
perfectly happy all the time it was coming.

Until I left school I had written poems fairly regularly. I wrote
half a dozen more while I was at Oxford, and another three or four,
widely spaced, when I was in my twenties. They were not good and
I did not suppose them to be good, but they were real in the sense
that they were pushed out of me by their own growth rather than
pulled out by my volition. They represented intensities of
experience, they were high points of my 'real' life, but they were
secret. I did not think of myself as someone whose intensities
deserved to be communicated, so when they stopped coming I was
regretful but not distressed.

Writing prose was something of which I had rarely thought
except as an enviable gift possessed by others. Two or three times,
when more than usually short of money, I had taken some incident
and tried to turn it into a 'travel piece' for the *New Statesman* or a
'funny piece' for *Punch*, without success. I was facetious when I
tried to be funny, high-flown when I tried to describe. I could see
clearly enough that I would dislike the results if they had been
produced by someone else. Three times during my adult life I had
scribbled a few pages for no purpose other than to put down what

I was feeling: once about Crivelli's *Annunciation*, once about Forster's *A Passage to India*, and once about my first visit to Florence. These I kept, but simply as reminders to myself. The 'feel' of the story triggered by Mr Mustafa Ali was entirely different. I did not bother to envisage a market for it, but it was, from the beginning, a story which I meant people to read.

As soon as that story was finished, another one began, and by the end of the year I had written nine. I did not think about them in advance: a feeling would brew up, a first sentence would occur to me, and then the story would come, as though it had been there all the time. Sometimes it would turn into 'work' halfway through and I would have to cast about for the conclusion to which the story must be brought, but more often it finished itself. Some of them connected very closely with my own experience, some of them, to my astonishment, depended on it so slightly that they might almost have been 'invented' (the 'invented' ones were the ones of which I felt most proud, although, with one exception, the others were better).

In March, when I was halfway through the third of these stories, I saw the announcement of the *Observer's* short-story competition for that year, the story to be called 'The Return' and to be three thousand words long. Neither of my finished stories had that title, but it could have made sense with either of them. One was too long, the other only needed cutting by a hundred words. Friends had encouraged me, so I put the shorter of the two in an envelope, chose for the necessary pseudonym the name of the horse which had just won the Grand National (Mr What, God bless him), posted it and forgot it. Or rather, I remembered it twice between then and December, when the results were to be announced, on selling two other stories to magazines. 'Perhaps,' I thought, 'if these have proved good enough to sell . . .' But both times I slapped myself down so firmly that when the literary editor of the *Observer* telephoned me at my office on December 21st, my birthday, the competition did not enter my head.

I had written to him a little earlier, asking him whether his paper had omitted to review one of our books because he did not like it, or because he had lost it – the sort of nagging a publisher only permits himself for a book he cares about. I was therefore pleased to hear that he was on the line, and more pleased when he said that he had good news for me. 'Hurrah,' I thought. 'He is going to send it out for review after all.'

'At least, I think I have good news,' he went on, 'if it *is* for you . . . Did you send in a story for our competition?'

The consolation prizes, I thought in a split second. There were several of them, of twenty-five pounds each. 'Yes,' I said.

'Then you have won first prize,' he said. 'You have won five hundred pounds.'

You do not look up because you know that you cannot climb the tree. You have forgotten, by now, that there is fruit hidden among its leaves. Then, suddenly, without a puff of wind, a great velvety peach falls plump into your hand. It happens to other people, perhaps; it never happens to oneself . . . I am still licking peach juice off my fingers.

Although, if the metaphor is to be exact, the peach does not fall into your hand so much as land on your head. It stuns you. Imagining such an event, I would have imagined blank incredulity followed by a clean burst of rapture, but the two emotions blurred together, there was no perfect moment. By the time I had gathered my wits to accept such a moment, I found that it was already in the past, I had had it. Something ought to *happen* at moments of delicious surprise: one ought to fly up into the air, one ought to change into music or light. I went on sitting at my desk, watching the cold pigeons huddling on a bit of roof outside my office window, and it was totally inadequate. Even when I was hurrying down Bond Street at lunch-time that day, buying prettier Christmas presents than I had planned, I found that frustration was mixed with my delight because none of the people in the street looked as though the world had changed. There were moments during that lovely day when I felt that I had better stop groping or I might touch a thread of real anguish in the evanescence of moments. For the first time in years I remembered

little Rosalba's song from *The Rose and the Ring*, and I was
humming it all day:

> Oh what fun
> To have a plum bun,
> *How I wish*
> *It never were done!*

But although at first it seemed as though nothing – or not enough –
had changed, two things did happen as a result of this event: one
of them no more than an amusing insight, the other with a value
hard to calculate.

'Poverty' is a word which should be forbidden to anyone who has
lived as comfortably as I have lived, with a family in the
background which, however ill it could afford it, could be counted
on to rescue me in an emergency. But I have never had any income
beyond my earnings, and my earnings have always been small.
(The small independent publisher who does not plough most of his
profits back into his firm will soon either dwindle to nothing, or
stop being independent.) Every penny I have earned I have always
spent at once, and always without having many of the things I
would have liked. To me, therefore, five hundred pounds tax-free
seemed wealth. I could go to Greece during the coming spring
without worrying – I could even travel *first-class*! I could buy a fitted
carpet, and new curtains which I really liked, and there would still
be money over. During that winter I felt rich, and because I felt it
I gave an impression of being it. A little while earlier I had been
looking at dresses in a large, smart shop, and when I had pointed
to a pretty one and said 'I'll try that,' the girl serving me had
answered in a tired voice: 'It's expensive. Why try on something
you can't afford?' In the same shop, wearing the same clothes, soon
after I had paid my five hundred pounds into the bank, I was
served with such civil alacrity that I could have ordered two grand
pianos to be sent home on approval and they would have offered
a third. Courteous men spent hours unrolling bolts of material for
me, urging me to consider another, and yet another. A pattern for

matching? Why, yes! And instead of the strip two inches wide which I was expecting, lengths big enough to make a bedspread were procured for me. For about a month I believe I could have furnished a whole house on credit, not because I was looking different, not because I could, in fact, afford it; simply because, for the first time in my life and for no very solid reason, I was feeling carefree about money. I learnt a great deal about the power of mood during that month.

The second happening was of more consequence. This plenty was the result of competent judges preferring my story to several thousand others, and my story was something I had done spontaneously, for the pleasure of it; something as much a part of me as the colour of my eyes. To have written one story considered good does not amount to much, but it does amount to something: it is not failure. It would be an absurd exaggeration to say that for twenty years I had been unhappy – I had enjoyed many things, and for most of the later years I had been contented enough – but it is the exact truth to say that if, at any minute during those years I had been asked to think about it, made to stop doing whatever was distracting me and pass judgment on my own life, I should have said without hesitation that failure was its essence. I had never really wanted anything but the most commonplace satisfactions of a woman's life, and those, which I had wanted passionately, I had failed to achieve. That I would have answered in such a way is not speculation. I *did* answer exactly that, to myself, over and over again, in the minutes before falling asleep, in the worse minutes of waking up, when I was walking down a street, when I looked up from a book, while I was stirring scrambled eggs in a pan. The knowledge was my familiar companion. It had been, at first, hot coals of pain and grief, and had later grown cold; but cold though it had become, its lumpy presence had still been there. My only pride had been that having by nature an easy disposition, and a fund of pleasure in life stored up from a happy childhood and youth, I was good at living with failure. I did not think that it had turned me disagreeable or mad, and that I considered an achievement.

And now something which did not go against my grain, something which was as natural to me as love, had worked. I believe that even had I never written another word, the success of that story alone would have begun to dissolve the lumps. Bury me, dear friends, with a copy of the *Observer* folded under my head, for it was the *Observer's* prize that woke me up to the fact that I had become happy.

It is surely important to make a few notes on that rare condition, happiness, now that I am in it. It began when I started to write, was fanned into a glorious glow when I won that prize, was confirmed when, soon afterwards, I began to love, and it shows no sign of altering.

A symptom of life: opening my eyes in the morning to wakefulness. The long hours of unconsciousness which I used to treasure are now meaningless. Even on Sundays I will sleep for no more than eight hours unless I am unusually and genuinely tired.

A symptom of life: not caring much where I live. Single women can root themselves in their rooms, their furniture, their ornaments, so that not to have the right things about them in the right order becomes intolerable to them. I love rooms and objects and materials; I love to choose them and to arrange them, and when – rarely – I have done it well, I am snug and satisfied. But I attach less importance to it now than I used to. Recently, being between flats, I have been camping here and there with friends, and once in a place which was everything I dislike. I expected to be uneasy and discontented, but found that while there was a table to write on, a stove to cook on, and a bed, I was at home.

A symptom of life: people saying 'What has happened to her? She looks so well,' or 'She looks so young.' My own sensation of physical well-being is perceptible to other people. 'She might be twenty-five,' said a woman in her seventies, and even allowing for the telescoping of the years when seen from that age,which would make thirty-five more accurate than twenty-five, some degree of physical rejuvenation is suggested. If it exists, it corresponds to an inward change towards the years. I was twenty-three when I began to be aware of ageing as something sad. While I had Paul every year passing carried me towards something better than I had hitherto known, possibilities proliferated, anything might happen to me. When I had accepted his disappearance the years became slow steps downhill. Common sense forbade me to consider myself old while still in my twenties, but I felt old, and once past my thirtieth birthday I began to accept the feeling as rational. Most of my thirties were overshadowed, when I allowed myself to notice it, not only by my forties but by my old age: by a sense that there was nothing ahead but old age, by an awareness of the disabilities of old age, a shrinking when I watched an old person stepping carefully, painfully on to the curb of a pavement, or noticed the round, puzzled eyes of old-age pensioners sitting on a bench in the sun, looking baffled by what had happened to them. Now that I am, in fact, several years nearer to them, have my first grey hairs, a neck less smooth and a waist considerably less slim – can observe in my own body the clear indications of time passing and know that they are there for good, not as a sign of a physical condition that could be cured – I have, perversely, stopped feeling old. The process of ageing is undeniable, but it no longer touches an exposed nerve. Being happy has made it unimportant.

This is because the present has become real. No one can be detached from his past, but anyone can come to see it as being past, and when that happens one is partly liberated from its consequences. I cannot only see mine as being past, but have become indifferent to it. *Then* is less real than *now*, and *now* has become potent enough to shape the future, who knows how, so that the future is no longer an immutable threat. Nothing is immutable: that is the thing. My condition has changed – even, to a small extent, my nature has changed – so possibilities exist again.

The sensation of happiness itself is one for which I have only a physical vocabulary: warmth, expansion, floating, opening, relaxation. This was so from its beginning, and has become more so with its confirmation in love. Unintellectual, unspiritual as I am, I have always identified closely with my body: for most of the time I am it and it is me. What happens to me physically is therefore of great importance to my general condition – a disposition threatening serious problems in illness or old age, but conducive to an especial happiness in love. To split the relationship of love into 'physical' and 'mental' is something which I cannot do. Making love is not a fugitive good, contained only in the time in which it is being done: it is, each time, an addition, an expansion of a whole happiness. I have never in the past known it to be quite wiped out by subsequent events, and I know that it will not be wiped out now. This final way of communication is one of the things which, like my feeling for Beckton and Oxford, I know to be stored in me: a *good* which I have experienced, which enters into and is entered by everything I see and hear and feel and smell, and of which I can only be deprived by the decay of consciousness. That when two people have lived together for several years their lovemaking loses its value is, in most cases, obvious, and I should expect it to do so with me: I should expect that only if the man I was living with and I were really as well suited as we had first believed would the habit of companionship and interdependence successfully supersede physical delight. But I do not see that this would discredit physical delight. If it exists, it will always *have existed*. Now, therefore, that it exists again for me, I am by that much richer to the end of my days.

So happiness, followed by love and increased by it, has for me the colour of physical pleasure although it embraces many other things and although it seems to me to mean something larger than my own emotions and sensations. This is a period in which many people are concerned with the difficulty of communication. Poetry, novels, plays, paintings: they emphasize this theme so constantly that anyone who feels that human beings *can* communicate is beginning to look naïve. But what is meeting a man from a different country, a different tradition, a different social and economic background, and finding that you and he can both speak about anything exactly as you feel, in perfect confidence of understanding even if not of agreement, if it is not communication? The discovery of trust and easiness which comes with such a meeting is another, and greater, enduring good.

On the face of it this love is of the same kind as others I have known and is no more likely to lead to a permanent companionship.

I must take my own word for it that it is not the same. It does not feel the same. *Then*, with a sort of despairing joy, I used to jump off cliffs into expected disaster; *now*, hardly knowing what I was doing, I slipped off a smooth rock into clear, warm water.

I have come to have a horror of many of the states to which human beings give the name of love – a horror at the sight of them, and at the knowledge that I have been in them. I feel like André Gide, when he wrote in *So Be It*, 'There are many sufferings I claim to be imaginary . . . few things interest me less than so-called broken hearts and sentimental affairs.' Gide, poor man, was not well equipped to talk about love, split as he knew himself to be between physical and mental to such an extent that both were crippled. (I know of no more striking example of the dependence of style on honesty than his descriptions of relationships with boys. Trying to write most honestly, he is betrayed by the sudden, tinny ring of his words because he is not writing honestly. He is persuading himself that a sick greed had beauty. I would have been prepared to believe that it *did* have beauty if it were not for the timbre of those sentences.) But the old man's impatience with sad love stories contains much truth. Hunger, possessiveness, self-pity, the stubborn obsession to impose on another being the image we ourselves have fabricated: good God, the torments human beings are impelled to inflict on themselves and each other!

I am frightened by my own arrogance in saying that now, because I had stopped expecting to love and had therefore almost stopped wanting to love, I love; but that is what it feels like. I do not want the man I love to be other than he is; I want more of his time and presence than he is free to give me, but not much more. I want him to exist as himself, without misfortune or unhappiness. Perhaps this is because I am too old and fixed in my habits to want anything more, or perhaps I am deceiving myself. If I am telling the truth – I must reread this in ten years' time! – I shall have been justified in calling my present condition happiness.

I do not think that I have become more agreeable for it. My relationship with other people has changed: they have, with one exception, become less important to me. In a sad or neutral condition I pored over my friends' lives almost to the extent of living them vicariously, whereas now I am more detached, particularly from their misfortunes. I have one friend, a woman, who is bound by some flaw in her nature to uncertainty and confusion so that she has rarely been able to know the rewards which her beauty, intelligence, and generous ways ought to have earned her. There have been times in the past when I was so concerned for her that I would lie awake puzzling her problems in real distress, but now, although I am still sorry for them, they no longer attack my own peace of mind. This increased selfishness both dismays and pleases me: dismays, because it is disagreeable to see in oneself so clear a demonstration of the limitations of sympathy; pleases, because I have suspected the motives of the concern I used to feel. A fictional character who has always made me uneasy is Sonia, in *War and Peace* – humble, unselfish Sonia, abdicating from her own claims on life, identifying so thoroughly with the Rostovs that their lives were substituted for hers. Tolstoy need do no more than present Sonia without comment to show that in spite of her virtues he dismisses her as a person incomplete, a failed human being. His attitude towards her has always made me wince: it is the right attitude, and there have been times when I myself was near deserving it. To grasp greedily is detestable; to abdicate is despicable. When unhappy, I have veered towards the despicable rather than the detestable, and if vanity must choose between the two evils, whose vanity would not prefer to be detested rather than despised?

In these circumstances happiness will, of course, end, in so far as it depends on a relationship. Or if not 'of course', then 'probably'. I have been puzzled because, in foreseeing this probability, I remain sure that I am not 'expecting disaster' as I used to do when I fell in love. If the man I love were to stop loving me, or were to go away, there would certainly be an eclipse of joy at first total: I should have a bad time to go through. Am I so far from being frightened by this only because I can see no reason why such a thing should happen *soon*? Is it because, growing old, I am used to the thought of the losses which come with age, so that I would see such a loss as just another of them? Or is it because I happen to trust the relationship as one in which no mystification is likely to enter (the worst part of Paul's disappearance was the silence)? No doubt these things contribute to my lack of 'disaster-expectation', but there is something else as well. It is embarrassing to revert to my writing when it still amounts to so little – to hardly more than a private satisfaction – but I believe that it is the impulse to write which underlies my peace of mind. If I ask myself, 'So what will become of me if *that* happens?' the answer is, 'I will be all right after a time. I will go on writing.' And because I can say that, I can live in the present with nothing but gratitude for and joy in what it offers.

It is now midnight, early in December. From this table, with this white tea-cup, full ashtray, and small glass half-full of rum beside me, I see my story, ordinary though it has all been and sad though much of it was, as a success story. I am rising forty-three, and I am happier in the present and more interested by the future than I have ever been since I was a girl: amused and delighted, too, because to find oneself in the middle of a success story, however modest, when one has for so long believed oneself a protagonist of failure, is bizarre. But is it a story which will seem worth having lived through, of value in itself, when I come to die? Will the question my grandmother asked – and I shall have no grandchild of whom to ask it – overshadow my last days?

17

THE THINGS WHICH I will not be able to claim for myself are easy to list.

I have not been beautiful. Looks do not matter, I was taught; indeed, handsome looks are even bad, tempting to vanity and silliness. This, for a woman, is a lie. If I had been beautiful I would not necessarily have been happier, but I would have been more important. Perhaps if I had been ugly I would also have been more important, an awkward body forced to build an awkward personality to protect grief. But my kind of looks – someone may say, surprised, 'How pretty you look in that colour,' or, if in love with me, 'You have lovely eyes' – that kind of looks cannot be accounted even momentarily a reason for existence, as beauty, so confusingly and sometimes so fatally, can be.

I have been intelligent only in comparison with dull people. Compared with what I consider real intelligence I am stupid, being unable to think. I do not even know what people do in their brains to start the process of thinking. My own brain has a door which swings backwards and forwards in the draught. Things blow into it – a lot of things, some of them good but none of them under my control as I feel they ought to be. I have intuitions, sympathies, a sense of proportion, and the ability to be detached, but nothing which goes click-click-click, creating structures of thought. In my work I am often humiliated by this inability to think. I do things, or leave them undone, purely through stupidity, and this hurts and puzzles me, so that each time it happens I turn quickly to something unconnected with the organization of facts or ideas. I am good at liking or not liking somebody's work or, at understanding what somebody means, or is trying to mean. If I am wrong about such things, it is for reasons other than stupidity. But because I see the ability to organize and to construct as something which it should be possible to learn, and I have not been able to learn it, I am more oppressed, in my work, by my lack than I am comforted by what I have. Outside work, in life, I do not mind being stupid in this way; it is sometimes inconvenient but that is my own business, and I get pleasure and interest enough from the blowing about of feelings. But clearly I shall not be able to claim intelligence of a high enough quality to justify a life.

I have not been good. My 'good', partly a legacy of my Christian upbringing and partly arrived at empirically, is one which centres on selflessness. I have seen few evils, and few ills, which could not be traced to the individual's monstrous misconceptions of his own value in relation to that of other individuals. But people are what they *do* more than what they believe; and over and over again my actions have been those of a woman who values things as trivial as her own comfort or convenience above another person's joy or sorrow.

I have not been brave or energetic. To push back the frontiers of experience is an activity which I believe to be essential, but lethargy and timidity have prevented my doing it to anything like the extent to which it would have been possible. For political engagement I have been too lazy; for exploratory travel I have been too unenterprising, fearing the insecurity in strange places which it would entail for someone with no money. My sympathies are with the hipster, but when I consider his techniques of broadening experience I can see myself in comparison, as square as a cube from a child's set of bricks: to me excesses bring discomfort and fatigue rather than freedom.

So I have not been beautiful, or intelligent, or good, or brave, or energetic, and for many years I was not happy: I failed to achieve the extremely simple things which, for so long, I wanted above all else: I found no husband and it is not likely that I shall ever have a child.

There is plenty of evidence, then, that my existence has been without value: that if, like my grandmother, I approach death slowly and consciously, I shall be driven to ask the question she asked: 'What have I lived for?' All that I shall be able to answer is that I have written a little, and I have loved, and if I do not die until am old, those things will have become too remote to count for much. I shall remember that they once seemed worth everything, but quite possibly the fact that by then they will be *over* will appear to have wiped out their value. It ought to be a frightening thought, but I am still not frightened.

I was looking through a dictionary of quotations in search of a title for a friend's play when I chanced on Carlyle and Ruskin, both saying something which caught my attention. Carlyle: 'No most gifted eye can exhaust the significance of any object.' Ruskin: 'The greatest thing a human soul does in this world is to see.'

Eyes are precarious little mechanisms, lodged in their sockets as though that were that. When I was living at Beckton we used to buy the heads of sheep for our dogs, boil them, then strip or gouge the meat from them. It was a horrifying job until you became used to it, then almost fascinating: the brain, the tongue, the eyes became meat of different textures. It was hard to believe that the rubbery globes of the eyes had ever been able to receive impulses and turn them into images; still harder to believe that when they had done that, they had filled even a sheep's head with the world. To me the mechanism of sight is the principal wonder of conscious living: the mechanism which, more than any other, brings into the mind that which is outside. Sight brings in objective reality. Sight is the proof that you are as real as I am, that a pencil is as real, that a tree, a bird, a typewriter, a flower, a stone is as real; that each object is as much the centre of its universe as I am, and that conscious, human objects have each a universe as enormous as my own.

'*You are not the only pebble on the beach*' was often said to me during my childhood: words with the force of the metaphor still strong in them, since the East Anglian beaches I knew were composed almost entirely of pebbles. I used to spend hours searching among them because I collected cornelians and amber, which I kept in a jam jar, with water to make them gleam. I knew pebbles well: the different shades of grey, the almost white, the mottled, the porous, the ones with microscopic sparkles in the graining of their surfaces, the flat, the round, the potato-shaped, the totally opaque, the almost translucent. It was obvious that there was an infinite number of them, and an infinite variety, and that they were all equally real. I handled them, but more often I looked at them. It was by looking at pebbles that I began to feel their nature, and it is by looking that I feel the nature of people. 'What are you thinking?' my lover asks, and often I am not thinking, I am looking. The way the hairs of an eyebrow grow along the ridge, the slight movement under the thin skin beneath the eyes, the folding of the lips, the grain of the skin behind the ear: what I am learning from them I am not sure, but the need to study them is imperative. No doubt I should still love if I were blind, with only my reason and my hands, but could I recognize a man's separate existence in the same way?

Marcel, the diamond-polisher whose recall by Mustafa Ali released my first story, did not find objective reality a comfort. Once he leant out of a window in the Savoy Hotel, looked down on trees in which starlings were bickering their way to bed, and pavements over which people were hurrying, then slammed the window shut and exclaimed, 'I can't bear it!'

'What can't you bear?'

'The thought that I might die in the night, and next morning everything would *still be going on*. All those bastards trotting up and down the street, and those silly damned birds chirping ... It's horrible! Sometimes, when I'm at home, I wake in the middle of the night and start thinking about it, and then I have to telephone my sister.'

'What does she do?'

'She comes over and makes tea for me, and talks. Sometimes I keep her there all night.'

He walked up and down the room, splashing whisky out of his glass in his agitation, his mouth twitching, his eyes bilious: a sad little figure for whom the world would not come to an end.

To me, on the other hand, the knowledge that everything will *still be going on* is the answer. If I die with my wits about me, not shuffled out under drugs or reduced to incoherence by pain, I want my last thoughts to be of plants growing, children being born, people who never knew me digging their gardens or telephoning their friends. It is in the existence of other things and other people that I can feel the pulse of my own: the pulse. Something which hums and throbs in everything, and thus in me.

Reading Aldous Huxley's account of his experiments with mescalin, I caught myself thinking that this exceptionally intelligent man was naive. The crease in his trousers, the chair and the bunch of flowers in which he discovered the vibrating truth of being: had he not known that they contained it? That every object contains it? It is true that one does not usually see it with the intensity he describes, but it is not necessary to see it in that way to know that it exists. Chemical vision-sharpeners are a luxury, not a necessity. My own (I have not seen this remarked by anyone else, but it cannot be a unique experience) comes with whatever change in glandular activity it may be that heralds menstruation, so that almost every month I have a day or two of heightened vision, a delicious spell in which to see things living.

This 'isness business' – what smartypants called it that? – is, to me, too obvious to be chic. Only the gifted mystic, in whom the necessary disciplines channel a power which already exists, is likely to get further in it by studying Buddhism: indeed, I suspect that in the East, as in the West, only the rare saints have gone beyond the man-invented paraphernalia with which the rest tag along in their wake for comfort and reassurance. It is the obviousness – the obviousness of the quiet throbbing of life in every object – which has filled for me the silence that should have been left by non-belief, and which makes me question whether I did, in fact, stop believing. Believing in what? God, I suppose, knows – if knowledge in a human sense is an attribute of whatever lies behind the throbbing, and I do not see why it should be. My senses tell me, not that 'God exists', but that 'it is'.

The test for anyone whose balance depends on messages received through the senses will come when the senses begin to atrophy. When I can no longer see (my grandmother had not seen the stars for ten years before she died), when I can no longer hear (larks dwindled away first, she said, then all other birds), when my body, which has not only given me all my most reliable and consoling pleasures but has also helped me to go out of its limits into other people and into things, becomes no more than a painful burden – and think only of what it can do to one under the influence of something so trivial as indigestion! – what will happen then? It may turn out that the throbbing was no more than the sound of my own blood in my ears. What I hope is that even if it does I shall not be afraid, because why should that blood have throbbed so steadily, for so long, in spite of so many reasons why I need not have lived, if it were not that I too have *been*, with the same intensity as any flower or matchbox or dog or other human being: all part of something which can only be expressed in the words 'I am that which I am', and which needs no further proof or justification?

I should like to appoint someone younger than myself to be a witness at my death: to record my success or lack of it in coming to terms with death, as I mean to do if I can, by simultaneously remembering the pulse in my self, and defeating the passion for self-preservation which makes death seem an outrage (easily said! Let the hum of an aeroplane's engine turn to a whine and my body stiffens, my stomach chills: 'Not *yet*!'). To die decently and acceptingly would be to prove the value of life, and that, in spite of limitations and inadequacy, is what I have felt inclined, still feel inclined, and have a hunch that I will always feel inclined to do.

STET

an editor's life

PART ONE

1

SOME YEARS AGO Tom Powers, an American publisher who is also a writer and historian, kindly told me I ought to write a book about my fifty years in publishing. He added: 'Put in all the figures – that is what one wants to know.' With those well-intentioned words he nearly finished off this book before it was begun.

Partly – as I shall explain – from conditioning, and more – I am pretty sure – because of some kind of mental kink, I cannot remember figures. When I recall the various houses I have lived in in London I can see the colours of their front doors, the way the steps leading to those doors were worn, what kind of railings guarded their areas; but not one of their numbers can I remember. My bank account has had the same number for years and years, but I still have to consult my chequebook every time I need to produce it. When I needed to tell one of my authors how many copies of his or her book we were printing, I could – having all the material to hand – tell them; but ask me three months later, was it three thousand or five, and I would not know. The only publishing figures that remain with me are the shaming £25 we paid Jean Rhys for an option to see her novel *Wide Sargasso Sea*, and the impressive (at that time) £30,000 we were paid for the serial rights of Franz von Papen's memoirs.

But surely I could research the figures?

No, I could not.

Soon after André Deutsch Limited, the firm of which I had been one of the directors since it was founded almost forty years earlier, was sold to Tom Rosenthal in 1985, Tom sold its complete archive to Tulsa University in Oklahoma, and I have neither the money nor the energy to go to Tulsa and dive into that mountain of paper. And I confess that I am grateful for those lacks because of another one: good researchers enjoy researching, which I have never done, and I am not going to develop the instinct for it now that I am in my eighties. So I am sorry that this will not be the useful kind of book which would interest Tom Powers, but there it is.

Why am I going to write it? Not because I want to provide a history of British publishing in the second half of the twentieth century, but because I shall not be alive for much longer, and when I am gone all the experiences stored in my head will be gone too – they will be deleted with one swipe of the great eraser, and something in me squeaks 'Oh no – let at least some of it be rescued!' It seems to be an instinctive twitch rather than a rational intention, but no less compelling for that. By a long-established printer's convention, a copy editor wanting to rescue a deletion puts a row of dots under it and writes 'Stet' (let it stand) in the margin. This book is an attempt to 'Stet' some part of my experience in its original form (which happens to be sadly short of figures). Other people have given better accounts of our trade (notably Jeremy Lewis in *Kindred Spirits*, which is not only a delight, but also says everything which needs saying about what has happened to publishing, and why). All this book is, is the story of one old ex-editor who imagines that she will feel a little less dead if a few people read it.

The story began with my father telling me: 'You will have to earn your living.' He said it to me several times during my childhood (which began in 1917), and the way he said it implied that earning one's living was not quite natural. I do not remember resenting the idea, but it was slightly alarming. This was because my great-grandfather on my mother's side, a Yorkshire doctor of yeoman stock, had made or married the money to buy a beautiful house in Norfolk with a thousand acres of land, which seemed to the children of my generation to have been 'ours' from time immemorial. It was largely because of this place that my mother's family was the one to which I felt that I belonged. My father's had lost money, not made it, so they had no land for us to feel rooted in. They had taken off from Norfolk to Antigua in the seventeenth century, had done very well as sugar planters, but had eventually fizzled out financially with their trade, so that by my time several generations of Athill men had taken the earning of livings for granted. But even on their more down-to-earth side, mine was the first generation in which this applied to daughters as well as sons. Daughters would not, of course, have to earn their livings if they got married, but (this was never *said*) now that they would have to depend on love unaided by dowries, marriage could no longer be counted on with absolute confidence.

Not until recently, when in my old age I began to ponder my career in publishing, did it occur to me that my family background had done a lot to determine the nature of that career.

In 1952, after working with André Deutsch for five years in his first publishing firm, Allan Wingate, I became a founding director with him of his second firm, to which we gave his name. I can therefore say that for nearly fifty years I was a publisher, but the truth is that I was not, and it was my background that prevented it.

Although for all my life I have been much nearer poor than rich, I have inherited a symptom of richness: I have a strong propensity for idleness. Somewhere within me lurks an unregenerate creature which feels that money ought to fall from the sky, like rain. Should it fail to do so – too bad: like a farmer enduring drought one would get by somehow, or go under, which would be unpleasant but not so unpleasant as having blighted one's days by bothering about money. Naturally I always knew that one did in fact have to bother, and to some extent I did so, but only to the least possible extent. This meant that although I never went so far as to choose to do nothing, I did find it almost impossible to do anything I didn't want to do. Whether it was 'cannot' or 'will not' I don't know, but it felt like 'cannot'; and the things I could not do included many of the things a publisher had to do.

A publishing firm is a complicated business which has to buy, sell and manufacture or cause to be manufactured. What it buys and sells is products of people's imaginations, the materials for making books, and a variety of legal rights. What it manufactures is never the same from one item to the next. So a publisher must be able to understand and control a complex financial and technical structure; he must be a smart negotiator, good at bargaining; he must have a shrewd instinct for when to lash out and when to penny-pinch; he must be able efficiently to administer an office full of people, or to see that it is efficiently administered; and above all he must be able to sell his wares in all their forms. Against this, all I have ever been able to do with money is spend it; I loathe responsibility and telling people what to do; and above all I am incapable of selling anything to anyone. Not being a fool, I was well aware of the importance of all the aspects of my trade which I couldn't and didn't want to master, and even came to know a fair amount about them. But although I felt guilty about my own incapacities, the only part of the business that I could ever bring myself *truly to mind about* was the choosing and editing of books. This is certainly a very important part of the publishing process, but without all the rest of it, it would amount to nothing.

So I was not a publisher. I was an editor.

And even as an editor, a job which I thoroughly enjoyed, I betrayed my amateurish nature by drawing the line at working outside office hours. The working breakfast, and taking work home at weekends – two activities regarded by many as necessary evidence of commitment, both of them much indulged in by that born publisher, André Deutsch – were to me an abomination. Very rarely someone from my work moved over into my private life, but generally office and home were far apart, and home was much more important than office. And whereas I was ashamed of my limitations within the office, I was not ashamed of valuing my private life more highly than my work: that, to my mind, is what everyone ought to do.

In spite of this, being an editor did enlarge and extend my life in a way for which I am deeply grateful. It gave me a daily occupation which brought in enough money to live on and which was almost always enjoyable, and it constantly proved the truth of that ancient cliché about working in publishing: You Meet Such Interesting People. The first part of this book is about the daily occupation. The second part is about some of the people.

2

ALTHOUGH MY FAMILY contributed to my limitations in publishing, they prepared me well for editing. Asking myself what were the most important things in my childhood, I get the answer 'Falling in love, riding and reading'.

They all started early. I can't have been more than four when I first fell in love, because surely someone who attempted communication with the beloved by leaning out of a window and spitting on his head can't have been older than that? He was the gardener's 'boy', his name was Denis, he had melancholy brown eyes, and every day he manned a green iron hand-pump by the back door to provide us with bath water. Each crank of the pump-handle was followed by a splosh in the tank in the attic above the lavatory – rich, cascading sploshes to start with, gradually turning to meagre little splishes. One day, hearing the pump at work, I went into the lavatory to lean out of the window and gaze fondly down on the flat cap below, until I became unable to resist the longing for communication, collected a mouthful of saliva, and spat. He felt it, looked up, those beautiful brown eyes met mine – and I shot out of the lavatory, scarlet and breathless with excitement. After which I was never, so far as I can remember, out of love.

The riding, too, started earlier than it could properly be done. When my mother, instead of Nanny, took me out she disliked pushing the pram, so a strange little saddle shaped like a miniature chair was strapped onto an aged pony and I was tied into it, to be led over grass instead of pushed along paths – a lovely improvement, heralding many years of being on a pony or a horse pretty well whenever I was out of doors.

And reading started with being read aloud to, which went on to overlap with one's own reading because my grandmother (we lived near her for many years) read aloud so beautifully that we never tired of listening to her. She might be doing a Beatrix Potter or the *Just So Stories* for the little ones, or *Uncle Remus* or *The Jungle Book* for the middle ones, or *Kim* or a Walter Scott (skipping the boring bits so cleverly that we never knew they were there) for the bigger ones, and whichever it was, everyone would be listening because she made them so marvellous. And everywhere we looked there were books. In our own house they were piled on tables and chairs, as well as on the shelves; and in Gran's house, where we so often were, they rose from floor to ceiling all round the library, along one whole wall in the morning-room, on three walls of my grandfather's study, along the full length of a passage called 'the corridor', and along three-quarters of a wall in the nursery. At Christmas and birthdays about eighty per cent of the presents we got were books, and no one was ever told not to read anything. My grandmother's father had been Master of University College, Oxford, and my grandfather, who wooed her when he was an undergraduate, had written several prize essays (which she kept and published privately after his death) which suggest by their distinction that he must have thought about becoming a professional historian before his father's death made him a contented landed gentleman. It never occurred to anyone in that family that reading could be a duty, so it never occurred to me. Reading was what one did indoors, as riding was what one did out of doors: an essential part of life, rather than a mere pleasure. As I grew older and 'You will have to earn your living' changed from being something my father said to being a real prospect, I was not bold enough to imagine myself worthy of work in publishing, but I would never have doubted that such work was the most desirable of all.

If publishing was too glamorous for me, what was I going to do? I was reasonably intelligent, I had been to Oxford . . . but I had certainly not qualified myself for anything while there. Indeed, it was at Oxford that my idleness found its fullest expression and all I did there was enjoy the best time of my life. Teaching was, I supposed, a possibility, or nursing; but both inspired in me the sensation of being faced with a bucket of cold porridge. And I didn't really know of any other kind of work. A vast difference between then and now is that then a middle-class Englishwoman in her early twenties could, without being exceptional, know not a single woman of her own age who was in a job. I had a fair number of friends, but to none of them could I turn for guidance.

Before the problem could become truly agitating it was blown away by the beginning of the Second World War, which made it unnecessary – even impossible – to think in terms of a career. You had to bundle into whatever war-work offered itself and get on with it. If you liked it, lucky you. If not, that was just a part of the general bloodiness of war and you expected yourself to endure it without making a fuss.

I was lucky. After a couple of false starts I was given a nudge towards the BBC by an Oxford friend who happened to have found a job in its recruitment office and thought I would have a chance of getting into a new information service that was to be attached to Overseas News. I did get in, and was allowed to stay there until the end of the war. I forget which Ministry it was that controlled the matter, but all jobs were reviewed from time to time, and if you were seen to be making no contribution to the war effort you were directed into something more useful. Telling the Overseas News Room who General de Gaulle was or how much oil was produced by the wells of Ploeşti was work classified as essential, so my wartime lot was an easy job shared with pleasant companions. The job was easy because an information service is only a matter of knowing where to look things up – and anyway, in those days the BBC confused *The Times* with Holy Writ: you showed someone a cutting from *The Times* and he believed it★.

★ The BBC's Information Services were initiated by a man called Bachelor, who had built up the same kind of service for *The Times*. We used to laugh at our customers' dependence on the newspaper, but the truth was that thanks to Mr Bachelor it was amazingly well-served with information. It had a slight edge on us because its press-cuttings library had been going for longer and was therefore larger; but we were no less admirably structured and no less keenly scrupulous. By the time I got there Batch, as we called him, had become too grand to be often seen by his minions, but he was undoubtedly brilliant at his job.

3

WITH ONE OF those BBC companions, after a while, I launched into flat-sharing. Until then I had lived in billets while our office was evacuated to Evesham in Worcestershire for safety's sake, and in a sequence of depressing bedsitters when we were brought back to London to await Hitler's secret weapons, the flying bombs and the long-range missiles. The flat was the two top floors of a stately house in Devonshire Place, one of the streets traditionally inhabited by England's most expensive doctors who had left a temporary vacuum in the neighbourhood when carried away by the war. Marjorie and I had the top floor, which included the kitchen. George Weidenfeld and Henry Swanzy had the floor below us.

The few young men in the BBC at that time had to be exempt from military service. George was exempt because he was still an Austrian, Henry because . . . and I suddenly see that I don't know why Henry was exempt, which speaks well for the Second World War compared with the First. In the First a feverish jingoism prevailed, with women thrusting white feathers on men simply because they were not in uniform. In the Second I never saw or heard of any jingoism. Perhaps Henry was disqualified for active service by some weakness in his health, or perhaps he was a conscientious objector who was considered more useful in the BBC than down a coal mine. Probably I once knew, but if so it was unimportant to me and my friends. Anyway, there he was, sharing the flat at first with George and a man called Lester Something, and when Lester moved away from London, with George, Marjorie and me. George was wooing Marjorie at the time, so our inclusion was probably his idea.

The men's floor had an enviable bathroom, all black glass and chrome, given extra distinction by containing a piano on which Henry often played moody music. Our bathroom was very mere – it had probably been the maids' – but the kitchen gave us an advantage since what communal living went on in the flat had necessarily to centre on it. Neither Marjorie's parents nor mine questioned the propriety of our ménage – but whether this was because they chose to believe us unshakeably chaste, or because we avoided mentioning George and Henry, I no longer remember.

The two of us who ended up in bed together were Marjorie and George. She fell seriously in love with him, causing some of our colleagues to exclaim 'Yuck!' and 'How could she?', because George at twenty-four already had a portly presence and a frog face. But he also had five times the intelligence of most of the young men we knew, and a great deal of sexual magnetism. I soon noticed – though Marjorie did not – that the women whose 'Yucks!' were the most emphatic were usually in bed with him before a month was out.

To be more exact, I did not notice this, but heard it from George himself, because in his early salad days he relished his sexual success too much to be discreet about it. He kept a list of his conquests at the back of his pocket diary, and would bring it out to show me when we were in the kitchen together without Marjorie. I remember him saying gleefully: 'Look – the fiftieth!'

At that time I was all but unsexed by sadness, because the man I was engaged to, who was serving in the Middle East, had first gone silent on me, then married someone else, then been killed. A little later I would start to find that promiscuity cheered me up, but our Devonshire Place days were too early for that. My inner life was bleak, which made surface entertainment all the more important. If Marjorie had been sailing into happiness with George I might have found the spectacle intolerably painful; but as it was, although I liked her and was far from wishing her ill, I found watching the relationship so interesting that it became enjoyable – the first time that I was shocked by my own beady eye.

After eight or nine months Lester came back and claimed his half of the apartment, so Marjorie went to live with her parents for a while and I returned to bedsitters. Just before we left, our kitchen witnessed a significant event: the four of us chose a name for the periodical which George would soon be editing. After much list-making and many disappointments when good names turned out to have been used already, *Contact* was picked. During one of our naming sessions, when we had drifted onto other subjects and one of us asked George what his central ambition was, he replied: 'Very simple – to be a success.' So that was where George's publishing career began, and where its direction first became apparent; and soon afterwards, because of someone I met through George, my own publishing career put out the first pale tip of an underground shoot, like a deeply buried bulb.

Before this happened I had begun to feel a good deal better, partly because I had the luck to fall into a frivolous and enjoyable affair, and partly because Marjorie's mother's dentist told her that he wanted to let the top floor of his house in Queen Anne Street, which is a few minutes from Devonshire Place, and Marjorie and I took it. The dentist had converted this floor into an elegant little flat for his son, who had killed himself in its kitchen by putting his head in the gas oven – which we did not at first enjoy using. But soon we began to think that the poor young man must have had a weak personality, because no flat could have had a pleasanter atmosphere. Devonshire Place had been fun, but also uncomfortable and shabby to the point of squalor. Queen Anne Street was a delight to come home to.

So we decided to celebrate it by giving a party. George came, of course, and brought André Deutsch, the man who had introduced him to the publishing firm which was going to produce and distribute *Contact*: a firm which would soon cease to exist, called Nicholson and Watson. André, a Hungarian the same age as

I was (twenty-six), had come to England to study economics, had been caught by the war, and had been interned as an enemy alien on the Isle of Man. The Hungarians were soon let out on condition that they reported regularly to the authorities, and André returned to London armed with a letter from a fellow internee to a well-known bookseller who had passed him on to John Roberts, managing director of Nicholson and Watson. Roberts, a kind, lazy, rather boozy man who was struggling to keep the firm going almost single-handed, took him on as a salesman and was pleased to discover that he had acquired an intelligent and energetic young man who was greedy to learn every aspect of the trade: who was, in fact, finding his vocation. By the time André came to our party he was doing much more for the firm than visiting booksellers and librarians – not that I was bothered about that. He could have been a junior packer for all I cared. His being the first person I had ever met who was 'in publishing' was enough to exalt him in my eyes.

He was small, trim and good-looking in a boyish way. I remember thinking that his mouth was as fresh and soft-looking as a child's, and being surprised that I found it attractive – usually I liked my men on the rugged side. He sat on the floor and sang 'The foggy foggy dew', which was unexpected in a Hungarian, and charming, so that I was more aware of him than of anyone else in the room. Two days later, when he asked me to dinner and a theatre, I was gratified. He was living in a tiny house in a Knightsbridge mews, and that was impressive, too. The possibility of having a house had never entered my head. André's had been lent him by a friend who was away on war-work, but it seemed like his, which made him more 'grown-up' than I was. In that little house, after the theatre, we ate an omelette and went to bed together, without – as I remember it – much excitement on either side.

In old age I can still remember the matchless intoxication of falling in love (which may well be a neurotic condition, but still nothing else lights up the whole of one's being in that way) and the more common but no less delicious sensations of a powerful physical attraction; but I have gone blurry about the kind of affair I had with André. I wonder what took me into such affairs, and what held me in them, almost always, until the man moved on. Rather than remembering, I have to work it out.

It was not thinking myself in love when I was not – I was too clear-sighted for that. And it was not simply the nesting instinct, because I was romantic enough (or perhaps realist enough?) to be sure that I couldn't marry a man I didn't love. To start with it was probably curiosity – a cat-like impulse to poke my nose round the next corner – combined with the emptiness of my emotional life at the time: this would at least seem to fill it. And once it had got going . . . well, perhaps the nesting instinct did start to come into it, after all. Although I knew from experience that whenever I genuinely fell in love it happened almost on sight, perhaps in this other kind of affair I allowed myself to slide into a vague hope that this time, given the chance, love might develop. And anyway I was pleased to be wanted; I liked the social and erotic occupations involved; I enjoyed being fond of someone; and I continued to be moved by curiosity. Quite early in my career the image of a glass-bottomed boat came to me as an apt one for sex; a lovemaking relationship with a man offered chances to peer at what went on under his surface. Once, listening to someone as he told me for the third time a story about his childhood, I caught myself thinking 'He's a squeezed orange' . . . oh dear, the beady eye again!

It was soon apparent that André and I would not be lovers for long. I felt that I could have enjoyed making love with him if he had been more enthusiastic about making love with me, and given my essential coldness since the shock of losing the man I really wanted, he probably felt the same about me: less than adequate grounds for an affair. And he was an insomniac whose bed, though a double one, was not wide. When I wanted to sleep, he wanted to sit up and read *The Times*, and what he wanted to do he did, with much uninhibited rustling: it was his house, his bed – and insomnia commands respect while somnolence is boring. Englishwomen are notorious for somnolence, he told me tetchily. He often remarked on the shortcomings of the English as lovers, a habit shared by many continental men with a touching failure to see how easily it can provoke the bitten-back response 'Who are you to talk?' Rather than enjoying the dozen or so nights we spent together, we went through them 'because they were there', and the only sadness I felt when he moved on to another bedfellow was the knee-jerk reaction 'There you are, you see – you're unable to keep *anyone*'. Understanding that I owed this droopy feeling to the fiancé who had jilted me, I didn't hold it against André. It turned out that the slightness of our affair did not matter because – mystifyingly given how unlike we are in temperament – we had ended it as friends.

We continued to meet, I became his confidante about his love-life, and he introduced me to his other friends: a handful of other Hungarians and three or four likeable and intelligent older women who had more or less adopted him. Two of the women ran an organization which helped to settle refugees, in which he had done part-time work before being interned; one – Sheila Dunn, who became a dear friend of mine – was the aunt of a girl he'd had an affair with; and one – Audrey Harvey – was an old friend of Sheila's. Because of my inwardly broken-spirited state, when we met I knew no one in London apart from the people I worked with; while my pre-war friends were scattered and out of reach. Even the merry lover who had done me (and was still intermittently doing me) so much good came from a neighbouring department of the BBC's Overseas Service; and anyway we saw each other only to dine and hop into bed because he was both married and busy. The sudden acquisition of a group shading from slight but amusing acquaintances to great friends was an important pleasure.

The first flying bomb came over while I was lying awake in André's bed. Its engine-sound was strange but we assumed that it was a plane, and that the sudden silence followed by an explosion as it landed meant that it had been shot down. The news next day that it was Hitler's 'secret weapon', which we had all been trying not to believe in, was the most frightening news that had yet hit us. As well as fearing the pilotless engine-driven bomb in itself, you feared the idea of being panicked by it; so it seemed best not to think about it, and that was how most people dealt with it, confining their fear to the short time between first hearing one of the horrible things approaching, and feeling guilty relief when it chuntered past without its engine cutting out, to fall on someone else. When the V2s took over – huge missiles launched at us from hundreds of miles away – I thought them less bad because they came down bang, without a whisper of warning, so you might be killed but you didn't have time to feel afraid. (In retrospect I find them the more frightening of the two.) To get a good night's sleep, André and I sometimes spent weekends with Audrey Harvey, who lived about an hour by train from Marylebone Station. Sheila would be there too, and usually one or two of the Hungarians: how dear generous Audrey found suppers and breakfasts for us in those tightly rationed days I can't remember: I suppose we took our rations with us. These were delightful occasions, which contributed a good deal to the feeling of being 'family' which grew up between André and me.

It was this feeling which made it natural for us both to expect me to be involved in his plans when he decided that he would start a publishing house as soon as the war ended . . . not that my own expectations, to begin with, were anything but provisional. He had no money and no connections: how could he possibly start a publishing house? It was like someone saying 'When I win the football pools'. But of course if he *did* win them, I would want to be in on it.

He asked me one day – we were walking arm in arm down Frith Street – 'What's the minimum you'd need to earn, to start with?' I didn't know what to say. I would like it to be more than the £380 a year I was getting from the BBC, but I didn't want to sound greedy. Impatient with my hesitation he said: 'What about £500?' and I replied: 'That would be lovely.' It sounded a lot to me, but we were only talking about a dream so what did it matter?

We spent VE Day (Victory in Europe) together, milling about the West End in a mass of people who mostly seemed deeply relieved rather than over the top with joy. Certainly my own feeling, which I had to keep stoking up to overcome incredulity, was 'It's over!' rather than 'We've won!' VJ Day (Victory over Japan) worked better – unlike more sensitive people among my friends I felt on that day no shadow of horror at the Atom Bomb: that came later. We were swept into the crowd which surged up the Mall to call the royal family out onto the balcony over and over again, and there was no resisting the mood engendered by that crowd. It was one of a joy so benign that it was no surprise to read in a newspaper report next morning that although people had stood all over the flower beds in front of the palace, they had placed their feet so carefully that hardly a single plant had been damaged.

4

ANDRÉ STARTED HIS first publishing house, Allan Wingate, late in 1945. I missed its first month or so because I did not leave the BBC until after July that year, then took a refreshing break at home in Norfolk. I know I was still in the BBC in July because a wonderfully exhilarating experience – more so, even, than VJ Day – was spending the whole night in the Overseas News Room when the results of the first post-war election were coming over the ticker-tape machine, and we gradually realized that Labour was winning. That *was* a matter of 'We've won!' Other people's memories of the years just after the war often stress the continuation of rationing and 'austerity', and a sense of fatigue, but it didn't feel like that to me. Recovery was slow – how could it be anything else? – but it was going on all the time. Why fret when it was evident that things were getting better and better, and that society was going to be juster and more generous than it had ever been before? And for many years to come the existence, and smooth functioning, of the National Health Service was by itself (how can people forget this?) enough to justify this now naive-seeming optimism.

One of the things I missed was the naming of André's firm. Before I left for Norfolk we had spent an evening together looking through the London telephone directory for a name beginning with D that he could feel at home with. (His father had written from Hungary, urging him not to use his own name, on the grounds that

English people would think he was German and would resent him.) His reason for wanting to keep his initials was that he had just had them embroidered on some new shirts, the logic of which was as obscure to me then as it is now, and proved too flimsy to overcome his lack of response to any of the D-names in the book. Although I disagreed with his father (what about Heinemann?), I liked the name he hit on while I was away. It sounded so convincing that people sometimes said they were glad to see the firm in business again, as though we were reviving a house that had existed before the war.

By the time I got back to London André had rented an office – the ground floor of a late Georgian house in Great Cumberland Place, near Marble Arch – and had moved into it with Mr Kaufmann who was to be our accountant; two secretaries; Mr Brown our packer; and Audrey Harvey who had put up some of the capital and was to edit *Junior*, a magazine for children, under our imprint. Sheila Dunn, who drew well and wittily and made her small living as a commercial artist, was to come in part-time as Audrey's art editor, and a gravely handsome man called Vincent Stuart was to design our books on a freelance basis. A figure in the background who remained shadowy to me was Alex Lederer, a manufacturer of handbags who had provided the greater part of the capital. My innate amateurishness is demonstrated by my lack of interest in how André persuaded this agreeable but alien being to cough up: it never occurred to me to ask. I did know, however, that our capital as a whole amounted to £3,000, and that it was generally held that no publishing company could make a go of it with less than £15,000: we were constantly reminded of that by André, as he urged us to recycle used envelopes, switch off lights behind us, and generally exercise the strictest economy in every possible way.

We had at our disposal a large front room, once the house's dining-room, with two tall windows and a pompous marble chimneypiece; a smaller back room – perhaps once the owner's study? – looking out into a well; a wide passage along the side of the well accommodating Mr Brown and his packing-bench; and at the end of the passage a lavatory and a small one-storey extension in which Mr Kaufmann lurked, which looked back across the well to the 'study'.

Although at the BBC I had shared an office with several other people, I was dismayed by the front room when I first saw it. André had his desk at one of the windows, Audrey hers at the other end of the room, and against the wall opposite the fireplace there was a rather handsome dining-room table almost hidden under piles of manuscripts, paper samples, reference books and so on – we had as yet no shelves, cupboards or filing cabinets. A corner of this table was to be mine, and Sheila was to use another corner on the two or three days a week when she would be in. It seemed likely that the work would need more concentration than anything I had done before, and here I would be, sandwiched in the exiguous space between the intense working lives of other people, with their animated telephone conversations and frequent visitors . . . would I be able to endure it?

The discomfort I went through to begin with – there must have been some – has faded from my mind, but I remember clearly a moment which occurred after three or four weeks. It was lunch-time; I pushed aside my work and looked round the room. There was André arguing for better terms with a printer's representative, Audrey talking to one of her authors who had two children in tow, Sheila going through a portfolio of drawings with an artist. 'How amazingly adaptable people are,' I thought. 'Until I happened to look round this room, I might have been alone in it.'

My job was to read, edit, copy-edit, proofread, and also to look after the advertising, which meant copy-writing and designing as well as booking space after André had told me which books he wanted advertised in which newspapers, and had given me a budget. Although reading and editing were by far the most interesting of my tasks, they did not at first seem the most important. This was because I could do them easily: I had read a lot and I was developing confidence in my own judgement. Against which I had never before even speculated as to how advertisements got into newspapers, and as soon as I had learnt what the process was I saw that I would be no good at an important part of it. Booking space was no problem, but after that was done I had to persuade the advertising manager of the paper concerned that although our space was a small one (usually a six or eight inch single column) it should be given the kind of conspicuous position usually occupied by much larger ads. This, to André's incredulous indignation, I hardly ever achieved, and almost every time I failed he would telephone the newspaper's man and tell him that next time he must give us an even better position to make up for his disgraceful failure this time – which the wretched man would usually do. But not without imploring me to keep André off his back because he couldn't go on inviting trouble for himself by granting such favours. I was soon feeling sick at the mere sound of the word 'advertising', and the fact that I continued to carry this albatross round my neck for several years is evidence of the power André could exercise by the simple means of being utterly convinced that what he wanted was *right*.

Over the advertising he was aided by my own guilt at evading so many other disagreeable things: it was ample expiation. But his power *was* extraordinary. Watching him use it I often thought I was witnessing the secret of the successful pathological liar: the one who persuades businessmen and politicians to back crackpot ventures. The liar is, of course, helped by the greed and gullibility of his victims, but he could not succeed on a grand scale without the 'magical' persuasiveness which comes from utter self-persuasion. How lucky, I used to think, that André is by nature an honest man, or where would we all be?

Another of his characteristics which I learnt at this time was less useful – indeed, it was to be his great weakness as a manager of people. He saw everything not done *exactly* as he himself would have done it as being done wrong – enragingly wrong – and anything that was done right as not worth comment. Things often were done wrong to begin with, and his vigilance taught us a lot, but the apparent indifference which took the place of carping when all was well was discouraging. Sheila and I often pointed out that praise and kindness made people work better as well as feel happier, and he would promise to mend his ways, but he never did.

For a while my experience of this in connection with the advertising was painful. I think I was brave in the way I plunged into the unfamiliar task, and showed fortitude in overcoming my nature and going on with it for years in spite of loathing it (except for the bits which involved messing about with pencil, ruler and eraser, which I quite liked).

True to form, André was always sharply critical, not only of my feebleness with the papers' advertising managers, but also of the wording and spacing within each ad. For some time this was helpful, then the implication that I was bad at this boring task into which he had shoved me began to get at me, so though I could soon see for myself that my ads didn't look too bad, a muted drone of guilt was gradually induced, to underlie this side of my work.

It threatened for a time to underlie everything, because once André's nagging focused on someone it did so with increasing intensity. I was sometimes slapdash about detail which struck me as unimportant. I might, for example, forget (not when dealing with a book's text, but perhaps when typing out an ad or the blurb for a jacket) that it was our house style to use single quotation marks, reserving double ones for quotations within quotations. When something like this happened André's shock would be extreme. 'How can I go to Paris next week if I can't trust you over something as simple as this? Don't you realize what it would cost to correct that if it got through to proof stage?' . . . and there would be a slight crescendo in guilt's drone. And a creepy result was that one began to make more and worse mistakes. I was to see this happening over and over again to other people after the nagging had swivelled away from me (I came to envisage it as a wicked little searchlight always seeking out a victim). It could escalate with mystifying speed until you began to dread going into the office. You knew that justice was really on your side in that he was making an absurd and sometimes cruel fuss over small matters, but you had been manoeuvred into a position where you couldn't *claim* this without appearing to be indifferent to the ideals of perfection to which we were all devoted. I can still recall the sensation of tattered nerves which came from the mixture of indignation and guilt which ensued.

To polish off this disagreeable subject, I must skip forward a few months to a time when he returned from one of those trips to Paris (they were book-hunting trips) and asked me for the key of his car. 'What do you mean? I haven't got it' – and he exploded. 'Oh my God – you're impossible! I gave it to you just before I left. What have you done with it?' I was stunned: how, in six short days, could I have forgotten something so important? I struggled to recall taking the key from him and was unable to summon up the least shadow of it, but his conviction was absolute and my own awareness of my shortcomings was inflamed: I had to believe that he had given me that key, and I truly feared that I might be losing my mind. I went home in misery, worried all night over this sudden softening of my brain, and next morning it was all I could do to crawl back to the office.

André's car was parked outside it, and he was at his desk looking cheerful. How, I asked tremulously, had he got it started? 'Oh that . . .' he said. 'I didn't leave the key with you after all, I left it with the man at the garage.'

That silenced the guilt drone for ever, and soon afterwards I learnt to disregard unnecessary fusses when what he was complaining of was something being done in way B instead of way A, and how to forestall his rage when I had genuinely erred. It was simple: a quick resort to *mea culpa*. 'Oh André – I've done such a dreadful thing. They've spelt Stephens with a v on the back flap of the jacket and I didn't notice!' – 'Is it too late to correct?' – 'Yes, that's what's so *frightful*.' – 'Oh well, worse things have happened. You'll have to apologize to Stephens – and *do* remember to get someone to give your jacket proofs a second reading.' End of scene. Once I had twigged that confession always took the wind out of his sails I had no more trouble from the 'searchlight'. But there would rarely be a time during the next fifty years when it was not making life a misery for someone, and working first in Allan Wingate, then in André Deutsch, would have been a great deal more pleasant if this had not been so.

One feels the lack of counterpoint when using words. Anyone reading the above account of André's nagging might wonder why I continued to work for him; but that was only one thread in many. I was doing and enjoying other parts of the job in addition to the advertising, while as for André . . .

It was not easy to summarize his activities. He read books; he hunted books; he thought books up; for several years he did all the selling of books, and the buying and selling of book rights; he bought paper; he dealt with printers, binders and blockmakers; he made all the decisions about the promotion of our books; he checked every detail of their design; he checked copy-writing, proofreading, important letters; he soothed and cajoled the bank; he persuaded suppliers to give us unprecedented credit; he raised capital out of the blue when we could no longer pay our bills; he delivered books in Aggie, his Baby Austin named after its AGY registration number (I did that, too); if we were sending out leaflets he sat on the floor stuffing them into envelopes until after midnight and always did more to the minute than anyone else; and his own pulse was no more part of him than his awareness of our turnover and overheads. He also did all the firm's remembering – the car-key incident was unique. Usually his memory for detail was so good as to be almost frightening. He had learnt his way about his trade so rapidly and so thoroughly, and had committed himself to it so whole-heartedly, that it is not fanciful to describe him as someone who had discovered his vocation. One never doubted that the firm, having been created by him, was now being kept going by him: if he had withdrawn from it, it would have ceased to exist.

Dictatorships work: that is why they are so readily accepted, and if they are demonstrably more or less just, as they can be to start with, they are accepted with a gratitude more personal than can be inspired by other kinds of regime. In its miniature way André's dictatorship was strong for the following reasons: he had already learnt so much about publishing while those working for him still knew nothing; it was his nature to turn ideas into action without delay, which is a rare gift; while he paid us mingy salaries he also paid himself a mingy salary, and the company was so small that we could all see with our own eyes that there was no money available for anything else; when he was mean, chiselling down payments, scrounging discounts, running after us to switch off lights and so on, even though he was certainly not offending against his nature, yet he was still always and evidently doing it for the company's sake; and when he nagged and raged, even when it was maddeningly out of proportion with the offence, that too was always and evidently for the company's sake. Reasonable explanation of errors and amiable encouragement to avoid them would have been more effective as well as pleasanter, but if such behaviour didn't come naturally to him, too bad: we would have to put up with him as he was which, on the whole, we were glad to do. Sheila and I, in particular, who were the people closest to him, had such a habit of fondness for him that it never occurred to us to do anything else.

So there we were, the strain and gloom of war gradually fading away behind us, starting on a delightful adventure supported and exhilarated by the energies and abilities of the man who had launched it. Even if the ride had its bumpy moments there was no question of wishing to climb down.

5

I REMEMBER ALLAN WINGATE'S first premises rather than its first books simply because the first books were so feeble that I blush for them. The firm kicked off with a list of four: *Route to Potsdam*, a piece of political journalism commenting on the Allies' plans for Europe, by Bela Ivanyi, one of André's Hungarian friends, the argument of which had no perceptible effect on anyone; *Beds*, a boring history of mankind's sleeping habits by Reginald Reynolds, to whom André had been introduced by George Orwell; *Fats and Figures*, a little book on diet, sensible but hardly more than a pamphlet, by a prison governor who was to become Lord Taylor; and the fourth has vanished from my mind. To start with André simply snatched at any homeless manuscript that happened to float by, and the reading public just after the war was so starved of books and so short of alternative forms of entertainment that almost anything (in our case almost nothing) could be presented by a publisher without looking silly.

A sad irony underlay this situation. While André was with Nicolson and Watson George Orwell submitted *Animal Farm* to them and John Roberts asked André to read it for him. André declared it wonderful, but Roberts, when he heard what it was about, said: 'Nonsense, laddie – no one nowadays wants to make fun of Uncle Joe.' André, who was determined to help the penniless and modest Orwell whom he saw as almost saint-like, decided that Jonathan Cape was the right publisher for him, and Orwell took his advice. Cape accepted the book, but shared Roberts's doubts to the extent of making a condition: it must be checked by some sort of official authority to make sure that it was not considered damaging to the war effort. And it was so considered: His Majesty's Government sincerely hoped that Mr Cape would refrain from publishing something so sharply critical of our Soviet Ally – and Mr Cape did refrain.

Orwell, who by this time was getting pretty desperate and who knew that André was planning to start his own firm as soon as he could raise a little capital, then said to André: 'Look, why don't *you* do it? Why don't you start off your firm with it?' And André, strongly tempted to pounce but still far from sure that he would be able to start a firm however much he wanted to, felt that he must not let a man he liked and respected so deeply take such a risk. No, he said. And the essential resilience of his nature was later to be well illustrated by the fact that the more famous *Animal Farm* became, the prouder he was of his own early recognition of it and of his not letting Orwell take the risk of giving it to him, with never a moan at having lost this prize.

The first book we took on because of me still sits on my shelves, and fills me with astonishment. André, through Hungarian friends in Paris, had come to know several people in the French literary world, among them Gerard Hopkins. Hopkins suggested that he should look at the work of a writer called Noël Devaulx, so André brought back from a visit to Paris *The Tailor's Cake*, a tiny volume of seven stories which he dumped on my corner of the table: he couldn't read French while I, though I had spent no time with French people so had no confidence in speaking it, had been taught it very well and could read it nearly as easily as English. So the decision was to be mine.

There was a solemn awareness of responsibility. There was bafflement for a while, then an increasing fascination. These were surreal stories in which characters who assumed you knew more about them than you did moved through strange places, such as a busy sea-port which was nowhere near the sea, or a village in which everyone was old and silent except for foolish laughter, and which vanished the morning after the traveller had been benighted in it. Everything in these stories was described with a meticulous sobriety and precision, which gave them the concentrated reality of dreams. Perhaps they were allegories – but of what? The only thing I felt sure of was that the author was utterly convinced by them – he couldn't have written them in any other way.

I would soon begin to find such fantasies a waste of time – of my time, anyway – but then, in addition to liking the sobriety and precision of the style, I felt the pull of mystification: 'I can't understand this – probably, being beyond me, it is very special.' This common response to not seeing the point of something has a rather touching humility, but that doesn't save it – or so I now believe – from being a betrayal of intelligence which has allowed a good deal of junk to masquerade as art. Whether that matters much is another question: throughout my publishing life I thought it did, so I am glad to say that the publication of *The Tailor's Cake* in 1946, beautifully translated by Betty Askwith, was the only occasion on which I succumbed to the charm of mystification.

A more amusing aspect of that publication is that even in those book-hungry days we would have had to go far to find a piece of fiction more obviously unsaleable than those stories, yet once I had pronounced them good we didn't think twice about publishing them. And they cannot have been a hideous flop: given my sense of responsibility for them, and André's tendency to attribute blame, I would surely remember if they had been. It is sad to think that we did not appreciate the luxury of not having to ask ourselves 'Is it commercially viable?' in those happy days before that question set in.

At Wingate I was André's employee, not his partner. My opinion of a book might or might not influence his decision, but if he took something on without asking my opinion I accepted without question that it was my job to work on it whether I liked it or not. Usually my attitude was 'No doubt he knows best'. Partly this was a hangover from my original feeling that working with books was something for people cleverer and more serious than I was; partly

it was a realistic assessment of my own inexperience; and partly –
something which shocks me now that I recognize it – it was that old
inherited idleness: it didn't really matter enough to me what he
brought in, provided a large enough proportion of our books struck
me as good enough.

The first of these to appear on our list were of a sober – almost
stately – kind, a result of the post-war book famine which meant
that the reissue of classics was felt as a need. Villon and Heine, for
example. André had met a man called Bill Stirling who considered
himself capable of translating all the major poets of Europe.
Although in this he was aiming too high, he did produce trans-
lations of those two which were up to appearing in good-looking
bilingual volumes with which we could justly be pleased. We also
produced a good edition of the novels and poems of the Brontë
sisters edited by Phyllis Bentley, whose introduction stands up well
against modern Brontë scholarship, and who included examples of
their important juvenilia – the first time that had been done in a
British edition.

Our first two money-spinners could hardly have been less like
the above, or each other. The first was *How to be an Alien* by
George Mikes. André had been at school in Budapest with
George's younger brother, when he had glimpsed George enviously
as a dashing grown-up. Meeting again in London, as exiles, they
found that the years between them had concertinaed, and became
friends. George's little squib on being a foreigner in England
had an extraordinary success. Its foreign rights seemed to sell
themselves, it is still in print today, and it was the foundation stone
of a career as a humorous writer that kept George going
comfortably until his death in 1990. It also brought in Nicolas
Bentley, who would become our partner when André Deutsch
Limited was founded. A book so short needed to be given a little
more bulk by illustrations, and an author so foreign and unknown
could do with a familiar British name beside his own on the title-
page. André persuaded Nick with some difficulty to do twelve
drawings for *Alien* – and was never to let him forget that he had
been dubious enough about an alliance with these two flighty

central Europeans to fight for an outright fee of £100 rather than a cut of the royalties. When André refused to give way over this, Nick almost backed out. I don't know exactly what he eventually made out of those twelve drawings, but it was certainly well over £10,000. Nick and his wife Barbara were soon close friends of André and the woman who became André's great love soon after he had launched Wingate, to whom he would remain loyal for the rest of his life.

Our second money-spinner was *The Reader's Digest Omnibus*: the first important chunk of loot brought home by André from New York. He had seen at once how important an annual shopping trip to the United States would be, and built up a network of good relationships there with amazing speed. Knowing that he would have trouble persuading Audrey and me that he was not disgracing us all for life by taking on this project, he made no attempt to do so but simply announced the *fait accompli* and told us we must lump it. We did indeed wince and moan – I more than Audrey, because I had to proofread the thing and write its blurb. *The Reader's Digest* may have changed by now – I have never looked at it again since that intensive experience of it – but at the end of the forties its central message could fairly be represented by the following little story. A man is faced with the choice between doing something rather dishonest and making a fortune, or refusing to do something rather dishonest and staying poor. Virtuously, he chooses to stay poor – whereupon an unexpected turn of events connected with this choice makes him a *much bigger fortune* than he would have gained by the dishonest act. Looking back, I think that having started off so prune-faced about it, the least I should have done for dignity's sake was keep up the disapproval; but in fact the book's success was so great, and so many people seemed to think that we had been clever to get hold of it, that I ended by feeling quite pleased with it.

Two other books from those distant days were important to my apprenticeship. One was a serious technical account of developments in modern architecture which revealed an incidental pleasure to be found in editing: the way it can teach you a lot about a subject unfamiliar to you, which you might not otherwise have approached. The other was about the discovery of Tahiti, which taught me once and for all the true nature of my job.

The latter book was by a man who could not write. He had clumsily and laboriously put a great many words on paper because he happened to be obsessed by his subject. No one but a hungry young publisher building a list would have waded through his typescript, but having done so I realized that he knew everything it was possible to know about a significant and extraordinary event, and that his book would be a thoroughly respectable addition to our list if only it could be made readable.

André had recently met an urbane and cultivated old man who had just retired from governing a British outpost in the Pacific, and who had said that he hoped to find the occasional literary task with which to fill his time. We brought the two men together, the author agreed to pay Sir Whatsit a reasonable fee for editing his book, and the latter carried it off, sat on it for three months, then returned it to its author with his bill which the poor man paid at once before forwarding his 'finished' book to us. To my dismay I found that lazy old Sir Whatsit had become bored after about six pages, and from then on had done almost nothing: the book was still unreadable. Either we had to return it to its author with a cheque to cover the expense we had let him in for, or I would have to edit it myself. We were short of non-fiction. I did it myself.

I doubt if there was a sentence – certainly there was not a paragraph – that I did not alter and often have to retype, sending it chapter by chapter to the author for his approval which – although he was naturally grouchy – he always gave. I enjoyed the work. It was like removing layers of crumpled brown paper from an awkwardly shaped parcel, and revealing the attractive present which it contained (a good deal more satisfying than the minor tinkering involved when editing a competent writer). Soon after the book's publication it was reviewed in the *Times Literary Supplement*: an excellent book, said the reviewer, scholarly and full of fascinating detail, and beautifully written into the bargain. The author promptly sent me a clipping of this review, pinned to a short note. 'How nice of him,' I thought, 'he's going to say thank you!' What he said in fact was: 'You will observe the comment about the writing which confirms what I have thought all along, that none of that fuss about it was necessary.' When I had stopped laughing I accepted the message: an editor must never expect thanks (sometimes they come, but they must always be seen as a bonus). We must always remember that we are only midwives – if we want praise for progeny we must give birth to our own.

The most important book in the history of Allan Wingate was Norman Mailer's first novel, *The Naked and the Dead*, which came to us from an agent desperate because six of London's leading publishers had rejected it in spite of its crossing the Atlantic on a wave of excitement (it was one of those books, always American at that time, which are mysteriously preceded by a certainty that they will cause a stir). Our list had gained substance and our sales organization was seen to be good, but we were still too small to be any agent's first choice for a big book – or indeed even their seventh choice, had they not concluded that none of the more firmly established houses was going to make an offer.

The book was a war novel, all its characters soldiers going through hell in the Pacific, where Mailer himself had served. He was bent on conveying the nature of these soldiers and their experiences accurately, so naturally he wanted the men in his novel to speak like the men he had known, which meant using the words 'fuck' and 'fucking', and using them often. His American publishers had told him that although they knew it to be a great book, they could not publish it, and nor would anyone else (which appeared to be true) with those words spelt out. I believe the use of 'f—' was suggested; but 'fuck' and 'fucking' occurred so often that this would have made the dialogue look like fishnet, so 'fug' and 'fugging' were agreed as substitutes.

It might be argued that the six English publishers who rejected the book because of the obscenity of its language were less ridiculous than the American publisher who accepted this solution. Given the premiss from which they were all working, that 'fuck' was unprintably obscene, how could another word which sounded so nearly the same, and which was loaded with the same meaning, not be equally obscene? There has never, I think, been a clearer demonstration of the idiocy of making words taboo.

We, of course, pounced. It is many years since I reread the book and much of it is now hazy in my mind, but I still have a strong memory of a passage in which exhausted men are struggling to manhandle a gun out of deep mud, which makes me think that I was right in feeling that it was very good – a book which had genuinely expanded the range of my imagination. We wanted to restore the 'fucks' but dared not; and as it turned out we were right not to dare.

Review copies went out to the press about three weeks before publication, and the literary editor of the *Sunday Times* left his lying about in his office. The newspaper's editor, who was an old man nearing retirement, ambled in and chanced to pick it up and open it. The first thing to meet his eye was 'fug' . . . followed by 'fug' and 'fug' again. So that Sunday, on the paper's front page, there appeared a short but furious protest, written by the editor himself, against the projected publication of a book so vile that (and he truly did use these words) 'no decent man could leave it where his women or children might happen to see it'.

As always on a Sunday I was sleeping late, so I was cross when I had to answer the front-door bell at eight-thirty. There stood André, unshaven, a pair of trousers and a macintosh pulled on over his pyjamas, and a copy of the *Sunday Times* in his hand.

'Read this!'

'Oh my God!'

I was as alarmed as he was. The book was printed and bound – the first printing was large – it was a long book, expensive to manufacture . . . close to the wind as the firm was still having to sail, if this book was banned we would go down.

'Hurry and get some clothes on,' said André. 'We must rush a copy to Desmond MacCarthy – I've got his address.'

MacCarthy was the most influential reviewer then writing. We scribbled a note begging him to read the book at once and to say publicly that it was not obscene, then we set off in Aggie to push it through his letter-box. To insist on seeing him so early on a Sunday morning might, we felt, put him off. In retrospect, the chief value of our outing was that it was something to *do* in this nerve-racking situation: I don't think that MacCarthy's eventual response can have been more than civil, or I would not have forgotten it.

Next morning orders started pouring into the office, and only then did it occur to us that if we were not heading for disaster, it might be a triumph. Meanwhile we were instantly served with an injunction against publishing *The Naked and the Dead* until the Attorney General, Sir Hartley Shawcross, had considered the case and had given us permission to do so (if he did). Whether the injunction was handed over by the large and apparently amiable police detective who spent the morning questioning us all, or whether it came separately, I do not know.

During the next two or three weeks the flood of orders nearly submerged us, the frustration of not being able to supply them became acute, and the encouragement we received from everyone we knew began to make triumph seem more likely than disaster. Finally André persuaded an MP of his acquaintance to ask a question in the House of Commons about the book's fate: was the Attorney General going to ban it or not? The answer was no – a rather grudging one in that Shawcross said that he thought it was a bad book, but still no. So we were off – into, ironically, quite worrying financial problems, because we were hard put to it to pay for the several reprints we had to order.

What we gained from this adventure was more than a good and best-selling novel; more, even, than the presence of Norman Mailer on our list from then on. Overnight we began to be seen as a brave and dashing little firm, worth serious attention from agents handling interesting new writers, and André's welcome when he visited New York became even more richly rewarding.

6

ALLAN WINGATE'S PERFORMANCE looked quite impressive from the outside. Our books soon became more interesting and we produced them well – even elegantly – within the limits imposed by continuing paper rationing. (The quality of paper was poor, and there were regulations controlling the use of white space in a layout and so on, which made good typography a challenge for several years after the war.) And we were good, by the cottage-industry standards of the day, at selling. André's work as a rep for Nicolson and Watson had taught him a lot about booksellers and librarians (the latter our chief customers for fiction), and he never underestimated the importance of good relations with them: again and again we were told how rare and pleasing it was for the head of a publishing house to visit and listen to booksellers, as he often did, and to be ready to negotiate directly with them about, for example, returning copies if they had over-ordered, instead of leaving such matters to a rep. To begin with he did this because we *had* no reps – no sales department, for that matter – but it was an attitude which stayed with him for all his career. He would always be liked by the people to whom we sold our wares – vital to a firm like ours, which remained short of books which the trade *had* to stock such as works of reference, how-to-do-its, and the cosier and flashier sorts of entertainment book.

From the inside, however, we looked wobbly. This was because the experienced people who said it was impossible to start a

publishing firm on £3,000 were right. We were always running out
of money.

Not being able to pay our bills used to give me horrible
sensations of hollowness mixed with nausea, and I think that poor
Mr Kaufmann, the man who actually had to do the desperate
juggling which was supposed to stave off disaster, felt much the
same. To André, on the other hand, these crises appeared to be
invigorating, chiefly because he didn't feel 'I have run up bills I
can't pay', but 'These idiotic printers and binders are trying to
prevent me from publishing truly essential books which the world
needs and which will end by making enough money to pay them all
and to spare'. So although he recognized that he would have to
raise some more money somehow, he was never debilitated. Instead
he was inspired. Never, at the time when a crisis struck, did we
know anyone who wanted to invest in a struggling new publishing
house; but always, in a matter of days, André found such a person.
My own way of weathering a panic was by thrusting it aside and
concentrating grimly on what was under my nose – reading a
manuscript, designing an advertisement or whatever – so instead of
following his manoeuvres with the intelligent interest which would
have made this account so much more valuable, I kept my eyes
tight shut; and when I next opened them, there would be André,
cock-a-hoop, with a new director in tow. This happened five times.

There was, however, an inconvenient, though endearing, weak
spot in André's otherwise impressive life-saving equipment. He had
come to England because he loved the idea of it. In the Budapest
of his schooldays the language you studied, in addition to Latin,
was either German or English, and he, influenced by a beloved and
admired uncle, had chosen English without a moment's hesitation,
and had found it greatly to his taste. The books he read as a result
must have been an odd selection, because they left him with a
romantic picture of a country remarkable for honesty and
reliability, largely inhabited by comic but rather attractive beings
known as English Gentlemen. I am sure that if, when he was
trawling for someone to invest money in his firm, his net had
caught a fellow-Hungarian, he would have insisted on their

agreeing a thoroughly businesslike contract; but each time what came up was an Englishman – an Englishman radiant with the glow which shines from the answer to a prayer, and coloured a becoming pink by his viewer's preconceptions. So – it is still hard to believe, but it is true – what existed between André and these five timely miracles was, in each case, nothing but a Gentleman's Agreement. You couldn't even say that it wasn't worth the paper it was written on, because there wasn't any paper.

Before this process began we lost Audrey, because André was unable to tolerate her husband Ronald. Her investment had been made largely to provide Ron with a job to come home to when he was demobilized from the Army, and within a few months of our opening he joined us as sales manager. He was a gentle, serene-looking person, a listener rather than a talker, and what his previous occupation had been I never knew. After he left us he trained as an osteopath, at which he was successful. There was nothing about him of the businessman – and certainly not of the salesman.

Because none of us had met him earlier, Ron was not strictly an example of André's inability to see what people were like. This weakness related to his impatient and clumsy handling of staff, both of them stemming from an absolute failure to be interested in any viewpoint but his own. It was quickly to become apparent that if he wanted a particular kind of person for his firm – a fireball of a sales manager, for example, or a scrupulously careful copy-editor – then he would see the next man or woman who approached him as that person, and would impatiently dismiss any dissenting opinion. Before he was done he would cram innumerable square pegs into round holes, and it is exhausting to remember the emotional wear and tear involved when, to his furious indignation (against the poor pegs) he began to see them for what they were and they had to be wrenched or eased out. But in Ron's case it was bad luck rather than bad judgement – bad luck, especially, for Ron, who was not with us three weeks before he was pinned helplessly in the eye of that alarming little searchlight, was seen to be doing nothing right, and as a consequence began doing more and more things wrong.

Sheila and I, who both loved Audrey and liked Ron, tried to make a stand, arguing and persuading as best we could, but in vain. I remember when Ron's sin was paying a bill on demand, as I would have done in his place. 'That blockhead! Doesn't he know what credit means?' – 'But you can't yell at a man like that – have you ever *explained* to him that their bills don't have to be paid for thirty days? Why should he know that? He's never done this sort of thing before.' – '*I* didn't have to have it explained to *me*.'

Ron *was* the wrong person for the job, but by the time he and Audrey decided that there was nothing for it but to pick up their money and go, what we would have to put up with for the sake of what we liked and admired in André had become uncomfortably evident.

Then the five timely miracles began, and brought us together again. They were all so astonishingly useless that it was impossible not to gang up against them. (Though none of them was quite so bad as one that got away because – by God's grace – he approached me not André. He was a charmingly camp old friend of my childhood who had married a very rich woman and wrote out of the blue to say that if we had a niche for him he would gladly put a lot of money into the firm. André quivered like a pointer, but it was I who was asked to lunch so it was I to whom my old friend said: 'Well, my dear, the chief object of this exercise is to give me something to do before lunch instead of getting drunk.' I often wondered how André would have managed to blank that sentence out if he had been sitting in my chair.)

Of the five, numbers one, two and three soon became discouraged, whereupon numbers four and five bought them out, thus ending up owning more of the firm than André did – and he with no scrap of paper to give him any rights at all. Neither of them was a crook; both of them to start with were ready to admit that André had created Wingate and that he was the person who put most into running it. With a lot of tolerance and tact it might have been possible for them and him to rub along together, but tolerance and tact were not at André's command.

Number four I shall call Bertie, because he looked and sounded exactly like P. G. Wodehouse's Bertie Wooster would have looked and sounded had he been in his forties. He was the son of a well-known middle-brow man of letters and had himself written several novels in which expensive sports cars figured more prominently than any human character (André used to say that the only thing that had ever given Bertie an erection was a Lagonda). He lacked business sense and common sense – indeed a nonsense was what he usually made of any of our daily tasks unless someone was breathing down his neck. I would take things away and quietly do them again, which naturally riled him, while André would attack him in an appallingly humiliating way.

Number five, whom I shall call Roger, had worked in publishing for years, but in an old-fashioned firm specializing in books on architecture and the British countryside, which had not demanded the expenditure of much energy. He knew the language of the trade, which was something, but he did not care to put himself out, and was often drunk (after, rather than before lunch, unlike my old friend). Occasionally he came in with a black eye, having been roughed up by an ill-chosen boyfriend, and he spent many of his afternoons in tears. (Roger was to end by killing himself – but at that time, on an acquaintance that was very superficial, I saw him only as foolish without understanding that he was also sad.) Perhaps he had thought he would work gently, between hangovers, on elegant books about eighteenth-century chinoiserie or Strawberry-Hill Gothick, but he never got round to signing up any such work and made no contribution to what we had on the stocks; so Roger, too, received short shrift from André. And, like Bertie, the more he was treated as an incompetent booby, the more he remembered that the two of them, not André, were now in financial control of Allan Wingate.

For a year or two this disastrous set-up bubbled and seethed, at first without the intervention of any outsider, then in the offices of lawyers. We had moved to more commodious offices near Harrods, and now had a sales department and a production department (but still no one in charge of publicity except me with my hateful ads). In spite of our problems we were producing about fifty books a year, most of them profitable, and we would have been exuberantly happy if we could have enjoyed Bertie's and Roger's money without their presence. It seemed impossible, with everything going so well, that André would be ousted from his own firm by these two fools . . . but the more expert advice he took, the clearer it became that this would happen. He hadn't a legal leg to stand on and the best his lawyer could do was to wangle a 'generous' gesture out of Bertie and Roger which allowed him, when he finally left, to take a few cookery books and three or four very unimportant others (he and I had agreed, once we had brought ourselves to face the facts, that there was nothing for it but to start another publishing house).

There was, however, one book due to be delivered quite soon, about which a decision was still to be reached. This was the memoirs of Franz von Papen. To quote my own catalogue description of it:

Franz von Papen's life has faithfully reflected the fortunes of his country for over half a century. As a boy, when he was a court page in the Kaiser's entourage, he witnessed the traditional pomp of imperialism. In his seventies, though cleared of war guilt by the Nuremberg Tribunal, he experienced defeat to the full when his own countrymen sentenced him to imprisonment. Between these extremes he was always at the centre of affairs in Germany, and whether the balance he maintained was the result of a clear or an ambivalent conscience is still a matter of conjecture.

His own interpretation of his career and the events with which it was so closely connected is of the greatest importance. He describes his activities as military attaché in the United States from 1913 to 1915; he gives an account of Allenby's campaign in the Middle East, as seen from 'the other side'; he analyses the decline of the Weimar Republic, which he knew both as a member of the Reichstag and as Reich Chancellor. On the subject of his collaboration with Hitler as Vice-Chancellor, his mission to Austria before the Anschluss, and his appointment as Ambassador in Ankara during the last war he is exhaustive. He does not shirk the central enigma of his career: his acceptance of further high office under the Nazis after his open criticism of their methods in his Marburg speech, the murder of his colleagues during the Roehm Putsch, and his own house arrest.

This book is of outstanding interest, both as a commentary on recent history from the German viewpoint, and as a personal record.

To which I would add, now, that no one who hadn't just lived through the Second World War can imagine how fascinating it was, so soon after it, to hear one of *them* speaking.

This book the old man had been persuaded to write by André, who had visited him in connection with *Operation Cicero*, the story of the valet to the British Ambassador in Ankara, who towards the end of the war had cheekily supplied the Germans with copies of the contents of the ambassadorial safe. Von Papen, having been our man's opposite number at the time, was in a position to confirm 'Cicero's' story (which at first sight seemed too good to be true), which he did. André might, of course, have written to him about it, but characteristically saw greater possibilities in a meeting. Capturing the Cicero story was already one of his more striking achievements, involving a lightning dash to Ankara, but the way he used that book as a lead into another and more important project was an even better example of his energy.

Technically the memoirs he had secured would, when completed, belong to Allan Wingate, but even the lawyers felt that André had a moral right to them; something which Bertie and Roger were reluctant to acknowledge. The wrangling was bitter, but they did finally accept a suggestion made by the lawyers on the Friday which was André's and my last day at Allan Wingate: that there should be a 'moratorium' on the subject of von Papen until the following Tuesday, during which everyone should calm down in preparation for a decisive meeting about it.

On the intervening Sunday I went to André's house at lunch-time, to discuss our next move. While I was there the telephone rang, and hearing André switch to talking German it dawned on me that von Papen was on the line. Who, he asked, was this person who had just called him to say that André had been sacked from Allan Wingate? How could he have been sacked? What on earth was happening?

André, always quick on his feet, was never quicker than at that moment. The call had come as a complete surprise, the situation he had to get across was not a simple one, and he was trembling with rage at this sudden revelation of Bertie and Roger's sneaky manoeuvre; nevertheless in little more than ten minutes he had explained what was up with perfect lucidity and in exactly the right tone, and by the time he hung up he had von Papen's assurance that in no circumstances would Allan Wingate ever set eyes on his manuscript, which would be André's just as soon as he had launched his new firm. Seeing that silly pair of English Gentlemen being hoisted so neatly by their own petard remains one of the choicest satisfactions of my career.

This event also provided a solid foundation for André's new firm, of which I was to become a director. Within a very short time he had sold the serial rights of von Papen's book to a Sunday paper called the *People* for the sum (peanuts now, but awe-inspiring then) of £30,000.

7

1952: TWO THINGS about the new firm were certain from the start: it would be called André Deutsch, and André would be its absolute boss. There would be other shareholders – eight of them including Nicolas Bentley and me, who would be working directors – but the value of each holder's shares would be limited so that even if one of them bought out all the others, he would not gain control. A loan, soon to be repaid, enabled André to ensure this satisfactory state of affairs, and the von Papen serial deal lifted the firm at once into profitability.

My own investment, the minimum necessary to qualify me for a directorship, was £350 given me by my godmother. Like Nick, I was in it for the job. The other shareholders were in it as a friendly gesture to André, not as a business venture, although all would end by making a modest but respectable profit. It was a sensible and pleasant arrangement, and a profound relief after Allan Wingate – which, gratifyingly, died a natural death about five years after André's departure.

From the five Wingate years we brought friends on both the manufacturing and retailing sides of the book trade, a good reputation with agents, and much useful experience. It hardly felt like starting a new firm, more like carrying on the old one in improved conditions: we now had the equivalent of Bertie's and Roger's money without Bertie and Roger – just what we had longed for. This was so delightful that it might have relaxed some people's moral fibre, but not ours. Perhaps the most useful thing gained from Wingate was a disposition shaped by poverty. It had always been natural to André to be careful, and those who had worked with him at Wingate, seeing that his attitude was strictly necessary for survival, had fallen into it themselves – even those like me, whose natural tendency was towards extravagance. Since then I have often noticed that it is not good for people to start a venture with enough – not to mention too much – money: it is hard for them to learn to structure it properly, simply because they are never forced to.

Even if we had been eager to relax we would not have been allowed to. André felt it to be a danger. He countered it by putting up a blood-chilling front of gloom about our prospects for the next forty years. However well we were doing, the slightest hint that expenditure of some sort would not come amiss (the redecoration of the reception area, perhaps, or thirty-two pages of illustrations in a book instead of sixteen, or – God forbid – a rise for someone) would bring on a fit of shocked incredulity at such frivolous heedlessness in the face of imminent disaster. Much though the rest of us used to complain about this frugality, it is a fact that our firm continued to make a profit every year until he sold it in 1985, in spite of the last five years of that time being hard ones for small independent publishing houses; and this might not have been – towards the end certainly would not have been – possible had his control of our overheads been less fierce.

For three years we rented the top two-thirds of a doctor's house in Thayer Street. They were happy years, but still a touch amateurish: did proper publishers have to put a board over a bath in order to make a packing-bench? Did proper editors and proper sales managers work together in the same small room? Our performance, nevertheless, was good enough to let us buy up Derek Verschoyle's firm in 1956, and move into its premises at 14 Carlisle Street in Soho.

Derek Verschoyle was a raffish figure, vaguely well-connected and vaguely literary, about whom I had first heard from my father who had encountered him as an agreeably picturesque feature of the *Spectator*. Verschoyle was its literary editor for a while. His room looked out over the mews behind that periodical's offices in Gower Street, and he, lolling with his feet up on his desk, used to take pot-shots at the local cats out of his window with a .22 which he kept on his desk for the purpose. He must have been able to raise a fair amount of money in order to set up his own publishing firm (its assets included the freehold of the house, which was very well placed) but it didn't take him long to get through it. We gained only two really valuable authors from him – Roy Fuller, whose novels and poetry added lustre to our list for a long time, and Ludwig Bemelmans, whose 'Madeline books' for young children did very well for us. One of the more burdensome books we inherited from him was a pointless compilation called *Memorable Balls*, a title so much tittered over that we thought of leaving it out when we were arranging our stand at the *Sunday Times*'s first book fair. Finally one copy was shoved into an inconspicuous corner – where the Queen Mother, who had opened the fair, instantly noticed it. Picking it up, she exclaimed with delight: 'Oh, what a tempting title!' André insisted that it was his confusion over this that made him drop her a deep curtsey instead of a bow.

Verschoyle was the kind of English Gentleman André seemed fated to meet, but although undeclared liabilities went on leaking out of crannies for a long time, and the bills which came in with despairing regularity from his tailor and his wine merchant used to make our eyes pop, he did us no harm and much good. Settled into his house, we ceased being promising and became pros.

There were two large and well-proportioned rooms, and the rest of the house rambled back from its narrow frontage in a haphazard but convenient jumble of partitioned spaces. André, as was only right, had the better of the two good rooms, and Nick Bentley had the other. I moved fast to secure the smallest room there was, knowing that only the physical impossibility of inserting a second desk would save me from having to share. If I had put up a fight for Nick's room I would have got it, because Nick was far too well-mannered to fight back; but André would quite certainly have seen it as a chance to squeeze two other people into it with me, neither of whom would have been my secretary because I didn't have one. It never entered his head to ask Nick to share it with anyone other than his secretary.

Nick edited our non-fiction – not all of it, and not fast. He was such a stickler for correctness that he often had to be mopped-up after, when his treatment of someone's prose had been over-pedantic, or when his shock at a split infinitive had diverted his attention from some error of fact. I don't think I am flattering myself in believing that I was busier and more useful than he was (though there was nothing to choose between us in uselessness when it came to exercising business sense – a fact often bewailed by André, although he enjoyed the jokes he could make about it). I certainly noticed the privileges enjoyed by Nick as a result of his gender, just as I noticed that his salary was a good deal larger than mine; but what I felt about it was less resentment than a sort of amused resignation. All publishing was run by many badly-paid women and a few much better-paid men: an imbalance that women were, of course, aware of, but which they seemed to take for granted.

I have been asked by younger women how I brought myself to accept this situation so calmly, and I suppose that part of the answer must be conditioning: to a large extent I had been shaped by my background to please men, and many women of my age must remember how, as a result, you actually saw yourself – or part of you did – as men saw you, so you knew what would happen if you became assertive and behaved in a way which men thought tiresome and ridiculous. Grotesquely, you would start to look tiresome and ridiculous in your own eyes. Even now I would rather turn and walk away than risk my voice going shrill and my face going red as I slither into the sickening humiliation of undercutting my own justified anger by my own idiotic ineptitude.

But one can, of course, always walk away. That I could easily have done, and never thought of doing; so I doubt that it was *only* the mixed vanity and lack of confidence of the brainwashed female which held me there in acceptance of something which I knew to be unjust and which other women, whom I admired, were beginning actively to confront.

Some time in January 1998 I read in the *Independent* an article about recent 'research' (it sounded small-scale and superficial) into the differences between the attitudes of men and those of women towards their jobs. Men had been found more likely to aim for promotion and increased pay, women to aim for work they would enjoy and the satisfaction of doing it well. As so often when industrious people 'discover' something obvious, my first reaction was 'You don't say!'; but this was followed by an oddly satisfying sense of agreement, because the article did so exactly sum up my own experience. I hadn't just loved being an editor, I had also positively liked not being treated as the director I was supposed to be. This was because, as I have explained, I loathed and still loathe responsibility, am intensely reluctant to exert myself in any way that I don't enjoy, and am bored by thinking about money (in spite of liking to spend it). So while it is true that André took advantage of my nature in getting me cheap and having to bother so little about my feelings, it cannot be said that *in relation to the job* he did any violence to those feelings.

Obviously it is true that indifference to status and pay is not found in all women, but I have seen it in a good many who, like me, enjoyed their work. All my colleagues during the sixties and seventies admired and sympathized with other women who were actively campaigning for women's rights, but none of them joined in as campaigners: we could see injustice, but we didn't feel the pinch of it, because we happened to be doing what we wanted to do. Lazy or selfish? Yes, I suppose so. But I have to say that when I search myself for guilt about it – and guilt comes to me easily – I find none. While conditioning must have played some part in the inertia displayed by myself and my friends, my own experience suggests that it was at work on an innate disposition to be satisfied with my lot. After all, there are *some* men who mind more about enjoying their work than about what they are paid for it and where they stand in the hierarchy; so why, when a woman does the same, should it be taken for granted that she is brainwashed?

8

THE CARLISLE STREET years hummed with possibility. Although we had now been in the game long enough to know that the majority of manuscripts received would disappoint, we still expected excitement daily, and among the seventy-odd books a year that we published, a fair number justified that expectation. To Mailer, Richler, Moore and Fuller we soon added Terry Southern, V. S. Naipaul, Jack Kerouac, Philip Roth, Mavis Gallant, Wolf Mankowitz, Jack Schaefer, Jean Rhys – the poets Stevie Smith, Elizabeth Jennings, Laurie Lee, Peter Levi, Geoffrey Hill – the non-fiction writers Simone de Beauvoir, Peggy Guggenheim, Sally Belfrage, Alberto Denti di Pirajno, Lionel Fielden, Clare Sheridan, Mercedes d'Acosta (not all of them names likely to be recognized now, but all remarkable people who wrote remarkably well).

By now I considered myself a proper editor, so perhaps this is the place to describe the job as I saw it. In many firms a distinction was made between editors and copy editors, the first being concerned with finding authors and keeping them happy, encouraging them in their projects and sometimes tempting them down this path or that; the second being the humbler but still essential people who tidy texts. In our firm a book's editor was responsible for both sides of the operation. Not until the eighties did we start farming out tidying jobs to freelance copy editors, and I doubt whether any Deutsch editor felt happy about doing so. I know I didn't.

The things which had to be done for all books were simple but time-consuming and sometimes boring (what kept one going through the boring bits was liking – usually – the book for which one was doing them). You had to see that the use of capital letters, hyphens, italics and quotation marks conformed to the house style and was consistent throughout; you had to check that no spelling mistakes had crept in, and make sure that if the punctuation was eccentric it was because the author wanted it that way; you had to watch out for carelessness (perhaps an author had decided halfway through to change a character's name from Joe to Bob: when he went back over the script to make the alteration, had he missed any 'Joes'?). You had to pick up errors of fact, querying ones you were doubtful about at the risk of looking silly. If your author quoted from other writers' work, or from a song, you had to check that he had applied for permission to do so – almost certainly he would not have done, so you would have to do it for him. If a list of acknowledgements and/or a bibliography and/or an index were called for you had to see that they were done. If the book was to be illustrated you might have to find the illustrations, and would certainly have to decide on their order and captioning, and see that they were paid for. And if anything in the book was obscene or potentially libellous you must submit it to a lawyer, and then persuade your author to act on his advice.

All that was routine, and applied to the work of even the most perfectionist of writers. Where the work became more interesting was when it was necessary to suggest and discuss alterations to the text.

Editorial intervention ranged from very minor matters (a clumsy sentence here, a slight lack of clarity there) to almost complete rewritings such as I did on the book about Tahiti (although I don't remember ever doing another rewrite as extensive as that one). Usually it would be on the lines of 'Wouldn't it work better if you moved the paragraph describing so-and-so's looks back to where he first appears?' or 'Could you expand a little on so-and-so's motive for doing such-and-such? It's rather arbitrary as it stands'. I can't remember anyone resenting such suggestions, though sometimes of course they would disagree for good reasons: mostly, if what is said by an obviously attentive reader makes sense, the writer is pleased to comply. Writers don't encounter *really* attentive readers as often as you might expect, and find them balm to their twitchy nerves when they do; which gives their editors a good start with them.

It was a rule with me that I must not overdo such tinkerings: it must always be the author's voice that was heard, not mine, even if that meant retaining something that I didn't much like. And of course it was an absolute rule with all of us that no change of any kind could be made without the author's approval. It was those two points which I considered my ground rules. The ideal was to receive a script which could go through unchanged (Brian Moore, V. S. Naipaul and Jean Rhys were outstanding providers of such scripts; and books already published in America were equally trouble-free, because such editorial work as they had needed would have been done over there). If, on the other hand, the text had needed work, then by the time it reached publication it must read as though none had been done on it, which could usually only be achieved by working closely with the author.

Writers varied greatly in their attitude to intervention. I never came across anyone who was anything but grateful at having a mistake, whether of fact or syntax, pointed out, but when it came to changes some weighed every word of every suggestion, many accepted suggestions cheerfully, a few asked for more, and a very few didn't seem to care one way or another.

George Mikes, for example, needed a lot of work done on his books. He was a lazy man, one of those people who, once they have become fluent enough in a foreign language to say what they want, can't be bothered to go the step further which would enable them to say it correctly. If his writing was to sound like natural, easy-going colloquial English, which he was aiming for, about one sentence in every three had to be adjusted. For the first two or three of the thirteen of his books that I edited, he took the trouble to read the edited script, but gradually he paid it less and less attention until, with the last three of his books, he would not even glance at the script – not even when I told him that I had put in a couple of jokes! Knowing him very well, I always felt quite sure that I had made his books sound just like he would have sounded if he had pushed his English up that last notch – that he was, in fact, right to trust me: but still I was slightly shocked at his doing so.

One kind of editing I did not enjoy: cookery books. We built up a list which eventually amounted to over forty titles, mostly about national cuisines or the use of a particular ingredient – rice cooking, mushroom cooking, cooking with yoghurt and so on. This list was André's idea – he it was who saw that as food supplies returned to normal, thousands of the British middle class would for the first time have to cook it with their own hands. I was too uninterested in food to have thought of it: in those days my notion of adventurous cooking was scrambling an egg instead of boiling it. But I was a woman, and where was the woman's place but in the kitchen? So the cookery list became 'mine'.

Luckily André capped his first inspiration by meeting Elizabeth David at a dinner party and inviting her to become our cookery-book consultant, and her year or so of doing this saved me. Quickly she taught me to look for authenticity, to avoid gimmicks, to appreciate how a genuine enjoyment of food made a book tempting without any self-conscious attempts at 'atmosphere'. Before long I could see for myself that Elizabeth would never have done as the sole editor of a cookery-book list because so many useful books would prove too coarse to get through the fine sieve of her rather snobbish perfectionism; but her respect for the art of cooking and the elegant sensuousness of her response to flavour and texture were an education in the enjoyment of eating, as well as in the production of cookery books, for which I am still grateful.

There is no kind of editing more laborious than getting a cookery book right. You cannot assume that a procedure described in detail on page 21 will be remembered by a cook using a recipe on page 37 or 102: it must be fully described every single time it is used. And never can you be sure that all the ingredients listed at the head of a recipe will appear in their proper place within it. You must check, check and check again, and if you slip into working automatically, without forcing yourself to imagine actually *doing* what you are reading, you will let through appalling blunders (oh those outraged letters from cooks saying 'Where do the three eggs go in your recipe for such-and-such'!). I did become proud of our cookery list, and fond of some of its authors – but even so, cookery books ran advertisements close as my least favourite things.

I suppose that when I started on them I had never come across any description of the traditional savagery of great chefs: I assumed that people, many of them comfortably built and rosy-faced, who wrote about what was evidently to them a great sensuous pleasure, would be by nature mellow and generous. When a West End bookshop devoted a week to promoting cookery books, and accepted our suggestion that it should open with a party for which six of our cooks should provide the food, I expected a merry evening. The six joined eagerly in the preliminary planning, which had to ensure that each would bring two dishes suitable for finger eating, which represented her own speciality and which didn't clash with the other cooks' contributions. They bravely undertook the task of transporting their delicate work to the shop, and all arrived in good time to set about arranging the food to its best advantage. Whereupon – crunch! and someone's tray landed on someone else's plate – splat! and a passing rump sent a dish flying to the floor – 'Oh do let me help!' and a knife was seized and brought to bear like a jolly hockey stick on a rival's exquisite confection . . . Never again did I allow any of our cooks to meet each other.

The kind of cookery book we brought out in the fifties, and which continued to do well in only slightly modified form during the sixties and seventies, would not get far today. It was an inexpensive, unillustrated collection of recipes which we assumed would sell (and which did sell) without being dressed up, because many of the new generation of middle-class cooks were enjoying holidays abroad for the first time and were therefore eager to make their meals more interesting by cooking dishes from foreign countries. As Britain's culinary revolution progressed (and you only have to look at a few of the cookery books published before the

Second World War to see that it was a real revolution), more publishers jumped on the bandwagon and more effort had to be put into making cookery books eye-catching. It was a good many years before the grand, glossy, lavishly illustrated tome swept the board, but the challenge became perceptible fairly soon, and we failed to rise to it.

Booksellers began to insist that they couldn't sell a cookery book unless it was illustrated in colour, so reluctantly we started to insert a few cheaply printed colour plates, the photographs usually scrounged from a tourist board, which was a waste of time and of the little money it cost. I knew this; it was obvious that the big successes were crammed with beautiful photographs specially taken for them and finely printed. They could only be so handsome because their publishers had the confidence to invest a lot of money in producing large editions, and printed their colour in even longer runs for several foreign editions as well as their own. To work on this scale they had to establish and cherish a Name – Carrier, Boxer and so on – culminating today in Delia, Queen of the Screen (one of the best things about cookery books is that no one who isn't a truly good cook can become a Name, because recipes are *used*). Then the book had to be planned so that the purchaser could feel 'That's it, I shall never need another!' (which didn't have to worry the Name, because once solidly established, collections of his or her Summer, Winter, Christmas, Birthday, Party or Whatever recipes would still sell merrily, even though a critical eye might detect signs of strain). Then photographers who could make food look eatable had to be found – a much rarer breed than the uninitiated would suppose, and worth their weight in caviar. And finally a network of international relationships had to be built up. This kind of investment was foreign to André's nature, and I certainly had not got the confidence to fight for it. Suppose we didn't get it right first time? We easily might not, and we could not afford such a disaster. So we settled for the modest success of our own kind of book, which slowly decreased until the early eighties, when the list faded out.

The stalest cliché about publishing – 'You meet such interesting 'people' – is true enough, but I think the greatest advantage it offers as a job is variety. Yes, I did find working on cookery books fairly boring, but how different it was from working on a novel or a book of poems. One was always moving from one kind of world into another, and that I loved.

I was nervous in the world of poetry. My mother used flatly to refuse to read it, declaring that it made no sense to her, and although I was shocked and embarrassed on her behalf in my teens, when I read poetry a good deal and wrote it too (though never supposing I was writing it well), I had in fact inherited her prosaic nature. Poetry moves me most sharply when it ambushes me from a moment of prose, and I can't really understand what it is that makes a person feel that to write it is his *raison d'être*.

Knowing this, all I could do while a volume of poetry was going through my hands was stand by – which, luckily, is all that an editor ought to do unless he is Pound working with Eliot: one poet rubbing sparks out of another in mutual understanding. I read the work carefully, tried to make the jacket blurb say what the author wanted it to say, was moved by some of the poems as wholes and by parts of other poems . . . all that was all right. But I also felt a kind of nervous reverence which I now find tiresome, because it was what I supposed one *ought* to feel in the presence of a superior being; and poets, although they do have a twist to their nature which non-poets lack, which enables them to produce verbal artefacts of superior intensity, are not superior beings. In the distant days when they were singing stories to their fellows in order to entertain and instruct them, they were useful ones: in the days when they devised and manipulated forms in which to contain the more common and important human emotions they were clever and delightful ones; and in the comparatively recent days when they have examined chiefly their own inner landscapes they have often become boring ones (I have stopped reading the *Independent*'s 'Poem of the Day' because of how distressingly uninteresting most of them are). And even when the poems are not boring, the poet can be far from superior – think of poor Larkin!

Naturally we did not think the poets we chose to publish

boring – except that I did become tired of Roy Fuller's meditations on his own ageing, sometimes found Elizabeth Jennings's thought less interesting than she did, and considered that 'Not Waving But Drowning' was the best-known of Stevie Smith's poems because it was the best of them. Peter Levi's early poems I found easy to love, but it was Geoffrey Hill's dense and knotty poems which were, for me, the richest in sudden flashes and enduring illuminations. 'If you are really without religious feelings,' he once said to me, 'how can you like my work?' To which the answer is: 'Does an agnostic have to dislike a Bach cantata or Botticelli's *Nativity*?' If an emotion or a state of mind has forced someone to give it intensely appropriate expression, that expression will have power enough to bypass opinion.

Geoffrey was a difficult writer to work with because of his anxiety: he was bedevilled by premonitions of disaster, and had to be patiently and repeatedly reassured although my own nerves, worked on by his, would be fraying even as I spoke or wrote my soothing words. Once something frightening happened. A book of his – I think it was *Mercian Hymns* – had been read in page proof by him and me, and I had just passed it to the production department to be sent to press. That same afternoon he telephoned apologetically, saying he was aware of how neurotic he was being and would I please forgive him, but he had suddenly started to worry about whether the copyright line had been included in the preliminary pages. I knew it had been, but I also knew how tormenting his anxieties were, so instead of saying 'Yes, of course it's there,' I said: 'Production probably hasn't sent it off yet, so hold on and I'll run down and check so that we can be a hundred per cent sure.' Which I did, and the line was there, and Geoffrey was comforted. And when the printed book was delivered to us there was no copyright line.

Whatever it may be that causes a poet to know himself one, Geoffrey was walking evidence of his own sense of vocation. Living seemed to be more difficult for him than for most people. Once he told me – wryly, not proudly – that he was hesitating about doing something which he passionately wanted to do because if he did it, and thus ceased to suffer, he might never write any more poems. And his prose seemed to illustrate the degree to which writing poetry was his *raison d'être*: it was so unconfident and clumsy that it made me think of a swan out of water.

Stevie Smith, too, in her different way, found life difficult; although she solved the problem cleverly and decisively by withdrawing from those parts of it that were too much for her and keeping to a well-defined territory of her own. She was amusing, and – strangely, given the cautious nature of her strategy – met one with a beguiling openness, so that I always started our meetings with the feeling that we were about to become close friends. We never did, and I think the reason was sexual. I was still young enough to be at heart more interested in my own sexual and romantic activities than in anything else (though mostly I kept them out of my office life), so Stevie's nervous asexuality distanced her. She almost fainted when she first came into my office, because I had on my wall a print of snakes. All the blood left her face and she could hardly make audible a plea that I should take the print down (after that I always removed it as soon as she was announced). Perhaps the notion that a phobia about snakes relates to their phallic quality is old-fashioned and misguided, but I supposed it to be true, and saw Stevie's phobia as revealing. I'm sorry to say that some part of me slightly despised the fear of sex I sensed in her; and I hope that she got her own back (this is far from unlikely) by slightly despising its opposite quality in me.

That we had a poetry list was almost accidental. While we were still at Thayer Street André had met Laurie Lee and had fallen in love with his *Cider with Rosie*, which was published by Chatto & Windus. Laurie must already have been dabbling in the manipulative games with publishers that he was to play with increasing zest in the future, because André was given to understand that Chatto's were in the doghouse for refusing to publish his poems, *My Many-Coated Man*, and who knew what might come the way, in the future, of the firm which took them on. So André snapped up the poems (and we did indeed get Laurie's next-but-one prose book). Six months later the acquisition of Derek Verschoyle's list landed us with five more books of verse. They were by Ronald Bottrall, Alan Ross, Roy Fuller, Diana Witherby and David Wright – Fuller was to continue with us for the next thirty years. Then Elizabeth Jennings came to us on Laurie's recommendation, and Peter Levi on Elizabeth's, and after that one poet led to another in a haphazard way, or sometimes an agent bobbed up with one, or sometimes one of our novelists was a poet as well (notably John Updike), and once there was a small infusion from another publisher, called Rapp & Whiting, whose list came our way . . .

In the almost fifty years I spent in publishing, poetry was never easy to sell, and we were not among the houses that were best at it. I find it hard to understand why we stayed with it as long as we did. Certainly I loved some of the books on our poetry list, but given my prosaic nature I would not have minded if we had never developed such a list: I edited most of the books on it, but I was not its instigator. It was André who liked to have it there. He had been an enthusiastic reader of poetry in his youth (Hungarians treasure their poets very earnestly), and was still, when I first knew him, reading Eliot's *Four Quartets* aloud to young women whenever they gave him the chance (and reading them well). Nor was Nick much interested in our poets – except for Ogden Nash who was a friend of his, and whom he edited. I suppose André simply thought that a proper publisher had a poetry list, rather as, in the past, an English country gentleman, even if he devoted all his leisure to shooting game birds or riding to hounds, thought that a proper house had a library. In retrospect I see it as interesting rather than praiseworthy, given the frugal habits insisted on by André. Poetry may not have lost us money (we paid poets minuscule advances and designed their books very economically), but it certainly didn't make us any, and none of us minded: an attitude which fifty – forty – thirty years ago was not worthy of remark, and now has become almost unimaginable.

To restore my balance after recalling the dutiful aspects of editing – the need to work conscientiously in spite of being bored, and to put oneself at the service of books that were not always within one's range – I shall now describe what was certainly the most absorbing of all the tasks that came my way: working with Gitta Sereny on *Into That Darkness*, which we published in 1974.

Gitta spent her childhood in Vienna, the daughter of a Hungarian father and an Austrian mother, neither of them Jewish. She was fifteen years old when Hitler took Austria over. She was sent to school in France and was caught there by the war. During the German occupation she looked after abandoned children in Paris and the Loire, then got out to America where, in 1945, she took a job in UNRRA (the United Nations Relief and Rehabilitation Administration) as a child welfare officer in camps for displaced people in southern Germany. Although many of the children were eventually reunited with their families, many more had no one and nowhere to go to: all had experienced unspeakable horrors. How could anyone have chosen to make concentration-camp and labour-camp victims of thousands of children, all under fourteen, many under ten? To quote from the preface of the paperback edition of *Into That Darkness* which we published in 1991: 'Over the months of the Nuremberg trials and our own increasing work with survivors, including a few from the extermination camps in occupied Poland, about which almost nothing had been known until then, we learnt more and more about the horrors which had been committed, and I felt more and more that we needed to find someone capable of explaining to us how presumably normal human beings had been brought to do what had been done.' Haunted by this question, she came to feel that 'it was essential to penetrate the personality of at least one such person who had been intimately associated with this total evil. If it could be achieved, an evaluation of such a person's background, his childhood, and eventually his adult motivation and reactions, as he saw them, rather than as we wished or prejudged them to be, might teach us to understand better to what extent evil in human beings is created by their genes, and to what extent by their society and environment.'

People sometimes ask why Gitta Sereny habitually writes about evil, but I do not see it as surprising that someone plunged into

such a scalding awareness of it so early in her life should be haunted
by it. It is only because it frightens us too much that we don't all
think about it much more than we do. Everything that makes life
worth living is the result of humankind's impulse to fight the
darkness in itself, and attempting to understand evil is part of that
fight. It is true that such understanding as has been achieved has
not made much – if any – headway against evil; and it is equally
true that horror and dismay at dreadful things are often used as
disguise for excitement; but if those facts are allowed to discourage
us from trying to understand how corruption comes about, what
hope have we? It seems to me that Gitta's need to seek explanations
has led her to do valuable work, none more so than when she seized
the chance, some twenty-five years after her experiences in
UNRRA, to penetrate one particular evil personality.

She had become a journalist. In 1967 she was commissioned by
the *Daily Telegraph* to write a series of pieces about West Germany,
including the Nazi crime trials then taking place. She was present
at the trial of Franz Stangl who had been Kommandant of
Treblinka, one of the four extermination (as opposed to
concentration) camps in German-occupied Poland, and who was
sentenced to life imprisonment for co-responsibility in the murder
of 900,000 people in that camp. There had been only four such
men: one of the others was dead, the other two had escaped.
Stangl, too, had escaped (to Brazil), but had been tracked down.
Gitta realized that he was the object for study that she had hoped
for, and that by now she herself felt capable of undertaking the task.

She was allowed to visit Stangl in prison and talked with him for
many hours over six weeks, at the end of which – the very end – he
reached the bottom of his guilt and admitted that he ought not still
to be alive. There was still a detail which he wished to confirm
about something he had said, so she agreed to return to the prison
in three days' time to collect the information. When she did so she
was told that he was dead. It had been heart failure, not suicide.
When the *Telegraph Magazine* published the interviews they refused
to include this fact, saying that no one would believe it.

Having read these interviews, we asked Gitta to come to the office and discuss the possibility of a book, whereupon she told us that she was already deep in the work for it, and would be glad to let us see it. I can't remember how long it was before she brought it in – or rather, brought in the raw material out of which it was to be shaped, but I shall never forget the sight of that mountain of script.

When I got it home that evening (it was far too unwieldy to deal with in the office) it covered the whole of my table. In addition to the central Stangl interviews there were interviews, many of them long, with at least twenty-four other people, and there was also much – though not all – of the material for the linking passages of description and explanation essential to welding the material into a whole.

No reading I have ever done has shaken me as much as the reading I did that night. Having seen the film of Belsen made when the Allies got there I thought I knew the nature of what had been done; but of course I didn't. Groping my way into the history of this ordinary, efficient, ambitious, uxorious Austrian policeman, through the astonishing material about Hitler's euthanasia programme to which he was transferred – all the men employed in the extermination camps, except for the Ukrainians, worked for that programme – was intensely interesting, but frightening because I knew where it was going. And then it got there. And then the voices began to tell me what it had really been like . . . I remember walking round and round the room as though I were trying to escape what was in that pile of paper, and I didn't sleep that night. But one editorial decision I was able to make then and there: we must use no adjectives – or very few. Words such as 'horrifying', 'atrocious', 'tragic', 'terrifying' – they shrivelled like scraps of paper thrown into a blazing fire.

After the enormous amount of source material she had dug into, and all those interviews which had taken her to Brazil and Canada and the United States as well as to Germany and Austria, and had plunged her ever deeper into the darkness that I had just glimpsed,

Gitta was near the end of her tether. She liked to have the support of an editor at the best of times, simply because, fluent though her English was, it was not her first language: she couldn't be absolutely confident in it – and did, in fact, sometimes slip into slightly Germanic rhythms and over-elaboration of syntax. But chiefly it was exhaustion, and being too close to the material, which made it essential for her to have help. Often it amounted to no more than me saying 'Let's put that bit here' so that she could say at once 'No no – it must go there'; but she was also enabled to reshape passages when she had seen them afresh through a new pair of eyes. I could point out where clarification, condensation, expansion were needed. I could say 'But you've said that already when you were describing such-and-such', or 'But wait a minute – I need reminding about that because it was so long ago that it first came up'.

It was clear enough that the Stangl interviews were the thread on which the rest must hang, but it was not easy to decide where to break them and introduce other voices: his wife's or his sister-in-law's, those of the men who worked under him, those of the five survivors, and many more. I have forgotten how long it took us, working usually in my flat (I had to take many days away from the office for this book); but I know it was months – Gitta often had to go back to her typewriter to provide links or expansions. From time to time we got stuck: there would be a chunk of material, fascinating in itself but seemingly impossible to fit in. 'Oh God, we'll just have to sacrifice it', I would say; and then, a little later, there would be some slight shift in the mass of the book, and click! in would go the problem piece, fitting exactly. This happened with almost uncanny regularity. Gitta *thought* she had just been collecting everything she could find, but the extent to which she had unconsciously been structuring her book became clearer and clearer. An interviewer does, after all, control the direction of an interview, and the further she had delved into Stangl's background, the more sure her touch had become at discovering what was relevant. We shortened a good deal, but we did not, in the end, have to leave anything out.

That was the most impressive thing about her work on this book: the way she knew, even when she felt as though she didn't, exactly what, in this most complicated operation, she was after. That, and her astonishing power as an interviewer which enabled her to draw out of people all that they had to give. And another thing which won my admiration was her lack of author's vanity. She would sometimes say 'no' to an alteration I suggested, on the grounds that it sounded too unlike her; but usually if a point were made more concisely or emphatically she appeared not to mind if I altered her original words. What she was committed to was *getting things said* rather than to making an impression as a wordsmith.

I could write at length about *Into That Darkness*, but it would make more sense for those of my readers who don't know it to get hold of a copy. The reason why working on it was so important to me was that its subject engaged me so completely. I still think – and often – of how that unremarkable man became a monster as the result of a chain of choices between right and wrong – some of the early ones quite trivial – and the way in which no one he respected intervened in favour of the right, while a number of people he respected (senior officers, a priest, a doctor – his idea of respectability was conventional) behaved as though the wrong were right. Chief among them, of course, the Führer. Stangl did not have a strong centre – had probably been deprived of it by a dreary childhood – so he became a creature of the regime. Other people without much centre didn't – or not to the same extent – so some quality inherent in him (perhaps lack of imagination combined with ambition) must have been evident to those who picked him for his appalling jobs. But it was surely environment rather than genes which made him what he became.

One good thing about being old is that one no longer minds so much about what people think of one. Boasting is disapproved of, but still I am going to quote the words with which Gitta acknowledged my help, because they gave me so much pleasure: 'Diana Athill edited *Into That Darkness*. She has lent it – and me – her warmth, her intelligence, her literary fluency, and a quality of involvement I had little right to expect. I am grateful that she has become my friend.' Which makes us quits, because I was and am grateful to my friend Gitta for allowing me that involvement.

Soon after the book was finished Gitta became ill: a cancer, discovered – thank God – early enough for complete extirpation. I know, of course, that there can be no proof of this, but I have always been convinced that it was a consequence of the strain she underwent when she had the courage to follow that man so closely into his dreadful night.

9

DOMESTIC LIFE AT Carlisle Street (and later) was as full of incident as professional life, and this was for two reasons: the first, André's weakness for the square peg; the second, love.

The square pegs were many, often harmless and soon remedied, sometimes dramatic. Two were actually deranged, one of them a sales manager, the other put in charge of publicity (I was at last allowed to hand over the advertising to a publicity department, such an overpowering relief that it was some time before I could believe it, and rejoice). The sales manager, who had been imported from Australia, was living in a hotel, and I remember going there with André, hoping to find out why he hadn't appeared at the office for three days, and being told by the receptionist in a hushed voice, as if he were divulging the movements of a celebrity: 'The Colonel left for Berlin two days ago.' The *Colonel*?? We were never to find out more about his attack of military rank, nor about his disappearance. The publicity lady simply suffered from *folie de grandeur*, which provided its own solution when she realized that the job was beneath her.

The square peg I remember most fondly I shall call Louise. André found her in New York, writing copy for Tiffany's catalogue, and saw in a flash that she was just the person to manage the editorial department: not to do editing, but to *organize the editors*. He had long nursed a dream of programming and wall-charts which would somehow overcome the hazards which beset a book's progress from typewriter to printing press: authors having second thoughts, indexers going down with flu, holders of copyright not answering letters and so on. Louise was going to cure him of this dream, but we were unable to foresee the happy outcome, and awaited her arrival with dread. He had announced her thus: 'You are all going to have to *obey* her absolutely. Even *I* am going to obey her.'

She did at first sight seem a little alarming – but only because she was so chic. She was willowy and fine-boned, and her clothes were almost painfully enviable: the sort of casual clothes at which classy New Yorkers excel, so simple that you can't pinpoint why you know they are very expensive, you just do know it. But her striking poise and confidence did not prevent her manner from being engaging, so I took her to lunch on her first day feeling warmer towards her than I had expected; and indeed, we had not finished the first course before every trace of alarm had been dispersed.

Louise couldn't wait to tell me why she had accepted André's offer. She had met Ken Tynan in New York (Tynan was even more famous there, both as theatre critic and as personality, than he was in London); she had fallen madly in love with him; when he had left for London she had been flat broke (*how did she get those clothes?*) so that she couldn't possibly follow him, and had been in despair . . . and then, out of the blue, came this God-sent chance. Did I think Ken would mind? She was almost sure he wouldn't, he had said this, that and the other, done this, that and the other . . . Surely that must mean that their affair was about to go from strength to strength . . . Or did I think, perhaps, that she had been *unwise*? I had never been nearer Tynan than the far side of a room at a drinks party, but it was impossible not to hear a great deal about him, and what I had heard made me pretty sure that she had been very unwise. I could already envisage mopping-up operations ahead, but what chiefly occupied my mind on that first day was the cheerful certainty that this charming but daft girl was never going to manage anything, not even her doomed love-life.

What still remained to be discovered was the extent of her curiously vulnerable recklessness – her almost heroic compulsion to plunge into disaster – and her total uselessness in an office. She was a brilliant con-artist as far as the first moves went – that first impression of exceptional poise and confidence never failed – but she couldn't follow through. I don't think she even tried to. I came to know her quite well, even had her to stay in my flat when her need to be rescued became acute, and often wondered how well she knew herself. Did she wake at night and start sweating at the thought of being found out, or did she simply blank out awkward facts such as that she had conned her way into a job she couldn't do and was now lying in her teeth to hide the fact that she wasn't doing it? Blank them out, and then switch on some kind of instinctive escape mechanism by which she would wriggle out of this situation and into another?

Not until she had left us did we discover that she had been hiding book-proofs behind a radiator instead of sending them out, as she had said that she had done, to distinguished persons in the hope that they would provide glowing quotes to go on book-jackets; but we did realize quite soon that when Louise said she had done something it didn't necessarily mean that she had, and it was only a matter of weeks before André was muttering and rumbling – though not to her. He was rarely able to sack a square peg. His method was to complain about them angrily to everyone from Nick and me to our switchboard operator (never, of course, admitting that he had brought the offender in) until he had created such a thick miasma of discomfort in the office that even the most obtuse peg would sense that something was amiss, and would eventually leave. (On one appalling, and unforgiven, occasion, much later, when a peg had failed to do this, André broke down, gulping: 'I can't – I *can't* – *You* do it!' And I had to.)

Luckily Louise had sensitive feelers and soon became aware that thin ice was melting under her feet. So when one evening she found herself next to Tom Maschler of Cape's at a dinner party, she switched on her act. And a few days later Tom called André to apologize for having done a wicked thing: he had poached our Louise! 'I hope to God,' said André, 'that I wasn't *too* gracious about it.' Luckily Tom suspected nothing, and that was that. I went on seeing Louise from time to time, but thought it better not to ask her about her new job – it was her love-life that I was following. She finally accepted rejection by Tynan, embarked on a therapeutic flutter with a man who didn't interest her at all, became pregnant by him, and had an excuse to flee back to New York just in time – or so I suspected – to avoid being sacked.

I didn't say to André 'I told you so' because I knew so well, by then, that it would have no effect whatsoever.

The love which most disturbed the office – this was both surprising and gratifying – was that which afflicted men, not women. Among people of my grandparents' generation and, to a slightly lesser extent, my parents' it was taken for granted that men were to be preferred to women in responsible jobs because they were in better control of their emotional lives. A woman might be as intelligent as a man, but her intelligence could not be relied on because if, for instance, she was crossed in love she would go to pieces. Menstrual moodiness was not actually mentioned, but the idea of it lurked: women, poor things, were so designed that they couldn't be expected to overcome their bodies' vagaries. To my generation this was not true, but it was still present as something which needed to be disproved. I was therefore delighted to find that while I and my woman colleagues at work sometimes endured gruelling emotional experiences in our private lives, we none of us ever allowed them to impinge on our work in anything like the shameless way that Nick and André did.

Nick, usually a pattern of gentlemanly reticence with an upper lip so stiff that it almost creaked, fell violently in love with a young woman who was working for us, and by the time he had left his wife, forced her into divorcing him, been dumped by his mistress, and returned to his wife, the amount of hysteria that had been unleashed left the onlookers prostrate with exhaustion. At the stage when Nick was alone in a dreary rented flat soon after his woman had decided that she didn't want him after all, I felt truly sorry for him: a man so dignified having been reduced to making such a pathetic exhibition of himself, and all for nothing – it was tragic. But his dignity and my sympathy were a good deal reduced when, less than a week later, André reported that Nick was back with his wife and that we were all being asked to behave as though nothing had happened. I couldn't see any explanation for such a rapid anti-climax other than an inability to imagine life without being cooked, cleaned and shopped for.

André's love trials, less severe than Nick's but no less hard on the audience, were incidental to a story which turned out to be life-long and – with ups and downs – happy.

Earlier, at the time when I first became his confidante, he used to get through women very quickly. There would be an earnest report of falling in love (it was always love, never liking, that he fell into), soon followed by the news that it was over. On one occasion only three days passed between the falling and the revelation that the woman was impossible because 'she keeps on telephoning'. 'But isn't that rather nice?' I asked. 'No, she wants to talk about her troubles.' Another time he invited someone he had just met to share a short holiday in Cornwall, only to see next day that this was a mistake; whereupon he bullied Sheila Dunn to go with them and she in turn had to bully him not to lock the girl out of his bedroom – a situation I remembered on reading in Liane de Pougy's *My Blue Notebooks* how an ex-lover of hers summoned her to his rescue because a new flame had trundled into his bedroom equipped with her pillow, obviously expecting (*quelle horreur!*) to stay in his bed all night.

This flightiness was soon to change. In 1949 André went on the first of the skiing holidays in Davos which he was to take every winter for the rest of his active life, asking me before he left to look after his latest girl. I spent an evening with her – and it seemed to me that she showed no sign of infatuation, which was lucky. As soon as André got home he called me, to announce: 'I'm in love!'

'I know you are – you left me in charge of her.'

'Not with *her*. This is the real thing.'

And it was. Staying at the same hotel in Davos was the woman who would put an end to his days of philandering.

Her dark-haired brown-eyed beauty was of the slightly sharp-featured kind which most excited him, so it was not surprising that she had appealed to him on sight, but why she was the one who caught him for keeps – and it was obvious from the start that this had happened – is more mysterious.

I thought about it a lot, and came to the conclusion that four things had combined to give her the unshakeable authority she was to hold over his imagination: she was ten years older than he was, she was married, she was shy and reserved by nature and she was seriously rich.

Glamour requires a certain distance, and this beauty's seniority, her married status and her reserve endowed her with it: André would never be able to feel in complete possession of her. And her – or rather her husband's – money, which I am convinced André never thought of as something from which he might profit, enhanced this slightly out-of-reach glamour a good deal – and did so all the more effectively because she herself made very little of having money. She was gloriously special in André's eyes less for her amazing richness than because she was *above* her amazing richness.

At first he longed to marry her and felt, when her husband made this impossible, that they were in a tragic plight. But they were able to go on seeing each other, and finally he seemed to become resigned to the situation. He was in fact far too single-minded in his self-absorption to be good at marriage, however sincerely he would have adored his wife, and no one could have spent many years of meeting him almost every day without seeing as much.

In almost fifty years I met his beloved no more than a couple of dozen times, because André insisted that she was fiercely jealous of me. To begin with that was not inconceivable – I was ten years younger than she was, shared his interests and was with him every weekday – but as the years passed it seemed less and less likely; and by the time he said it (as he did) to an eighty-year-old me of a ninety-year-old her, it had become no more than an automatic twitch of an ossified male vanity. The truth was more likely to be that she had no intention of being lumbered with her lover's hangers-on. I believe she never once met his mother (for which no one who knew Maria Deutsch would dream of blaming her).

In any relationship as long as theirs there are ups and downs, and twice during our Carlisle Street days André was overtaken by fits of jealousy. Neither time, as far as I could see, did he have good reason for it, though that was not from want of trying to find one. Because both times, in addition to collapsing into a melting jelly of woe, unable to think or talk for days on end about anything else ('How can you expect me to think about print-runs when *this* is going on?' – which was hard to take given the degree of commitment he demanded from everyone else), he devoted evening after evening to what he called 'driving round', which meant spying, and for 'driving round' he insisted on a companion. He would endlessly circle whatever restaurant he thought she might be dining at; and having failed to catch her coming or going would then drive up and down the street where his suspected rival lived, hoping (or dreading) to see her car parked on it. Which he never did. If he had I would have known, because although I soon went on strike about 'driving round' with him, finding it as disgusting as it was boring, and was succeeded by other reluctant attendants, I still had to hear a blow-by-blow account of every evening, together with all the other moaning.

Why did I feel that I must go on listening? Nowadays, of course, I would soon find a way of escaping from such a desperately boring ordeal, but at the time it seemed to me that listening was what friends are for . . . which is, I suppose, true enough up to a point, and it is not easy to draw a line between a genuine need for sympathy and greedy self-indulgence. I could and did draw it, but still I felt that André couldn't help crossing that line so that I *must* bear with him. I remember a particularly violent spasm of impatience, and thinking 'Hang on, don't let it rip, if he knew what I'm really feeling how could our friendship survive?'.

And in fact it was to be given a rude shock – though by André's impatience, not mine.

At about the time when he was going through his paroxysms of jealousy, and just before Nick's debacle, I fell in love with a man who had the courage, when he realized what had happened, to tell me that he was unable to fall in love with me. Even then I was grateful for his honesty because experience had already taught me a good deal about broken-heartedness, and I knew that the quickest cure is lack of hope. If mistaken kindness allows you the least glimmer of hope you snatch at it and your misery is prolonged: but this man (this dear man whom I continued to like very much after I was cured) made it impossible for me to fool myself, so I was able to set about getting better without delay and in the end was left without a scar. But although the process was steady it was not quick, and for about a year I had nothing to take my mind off sadness but my work, so that my evenings were often desolate.

Those enjoyed by André, his beloved, Nick and his wife Barbara seemed, on the other hand, to be all that evenings should be. They made a foursome and went to theatres, concerts, exhibitions and movies together two or three times a week. 'I wish that they would sometimes ask me to go with them,' I thought on one particularly dreary evening; and went on to wonder if it would be importunate to suggest as much to André. It would go against the grain to do so because I had fallen into the habit of keeping my love troubles to myself – and perhaps that was why it had not occurred to him that I could do with cheering up. If he knew . . . and we were, after all, friends: think of all the listening I'd done to *his* love troubles; think of all that 'driving round' for heaven's sake! Surely after all that I could bring myself to confess that I was going through a bad time and that an occasional evening at the cinema with him and the others would be very welcome.

So I did – probably, after all the screwing up to it which had gone on, in a tiresomely self-conscious voice. And what he said, very crossly, was: 'Oh for God's sake! Don't be so sorry for yourself.'

10

IN 1961 WE BOUGHT 105 Great Russell Street, where the firm was to spend the rest of its days. André pounced on it less because we needed a bigger house, although we did, than because it came with Grafton Books, a small firm specializing in books on librarianship, which he felt would contribute a ballast of bread and butter to our list in the future. In our early days we used to look respectfully at Faber & Faber because, as André often pointed out, their distinguished list of literary books was supported by others less glamorous – I think there were references to books about nursing – and we all felt slightly worried by our own lack of such reliable 'back-list' material. The cookery list was an attempt to remedy this, and so was the Language Library, a series of books on the nature and history of language which the lexicographer Eric Partridge thought up for us, and which he edited first entirely, then in an advisory capacity, until his death. Grafton seemed a timely expansion of this policy, and its house was splendid: a decent though often-adapted Georgian building, which bore a plaque announcing that the architect A. W. N. Pugin once lived in it, and which we saw at first as huge. The street on which it stood was drab, catering for the kind of tourist who, clad in anorak and trainers, is in pursuit of culture; but the British Museum still looks out on it through its noble gates and a screen of plane trees, bestowing enough dignity to make it a good address for a publisher.

Here we settled down to enjoy the sixties which were, indeed, good years for us; although they never seemed to me essentially different from any other decade. Perhaps they would have done if I had been younger and still fully responsive to the pull of fashion, but as it was I saw them as an invention of the media. Most of the people I knew had been bedding each other for years without calling it a sexual revolution. Jean Rhys agreed, saying that people were using drugs like crazy when she first came to London before the First World War, the only difference being that the papers didn't go on about it. But of course the fact that we now felt that we had finished recovering from the Second World War did make for cheerfulness.

Because we had more space in which to accommodate more people we began to feel less like a family and more like a firm. For some time we stuck at twenty-four people, not counting packing and dispatch which was always under a separate roof and functioned efficiently and happily in the hands of an earnest Marxist and various members of his family (until the fatal day when André caught the suddenly-fashionable Management Consultant bug, after which they became less efficient, and unhappy). Then the production department grew from two to three to four; publicity and rights each managed to convince André that they needed a secretary of their own; Pamela Royds, our children's books editor, forced herself to confess that she really did *have* to have an extra hand (long overdue, given the size and importance of her list) . . . By the time we reached full strength we were using windowless passages as rooms and every real room was subdivided to the limit. Because my little room looked out of a window on the house's quiet side I felt guiltily privileged. Poor Esther Whitby and the other three of the editorial department were, for several years, entombed in the cellar.

I often wondered whether other businesses above the level of sweated labour imposed on their personnel the degree of discomfort we got away with. The country seemed to teem with people, most of them young women, so eager to work with books that they would endure poverty and pain to do so: a situation which we certainly exploited. The only people paid salaries commensurate with the value of their labour were our sales manager, our production manager and our accountant – all usually married men who would very properly not have taken the job for less. The rest of us, in spite of mopping and mowing fairly steadily about our pitiful lot . . . well, we could have left but we did not, and the atmosphere was usually cheerful.

Since I was always down among the common people as far as salary was concerned (several women who came to work for us after 1962 had the sense to insist on pay higher than mine), I felt like one of the employed rather than one of the employers. We were well into the nineteen-seventies before I reached £10,000 a year and I was never to be paid more than £15,000 – though some time in the late seventies I did get a company car (I remember André failing to convince me that a *deux chevaux* had a lot of throw-away chic). By the time we reached Great Russell Street I was no longer even noticing the extent to which the title 'Director', applied to me, meant next to nothing. When it came to buying property, increasing or not increasing staff, deciding where our books should be printed and what people should be paid, André made no pretence of preliminary discussion with anyone: which I accepted, so long as I was listened to – as I was – about books.

In only one respect do I now regret my attitude. If I had instinctively felt myself to be a senior officer rather than one of the crew I would have kept André in better order: would, for instance, have said 'Nonsense, of course we must buy them proper chairs and desk lamps – and *so what* if they cost as much as the ones you have just bought for yourself'. Instead of which I just, like everyone else, put up with the junk available, thinking 'What a mean old bastard he is' with the reluctant resignation of one complaining about bad weather.

Grafton Books was a good thing as far as it went, but it did not go very far: we were mistaken in thinking that it and the Language Library would keep us in bread and butter should we ever hit hard times. Grafton was run for us by Clive Bingley (who was to buy it from us in 1981) with the support of a small advisory committee, and he tended it through a growth as vigorous as a narrow field allowed; but few people had less interest in the technicalities of librarianship than André, Nick and me, so Clive must often have felt unsupported. When André sold it to him I think it was because of lack of interest in it rather than because it was losing us money, but it certainly was not bringing in a missable amount. And similarly, the Language Library would probably have done much better if one of us had cared about linguistics (for my part, having brushed the fringes of the subject at Oxford, I had moved rapidly through ignorance to abhorrence). It remained respectable, but it was unadventurous: we might, after all, have become the British publishers of Chomsky, but no one even thought about it. We hung on to the Language Library until 1984, and when we shunted it off onto Basil Blackwell Ltd of Oxford no one in the house noticed that it had gone. The truth is that a specialized list, if it is to succeed, must be published by a specialist: someone who will bring to it the energy and enthusiasm that we put into the rest of our list. Grafton and the Language Library made a modest but real contribution to the golden glow of our best years, but by the time we began to see rough weather ahead both of them, for lack of love, had become the kind of cargo that can be jettisoned.

The books that did well for us in the next thirty years were the books we liked – not, of course, that they were all liked equally, or all by all of us, but all of them more or less 'our sort of book'. Among the more conspicuous of our novelists (I put them in alphabetical order to disguise preference) were Margaret Atwood (her three earliest), Peter Benchley (all his novels, but *Jaws* was the one which struck gold), Marilyn French (two of her novels, but it was *The Women's Room* which counted), Molly Keane (her three last, *Good Behaviour* supreme among them), Jack Kerouac, Norman Mailer (up to and including *An American Dream*), Timothy Mo (his first two), V. S. Naipaul (eighteen of his books, including non-fiction), Jean Rhys (all), Philip Roth (his first two), and John Updike (up to and including the collection of essays, *Odd Jobs*).

There were a great many others, a few of which I have forgotten, many of which I enjoyed, some of which I loved – and I shall insert here a note to those readers who like to poke about in second-hand bookshops: if you come across any of the following, *buy them*:

Michael Anthony's *The Year in San Fernando*. Michael came from a remote Trinidadian village. His mother was very poor, and when offered the chance to send her boy to work for an old woman in San Fernando, she couldn't afford to turn it down. So the ten-year-old was dispatched to a small provincial town which seemed to him a thrilling and alarming metropolis; and Michael's novel is based on this experience. It is a wonderfully true and touching child's-eye view of life.

John Gardner's *Grendel*. A surprising novel to come out of Tennessee, by the man Raymond Carver acknowledged gratefully as a major influence. It is the Beowulf story told from the monster's point of view. Having to read *Beowulf* almost turned me against Oxford, so when a New York agent offered me this novel I could hardly bring myself to open it. If I hadn't I would have missed a great pleasure – a really powerful feat of imagination.

Michael Irwin's *Working Orders* and *Striker*. Two of the best novels of British working-class life I know – particularly *Striker*, which is about the making and breaking of a soccer star.

Chaman Nahal's *Azadi*. A superb novel about a Hindu family's experience of the partitioning of India, which ought to be recognized as a classic.

Merce Rodoreda's *The Pigeon Girl*. An extremely moving love story translated from the Catalan, which reveals much about the Spanish civil war as ordinary, non-political people had to live it.

It must seem to many readers that if someone was lucky enough to publish Roth's first books and almost all of Updike's, those two writers ought to figure largely in her story, but they are not going to do so. We lost Roth early through lack of faith, although I still think it was excusable. He, even more than Mailer, was a writer whose fame preceded his work: when his very gifted little first novel, *Goodbye, Columbus*, crossed the Atlantic it was all but invisible for the haze of desirability surrounding it, so that no one doubted for a moment that we had made a valuable catch. Then came *Letting Go* which I thought wonderful, although I agreed with André that it was too long – not 'by a third', as he said, but still too long. So we asked each other whether we should raise the matter with Philip and agreed that it would be too dangerous; there was such a buzz going on about him, everyone was after him – annoy him and he would be gone in a flash. And anyway it would be difficult to cut because it was all so good – there was not a dead line in it. Much of that novel is dialogue and I got the impression that Philip's brilliance with dialogue had gone to his head: he had enjoyed doing it so much that he couldn't bring himself to stop. So we accepted the novel as it was and it didn't earn its advance. (Imagine my feelings when he said to me, several years later: 'The trouble with *Letting Go* is that it's far too long.') Then came a novel called *When She Was Good*, told from the point of view of a young woman from the Middle West, non-Jewish, who struck me as being pretty obviously Philip's first wife. I never talked to him about this book, so what I say here is no more than my hunch, but I thought 'This is an exercise – he is trying to prove to himself that he doesn't *have* to write as a Jew and a man'. And as I read I kept telling myself 'It must soon come alive – it must'. And it didn't.

So we thought 'No more silly money' and decided to calculate the advance on precisely what we reckoned the book would sell – which I think was four thousand copies at the best – and that was not accepted. As far as I know *When She Was Good* was not a success – but the next novel Philip wrote was *Portnoy's Complaint*.

This space represents a tactful silence.

John Updike, on the other hand, was never set up as a star and never disappointed. From a publisher's point of view he was a perfect author: an extremely good writer who knows his own worth but is also well-informed about the realities of the publishing and bookselling trades. And from a personal point of view he is an exceptionally agreeable man, interesting, amusing and unpretentious, who knows how to guard his privacy without being unfriendly. I like John very much, always enjoyed meeting him, and never felt inclined to speculate about whatever he chose to keep to himself, so I have nothing to say about him except the obvious fact that we would have been a *much* less distinguished publishing house without him.

The strangest of my Great Russell Street experiences came in the mid-eighties, and did not result in a book. David Astor, the then retired editor of the *Observer*, and Mr Tims, a Methodist minister who had been a prison chaplain and had acted as counsellor to Myra Hindley, wanted her to write a truthful account of her part in the 'Moors Murders'. Mr Tims's motive was that of a Christian believing in redemption through penitence: he wanted, as a man in his position ought to want, to see this woman save her soul by plumbing the darkest depths of her guilt. Whether David Astor was at one with him about the soul-saving I am not sure, but he was convinced that if she could get to the bottom of her actions it would provide information valuable to sociologists and psychologists. Encouraged by these two men, she had written about her childhood and about meeting Ian Brady, falling in love with him and starting to live with him; but when she approached the murders, she stuck. She needed help. She needed an editor.

David Astor invited André and me to his house to meet Mr Tims and discuss the matter. It was soon after Tom Rosenthal had joined us, in the first stage of his buying the firm when he and André were to go through a period of joint management, so he too knew about the proposal. Our reactions to it had been characteristic: Tom's was instant and uncomplicated – he wouldn't touch anything to do with that monstrous woman with a bargepole; André's was uncomfortable but respectful, because he greatly admired David Astor and felt that any suggestion of his must be taken seriously; mine was a mixture of dismay and a curiosity too strong to be withstood. As we talked it over with the two men I became more and more sure that I wouldn't do it; but, having read the material they had persuaded her to write, I was ready to postpone my decision until after I had met her. She wrote simply and intelligently, making it clear how an ambitious nineteen-year-old with very little education, feeling herself to be more interesting than the rest of her family but frustratingly cut off from ways of proving it, could not fail to respond to the man she met at her work-place: the reserved austere man who quite obviously despised nearly everyone, but who *chose her*; who then went on to introduce her to frightening but fascinating books unknown to anyone else of her acquaintance; and who believed that it was necessary to be above the petty considerations which governed most people's despicable little lives. It was easy enough to see how that particular girl, falling in love with that particular man, would soon start to feel privileged, and to enjoy the sense of superiority gained by flouting ordinary people's timid limitations on behaviour. It was certainly not surprising that when she tried to confront the appalling results of following this line to its end, she couldn't. And I didn't see how anyone could help her do it – nor was I convinced that anyone ought to try. But given the chance to meet her, I was going to take it.

Mr Tims took me to the prison, a modern one, surrounded not by a wall but by a very high mesh fence. Its windows were of a normal size, out of which people could see grass and trees. Its only strangeness was that none of its inhabitants was visible: nobody was walking across those lawns or leaning out of those windows. No one but David Astor, André and Tom knew I was there – but I had not been in that prison fifteen minutes before a representative of a newspaper – I think the *Mail*, though I'm not sure – was on the telephone to the office asking if we were signing Myra Hindley up for a book. This, I was told later, always happened: wherever Hindley has been held, it seems there has been someone ready to keep the press informed of what is going on. To the British press, even after twenty-two years, Myra Hindley was firmly established as a kind of sacred monster, the least twitch of whose tail *had* to cause a ritual frenzy.

I spent about an hour with Myra Hindley, in a small room outside the open door of which sat a bored-looking wardress. If I had not known who the woman opposite me was, what would I have thought of her? I would have liked her. She was intelligent, responsive, humorous, dignified. And if someone had then informed me that this unknown woman had been in prison for twenty-two years I would have been amazed: how could a person of whom that was true appear to be so little institutionalized?

We talked about writing, of course – she had just taken a degree in English from the Open University – and about her conversion to Catholicism. She described how nightmarish it was to have the press breathing down the back of her neck all the time, and how boring to be short of intelligent talk. She was flippant rather than grateful about what she called 'my old men' – Lord Longford, David Astor, and Tims. To begin with her speech was very slightly slower than normal, so that I wondered if she was on tranquillizers – and Mr Tims was to say yes, she would have been: she had had to use them a lot since she had agreed to visit the moors with the police in an attempt to find the place where Brady had buried a victim whose remains had never been recovered. By the end of the hour she was speaking quite normally, and we could easily have gone on talking. I still liked her – and I had become quite sure that I was not going to become her editor.

The reason for this was two-fold: I could not believe that such a book would in fact teach anyone anything that could not already be inferred from the events, and I was also unable to believe that forcing herself to write it would help Myra Hindley. I was not a believer like Mr Tims, so about her soul I did not know: I was capable of envisaging the healing of guilt only in terms of *tout comprendre c'est tout pardonner*, and I did not think that this woman, if she compelled herself fully to acknowledge what she had done, would be able to grant herself pardon. When she did what she did, she was not mad – as Ian Brady was – and, although she was young, she was an adult, and an intelligent one. It seems to me that there are extremes of moral deformity which cannot be pardoned: that Stangl was right when, having faced the truth about himself, he said 'I ought to be dead'. He then had the luck to die, but that is not a conclusion that can be counted on. By the law of our land Myra Hindley had been condemned to live with what she had done, and she had contrived for herself a probably precarious way of doing so: admitting guilt, but blurring it by exaggerating her youth at the time and keeping the extent to which she had been influenced by, and eventually frightened by, Brady to the fore. What would society gain if she were made to live through those murders again as the sane adult she had in fact been, and ended by saying 'I ought to be dead', or by breaking down completely, which seemed to me the likely conclusion? Nothing. So if I enabled her to write the proposed book, and André Deutsch Limited published it, we would simply be trading in the pornography of evil, like the gutter press we despised. No, it could not be done.

Much of our non-fiction came in as a result of André's visits to New York: for example, John Kenneth Galbraith's books about economics, Arthur Schlesinger's about the Kennedy presidency, Joseph P. Lash's two about the Roosevelts. He also harvested many unexpected books such as Eric Berne's account of transactional analysis, *Games People Play*, very modish in its day, George Plimpton's funny stories about taking on professional sportsmen at their own games, and Helene Hanff's almost absurdly successful little collection of letters to a London bookseller, *84 Charing Cross Road*. Quickies by Daniel Cohn-Bendit and Bernadette Devlin resulted from his rapid response to whatever happened to be going on in the world; books by Gitta Sereny from his inability to read a newspaper without asking 'Is there a book in it?'. Simone de Beauvoir's books came from his flirtation with his old friend George Weidenfeld, with whom he had almost yearly meetings at which they discussed collaboration (sharing a warehouse, perhaps?), always to no avail except (mysteriously) in the case of joint publication of de Beauvoir. And it was André who launched us into our lively and profitable series of 'Insight Books' from the *Sunday Times*.

In the sixties Harold Evans made his name as the inspiring

young editor of that paper, piloting it to the forefront of investigative journalism. His literary editor Leonard Russell, an old friend of Nick's and newer friend of André's, called André one day in 1967 to consult him about an offer the paper had just received. The Insight Team was doing an investigation of the Philby affair, it had occurred to them that there might be a book in it, and George Weidenfeld had offered £10,000: did André think this was about right? 'No,' said André. 'I will give you £20,000.' And that was that.

We had a slightly proprietorial feeling about Philby, because he had been introduced to us during his curious limbo-years between the defection of Burgess and Maclean to the Soviet Union and his own uncovering as a spy. Since 1949 Philby had been the top British Secret Intelligence Service man in Washington, liaising with the FBI and the CIA, and he and Burgess were colleagues both in their above-ground roles in the British secret service and in their underground roles as spies for Russia – he had even had Burgess to stay with him in Washington. He was therefore recalled to London for investigation and, although nothing could be proved against him, left his masters so uneasy that he was asked to resign. Soon afterwards a friend of Nick's, a rich picture dealer called Tommy Harris who had also been in the British Secret Service, came to us and suggested that we should commission Philby's life story: the poor man was now short of an occupation and of money, and of course there was nothing in the very unjust rumours which had followed his resignation. Tommy Harris brought him to meet Nick and André, who found him impressive and congenial, as did most of the people who met him, and who signed him up, agreeing to let him have his advance in instalments to keep him going during the writing. None of which was done, of course – I think Tommy Harris repaid the advance. Philby's failure to deliver was attributed to his finding, when he came to it, that he was not a writer. Another five years were to pass before the true reason emerged, on his disappearance to Russia. While it is possible for a dedicated professional spy to *live* a life of deceit – an effort constantly rewarded by the achievement of specific ends, and probably by the feeling that you are being cleverer than the enemy – it would be unutterably boring to *write* it: to slog away at a story completely lacking in the one element which gave it, from your point of view, meaning. Once Philby had 'come out' he was able to write what he felt to be the true story of his life very well.

There were to be five more 'Insight Books': a detailed analysis of a presidential election in America (Nixon's); a hair-raising account of how a financial colossus (Bernard Cornfeld) rose and fell; an overview of the Middle Eastern war of 1973; the inside story of the Thalidomide disaster; and (the tail-end of the series, lacking the zing of its predecessors) *Strike*, the story of Thatcher, Scargill and the miners. All of them were team books produced by a group of exceptionally brilliant journalists in different combinations, chief among them Bruce Page, David Leitch, Phillip Knightley, Lewis Chester, Godfrey Hodgson and Charles Raw. The books emerged from a room at the *Sunday Times* so throbbing with activity that it was hard to imagine how a single paragraph of lucid prose could be written in it. It was Piers Burnett who edited them all for us, and he tells me that no experience in his long and varied publishing career was more entertaining.

In spite of André's record as a collector of square pegs, he did, of course, hit on many more round ones, and Piers was probably the roundest of them all. I think he was taken on as another attempt to impose on the editorial department that illusory orderliness and method of which André still spasmodically dreamt, and Piers did continue to function as an editor all the time he was with us; but quite soon his practicality, good sense and astonishing appetite for hard work got through to André. He had long nursed another dream in addition to that of the Editorial Manager; the dream of a Right Hand Man who would relieve the weight on his own shoulders by taking on at least some of the planning, negotiating and calculating with which he was burdened. He had recently made two attempts to bring this dream person in from outside, neither of which had worked – and very few of his onlookers would have been prepared to bet so much as a penny on any such attempt working.

But now it dawned on him that perhaps what he needed was already in the house. He hesitated; he seemed for a while to be almost disgruntled at the prospect of anything so *easy*; and then the decision was made and Piers moved downstairs to the little room next to André's, and there, at last, was the Right Hand Man who suited possibly the most difficult man in London.

The most spectacular thing that Piers did for us was to bring in Peter Benchley's *Jaws* on his first visit to New York; but he was not ordinarily much at home with fiction, and when from '79 to '81 a small list under his own imprint came out under our wing it specialized in psychology and sociology. Nowadays his own publishing firm, Aurum Press, which he runs with Bill McCreadie (once our sales manager) and Sheila Murphy (once our publicity manager), has a much wider focus but still avoids fiction. Otherwise it is the nearest thing going to a 'Son of Deutsch': much nearer than the firm which now bears our name.

An aspect of our activities which seemed in the sixties to be very important was André's adventures in Africa. In '63 we declared: 'We are proud to announce that we are working in close association with AUP (African Universities Press, Lagos), the first indigenous publishing house in free Africa, the foundation of which was announced in Lagos in April this year. The greater part of AUP's output will be educational books chosen to answer the needs of Nigerian schools and colleges. It will, however, have a general list as well. Books on this list likely to appeal to readers outside Nigeria will be published simultaneously by us.' Two years later a similar announcement was made about the East African Publishing House in Kenya. Both publishing houses were started by André, who had chased up the local capital and editorial board for them and had found them each a manager. As a result we secured some good African novelists (my own favourites were *The Gab Boys* by Cameron Duodu and *My Mercedes Is Longer than Yours* by Nkem Nwankwo), and a number of intelligent books about African politics and economics – and André enjoyed some exciting trips. (One of them was too exciting. Meeting a seductive young woman at a party, he took her for a midnight stroll on a beautiful beach near Lagos, and they were hardly out of his hired car before he was flat on his face in the sand being knelt on by two large ragged men with long knives who slit his trousers pocket to get his wallet and car-keys, and might well have slit *him* if another large ragged man had not loomed out of the darkness to intervene. The thieves fled, the young woman was in hysterics, they were miles from the city centre or a telephone . . . all André could do was ask their rescuer to lead them to the nearest police station – at which all three of them were instantly arrested and the policemen started beating up the poor rescuer. It took André four hours to get the facts into the heads of the Law and procure a lift back to town – having not a penny left on him he couldn't offer a bribe. Nor could he give his rescuer a reward. He delivered the reward to the police station next day but was pretty sure it would not be passed on.)

Most of his African experiences, however, were pleasant and productive, and I admired him for having taken the current interest among publishers in the newly freed countries a step further than anyone else. Most of the people in our trade were more liberal than not, feeling guilty at being subjects of an imperial power and pleased that with the war's end Britain began relinquishing its so-called 'possessions' overseas. And many of them were genuinely interested in hearing what writers in those countries had to say now that they were free. For a time during the fifties and early sixties it was probably easier for a black writer to get his book accepted by a London publisher, and kindly reviewed thereafter, than it was for a young white person.

There was, of course, something else at work as well as literary and/or political interest. There are, after all, a vast number of Indians, Africans and West Indians in the world – a potential reading public beyond computation – and nowhere, except in India on a tiny scale, were these masses able to produce books for themselves. Certainly no British publisher was foolish enough to suppose that more than a minuscule fringe of that great potential market was, or would be for years, accessible, but I think most of us thought it would become increasingly accessible in the foreseeable future. The feeling in the air was that freedom would mean progress; that the market out there was certainly going to expand, however slowly, so that it would not only be interesting to get in on the ground floor of publishing for and about Africa: it would also prove, in the long run, to be good business. Longman's and Macmillan's, with their specialized educational lists, were the firms which addressed the situation most sensibly, in ways helpful to their customers and profitable to themselves. André was the one who did it most romantically. Instead of providing Nigeria and Kenya with books made in Britain, he felt, Britain should help them develop publishing industries of their own. André Deutsch Limited was a shareholder in both the African houses he got off the ground, but not a major shareholder; and it claimed no say in what they were to publish. It was a generous enterprise, which seemed for a while to work well in a rough and ready way . . .

History, alas, has not left many traces of it, nor of the often wise and persuasive thinking in the non-fiction books about African affairs, particularly those of the French agronomist René Dumont, which we were so proud of. In Tanzania Julius Nyerere ordered a copy each of Dumont's *False Start in Africa* for every member of his government. He might as well have tossed them into Lake Victoria. But in the sixties it would have felt not only defeatist, but *wrong*, to foresee that the dangers Dumont warned against were not to be avoided.

Now I wonder whether we were expecting history to move faster than it can because we were witnesses of how fast an empire can crumble, and did not stop to think that falling down is always more rapid than building up . . . and what, anyway, were we expecting the multitude of tribal societies in that continent, many of them with roots more or less damaged by European intrusion, to build up *to*? Perhaps our concern was, and is, as much an aspect of neo-colonialism as American investment in Nigerian oil-wells.

André, and to some extent Piers, were the people who dealt with the African houses. My only brush with them came when we published a book by Tom Mboya jointly with EAPH and he came to London for its launching. For some reason André was prevented from meeting him at the airport. Feeling that it would be rude just to send a limousine for him, he asked me to go in his stead. I had a clearer idea than he had of the value a Kenyan VIP would attribute to a middle-aged female of school-marmish appearance as a meeter, but André pooh-poohed my doubts and feebly I gave in. The drive from Heathrow to Mboya's hotel was even less agreeable than I expected. Almost all of it was spent by him and his henchmen discussing, with a good deal of sniggering and in an extemporized and wholly transparent code, how and where they were going to find fuckable blondes. But that little incident did not prevent me from feeling pleased about our African connection, seeing it as adding stature to our house.

Although I did not get to Africa, I did to the Caribbean: the only 'perk' of my career, but such a substantial one that I am not complaining. Among our several Caribbean writers was the prime minister of Trinidad & Tobago (two islands, one country), Eric Williams, with his *Capitalism and Slavery* and *From Columbus to Castro*. Such editorial consultation as was necessary could easily have been done by letter, but André delighted in collecting freebies. He saw journeys as a challenge, the object of the challenge being to get there without paying. At a pinch he would settle for an upgrading rather than a free flight – or even, if he was acting on someone else's behalf, for an invitation into the VIP lounge; but he was not often reduced to spending the firm's money on an economy fare. Acting on someone else's behalf gave him a cosy feeling of generosity, so when Eric Williams's proofs came in he staggered me by suggesting that I should take them to Port of Spain, and he wangled the works out of Eric: VIP lounge, first class, and free. I had to get to New York on the cheapest charter flight I could find (quite a complicated and chancy business in those days), but from New York to Port of Spain it was champagne all the way. And once there, after a short session with that aloof, almost stone-deaf man whose only method of communication was the lecture, I could extend the visit into a holiday.

And even that was free to begin with, because we were doing a book about the islands for tourists, and the owners of the biggest hotel on Tobago, confusing the word 'publishing' with 'publicity', invited me to stay there. It was a luxurious hotel, but the people staying in it were very old. The men played golf on its lovely links all day, the women sat by its swimming-pool, apparently indifferent to the emerald and aquamarine sea being fished by pelicans a stone's throw away, and the 'tropical fruit' announced on its menus turned out to be grapefruit. I retired to my pretty cabin in a gloomy state – and became much gloomier when I read the little notice on the back of the door listing the hotel's prices. I did know, really, that I was there as a guest, but it had not been put into words, and the question 'Supposing I'm not?' seized on my mind. If I wasn't I'd have to be shipped home in disgrace as an indigent seaman (when I was a child my father told me that that was what consuls did to people who ran out of money abroad). So next morning I took to the bush with that irrational worry still gnawing, and had the luck to hit on Tobago's Public Beach.

This was a folly wished on the island by the government in Port of Spain. Tobago was girdled by wonderful beaches open to everyone, and would have preferred the money to be spent on something useful, such as road-repairs. So nobody went to the Public Beach, and Mr Burnett, who ran it, had such a boring time that he couldn't wait to invite me to join him and his assistant for a drink on the verandah of his little office. I told him my worry about the big hotel, and said: 'Surely there must be a hotel somewhere on the island where ordinary people stay?' There was a tiny pause while the two men avoided exchanging glances and I remembered with dismay that when people here said 'ordinary' they meant 'black' in a rude way; then Mr Burnett kindly chose to take the word as I had intended it, and said of course there was: his old friend Mr Louis was opening one that very week, and he would take me there at once.

So I became – it seemed like a dream, such a delightful happening coming so pat – Mr Louis's first guest in the Hotel Jan de Moor: a former estate house in pretty grounds, scrupulously run and not expensive. Mr Louis had reckoned that American tourists would soon include American black people – school teachers and so on – who would expect comfort but would be unable to pay silly prices, so he had decided to cater for the likes of them. In that first week the only people who visited were his neighbours, dropping in for a drink in the bar as dusk fell, which made it almost as friendly as staying in a private house, and I have never enjoyed a hotel more.

That whole holiday was a joy, not only because it was my introduction to the beauties of tropical seas, shores and forests, but because I *knew the place so well*. Of course I had always been aware of how well V. S. Naipaul and Michael Anthony wrote, but until I had stepped off an aeroplane into the world they were writing about I had not quite understood what good writing can do. There were many moments, walking down a street in Port of Spain, or driving a bumpy road between walls of sugar cane or under coconut palms, when I experienced an uncanny twinge of *coming home*; which made the whole thing greatly more interesting and moving than even the finest ordinary sightseeing can be. And after that I was always to find what I think of as the anti-Mustique side of the Caribbean, dreadful though its problems can be, amazingly congenial.

In the nineteen-seventies we went through an odd, and eventually comic, experience: to the outward eye we were taken over by Time/Life. 'Synergy' had suddenly become very much the thing among giant corporations, and on one of his New York trips André had allowed himself to be persuaded that we would benefit greatly if he sold a considerable chunk of shares in André Deutsch Limited to that company. Piers and I both think it must have been about forty per cent, but we were never told. The chief – indeed, the only – argument in favour of doing so was that already the advances being paid for important books were beginning to sky-rocket beyond our reach, and with Time/Life as our partners we could keep up with that trend.

I was present at the London meeting where the beauties of the scheme were explained to our board by two or three beaming Time/Lifers who appeared to be describing some mysterious charity founded for the benefit of small publishers. At one point I asked a question which was genuinely puzzling me: 'But what do you see as being in it for *you*?' After a fractional pause, a gentle blast of pure waffle submerged the question, and I was left believing what in fact I continued to believe: *that they didn't know*. Shrewd predatory calculations *might* be underlying all this, but it seemed unlikely. 'Can it be,' I asked André after the meeting, 'that they are just silly?' To which he answered crisply: 'Yes.' I think he had already started to wonder what on earth he was doing, but couldn't see how to back out of it.

Oh well, we all thought, perhaps we *will* get some big books through them, and they don't seem to intend any harm – and the truth was, they did not. We got one big book through them – Khrushchev's memoirs in two volumes, the first of which was sniffed at suspiciously by reviewers who thought it was written by the CIA, and the second of which was claimed by Time/Life to be proved genuine by scientific means, but who cared? They made no attempt to intervene in any of our publishing plans. And they drove André mad.

This they did by writing to him from time to time, asking him for a detailed forecast of our publishing plans for the next five years. The first time they did this he sent a civil reply explaining that our kind of publishing didn't work like that, but gradually he became more and more enraged. I remember being taken aside at a New York party by the man who functioned as our link with Time/Life, and asked to calm André and explain to him that all he need do to keep the accounts people happy was *send a few figures*. He didn't say in so many words 'It doesn't matter if they make sense or not', but he very clearly implied as much, and that was the message I carried home . . . which made André even madder. It was their silliness that was getting to him, not their asking for information. Our accountant Philip Tammer (who, by the way, was the dearest, kindest, most long-suffering, most upright and most loyal accountant anyone ever had) once wrote to their accountants: 'What we will be publishing in five years' time depends on what's going on in the head of some unknown person probably sitting in a garret, and we don't know the address of that garret.' André was feeling about Time/Life very much what I felt about André when he nagged the editorial department about lack of method.

The other cause of indignation was the Annual Meeting of the Associates (there were ten or so other companies linked to Time/Life, like us). Sales conferences in exotic venues were much indulged in during the seventies – perhaps they still are? They were justified on the grounds that giving the reps a treat would improve their morale. This was not a belief subscribed to by anyone in our firm. On one occasion we ventured as far as a pub outside Richmond, but usually at the end of the conference we all sloped off to dinner at an inexpensive restaurant, the meal (if André had managed to get his oar in) ordered in advance so that no one could start getting silly with the smoked salmon (and they were fun, those evenings). So the idea of traipsing off to *Mexico* for what amounted to a glorified sales conference, as he had to do in the first year of this alliance, seemed to André an outrage. For the second year they announced that the venue would be Morocco, and he struck. He wrote to them severely, pointing out that all the Associates would be going, like him, to the Frankfurt Book Fair, so the obvious time and place for their meeting would be the weekend before the Fair, somewhere in Germany within easy reach of Frankfurt. I distinctly heard the sound of gritted teeth behind the fulsome letter received in return, which assured him that 'this is exactly the kind of input we were hoping to gain from our Associates'.

Before each meeting all the Associates were asked to think up ten Publishing Projects (which meant books), and to send their outlines to New York, where they would be pooled, printed, and bound in rich leather, one copy each for every delegate with his name impressed on it in gold, to await him on the conference table. 'Thinking up' books on demand is one of the idlest occupations in all of publishing. If an interesting book has its origins in a head other than its author's, then it either comes in a flash as a result of compelling circumstances, or it is the result of someone's obsession which he has nursed until just the right author has turned up. Books worth reading don't come from people saying to each other

'What a good idea!' They come from someone knowing a great deal about something and having strong feelings about it. Which does not mean that a capable hack can't turn out a passable book-like object to a publisher's order; only that when he does so it ends on the remainder shelves in double-quick time.

So we asked each other 'Do you think that all the other Associates are feeling just like us?' – and what we were feeling was a blend of despair and ribaldry. We had a special file labelled 'Stinkers', kept in a bottom drawer of André's desk, which contained a collection of all the most appalling ideas that had been submitted to us over the years, and I dug this out . . . But finally sobriety prevailed and we settled for two or three notions so drab that I have forgotten them. No one else, André reported, did any better, so they *had* all been feeling like us.

Two years were as many as André could stand of Time/Life – and probably as much as they could stand of him. He never divulged which side it was who first said 'Let's call it a day', nor how much money was lost on the deal when he bought the shares back, but his delight at being free of them was manifest. I thought of pressing him for details, and so, I think, did Piers, but it would have been too unkind. The silliness had not all been on the other side.

Since starting this chapter about our long and mostly happy time in Great Russell Street I have spent hours remembering colleagues, remembering authors, remembering books . . . colleagues, especially. I suppose people who choose to work with books and are good at their jobs are not inevitably likeable, but they very often are; and if you see them every day over long periods of time, collaborating with them in various ways as you do so, they become more than likeable. They become a pleasing part of your life. Esther Whitby, Ilsa Yardley, Pamela Royds, Penny Buckland, June Bird, Piers Burnett, Geoff Sains, Philip Tammer . . . : I can't write about them in the sense of making them come alive and interesting to people who know nothing about them, without embarking on a different kind of book, and one which is, I fear, beyond my range, so I will just have to go on carrying them, and others, in my head for my own pleasure. And it's for my own satisfaction that I now say how glad I am to have them there.

The authors: well, about a few of them I shall write in Part Two. And the books: there were too many of them, and anyway nothing is more boring than brief descriptions of books which one has not read. But two of them have floated to the surface as being of great value to me. Neither of them was part of a literary career; neither of them sold well; neither of them will be remembered by many readers. What is remarkable about both of them is the person who speaks.

Over and over again one sees lives which appear to have been shaped almost entirely by circumstances: by a cruel childhood, perhaps, or (like Franz Stangl's) by a corrupt society. These two stories are told by a man and a woman who, if shaping by circumstances were an immutable law, would have been hopeless wrecks. They did not just survive what would have finished off a great many people: they survived it triumphantly.

The first of these books is *Parents Unknown: A Ukrainian Childhood*, by Morris Stock. He was found as a newborn baby on the steps of a synagogue in a small Ukrainian town; was shunted around the Jewish community to various foster parents, ending with a brutal couple who almost killed him. If an interfering peasant woman hadn't made a fuss when she noticed a little boy almost dead with cold, waiting on a wagon outside an inn, they would quite have done so. The community stepped in again, and he was passed on to a grain-merchant who was eventually to work him very hard, but who treated him well. Almost at once he began to be liked and trusted, learning how to read and write and mastering his trade: it seems that as soon as he was free to be himself he revealed intelligence, resilience and generosity. Before he was twenty he had set up business on his own, married a girl he was to love for the rest of her life, and decided to move to London, where he spent the next fifty years prospering, and raising a family remarkable for talent and ability. He was an old man when his daughter persuaded him to write his story, which he did with vigour and precision – a very charming old man. Some quality at the centre of Morris Stock had been able to triumph over formidable odds.

And the same was true of Daphne Anderson, who wrote *The Toe-Rags*. By the time I met her Daphne was the beautiful wife of a retired general, living in Norfolk, better-read and more amusing in a gentle way than I expected a general's wife to be. It was astounding to learn that this woman had once been a barefoot, scabby-legged little girl whose only dress was made from a sugar-sack, knowing nothing beyond the Rhodesian bush and speaking an African language – Shona – better than she spoke English. Her parents were the poorest of poor whites, victims of her father's uselessness: he was stupid, bad-tempered, utterly self-centred, incompetent and irresponsible. He dumped her wretched mother, with three children, in the bush and left them there for months on end, sending no money. She scraped by, by allowing occasional favours to such men as were about, and the children were looked after by Jim, their Shona servant (no white could be so poor as not to have a servant: it was like Charles Dickens's family taking their little maid into debtors' prison with them). Jim saved not only Daphne's life, but also her spirit, being a rock of kindness and good sense for the children to cling to.

Not surprisingly, when a decent man asked the mother to go off with him she did, taking her new baby but leaving the three other children in the belief that their father would be arriving next day. She thought that if no one else was there he would *have* to cope. He did not turn up. Three days later Jim, having run out of food, walked them to the nearest police station. They never saw their mother again, and had the misfortune to be delivered into the hands of their father's sister. She was like him in every way except in being (although unable to read) ruthlessly competent, so that she had become rich by running a brick kiln. She took the children in because of 'What would the neighbours say?', then took it out on them by consigning them to the kitchen: where, once again, they were saved by an African man – her cook. He provided kindness, common sense about good behaviour, and a comforting sense of irony. Their aunt it was who dubbed them the Toe-Rags.

There followed, until Daphne was in her twenties, a long chain of deprivation and disturbing events, with one blessing in their midst: Daphne was sent to a convent school. Right from the beginning the child had fallen on every tiny scrap of good that came her way – every kindness, every chance to learn, every opportunity to discriminate between coarse and fine, stupid and wise, ugly and beautiful, mean and generous. School came to her – in spite of agonizing embarrassment over unpaid bills and having no clothes – as a feast of pleasure. She does not, of course, tell her story as that of an astonishing person. She tells it for what happened, and out of delighted amazement at her own good luck. It is the reader who sees that this person who should have been a wreck had somewhere within her a centre so strong that all she needed were the smallest openings in order to be good and happy.

I loved that book even more than I loved Morris Stock's; and both of them I loved not for being well-written (though both were written well enough for their purposes), but because of what those two people were like. They brought home to me the central reason why books have meant so much to me. It is not because of my pleasure in the art of writing, though that has been very great. It is because they have taken me so far beyond the narrow limits of my own experience and have so greatly enlarged my sense of the complexity of life: of its consuming darkness, and also – thank God – of the light which continues to struggle through.

11

ALTHOUGH ANDRÉ'S CHIEF instrument for office management was always, from 1946 to 1984, the threatening of Doom, he was slow to recognize its actual coming. For a long time he preferred to interpret its symptoms as temporary blips.

The demise of our house, a slow process, was caused by a combination of two things: the diminishing number of people who wanted to read the kind of book we mostly published, and the recession.

Ever since we started in business books had been becoming steadily more expensive to produce: the eight and sixpenny novel became the ten and sixpenny novel, then the twelve and sixpenny, then the fifteen shilling (that seemed a particularly alarming jump) – after which the crossing of the hitherto unthinkable one pound barrier came swiftly. (What would we have thought if some Cassandra had told us that soon eight, ten, twelve, fifteen, twenty would be enumerating pounds, not shillings?) After each rise people continued to buy books – though not quite so many people. André was impatient of the idea that the falling-off was caused by anything other than the rise in price . . . But *everything* was costing more – that was life, people were used to it: it seemed to me that something else was at work. Which was proved true by several attempts, made by ourselves and others, to bring out cheap editions of first novels of a kind categorized as 'literary': making them cheaper did not make them sell better.

People who buy books, not counting useful how-to-do-it books, are of two kinds. There are those who buy because they love books and what they can get from them, and those to whom books are one form of entertainment among several. The first group, which is by far the smaller, will go on reading, if not for ever, then for as long as one can foresee. The second group has to be courted. It is the second which makes the best seller, impelled thereto by the buzz that a particular book is really something special; and it also makes publishers' headaches, because it has become more and more resistant to courting.

The Booker Prize was instigated in 1969 with the second group in mind: make the quality of a book *news* by awarding it an impress-ive amount of *money*, and *hoi polloi* will prick up their ears. It worked in relation to the books named; but it had been hoped that after buying the winner and/or the runners-up, people would be 'converted' to books in general, and there was no sign of that. Another attempt to stir the wider public's consciousness resulted in the slogan 'Books are Best' which still chirps its message from booksellers' carrier bags – and is surely the kind of advertising that is not even *seen* by those who do not want the advertised object.

What has been happening is that slowly – very slowly, so that often the movement was imperceptible – group number two has been floating away into another world. Whole generations have grown up to find images more entertaining than words, and the roaming of space via a computer more exciting than turning a page. Of course a lot of them still read; but progressively a smaller lot, and fewer and fewer can be bothered to dig into a book that offers any resistance. Although these people may seem stupid to us, they are no stupider than we are: they just enjoy different things. And although publishers like André Deutsch Limited went on having a happy relationship with group number one, and still, throughout the seventies, hit it off quite often with group number two, the distance between what the publisher thought interesting and what the wider public thought interesting was widening all the time.

Surely, I used to think as we moved into the eighties, we ought to be able to do something about this? Look at Allen Lane, in the thirties, thinking up Penguin Books: that had been a revolution in publishing to meet a need . . . couldn't we do something like it in a different way? Piers and I discussed it occasionally (André couldn't be bothered with such idle speculation), but we never got anywhere. Piers thought we should cut down on fiction and look for serious non-fiction of a necessary kind, and he was right; but it was easier said than done. I just went blank. I was too stuck in my ways to want to change, that was my trouble. We had been publishing books we liked for so long that the thought of publishing any other kind was horrible. So let's talk about something else . . . Which must have been more or less what André was feeling under his irritability.

Meanwhile recession was approaching. The first time it sent a shiver down my spine was when Edward Heath ordained a three-day week. Down we go, I thought, and how could anyone expect anything else when a country which was once the centre of a vast empire had become a little island off the shores of Europe? Gone are the days when we could buy cheap and sell dear – other people are going to pinch our markets . . . Perhaps this crisis will pass, but it would be foolish to suppose that it is going, in any permanent way, *to get better.*

The feeling was so similar to those moments before the Second World War when one suddenly saw that it was going to happen, that all I could do was react as I had reacted then: shut my eyes tight and think of something else. André, after all, said that I was exaggerating, and he was much better at economic matters than I was . . . I managed to avert my mind from the depressing prospect so successfully that the rest of the seventies and the early eighties passed quite cheerfully; but I was not in the least surprised when recession was declared.

André talked very little about selling the firm. I knew, quite early in the eighties, that he was half-heartedly sniffing around for an offer, and he had stated his reason as clearly as he would ever do: 'It's not any fun any more,' is what he said.

And it was not. He could no longer make those exciting swoops on 'big' books because the firms which had combined into conglomerates could always outbid us; and the 'literary' books at which we had been good . . . well, I was beginning to hope, when a typescript arrived on my desk, that it would be bad. If it was bad, out it went and no hassle. If it was good – then ahead loomed the editorial conference at which we would have to ask ourselves 'How many do you reckon it will sell?', and the honest answer would probably be 'About eight hundred copies'. Whereupon we would either have to turn down something good, which was painful, or else fool ourselves into publishing something that lost money. We still brought out some good things – quite a number of them – during those years, and by careful cheese-paring André kept the firm profitable (just) until at last he did sell it; but there are some embarrassing books on our eighties lists: obvious (though never, I am glad to say, shameful) attempts to hit on something 'commercial' which only proved that we were not much good at it. And André was already starting to fall asleep during editorial conferences.

He never surprised me more than when he announced, on returning from the annual book-trade jamboree in the United States, that he had found the right person to buy the firm.

'Who?'

'Tom Rosenthal.'

'Are you mad?'

This reaction was not dictated by my own feelings: I had glimpsed Tom only occasionally at parties. It was because André had always seemed to dislike him. Tom began his career in 1959 with Thames and Hudson, which specialized in art books, and why he left them in 1970 I don't know. Probably it was because he felt drawn to a more literary kind of publishing, since his next job, starting in 1971, was managing director of Secker & Warburg, and in the short interval between the two he had played with the idea of launching his own list, and had visited André to discuss the possibility of doing it under our wing. It was then that André had been rude – not to him, but about him. It seemed to be simply the dissimilarity of their natures that put him off.

André was small and dapper; Tom was large, with the slightly rumpled look of many bearded men, though he was far from being among the seriously shaggy. André was a precise and dashing driver; Tom was too careless and clumsy to trust himself to drive at all. André, without being prissy, was nearer to being fastidious in his speech than he was to being coarse; Tom evidently liked to shock. And above all, André abhorred extravagance, while Tom enjoyed it. They were also very different in their pleasures. André had no important pleasures outside his work except for going to the theatre (he never missed a well-reviewed West End play, and adventured into the fringe quite often), and skiing, which he adored; Tom took no exercise except for a daily swim for his health (his back had been badly damaged in a traffic accident), preferred opera to plays, gave much time and thought to his collection of first editions, and had also built up an impressive collection of paintings – many of which André thought were ugly. They were not designed to be friends.

But now André *needed* someone to buy the firm, so when Tom, who had become a director of the Heinemann group in 1972, told him that he was fed up with administration and longed to get back into hands-on book producing, he suddenly saw that he had been wrong about this brilliant publisher who was a much nicer man than anyone realized, and who – best of all – was our kind of person, so would not want to turn our firm into something else . . . As it would turn out, that 'best of all' summed up precisely why Tom was the *wrong* man, but the fact escaped us all: I can't think why, given that most of us were well aware that the firm needed to change.

The negotiations, which took place under the guidance of Arnold (Lord) Goodman, the ubiquitous fixer and smoother, lasted a long time. André never told anyone how much Tom paid for the firm, but we all knew that he was to pay in two stages. On putting down the first half of the money he would come in as joint managing director with André, and two years later (or perhaps it was three), when he put down the rest, he would become the sole managing director and André would be awarded the title of President and continue to have a room in the office if he wanted it, but would cease to have any say in its affairs. I remember André telling me: 'Last week Arnold said I must remember that now the agreement has been signed the firm is *no longer mine*. He must think I'm dotty – of course I know that.'

But alas, alas! Of course he didn't.

Tom made the sensible suggestion that they should divide our authors between them and each be responsible for his own group without interfering in the other's. André agreed, but he was unable to keep to it. Over and over again he would pick up the intercom, or (worse) amble into Tom's room, to say something on the lines of 'If you are thinking of selling the German rights of such and such a book to Fischer Verlag, would you like me to drop a line to so-and-so?' To start with Tom was civil: 'That's very kind, but I've done it already.' But he is a man with a short fuse and it was not long before he was snapping . . . and not long again before he was yelling. Whereupon André would come into my room and report querulously 'Tom *yelled* at me!' And when I had extracted the details of the incident, and told him that it was his own fault for sticking his nose in when he knew how much it maddened Tom, in an even more querulous, almost tearful voice: 'But I was only trying to *help*!'

'Well, for God's sake *stop* trying to help. You know it doesn't do any good . . . and he doesn't do it to you.' And a few days later it would happen all over again.

Then André's pain began to turn into anger. He began to see almost everything that Tom did as wrong, and to complain endlessly – first to me, then to those other people in the office who were concerned with whatever he was complaining about, then to everyone in the office, putting out feelers for Tom's sins in the accounts department, the production department, even to the switchboard. Nearly everyone in the place was fond of André, and felt for him now that he was losing the firm that had so obviously meant so much to him for so long; but people began to be embarrassed by his behaviour and to lose sympathy with him. Burly, bluff, bearded Tom was not a man of delicate sensibility (was even inclined to boast of that fact, as he boasted about many things), and he *was* extravagant, so people had reservations about him; but they didn't feel he deserved this campaign against him. In fact, for quite a while after his arrival he cheered us up. If someone says loudly 'Though I say it myself, I'm a bloody good businessman', you tend to believe him simply because you can't believe anyone would be so crass as to say that, if he wasn't. Or at least I tended to believe it, and I think others did too. Tom liked to think big and generously, so if you said, for instance, that a book would be better with sixteen pages of illustrations – or even thirty-two – instead of the eight pages which André would have grudgingly allowed if he absolutely had to, Tom would say 'My dear girl, let it have as many as it *needs*', and that sort of response was invigorating. He brought in some interesting books, too – notably the first volume of David Cairns's magnificent biography of Berlioz – and a few big names including Elias Canetti and Gore Vidal; so for a year or so it was possible to believe that, given his flair as a businessman, he was going to revitalize the firm. You did not have to be particularly drawn to him to be pleased about that – or to be shocked when André began to extend his campaign outside the office. For some time I hoped it was only old friends to whom he was confiding his grievances, but gradually it became clear that he was going on and on and on to *everyone he met*.

And then came a substantial feature article in the *Independent* about the situation, telling the story entirely from André's point of view, with all its distortions, and making Tom look silly as well as disagreeable. Even the illustrations were slanted: André looking young and handsome, Tom, in a really unforgivable photograph, looking grotesque. Tom was convinced that the story must have come from interviews with André, and no one could deny that it did represent his opinions and emotions with remarkable fidelity. I have never been able to blame Tom for his fury. It was some time since they had spoken to each other. Now Tom forbade André to set foot in the office ever again, and be damned to the agreement about his continuing to have a room there. What else could he have done?

I have been reminded that I wrote funny letters to friends about all this – indeed, that one friend kept them for their funniness. But in retrospect it was far from funny. It became evident quite soon after André had been thrown out that his health had begun a long process of deterioration, and I now think this had started several years earlier, even before he sold the firm, when we first noticed him falling asleep during editorial conferences. He had always cried wolf about his health (you could safely bet that if you were just about to tell him that you were going down with flu, he would nip in ahead of you with angina pains), so I had a long-established habit of disregarding his complaints . . . But this time he would have denied that anything was wrong with him, so even if all of us had recognized that his ugly but pathetic campaign against the man he himself had chosen was not waged by a well man, we could have done nothing about it.

My shares in André Deutsch Limited were so few that I made very little money from the sale of the company, and I had hardly any other income, so I was grateful when Tom told me that if I were willing to stay on at the salary I was earning when he took over, he would be glad to have me for as long as I could keep going. I was seventy by then, and would not start feeling like an old woman till I turned eighty; but in spite of that comparative spryness, having never been a specially good copy editor (picker-up of spelling mistakes and so on), I was now a bad one, and often alarmed myself when I read something a second time and saw how many things I had missed on the first run-through. I was therefore less valuable than I should have been at that side of the job; and in its larger aspects . . . well, I was still sure that I could tell good writing from bad, but was I able to judge what people the age of my grandchildren, if I'd had them, would want to buy? No – no more able than Tom was. We often liked the same books, among them Pete Davies's *The Last Election*, Boman Desai's *The Memory of Elephants*, David Gurr's *The Ring Master*, Llorenç Villalonga's *The*

Doll's Room, Chris Wilson's *Blueglass* – each in its own way, I am still prepared to swear, very good: but none of them money-makers. So I could make no contribution in that way. Friends said 'He's getting you cheap', but I didn't think he was. I thought I was lucky in still earning money, and that although the job was 'not any fun any more', it could have been much worse.

But quite soon three depressing things happened: Tom sold the whole of the André Deutsch Limited archive; he sold the children's books; and he got rid of warehousing and sales, handing all that side of the publishing operation over to Gollancz.

It was sentimentality to feel the loss of that intractable mountain of old files so keenly – we had kept copies of essential matter such as contracts, and never suffered in any practical way from the absence of the rest; but it did, all the same, give me a most uncomfortable feeling. A publishing house without its archive – there was something shoddy about it, like a bungalow without a damp course. And where was the money which came in as a result? – a question even more obtrusive when it came to the sale of the children's books, for which he got a million pounds. We all supposed, in the end, that Tom must have had to borrow heavily in order to buy us, and was now selling off bits of us in order to pay off his debt – which, naturally, he had a perfect right to do; he would have had the right to spend the money on prostitutes and polo ponies, if he liked. But he had given us the impression that he had sold the children's books in order to get the firm back onto an even keel, and that was only too evidently not happening. Fortunately Pamela Royds and the list which she had built up single-handed with so much loving care and unremitting labour (the most profitable thing under our roof, into the bargain!) were well-served by the change. Scholastic Press, which bought them, was a prosperous firm specializing in children's books, which had a first-rate sales organization, and Pam reported that it was delicious to breathe such invigorating air after the oppressive atmosphere of the last few years at Deutsch. While for us . . . It was like having a hand chopped off with a promise that it would result in a magic strengthening of the rest of the body, and then finding oneself as wobbly as ever and minus a hand into the bargain.

While as for losing control of one's sales organization . . . Surely Tom must know that however good the intentions, no one ever ran someone else's sales as well as they ran their own? Surely he must know that this move is the beginning of the end? When asked what the situation was, all he would ever answer was 'It would be fine if it weren't for *the bloody bank*'. From which we all concluded that they had over-indulged the firm hideously with a gigantic overdraft, which now he had somehow got to pay off, or else!

And indeed, there was soon a man from the bank sitting in on meetings, and any number of little chisellings going on: people who left not being replaced, books postponed because printers couldn't be paid, lies being told for fear of loss of face . . . It is depressing to remember that time, and pointless to describe it in detail. What it boiled down to was that Tom's claim to be a bloody good businessman was poppycock, because no businessman who was any good would have bought our firm at that time, and then imagined that he could go on running it as the same kind of firm only more so. It was a fantasy, and he was lucky to get clear of it in the end, having at last found someone willing to buy the firm for, I suppose, the name and the building. To a man unable easily to admit, or even discuss, failure, the experience must have been excruciating.

While those two last years were going on I did not allow myself to know how much I was hating them. I was frightened by the thought of living without my salary, and had become hypnotized, like a chicken with its beak pressed to a chalk line, by the notion of continuing to work for as long as possible. And when some quite minor incident jerked my beak off the line, and I thought 'This is absurd – I don't have to go on with this', elation was mixed with further alarm. I did not expect to be one of those people who find themselves at a complete loss when they retire – I would have a companion, a place that I loved, things to do – but my days had been structured by a job for all my adult life, and it seemed possible that freedom, at first, would feel *very odd*. I even had one fit of 3 a.m. angst, thinking 'This is like standing on the edge of a cliff with a cold wind blowing up my skirt!'

But I was overlooking the extent to which I had been drained and depressed by trying not to admit how miserable I was, and as it turned out there was no cold wind at all. When I woke up to my first morning as a retired person, what I thought *at once* was 'I am happy!' Happy, and feeling ten years younger. Instead of being sad that my publishing days were over, it was 'Thank God, thank God that I'm out of it at last'. And then, gradually, it became even better, because the further I move from the date of my retirement, the less important those last sad years in the office become, and the luckier I know myself to be in having lived all the years that went before them.

PART TWO

IN 1962 I wrote – and meant – the following description of the relationship between publisher and writer.

It is an easy one, because the publisher usually meets his writers only after having read something they have written, and if he has thought it good it does not much matter to him what the man will be like who is about to come through his door. He is feeling well-disposed for having liked the work; the writer is feeling well-disposed for his work having been liked; neither is under obligation to attempt a close personal relationship beyond that. It is a warm and at the same time undemanding beginning, in which, if genuine liking is going to flower, it can do so freely.

That is true, but only as far as it goes. I find it surprising – perhaps even touching – that after sixteen years in the trade I was still leaving it at that, because although the beginning is, indeed, nearly always easy, the relationship as a whole is quite often not. I would now say that a friendship, properly speaking, between a publisher and a writer is . . . well, not impossible, but rare.

The person with whom the writer wants to be in touch is his reader: if he could speak to him directly, without a middleman, that is what he would do. The publisher exists only because turning someone's written words into a book (or rather, into several thousand books) is a complicated and expensive undertaking, and so is distributing the books, once made, to booksellers and libraries. From the writer's viewpoint, what a mortifying necessity this is: that the thing which is probably more important to him than anything else – the thing which he has spun out of his own guts over many months, sometimes with much pain and anxiety – should be denied its life unless he can find a middleman to give it physical existence, and will then agree that this person shall share whatever the book earns. No doubt all writers know in their heads that their publishers, having invested much money and work in their books, deserve to make a reasonable profit; but I am sure that nearly all of them feel in their hearts that whatever their books earn *ought* to belong to them alone.

The relationship is therefore less easy than I once supposed. Taking only those cases in which the publisher believes he has found a truly good writer, and is able to get real pleasure from his books, this is how it will go. The publisher will feel admiration for this man or woman, interest in his or her nature, concern for his or her welfare: all the makings of friendship. It is probably no exaggeration to say that he would feel honoured to be granted that person's friendship in return, because admiration for someone's work can excite strong feelings. But even so, part of the publisher's concern will be that of someone who has invested in a piece of property – how big a part depending on what kind of person the publisher is. With some people it would preponderate; with me, because of how useless I am as a business woman, it was very small indeed, but it was never non-existent. So there is potential complication, even looking at only one side of the relationship; and looking at the other side there is a great deal more.

In the writer the liking inspired by the publisher's enthusiasm may well be warm, but it will continue only if he thinks the publisher is doing a good job by making the book look pleasing and selling enough copies of it; and what the writer means by 'enough' is not always what the publisher means. Even if the publisher is doing remarkably well, he is still thinking of the book as one among many, and in terms of his experience of the market; while the writer is thinking in terms of the only book that matters in the world.

Of course writers' attitudes vary. I have known a few who, behind a thin veneer of civility, see their publisher in the way a man may see his tailor: a pleasant enough person while he is doing a good job, allowed a certain intimacy in that he has to know things the equivalent of your inner-leg measurement and whether you 'dress' to the left or the right – but you wouldn't ask him to dinner (such a writer is easy to work with but you don't like him). I have known others whose dependence on their publisher is as clinging as that of a juvenile tennis star on her parent (very boring). But generally the writer likes to like his publisher, and will go on doing so for years if he can; but will feel only mildly sorry if the publisher's poor performance, or what he sees as such, causes him to end the relationship. When the ending of a relationship causes no serious personal disturbance it cannot be called a friendship. The only André Deutsch authors whom I count among my real friends opened the way to that friendship by going off to be published by someone else.

But this is not to say that I haven't been *more interested* in some of 'my' authors than I have been in anyone else: haven't watched them more closely, speculated about them more searchingly, wondered at them with more delight – or dismay. Only two of them have actually played a part in my life (I have written books about both of them, *After a Funeral* and *Make Believe*). But several of them have enlarged my life; have been experiences in it in the way, I suppose, that a mountain is an experience to a climber, or a river to an angler; and the second part of this book is about six of those remarkable people.

MORDECAI RICHLER AND
BRIAN MOORE

A FEW DAYS AGO I read *The Acrobats* again: Mordecai Richler's first novel which we published in 1954. I had not looked at it for forty-five years. 'Talk about a young man's book!' I said to myself. 'What on earth made us take it on?' It really is very bad; but something of its author's nature struggles through the clumsiness, and we were in the process of building a list, desperate for new and promising young writers. I must say that I congratulate André and myself for discerning that underpinning of seriousness and honesty (there was no hint of his wit), and think we deserved the reward of his turning out to be the writer he is.

Mordecai in himself presented rather the same kind of puzzle, in those days. I liked him very much from the moment of meeting him, but sometimes found myself asking 'Why?', because he hardly ever spoke: I have never known anyone else so utterly unequipped with small-talk as he was then. How could one tell that someone was generous, kind, honest and capable of being very funny if he hardly ever said a word? I still don't know how, but it happened: I was always sure that he was all those things, and soon understood that his not saying anything unless he had something to say was part of what made me so fond of him. He was the least phoney person imaginable, and still is today (though he has become much better at talking).

He and Brian Moore, to whom he introduced me, were the

writers I had in mind when I wrote the optimistic paragraph quoted five pages back. I was thirty-seven by then, but the war had acted on time rather as brackets act on a text: when one got back to normal life it felt in some ways like a continuation of what had preceded the interruption, so even if you carried wartime scars you were suddenly younger than your actual years. When those two men were new on our list and in my life, the days had a flavour of discovery, amusement and pleasure which now seems odd in the light of chronology, but was very agreeable. By then, of course, I had already met a number of writers whom I admired, but those two were the first good writers I thought of as friends; and also (although I didn't notice this at the time) the first two men I had ever deeply liked without any sex in the relationship. Our relationship depended on their writing – something which mattered to each of them more than anything else, and which happened to interest me more than anything else: that was what created the warmth and made the absence of sexual attraction irrelevant.

Although I felt more attached to Mordecai than to Brian, I got to know Brian better – or so I thought. This was partly because I was more aware of being older than Mordecai, partly because of Mordecai's taciturnity, and partly because of his women. His first wife combined a good deal of tiresomeness with many endearing qualities, so that impatience with her was inevitably accompanied by guilt – an uncomfortable state, so that I sought their company less often than I might have done. And Florence, his second wife, was so beautiful that she used to daunt me. I am happy to say that I have become able to see through Florence's beauty (which endures) to all the other reasons why she remains the best-loved woman of my acquaintance; but in the past Mordecai did rather disappear into his marriage with this lovely person (you only have to read *Barney's Version* – the latest, and to my mind best, of his novels – to see that Mordecai knows all about *coups de foudre*). Added to which they went back to Canada: a distancing which certainly made it easier to accept his leaving us without bitterness.

And before he left I had the delight of seeing him come into his own. Both his second and third novels had been better than his first, but both were still dimmed by a youthful earnestness, so *The Apprenticeship of Duddy Kravitz*, in which he broke through to the wit and ribaldry that released his seriousness into the atmosphere, so to speak, was a triumph. If it had come after his leaving us, I would have been sad; instead, I was able to be proud. And the last of his books with us (until, much later, he invaded our children's list), *The Incomparable Atuk*, although it wilted a little towards its end, was for most of its length so funny that it still makes me laugh aloud. So he left pleasure behind him. And – this was the most important specific against bitterness – I understood exactly why he went, and would even have thought him daft if he had not done so. Mordecai was living by his pen; he had a growing family to support; and someone else was prepared to pay him more money than we did. A great advantage of not being a proper publisher with all a proper publisher's possessive territorial instincts is that what you mind about most is that good books should get published. Naturally you would like the publisher to be yourself, but it is not the end of the world if it is someone else.

It was Mordecai who introduced me to Brian Moore in that he told me that this friend of his had written an exceptionally good book which we ought to go after; but I must not deprive André of his discovery of *Judith Hearne*. As André remembers it, he was given the book by Brian's agent in New York on the last day of one of his – André's – visits there; he read it on the plane on the way home and decided at once that he must publish it. I think it likely that he *asked* to see it, having been alerted, as I had been, by Mordecai. But whether or not he asked for it, he certainly recognized its quality at once; and when he handed it over to me, it came to me as something I was already hoping to read, and its excellence was doubly pleasing because Brian was a friend of Mordecai's. The two had got to know each other in Paris, and in Canada, where Mordecai was a native and Brian, an Ulsterman, had chosen to live in common – although the Moores moved to New York soon after we met.

Before Brian wrote *Judith Hearne* (later retitled *The Lonely*

Passion of Judith Hearne for publication in paperback and in the United States), when he was scrabbling about to keep a roof over his head, he had written several thrillers for publication as pocketbooks, under a pseudonym, which he said had been a useful apprenticeship in story-telling because it was a law of the genre that something must happen on every page. But however useful, it came nowhere near explaining *Judith*. With his first serious book Brian was already in full possession of his technical accomplishment, his astounding ability to put himself into other people's shoes, and his particular view of life: a tragic view, but one that does not make a fuss about tragedy, accepting it as part of the fabric with which we all have to make do. He was to prove incapable of writing a bad book, and his considerable output was to include several more that were outstandingly good; but to my mind he never wrote anything more moving and more true than *Judith Hearne*.

When he came to London in 1955 for the publication of *Judith*, he came without his wife Jackie – perhaps she was in the process of moving them to New York. He was a slightly surprising figure, but instantly likeable: a small, fat, round-headed, sharp-nosed man resembling a robin, whose flat Ulster accent was the first of its kind I had heard. He was fat because he had an ulcer and the recommended treatment in those days was large quantities of milk; and also because Jackie was a wonderful cook. (Her ham, liberally injected with brandy before she baked it – she kept a medical syringe for the purpose – was to become one of my most poignant food memories.) When I asked him home to supper on that first visit he was careful to explain that he was devoted to his wife – a precaution which pleased me because it was sensible as well as slightly comic.

Few men would be considerate enough to establish their unavailability like that. (Perhaps I was flattering him: it may have been a touch of puritanical timidity that he was exhibiting, rather than considerateness. But that was how I saw it.) Once he was sure that I was harbouring no romantic or predatory fancies, the way was opened to a relaxed friendship, and for as long as I knew him and Jackie as a couple there seemed to be nothing that we couldn't talk about. They were both great gossips – and when I say great I mean great, because I am talking about gossip in its highest and purest form: a passionate interest, lit by humour but above malice, in human behaviour. We used often, of course, to talk about writing – his and other people's, and eventually mine – but much more often we would talk with glee, with awe, with amazement, with horror, with delight, about what people had done and why they had done it. And we munched up our own lives as greedily as we did everyone else's.

In addition to seeing the Moores when they came to England (once they rented a house in Chelsea which had a Francis Bacon hanging in the drawing-room) I spent half a holiday with them in Villefranche (the other half had been with the Richlers in Cagnes), crossed the Atlantic with them on board the *France*, stayed with them in New York and twice in their summer house in Amagansett. It was from Brian himself that I heard, in Villefranche, the story of how he came to move to Canada.

It was a painful and romantic story. Immediately after the war Brian had got a job in the relief force, UNRRA, which had taken him to Poland, and there he fell in love with a woman older than himself (or perhaps he had fallen already and went there in pursuit of her). It was a wild passion, undiminished by the fact that she was an alcoholic. The only effect of that misfortune was to make him drink far beyond his capacity in an attempt to keep up with her: he described with horror waking up on the floor of a hotel bedroom lying in his vomit, not knowing what day it was; crawling on his hands and knees to the bathroom for a drink of water; getting drunk again as the water stirred up the vodka still in him; and finally discovering that he had been unconscious for two whole days. And there had never been anything but flashes of happiness in the affair because he had never known where he was with her, whether because of the swerving moods of drunkenness, or because she despised the abjectness of his obsession, I am not sure. He remembered it as an agonizing time, but when she told him it was over and went away to Canada, although he tried to accept it, he couldn't. He followed her – and she refused even to see him. And thus, he said, he learnt to detest the very idea of romantic passion.

Thus, too, he made his break with his native Ulster, and became distanced from (he never broke with) his rather conventional Catholic family, which gave him the necessary perspective on a great deal of the material he was to use in his novels. Not that he began at once to write seriously. Among the ways he earned his living during those early days in Canada was proofreading for a newspaper, during which he met Jackie, who was a journalist. Then came those useful pocketbook thrillers – which must have paid pretty well, because by the time he felt secure enough to settle down to writing what he wanted to write, Jackie was able to stop working. Their son Michael was about two when I first met them, and although the comfort the Moores lived in was modest, it *was* comfort.

They gave the impression of being an exceptionally compatible pair: as good an advertisement as one could hope to find for *liking* one's spouse as opposed to being mad about him/her. They got on well with each other's friends; they shared the same tastes in books, paintings, household objects, food and drink – and, of course, gossip. They laughed a lot together and they loved Michael together. They were delightful to be with. I remember trying to decide which of them I found the better company and settling for a dead heat: with Brian there was the extra pleasure of writing talk, in which he was simultaneously unpretentious and deeply serious; with Jackie the extra amusement of woman talk, in which she was exceptionally honest and funny. I used to look forward to our meetings with wholehearted pleasure.

We were to publish five of Brian's books: *Judith Hearne* in '55, *The Feast of Lupercal* in '58, *The Luck of Ginger Coffey* in '60, *An Answer from Limbo* in '63 and *The Emperor of Ice Cream* in '66. Why, having made this good start with him, did we not go on to publish all his books?

Well, we might have lost him *anyway* because of the frugality of our advertising. Book promotion, before the ways of thinking and behaving bred by television became established, depended almost entirely on reviews, which we always got; and on advertising in newspapers. Interviews and public appearances were rare, and only for people who were news in themselves, as well as writers, like our Alain Bombard who crossed the Atlantic in a rubber dinghy to prove that shipwrecked sailors could live off the sea if they knew how. A novelist had to stab his wife, or something of that sort, to get attention on pages other than those devoted to books. So when a novelist felt that his publisher sold too few copies, what he complained about was always under-advertising.

Publishers, on the other hand, knew that the sort of advertisements that books – even quite successful ones – could pay for were almost useless. Inflate them to the point at which they really might shift copies, and they would then cost more than the extra copies sold could bring in. Two kinds of advertisement did make sense: descriptions of all your forthcoming books in the trade papers, to which booksellers and librarians turned for information; and conspicuous announcements in big-circulation broadsheets, devoted to a single book provided it was by an already famous author. The run-of-the-mill ad, a six or eight or ten inch column (sometimes double, more often single) into which as many books as possible had been squashed . . . For my part, I only had to ask myself: when had I even looked at such an ad (except for one of our own, to check that nothing had gone wrong with it), to say nothing of buying something because of it? It was reviews, and people talking enthusiastically about books that made me buy them, and why should other people be different? Yet we went on running those pointless, or almost pointless, ads – as few of them as we could get away with – simply so that we could keep our authors happy by reporting 'Your book was advertised in newspapers A, B, C, D, E and F', hoping they would be enough impressed by this true statement not to ask 'And how many other books were in the same ad, and how big was the space, and where was it on the page?' Often they were sufficiently impressed; but Brian quite soon began to be not impressed enough. By his third novel he had started to think that it ought to be treated like a novel by Graham Greene.

Given the quality of Brian's books, if we had indeed given them big solo ads in big-circulation newspapers, and done it often enough, we would no doubt have made him as famous as Greene. But a) it would have taken quite a long time to work, b) all our other writers would meanwhile be going into conniptions, and c) we could not afford it. Or so André was convinced. And in André Deutsch Limited no one but André Deutsch himself had a hope in hell of deciding how much money was to be spent on what. When André dismissed the idea of shifting the advertising of Brian's work into the big-time category as nonsense, all I could do – all, I must admit, I ever dreamt of doing – was convey his opinion to Brian in less brutal words. And up to the publication of *The Emperor of Ice Cream* in 1966 Brian did no more than mutter from time to time, and then appear to forget it.

Not long after that publication I went to New York for the firm, saw the Moores as usual, and was invited by them to spend a few days in Amagansett. The misery of New York in a heatwave gives those easygoing Long Island seaside towns great charm: their tree-shaded streets, their shingled houses set back from the streets and far apart, among more trees – how pretty and restful they are! The English pride themselves on having evolved in the eighteenth century a perfect domestic architecture, but I think the Americans beat them at it with the unpretentious, graceful, welcoming wooden houses that are so respectfully and unpompously preserved in New England. The house rented by the Moores was not particularly distinguished, but the moment you were through the front door you were comfortable in it – and 'comfortable' was the word for Amagansett as a whole. It has (or had then) a life of its own apart from accommodating summer visitors, although that was what it chiefly did; and it wasn't smart. Its regular visitors insisted a little too much on how they preferred it to the snobby Hamptons, where the vast country retreats of the robber barons still stood, and where the big money still tended to go; but I thought Amagansett really did deserve preference. It was favoured by writers and medical people, particularly psychiatrists. When I arrived this time Brian and Jackie were full of a party ending with a moonlit swim, during which four or five drunk psychiatrists had been so relaxed and happy that, as they bobbed about in the sea, they had confided in each other their most intimate secrets: which were not, as ordinary people's might have been, what they did in bed, but *how much they earned*.

I was not the Moores' only guest. They had become friends with a couple whom I had met a year or so before, and liked: Franklin Russell, who wrote good and successful nature books, and his very attractive Canadian wife Jean, who was an actress – a good one according to the Moores, although she found it impossible to get parts in New York because Americans never took Canadians seriously. Frank was travelling in some inhospitable place for one of his books, so Jean needed cheering up and was therefore with us. The two couples had become so close that they had just pooled their resources and bought a country place in New Jersey: the Moores were going to live in the old farm house, the Russells were converting its barn. This venture was the summer's big excitement.

I was there for three or four days which were as enjoyable as our times together always were. On one of the days Jean took over the kitchen and cooked a supremely delicious shrimp dish, for which she was famous, and on another day she and Brian had to make the long drive to the new property, to sort something out with the builders, so Jackie and I made an outing to Sag Harbor. On my last day, as we were all strolling to the beach, Jackie and ten-year-old Michael leading the way, I caught myself thinking 'Perhaps darling Jackie is letting her indifference to appearance go a bit far'. Like Brian, she was fat, and she had recently become fatter – her ragged old denim shorts were too tight. And she had been neglecting her roughly blonded hair, which looked chopped rather than cut and was stiff from sea-bathing so that it stuck out like straw. When you couldn't see her vivid face and the brightness of her hazel eyes, you noticed that she was looking a mess. I don't recall making the comparison, but the always remarkable and apparently effortless physical elegance of Jean, who was walking beside me, may well have triggered the thought.

It was, however, a passing one: something which I would not have remembered if I had not received a letter from Jackie about a month later, telling me that Brian and Jean had run away together.

My first reaction was a shock of shame at my own obtuseness. Did I not pride myself on being a shrewd observer of people's behaviour? How could I possibly have registered no more than that one tiny flicker of foreboding, and then dismissed it? So much for perceptiveness! And so much for Brian's detestation of romantic passion!

My next, and enduring, reaction was one of acute consternation on Jackie's behalf. She, too, had failed to pick up any hint of what was going on. She had made her discovery through some cliché of marital disaster such as finding a note in a pocket when sending a jacket to the cleaner. Trying not to be entirely sure of its implications, she had asked Brian for an explanation: out it all came, and off they went. She was still in shock when she wrote, and all my feelings of sympathy were for her and Michael.

It was only for a few days, however, that I felt Brian to have transmogrified into a villain. It did seem extraordinary that he and Jean had been prepared to continue with the property-sharing plan once they had fallen in love, abandoning it only on being discovered. That was what it looked like then, to both Jackie and me. Later it occurred to me that they might well have been less cold-blooded towards Frank and Jackie than they seemed: that they might not have realized how irresistible their passion had become until that day they spent together 'sorting things out with the builders', or even after that. But even while I was still being shocked by their ruthlessness, I knew that falling in love happens, and once it has happened it can't be undone. And I also acknowledged that I and their other friends must have been wrong in seeing the partnership between Brian and Jackie as cloudless. Little though he had shown it, he must have been finding it oppressive for some time. It is absurd for anyone to believe himself aware of the ins and outs of other people's relationships, so it was absurd to blame Brian for finding in Jean something which he needed, and which Jackie could not give. (That he had done so was true, and remained true for the rest of his life.)

So I expected soon to emerge from total dismay at the Moores' break-up, and to see Brian again as himself. But for the moment the person I couldn't stop thinking about was Jackie. *She* had not wanted anything from the marriage that it didn't give her: she had been as proud of Brian as a writer as she had been happy with him as a companion, and now all that was gone. Ahead of her stretched emptiness; above and below and within and without was the horrible miasma of the humiliation which comes from rejection. Then there was the anxiety of how to bring Michael through this debacle – and, for that matter, of how he and she were going to manage on their own . . . if ever anyone deserved sympathy, she did. Whereas Brian had seen what he wanted and had taken it, while remaining perfectly secure in the part of his own territory that was most important to him: his writing. No one need feel sorry for Brian. So it was Jackie I wanted to support, which meant writing to her often; whereas if I wrote to Brian, I wouldn't know what to say.

I ought, therefore, to have kept silent, but I did not. On getting a brief note giving me an address for him (whether this came from him or his agent I can't remember), I answered it almost as briefly, saying that although I was sure that we would soon be back on our old footing, for the present I was feeling for Jackie so strongly that I would prefer it if he and I confined ourselves to business matters.

How I regret not keeping his reply; because its strangeness is far from being communicable by description. I did not keep it because, having shown it to André, I wanted never to see it again.

It began disagreeably but rationally: there would be no business letters because there would be no further business. He had been displeased for some time by our failure to advertise his books properly, so now he was finding a new publisher. Upsetting, but sensible: if the letter had ended there we would have come back with some kind of undertaking to improve our performance, and if that had failed to mollify him André would have written him off as an example of the greed and folly of authors, and I would have known sadly that we had lost him through our own fault. But the letter did not end there. It went on for another page and a half, and what it said, in what appeared to be a fever of self-righteous spite against the woman he had dumped, was that I had sided with Jackie, and no one who had done that could remain his friend. The tone of that letter left André as shocked as it left me: so shocked that Brian's was the only departure from our list that he made no attempt to prevent.

Mordecai told me at the time that other friends of the Moores had been taken aback by this 'He who is not with me is against me' attitude, which made it seem all the more extraordinary. I had never encountered what I now know to be quite a common phenomenon: a person who has smashed a partnership trying to shift the whole blame for the break onto the one he or she has abandoned. It is natural, I suppose, to recoil from guilt – especially so, perhaps, in someone who was raised, as Brian was, to have a sharp sense of sin. But I still think that such a blind determination to have your omelette without breaking your eggs is ugly – and stupid, too – and this first example of it to come my way seemed impossible to believe. And it still seems nearly so. That Brian, with his wonderfully benign relish for human follies and failings, should have flumped into gross self-deception in this way . . . It seemed that I was losing him twice over, first as my friend (and that was very painful), then as himself. That letter could not have been written by the man I had thought Brian to be.

It often happens in old age that when one looks back on events which once seemed amazing, they now seem explicable and even commonplace: a depressing consequence of responses made blunt by the passing of time. Perhaps I should be grateful to Brian for having done something which still gives me a jab of genuine dismay.

Jackie is dead. For a time it looked as though the story, for her, had taken an astonishingly happy turn – and a comic one, into the bargain. She and Franklin Russell, left with the task of sorting out the shared-property plan, became closer friends than ever, had an affair – and ended up married. She was not a spiteful person. I never heard her say a word against Brian stronger than an expression of puzzlement. But she did evidently enjoy telling me, just once, that in fact Frank had been quite glad to get rid of Jean. I got the impression that she was comfortable with Frank in rather the same way that Brian had, to begin with, been comfortable with her when recovering from his passion for his drunken love. I stayed with them once in the New Jersey house (they had sold the barn), and saw them happy enough together to be dealing bravely with the first of the disasters which hit them: the fact that their son Alexander had been born with spina bifida. He had by then reached the end of a long chain of operations, and was an enchanting little boy who seemed to be as active and cheerful as any other child of his age; and the core of Jackie's emotional life had obviously become her pride in him, and her happiness at having got him through to this state.

Soon after that visit she went with Frank on one of his journeys – I think it was the first time they had felt that they could briefly leave Alexander in other hands. On that journey she fell ill, and when she got home the illness was diagnosed as cancer of the pancreas. She fought it gallantly and died cruelly.

Frank and I did not know each other well enough to keep in touch, but I did run into him by chance about two years after her death. He had looked after her at home until the end and had been terribly shaken by what he had been through. I know that Michael Moore came together with his father after his mother's death, but what has happened to Franklin and Alexander Russell I do not know.

Although Brian's departure from our list was more painful than any other, it has never prevented me from remembering the years when he was with us with pleasure; and it made a substantial and valuable contribution to many a subsequent gossip-fest. There was very much more gain than loss in having published him. And my regret at hardly ever seeing Mordecai since he made that sensible move in his career, though very real, is softened by being able to read his books and being proud that we were his first publisher. When I finished reading *Barney's Version* I felt nothing but delight at his having so triumphantly outlived his first publishing house; and I am happy to end this chapter remembering that I once said to him 'You are going to end up as a Grand Old Man of Canadian Literature'. That is exactly what he would have done, if it were possible for a Grand Old Man to be wholly without pomposity.

JEAN RHYS

No one who has read Jean Rhys's first four novels can suppose that she was good at life; but no one who never met her could know how very bad at it she was. I was introduced to the novels quite early in the fifties, by Francis Wyndham, who was one of their very few admirers at that time, and I started corresponding with her in 1957; but I didn't meet her until 1964; and as a result I did almost nothing to help her during a long period of excruciating difficulty.

It was not, perhaps, her very worst time. That must have been the last three years of the forties, when she and her third husband, Max Hamer, were living at Beckenham in Kent, their money had run out, and Max, a retired naval officer, became so desperate that he stumbled into deep trouble which ended in a three-year prison sentence for trying to obtain money by fraudulent means. During that nightmare Jean, paralysed by depression, could do nothing but drink herself into a state so bad that she, too, was several times in court and once in jail. By the time we were in touch Max had served his sentence, they had crept away to a series of miserable lodgings in Cornwall, and Jean was no longer quite at rock-bottom; but she still had nine terribly difficult years ahead of her before re-emerging as a writer.

She had always been a very private person, but she was known in literary circles when her fourth novel, *Good Morning, Midnight*, came out in 1939. When the war began a lot of people 'disappeared' in that they were carried away from their natural habitat on joining the forces or taking up war-work. Jean followed her second husband out of London, so when he died, and she slithered with Max into their misfortunes, she was no longer in touch with former acquaintances and became 'lost'. Francis tried to find out what had happened to her and was told by one person that she had drowned herself in the Seine, by another that she had drunk herself to death. People expected that kind of fate for her.

It was the BBC which found her, when they were preparing to broadcast an adaptation of *Good Morning, Midnight* made and performed by the actress Selma vaz Dias. They advertised for information about 'the late Jean Rhys', and she answered. Learning of this, Francis wrote to her, and she replied, saying that she was working on a new book. Responding to Francis's and my enthusiasm, André Deutsch agreed that we should buy the option to see it – for £25.

When people exclaim at how mean this was I no longer blush simply because I have blushed so often. I tell myself that the pound bought much more in the fifties than it does now, which is true; that this was not, after all, an advance, only an advance on an advance, which is true; and that no one else in those days would have paid much more for an option, and that, too, is true. But it is inconceivable that anyone would have paid less – so mean it was. If we had known anything about Jean's circumstances I am sure that Francis and I would have fought for more, but it would be a long time before we gained any idea of them.

The trouble was, she kept up a gallant front. In the letters we exchanged between 1957, when she said that her book would be finished in 'six or nine months', and March 1966, when she announced that it *was* finished, she would refer to being held up by domestic disasters such as leaking pipes, or mice in the kitchen, and she would make the disasters sound funny. Not until I met her did I understand that for Jean such incidents were appalling: they knocked her right out because her inability to cope with life's practicalities went beyond anything I ever saw in anyone generally taken to be sane. Max's health had given out, but her loyalty to him extended beyond keeping silent about his prison sentence to disguising his subsequent helplessness. It was years before I learnt how dreadful her seventies had been as she alternated between the struggle to nurse him and bleak loneliness when he was in hospital. She ate too little, drank too much, was frightened, exhausted and ill – and paranoid into the bargain, seeing the village of Cheriton FitzPaine (to which they moved during these years) as a cruel place. So any little horror on top of all this would incapacitate her for weeks. And when it passed a certain point she would crack.

For example: she told me that neighbours were saying that she was a witch, and she told it lightly, so that I thought she was making a funny story out of some small incident. But Mr Woodward, the rector, was to say that indeed she had been so accused, and that anyone who thought such beliefs were extinct didn't know Devon. Jean, driven frantic, had run out into the road and attacked the woman who originated the charge with a pair of scissors, which led to her being bundled for a week or so into a mental hospital. 'And if you ask me,' said Mr Greenslade, one of her few friends in the village, as he drove me from Exeter in his taxi, 'it was the other one who ought to have been shut up, not poor Mrs Hamer.' And not a word of all that appeared in her letters.

Luckily she gradually became less inhibited with Francis – partly, no doubt, because he was a man, and partly because he wrote to her as a friend from his own home, not as her publisher from an office (he worked with us only part-time). To him she owed the fact that a publisher was waiting for her book, and in him (this was probably more important to her) she had found someone who understood and loved her writing, who was sympathetic, amusing, kind, anxious to help. He made her dig out stories and found magazines to publish them, and when at last she let him know that she was on the verge of collapse, he sent her £100 so that she could go to a hotel or into a nursing-home for a rest. Her letters to me during those years are those of a writer glad to have a sympathetic editor; her letters to Francis are those of someone luxuriating in the unexpected discovery of a friend. Had it not been for his support she would not have been able to finish the book through which, in spite of such heavy odds against it, she was slowly, slowly, slowly inching her way.

People are not, thank God, wholly explicable. Carole Angier's biography of Jean does as much as anything ever will to explain the connections between the life and the work, but how this hopelessly inept, seemingly incomplete woman could write with such clarity, power and grace remains a mystery. I have long since settled for this fact; but I think I have reached a better understanding of the bad-at-life side of Jean since coming to know Dominica*, the island in the eastern Caribbean where she was born.

I have been given an unusually close view of the island by a piece of great good fortune: becoming friends (through having been Jean's publisher) with a Dominican family which includes the man who knows more than anyone else about every aspect of it. In Lennox Honychurch one of the Caribbean's smallest islands has produced the region's best historian, and it is through mental spectacles borrowed from him that I suddenly saw how *foreign* Jean was when she came to England in 1906, at the age of sixteen.

The British, thinking 'West Indies', mostly envisage a mixture of Jamaica and Barbados with a touch of Mustique. My own image, which I considered well-founded because I had been there, was Trinidad & Tobago plus Jamaica. So Dominica surprised me.

In the first place, no one had seriously wanted to make a colony of it. Columbus hit on it in 1493, and once described it by scrunching up a sheet of paper and tossing it onto a table: an inadequate image, but one can see what he meant. It consists of thirty by sixteen miles of densely packed volcanic mountains separated by deep valleys into which waterfalls roar and down which little rivers, often turbulent, run. The whole of it is clad in exuberant forest and some of it is given to steaming and shuddering. The dramatic nature of its conformation, and the

---

* Dominica has adopted the appellation 'The Commonwealth of Dominica'. The Dominican Republic, also in the Caribbean, is a different country, which shares an island with Haiti.

tropical richness of its forest (much of it rain forest) make it wonderfully beautiful, but it is hardly *useful-looking*.

Human beings have two ways of relating to such terrain. If, like the Caribs, who were there when Columbus turned up, you are the kind of human who lives with nature rather than on or against it, you find it hospitable: you can't freeze in it, you can't starve in it, there is plenty of material for building shelters and a vast number of mighty trees out of which to make canoes; and if hostile humans invade they find it extremely difficult to move about in, while you can very easily hide, and then ambush them. (There are still more Caribs living in Dominica than anywhere else, and it enabled escaped slaves to put up a more impressive resistance to vengeful slave-owners than they could do on any other island.) But if you are the kind of human who likes to control nature, and hopes to make a profit from it, then you must either leave such an island alone, as the Spanish sensibly did, or else steel yourself to work very hard for sadly little return. Dominica's settlers have tried planting a variety of crops – coffee, cocoa, a very little sugar (not enough flat ground), lots of bananas and citrus fruit, vanilla, bay rum . . . all of them reasonably profitable for a time, then wiped out or greatly reduced by hurricanes, blights, or shifts in the market. In many parts of the Caribbean planters made fortunes; in Dominica with luck you got by, but rich you did not get.

It was the French who first, early in the eighteenth century, edged themselves in to start plantation life: the Dominicans of today, almost all of them of African descent, still speak the French-based patois introduced by the slaves of the French planters, and Catholicism remains the island's predominant religion. The English took the place over in 1763 as part of the peace settlement at the end of the Seven Years War between France and England, and were not excited by it. 'These islands', said a booklet for investors in 1764, 'are not the promised land, flowing with milk and honey . . . Of those who adventure, many fall untimely. Of those who survive, many fall before enjoyment . . .'* Most

---

* I owe both this and the next quotation to Lennox Honychurch's *The Dominica Story*.

plantation owners from then on were absentees who left managers in charge – men who had a bad reputation. A coffee planter in the eighteenth century wrote: 'When we look around and see the many drunken, ignorant, illiterate, dissolute, unprincipled Characters to whom the charge of property is confided . . . it is no wonder that the Estate goes to ruin and destruction.' But the managers deserve some sympathy: it was a lonely life. The small and rustic estate houses were separated from each other not by great distances, but by impassable terrain.

To this day the abruptness with which mountains plunge into sea at each end of the island has defeated road-builders, so that no road runs right round it; and only since 1956 has it been possible to drive obliquely across it from the Caribbean to the Atlantic on a road forced by mountains to be much longer than the distance straight across. This trans-insular road, grandly named the Imperial Road, was officially 'opened' in about 1900, but in fact petered out halfway across, with only the first five or six miles surfaced. In Jean's day you either sailed round the island, or rode a very difficult track often interrupted by flood or landslip. Even the flat coast road linking Roseau and Portsmouth, the two main towns on the Caribbean side, was non-existent until 1972. Nowadays a few narrow metalled roads run up into the mountains from the coast, so that farmers can truck their produce down to be shipped; but when Jean went to visit her grandmother at Geneva, the family's estate, she rode nine miles of stony track.

Except for the one between Roseau and Portsmouth, Dominica's narrow bumpy roads still inspire awe just by existing: so much forest to be cleared, so many ups and so many downs to be negotiated hairpin after hairpin after hairpin, so many tropical downpours to wash away what has just been achieved . . . and so little money and no earth-moving equipment! They are valiant little roads, and keeping them in repair is a heavy task.

So it is not surprising that few white people settled in Dominica. In Jean's girlhood an energetic Administrator tempted in a new generation of English planters, and briefly the white population soared . . . from forty-four in 1891 to three hundred and ninety-nine in 1911*. But the new planters soon gave up, and now it is under a dozen. Jean's parents lent her elder sister to rich relations to be brought up, and I can see why. White middle-class girls didn't work, they got married, and who was there in Dominica for a girl to marry? No one. In those days British neglect of the island had been so scandalous regarding schools that hardly any black Dominicans had any schooling at all. Racial prejudice would, anyway, have made a black husband for a white girl seem impossible, but there would also have been real incompatibility. White education was nothing to boast of, but even the least polished white daughter could read.

In a colonial society people only had to be white to feel themselves upper-class, in addition to which they hung on with determination to awareness of gentlemanly forebears if they had them, as the Lockharts (Jean's mother's family) did. So normal life to the child Jean was life at the top of the pile. Against which, the pile was no more than a molehill. Such a very small and isolated white society was less than provincial – less, even, than parochial, since there was considerably less enduring structure to it than to an average English village. It was threatened from below, which Jean sensed while still very young; but that pushed her in the direction of her family's attitudes, rather than away from them (not until she had worked her way through to the writer in herself – the seeing eye – would she, almost in spite of herself, reflect back an image of white Dominican society as it really was). As she approached the age of sixteen, when she would leave for England, her life was that of a tiny group of people whose experience was considerably narrower than they liked to think, combined with life in the head: dream life.

Part of the dream was of Dominica itself, because its combination of beauty and untameability exerts a strong pull on the imagination. Jean wrote**

---

* Figures from Peter Hulme's essay 'Islands and Roads', *The Jean Rhys Review*.
** In *Smile Please*, her last book. The writing is less taut and evocative than it used to be.

. . . It was alive, I was sure of it. Behind the bright colours the softness, the hills like clouds and the clouds like fantastic hills. There was something austere, sad, lost, all these things. I wanted to identify myself with it, lose myself in it. (But it turned its head away, indifferent, and that broke my heart.)

The earth was like a magnet which pulled me and sometimes I came near it, this identification or annihilation that I longed for. Once, regardless of the ants, I lay down and kissed the earth and thought, 'Mine, mine.' I wanted to defend it from strangers . . .

Outsiders, too, respond to it romantically. I know others beside myself who try to play down the intensity of their infatuation with it for fear of seeming absurd. I was charmed by Tobago, but it did not haunt my imagination as Dominica does. Perhaps it has to do with its volcanic nature. In addition to the Boiling Lake, steaming and gulping in its impressive crater, it has several lesser fumaroles, sulphur springs, earth tremors . . . vulcanologists say that at least four of its centres of volcanic activity might blow at any time. The inconceivable violence barely contained within our planet can't be forgotten on Dominica. It is a place so far from ordinary in the mind's eye that belonging to it, as Jean so passionately felt she did, must set one apart.

Her other dream was of England, bred partly from the way that colonial families of British origin idealized it, more from the books which were sent her by her grandmother on her father's side. From this material she created a promised land even more seductive than her beloved Dominica. Her father had an inkling of what would happen when she got there: he warned her that it would be 'very different', and told her to write directly to him if she was unhappy – 'But don't write at the first shock or I'll be disappointed in you.' But when they said goodbye, and he hugged her tightly enough to break the coral brooch she was wearing, she was unmoved by his emotion and felt very cheerful, 'for already I was on my way to England'. At which she arrived knowing so little about it that she might have been landing from Mars.

It was not just a matter of the obvious ignorances, such as not knowing what a train looked like (put into a little brown room at her first railway station she didn't realize what it was), or supposing that the hot water gushing from bathroom taps was inexhaustible (she was scolded for using it all up when she took her first bath, and how could she have known?). And of course she had never dreamt of endless streets of joined-together brick houses, all grey . . . All that was bad enough, but worse was having none of the instinctive sense of give and take that is gained from living in a complex society surrounded by plenty of people like oneself. The older women she had known had been given no more opportunity than she had to acquire this . . . She could hardly have known what it was that she lacked, but she did know how badly she was at a loss.

In England *everyone she met* knew things she didn't know – not just the things taught in schools, but baffling ordinary, everyday things. Many young women are nimble face-savers, able to learn ways out of difficult situations, but Jean was not. Already, for whatever reason, she was in some ways trammelled in childishness; already paranoia threatened. It did not occur to her to learn, all she could do was hate. She hated this country which was so far from resembling her dream, and even more fiercely its inhabitants, for despising (as she was sure they did) her ignorance and her home. This feeling persisted into her old age: I saw it flare up when a woman spoke of Castries, in St Lucia, as 'a shanty town'. Instantly Jean assumed that this sneering woman – these sneering English – would see Roseau in the same way, and Roseau was not a shanty town – it was *not* – they were not seeing it right. She sprang to defend it against strangers – hateful strangers. She had always hated them with their damned cold competence and common sense: never would she dream of trying to be like them. Probably she could not have been, anyway; but her abhorrence of what she saw as Englishness did make her *embrace* her own incompetence.

The book she was trying against such heavy odds to finish was inspired by this hate. At first it was called 'The First Mrs Rochester'. Charlotte Brontë's *Jane Eyre* had always filled her with indignation on behalf of the mad West Indian wife shut up in the attic of Thornfield Hall. She knew that Englishmen had sometimes married West Indian heiresses for their money, and suspected that Brontë had based her story on local gossip about such a marriage; and to Jean such gossip could only have been spiteful and unfair. For years she had wanted to write a novel showing the wife's point of view, and for almost as many years again that was what – with long and painful interruptions – she had been doing.

We had not been corresponding for long before she admitted that her worry about Part Two of *Wide Sargasso Sea* (as it had become) was exhausting her. In this Part Mr Rochester turns up and marries Antoinette (disliking the name Bertha, which Brontë gave the wife, Jean chooses to call her heroine by her second name). Their relationship has to be established and the reason why this marriage of convenience goes so terribly wrong has to be explained. For Antoinette's childhood and schooling, Jean said in letters, she could draw on her own, and 'the end was also possible because I *am* in England and can all too easily imagine being mad'. But for the wedding and what followed she had nothing to go on, and she went through agonies of uncertainty: 'Not one real fact. Not one. No dialogue. Nothing.'

She sent an early version of Parts One and Two to Francis, who showed them to me, and in that version Part Two was indeed thin: the marriage became a disaster almost immediately, before it had been given time to exist. About this I wrote to her – nervously, because Part One was so marvellous that the book I was meddling with could obviously become a work of genius. I was relieved when she accepted what I had said; but not until much later, when I read one of her letters to Francis*, did I see that my suggestion had been of real use.

She told him of certain 'clues' that had led her forward. The first was obeah, and how it must have played its ambiguous part in the story. 'The second clue was when Miss Athill suggested a few

* In *Jean Rhys: Letters 1931–1966*, edited by Francis Wyndham and Diana Melly, André Deutsch, 1984.

weeks' happiness for the unfortunate couple – before he gets disturbing letters.' Starting to follow this suggestion, she saw at once that 'He must have fallen for her, and violently too', and at once the marriage came alive and was launched on its complex and agonizing course.

That was to remain my only editorial intervention, strictly speaking, in Jean Rhys's work: on points of detail she was such a perfectionist that she never needed 'tidying up'.

Jean and I met for the first time in November 1964, when, after the support she had received from Francis, and also from another Deutsch editor, Esther Whitby, who had volunteered to spend a weekend at Cheriton FitzPaine to help her sort out and arrange what she had written, she felt able to bring the finished book to London. Or rather, the almost finished book: there were still a few lines which she would have to dictate to the typist to whom we had given the material brought back by Esther. We would meet, Jean and I, for a celebratory lunch the day after she arrived . . . Instead, I was called to her hotel by an agitated manageress, who reported that she had suffered a heart attack during the night. So there was no triumph over a bottle of champagne. I had to pack her into an ambulance and take her to hospital. This, followed by three or four weeks of hospital visiting, with all the usual intimacies of nightdress washing, toothpaste buying and so on, plunged us into the deep end of friendship – though I soon learnt that it would be a mistake to suppose that meant trust. Jean never entirely trusted anybody. But she was never thereafter to show me an unfriendly face.

At the end of her first day in hospital she presented me with what might have become a painful moral problem: she asked me for a solemn promise that the book would never be published in its unfinished state – without, that is, the few lines she had been intending to dictate. Naturally I gave it. And then I went home to think 'What if she dies?' It seemed quite likely that she would. The book was publishable as it stood – perhaps a footnote or two would be necessary at the places where the lines were to go, but that was all. If she died would I be able to – would it even be right to – keep my promise? Now I know there would have been no question about it: of course we would have published. But at the time, in all the disturbance and anxiety caused by her illness, my sense of the terrifyingly treacherous world in which Jean's paranoia could trap her (I'd picked that up at once) was so strong that I felt any promise given her *must* be real.

A possible solution occurred to me. Esther had described how Jean kept her manuscript in shopping-bags under her bed, a hugger-mugger of loose sheets and little notebooks which Jean had said only she herself could make sense of. I knew that her brother, Colonel Rees-Williams, was coming up from Budleigh Salterton to visit her in hospital. Why not ask him to collect every bag of writing he could find in her cottage and bring it to me, without telling her (she was too ill to deal with it herself)? I would then go through it, returning everything meticulously to the order in which I found it, hoping to find clues to what she intended to insert; so that, if the worst happened, I could follow, at least approximately, her intentions.

Colonel Rees-Williams did his part, but in vain. Jean had been right: she *was* the only person who could make sense of the amazing muddle seething in those bags. So I gave up, her brother put the bags back exactly where he found them, and Jean never knew what we had done.

It took her nearly two years to regain enough strength to look at the book again, and to add the scraps of material she felt to be necessary. She could do it, she said, because of a new pill prescribed, I think, by a new doctor – though it may have been her old doctor trying something new. Perhaps he was the most important contributor to the conclusion of that novel, so I am sorry I cannot name him.

It was on March 9th 1966 that she wrote to tell me that the book was finished – and that Max was dead.

My dear Diana

Thank you for your letter [knowing that Max was dying I had just written her a letter of affection and anxiety]. I don't know what else to say. Max died unconscious, and this morning very early we went to Exeter crematorium.

A sunny day, a *cold* sun, and a lot of flowers but it made no sense to me.

I feel that I've been walking a tight rope for a long time and have finally fallen off. I can't believe that I am so alone and there is no Max.

I've dreamt several times that I was going to have a baby – then I woke with relief.

Finally I dreamt that I was looking at the baby in a cradle – such a puny weak thing.

So the book must be finished, and that must be what I think about it really. I don't dream about it any more.

Love from Jean

It's so *cold*.

I asked if I could come to Cheriton to collect the book, which seemed to please her; that first visit was when Mr Greenslade, sent by Jean to pick me up at Exeter, told me about her attack on her disagreeable neighbour.

She had booked me a room at the Ring of Bells, the village pub, because although she had a tiny extra room it would be another two years before it was inhabitable. Her letters always bewailed the weather, and sure enough, when I walked the length of the village to Landboat Bungalows, where she lived in number 6, it was raining and windy; and the village, too, behaved as she always said it did. On a walk of about half a mile I saw not a single person, the houses all stood with their backsides to the road, and the two dogs I met – mongrels of a sheepdog type – peered at me with hostile yellow eyes through their sodden shagginess and sidled away as though they expected me to stone them. Later I would see Cheriton looking quite normal (though the houses turning their backs to the road on that stretch of it remained odd); but that day I thought 'What a depressing place – she hasn't been exaggerating at all'.

I had always thought of a bungalow as a detached dwelling sitting on its own little plot, but Jean's was the last in a joined-together row of one-storey shacks, crouching grey, makeshift and neglected behind a hedge which almost hid them. They looked as though corrugated iron, asbestos and tarred felt were their main ingredients, and if I had been told that I must live in one of them I would have been appalled.

Jean could not afford to heat, and so didn't use, the only decent room which, like her bedroom, looked out over what would have been the garden had it been cultivated, towards some fields. On the road side there was a strip of rough grass shaded by the hedge, and the door opened into a narrow unlit passage, bathroom on the left, kitchen – into which I was immediately steered – on the right. It was about ten feet by ten, and it was just as well that it was no bigger; the only heating, apart from the two-burner gas cooker, was an electric heater of the kind which has little bars in front of a concave metal reflector, which scorches the shins of the person just in front while failing to warm the space as a whole. The small table at which Jean worked and ate, two upright chairs, a cupboard for food and another for utensils were all the furniture, and this was the room in which Jean spent all day, every day.

I doubt whether she could have survived another year in Landboat Bungalows if she had not managed to finish *Wide Sargasso Sea*.

Its publication, followed by the reissue of all her earlier work except for two or three stories which she didn't consider good enough to keep, brought her money: not a great deal of it, but enough to keep her warm and comfortable for the rest of her life. It also brought her fame, to which she was almost completely indifferent but which must have been better than being forgotten, and friends. Among the friends was Sonia Orwell, who made more difference to her life than anyone else.

Sonia struck me as tiresome. She often drank too much, was easily bored, which made her tetchy and sometimes rude, and was an intellectual snob without having, as far as I could see, a good enough mind to justify it. But although I suspect it was Jean's sudden fame, rather than her writing in itself, which made Sonia take her up, once she had been moved to do so she was amazingly generous about it.

She financed long winter holidays in London for Jean every year from the publication of *Wide Sargasso Sea* in 1966 to the end of her life, and she gave her many expensive presents. When I remarked on the amount she was spending she told me that she had always felt embarrassed at having inherited George Orwell's literary income, and had decided that she must use it to help writers who were hard up. This she said shyly and apologetically, to stop me thinking she was more generous than she was, not to take credit for it. And more impressive than the money she spent was the sensitivity she showed in her determination to give Jean a good time. She didn't just pay hotel bills: she did all the tipping in advance, she explained to the management the special kinds of attention this old lady would need, she booked hairdressers and manicurists, she bought pretty dressing-gowns, she saw to it that the fridge was full of white wine and of milk for Jean's nightcap, she supplied books, she organized visitors . . . From time to time she even did the thing she most hated (as I did too): took Jean shopping for clothes. This was so exhausting and so boring that eventually we both went on strike – and it was Sonia who then saw to it that younger and stronger spirits took our place. It was also she who was the most active member of what we called 'the Jean Committee' – the meetings at which she, Francis and I discussed 'Jean problems', such as getting her finances in order, or trying to find her somewhere to live nearer London, and less mingy, than Landboat Bungalows. (In this we did not succeed: whenever we came up with a real possibility Jean would jib: 'Better the devil I know', she would say.)

My gratitude for all this was profound, because quite early on I had been faced with a daunting prospect.

Jean loved her daughter, Maryvonne Moerman. She longed for her visits, grieved when she left, talked about her often with pride and admiration. During her bad times she had never burdened Maryvonne with worrying facts, and when she had money she constantly pondered ways of leaving her as much of it as possible. Several times she asked me to find answers to questions about the inheritance of money from England by someone living in Holland, as the Moermans did after returning from some years in Indonesia; and she often spoke about writing an account for Maryvonne of how the past had really been. If she could get it right, she said, then Maryvonne would at last understand.

What was it that she so urgently wanted her daughter to understand – and, by unmistakable implication, to forgive?

How much of Maryvonne's infancy was spent with her mother I do not know exactly, but I think it was almost none. Certainly she was for a time in 'a very good home run by nuns', and other nurseries were also involved. Fairly soon after her birth Jean got a job ghost-writing an autobiography in the south of France, one of its attractions being that if it worked she would be able to have her baby with her – but it didn't work. And when Maryvonne was about four years old Jean went away to England, leaving her to be raised in Holland by her father. Maryvonne adored her father, and arrangements were made later for her to spend school holidays in England with Jean, which she remembers as enjoyable: but it is hard for any small child not to feel, if her mother vanishes, that she has been abandoned.

This Jean could never undo, whatever she wrote, because the person she wanted forgiveness from was the abandoned child. Maryvonne the grown-up woman understood very well that she must accept her mother's nature – her absolute inability to behave like a capable adult in the face of practical difficulties – and she was generous enough to forgive it; but nothing could change what Maryvonne the child had experienced. This cruel fact brought Jean to a halt each time she approached it, and did more than the weakness of old age to explain why *Smile Please*, the autobiography she attempted in her late eighties, ended where it did. And no doubt it was this haunt between them that caused Maryvonne's longed-for visits always to end in some kind of pain and bitterness.

So after one of her visits to Cheriton, Maryvonne came to London and asked me to lunch with her. Jean had been talking of moving to Holland, and Maryvonne had decided that she must quickly establish that this was impossible. She told me that she would keep in touch with her mother and visit her from time to time, and that I could count on her to come over in an emergency, but that she could not have her with or near her all the time. I would have to take on the responsibility of looking after Jean, because she simply couldn't do it. 'It would wreck my marriage,' she said.

I cannot deny that my heart sank, all the more so because I could see exactly what Maryvonne meant. I knew less about Jean then than I do now, but I knew enough to see that she could not be lived with; certainly not by a daughter she had dumped at the age of about four. All editors have, to some extent, to play the role of Nanny, and I saw that in this case it was about to expand – in terms of size, not of glamour – into a star part. And so it would most onerously have done if it had not been for Sonia's invaluable help, and that of Francis. But he was soon to have his mother's old age to deal with, so he had gradually to withdraw from practical involvement, whereas it was many years before a combination of financial trouble and ill-health caused Sonia to flag.

It was thanks to her that I got a glimpse of how enchanting Jean must have been as a young woman (when happy). Sonia had taken her out to lunch and they had drunk enough champagne to make them both giggly – 'tipsy' would be the word rather than 'drunk'. When Jean got drunk (which I was not to witness until the last two years of her life) it was usually a disastrous release of resentment and rage; but this time her tipsiness hit the level which is exactly right. Everything became comic: she remembered – and sang – delightful songs; she told jokes; she liked everyone. She might have been enclosed in a pink bubble of Paris-when-she-was-happy-there, and it lasted until I had filled her hot water bottle and steered her into bed (I was taking the late afternoon and evening shift, as I usually did). Jean and I often spent enjoyable times together, but only with Sonia did she taste that sort of fun. Sonia, who knew Paris intimately, brought a whiff of Jean's favourite city with her, and she drank too much; whereas I was so undeniably English, and liked to stay sober. With me Jean couldn't quite let herself go.

That occasion was at the Portobello Hotel: the Portobello winter was the best of the treats provided by Sonia. The hotel was small, elegant in an informal way, and favoured by French theatre people. At that time it was being managed by a young woman recently celebrated in a Sunday newspaper as one of 'the new Fat' – a despiser of dieting who liked to wear flamboyant clothes and enjoy her own amplitude. She had, Sonia told me, made a special price for Jean because she loved her books (unfortunately she was no longer in charge when the next winter came round, perhaps because of her amiable tendency to make such gestures). The first time I visited Jean there I was greeted at the reception desk by a faun-like being in a pink T-shirt trimmed with swansdown which had little zipped slits over each breast, both of them unzipped so that his nipples peeped out. This seemed such a far cry from Cheriton FitzPaine that I wondered whether Jean, much as she longed for a change, would find it upsetting; but she loved it, was fussed over charmingly by both the manageress and the saucy faun, and would have been happy to spend the rest of her days at the Portobello. I think it was during that holiday that she played with the idea of dyeing her hair red. I protested, because bright hair-dyes make one's skin look old, and she said: 'But it's not other people I want to fool – only myself.'

Where Jean was *not* happy was in a hotel which Sonia fell back on later, when she was beginning to feel the financial pinch which, together with illness, made her last years miserable. It was one of those comfortable but drab places near the Cromwell Road which are chosen as permanent homes by elderly widows, and Jean made her loathing of it brutally clear. Generosity inspired in her no more sense of obligation than it would have done in a six-year-old, and even after Sonia had moved her (as she quickly did) into a vastly chic and expensive establishment, she remained slightly sulky. It was to Sonia, not to her, that the manager of the rejected hotel had said that they were accustomed to – indeed, specialized in – elderly people, but Jean had picked it up the moment she crossed the threshold, and was not going to forgive the making of such a choice for her. Later still, when Sonia left London for a cheaper life in Paris, I and others often explained to Jean how her circumstances had changed. Jean would acknowledge her friend's misfortunes with a ritual 'Poor Sonia', but her voice would be indifferent and there would be a distant look in her eyes. For her, inevitably, a friend who had gone away was a friend who was rejecting her.

Jean's comparative sedateness with me made it a shock when I received a letter from a man who had been her neighbour in Beckenham, and who resented the acclaim she was getting for *Wide Sargasso Sea*. He wrote an unsparing, and horridly convincing, description of the aggressive drunken behaviour which had led to her arrests, and he also took it on himself to tell me about Max's disaster, which Jean had never mentioned. I was able, therefore, to explain Jean's lapses as a breakdown under strain. Only in her last few years did I begin to understand that ugly drunkenness had been her downfall, on and off, for most of her adult life. Before that, my personal experience of her had revealed her incompetence, her paranoia, her need for help and reassurance, and the superficial nature of her gratitude ('I've got hold of some money' was how she told Maryvonne of Francis's gift, and glimpses of that attitude were not infrequent through the chinks in her politeness). But I also knew that she was very often charming, had an old-fashioned sense of decorum and good taste (she hated unkind gossip), and that however tiresome her muddles could be, I enjoyed being her nanny more often than I found it wearisome.

It did not really matter that the Jean Committee failed to find her a new house. Her bungalow was made so much more comfortable and pleasant by the hard work and ingenuity of two of her new friends, Jo Batterham and Gini Stevens, that – given more visitors, and the daily help which Sonia and I were at last able to find for her – she was probably as well off there as anywhere. Gini even took over the role of amanuensis for a while (Jean couldn't type and was frightened of tape-recorders, so she always had to have that kind of help). Like so many of Jean's relationships, this one ended in tears; but not before it had enabled her to put together the collection of stories, *Sleep it Off, Lady*, which would have been impossible without it.

Meanwhile Jean's finances were, by a miracle, kept in order by an accountant recommended by Sonia on the grounds that he liked good writing and drank a lot.

A good example of a Jean muddle was the case of Selma vaz Dias, the actress who had adapted *Good Morning, Midnight* for the radio, and who saw herself, not without reason, as Jean's true 'rediscoverer'. The trouble with Selma was not that she made that claim, but that she thought herself entitled by it to become a bandit.

Although middle-aged and rather stout, she was a striking woman with bold dark eyes who wore clothes to suggest a dash of the Spanish gypsy, and was an ebullient talker. Jean had been delighted and grateful on learning of her plans for *Good Morning, Midnight*, had enjoyed her company when they met, and loved her infrequent letters. Knowing they had planned to meet when Jean brought the manuscript of *Wide Sargasso Sea* to London, I telephoned Selma to report that she had been taken to hospital . . . and began almost at once to doubt the worth of her friendship. First, a surprising amount of prodding was necessary to make her visit Jean; then the visit turned out to be extremely short and to consist mostly of Selma complaining of its inconvenience to herself; and lastly, when I was giving her a lift home after it, she said almost nothing about Jean except: 'You know, of course, that she used to work as a prostitute?'

Worse was to emerge. After the publication of *Wide Sargasso Sea* Jean confessed to worry about something which Selma had made her sign. It then came out that in 1963, on a visit to Cheriton, Selma had produced 'a bit of paper' which Jean understood to concern the broadcast rights of *Good Morning, Midnight*, *Voyage in the Dark* and *Wide Sargasso Sea*, but which was in fact an agreement to give Selma fifty per cent of the proceeds from any film, stage, television or radio adaptation of any of Jean's books, anywhere in the world, for so long as the books were in copyright, and granting Selma sole artistic control of any such adaptation.

Jean was to say repeatedly that she thought being made to sign it was a joke – 'I was a bit drunk, you see . . . well, a bit, very.' However, two years later, when Selma got an agent to recast this same agreement in more formal terms, and he wrote to ask Jean whether she really did want to sign it again, she apparently felt that she must, and did so. (The agent had never met her, so I suppose was unaware of her near-idiocy in practical matters; otherwise he would, I hope, have taken a stronger line.)

At first I was not too worried, because I was unable to believe that anything so outrageous could stand. Selma herself, I thought, could surely be made to see as much: a foolish thought, that one turned out to be. Then André Deutsch and I talked to her husband who, though obviously deeply embarrassed, insisted there was nothing he could do. So – 'Write a full account of the whole thing,' said André to me, 'and I'll send it to Arnold.'

'Arnold' was Arnold Goodman, not yet a lord but already the most famous lawyer in the United Kingdom and André's guru. Hope revived: *of course* Arnold would save the day. But all he could say was that this was a contract, and if someone was daft enough to sign a contract without understanding it, whether drunk or sober, too bad for them. My inability to expect anything good from lawyers was born out of that day's impotent rage.

I have forgotten how I knew that the theatrical agent Margaret Ramsay had once been Selma's agent and friend, but I did know it, and inspiration hit me. 'If anyone can deal with this it will be that little war-horse.' Peggy always talked without drawing breath, so when she heard me name one of my authors it was a minute or two before I could stem the torrent of her refusal even to think about taking on another writer, and explain our problem. Once she had taken it in: 'GOOD GOD! That's perfectly appalling! Selma can't be allowed to get away with that. LEAVE HER TO ME!' Oh, the gratitude.

Even Peggy couldn't make Selma cancel the contract, but she did get her to reduce her fifty per cent to thirty-three and a third; and – far more important – she did make her cancel the clause giving her artistic control by somehow drilling into her mulish head that such a clause would forever prevent the sale of any such rights to anyone.

From then on Peggy Ramsay handled all Jean's film, stage, television and radio rights; and a few years later we steered her other literary affairs into the hands of the agent Anthony Sheil – a belated and profound relief. Because until then almost anyone Jean met could, and only too often did, become her agent, with results which – though never so dire as the Selma affair – were often maddeningly confusing and counter-productive.

Although I never had to do any work on a text by Jean, I did once intervene by discouraging the inclusion of one of her stories in the collection *Sleep it Off, Lady*. Francis, too, advised her to leave it out; I can't now remember which of us was the first to raise the matter. In a catalogue of her private papers, appended to the typescript of the story 'The Imperial Road', there is this note: 'Miss Rhys has stated that her publishers declined to include this story in *Sleep it Off, Lady*, considering it to be too anti-Negro in tone.' True, but over-simplified.

Jean shared many of the attitudes of other white Dominicans born towards the end of the nineteenth century. It is true that she often spoke of how, as a child, she longed to be black, because black people's lives were so much less cramped by boring inhibitions than those of the whites; but this was a romantic rebellion within the existing framework, not a rejection of the framework. When I knew her she talked – sometimes unselfconsciously, sometimes with a touch of defiance – like any other old member of the Caribbean plantocracy, describing black people she liked as 'loyal'; saying what a mess 'they' had made of things once 'we' were no longer there (that was the burden of 'The Imperial Road') and so on. Typical white liberal of the sixties that I was, I disliked hearing her talk like that, but it seemed natural: and it never failed to make me marvel that in *Wide Sargasso Sea* she had, by adhering to her creed as a writer, transcended her own attitude.

Her creed – so simple to state, so difficult to follow – was that she must tell the truth: must get things down *as they really were*. Carole Angier, in her biography, has demonstrated how this fierce endeavour enabled her to write her way through to understanding her own damaged nature; and it also enabled her, in her last novel, to show Dominica's racial pain as it really was. But it didn't work in 'The Imperial Road'.

Oddly enough neither Francis nor I was then aware of how far it was from working. We were simply uneasy at the story's tone, without realizing that it was the consequence of a major (though explicable) misunderstanding on Jean's part. In the story the Jean-figure sets out to cross Dominica on the Imperial Road – the trans-insular road built in her childhood. Revisiting the island many years later she wants to follow the road. To her incredulous dismay she finds that 'they' have let it be swallowed up by the forest: it is no longer there.

Jean herself had been present, as a child, at the opening of the Imperial Road, and had not unnaturally supposed that if a trans-insular road is declared open, it must have been built. No one had explained to her that it had in fact been built only to a point half-way across, where the Administrator's estate happened to be, and that even that stretch of it was metalled for only five miles. What she thought, thirty years later, to have vanished as a result of 'their' neglect, had never in fact been built by 'us'. So the story was even more 'wrong' than it smelled to Francis and me; and once I had learnt the historical facts I became even gladder that she did not dig in her heels and insist on including it (which, of course, she could have done if she had really wanted to).

The contrast with *Wide Sargasso Sea* is striking. In that novel the story is told from the point of view of someone whose life was wrecked by the emancipation of the slaves, and who is puzzled and angry, as well as grieved, by the hostility which blacks are now free to show against whites. But because the observation is so precise, and the black and mixed-blood people are allowed their own voices when they speak, the reader understands why Coulibri is burnt down; why Daniel Cosway has become the very disagreeable person he is; why the child Tia turns against Antoinette – indeed, has never really been able to be her friend, which is a fact equally cruel to both of them. Antoinette's world has been poisoned, not by these people's malice, but by their having been owned, until very recently, by her family as though they were cattle. Nowhere does Jean say this, but she shows it: Jean writing at her best knew more than the Jean one met in everyday life. I did not want her to publish 'The Imperial Road' because I did not want anyone to despise as racist a writer who could, when it mattered, defeat her own limitations with such authority.

By the time Jean started work on her last book, the autobiographical *Smile Please*, she was too old to do without help; but it was not I who gave it (apart from reading and making encouraging noises as it progressed) . . . She had always had to find someone to type her books for her, and continued to think of the person helping her as doing no more than that. But the novelist David Plante, who had offered to be her amanuensis for this book, did a good deal more to coax material out of her, and organize it, than she acknowledged. There was an anxious time when she panicked at what he was doing, telling me that he was taking the book over and trying to make it his own; but he had only been using scissors and paste on a few pages, to get the material into its proper sequence. Once she had been persuaded to read it and see her own words still saying what she wanted them to say, she relaxed. More or less. That was a difficult time: her last winter in London, when she proved to be beyond coping with a hotel, and Diana Melly, with incomparable generosity, took her into her house (indeed, gave up her own bedroom to her) for three months. After a few weeks of great pleasure, Jean began to slide into a sort of senile delinquency, and to drink too much: one of David's problems was steering his way between the disintegration which soon followed if he joined her in a drink, and the mutinous rage if he refused to. I remember huddling round the kitchen table with him and Diana, all of us agreeing that it was just a matter of one of us going upstairs and *taking the drinks tray out of her room* . . . a discussion which ended in Diana saying: 'Oh God – we're none of us any more use than a wet Kleenex.' But the book did get done, all the same: it was not what she wanted it to be, but it had a good deal more value than she feared.

In fact *Smile Please* is an extraordinary example of Jean's ability to condense: everything about her that matters is in it, though sometimes touched in so lightly that it can escape the notice of a reader who is less than fully attentive. It was as though something in her quite separate from her conscious mind was still in control, still making choices and decisions; and I have always thought that, about a year earlier, I was granted a glimpse of that something at work.

The proofs of *Sleep it Off, Lady* came in from the printer while Jean was in London, and she told me she was worried about checking them because she feared she was no longer capable of the necessary concentration. So I suggested that I should read them aloud to her, going very slowly, and doing no more than twenty minutes at a time. As soon as we began she became a different person, her face stern, her eyes hooded, her concentration intense. When I was halfway down the first galley-proof she said: 'Wait – go back to the beginning – it must be about three lines down – where it says "and then". Put a full stop instead of the "and", and start a new sentence.' She was carrying the whole thing in her mind's eye.

This tiny incident seemed to me to give a clear glimpse of the central mystery of Jean Rhys: the existence within a person so incompetent and so given to muddle and disaster – even to destruction – of an artist as strong as steel.

It was that incident which made me write the following lines, which I think of as 'Notes for a biography which will never be written'.

THE MOTHER A woman wearing corsets under a dark serge riding habit, cantering over sand under palm trees, up a track through the forest of leaves like hands, saws, the ears of elephants.

She banished mangoes from the breakfast table and gave her children porridge, lumpy because it was cooked by long-fingered brown hands more adept at preparing calaloo. She made the children wear woollen underwear the colour of porridge.

'What will become of you?' she said.

For all her care they were in danger of not seeming English. Her grandfather had built his house in the forest and taken a beautiful wife whose hair was straight and fell to her waist. But it, and her eyes, were very black.

Only one child was pink and white, with blue eyes, the proof. Why was she the one so difficult to love?

That child never asked and never told. She listened hungrily to the laughter in the kitchen, was locked in sulky silence when the Administrator's wife came to tea, and let the eyes of old men dwell on her.

'What will become of you?' Addressed to this one the question was more urgent, even angry; and after a while was not asked because what was the good? Who is not annoyed and fatigued by perversity?

But the child obeyed her mother. Bidden to dream of England, she dreamt. 'When I get there,' she dreamt, 'it will be like the poems, not like she says.' When she got there she found dark serge, porridge and porridge-coloured underwear. 'My poor mother,' she said later. She had decided long ago never to forgive a country's whole population, so she could afford to say no more than that about one woman.

THE FATHER A man in a panama hat and a white linen suit, leaving the house to make people better. 'Is the doctor in?' The voices were sometimes frightened and only he could help. He was often out, often had to be spared trouble when he was in, so it was a long time before he came into the room and found the child crying over her plate of lumpy porridge. 'In this climate!' he said. And after that her breakfast was an egg beaten up in milk, flavoured with sugar and nutmeg.

He liked her to mix his evening drink, and as she carefully measured out the rum and lime juice, and grated a little nutmeg over the glass, she knew she was a pretty sight in her white frock which hid the woollen vest.

It was his mother who sent the child books for Christmas and all the grown-up books in the glass-fronted case were his, except *The Sorrows of Satan* which was her mother's. And when he was a boy he ran away to sea because people were unkind and he couldn't bear it.

When he died there was no more money and no more love, and no one, she saw after that, could be relied on. But: 'I have always been grateful to my father,' she said later, 'because he showed me that if you can't bear something it's all right to run away.'

<u>THEIR DAUGHTER</u> She didn't want to hurt the man, but she went with him. Her new dream was Paris and he could take her there. He came at a time when her bad luck was so bad that she deserved a little good luck for a change. She thought: 'Poor man, I am sorry about this, but I would have been done for if he had not turned up to make life less difficult.'

She didn't want the child to die, but when it went a strange colour and wouldn't eat she thought: 'This baby, poor thing, has gone a strange colour and won't eat and I don't know what to do. I'm no good at this.' So she took it to a hospital and left it there. When they wrote to tell her it had died she saw that life was as cruel as she had always believed. But it did become less difficult.

She wanted to keep the other child, but where could she have put her? How could she have fed her? She thought: 'Perhaps one day my luck will change and I will get her back.' Her luck did change, and after that she saw the child from time to time; but the child loved her father better than she loved her. That was unfair. But it did make life less difficult.

Cruelty had never surprised her because she had always heard it sniffing under the door; and the exhausting difficulty was her own fault. She knew that others who wanted blue skies, pretty dresses, kind men, went out to find what they wanted, but she was no good at that, she never had been. So all she could do was wait for her luck to change. And dream. 'If you dream hard enough, sometimes it comes true.' She could dream very hard, and when it failed to work she dreamt harder. But never hard enough to dream away one thing: her gift. She ran away, she dodged, she lay low, but her gift was always there. Over and over again it forced her to stand, to listen to the rattling door and put what she heard into words which were as nearly precisely true as she could make them. She said about her gift: 'I hate it, for making me good at this one thing which is so difficult.'

Perhaps she thought that true. She could not see herself when she was working. Out of her eyes, then, looked a whole and fearless being, without self-pity, knowing exactly what she wanted to do, and how to do it.

ALFRED CHESTER

IT IS POSSIBLE that I am the only person in the United Kingdom who remembers Alfred Chester and his books: what he wrote was too strange to attract a large readership, and we did not overcome this problem. But he remains the most remarkable person I met through publishing and I, and his friends in the United States who, since his death in 1971, have been finding new readers for him, continue to think and talk about knowing him as one of our most important experiences.

He was twenty-six when I first met him in 1956, the year we published his novel *Jamie Is My Heart's Desire* and his stories *Here Be Dragons*. First impressions? The very first was probably of ugliness – he wore a wig, his brows and eyelids were hairless, his eyes were pale, he was dumpy – but immediately after that came his openness and funniness. It didn't take me long to become fond of Alfred's appearance.

He also inspired awe, partly because of his prose and partly because of his personality. Alfred wore a wig, but never a mask: there he sat, being Alfred, and there was nothing anyone could do about it. He was as compactly himself as a piece of quartz.

He had come to London from Paris, where he had been kicking up his heels in green meadows of freedom from his conventional, even philistine, Jewish family in Brooklyn. Already brilliant young New Yorkers such as Susan Sontag and Cynthia Ozick, who had known him when they were students together, were eyeing him nervously as one who might be going to outshine them, but he had needed to get away. And now he was in a stage of first-novel euphoria, ready to enjoy whatever and whoever happened. Meeting him, whether alone or at parties, reminded me of the excitement and alarm felt by Tolstoy's Natasha Rostov on meeting her seducer and knowing at once that between her and this man there were none of the usual barriers. Something like that shock of sexual accessibility can exist on the level of friendship: an instant recognition that with this person nothing need be hidden. I felt this with Alfred (though there was a small dark pit of secrecy in the middle of the openness: I would never have spoken to him about his wig).

On his second visit he was with his lover, a very handsome young pianist called Arthur. When I went to supper with them in the cave-like flat which they had rented or borrowed, Arthur spent much time gazing yearningly at a portrait of Liszt, and I wondered whether Alfred was husband or wife in this ménage (heterosexuals are always trying to type-cast homosexuals). I decided eventually that, on that evening, anyway, what he mostly was was Mother.

That was the first time he talked to me about identity, explaining how painful it was not to have one: to lack a basic 'I' and to exist only as a sequence of behaviours. Did I have a basic and continuous sense of identity, he asked, and I was tempted not to say 'Yes' because such a commonplace lack of anxiety seemed uninteresting compared with the condition he was claiming. I think I put the temptation aside because I didn't take him seriously. How could quartz-like Alfred feel, even for a second, that he had no basic identity?

Nevertheless I remember that long-ago talk very clearly. Perhaps I am being wise after the event, but it seems to me there was a slight judder of uneasiness under the surface which fixed it in my head.

Through '56 and '57 we exchanged letters, and one of his contained a passage which now seems obviously deranged.

I was running away from the police, through Luxembourg which is incredibly beautiful (a valley in the midst of a city), then to

Brussels and back to Paris in thirty-six hours without sleep only to find that no one was chasing me after all. Unless they are being incredibly clever. You see, I'll be able to do things like that when I finish my book.

That sounds like paranoia. And how does the last sentence connect with the first two? But I was not much disturbed by this letter at the time. The rest of it was cheerful and normal, and the sobriety of my own life compared with Alfred's must have made me assume that his might well include mystifying events.

A letter of mine dated July 1959 reminds me that one of his London visits ended when he disappeared without a word.

. . . at one time, a long time ago, there was an extraordinary panic in London. John Davenport kept calling me and Elizabeth Montagu kept calling and I kept calling J.D. and E.M. and they kept calling each other and at one point an excursion was organised to Archway to confirm that you really had vanished and were not lying there sick unto death, or dead, or were not under arrest. After a while we said to each other 'Look, if any of those things had happened we'd have heard *somehow*. Wherever he is he must be all right.' So we gave up.

It was about a year after this disappearance that a visiting New Yorker let fall that Alfred was back in New York, and gave me the address to which I sent the above, whereupon Alfred replied that yes indeed, he'd become fed up with Greece and was now installed in a Greenwich Village apartment 'with a *roof garden!*' And that was where I next saw him when I was on a business visit to New York: in almost unfurnished rooms above the theatre in Sullivan Street, where I found our friendship in good health.

Alfred had to lead the way up the stairs because he was feuding with the landlord who had taken to leaving brooms and buckets in the darkness, to trip him and send him crashing through the frail and wobbly banisters. As we climbed he described the feud with great relish. It was still daylight, so he took me right to the top to show me the roof garden – the heat-softened asphalt of the roof's surface, thickly studded with dog turds. Dutifully I leant over the parapet to admire the view and the freshness of the breeze, but I was shocked. Dogs are quasi-sacred in my family, and I had been raised in the understanding that they don't ask to belong to people, so – given that we have taken them over for our own pleasure – it is our duty not only to love them but to recognize their nature and treat them accordingly. Never have I denied a dog exercise and the chance to shit in decent comfort away from its lair – adult dogs, except for half-witted ones, dislike fouling their own quarters. I saw soon enough that Alfred's beloved Columbine and Skoura, whom he had rescued in Greece, were a barbaric pair, perfectly happy to shit on the roof – and indeed on the floors, and the mattresses which lay on the floors to serve as beds. They had never been house-trained, and Skoura, anyway, *was* half-witted. But still I was disconcerted that Alfred was prepared to inflict such a life on his dogs.

It was dark by the time we sat down by candlelight (the electricity may have been cut off) to eat mushrooms in sour cream and some excellent steak, and the dim light concentrated on the carefully arranged table disguised the room's bareness and dirt. Halfway through the meal we heard someone coming up the stairs. Alfred hushed me and blew out the candles. A knock, a shuffling, breathing pause; another knock; another pause; then the visitor retreated. When Alfred relit the candles he was looking smug. 'I know what *that* was. A boy I don't want to see any more.'

That led to talk of his unhappiness. Arthur, the most serious and long-lasting of all his loves, had left him. He was trying to force himself into an austere acceptance of solitude, but like a fool kept on hoping, kept on falling into situations which ended in disappointment, or worse. The boy on the stairs was the latest disappointment, a chance pick-up who turned out to be inadequate. I said: 'But Alfred, dear heart, what makes you think it *likely* that someone you pick up in a urinal will instantly turn into your own true love?'; to which he replied condescendingly that I had no sense of romance.

My two favourite memories of New York were given me by
Alfred during my visit: he showed me the only pleasure in the city
which could still be had for a nickel, and he took me to Coney
Island. The nickel pleasure was riding the Staten Island ferry there
and back on a single fare, which meant hiding instead of landing at
the end of the outward journey. Early on a summer evening, when
the watery light and the ting-tong of a bell on a marker-buoy almost
turned Manhattan into Venice, it was indeed a charming thing to
do. And Coney Island was beautiful too, the water sleepy as it
lapped the dun-coloured sand, the sound of the boardwalk
underfoot evoking past summers which seemed – mysteriously – to
have been experienced by me. Sitting on the beach, we watched the
white flower of the parachute jump opening and floating down,
opening and floating down . . . Alfred teased me to make the jump
but I'm a coward about fairground thrills, and jibbed. He was
afraid, too, and told stories about famous accidents. He showed me
where, when he was a child, he used to climb down into the secret
runways under the boardwalk, and instructed me in methods of
cheating so that this or that could be seen or done without paying.
He was fond and proud of the child who used to play truant there
and had become so expert at exploiting the place's delights, and as
we sat beside each other in the subway, going home, I felt more
comfortably accepted by New York than I had ever done before. I
don't remember him ever talking about the pleasures of being an
enfant terrible reviewer, capable of causing a considerable frisson in
literary New York, which he was at that time.

Being the publisher of someone whose books are good but don't
sell is an uncomfortable business. Partly you feel guilt (did we miss
chances? Could we have done this or that more effectively?), and
partly irritation (does he really expect us to disregard all
commercial considerations for the sake of his book?). Alfred gained
a reputation for persecuting his publishers and agents with
irrational demands, but with us he was never more than tetchy, and
most of the uneasiness I felt came from my own disappointment
rather than from his bullying. In England he was all but overlooked:

a few reviewers made perfunctory acknowledgement of his cleverness and the unusual nature of his imagination, but many more failed to mention him. Our fiction list was well thought of by literary editors, and I had written them personal letters about Alfred. I was driven to wondering whether the favour we were in had backfired: had they – or some of them – taken against his work and decided that it would be kinder to us not to review it at all, rather than to review it badly? Only John Davenport, a good critic who had become Alfred's friend out of admiration for his writing, spoke out with perceptive enthusiasm.

I have forgotten when Alfred moved to Morocco and whether he told me why he was doing so (Paul Bowles had suggested it at a party in New York). The first letter that I still have with a Tangier address was written soon after the publication in England of his collection of stories, *Behold Goliath*, early in 1965.

Dear Rat

Why haven't you written?

Why didn't you let me know about publication?

Why haven't you sent me copies?

Why haven't you sent me reviews?

I will not make you suffer by asking why you didn't use the Burroughs quote, though I would like you to volunteer an explanation. I hope you will write me by return of post.

I'm coming to England, either driving in my trusty little Austin or by plane which terrifies me. I'm coming with my Moroccan boyfriend, and the real reason for the trip is to get his foot operated on. He has a spur, an excrescence of bone on the left heel, due to a rheumatic process. I'm afraid of doctors here. But please keep this a secret as they probably won't let us into England if they find out . . . I would appreciate it if you would check up on surgeons, bone surgeons or orthopedic specialists. I have some money so it doesn't have to be the health insurance thing, though that would help . . . They always used to fuss about me at the frontier, so there's bound to be a fuss about Dris. I am going to tell them that we are going to be your guests over the summer. I hope this is okay with you (for me to say so, not for us to stay) and that if they phone you or anything you will say yes it's true. Please reply at once.

Oh, I don't know if Norman [Glass] mentioned it, but I don't wear a wig any more. I thought I'd better tell you in advance so you don't go into shock. I like it better this way, but I'm still somewhat self-conscious.

Edward [Field] says I must give you and Monique Nathan* a copy of *The Exquisite Corpse* immediately. Epstein** says: 'I doubt very much that I can publish the book in a way that will be satisfactory to you, and I don't want to compound our joint disappointment in *Goliath*. The other reason has to do with the book itself. I recognize its brilliance – or more accurately I recognize your brilliance – but I confess that I'm baffled by your intentions, and I'm concerned that I would not know how to present the book effectively. I don't mean that for me the book didn't work; simply that it worked in ways I only partly understood. Or in ways that suggest it is more a poem than a novel, though whether this distinction clarifies anything is a puzzle.'

The book is too simple for him. It reads like a children's book and requires innocence of a reader. Imagine asking Jason Epstein to be innocent . . .

Will let you see it when I come. PLEASE REPLY BY RETURN OF POST. Love.

My answer:

I did tell you publication date, I have sent you copies – or rather, copies were sent, as is customary, to your agent (if A. M. Heath is still your agent – they are on paper. I called them this morning and they said they'd post your six copies today, and I don't know why they haven't done this before). Here are copies of the main

---

* His editor at Editions du Seuil, Paris
** His editor at Random House, New York

reviews [my lack of comment makes their disappointing nature evident]. And I didn't put the Burroughs quote on the jacket because no one in Sales wanted me to, Burroughs being thought of here except by the few as dangerously far out and obscene, and they not wanting to present you as more for the few than you are. Should have told you this. Sorry.

I am enclosing a letter of invitation in case it may be useful with the visa people or at frontiers. It's marvellous that you are coming . . .

Your quote from Jason Epstein made me laugh – there's a nervous publisher backing against a wall if ever there was one. I was also, of course, scared by his reaction because there is nothing more twitch-inducing than waiting for something to come in which you know is going to be unlike anything else, for fear that it is going to be so unlike that one will have hideous forebodings about its fate. I'm dying to read it. Hurrah hurrah that you'll soon be here. Love.

His answer, written in a mellow mood, ended with the words: 'As for *The Exquisite Corpse* being unlike, yes, it is probably the most unlike book you've read since childhood. And probably, also, the most delicious.'

I could not have rejected *The Exquisite Corpse*, because it seemed – still seems – to me to draw the reader into itself with irresistible seductions. Alfred was right: you must read it as a child in that you must read it simply for what happens next, without trying to impose 'inner meanings' on it. The title comes from the game called in England 'Consequences' – it was the Surrealists who gave it the more exotic name. Do people still play it? A small group of people take a sheet of paper, the first person writes the opening line of a miniature story, then folds the paper so that the next person can't see what he has written; the next person writes the next line, and folds – and so on to the last person, whose line must start 'and the consequence was . . .' Unfold the paper and you have a nonsense story which is often delightfully bizarre. You can do it with drawing, as well as with words: I can still remember a sublime monster produced that way by my cousins and me when I was a child, far more astonishing than anything any of us could have thought up on our own, yet perfectly convincing. Alfred followed the 'consequences' principle – it's as though the paper were folded between each chapter, and when people you have already met reappear you are not always sure that they are the same people – perhaps the name has been given to someone else? Sometimes appalling or obscene things happen to them (I still find it hard to take the scene in which the character called Xavier watches his papa dying). Often it is monstrously funny. In no way is the writing 'difficult'. There is nothing experimental about the syntax; you are not expected to pick up veiled references or make subtle associations; and there can never be a moment's doubt about what is happening to the characters. The writing – so natural, so spontaneous-feeling, so precise – makes them, as Alfred claimed, delicious. The book's strangeness lies entirely in the events, as it does in a fairy story, remote though Alfred's events are (and they could hardly be remoter) from those of Hans Andersen.

I was captivated, but two things disturbed me. The first was that we would be no more able than Jason Epstein to turn this extremely 'unlike' book into a best seller, so Alfred was bound to be disappointed. And the second was that it left me feeling 'one inch madder, and it would have been too mad'.

This was something to do with the contrast between the perfection and airiness of the writing and the wildness of the events. The easy elegance, the wit, the sweet reason of the style are at the service of humour, yes; of inventiveness, yes; but also of something fierce and frightening. A fierce – an aggressive – despair? If aggressive despair is screamed and thumped at you it is painful, but it makes sense. When it is flipped at you lightly, almost playfully . . . Well, it doesn't make nonsense, because nothing so lucid could be called nonsensical, but (like Jason Epstein) I don't know for sure what it does make. I am captivated, but I am uneasy. I am uneasy, but I am captivated. The balance wobbles and comes to rest on the side of captivation. I use the present tense because I have just reread it for the first time in years, and reacted to it exactly as I did at the first reading.

When Alfred arrived with Dris he was wigless. He looked impressive, face, scalp, ears, neck all tanned evenly by the Moroccan sun. Although he himself had already broken the taboo, I still felt nervous and had to screw up my courage in order to congratulate him on his appearance. I don't think I am inventing the shyly happy expression on his face as he accepted the congratulations. As I learnt later, having to wear a wig because a childhood illness had left him hairless was the most terrible thing in his life, an affliction loaded almost beyond bearing with humiliation and rage; so throwing it off, which had taken great courage, was a vastly important event to him.

Morocco, I thought, had given him a new calm and freedom, and he agreed. The version he gave me of the place was all liberation and gentleness: you could smoke delicious kif there as naturally as English people drink tea; no strict line was drawn between hetero- and homosexual love; and you didn't have to wear a wig – you could be wholly yourself. I rejoiced for him that he had found the place he needed.

A couple of days later he brought Dris to dinner at my place: handsome, cheerful Dris, with whom I could communicate only by smiling because I have no Spanish. After dinner Alfred sent him into the kitchen to wash the dishes, which shocked me until they had both convinced me that it was dull for him to sit listening to incomprehensible English. Soon Dris stuck his head round the door and offered me his younger brother – he thought it wrong that I should have no one to do my housework. Alfred advised against it, saying that the boy was beautiful but a handful and that Dris constantly had to chivvy him out of louche bars. Dris himself had become a model of respectability now that he had a loving and reliable American, and Alfred – so he said – would one day be the guest of honour at Dris's wedding. That would be recognized in Morocco as the proper conclusion of their relationship, and probably Dris's wife would do Alfred's laundry while their children would be like family for him. It sounded idyllic.

The high point of the evening was the story of their adventures on their drive to England, told with parentheses in Spanish so that Dris could participate. Alfred had crashed the car in France. When the police came Dris was lying on the ground with blood on his head. It was really only a scratch but it looked much worse and Dris was groaning and rolling up his eyes so that only the whites were visible. Yes, yes, Dris intervened, sparkling with delight, with Alfred interpreting in his wake. He had suddenly remembered that a friend of his had been in an accident in France, and was taken to hospital, and when he got there he *was given all his meals for free*! So Dris decided in a flash to get to hospital where he would save Alfred money by getting fed, and also – this was the inspiration which filled him with glee – by complaining piteously about his foot, as though it had been hurt in the accident, he would make them X-ray his foot, as well as feed him, so that Alfred would not have to pay for an X-ray in London. Unfortunately this brilliant wheeze came to nothing because he was not allowed to smoke in the ward, so before he could be X-rayed he became too fed up to endure it, and walked out. It was pure luck, Alfred said, that they had run into each other as they wandered the streets.

Alfred's gloss to the story was that the police and ambulance men had been fussing around so that Dris had no chance to explain his plan. Alfred had seen him whisked away without knowing where to, and had spent a day and a night adrift, wondering how the hell he was going to find Dris – and, indeed, whether Dris was still alive. Later this struck me as odd. It is not difficult to ask a policeman where an ambulance is going, nor to find a hospital. I supposed he must have been stoned out of his mind at the time of the accident, although I had never seen him more than mildly high and he was always careful to give me the impression that mildly high was as far as he went. I sometimes thought that Alfred tended to see me as slightly Jane-Austenish, which caused him to keep his less Jane-Austenish side averted from my view.

I didn't see much of him on that visit. He was affectionate and easy, but after a couple of hours I would know that I was becoming an inhibiting presence, and assume that he wanted to bring out the kif – I was unaware, then, that he also used other drugs – which I didn't use, so I would say goodnight and leave, feeling that the real evening was starting up behind me. Dris's foot remained a mystery. He saw a doctor, he did not have an operation, someone told me that the spur had been diagnosed as a result of gonorrhoea; and Alfred, when questioned, was vague, as though the matter had become unimportant.

Alfred's next visit, two years later, came out of the blue. As I came into the office one morning the receptionist behind her keyboard half rose from her chair and signalled that someone was waiting to see me. I peeked round the corner, and there was Alfred, sitting in a hunched position, staring into space. 'Oh my God, trouble' . . . the reaction was instantaneous, although his attitude might, I suppose, have been attributed to weariness.

I welcomed him and took him to my room, asking the usual questions and getting the information that he was on his way back to Morocco from New York and had stopped off because he needed to see a dentist. Would I find him one, and would I give him some typing to do so that he could earn a little money while he was here? Of course I would. And then, in a tone which indicated that this was the visit's real purpose: 'Will you call the Prime Minister and tell him to stop it.'

Stop what?

The voices.

I must not attempt dialogue or I will start cheating. The voices had been driving him mad. They gave him no peace, and the most dreadful thing about them was that they, not he, had written every word of his work. Did I see how appalling it was: learning that he had *never* existed? And even Dris was on their side. They often came at night, very loud. Jeering at him. Dris, in bed beside him, *must* have heard them. He could only be lying when he insisted that he didn't. It was not really for the money that Alfred needed the typing, it was because it might drown the voices.

He had been to New York, where he had attacked his mother with a knife (he had attacked Dris, too; though whether it was at this point, or a little later, that I learnt about these attacks I cannot remember). He was in London now because of what I had told him in Fez. But I had never been to Fez. Oh yes, I had, last week. Alarm became more specific because of the stony way he looked at me: I saw that it was possible to become one of 'them', an enemy, at any moment. I said cautiously that this Fez business puzzled me, because certainly my *physical* self had been in London last week.

I told him I had never met the Prime Minister (Harold Wilson it was then), and would not be put through to him if I called him, but that I could approach a Member of Parliament if that would do. I also told him that I was sure the voices were a delusion. He replied that he could understand my disbelief, and that I thought he was mad, so could I not in return understand that to him the voices were real: 'As real as a bus going down the street'? Yes, I could grant that, which seemed to help. It enabled him to make a bargain with me. If I proved that I was taking him seriously by approaching an MP, he would take me seriously enough to see a doctor.

That settled, things began to go with astonishing slickness. When I called my dentist I got through in seconds and he was able to see Alfred that afternoon; and it turned out that we had in the office a manuscript which genuinely needed to be retyped. Both these pieces of luck seemed providential, because I was sure that Alfred would have interpreted delay or difficulty as obstruction. (He kept all his appointments with the dentist, behaving normally while there, and he typed the manuscript faultlessly.)

After he had gone I sat there shaking: it would not have been very much more of a shock if I had come across someone dead. Then I pulled myself together and went to discuss the crisis with the person in the office most likely to know something about madness, who recommended calling the Tavistock Clinic for advice. At that time Doctors Laing and Cooper were in their heyday, and someone at the clinic suggested that I should get in touch with Laing. He was away, so his secretary passed me on to Cooper.

Dr Cooper agreed to see Alfred, told me that having offered to speak to an MP I must do so – it would be a bad mistake to cheat –

and asked me who would be paying him. Alfred's family, I extemporized, hoping devoutly that it would not end by being me; and when, next day, I managed to speak to Alfred's brother in New York, he agreed. He sounded agitated, but a good deal nicer than Alfred's rare references to him had suggested. Then I called an MP of my acquaintance who said: 'Are you out of *your* mind? If you knew the number of nuts we get, asking us to stop the voices . . .'

The thought of telling Alfred that afternoon that the MP would not play worried me enough for me to ask someone to stay within earshot of my room while he was with me. To my surprise he took the news calmly, and agreed to visit Dr Cooper in spite of my failure. I began to see what I had been doing, talking to him in Fez: of all his friends I was probably the one most likely to think of madness in terms of illness, and of illness in terms of seeing a doctor, and because we saw little of each other I had not yet turned into an enemy. Alfred *wanted* to be proved wrong about the voices, he *wanted* someone to force him into treatment. I had been chosen as the person most likely to do that.

Nevertheless he could bring himself to visit Dr Cooper only once, because: 'I don't like him, he looks like an Irish bookmaker.' Cooper then volunteered to find a psychiatric social worker to talk him through this crisis, telling me that if this one could be overcome, Alfred would be less likely to experience another – perhaps. A pleasant, eager young man came to me for a briefing, then started to make regular visits to Alfred who had found himself a room in a remote suburb – I think it was lent to him by friends, but I didn't know them. What Alfred thought of his conversations with the psychiatric social worker I never heard, but the young man told me that he felt privileged to be in communication with such a mind. I remember fearing that Alfred would draw the young man into his world before the young man could draw him back into ours.

Two, or perhaps three weeks went by, during which I called Alfred a couple of times – he sounded lifeless – but did not ask him to my place or visit him at his. I knew I ought to do so, but kept putting it off. This was my first experience of mental illness, and

I felt without bearings in strange and dangerous territory. Having taken such practical steps as I was able to think of, I found to my shame that the mere thought of Alfred exhausted me and that my affection was not strong enough to overcome the exhaustion. Not yet . . . next week, perhaps . . . until the telephone rang and it was the psychiatric social worker reporting that Alfred had left for Morocco – and I felt a wave of guilty relief. Asked whether he was better, the young man sounded dubious: 'He was able to make the decision, anyway.' And after that I never heard from Alfred again.

I suppose it was his New York agent who sent me a copy of *The Foot*, his last novel, which has never been published. There was wonderful stuff in it, particularly about his childhood and losing his hair – when the wig was first put on his head, he wrote, it was as though his skull had been split with an axe . . . But much of the book had gone over the edge into the time of the voices. After reading *The Foot* I saw why *The Exquisite Corpse* is so extraordinarily vivid: more than anyone had realized at the time, its strange events had been as real to Alfred 'as a bus going down the street'. He was already entering the dislocated reality of madness, but was still able to keep his hold on style: instead of leaving the reader, flustered, on the edge of that reality, he could carry us into it. When he came to write *The Foot* his style had started to slither out of his grasp. By that time the sickness which found such nourishment in the 'liberation and gentleness' of Morocco, with its abundance of delicious kif, had won.

Without knowing it, Alfred left me a delightful legacy: his oldest and truest friend, the poet Edward Field. Some years ago Edward's tireless campaign to revive Alfred's reputation in the United States caused him to get in touch with me, and almost instantly he and his friend, the novelist Neil Derrick, took their place among my most treasured friends. It is Edward who told me about Alfred's last, sad years.

Back in Morocco, his behaviour became so eccentric that he lost all his friends and alarmed the authorities. He was thrown out, and moved with his dogs – new ones, not Columbine and Skoura – to

Israel, where he survived by becoming almost a hermit, still tormented by the voices and trying frantically to drown them with drink and drugs. I was shown by Edward what was probably the last thing he ever wrote: a piece intended to be published in a periodical as 'A Letter from Israel'. It was heartbreaking. Gone was the sparkle, gone the vitality, humour and imagination. All it contained was baffled misery at his own loneliness and hopelessness. The madness, having won, had turned his writing – a bitter paradox – far more *ordinary* than it had ever been before. The world he was describing was no longer magical (magical in horror as well as in beauty), but was drab, cruel, boring – 'mad' only in that the mundane and tedious persecutions to which he constantly believed himself subject were, to other people, obviously of his own making. When he died – probably from heart failure brought on by drugs and alcohol – he was alone in a rented house which he hated. It is true that his death cannot be regretted, but feeling like that about the death of dear, amazing Alfred is horribly sad. However, other people are now joining Edward in keeping his writing alive in the United States: it is still a small movement, but it is a real one. May it thrive!

V. S. NAIPAUL

GOOD PUBLISHERS ARE supposed to 'discover' writers, and perhaps they do. To me, however, they just happened to come. V. S. Naipaul came through Andrew Salkey who was working with him at the BBC, and Andrew I met through Mordecai Richler when he took me for a drink in a Soho club. When Andrew heard that I was Mordecai's editor he asked me if he could send me a young friend of his who had just written something very good, and a few days later Vidia came to a coffee bar near our office and handed me *Miguel Street*.

I was delighted by it, but worried: it was stories (though linked stories), and a publishing dogma to which André Deutsch strongly adhered was that stories didn't sell unless they were by Names. So before talking to him about it I gave it to Francis Wyndham who was with us as part-time 'Literary Adviser', and Francis loved it at once and warmly. This probably tipped the balance with André, whose instinct was to distrust as 'do-gooding' my enthusiasm for a little book by a West Indian about a place which interested no one and where the people spoke an unfamiliar dialect. I think he welcomed its being stories because it gave him a reason for saying 'no': but Francis's opinion joined to mine made him bid me find out if the author had a novel on the stocks and tell him that if he had, then that should come first and the stories could follow all in good time. Luckily Vidia was in the process of writing *The Mystic Masseur*.

In fact we could well have launched him with *Miguel Street*, which has outlasted his first two novels in critical esteem, because in the fifties it was easier to get reviews for a writer seen by the British as black than it was for a young white writer, and reviews influenced readers a good deal more then than they do now. Publishers and reviewers were aware that new voices were speaking up in the newly independent colonies, and partly out of genuine interest, partly out of an optimistic if ill-advised sense that a vast market for books lay out there, ripe for development, they felt it to be the thing to encourage those voices. This trend did not last long, but it served to establish a number of good writers.

Vidia did not yet have the confidence to walk away from our shilly-shallying, and fortunately it did him no real harm. Neither he nor we made any money to speak of from his first three books, *The Mystic Masseur*, *The Suffrage of Elvira* and *Miguel Street*, but there was never any doubt about the making of his name, which began at once with the reviews and was given substance by his own work as a reviewer, of which he got plenty as soon as he became known as a novelist. He was a very good reviewer, clearly as widely read as any literary critic of the day, and it was this rather than his first books which revealed that here was a writer who was going to reject the adjective 'regional', and with good reason.

We began to meet fairly often, and I enjoyed his company because he talked well about writing and people, and was often funny. At quite an early meeting he said gravely that when he was up at Oxford – which he had not liked – he once did a thing so terrible that he would never be able to tell anyone what it was. I said it was unforgivable to reveal that much without revealing more, especially to someone like me who didn't consider even murder literally unspeakable, but I couldn't shift him and never learnt what the horror was – though someone told me later that when he was at Oxford Vidia did have some kind of nervous breakdown. It distressed me that he had been unhappy at a place which I loved. Having such a feeling for scholarship, high standards and tradition he ought to have liked it . . . but no, he would not budge. Never for a minute did it occur to me that he might have felt at a loss when he got to Oxford because of how different it was from his background, still less because of any form of racial insult: he appeared to me far too impressive a person to be subject to such discomforts.

The image Vidia was projecting at that time, in his need to protect his pride, was so convincing that even when I read *A House for Mr Biswas* four years later, and was struck by the authority of his account of Mr Biswas's nervous collapse, I failed to connect its painful vividness with his own reported 'nervous breakdown'. Between me and the truth of his Oxford experience stood the man he wanted people to see.

At that stage I did not know how or why he had rejected Trinidad, and if I had known it, would still have been unable to understand what it is like to be unable to accept the country in which you were born. Vidia's books (not least *A Way in the World*, not written until thirty-seven years later) were to do much to educate me; but then I had no conception of how someone who feels he doesn't belong to his 'home' and cannot belong anywhere else is forced to exist only in himself; nor of how exhausting and precarious such a condition (blithely seen by the young and ignorant as desirable) can be. Vidia's self – his very being – was his writing: a great gift, but all he had. He was to report that ten years later in his career, when he had earned what seemed to others an obvious security, he was still tormented by anxiety about finding the matter for his next book, and for the one after that . . . an anxiety not merely about earning his living, but about *existing as the person he wanted to be*. No wonder that while he was still finding his way into his writing he was in danger; and how extraordinary that he could nevertheless strike an outsider as a solidly impressive man*.

This does not mean that I failed to see the obvious delicacy of his nervous system. Because of it I was often worried by his lack of

---

* Since writing this I have read the letters which Vidia and his father exchanged while Vidia was at Oxford. *Letters Between a Father and Son* fully reveals the son's loneliness and misery, and makes the self he was able to present to the world even more extraordinary.

money, and was appalled on his behalf when I once saw him risk losing a commission by defying the *Times Literary Supplement*. They had offered their usual fee of £25 (or was it guineas?) for a review, and he had replied haughtily that he wrote nothing for less than fifty. 'Oh silly Vidia,' I thought, 'now they'll never offer him anything again.' But lo! they paid him his fifty and I was filled with admiration. Of course he was right: authors ought to know their own value and refuse the insult of derisory fees.

I was right to admire that self-respect, at that time, but it was going to develop into a quality difficult to like. In all moral qualities the line between the desirable and the deplorable is imprecise – between tolerance and lack of discrimination, prudence and cowardice, generosity and extravagance – so it is not easy to see where a man's proper sense of his own worth turns into a more or less pompous self-importance. In retrospect it seems to me that it took eight or nine years for this process to begin to show itself in Vidia, and I think it possible that his audience was at least partly to blame for it.

For example, after a year or so of meetings in the pubs or restaurants where I usually lunched, I began to notice that Vidia was sometimes miffed at being taken to a cheap restaurant or being offered a cheap bottle of wine – and the only consequence of my seeing this (apart from my secretly finding it funny) was that I became careful to let him choose both restaurant and wine. And this carefulness not to offend him, which was, I think, shared by all, or almost all, his English friends, came from an assumption that the reason why he was so anxious to command respect was fear that it was, or might be, denied him because of his race; which led to a squeamish dismay in oneself at the idea of being seen as racist. The shape of an attitude which someone detests, and has worked at extirpating, can often be discerned from its absence, and during the first years of Vidia's career in England he was often coddled for precisely the reason the coddler was determined to disregard.

Later, of course, the situation changed. His friends became too used to him to see him as anything but himself, and those who didn't know him saw him simply as a famous writer – on top of which he could frighten people. Then it was the weight and edge of his personality which made people defer to him, rather than consideration for his sensitivity. Which makes it easy to underestimate the pain and strain endured by that sensitivity when he had first pulled himself up out of the thin, sour soil in which he was reared, and was striving to find a purchase in England where, however warmly he was welcomed, he could never feel that he wholly belonged.

During the sixties I visited the newly independent islands of Trinidad & Tobago twice, with intense pleasure: the loveliness of tropical forests and seas, the jolt of excitement which comes from *difference*, the kindness of people, the amazing beauty of Carnival (unlike Vidia, I like steel bands: oh the sound of them coming in from the fringes of Port of Spain through the four-o'clock-in-the-morning darkness of the opening day!). On my last morning in Port of Spain I felt a sharp pang as I listened to the keskidee (a bird which really does seem to say *'Qu'est-ce qu'il dit?'*) and knew how unlikely it was that I should ever hear it again. But at no time was it difficult to remember that mine was a visitor's Trinidad & Tobago; so three other memories, one from high on the country's social scale, the others from lower although by no means from the bottom, are just as clear as the ones I love.

One. Vidia's history of the country, *The Loss of El Dorado*, which is rarely mentioned nowadays but which I think is the best of his non-fiction books, had just come out. Everyone I had met, including the Prime Minister Eric Williams and the poet Derek Walcott, had talked about it in a disparaging way and had betrayed as they did so that they had not read it. At last, at a party given by the leader of the opposition, I met someone who had: an elderly Englishman just retiring from running the Coast Guard. We were both delighted to be able to share our pleasure in it and had a long talk about it. As we parted I asked him: 'Can you really be the only person in this country who has read it?' and he answered sadly: 'Oh, easily.'

Two. In Tobago I stayed in a delightful little hotel where on most evenings the village elders dropped in for a drink. On one of them a younger man – a customs officer in his mid-thirties seconded to Tobago's chief town Scarborough, from Port of Spain – invited me to go out on the town with him. We were joined by another customs officer and a nurse from the hospital. First we went up to Scarborough's fort – its Historic Sight – to look at the view. Then, when conversation fizzled out, it was suggested that we should have a drink at the Arts Centre. It looked in the darkness little more than a shed, and it was shut, but a man was hunted up who produced the key, some Coca-Cola and half a bottle of rum . . . and there we stood, under a forty-watt lamp in a room of utter dinginess which contained nothing at all but a dusty ping-pong table with a very old copy of the *Reader's Digest* lying in the middle of it. We sipped our drinks in an atmosphere of embarrassment – almost shame – so heavy that it silenced us. After a few minutes we gave up and went to my host's barely furnished but tidy little flat – I remember it as cold, which it can't have been – where we listened to a record of 'Yellow Bird' and drank another rum. Then I was driven back to the hotel. The evening's emptiness – the really frightening feeling of nothing to do, nothing to say – had made me feel quite ill. I knew too little about the people I had been with to guess what they were like when at ease: all I could discern was that my host was bored to distraction at having to work in the sticks; that he had been driven by his boredom to make his sociable gesture and had then become nervous to the extent of summoning friends to his aid; and that all three had quickly seen that the whole thing was a mistake and had been overtaken by embarrassed gloom. And no wonder. When I remember the Arts Centre I see why, when Vidia first revisited the West Indies, what he felt was fear.

Three. And it is not only people like Vidia, feverish with repressed talent, who yearn to escape. There was the conversation I overheard in the changing-cubicle next to mine when I was trying on a swimsuit in a store in Port of Spain. An American woman, accompanied by her husband, was also buying something, and they were obviously quite taken by the pretty young woman who was serving them. They were asking her questions about her family, and the heightened warmth of their manner made me suspect that they found it almost exciting to be kind to a black person. When the customer had made her choice and her husband was writing a cheque, the saleswoman's voice suddenly changed from chirpiness to breathlessness and she said: 'May I ask you something?' The wife said: 'Yes, of course,' and the poor young woman plunged into desperate pleading: please, please would they help her, would they give her a letter inviting her to their home which she could show to the people who issued visas, she wouldn't be any trouble, and if they would do this for her . . . On and on she went, the husband trying to interrupt her in an acutely embarrassed voice, still wanting to sound kind but only too obviously appalled at what his entirely superficial amiability had unleashed. Soon the girl was in tears and the couple were sounding frantic with remorse and anxiety to escape – and I was so horrified at being the invisible and unwilling witness of this desperate young woman's humiliation that I abandoned my swimsuit, scrambled into my dress and fled, so I do not know how it ended.

Vidia had felt fear and dislike of Trinidad ever since he could remember. As a schoolboy he had written a vow on an endpaper of his Latin primer to be gone within five years (it took him six). He remembered this in *The Middle Passage*, his first non-fiction book, published in 1962, in which he described his first revisiting of the West Indies and did something he had never done before: examined the reasons why he feared and hated the place where he was born.

It was a desperately negative view of the place, disregarding a good half of the picture; and it came out with the fluency and force of something long matured less in the mind than in the depths of the nervous system. Trinidad, he said, was and knew itself to be a mere dot on the map. It had no importance and no existence as a nation, being only somewhere out of which first Spain, then France, then Britain could make money: grossly easy money because of using slaves to do the work, and after slaves indentured labour which was almost as cheap. A slave-based society has no need to be efficient, so no tradition of efficiency exists. Slave-masters don't need to be intelligent, so 'in Trinidad education was not one of the things money could buy; it was something money freed you from. Education was strictly for the poor. The white boy left school "counting on his fingers" as the Trinidadian likes to say, but this was a measure of his privilege . . . The white community was never an upper class in the sense that it possessed superior speech or taste or attainments; it was envied only for its money and its access to pleasure.'

When this crude colonial society was opened up because the islands were no longer profitable and the British pulled out, what Vidia saw gushing in to fill the vacuum was the flashiest and most materialistic kind of American influence in the form of commercial radio (television had yet to come) and films – films at their most violent and unreal. ('British films', he wrote, 'played to empty houses. It was my French master who urged me to go to see *Brief Encounter*; and there were two of us in the cinema, he in the balcony, I in the pit.') Trinidad & Tobago was united only in its hunger for 'American modernity', and under that sleazy veneer it was split.

It was split between the descendants of slaves, the African Trinidadians, and the descendants of indentured labourers, the Indians; both groups there by an accident of history, neither with any roots to speak of. In *The Middle Passage* Vidia called the Africans 'Negroes', which today sounds shocking. Reading the book one has to keep reminding oneself that the concept of Black Power had yet to be formulated. Black people had not yet rejected the word 'Negro': it was still widely used and 'black' was considered insulting. And in this book his main criticism of Trinidadians of African descent is that they had been brainwashed by the experience of slavery into 'thinking white' – into being ashamed of their own colour and physical features. What he deplored – as many observers of West Indian societies had done – was precisely the attitudes which people of African descent were themselves beginning to deplore, and would soon be forcing themselves to overcome.

The Indians he saw as less unsure of themselves because of the pride they took in the idea of India; but he also saw that idea as being almost meaningless – they had no notion of what the sub-continent was really like. It was also dangerous in that it militated against attempts to bridge the rift. The Indians were 'a peasant-minded, money-minded community, spiritually static, its religion reduced to rites without philosophy, set in a materialist, colonialist society; a combination of historical accident and national temperament has turned the Trinidadian Indian into the complete colonial, even more philistine than the white.'

He sums up his account of racial friction thus: 'Like monkeys pleading for evolution, each claiming to be whiter than the other, Indians and Negroes appeal to the unacknowledged white audience to see how much they despise one another. They despise one another by reference to the whites; and the irony is that their antagonism should have reached its peak today, when white prejudices have ceased to matter.'

This was a fair assessment: everyone, apart from Tourist Board propagandists, to whom I talked about politics deplored this racial tension, and most of them either said outright, or implied, that blame lay with the group to which they did not belong. No one remarked on the common sense which enabled people to rub along in spite of it (as they still do), any more than Vidia did. The rift, which certainly was absurd and regrettable, became more dramatic if seen as dangerous, and therefore reflected a more lurid light on whoever was being presented as its instigator. People did make a bid for the outsider's respect – did 'appeal to the unacknowledged white audience'. But to what audience was Vidia himself appealing? It was *The Middle Passage* which first made black West Indians call him 'racist'.

The book was admired in England and disliked in Trinidad, but it was not addressed to the white audience in order to please it. Its whole point was to show that Caribbean societies are a mess because they were callously created by white men for the white men's own ends, only to be callously administered and finally callously abandoned. Vidia was trying to write from a point of view above that of white or brown or black; he was trying to look at the people now inhabiting the West Indies with a clear-sighted and impartial intelligence, and to describe what he saw honestly, even if honesty seemed brutal. This he felt, and said, had to be done because a damaged society shuffling along with the help of fantasies and excuses can only become more sick: what it has to do is learn to know itself, and only its writers can teach it that. Caribbean writers had so far, he claimed, failed to do more than plead their own causes. If he expected Trinidadians to welcome this high-minded message he was naive – but I don't suppose he did. He was pursuing his own understanding of the place, and offering it, because that is what a serious writer can't help doing. If anyone resented it, too bad.

Of course they did resent it – who doesn't resent hearing disagreeable truths told in a manner verging on the arrogant? But I think the label 'racist' which they stuck on him was, so to speak, only a local one. I saw him as a man raised in, and frightened by, a somewhat disorderly, inefficient and self-deceiving society, who therefore longed for order, clarity and competence. Having concluded that the lack of these qualities in the place where he was born came from the people's lack of roots, he over-valued a sense of history and respect for tradition, choosing to romanticize their results rather than to see the complex and far from admirable scenes with which they often co-exist. (His first visit to India, described in *An Area of Darkness*, left him in a state of distress because it showed him that an ancient civilization in which he had dared to hope that he would find the belonging he hungered for could be just as disorderly and inefficient as the place where he was born.) Although both England and the United States were each in its own way going to fall short of his ideal society, Europe as a whole came more close, more often, to offering a life in which he could feel comfortable. I remember driving, years ago, through a vine-growing region of France and coming on a delightful example of an ancient expertise taking pleasure in itself: a particularly well cultivated vineyard which had a pillar rose – a deep pink pillar rose – planted as an exquisite punctuation at the end of every row. Instantly – although it was weeks since I had seen or thought of him – he popped into my head: 'How Vidia would like that!'

But although I cannot see Vidia as racist in the sense of wanting to be white or to propitiate whites, I do think it is impossible to spend the first eighteen years of your life in a given set of circumstances without being shaped by them: and Vidia spent the first eighteen years of his life as a Trinidadian Indian*. Passionate though his determination to escape the limitations imposed by this fate was, and near though it came to achieving the impossible, it could not wholly free him from his conditioning.

In Chapter One of *The Middle Passage*, when he has only just boarded the boat-train which will take him to Southampton, there begins the following description. Into the corridor, out of the compartment next to Vidia's, had stepped 'a very tall and ill-made Negro. The disproportionate length of his thighs was revealed by his baggy trousers. His shoulders were broad and so unnaturally square that they seemed hunched and gave him an appearance of fragility. His light grey jacket was as long and loose as a short top-coat; his yellow shirt was dirty and the frayed collar undone; his tie was slack and askew. He went to the window, opened the ventilation gap, pushed his face through, turned slightly to his left, and spat. His face was grotesque. It seemed to have been smashed in from one cheek. One eye had narrowed; the thick lips had bunched into a circular swollen protuberance; the enormous nose was twisted. When, slowly, he opened his mouth to spit, his face became even more distorted. He spat in slow, intermittent dribbles.'

Vidia makes a slight attempt to give this man a role in the story of his journey by saying that he began to imagine that the poor creature was aware of him in a malign way, that at one moment their eyes met, that in the buffet car there he was again . . . but in fact once he has been described the man has no part to play, he is

---

* Only one of his father's letters refers to anyone of African descent – and that one letter is frantically agitated: a niece has started to date a man half-Indian, half-African; how should he deal with this frightful event?

done with; in spite of which Vidia could not resist placing him right at the start of the book and *describing him in greater physical detail than anyone else in all its 232 pages*. I am not saying that this man was invented or that he may have been less dreadfully unattractive than we are told he was; but by choosing to pick him out and to *fix* on him, Vidia has given an indelible impression less of the man than of his own reaction: the dismayed recoil of a fastidious Trinidadian Indian from what he sees as an inferior kind of person. And I believe that if I were black I should from time to time, throughout his work, pick up other traces of this flinching presence hidden in the shadow behind one of the best English-language novelists we have. And even as part of the white audience I cannot help noticing the occasional touch of self-importance (increasing with the years) which I suspect to have its roots far back in the Trinidadian Indian's nervous defiance of disrespect.

Vidia's mother, handsome and benignly matronly, welcomed his publishers very kindly when they visited Trinidad, and gave the impression of being the beloved linchpin of her family. When I first met them, long before they had been stricken by the close-together deaths of one of the daughters and of Shiva, Vidia's younger and only brother, they impressed me as a flourishing lot: good-looking, intelligent, charming, successful. A married daughter told me that Mrs Naipaul 'divides her time between the Temple and the quarry' – the latter being a business belonging to her side of the family, in which she was a partner. That she was not simply a comfortable mother-figure became apparent when she told me that she had just got home from attending a seminar on welding and was very glad that she hadn't missed it because she had learnt enough at it to be able to cut the number of welders they employed at the quarry by half. Soon afterwards she threw more light on her own character by making a little speech to me, after noticing my surprise when she had appeared to be indifferent to some news about Vidia. She had been, she said, a well-brought-up Hindu girl of her generation, so she had been given no education and was expected to obey her parents in everything, and that was what she did. Then she was married ('And there was no nonsense about falling in love in those days'), whereupon it was her husband she had to obey in everything, and that was what she did. Then she had her children, so of course it was her job to devote herself entirely to them and bring them up as well as possible, and that was what she did ('and I think I can say I made a good job of it'). 'But then I said to myself, when I am fifty – FINISH. I will begin to live for myself. And that is what I am doing now and they must get on with their own lives.'

It was an impressive little thumbnail autobiography, but it left questions in my mind. I had, after all, read *A House for Mr Biswas*, the novel Vidia had based on his father's life, and had gained a vivid picture of how humiliated Mr Biswas had been after his marriage into the much richer and more influential Tulsi family – although I don't think I knew at that stage that Seepersad Naipaul, Vidia's father, had once had a mental breakdown and had vanished from his home for months. Clearly this attractive and – I was now beginning to think – slightly formidable woman was greatly over-simplifying her story, but I liked her; as I told Vidia when, soon after this, he asked me if I did. 'Yes, very much,' I said; to which he replied: 'Everyone seems to. I hate her.'

I wish I had asked him what he meant by that. It was not the first time that I heard him, in a fit of irritation, strike out at someone with a fierce word, so I didn't think it was necessarily true (and anyway, dislike of a mother usually indicates damaged love). But uncertain though I remained about his feelings towards his mother, I knew that he loved his father, who had died soon after Vidia left Trinidad to come to Oxford. He wrote a moving introduction to the little volume of his father's stories which he gave us to publish in 1976, and he spoke about the way his father had introduced him to books. Seepersad Naipaul had possessed a remarkably strong and true instinct for writing which had overcome his circumstances to the point of giving him a passion for such English classics as had come his way, and steering him into a writing job on the local newspaper. He had passed his passion on by reading aloud to Vidia and Kamla, the sister nearest to him, making the children stand up as he read to keep them from falling asleep – which seems to have impressed the importance of the ritual on them rather than to have put them off. Seepersad's own few stories were about Trinidadian village life, and the most important lesson he gave his son was 'Write about what you know', thus curing him of the young colonial's feeling that 'literature' had to be exotic – something belonging to the faraway world out of which came the books he found in the library. And I know of another piece of advice Seepersad gave his son which speaks for the truth of his instinct. Vidia had shown him a piece of would-be comic writing, and he told him not to strive for comedy but to let it arise naturally out of the story. It is sad to think of this man hobbled by the circumstances of his life (see *A House for Mr Biswas*) and dying before he could see his son break free. The mother was part of the 'circumstances' and the child sided with his father against her, of that I feel sure.

I cannot remember how long it was – certainly several months, perhaps even a year – before I learnt that Vidia was married. 'I have found a new flat', he would say; 'I saw such-and-such a film last week'; 'My landlady says': not once had he used the words 'we' or 'our'. I had taken it for granted that he lived in industrious loneliness, which had seemed sad. So when at a party I glimpsed him at the far end of a room with a young woman – an inconspicuously, even mousily pretty young woman – and soon afterwards saw him leaving with her, I was pleased that he had found a girlfriend. The next time he came to the office I asked who she was – and was astounded when he answered, in a rather cross voice, 'My wife, of course.'

After that Pat was allowed to creep out of the shadows, but only a little: and one day she said something that shocked me so much that I know for certain that I am remembering it word-for-word. I must have remarked on our not meeting earlier, and she replied: 'Vidia doesn't like me to come to parties because I'm such a bore.'

From that moment on, whenever I needed to cheer myself up by counting my blessings, I used to tell myself 'At least I'm not married to Vidia'.

It did not exactly turn me against him, I suppose because from the beginning I had thought of him as an interesting person to watch rather than as a friend. The flow of interest between us had always been one-way – I can't remember ever telling him anything about my own affairs, or wanting to – so this odd business of his marriage was something extra to watch rather than something repellent. Had he ever loved her – or did he still love her in some twisted way? They had married while he was at Oxford: had he done it out of loneliness, to enlarge the minuscule territory he could call his own now that he was out in the world? Or was it because she could keep him? She was working as a teacher and continued to do so well into their marriage. Or was it to shelter him from other women? He had once asked a man of my acquaintance: 'Do you know any *fast* women?', which my friend found funny (particularly as he was gay) but which seemed touching to me. As did Vidia's only attempt to make a pass at me. Pat was away and I had asked him to supper. Without warning he got to his feet, came across the room and tried to kiss me as I was coming through the door carrying a tray loaded with glasses. It hardly seemed necessary to put into words the rebuff which most of him was clearly anxious for, but to be on the safe side I did. Our friendship, I said gently, was too valuable to complicate in any way – and his face brightened with relief. That someone so lacking in sexual experience and so puritanical should have to resort to prostitutes (as he told the *New Yorker* in 1994, and as a passage in *The Mimic Men* suggests) is natural; though I guess he did so infrequently, and with distaste.

The little I saw of Vidia and Pat together was depressing: there was no sign of their enjoying each other, and the one whole weekend I spent with them they bickered ceaselessly, Pat's tetchiness as sharp as his (developed as a defence, I thought). When he was abroad she was scrupulously careful of his interests; she did research for him; sometimes he referred to showing her work in progress: he trusted her completely, and with reason, because he was evidently her *raison d'être*. And she made it unthinkable to speak critically of him in her presence. But always her talk was full of how tiresome it was for him that she was sick in aeroplanes, or fainted in crowds, or couldn't eat curries . . . and when I tried to introduce a subject other than him that would interest us both, such as West Indian politics or her work as a teacher, she never failed to run us aground yet again on some reference to her own inadequacy. At first I took it for granted that he had shattered her self-confidence, and I am still sure he did it no good. But later I suspected that there had always been something in her which accepted – perhaps even welcomed – being squashed.

In *A Way in the World*, writing (as usual) as though he were a single man, Vidia described himself as 'incomplete' in 'physical attractiveness, love, sexual fulfilment'. How terrible for a wife to be publicly wiped out in this way! Everyone who knew the Naipauls said how sorry they were for Pat, and I was sorry for her, too. But whatever Vidia's reason for marrying, he cannot have foreseen what their marriage, for whatever reason, was going to be like. He, too, probably deserved commiseration.

When his Argentinian friend Margaret first came to London he brought her to lunch with me. She was a lively, elegant woman who, though English by descent, was 'feminine' in the Latin-American style, sexy and teasing, with the appearance of having got him just where she wanted him. And he glowed with pride and pleasure. Afterwards he said he was thinking of leaving Pat, and when I was dismayed (could she exist without him?) said that the thought of giving up 'carnal pleasure' just when he'd discovered it was too painful to bear. Why not stay married and have an affair, I asked; which he appeared to think an unseemly suggestion, although it was what he then did for many years. What happened later I don't know, but in the early years of their relationship there was no sign of his squashing Margaret. He did, however, make one disconcerting remark. Did I not find it interesting, he asked, that there was so much cruelty in sex?

What began to wear me down in my dealings with Vidia (it was a long time before I allowed myself to acknowledge it) was his depression.

With every one of his books – and we published eighteen of them – there was a three-part pattern. First came a long period of peace while he was writing, during which we saw little of him and I would often have liked to see more, because I would be full of curiosity about the new book. Then, when it was delivered, there would be a short burst of euphoria during which we would have enjoyable meetings and my role would be to appreciate the work, to write the blurb, to hit on a jacket that pleased both him and us, and to see that the script was free of typist's errors (he was such a perfectionist that no editing, properly speaking, was necessary). Then came part three: post-publication gloom, during which his voice on the telephone would make my heart sink – just a little during the first few years, deeper and deeper with the passing of time. His voice became charged with tragedy, his face became haggard, his theme became the atrocious exhaustion and damage (the word *damage* always occurred) this book had inflicted on him, and all to what end? Reviewers were ignorant monkeys, publishers (this would be implied in a sinister fashion rather than said) were lazy and useless: what was the point of it all? Why did he go on?

It is natural that a writer who knows himself to be good and who is regularly confirmed in that opinion by critical comment should expect to become a best seller, but every publisher knows that you don't necessarily become a best seller by writing well. Of course you don't necessarily have to write badly to do it: it is true that some best-selling books are written astonishingly badly, and equally true that some are written very well. The quality of the writing – even the quality of the thinking – is irrelevant. It is a matter of whether or not a nerve is hit in the wider reading public as opposed to the serious one which is composed of people who are interested in writing as an art. Vidia has sold well in the latter, and has pushed a good way beyond its fringes by becoming famous – at a certain point many people in the wider reading public start to feel that they *ought* to read a writer – but it was always obvious that he was not going to make *big* money. An old friend of mine who reads a great deal once said to me apologetically: 'I'm sure he's very good, but I don't feel he's for me' – and she spoke for a large number of reading people.

Partly this is because of his subject matter, which is broadly speaking the consequences of imperialism: people whose countries once ruled empires relish that subject only if it is flavoured, however subtly, with nostalgia. Partly it is because he is not interested in writing about women, and when he does so usually does it with dislike: more women than men read novels. And partly it is because of his temperament. Once, when he was particularly low, we talked about surviving the horribleness of life and I said that I did it by relying on simple pleasures such as the taste of fruit, the delicious sensations of a hot bath or clean sheets, the way flowers tremble very slightly with life, the lilt of a bird's flight: if I were stripped of those pleasures . . . better not to imagine it! He asked if I could really depend on them and I said yes. I have a clear memory of the sad, puzzled voice in which he replied: 'You're very lucky, I can't.' And his books, especially his novels (after the humour which filled the first three drained away) are coloured – or perhaps I should say 'discoloured' – by this lack of what used to be called animal spirits. They impress, but they do not charm.

He was, therefore, displeased with the results of publication, which filled him always with despair, sometimes with anger as well. Once he descended on me like a thunderbolt to announce that he had just been into Foyles of Charing Cross Road and they didn't have a single copy of his latest book, published only two weeks earlier, in stock: not one! Reason told me this was impossible, but I have a lurking tendency to accept guilt if faced with accusation, and this tendency went into spasm: suppose the sales department really had made some unthinkable blunder? Well, if they had I was not going to face the ensuing mayhem single-handed, so I said: 'We must go and tell André at once.' Which we did; and André Deutsch said calmly: 'What nonsense, Vidia – come on, we'll go to Foyles straight away and I'll show you.' So all three of us stumped down the street to Foyles, only two minutes away, Vidia still thunderous, I twittering with nerves, André serene. Once we were in the shop he cornered the manager and explained: 'Mr Naipaul couldn't find his book: will you please show him where it is displayed.' – 'Certainly, Mr Deutsch': and there it was, two piles of six copies each, on the table for 'Recent Publications'. André said afterwards that Vidia looked even more thunderous at being done out of his grievance, but if he did I was too dizzy with relief to notice.

Vidia's anxiety and despair were real: you need only compare a photograph of his face in his twenties with one taken in his forties to see how it has been shaped by pain. It was my job to listen to his unhappiness and do what I could to ease it – which would not have been too bad if there had been anything I *could* do. But there was not: and exposure to someone else's depression is draining, even if only for an hour or so at a time and not very often. I felt genuinely sorry for him, but the routine was repeated so often . . . The truth is that as the years went by, during these post-publication glooms I had increasingly to force myself into feeling genuinely sorry for him, in order to endure him.

Self-brainwashing sometimes has to be a part of an editor's job. You are no use to the writers on your list if you cannot bring imaginative sympathy to working with them, and if you cease to be of use to them you cease to be of use to your firm. Imaginative sympathy cannot issue from a cold heart so you have to like your writers. Usually this is easy; but occasionally it happens that in spite of admiring someone's work you are – or gradually become – unable to like the person.

I thought so highly of Vidia's writing and felt his presence on our list to be so important that I simply could not allow myself not to like him. I was helped by a foundation of affection laid down during the early days of knowing him, and I was able to believe that his depressions hurt him far more than they hurt me – that he could not prevent them – that I ought to be better at bearing them than I was. And as I became more aware of other things that grated – his attitude to Pat and to his brother Shiva (whom he bullied like an enraged mother hen in charge of a particularly feckless chick) – I called upon a tactic often employed in families: Aunt Emily may have infuriating mannerisms or disconcerting habits, but they are forgiven, even enjoyed, because they are *so typically her*. The offending person is put into the position of a fictional, almost a cartoon, character, whose quirks can be laughed or marvelled at as though they existed only on a page. For quite a long time seeing him as a perpetrator of 'Vidia-isms' worked rather well.

In 1975 we received the thirteenth of his books – his eighth work of fiction – *Guerrillas*. For the first time I was slightly apprehensive because he had spoken to me about the experience of writing it in an unprecedented way: usually he kept the process private, but this time he said that it was extraordinary, something that had never happened before: it was as though the book had been *given* to him. Such a feeling about writing does not necessarily bode well. And as it turned out, I could not like the book.

It was about a Trinidad-like island sliding into a state of decadence, and there was a tinge of hysteria in the picture's dreadfulness, powerfully imagined though it was. A central part of the story came from something that had recently happened in Trinidad: the murder of an Englishwoman called Gail Benson who had changed her name to Halé Kimga, by a Trinidadian who called himself Michael X and who had set up a so-called 'commune'. Gail had been brought to Trinidad by her lover, a black American known as Hakim Jamal (she had changed her name at his bidding). Both of the men hovered between being mad and being con-men, and their linking-up had been Gail's undoing. I knew all three, Gail and Hakim well, Michael very slightly: indeed, I had written a book about them (which I had put away – it would be published sixteen years later) called *Make Believe*.

This disturbed my focus on large parts of *Guerrillas*. The people in the book were not meant to be portraits of those I had known (Vidia had met none of them). They were characters created by Vidia to express his view of post-colonial history in places like Trinidad. But the situation in the novel was so close to the situation in life that I often found it hard to repress the reaction 'But that's not true!' This did not apply to the novel's Michael X character, who was called Jimmy Ahmed: Jimmy and the half-squalid half-pathetic ruins of his 'commune' are a brilliant and wholly convincing creation. Nor did it apply to Roche, Vidia's substitute for Hakim Jamal. Roche is a liberal white South African refugee working for a big commercial firm, whose job has involved giving cynical support to Jimmy. Roche was so evidently not Hakim that the question did not arise. But it certainly did apply to Jane, who stood in for Gail in being the murdered woman.

The novel's Jane, who comes to the island as Roche's mistress, is supposed to be an idle, arid creature who tries to find the vitality she lacks by having affairs with men. Obtuse in her innate sense of her superiority as a white woman, she drifts into such an attempt with Jimmy: an irresponsible fool playing a dangerous game for kicks with a ruined black man. Earlier, Vidia had written an account for a newspaper of Gail's murder which made it clear that he saw Gail as that kind of woman.

She was not. She was idle and empty, but she had no sense of her own superiority as a white woman or as anything else. Far from playing dangerous games for kicks, she was clinging on to illusions for dear life. The people she had most in common with were not the kind of secure Englishwomen who had it off with black men to demonstrate their own liberal attitudes, but those poor wretches who followed the American 'guru' Jones to Guyana in 1977, and ended by committing mass suicide at his bidding. She was so lacking in a sense of her own worth that it bordered on insanity.

It was therefore about Jane that I kept saying to myself 'But that's not true!' Then I pulled myself together and saw that there was no reason why Jane should be like Gail: an Englishwoman going into such an affair for kicks was far from impossible and would be a perfectly fair example of fraudulence of motive in white liberals, which was what Vidia was bent on showing.

So I read the book again – and this time Jane simply fell to pieces. Roche came out of it badly, too: a dim character, hard to envisage, in spite of revealing wide-apart molars with black roots whenever he smiled (a touch of 'clever characterization' which should have been beneath Vidia). But although he doesn't quite convince, he almost does; you keep expecting him to emerge from the mist. While Jane becomes more and more like a series of bits and pieces that don't add up, so that finally her murder is without significance. I came to the conclusion that the trouble must lie with

Vidia's having cut his cloth to fit a pattern he had laid down in advance: these characters existed in order to exemplify his argument, he had not been *discovering* them. So they did not live; and the woman lived less than the man because that is true of all Vidia's women.

We have now reached the second of my two shocking failures as an editor (I don't intend ever to confess the other one). From the professional point of view there was no question as to what I ought to do: this was one of our most valuable authors; even if his book had been really bad rather than just flawed we would certainly have published it in the expectation that he would soon be back on form; so what I must say was 'wonderful' and damn well sound as though I meant it.

Instead I sat there muttering: 'Oh my God, what am I going to say to him?' I had never lied to him – I kept reminding myself of that, disregarding the fact that I had never before needed to lie. 'If I lie now, how will he be able to trust me in the future when I praise something?' The obvious answer to that was that if I lied convincingly he would never know that I had done it, but this did not occur to me. After what seemed to me like hours of sincere angst I ended by persuading myself that I 'owed it to our friendship' to tell him what I truly thought.

Nothing practical would be gained. A beginner writer sometimes makes mistakes which he can remedy if they are pointed out, but a novelist of Vidia's quality and experience who produces an unconvincing character has suffered a lapse of imagination about which nothing can be done. It happened to Dickens whenever he attempted a good woman; it happened to George Eliot with Daniel Deronda. And as for my own attitude – I had often seen through other people who insisted on telling the truth about a friend's shortcomings: I knew that *their* motives were usually suspect. But my own were as invisible to me as a cuttlefish becomes when it saturates the surrounding water with ink.

So I told him. I began by saying how much I admired the many things in the book which I did admire, and then I said that I had to tell him (*had to* tell him!) that two of his three central characters had failed to convince me. It was like saying to Conrad '*Lord Jim* is a very fine novel except that Jim doesn't quite come off'.

Vidia looked disconcerted, then stood up and said quietly that he was sorry they didn't work for me, because he had done the best he could with them, there was nothing more he could do, so there was no point in discussing it. As he left the room I think I muttered something about its being a splendid book all the same, after which I felt a mixture of relief at his appearing to be sorry rather than angry, and a slight (only slight!) sense of let-down and silliness. And I supposed that was that.

The next day Vidia's agent called André to say that he had been instructed to retrieve *Guerrillas* because we had lost confidence in Vidia's writing and therefore he was leaving us.

André must have fought back because there was nothing he hated more than losing an author, but the battle didn't last long. Although I believe I was named, André was kind enough not to blame me. Nor did I blame myself. I went into a rage. I fulminated to myself, my colleagues, my friends: 'All those years of friendship, and a mere dozen words of criticism – *a mere dozen words!* – send him flouncing out in a tantrum like some hysterical prima donna!' I had long and scathing conversations with him in my head; but more satisfying was a daydream of being at a huge and important party, seeing him enter the room, turning on my heel and walking out.

For at least two weeks I seethed . . . and then, in the third week, it suddenly occurred to me that never again would I have to listen to Vidia telling me how damaged he was, and it was as though the sun came out. *I didn't have to like Vidia any more!* I could still like his work, I could still be sorry for his pain; but I no longer faced the task of fashioning affection out of these elements in order to deal as a good editor should with the exhausting, and finally tedious, task of listening to his woe. 'Do you know what,' I said to André, 'I've begun to see that it's a release.' (Rather to my surprise, he laughed.) I still, however, failed to see that my editorial 'mistake' had been an act of aggression. In fact I went on failing to see that for years.

Guerrillas was sold to Secker & Warburg the day after it left us.

A month or so after this I went into André's office to discuss something and his phone rang before I had opened my mouth. This always happened. Usually I threw myself back in my chair with a groan, then reached for something to read, but this time I jumped up and grabbed the extension. 'Why – Vidia!' he had said. 'What can I do for you?'

Vidia was speaking from Trinidad, his voice tense: André must call his agent *at once* and tell him to recover the manuscript of *Guerrillas* from Secker & Warburg and deliver it to us.

André, who was uncommonly good at rising to unexpected occasions, became instantly fatherly. Naturally, he said, he would be delighted to get the book back, but Vidia must not act too impetuously: whatever had gone wrong might well turn out to be less serious that he now felt. This was Thursday. What Vidia must do was think it over very carefully without taking action until Monday. Then, if he still wanted to come back to us, he must call his agent, not André, listen to his advice, and if that failed to change his mind, instruct him to act. André would be waiting for the agent's call on Monday afternoon or Tuesday morning, hoping – of course – that it would be good news for us.

Which – of course – it was. My private sun did go back behind a film of cloud, but in spite of that there was satisfaction in knowing that he thought himself better off with us than with them, and I had no doubt of the value of whatever books were still to come.

Vidia never said why he bolted from Secker's, but his agent told André that it was because when they announced *Guerrillas* in their catalogue they described him as 'the West Indian novelist'.

The books still to come were, indeed, worth having (though the last of them was his least important): *India, a Wounded Civilization*, *The Return of Eva Perón*, *Among the Believers*, *A Bend in the River* and *Finding the Centre*. I had decided that the only thing to do was to behave exactly as I had always done in our pre-*Guerrillas* working relationship, while quietly cutting down our extracurricular friendship, and he apparently felt the same. The result was a smooth passage, less involving but less testing than it used to be. Nobody else knew – and I myself was unaware of it until I came to look back – that having resolved never again to utter a word of criticism to Vidia, I was guilty of an absurd pettiness. In *Among the Believers*, a book which I admired very much, there were two minor points to which in the past I would have drawn his attention, and I refrained from doing so: thus betraying, though luckily only to my retrospecting self, that I was still hanging on to my self-righteous interpretation of the *Guerrillas* incident. Vidia would certainly not have 'flounced out like some hysterical prima donna' over matters so trivial. One was a place where he seemed to draw too sweeping a conclusion from too slight an event and could probably have avoided giving that impression by some quite small adjustment; and the other was that when an Iranian speaking English said 'sheep' Vidia, misled by his accent, thought he said 'ship', which made some dialogue as he reported it sound puzzling. To keep mum about that! There is nothing like self-deception for making one ridiculous.

When Vidia really did leave us in 1984 I could see why – and even why he did so in a way which seemed unkind, without a word of warning or explanation. He had come to the conclusion that André Deutsch Limited was going downhill. It was true. The recession, combined with a gradual but relentless shrinkage in the readership of books such as those we published, was well on the way to making firms of our size and kind unviable; and André had lost his vigour and flair. His decision to sell the firm, which more or less coincided with Vidia's departure, was made (so he felt and told me) because publishing was 'no fun any more', but it was equally a matter of his own slowly failing health. The firm continued for ten years or so under Tom Rosenthal, chuntering not-so-slowly downwards all the time (Tom had been running Secker's when they called Vidia a West Indian, so his appearance on the scene did nothing to change Vidia's mind).

A writer of reputation can always win an even bigger advance than he is worth by allowing himself to be tempted away from publisher A by publisher B, and publisher B will then have to try extra hard on his behalf to justify the advance: it makes sense to move on if you time it right. And if you perceive that there is something going seriously wrong with publisher A you would be foolish not to do so. And having decided to go, how could you look in the eye someone you have known for over twenty years, of whom you have been really quite fond, and tell him 'I'm leaving because you are getting past it'? Of course you could not. Vidia's agent managed to conceal from André what Vidia felt, but André suspected something: he told me that he thought it was something to do with himself and that he couldn't get it out of the agent, but perhaps I might have better luck. I called the agent and asked him if there was any point in my getting in touch with Vidia, and he – in considerable embarrassment – told me the truth; whereupon I could only silently agree with Vidia's silence, and tell poor André that I'd been so convincingly assured of the uselessness of any further attempt to change Vidia's mind that we had better give up.

So this leaving did not make me angry, or surprised, or even sad, except for André's sake. Vidia was doing what he had to do, and it seemed reasonable to suppose that we had enjoyed the best of him, anyway. And when many years later Mordecai Richler (in at the story's end, oddly enough, as well as its beginning) told me that he had recently met Vidia with his new wife and had been pleased to see that he was 'amazingly jolly', I was very glad indeed.

MOLLY KEANE

I KNOW THAT I have sometimes been described as 'one of the best editors in London', and I can't deny that it has given me pleasure; but I also know how little I had to do to earn this reputation beyond routine work and being agreeable to interesting people. And another example of this is my dealings with the person I liked best among those I came to know on the job: the Irish novelist Molly Keane.

It is common knowledge that after establishing herself in her youth as a novelist and playwright, Molly went silent for over thirty years and was 'rediscovered' in 1981 when André Deutsch Limited published *Good Behaviour*. Because I was her editor I was often congratulated on this 'rediscovery' – which is nonsense. We got the book by pure luck.

The person who persuaded Molly to offer it for publication was Peggy Ashcroft, who had remained a close friend of hers since acting in one of her plays, and who said one day, when staying with her, how sad it was that she had stopped writing. Molly told her that she had recently started again and had a novel which she was unsure about tucked away in a drawer. Peggy insisted on taking it to bed with her that night, and as a result of her enthusiasm Molly sent it to Ian Parsons of Chatto & Windus. That was where our good luck began: Ian didn't like it. Worse mistakes have been made – publishers often used to console themselves by remembering that André Gide, reading Proust's *Remembrance of*

Things Past, turned it down . . . although if you envisage that enormous manuscript, and discovering that many of its sentences are as long as most people's paragraphs, that mistake was perhaps less *odd* than failing to respond to a novel as accessible as *Good Behaviour*.

Our next stroke of luck was that Molly then chose Gina Pollinger as her agent. Gina had been an editor before she married into agenting, and her last job as such had been with us. When she called me to say that she had just read something she loved, and felt sure I would love it too, I was hearing from someone whose taste I knew and respected, rather than listening to a sales spiel, so naturally I read the book at once – and it happened that I, unlike Ian Parsons, had not fallen on my head. So much for being Molly's rediscoverer.

Molly did usually need a little editing because she could get into muddles about timing – make, for instance, an event happen after an interval of two years when something in the text revealed that at least three years must have passed – and she had little tricks of phrasing, such as describing a person's interests as her 'importances', which she sometimes overdid. (Such tricks are part of a writer's 'voice', so it is usually best to leave some of them in – but not enough of them to be annoying.) She was always glad to have such things pointed out, and she was equally co-operative over the only big question that needed solving in the course of her last three novels.

This occurred in *Good Behaviour*, at a point where a small English boy is discovered hiding up a tree in order to read poetry, which causes his extremely upper-class parents to go into paroxysms of dismay. At that point Molly's sense of comedy had taken the bit between its teeth and bolted, carrying the story off into the realm of the grotesque. It was wildly funny, but funny in a way at odds with the rest of the book so that it fractured its surface. I asked her to cool it, which she did. She was always 'splendidly co-operative to work with', as John Gielgud was to say in a letter to the *Daily Telegraph* after her death, remembering the days when he directed the four plays which she wrote in the thirties.

He also paid a warm tribute to her charm and wit, adding that 'she was endlessly painstaking and industrious' – slightly surprising words applied to someone as sparkly as Molly, but they do catch the absence of pretentiousness in her attitude to her work. Her background was that of the Irish landed gentry, whose daughters were lucky, in her day, if they got more than a scrappy education. Not that most of them, including Molly, were likely to clamour for more, since horses and men interested them far more than anything else; but Molly had come to feel the lack and it made her humble: she needed to be convinced that she was a good writer.

She was well aware, however, that *Good Behaviour* was different from the eleven early novels which she had written under the pen-name M. J. Farrell – a pen-name because who would want to dance with a girl so brainy that she wrote books? (You probably need to have had a 'county' upbringing fully to feel the withering effect of that adjective: 'You're the brainy one, aren't you?' It still makes me flinch.) Molly always said that she wrote the early books simply for money, because her parents couldn't afford to give her a dress allowance – though the verve of the writing suggests that she must have enjoyed doing it. *Good Behaviour*, on the other hand, had insisted on being written. She described it as a book that 'truly interested and involved' her: 'Black comedy, perhaps, but with some of the truth in it, and the pity I feel for the kind of people I lived with and laughed with in the happy maligned thirties.' She said that she dropped the pen-name because so much time had gone by; but in fact she took a lot of urging, and left me with the impression that she finally agreed because she had allowed herself to be persuaded that this one was the real thing.

The reason why *Good Behaviour* is so gripping is that Molly brings off something much cleverer than she had ever attempted before: she manoeuvres her readers into collaboration. Her narrator, Aroon St Charles, the large, clumsy daughter of a remote and elegant little mother who finds her painfully boring, tells us everything she sees – and often fails to understand what she is telling. It is up to us, the readers, to do the understanding – most crucially concerning Aroon's beloved brother Hubert and the friend he brings home from Cambridge, Richard Massingham (once the little boy who read poetry up a tree). Aroon has never heard of homosexuality, because the rules of Good Behaviour are the rules of behaving 'as if'. You may be afraid but you must behave as if you were brave; you may be poor but you must behave as if you can afford things; your husband may be randy but you must behave as if he wasn't; embarrassing things such as men falling in love with men may happen, but you must behave as if they don't. How could Aroon, who doesn't read and has few friends, know anything about being gay? But in spite of all the 'as iffing', her father starts to feel uneasy about the two young men, they become alarmed – and Hubert has a brilliant idea: Richard must start behaving as though he were courting Aroon. He must even go into her bedroom one night, and make sure that her father hears him leaving it . . . We hear nothing of all this but what Aroon tells us: that Richard does this, and Richard does that, so surely he must like her – must even be finding her attractive – must *love* her! After he has been to her room we see her half-sensing that something is wrong (his Respecting her Virginity is acceptable, but there is something about his manner . . .). And we see her, very soon, working herself into a blissful daze of happiness at having a lover. And all the time, as though we were observant guests in the house, *we can see what is really going on.* It is powerfully involving, and it continues throughout the book: at one point thirty pages go by before we are allowed a flash of understanding (the family lawyer has made a tentative pass at Aroon, which seems a bit odd – until the times comes, as it would do in 'real life', when one exclaims 'But of course! He knew what was in her father's will!').

Molly called this book 'black comedy', and comic it often is – brilliantly so. She is studying tribal behaviour, and no one could hit off its absurdities to better effect. But its strength comes from her fierce, sad knowledge of what underlies Good Behaviour, and is crippled by it; and she once told me something about herself which struck me as the seed from which this novel's power grew.

Molly's husband Robert Keane died in his thirties, with appalling suddenness, when they were visiting London with their two little daughters, having a very good time. He became violently ill so that he had to be rushed to hospital, but once he was there everything seemed to be under control, so she went back to the children for the night, worried but not really frightened. During the night the telephone rang. It was the hospital matron, who said: 'Mrs Keane, you must be brave. Your husband is dead.' Molly had friends in London, but they were busy theatre friends, and she was seized at once by the thought 'I must not be a nuisance. I must not make scenes' – the quintessential Good Behaviour reaction. And some time during those terrible first days her eldest daughter, Sally, who was six, clutched her hand and said: 'Mummy, we mustn't cry, we mustn't cry.'

And Molly never did cry. Forty years later, telling me that, her voice took on a tone of forlorn incredulity. There was, indeed, nothing she didn't know about her tribe's concept of good behaviour, in all its gallantry, absurdity and cruelty.

The part of the novel which calls most directly on her personal experience of clamping down on pain is so quietly handled that I believe it sometimes escapes quick readers. On their way back to Cambridge in Richard's car the boys are involved in a crash and Hubert is killed. It is easy to see that when the news comes his stricken parents behave impeccably according to their lights: no scenes, not a tear – the deep chill of sorrow evident only in the rigidity of their adherence to the forms of normality. But there comes a day when Aroon can't resist pretending to her father that Richard truly was her lover and he says 'Well, thank God' which puzzles her a little; but his leaving her rather suddenly to visit the young horses down on the bog (so he says) ends their talk. And on that same day her mother has gone out, carrying a little bunch of cyclamen, and Aroon has wondered where she is off to. And it never occurs to her that both parents are slipping off to visit Hubert's grave in secret; that only guiltily can they allow their broken hearts this indulgence. That her father is felled by a stroke in the graveyard, not the bog, and that her mother, who comes screaming back to the house in search of help, was there with him . . . in the commotion and horror of it all Aroon makes no comment on this, and again it is left to the reader to understand.

It is impossible for someone of great natural charm to remain unaware of the effect he or she has on others, which makes the gift a dangerous one: the ability to get away with murder demands to be exploited, and over-exploited charm can be less attractive than charmlessness. Molly Keane was remarkable in being both one of the most charming people I ever met, and an entirely successful escaper from that attendant danger.

Of course she knew how winning she could be. She once said to me: 'When I was young I'm afraid I used to sing for my supper,' meaning that when she first met people more interesting and sophisticated than her own family she won herself a warm welcome, in spite of being neither pretty nor well-dressed, by her funniness and charm. She needed to do this because she was too intelligent for her background and her mother had made her feel an ugly duckling, and a delinquent one at that (probably, like many unloved children, she did respond by being tiresome from her parents' point of view). Being taken up by people who were charmed by her was her salvation, and winning them over did not end by making her unspontaneous or manipulative because her clear sight, sensitivity, honesty and generosity were even stronger than her charm. By the time I knew her, when she was in her seventies, she would occasionally resort to 'turning it on' in order to get through an interview or some fatiguing public occasion, and very skilfully she did it; but otherwise she was always more interested in what was happening around her, and in the people she was meeting, than she was in the impression she was making, so even on a slight acquaintance it was the woman herself one saw, not a mask, and the woman was lovable.

In spite of liking her so much I have to consider my acquaintance with her as less than a friendship, properly speaking. Someone in her seventies with two daughters to love, a wide circle of acquaintances and an unusually large number of true and intimate friends of long standing, hasn't much room in her life for new close friends. I see that only too clearly now that I have overtaken the age Molly had reached when we met: one feels almost regretful on recognizing exceptionally congenial qualities in a newly met person, because one knows one no longer has the energy to clear an adequate space for them. When Molly and I exchanged letters about her work I was always tempted by her image in my mind to run on into gossip and jokes, while hers were quick scrawls about the matter under discussion; and enjoyable though our meetings were when she came to London, they didn't much advance the intimacy between us, and I sometimes thought I discerned in them a courteously disguised distaste for an important aspect of my life: the fact that I live with a black man. Molly was well aware of how others could see attitudes belonging to her background and generation, such as disliking left-wing politics and mixed marriages; but an attitude is not necessarily *quite* expunged by knowing that it is not respectable.

Only once did I spend more than a meal-time with her. We gave a launching party for *Good Behaviour* in Dublin, I decided to take my car over and stay on for a ten-day holiday, and Molly invited me to stay with her for (I thought) the weekend at the start of the holiday. After the party I drove her to her home in Ardmore, and learnt on the way that she had arranged parties for me on every day of the coming week and had told a friend that she was bringing me to stay with him for two nights at the end of it. At first I was slightly dismayed by this unexpected abundance of hospitality, but I was soon enjoying every minute of it.

Partly this was because of the difference between Counties Cork and Waterford and my native East Anglia. Most of the people we met were the Irish equivalent of my family's friends: country gentlefolk preoccupied with hunting, shooting, farming, gardening . . . the very people I had escaped from (so I had felt, fond though I was of many of them) when I moved on from Oxford to earn my living in London. Had I been faced with a week of parties given by Norfolk people of that kind who were strangers to me I would have seen it as a grim ordeal by boredom – and it *would* have been pretty boring because my hosts, given the tedious duty of entertaining a foreign body, and I as the reluctant victim of their hospitality, would between us have erected an impenetrable wall of polite small-talk from which eventually both sides would have retreated in a state of exhaustion. But in Ireland . . . much as I distrust generalizations about national characteristics, there's no denying that most Irish people are more articulate than the English, appearing to see talk as a positive pleasure rather than a tiresome necessity. I don't suppose I shared many more interests with my Irish hosts than I would have done with English ones (although I did know quite a lot about theirs) – but they were so much more lively and witty, and so much readier to start or to follow a new trail, than the people among whom I was raised, that whether or not interests were shared didn't seem to matter. All the parties were thoroughly enjoyable.

They were given an appetizing touch of spice by the stories Molly told on the way to them about the people we were going to meet, which were splendidly indiscreet. If she disliked someone she either kept silent or spoke briefly with indignant disapproval; with the rest she rejoiced in their follies, if follies they displayed, but as a fascinated observer rather than a censorious judge. Perhaps novelists are so often good at gossip because – like God with forgiveness – *c'est leur métier.*

On one of those drives she gave me a gleeful glimpse of local standards of literary criticism. An elderly neighbour, blue-blooded but rustic in her ways (I gathered that she usually kept her gum-boots on and her false teeth out) had said to her: 'I read your book, Molly, and I absolutely *hated* it – but I must say that it was very well written. I didn't find a single spelling mistake.'

The drives, and the time spent alone with Molly in her house tucked into the hillside overlooking Ardmore and its bay, were even better than the parties. She was an exquisitely kind and considerate hostess, but it wasn't that which made the visit so memorable. It was the extent to which Molly was alive to everything around her – to the daughters she worried about and adored, the people she knew, the events she remembered, her garden, the food she cooked, the problems and satisfactions of writing. And it was also the fact that day by day I became more aware of the qualities she kept hidden: her courage, her unselfishness – simply her goodness.

The chief difference, it seems to me, between the person who is lucky enough to possess the ability to create – whether with words or sound or pigment or wood or whatever – and those who haven't got it, is that the former react to experience directly and each in his own way, while the latter are less ready to trust their own responses and often prefer to make use of those generally agreed to be acceptable by their friends and relations. And while the former certainly include by far the greater proportion of individuals who would be difficult to live with, they also include a similarly large proportion of individuals who are exciting or disturbing or amusing or inspiring to know. And Molly, in addition to having charm and being good, was also a creator.

I am glad, therefore, that our last exchange of letters was about her writing, and not just one of general well-wishing (as they had been for some years, since she became seriously ill with heart trouble). I had just reread *Good Behaviour* for some forgotten reason, and on meeting Molly's daughter Virginia as we walked our dogs, had told her how greatly I had re-enjoyed it. Virginia urged me to write and tell Molly, saying that although the worst of her depression at being weak and helpless had lifted, she still needed cheering up. So I wrote her a long letter about why I love that book so much, and also her last book, *Loving and Giving*, and said that although I knew she was downcast at not having been able to write another book, she surely must acknowledge that what she had done had been marvellously well done – that her writing had, in fact, won laurels on which anyone should be proud to rest. She replied that my letter had done her good and had lifted her depression about her writing 'right off the ground', then went on to say very sweetly how much she valued my opinion, ending with words which I knew to be valedictory, of such generosity that I can only treasure them.

> I feel a real loss at losing your company. I shan't get to London again and I'm too weak and foolish to ask you to come here. But we have had many good moments together and you have done

everything for my books – *think* what that has meant to me, to my life. With my love and thanks. Molly

By 'doing everything' for her books she meant that if we had not published *Good Behaviour*, *Time After Time* and *Loving and Giving*, her earlier books would not have been reissued in paperback by Virago. The real originator of this sequence (not counting Ian Parsons) was Gina Pollinger, as I am sure Molly recognized and must have acknowledged with a similar generosity and more reason; but I do still get great satisfaction from remembering that Molly's reappearance under our imprint brought her serious recognition as a writer, and also put an end to the money problems that had harassed her throughout her long widowhood. I do think of it, as she bade me, and it makes me happy. Remembering that outcome, and the pleasure of knowing her, is a good way to end this book.

POSTSCRIPT

Having seen André Deutsch Limited fade out, why am I not sadder than I am?

I suppose it is because, although I have often shaken my head over symptoms of change in British publishing such as lower standards of copy-preparation and proofreading, I cannot feel that they are crucial. It is, of course, true that reading is going the same way as eating, the greatest demand being for the quick and easy, and for the simple, instantly recognizable flavours such as sugar and vinegar, or their mental equivalents; but that is not the terminal tragedy which it sometimes seems to the disgruntled old. It is not, after all, a new development: quick and easy has always been what the majority wants. The difference between my early days in publishing and the present is not that this common desire has come into being, but that it is now catered for more lavishly than it used to be. And that is probably because the grip on our trade of a particular caste has begun to relax.

Of that caste I am a member: one of the mostly London-dwelling, university-educated, upper-middle-class English people who took over publishing towards the end of the nineteenth century from the booksellers who used to run it. Most of us loved books and genuinely tried to understand the differences between good and bad writing; but I suspect that if we were examined from a god's-eye viewpoint it would be seen that quite often our 'good' was good only according to the notions of the caste. Straining for that god's-eye view, I sometimes think that not a few of the books I once took pleasure in publishing were pretty futile, and that the same was true of other houses. Two quintessentially 'caste' writers, one from the less pretentious end of the scale, the other from its highest reaches, were Angela Thirkell and Virginia Woolf. Thirkell is embarrassing – I always knew that, but would have published her, given the chance, because she was so obviously a seller. And Woolf, whom I revered in my youth, now seems almost more embarrassing because the claims made for her were so high. Not only did she belong to the caste, but she was unable to see beyond its boundaries – and that self-consciously 'beautiful' writing, all those adjectives – oh dear! Caste standards – it ought not to need saying – have no right to be considered sacrosanct.

Keeping that in mind is a useful specific against melancholy; and even better is the fact that there are plenty of people about who are making a stand against *too much* quick-and-easy. The speed with which the corners of supermarkets devoted to organic produce are growing into long shelves is remarkable; and there are still publishers – not many, but some – who are more single-mindedly determined to support serious writing than we ever were.

I have just visited one: the first time in seven years that I have set foot in a publisher's office. It astonished me: how familiar it was, the way I knew what was happening behind its doors . . . and how much I loved it. 'It's still there!' I said to myself; and on the way home I saw that by 'it' I meant not only publishing of a kind I recognized, but something even more reassuring: being young. Old people don't want to mop and mow, but age has a blinkering effect, and their narrowed field of vision often contains things that *are* going from bad to worse; it is therefore consoling to be reminded that much exists outside that narrow field, just as it did when we were forty or thirty or twenty.

Finding myself not gravely distressed by the way publishing is changing seems reasonable enough. I am harder put to understand how anyone can feel in their bones, as I can, that life is worth living when every day we see such alarming evidence that a lot of it is unacceptable: that idiocy and cruelty, far from being brought to heel by human ingenuity, are as rampant as ever. I suppose the answer lies in something of which that small publishing house is a part.

Years ago, in a pub near Baker Street, I heard a man say that humankind is seventy per cent brutish, thirty per cent intelligent, and though the thirty per cent is never going to win, it will always be able to leaven the mass just enough to keep us going. That rough and ready assessment of our plight has stayed with me as though it were true, given that one takes 'intelligence' to mean not just intellectual agility, but whatever it is in beings that makes for readiness to understand, to look for the essence in other beings and things and events, to respect that essence, to collaborate, to discover, to endure when endurance is necessary, to enjoy: briefly, to co-exist. It does, alas, seem likely that sooner or later, either through our own folly or a collision with some wandering heavenly body, we will all vanish in the wake of the dinosaurs; but until that happens I believe that the yeast of intelligence will continue to operate one way or another.

Even if it operates in vain, it remains evolution's peak (as far as we can see): something to enjoy and foster as much as possible; something not to betray by succumbing to despair, however deep the many pits of darkness. It even seems to me possible dimly to perceive it as belonging not to a particular planet, but to universal laws of being, potentially present anywhere in the universe where the kind of physical (or should it be chemical?) conditions prevail which kindle life out of dust: an aspect of something which human beings have called by the various names of god, because having no name for it made them feel dizzy.

In the microscopic terms of my own existence, believing this means that in spite of reading the newspapers, and in spite of seeing the sad end of André's brave endeavour, and in spite of losing a considerable part of my youth to heartbreak, I wake up every morning *liking* being here. (I apologize to André, and to my young self, for being able to dismiss so lightly events which were once so painfully heavy.) I also wake up knowing that I have been extraordinarily lucky, and a good chunk of that luck came with the job. When I was moved to scribble 'Stet' against the time I spent being an editor it was because it gave so many kinds of enlargement, interest, amusement and pleasure to my days. It was a job on the side of the thirty per cent.

5. LONG LIFE:
TOWARDS THE END

SOMEWHERE
TOWARDS THE END

1

NEAR THE PARK which my bedroom overlooks there came to stay a family which owned a pack of pugs, five or six of them, active little dogs, none of them overweight as pugs so often are. I saw them recently on their morning walk, and they caused me a pang. I have always wanted a pug and now I can't have one, because buying a puppy when you are too old to take it for walks is unfair. There are dog-walkers, of course; but the best part of owning a dog is walking with it, enjoying its delight when it detects the signs that a walk is imminent, and its glee when its lead is unsnapped and it can bound off over the grass, casting cheerful looks back at you from time to time to make sure that you are still in touch. Our own dog is as old in dog years as I am in human ones (mine amount to eighty-nine), and wants no more than the little potter I can still provide, but I enjoy watching other people's animals busy about their pleasures.

Brought up with dogs, I am baffled by those who dislike them. They have been domesticated for so long that cohabiting with us is as natural to them as the jungle is to the tiger. They have become the only animal whose emotions we can truly penetrate: emotions resembling our own excepting in their simplicity. When a dog is anxious, angry, hungry, puzzled, happy, loving, it allows us to see in their purest form states which we ourselves know, though in us they are distorted by the complex accretions of humanity. Dogs and humans recognize each other at a deep and uncomplicated level. I would so like to begin that process all over again with a little black-velvet-faced pug – but no! It can't be done.

And another thing that can't be done became apparent this morning. I had seen in Thompson & Morgan's plant catalogue a photograph of a tree fern which cost £18, reasonable for something so exotic. A few years ago I fell in love with the tree ferns in the forests of Dominica, and since then I learnt that they, or their cousins, can survive in English gardens, so now I ordered one from that catalogue by phone. It arrived today. Of course I knew that I would not receive a mature tree as shown in the photograph, but I was expecting a sizeable parcel, probably by special delivery. What came, by ordinary post, was a box less than twelve inches long containing a three-inch pot, from which four frail little leaves are sprouting. Whether tree ferns grow quickly or slowly I don't know, but even if it is quickly, it is not possible that I shall ever see this one playing the part I envisaged for it in our garden. I shall pot it on towards that end as far as I can, hoping to see it reach a size at which it can be planted out, but virtuous though planting for the future is supposed to be, it doesn't feel rewarding. It made me think of a turn of phrase often used by Jean Rhys, usually about being drunk: 'I was a bit drunk, well very.' She never in fact said 'I was a bit *sad*, well very' about being old, but no doubt she would have done if she had not hated and feared it too much to speak of it.

Jean was one of my object lessons, demonstrating how not to think about getting old. The prospect filled her with resentment and despair. Sometimes she announced the defiant intention of dyeing her pretty grey hair bright red, but she never did so; less, I think, for the sensible reason that it would have made her look grotesque than because she lacked the energy to organize it. Sometimes – very rarely – drink made her feel better, but more often it turned her querulous and tetchy. She expected old age to make her miserable, and it did, although once she was immersed in it she expressed her misery by complaining about other and lesser things, the big one itself being too much to contemplate – although she did once say that what kept panic at bay was her suicide kit. She had depended on sleeping pills for years and had saved up a substantial cache of them in the drawer of her bedside table, against the day when things got too bad. They did get very bad, but after her death I checked that drawer and the cache was intact.

My second object lesson was the Bulgarian-born, Nobel-Prize-winning writer, Elias Canetti, whose defiance of death was more foolish than Jean's dismay. He had a central European's respect for the construction of abstract systems of thought about the inexplicable, which is uncongenial to many English minds, and which caused him to overvalue his own notions to the extent of publishing two volumes of aphorisms. I never met him, but I knew those books because André Deutsch Limited, the firm in which I worked, published them. During the long years he spent here as a refugee from Nazi Germany, Canetti had taken so violently against the British, I think because they had failed to recognize his genius (the Nobel Prize was yet to come), that he determined never to be published in this country. However Tom Rosenthal, who took over our firm towards the end of its days, had once done him a kindness which he remembered, so he finally agreed to let us have his books on condition that we began with the two lots of aphorisms and followed the American editions, which he had approved, to the last comma, including the jacket copy. This left his English editor (me) nothing to do except read the books, but that was enough to get my hackles up. Many of the aphorisms were pithy and a few were witty, but as a whole what pompous self-importance! The last straw was when his thinking turned to nonsense and he declared, as he did in several of these snippets, that he 'rejected death'.

Later I came to know a former lover of his, the Austrian painter Marie-Louise Motesiczky, a woman who sailed into her eighties gracefully in spite of much physical pain as a result of a severe case of shingles, and a life-story that might well have flattened her. She deserves more than passing attention.

I met her by chance. Mary Hernton, a friend who was looking for a bedsitter in Hampstead, told me she had found a wonderful room in the house of an extraordinary old woman. The room, though wonderful, was not right for her purposes, but the woman had impressed Mary so much that she had invited her to tea and wanted me to meet her. What was so remarkable about her? I would see when I met her, and anyway Mary thought she had been Canetti's mistress: her shelves were full of books owned by him and the room had once been his. I did join them for tea, and I too was impressed by Marie-Louise. She was funny, warm, charming and indiscreet. When she learnt that I published Canetti she became excited, disregarding the fact that I had never met him, and plunged at once into telling me how they had been friends and lovers for over twenty years before she learnt that he had a wife and daughter. She knew it sounded improbable, but she had lived a secluded life looking after her mother, who had come with her to England from Vienna just before Hitler invaded Austria (they were members of a rich and distinguished Jewish family). Her seclusion seemed to have spared her the knowledge of Canetti's many other women: she never said anything to me suggesting that she knew about them, only that the revelation of his being married had brought their affair to a sudden and agonizing end. The more she told me, the more it seemed to me that Canetti and her mother, who had died quite recently at a great age, had consumed her life and had left her in emptiness . . . except that there was no real feeling of emptiness about Marie-Louise.

Mary had told me that she thought Marie-Louise painted, but when quite soon I visited her in her large Hampstead house, which was full of interesting objects and paintings, I could see nothing that looked as though it had been done by her. She did, however, make a passing reference to her work, so I asked if I might see some of it. I asked nervously – very nervously – because nothing is more embarrassing than being shown paintings that turn out to be dreadful. She led me – and this boded ill – into her bedroom, a large, high-ceilinged room, one whole wall of which was an enormous built-in cupboard. This she opened, to reveal racks crammed with paintings, two of which she pulled out. And I was stunned.

This sweet, funny, frail old woman was indeed a painter, the real thing, up there with Max Beckmann and Kokoschka. It was difficult to know how to take it, because one couldn't say 'Oh my god, you really are a painter!', while if one took her for granted as what she was, one would feel impertinent commenting on her work. I can't remember what I did say, but I must have scrambled through it all right because thereafter she was always happy to talk about her work, for which I was grateful. She was wonderful to talk with about painting, and it explained why there was no feeling of emptiness about her. She was an object lesson on the essential luck, whatever hardships may come their way, of those born able to make things.

There was, however, something to worry about, because what were all those paintings doing, languishing in a bedroom cupboard? It turned out that there were two or three in European public collections and that there had been a show of her work at the Goethe Institute not long ago, but still it was a ridiculous situation for which one couldn't help concluding that Canetti and her mother had been largely responsible. Both were cannibals, Canetti because of self-importance, her mother because of dependence. (Once, she told me, when she said to her mother that she was going out for twenty minutes to buy some necessity, her mother wailed 'But what shall I do if I die before you get back?') Though the fact that during the years of her life in England, German expressionist painting, to which her work was related, had been held in little esteem, may also have contributed to her abdication from the art scene.

But worry was wasted. Although she had been taken advantage of by her two loves, Marie-Louise was a skilful manipulator of everyone else. No sooner did she meet anyone than she began diffidently asking them for help. Could you tell her a good dentist, or plumber, or dressmaker? Might she ask you to help her with this tax return? Always in a way suggesting that you were her only hope. It was quite a while before it dawned on me that a considerable part of the population of Hampstead was waiting on her hand and foot, so that worry wasn't really necessary, and by the time I met her a young friend of hers called Peter Black was well on the way to convincing a great Viennese gallery, the Belvedere, that it must give her the major exhibition that she deserved. I was able to help her write tactful letters to them when she disliked the catalogue descriptions they were providing, which earned me an invitation to the opening. (I also, which pleased me even more, persuaded our National Portrait Gallery to reverse its rejection of her portrait of Canetti. They had told her coldly that they were not interested in portraits of unknown people, and – although I ought not to say it – the letter in which I told them who Canetti was without showing that I knew they didn't know, was a masterpiece. I wish I had kept a copy. The portrait is now there.)

The exhibition in Vienna was a wonderful occasion. Seeing those paintings hung where they ought to be was like seeing animals which had been confined in cages at a zoo released into their natural habitat. I am sure Marie-Louise did not wish to be pleased with anything that her native city did for her (it had murdered her beloved brother, who had stayed behind to help his fellow Jews), but although she made a game attempt at dissatisfaction with details, she could not conceal her pleasure at the whole.

At one of our last meetings before her death I asked her if Canetti had meant it literally when he declared that he would not accept it. Oh yes, she said. And she confessed that there was a time when she was so enthralled by the power of his personality that she had allowed herself to think 'Perhaps he will really do it – will become the first human being not to die.' She was laughing at herself when she said this, but a little tremulously. I think she still felt that his attitude was heroic.

To me it was plain silly. It is so obvious that life works in terms of species rather than of individuals. The individual just has to be born, to develop to the point at which it can procreate, and then to fall away into death to make way for its successors, and humans are no exception whatever they may fancy. We have, however, contrived to extend our falling away so much that it is often longer than our development, so what goes on in it and how to manage it is worth considering. Book after book has been written about being young, and even more of them about the elaborate and testing experiences that cluster round procreation, but there is not much on record about falling away. Being well advanced in that process, and just having had my nose rubbed in it by pugs and tree ferns, I say to myself, 'Why not have a go at it?' So I shall.

2

ALL THROUGH MY sixties I felt I was still within hailing distance of middle age, not safe on its shores, perhaps, but navigating its coastal waters. My seventieth birthday failed to change this because I managed scarcely to notice it, but my seventy-first did change it. Being 'over seventy' is being old: suddenly I was aground on that fact and saw that the time had come to size it up.

I have lived long enough to have witnessed great changes in being old as far as women are concerned – smaller ones for men, but for them less was needed. In my grandmothers' day a woman over seventy adopted what almost amounted to a uniform. If she was a widow she wore black or grey clothes that disregarded fashion, and even if she still had a husband her garments went a bit drab and shapeless, making it clear that this person no longer attempted to be attractive. My paternal grandmother, who was the older of the two, wore floor-length black garments to her dying day, and a little confection of black velvet and lace on her head, a 'cap' such as full-blown Victorian ladies wore. (Judging by the skimpiness of my own hair in old age, which comes from her side of the family, she had good reason for adhering to that particular fashion.) Even one of my aunts, my mother's eldest sister, never wore anything but black or grey after her husband's death in the 1930s, and deliberately chose unsmart shapes for her garments. The abrupt shortening of skirts in the 1920s contributed to the preservation of this 'uniform', because no one at any age wants to look grotesque, and grotesque is what old legs and bodies would have looked in 'flapper' fashions, so in my youth old women were still announcing by their appearance that they had become a different kind of person. After the Second World War, however, reaction against the austerity it had imposed led to far greater flexibility. For a while *Vogue* ran a feature called 'Mrs Exeter' to persuade elderly women that they could wear stylish clothes, and this demonstration soon became unnecessary, so pleased were women to choose clothes to suit their shapes and complexions rather than to conform to a convention. Nowadays an old woman would obviously be daft if she dressed like a teenager, but I have a freedom of choice undreamt of by my grandmothers. There have been days when I went shopping in my local Morrisons wearing something a bit eccentric and wondered whether I would see any raised eyebrows, only to conclude that I would probably have to wear a bikini before anyone so much as blinked.

Even more than clothes, cosmetics have made age look, and therefore feel, less old. Until quite recently they could be a danger, because women who had always worn a lot of make-up tended to continue to do so, blind to the unfortunate effect it could have on an inelastic and crêpy skin. One of my dearest old friends could never get it into her head that if, when doing herself up for a party, she slapped on a lot of scarlet lipstick, it would soon come off on her teeth and begin to run into the little wrinkles round the edge of her lips, making her look like a vampire bat disturbed in mid-dinner. Luckily today's cosmetics are much better made and more subtle in effect, so that an ancient face that would look absurd if *visibly* painted can be gently coaxed into looking quite naturally better than it really is. Having inherited a good skin from my mother, I still receive compliments for it, but nowadays I know that at least half its 'goodness' is thanks to Max Factor. Appearance is important to old women, not because we suppose that it will impress other people, but because of what we ourselves see when we look in a mirror. It is unlikely that anyone else will notice that the nose on an old face is red and shiny or the broken veins on its cheeks are visible, but its owner certainly will, and will equally certainly feel a lift in her spirits when this depressing sight is remedied. And even if how one sees oneself is not wholly how one is, it does contribute a great deal towards it. I know for sure that I both feel and behave younger than my grandmothers did when they were old.

In spite of this, however, the most obvious thing about moving into my seventies was the disappearance of what used to be the most important thing in life: I might not look, or even feel, all that old, but I had ceased to be a sexual being, a condition which had gone through several stages and had not always been a happy one, but which had always seemed central to my existence.

It had started when I was four or five in a way which no doubt appeared comic to onlookers but which felt serious enough to me, with the announcement that I was going to marry John Sherbroke. He was a little boy who lived a few houses up from us on the street beside Woolwich Common (my father, an officer in the Royal Artillery, was presumably an instructor at the Military Academy there at the time, and John's father was also a Gunner). I can't remember John at all, except for his name, and that he was my Intended. His successor is clearer in my memory because of his beautiful, sad brown eyes and the glamour bestowed on him by his great age – he was Denis, the gardener's boy at the Hall Farm where we had gone to live under the wing of my mother's parents. I doubt whether I ever spoke to Denis, but I did, with great daring, spit on his head out of the lavatory window when he was working the pump by the back door. He was followed by loves with whom I did communicate – indeed I and my brother spent much time with them: Jack and Wilfred, sons of the head cow-man at the farm, remembered even more clearly than Denis because of the amount of time I put into trying to decide which I loved best.

Those two were the first beneficiaries of my romantic phase, in which love took the form of daydreams. The object of my passion would be placed in a situation of great danger – his house on fire, perhaps, or he was being swept away in a flood – and I would rescue him, the dream's climax being that when he recovered consciousness he would open his eyes to find me leaning over him, my cloud of black hair enveloping him like a cloak (I was a skinny child with a mouse-coloured bob, but I confidently expected to improve with time). Jack and Wilfred lasted until I was nine, when they were ousted by the first love I chose for real reasons: David, who was far kinder, braver and more sensible than the rest of us and was also a familiar friend and companion. He, too, was liable to be rescued, though rather guiltily because of how silly he would have thought it, had he known. He told his mother I was a good sport, which was thrilling at the time, though as I entered my teens it did begin to pall.

Then, at fifteen, I fell in love as an adult. It was with Paul (I called him that in *Instead of a Letter*, so he can keep the name here), who came during one of his Oxford vacations to earn a bit of money by coaching my brother for an exam. He dispelled daydreams by being the real thing, but he did not dispel romance. I loved, I assumed love equalled marriage, and I was certain that once I was married to the man I loved I would be faithful to him for the rest of my life. I did have the occasional, fleeting daydream about my beautiful white wedding, but to embroider my romanticism beyond that, once I was old enough to hold Paul's attention and we became engaged, was not easy, partly because of how everyone went on at me about how poor we would be and how I would have to learn to be a good housewife. Paul, who had gone into the RAF, was still only a pilot-officer whose pay was £400 a year, which seemed to him and me enough to have a good time on, whatever 'they' said, but still the warnings were sobering; though less so than something which happened about six months after we announced our engagement.

We went, with his sister, to a party with a group of rather louche friends of Paul's – I didn't know where he had picked them up, and was disconcerted by them from the start because they were drinking harder and talking more crudely than anyone I had met hitherto. One of them had brought along an extravagantly sexy-looking girl who made a dead set at Paul the moment she saw him, and to my incredulous dismay he responded. After an extremely uncomfortable hour or two he shovelled the task of seeing me home onto his embarrassed sister, and he ended the evening, I was sure, in bed with that girl. During the following two weeks I heard nothing from him, and felt too crushed to write or call myself, and when he let me know that he was about to fly down from Grantham to spend the weekend at Oxford with me, as he often did, I was more anxious than relieved.

During the Saturday evening we drank too much and he collapsed into almost tearful apology. He had behaved horribly, he was so ashamed of himself he couldn't bear it, I must, must believe that it had meant absolutely nothing, that girl had turned out to be a ghastly bore (what a slip-up! Suppose she hadn't been?). Never again would he do anything like that because I was and always would be the only woman he really loved, and so on and so on. It was better than silence had been, but it was not good.

Next morning we took a taxi to 'our' pub in Appleton and dismissed it before we got there in order to dispel our headaches by walking the last mile, although it was a bitterly cold and windy winter day. Paul seemed relaxed, scanning the fields on either side of the muddy lane for fieldfares; I was dismally silent, mulling over his apology. It had meant nothing: yes, I accepted that. But his declaration that such a thing would never happen again: no, that I was unable to believe. I don't remember being as shocked as I ought to have been at his doing it under my nose, thus betraying a really gross indifference to my feelings. I had a humble opinion of my own importance, carefully fostered by a family which considered vanity a serious sin, so in such a situation I tended to blame myself as not being worthy of consideration, and I wasn't consciously thinking of that although I am now sure that it was gnawing away at me. What I knew I was thinking about was how this flightiness of Paul's must be handled. I remember thinking that once we were married I would have to learn to be *really clever*. 'It will be all right for quite a time,' I thought. 'He will go on coming back to me while we are like we are now. But when I get old – when I'm *thirty*' – and I saw a flash of my own face, anxious and wrinkled under grey hair – 'then it will be dangerous, then he could fall in love with one of them.' Would I learn to be clever *enough*? I'd have to. The whole of that day remained dismal, but not for a moment did it occur to me that I might not want to marry him, and soon our relationship was restored to its usual enjoyable state.

So I don't think there was ever a time in my adult life when I didn't realize that men were quite likely to be technically unfaithful to women, although it was not until Paul had finally jilted me that I saw that women, too, could be cheered up by sex without love. I 'recovered' from Paul in that I fell in love again, twice, and heavily, but both times it felt 'fatal', something impossible to avoid, and anyway I longed for it, but which was bound to bring pain. The first time it was with a married man much older than myself, and I never envisaged him leaving his wife for me. No doubt if he had suggested it I would have accepted, but I admired him far too much to expect it: I was his wartime fling, or folly (there's nothing like a whiff of death in the air to intensify desire, the essence of life – I remember him whispering in amazement 'I'd resigned myself to never feeling like this again'), while she was his good and blameless wife who had just become the mother of their first child, so leaving her would prove him cruel and irresponsible which I was sure he was not. I would not have loved him so much if he had been.

My second after-Paul love was available, even eligible, but his very eligibility seemed to make him too good to be true. He liked me a lot. For a time he almost thought he was in love with me, but he never quite was and I sensed almost from the beginning that it was going to end in tears, whereupon I plunged in deeper and deeper. And it did end in tears quite literally, both of us weeping as we walked up and down Wigmore Street on our last evening together. With masochistic abandon I loved him even more for his courage in admitting the situation and sparing me vain hopes (and in fact such courage, which takes a lot of summoning up, is something to be grateful for, because a broken heart mends much faster from a conclusive blow than it does from slow strangulation. Believe me! Mine experienced both.).

That, for me, was the end of romantic love. What followed, until I met Barry Reckord in my forty-fourth year, was a series of sometimes very brief, sometimes sustained affairs, always amiable (two of them very much so), almost always cheering-up (two of the tiny ones I could have done without), and none of them going deep enough to hurt. During those years, if a man wanted to marry me, as three of them did, I felt what Groucho Marx felt about a club willing to accept him: disdain. I tried to believe it was something more rational, but it wasn't. Several of the painless affairs involved other people's husbands, but I never felt guilty because the last thing I intended or hoped for was damage to anyone's marriage. If a wife ever found out – and as far as I know that never happened – it would have been from her husband's carelessness, not mine.

Loyalty is not a favourite virtue of mine, perhaps because André Deutsch used so often to abuse the word, angrily accusing any writer who wanted to leave our list of 'disloyalty'. There is, of course, no reason why a writer should be loyal to a firm which has supposed that it will be able to make money by publishing his work. Gratitude and affection can certainly develop when a firm makes a good job of it, but no bond of loyalty is established. In cases where such a bond exists – loyalty to family, for example, or to a political party – it can become foolishness if betrayed by its object. If your brother turns out to be a murderer or your party changes its policies, standing by him or it through thick or thin seems to me mindless. Loyalty unearned is simply the husk of a notion developed to benefit the bosses in a feudal system. When spouses are concerned, it seems to me that kindness and consideration should be the key words, not loyalty, and sexual infidelity does not necessarily wipe them out.

Fidelity in the sense of keeping one's word I respect, but I think it tiresome that it is tied so tightly in people's minds to the idea of sex. The belief that a wife owes absolute fidelity to her husband has deep and tangled roots, being based not only on a man's need to know himself to be the father of his wife's child, but also on the even deeper, darker feeling that man *owns* woman, God having made her for his convenience. It's hard to imagine the extirpation of that: think of its power in Islam! And woman's anxious clamour for her husband's fidelity springs from the same primitive root: she feels it to be necessary proof of her value. That I know only too well, having had the stuffing knocked out of me so painfully when Paul chose to marry someone else. But understanding doesn't mean approving. Why, given our bone-deep, basic need for one another, do men and women have to put so much weight on this particular, unreliable aspect of it?

I think now of Isaac Bashevis Singer's story, 'The Peephole in the Gate', about a young man who saw his sweetheart home on the eve of their marriage, couldn't resist taking one last look at her through the peephole – and there she was, being soundly and obviously enjoyably kissed by the porter. End of betrothal – though the narrator does slyly remind the young man that he had it off with a serving maid that same afternoon. The story goes on to suggest how much simpler, and probably better, two people's lives would have been if that sexual infidelity had never come to light: a theme which Singer, that wise old bird, returns to several times, always with his characteristic trick of leaving the pronouncement of a moral judgement in the hands of the reader. Given his deep attachment to his religious background, I can't be sure that he would have agreed with the judgement I produce – but after all, he *does* ask for it. Yes, there are some things, sexual infidelities among them, that do no harm if they remain unknown – or, for that matter, are known and accepted, and which is preferable depends on the individuals and their circumstances. I only have to ask myself which I would choose, if forced to do so, between the extreme belief that a whole family's honour is stained by an unfaithful wife unless she is killed, and the attitude often attributed to the French, that however far from admirable sexual infidelity is, it is perfectly acceptable if *conducted properly*. Vive la France!

This attitude I shared, and still share, with Barry, with whom, after I had finally shed the scars of a broken heart (by 'writing them out', as I will explain later), I eventually settled down into an extraordinarily happy loving friendship, which remained at its best for about eight years until it began to be affected not by emotional complications, but by Time. This was not a sudden event, but its early stage, which took place during my mid- and late fifties, was followed by a reprieve, which made it possible to ignore its significance. Gradually I had become aware that my interest in, and therefore my physical response to, making love with my dear habitual companion, was dwindling: familiarity had made the touch of his hand feel so like the touch of my own hand that it no longer conveyed a thrill. Looking back, I wonder why I never talked about this with him, because I didn't. I simply started to fake. Probably this was because the thought of 'working at' the problem together, as I supposed a marriage counsellor would suggest, struck me as unlikely to solve it. Tedious and absurd: that was how I envisaged such a procedure. If something that had always worked naturally now didn't work – well, first you hoped that faking it would bring it back, which sometimes it did, and when that stopped happening you accepted that it was over.

That acceptance was sad. Indeed, I was forced into it, at a time when our household was invaded by a ruthless and remarkably succulent blonde in her mid-twenties and he fell into bed with her. There was one sleepless night of real sorrow, but only one night. What I mourned during that painful night was not the loss of my loving old friend who was still there, and still is, but the loss of youth: 'What she has, god rot her, I no longer have and will never, never have again.' A belated recognition, up against which I had come with a horrid crunch. But very soon another voice began to sound in my head, which made more sense. 'Look,' it said, 'you know quite well that you have stopped wanting him in your bed, it's months since you enjoyed it, so what are you moaning about? Of course you have lost youth, you have moved on and stopped wanting what youth wants.' And that was the end of that stage.

Soon afterwards came the reprieve, when I found, to my amusement and pleasure, that novelty could restore sex. I described in *Instead of a Letter* how after an early, real and long-lasting sorrow my morale had begun to be restored by an affair with a man I called Felix, which did not involve love but was thoroughly enjoyable otherwise. Now, as I approached my sixties, it happened again, and my life as a sexual being was prolonged by seven years while Barry went his own way, our companionship having become more like that of brother and sister than of lovers. A second man with whom I had little in common won himself a place in memory made warm by gratitude. After him there was no reprieve, nor did I want one.

3

THE LAST MAN in my life as a sexual being, who accompanied me over the frontier between late middle-age and being old, was Sam, who was born in Grenada in the Caribbean. Whether he had come to England in order to volunteer for the war, or his arrival just happened to coincide with its outbreak, I don't know. He joined the RAF Regiment, in which he worked as a clerk, and in his own time came to know Padmore and other black elders of that day who were concerned with establishing the black man's rights in Britain. He gained a good deal of experience in broadcasting at this time, which served him well later, when he moved on to Ghana and soon attracted the attention of Kwame Nkrumah, who put him in charge of his government's public relations so that he became in effect a member of it, although he was never a minister. He remained Nkrumah's trusted servant and friend until the coup which brought the Redeemer down, simultaneously putting an end to Sam's palmy days in Africa. Because he was known in Accra as an honest man who took no bribes he escaped prison, but he had to leave the country at four days' notice taking nothing but his clothes. When I met him, all he had left from those palmy days was a beautiful camel-hair overcoat with a sable collar, and the gold watch on a handsome bracelet given him by Haile Selassie.

Being an impressive-looking man, very tall, with pleasant manners, easygoing but sensible, clearly on the side of good sense and decorum, he had no trouble getting a job almost at once in the

British Government's organization concerned with race relations. He was just settling into it when we met at a party at which there were several old African hands of one sort and another. My partner at André Deutsch had kick-started a publishing firm in Nigeria during the 1960s and we had some African writers on our list, so the newly independent countries, and race relations, were part of the landscape in which I existed at that time.

In addition to that, in the course of my close and happy relationship with Barry, which had by then lasted about eight years, I had come to feel more at home with black men than with white. Barry, having been educated by English schoolmasters at his Jamaican school and by English dons at Cambridge, used sometimes to say that his fellow Jamaicans saw him as 'a small, square, brown Englishman', and some of them may have done so, but he was black enough to have received his share of insults from white men; and one can't identify with someone of whom that is true without feeling more like him than like his insulters.

The first black person with whom I was ever in the same room was an African undergraduate at a party during my first term at Oxford in 1936. Dancing was going on, and I was deeply relieved at his not asking me for a dance. I knew that if he asked I would have to say yes, and I hadn't the faintest idea why the prospect seemed so appalling. It was just something which would have appalled my parents, so it appalled me. But I am glad to say that when, a week later, a friend said to me, 'I think I would be sick if a black man touched me,' I was shocked. I don't remember thinking about it in the intervening days, but somehow I had taken the first tiny step of seeing that my reaction to the idea of dancing with that man had been disgusting.

After that I must gradually have given the matter enough thought to get my head straight about it, because when I next came in touch with black people, which didn't happen for some years, I was able to see them as individuals. The first time I was kissed by a black man – a friendly peck at the end of a taxi-ride from one pub to another – I did note it as an occasion, because the fact that it was just like being kissed by anyone else proved me right in a satisfactory way: I was still feeling pleased with myself for not having racist feelings. But by the time I met Barry, although I had never had occasion to make love with a black man I had met many black people and worked with some of them, so clicking with him at a party and soon afterwards going to bed with him didn't seem particularly noteworthy except for being much more fun than the last such encounter I'd had, because this time we liked each other so well. It was only after we had settled into togetherness that I started expecting to like black men better than whites. I always might, of course, end up disliking the one or liking the other contrary to expectation, but I did, from then on, start out with a bias towards the black, or at any rate the un-English.

So when at our first meeting Sam made a stately swoop, I was pleased: it was both funny and revivifying to be seen as attractive by this agreeable and sexy person, just after concluding that my lovemaking days were over. Soon after that he moved into a flat near Putney Bridge, and for the next seven years I spent a night with him there about once a week.

We rarely did anything together except make ourselves a pleasant little supper and go to bed, because we had very little in common apart from liking sex. Sam had an old-fashioned sense of what was proper, but I am sure it had never entered his head to think of sex in connection with guilt. As well as *The Pickwick Papers*, *The Bab Ballads* and several booklets about the Rosicrucians and the Christian Scientists, *The Kama Sutra* was among the books permanently entangled in his bedclothes. We also shared painful feet, which was almost as important as liking sex, because when you start feeling your age it is comforting to be with someone in the same condition. You recognize it in each other, but there is no need to go on about it. We never mentioned our feet, just kicked our shoes off as soon as we could.

To be more serious, the really important thing we had in common was that neither of us had any wish to fall in love or to become responsible for someone else's peace of mind. We didn't even need to see a great deal of each other. We knew that we would give each other no trouble.

So what did we give each other?

I gave Sam sex that suited him. The first, but not most enduring, attraction was that I was white and well-bred. Sam had nothing against black women (except his wife, whom he saw as a burden imposed on him by his mother before he'd developed the sense to understand what a mistake it was); but since he came to England at the end of the 1930s all his most important women had been white. He had been bettering himself ever since his mother urged him to work hard at school, and claiming a white woman for yourself would, alas, be recognized by most black men from his background, at that time, as part of that process. This was a fact that gave older and/or not particularly glamorous white women an edge with black men that they hadn't got for white ones, which is evidently deplorable although I can't help being grateful for it. Sam was not a man of vulgar instincts so he didn't want to show his woman off, but it gave him private satisfaction to feel that she was worth showing. Then it turned out that physically I was right for him, and that I could be good company. So I was satisfying as a status symbol, agreeable as a companion in so far as he wanted one, and was able and willing to play along with him in a way he enjoyed. He obviously felt he need look no further.

Sam's chief attraction to me was that he wanted me: to be urgently wanted at a time when I no longer expected it cheered me up and brought me alive again – no small gift. Also, I am curious. His background and the whole course of his life, being so different from mine, seemed interesting even when he was being dull. A middle-class Englishman with his nature would have bored me because I would have known too much about him. Sam I wanted to find out about, and what I found out was likeable. Even when I was thinking 'What an old noodle!' I liked him, and what I liked best was the sense I picked up of the boy he used to be.

He had the calm self-confidence and general benevolence bestowed by a secure and happy childhood. A middle-class adoring mother can sometimes damage her child, but in a peasant family she is more likely to make him: she must get him out of this hard life if she possibly can, even if she loses him in the process. Sam's father owned the patch of land on which they lived (and that, too, contributed to self-confidence, because being raised on your own place, however small, is stabilizing), but it was a property too small to support a family so he had to find work in Trinidad, and then in Venezuela. It was the mother who ran the home, and she gave her son unquestioned precedence over her two daughters (Barry's mother did the same thing and her daughter never quite forgave her).

'We didn't know it,' Sam told me, 'but the food we ate was just what everyone says nowadays is the healthiest: fish, fruit and vegetables, we were never short of those.' They lived right on the sea so escaped the common West Indian overdependence on root vegetables. 'And all that air and exercise. I thought nothing of running five miles to school and five miles back – long-distance running was a craze with us boys, we ran everywhere.' They rode, too. Most people kept a horse (this surprised me) and if a boy wanted to get somewhere in a hurry he could jump on to some neighbour's bare-backed nag without having to ask. And they swam as much as they ran. He marvelled when he remembered how no one fussed when they used to swim out to a little islet about two miles offshore. A very tall, good-looking, even-tempered boy, good at all the local pastimes, crammed with healthy food and plunged by his fond mother into herb baths of which she knew the secrets, Sam was evidently secure among his friends as a leader. When he recalled those happy times he seemed to bring glimpses of them into the room – a whiff of nutmeg-scented sea-breeze, very endearing.

His mother lost him, of course – that wife was her big mistake. He begot two children on her, then could stand it no longer, left for England and his mother never saw him again. She died asking for him, people wrote and told him that. He spoke of it solemnly but placidly: it was a mother's fate, he implied, sad but inevitable.

He did not consider himself a bad son, husband or father for having left. He had kept in touch, sent money, seen to it that his children were educated: he had done what was proper. His son became a doctor and moved to the United States, and they saw each other from time to time. His daughter was unforgiving, 'a stupid girl'. And his wife . . . Thirty-five years after he left Grenada he returned for the first time, for a three-week visit at the invitation of the prime minister. He didn't let his wife know he was coming, but after the first week it occurred to him to drop in on her, still without warning. 'So what happened?' I asked. He shook his head, clicked his tongue, and said slowly and disapprovingly: 'That's a very *cantankerous* woman'. This made me laugh so much that he took offence and provided no more details. Not that he would have been able to provide any of real interest, since he obviously had no conception of the life to which he had condemned that 'stupid' daughter and that 'cantankerous' wife: a convenient ignorance shared by a great number of West Indian husbands and 'baby-fathers' – though many of the women left behind seem to take it calmly.

Our relationship ended gently, the gaps between our meetings becoming gradually longer. The last time we met, after an especially long one (so long that, without regret, I had thought it final), he was slower than usual and seemed abstracted and tired, but not ill. Although we had agreed already that our affair was over, he said 'What about coming to bed?' but I could see he was relieved when I said no. 'The trouble with me,' I said, 'is that the spirit is willing but the flesh is weak. My body has gone against it.' He didn't say 'Mine too', he wouldn't want to go as far as that, but he did say: 'I know, the body does go against things. You can't do anything about that.' And the next thing I heard about him, not very much later, was that he had died suddenly of a heart attack.

You can't miss someone grievously if you haven't seen them or wanted to see them for several months and they had touched only a comparatively small corner of your life, but after his death Sam became more vivid in my mind than many of my more important dead. I saw him with photographic clarity – still can. His gestures, his expressions, the way he walked and sat, his clothes. The seven years of him played through my head with the immediacy of a newsreel: all we said, all we did, perhaps the pattern of our meetings was so repetitive that I couldn't help learning him by heart. I particularly remember the feel of him. His skin was smooth and always seemed to be cool and dry, a pleasant, healthy skin, and his smell was pleasant and healthy. I feel him lying beside me after making love, both of us on our backs, hands linked, arms and legs touching in a friendly way. His physical presence is so clear, even now, that it is almost like a haunt (an amiable one).

The faith Sam had decided to favour was in the transmigration of souls because, he said, how else could one explain why one person had a good life and another a horrid one: they were getting what they had earned in their previous lives, it was obvious. He was displeased when I said that if that were so, how odd that so many black people must have been very wicked in the past. He refused to take it up because, I think, transmigration was promising to him personally. He had, after all, been uncommonly lucky: a little refinement of the soul towards the end and up he would go. That, he once explained to me, was why he had given up meat and hard liquor once he was past sixty. I wish I could hope that Sam was right in expecting to come back to earth for another life. If he could, I doubt whether it would be so rarefied a life as he had aimed for, but it would certainly be several degrees more enjoyable than the one he left, which would make it much better than most. Meanwhile, perhaps because he carried into the beginning of my old age something belonging to younger days, he is still alive in my head, and I am glad of it. Dear Sam.

4

A N IMPORTANT ASPECT of the ebbing of sex was that other things became more interesting. Sex obliterates the individuality of young women more often than it does that of young men, because so much more of a woman than of a man is used by sex. I have tried to believe that most of this difference comes from conditioning, but can't do so. Conditioning reinforces it, but essentially it is a matter of biological function. There is no physical reason why a man shouldn't turn and walk away from any act of sex he performs, whereas every act of sex performed by a woman has the potential of changing her mode of being for the rest of her life. He simply triggers the existence of another human being; she has to build it out of her own physical substance, carry it inside her, bond with it whether she likes it or not – and to say that she has been freed from this by the pill is nonsense. She can prevent it, but only by drastic chemical intervention which throws her body's natural behaviour out of gear. Having bodies designed to bear children means that many generations will have to pass before women are freed from the psychic patterns dictated by their physique, however easy it is for them to swallow a pill; and it is possible that they will never be able to achieve such psychic freedom. Exactly how much of personality is determined by chemistry is at present beyond assessment, but that some of it is can't be doubted. Because of all this, when they are at the peak of their physical activity women often disappear into it, many of them discovering what kind of people they are apart from it only in middle age, some of them never. I had started to have glimpses of myself earlier than most, as a result of being deprived of marriage and child-bearing, but not with the clarity I discovered once sex had fallen right away. My atheism is an example: it became much more firmly established.

I had known for a long time that I did not believe in a god, an attitude which had crystallized when I was at Oxford towards the end of the 1930s and met a man called Duncan at a party. We were not to become friends because it was the end of term, and the term was Duncan's last. He had finished his final exams that day, had already been accepted by the Colonial Service, and would be taking up a post in Cyprus in a few weeks' time. We were drawn to each other, however, left the party together, had dinner and went punting on the river, and the next day we met again and spent the afternoon in his rooms. At that time I was stuck in the unhappiness of betrayed love, feeling shrivelled because it was months since I had heard from Paul. Being in the habit of considering myself unavailable to other men, I told Duncan I was engaged, but I am sure that if we had gone on seeing each other I would have been rescued: he was the most agreeable and intelligent man I had met at Oxford, and the morning after our afternoon together he sent me flowers with a note saying, 'We will see each other again'. We never did. I had two letters from him, the second from Cyprus, and then the war began and I forgot him. Except that I kept, and still keep, one thing he said.

We must have talked at supper about what we believed, because after it, as we walked over grass through the sweet summer night to the place where the punts were moored, I said that though I was unable to believe in the god I had been taught to believe in, I supposed that some kind of First Cause had to be accepted. To which Duncan replied 'Why? Might it not be that beginnings and endings are things we think in terms of simply because our minds are too primitive to conceive of anything else?'

Did I answer? I can remember only tilting my head back and gazing up into the star-filled sky with a feeling of extreme, almost dizzy elation, as though for the first time my eyes were capable of seeing space as it deserved to be seen. I made no attempt to plumb the implications of this idea, but neither did I hesitate to accept it as the truth. And for a long time that was the extent of my thinking about religion.

I was brought back to it when I was beginning to be old by John Updike, when he was analysing (I don't remember where) his own religious belief, and said, or rather wrote: 'Among the repulsions of atheism for me has been its drastic uninterestingness as an intellectual position. Where was the ambiguity, the ingenuity, the humanity (in the Harvard sense) of saying that the universe just happened to happen and that when we're dead we're dead?' This baffled me. Perhaps it is uninteresting intellectually to believe that the nature of the universe is far, far beyond grasping, not only by oneself as an individual but by oneself as a member of our species; but emotionally, or poetically, it seems to me vastly more exciting and more beautiful than exercising any amount of ingenuity in making up fairy stories.

John Updike would agree that our planet is a mere speck in that small part of the universe which we are capable of perceiving, and that *Homo sapiens* has existed for only a tiny fraction of that planet's tiny time, and has not the slightest idea of what 90 per cent of the universe is made of (I like scientists calling what they don't know 'dark matter'); so how can he, or any other intelligent person, fail to agree that men are being absurdly kind to themselves when they suppose that something thought by them is universally relevant (those religious people who believe in one god do seem to see him as universal, not as local to Earth)? Faith – the decision to act as though you believe something you have no reason to believe, hoping that the decision will bring on belief and then you will feel better – that seems to me mumbo-jumbo. I can't feel anything but sure that when men form ideas about God, creation, eternity, they are making no more sense in relation to what lies beyond the range of their comprehension than the cheeping of sparrows. And given that the universe continues to be what it is, regardless of what we believe, and what it is has always been and will continue to be the condition of our existence, why should the thought of our smallness in it be boring – or, for that matter, frightening?

I have heard people bewailing man's landing on the moon, as though before it was touched by an astronaut's foot it was made of silver or mother-of-pearl, and that footprint turned it into grey dust. But the moon never was made of silver or mother-of-pearl, and it still shines as though it were so made. Whether we know less or more about it, it remains itself and continues to reflect the sun's light in a way that is beautiful in men's eyes. Surely the part of life which is within our range, the mere fact of life, is mysterious and exciting enough in itself? And surely the urgent practical necessity of trying to order it so that its cruelties are minimized and its beauties are allowed their fullest possibly play is compelling enough without being seen as a duty laid on us by a god?

People of faith so often seem to forget that a god who gives their lives meaning too often provides them with justification when they want to wipe out other people who believe in other gods, or in nothing. My own belief – that we on our short-lived planet are part of a universe simultaneously perfectly ordinary in that *there it is* and incalculably mysterious in that it is beyond our comprehension – does not feel like believing in nothing and would never make me recruit anyone for slaughter. It feels like a state of infinite possibility, stimulating and enjoyable – not exactly comforting, but acceptable because true. And this remains so when I force myself to think about the most alarming aspect of what I can understand, which is that we will eventually become extinct, differing from the dinosaurs only in contributing a good deal more than they did to our own fate. And it also remains so when I contemplate my personal extinction.

I once had a favourite image for falling asleep which I used when getting into bed felt particularly good. After waiting a minute or two before switching off my lamp, collecting awareness so that I would fully appreciate the embrace of darkness, I turned face downwards, sprawled my arms and legs, and my bed became a raft which floated me out onto the sea of night. It produced a sensation of luxury, the more seductive for being enlivened by an almost imperceptible thread of risk.

Once we at André Deutsch brought out a coffee-table book about beds prefaced by an oddly inappropriate essay by Anthony Burgess. The book was supposed to be in praise of beds, but Burgess said he loathed them because he was afraid of going to sleep and needed to outwit his fear by letting sleep catch him unexpectedly in a chair or on the floor. Lying down on a bed, he felt, was like lying down on a bier from which, if he lost consciousness, he might never get up. (I did question this preface, but André's view was that no one bothered to read prefaces, what mattered was having the man's name on the book, not what he said – a bit of publisher-think which I deplored, but not strongly enough to make a stand.) I have read of people undergoing many things worse than this quirk of Burgess's, but of no ordeal that was harder for me to imagine sharing. Being forced to deny oneself one of the greatest pleasures of everyday life, the natural seal of happiness, the sure escape from sorrow or boredom, the domestication of mystery . . . What an affliction! Could the poor man really have been so savagely haunted by the fear of death? From which it may correctly be deduced that I myself have never been enough troubled by it to want to envisage an afterlife.

What explains irreligiosity? Lack of imagination? Courage? A genetically bestowed pattern of temperament? The first two occur in the religious as well as the irreligious, and the third only shunts the question back through the generations. Religious people of limited intelligence often think that the explanation is licentiousness, a naughty refusal to accept restraints; but many an unbeliever is as scrupulous as any religious person in acknowledging the restrictions and obligations laid on us by sharing the world with others. To the irreligious person the answer seems simple enough, though embarrassing to pronounce: he is more intelligent than his religious brother. But his religious brother sees with equal clarity that the opposite is true, and where is the neutral referee? We must settle, I suppose, for there being in this respect two kinds of person.

My kind enjoys an unfair advantage. In the Western world there are probably nowadays as many people without the religious instinct as with it, but all of them live in societies which developed on lines laid down by believers: everywhere on earth men started by conjuring Powers into being to whom they could turn for direction and control of their behaviour. The mechanism was obviously a necessary one in its time. So we, the irreligious, live within social structures built by the religious, and however critical or resentful we may be of parts of them, no honest atheist would deny that in so far as the saner aspects of religion hold within a society, that society is the better for it. We take a good nibble of our brother's cake before throwing it away.

Right behaviour, to me, is the behaviour taught me by my Christian family: one should do unto one's neighbour as one would like him to do unto one, should turn the other cheek, should not pass on the other side of those in trouble, should be gentle to children, should avoid obsession with material possessions. I have accepted a great deal of Christ's teaching partly because it was given me in childhood by people I loved, and partly because it continues to make sense and the nearer people come to observing it the better I like them (not that they come, or ever have come, very near it, and nor have I). So my piece of my brother's cake is a substantial chunk, and it is covered, what's more, with a layer of icing, because much of the painting and sculpture I love best (and such things matter a lot to me) was made by artists who lived long enough ago to believe that heaven and hell were real. In the Correr Museum in Venice, coming suddenly on Dieric Bouts's little *Madonna Nursing the Child*, I was struck through with delight as I never was by a mother and child by, for example, Picasso or Mary Cassatt, and I cannot remember being more intensely moved by any painting than by Piero della Francesca's *Nativity*.

It is not the artist's skill that works the spell, charming though it is in Bouts's case and awe-inspiring in della Francesca's. It is the selflessness of such art that is magnetic, as it is in a Chinese bronze of the Buddha, a medieval wood-carving of an angel, or an African mask. The person making the object wasn't trying to express his own personality or his own interpretation of appearances; he was trying to represent something outside himself for which he felt the utmost respect, love or dread – to show us this wonderful thing as well as he possibly could. How the purity of this intention makes itself felt in the artefact I don't understand, but it does. You need only compare any halfway respectable Madonna and child from the fourteenth or fifteenth century with even the best modern one to see that it does, and that it is something to do with the artist's taking for granted the truth of what he is representing. From the seventeenth century on there is always a taint of sentimentality or hysteria in religious art, however splendid the technique, and by the twentieth century it soaks the object right through: think of the junkety smugness of Eric Gill! Of course great artists painting non-religious works often attend to what they are making with a respect and love which takes them beyond self and approaches the same purity, but there is no longer a subject strong enough to save the bacon of an artist less than great (Bouts was good, not great).

Early religious music, lovely though much of it is, has a less powerful effect on me: I prefer Bach's instrumental music to his cantatas. The words, I suppose, make the cantatas too dogmatic for me: even the greatest religious poetry and prose leaves me unmoved. The painter of a triptych for an altar did it with dogmatic intent, but his medium is less suited to teaching than words are. Dogmatically, painting is a blunt instrument, so the lily, the goldfinch, the pomegranate, the dove, the mother, the child can all be taken to exist for their own sakes, regardless of their message. Although – baffling paradox – it is precisely their creator's belief in the truth of the message that gives them their force.

My indifference to religious writing is overcome by one majestic exception: the Bible. I was brought up to know both the Old Testament and the New fairly well, and am still glad of it. The beauty of the language has much to do with this, but my maternal grandmother's gift for reading aloud to children has much more. She left us in no doubt that we were listening to very *special* true stories – special because their truth concerned us closely. Nowadays, if I read the story of Joseph and his brethren, or of Shadrach, Meshach and Abednego, or of the nativity, or of the raising of Lazarus, something odd but enjoyable happens. This laptop offers the choice of a number of different typefaces and I can tell it which to use with a touch of a finger. When I read those stories it is as though at a finger-touch my adult mind is replaced by my child mind. There go the familiar stories, unfolding before my eyes, sounding and looking just as they sounded and looked when Gran read them to me. Of course I can still think about them in an adult way and of course it does not mean that I kneel down and worship God: I love the story of how he called Samuel in the night, but he still doesn't call me. It is simply that those stories are engraved in my imagination so deeply that they can't be erased by disbelief. They have, in fact, nothing to do with belief or disbelief as I mean the words now, but they restore the sensation of belief as it used to be in the same way that Christmas carols do. They still trail a whiff of that old special importance, to be caught by some part of my awareness which is usually dormant. The Bible was shown to me through the prism of belief, the absolute belief of those who wrote it and the diluted but still real belief of my grandmother, who did not think God was like the Jehovah of the Jews but still believed that he existed, and who probably saw Jesus's son-ship, immaculate conception and so on as metaphor but still held that in order to be good people we must believe in his divinity. Coming to me in this persuasive way it did certainly influence the way I was to see life; yet it failed to convince me of its central teaching. How, then, does the written word work? What part of a reader absorbs it – or should that be a double question: what part of a reader absorbs what part of a text?

I think that underneath, or alongside, a reader's conscious response to a text, whatever is needy in him is taking in whatever the text offers to assuage that need.

For example, I have a much younger friend, Sally, who when her children were just beginning to read became annoyed because so many of the books written for them were about animals: it was a mouse, not a child, which disobeyed its mother and got into trouble, a rabbit who raided the kitchen garden, an elephant who became king. Why, she asked, was she expected to feed her children on this pap of fantasy instead of on stories about real life? The answer, it seems to me, is that children respond to animal protagonists because when very small what they need is not to discover and recognize 'real life', but to discover and recognize their own feelings. Take a pair of well-known animal characters, Piglet and Tigger, in *The House at Pooh Corner*. Piglet is an anxious, timid little person, capable of being brave if he absolutely has to be, but only at great cost to himself, and Tigger is so exuberantly bouncy that he can be a nuisance. Both of them express things which a child discovers and recognizes with pleasure because they exist within himself. If those characteristics were expressed on the page by a child, they would belong to that child and would call for the use of the kind of critical faculty one employs vis-à-vis another person. Expressed by a 'made up' animal (I have yet to meet a child so simple-minded that it doesn't know perfectly well that animals don't talk in human language), they slip past the critical faculty into the undergrowth of feelings which need so urgently to be sorted out and understood. (When a story about people, not animals, is *popular* with the very young – the Postman Pat stories, for example – the people are drawn in such an unrealistic way that they might as well be animals.) What was important for Sally's little children was not to be given only sensible, real-life stories, but to have plenty of them about for when they began to need them.

When I was in my early teens I used to sink luxuriously into a romantic novel as though into a hot bath, and couldn't have too many of them. I never believed, however, that anyone in real life looked or behaved like the heroes and heroines of those books. What I needed was to practise the sensations of sex – to indulge in a kind of non-genital masturbation – because I was a steamy girl forbidden by the society in which I lived to make love. Perhaps because I was lucky enough also to have plenty of good writing at my disposal, the romantic novels did not make a romantic lover of me: it was only the 'nyum-nyum' sensations I needed, and I gave no more credence to their soppy message than a young child gives to a rabbit's little blue coat. Or than I myself gave to the Holy Trinity, first met at a time when I had taken my fill of baby-stories about animals and before I had begun to hunger for the sexy taste of romances, when I was just starting to feel my appetite for real life.

5

SO HERE I go, into advanced old age, towards my inevitable and no longer distant end, without the 'support' of religion and having to face the prospect ahead in all its bald reality. What are my feelings about that? I turn for enlightenment to the people I know who have gone ahead of me.

Most of the women on both sides of my family live into their nineties, keeping their wits about them. None of them has ever had to go into an old person's home, or has even had to employ live-in carers. All the married ones outlived their husbands and had daughters to see them through their last days, and the few who did their dying in hospital were there for only a day or two. I have become sharply aware of how lucky we have been in that respect, since the old age and death of my closest friend has taught me how much it costs to employ skilled home nursing, or to take refuge in a 'home' with staff as kind and understanding as they are efficient (no such place exists but some are nearer to it than others, usually because they cost hair-raising sums). No one in my family could have afforded either alternative for more than a week or so. What everyone wants is to live until the end in their own home, with the companionship of someone they love and trust. That is what my lot wanted and achieved, including my widowed mother, although I still feel guilty at the knowledge that in her case this happy conclusion was achieved by a narrow squeak.

By the time she was ninety-two I was seventy. She was deaf,

blind in one eye and depending on a contact lens for sight in the other, so arthritic in her hips that she could hardly walk, and in her right arm that it was almost useless. She also had angina (still mild and infrequent) and vertigo (horribly trying and not infrequent). I was living in London, still by great good luck working, sharing a flat with an old friend who had barely enough money to cover his keep, while I had never earned enough to save a penny. Nothing would have made my mother confess that she longed to have me at home with her in Norfolk, but I knew that she did, and I believed that if you are the child of a loving, reliable and generously undemanding woman you owe her this consolation in her last years. I think that for people to look after their children when they are young, and to be looked after by them when they are old, is the natural order of events – although stupid or perverse parents can dislocate it. My mother was not stupid or perverse.

I ought, of course, to have seen to it that in the past I was paid what was due to me for my skills so that I could have bought a house in which, eventually, I could have accommodated my mother, instead of continuing in a small flat which an extraordinarily generous cousin let me have for a peppercorn rent. Foreseeing my mother's old age, I did once raise the matter with André Deutsch (who was justified in taking more out of our firm than he allowed me because without him it would not have existed, but who allowed the discrepancy to become too great, being unable to resist taking advantage of my idiocy about money. No doubt if I had kicked and screamed I could have brought him to heel, but I was too lazy to face the hassle.). He thought, as usual, that the firm could not afford to increase my salary, but he consulted a money-wise friend who said that if I could find a suitable house, he could arrange for an insurance company to buy it, whereupon I could occupy it while I lived on advantageous terms which I have now forgotten. I found a charming little house with a surprisingly large garden and a ground floor which could become a flat for my mother, but the insurance company's surveyor declared it a bad risk because it was at the end of a row and had a bulge. It did not have even a hint of a bulge, nor has it now, a great many years later

(I look carefully whenever I pass it), but I was not unwilling to be discouraged. Given support in this sensible project I would have pursued it happily enough, but without support my underlying reluctance to change my congenial way of life won the day, and I failed to look for another house.

·And that is where the guilt is. There was a real, financial reason why it would have been unwise to give up my job and my London life; but no doubt my mother and I could have managed if we had absolutely had to. The reason was not as compelling as my strong disinclination to do so.

I was being no more selfish than my mother had been when her mother, at the age of ninety-four, was approaching death. My mother wanted to visit my sister in Southern Rhodesia, as it then was. Ought she to postpone the visit, given Gran's condition? She asked herself the question, then reported that Aunt Joyce, who lived with Gran and was carrying the full weight of her illness, had agreed that the postponement might alarm Gran by betraying that she was expected to die. I knew this was rationalization: that my mother was terrified of being there for the death and was hoping it would happen in her absence, as it did. All her life she had been the spoilt youngest daughter, the wilful one who could get away with things, unlike her responsible elders. I felt ashamed for her – perhaps even shocked – but not able to blame her. I was not seeing much of her at the time and thought I was free of family dependency, but that uncanny genetic closeness which forces one to feel in one's nerves what one's nearest kin are feeling in theirs was at work. And I am still unable to make her selfishness then feel like an excuse for my own.

Finally, however, the discomfort of guilt became too much for me, so I decided on a compromise between my disinclination to uproot and what I couldn't help seeing as my duty. I decided to spend four days – the weekend and a shopping day – with my mother for every three days in London, shuttling by car in good weather and by rail when the roads threatened to be bad. She had people to keep an eye on her during the week: Eileen Barry, a home help kind and reliable far beyond the call of duty, every morning;

Sid Pooley, who chopped logs and did rough work in the garden every afternoon, while his wife Ruby mowed the lawns, picked and arranged flowers, and kept the bird-table supplied; and Myra, who cooked her supper, did her washing and ironing, and shopped for her (though rarely to my mother's satisfaction because, naturally enough, she bought things at shops she would visit anyway while catering for her family, and they were not to my mother's taste). At that time, in the country, such unprofessional but reliable help was not expensive – indeed, the home help was supplied free by the social services (this, I hear, has been discontinued).

Having announced my four-nights/three-nights plan I returned to London and collapsed into bed feeling horribly ill, with a temperature so low that I thought the thermometer must be broken; but once that involuntary protest was over I hit my stride, becoming quite good at suspending my life, which is what has to be done when living with an old person. You buy and cook the food that suits her, eat it at her set mealtimes, work in the garden according to her instructions, put your own work aside, don't listen to music because her hearing aid distorts it, and talk almost exclusively about her interests. She is no longer able to adapt to other people's needs and tastes, and you are there to enable her to indulge her own. Luckily gardening, my mother's great passion, is genuinely an interest of mine, and so is making things. All she could make by then, because of limited eyesight and rheumatic hands, was knitted garments, but her knitting was adventurous and I truly enjoyed discussing whether purple should be introduced, or a new pattern embarked on for the yoke. While my mother was well there was real pleasure in seeing her contented, and knowing she was more fully so because of my presence.

But she was not always well. Sometimes she went grey in the face and quietly slipped one of her 'heart pills' under her tongue; more often she had a less dangerous but more distressing attack of vertigo. She was clever at keeping her medicaments for this in strategic places, so that whether a 'dizzy' came on in the drawing room, the kitchen, her bedroom or the bathroom she could get herself without too much trouble into a chair with the necessary equipment. But gradually the length and intensity of the attacks increased, and the occasions on which I was thankful that I had been there to help her became more frequent. This did not lessen my anxiety at the prospect of such crises – indeed, it increased. If I woke during the night worry would start to nag, and I could rarely go to sleep again. I knew her usual movements very well: how she almost always shuffled along to the lavatory at about four in the morning (only the most acute emergency could make her use the commode I persuaded her to keep in her bedroom); how she began the slow process of washing and dressing at about six-thirty. If I didn't hear these sounds . . . was it because I had missed them, or was something wrong? I would have to get up and check. If I heard her cough, was it just an ordinary cough or was it the first retching of a vertigo? I had to listen tensely until its nature became clear. The anxiety seemed nearer to some kind of animal panic than anything rational. After all, I knew that I could help her through a vertigo, and even supposing it were a heart attack and she died of it, I knew that this sooner-rather-than-later inevitable event would be the timely conclusion of a long and good life, not a tragedy. But still, the way she was a little older, a little more helpless, a little more battered by that wretched vertigo with every week that passed – the fact that death was, so to speak, up in the attic of her house, waiting to come down and do something cruelly and fatally painful to her – frightened me.

I had been observing the four-night/three-night plan for about a year before I realized quite how much it frightened me. Of course it was tiring, even without the worry. I was working hard on my London days, so I never had time to be on my own and do my own things in my own home. I began to feel heavily weary. I drove to work every day, leaving my car in a garage about fifteen minutes walk away from the office – a pleasant walk, taking me through Russell Square, which I had always enjoyed. Now it began to seem exhausting; my feet seemed less manageable than they ought to be so I had to be careful not to stumble; I even began to dread it. And one weekend with my mother I felt so bad-tempered, so dreary, so near to irrational tears, that I decided I must see my doctor as soon as I got home. High blood pressure, he said: very much too high. This was both alarming and a relief: alarming because I had a secret dread of having a stroke, a relief because there was a real reason for feeling lousy, it was not just my imagination. The doctor said it was not surprising that I was suffering from stress and that I must take a proper holiday, and I added a scold to myself about my weight, which I hadn't bothered to check for months: it had gone up to twelve and a half stone! So my sister kindly came over from Zimbabwe for five weeks to be with my mother, and I stayed in my own dear bed for a week, then went for a week to a luxurious health clinic to start the process of weight-loss (successfully continued on my own). Once my blood pressure was back to normal and I was feeling well again – better than I had felt for years – I decided that I would not go on with the unbroken four/three plan, but would keep every third weekend to myself in London. This made sense, but it renewed guilt. In London I was able to shrug off anxiety and think about my own concerns (even enjoy them more than I used to because of having had to turn my back on them), but the night-time worries when I was staying with my mother were sharper than ever.

'I am not afraid of death.' My mother said this, and showed that she really was less afraid than many people by the calm way she discussed what would happen once she was gone. I believe the same is true of myself – but there are words which follow that statement so often that they have become a cliché: 'It's dying that I'm afraid of.' When dying is actually in sight, those words become shockingly true. My mother was not afraid of being dead, but when an attack of angina made her unable to breathe she was very frightened indeed. I was not afraid of her being dead, but I was terrified of the process of her dying.

I had seen only one dead person – and what a ridiculous state of affairs that was: that a woman in her seventies should have seen only one cadaver! Surely there has never been a taboo more senseless than our modern one on death. My only dead person was André Deutsch's ninety-two-year-old mother, who was found dead by her home help when André happened to be abroad. After the police had her body carried off to the coroner's mortuary they tracked down André's secretary and me and asked if one of us would identify the body. We decided to do it together.

On the way to the mortuary I recalled various reassuring descriptions of dead bodies: how they seemed empty and nothing to do with the person who had left them, and how beautiful faces become in the austere serenity of death. I wanted reassurance because I expected us to be in the same room as the body and to stand beside it while an attendant turned back a sheet covering its face, but that was not how it was done. We were taken into a narrow room with a large plate-glass window curtained with cheap sage-green damask. The curtain was drawn back and there was the body on the other side of the glass, lying in a box and covered up to the neck with a kind of bedspread of purple velour.

The words I spoke involuntarily were: 'Oh *poor* little Maria!' It did not look as though it had nothing to do with her, nor was it austerely serene. What was lying there was poor little Maria with her hair in a mess and her face grubby, looking as though she were in a state of great bewilderment and dejection because something too unkind for words had been done to her. It was a comfort to remember that she was dead, and therefore couldn't possibly be feeling how she looked. But it was not a comfort to be shown so clearly that my favourite image of floating out to sea at night was nonsense. What Maria's body demonstrated was that even a quick dying can be *very nasty*.

In other ways the coroner's domain was surprisingly bracing. We approached it through a walled yard where white vans with their rear windows painted out were coming and going. One of them was backed up close to a small unloading bay. It might have been delivering groceries, but was in fact delivering a body. The men who drove, loaded and unloaded the vans, several of whom were drinking tea in a room off the passage through which we entered, were middle-aged to elderly and looked tough and slightly ribald. They glanced at us sideways as we passed the door of their room, and in their eyes was the faintest hint – an almost imperceptible gleam – of mockery. *They knew.* They knew that however nasty death may be while it is happening, it is too ordinary an event to make a fuss about. Most of them, no doubt, went about their work soberly, but that hint of a gleam suggested that some of them might enjoy doing some flippancy to a corpse – using its navel as an ashtray, perhaps – imagining as they did it the horror of a squeamish observer. They would probably respect the grief of the bereaved, but squeamishness they would despise. Having shed it, they had moved into a category apart.

My own reaction to this place where dead bodies were all in the day's work had something prurient about it. If the men in the room off the entrance passage looked at me out of the corners of their eyes, so did I at them: I did not want to betray the extent of my curiosity, did not want to be caught at it. My awareness of the cadavers hidden in the white vans and in the accommodation specially designed for them on Maria's side of the plate-glass window, was sharp. Had I been a dog my ears would have been pricked and my hackles up. I think this odd excitement was connected at some level with the violent recoil from dead animals which seized me in childhood when I unexpectedly came on a decaying corpse hidden in long grass, or caught in a trap, or on one of those macabre gamekeeper's 'larders', the wires on which they strung up the corpses of 'vermin' they had trapped or shot. I often went a long way round to avoid passing one of those – in fact I think they are the reason why I have never much enjoyed walking through a wood. The two reactions seem like opposites, but could be the opposite sides of the same coin. Whatever the truth, I did call up that mortuary and those dead animals when trying to reason myself out of the night terrors in my mother's house: 'Calm down, this is not a matter of the mind saying "Alas, she will soon be dead and gone" – to that there is a whole set of other reactions of quite a different kind. This is simply a matter of flesh shuddering because flesh rots, and it is possible not only to acknowledge the ordinariness of that dissolution, but also to feel it.' Not long afterwards I wrote a poem – or perhaps more accurately a short statement – as a result of that visit to the mortuary, which had contributed a good deal to my attitude towards death.

I have learnt to recognize the plain white vans with painted-out
    back windows
and the black ones, equally discreet, standing at those back-
    street doors
which have a never-opened look (misleading).

The white vans carry dead junkies picked up in alleys, old
    women
found frozen when the neighbours began to wonder and called
    the cops,
the man who stayed late at his office to hang himself, the boy
stabbed in a sudden brawl outside a disco.

The black vans, early every morning, deliver coffins to
    mortuaries.

Men who handle corpses despise people who don't.
Why? How? What? Where? cry the hearts of the bereaved,
and the men who handle corpses lower their eyelids over
looks of secret but impatient ribaldry.
A few of them are necrophiliacs onto a good thing, but most
are normal men who have learnt from handling death
that it tells nothing because it has nothing to tell, there is
    nothing to it.

When I first recognized those vans I waited for my skin to
    crawl.
I am still surprised that they cheer me up.
'There goes death' I think when I see one. 'There it goes about
    its daily work,
and they think I don't see it. They think they are the only ones
with the nerve to know how ordinary it is.'

Recognition of a van: no more familiarity than that,
and already the look I give my unrecognizing friend
has in it, I suspect, a touch of secret but impatient ribaldry.

When the time came for my mother to die, she was almost unbelievably lucky – and therefore I was, too. On the day before her ninety-sixth birthday she walked on her two sticks down to the end of her garden, to oversee the planting of a new eucalyptus tree by Sid Pooley. Halfway through the planting he thought she looked not quite herself. 'Are you all right?' he asked, and she said she was feeling a bit unsteady and had better go back to the house. He helped her back, settled her in her chair, and called Eileen Barry, her home help, who came at once and recognized heart failure when she saw it. Eileen got her to the local cottage hospital and called me – by then it was 8.30 in the evening – saying it would probably be a good thing if I got there first thing next morning: no, she didn't think it was necessary for me to come straight away. I reached the hospital very early and found that my brother and my mother's favourite niece, both of whom lived fairly near, were already there. Soon after her death I again wrote a kind of poem describing it, which seems to me to belong here.

THE GIFT

It took my mother two days to die, the first of them cruel
as her body, ninety-five years old, crashed beyond repair.
I found her, 'an emergency' behind screens in a crowded ward,
jaw dropped, tongue lolling, eyes unseeing.
Unconscious? No. When about to vomit she gasped 'Basin!'
She was aware of what she was having to endure.

I put my hand on hers. Her head shifted, eyelids heaved up.
Her eyes focused.
Out of deep in that dying woman came a great flash
of recognition and of utmost joy.

My brother was there. Later he said,
'That was a very beautiful smile she gave you.'
It was the love I had never doubted flaming into visibility.
I *saw* what I had always believed in.

Next morning: quietness, sleep,
intervals of murmured talk.
'She is better!'
'She is feeling much better,' said the kind nurse,
'but she is still very very ill.'
I understood the warning and that what seemed miracle was
    morphine.

What did I feel? Like Siamese twins, one wanting her never to
    die,
the other dismayed at the thought of renewed life,
of having to go on dreading pain for her, go on foreseeing
her increasing helplessness and my guilt
at not giving up my life to be with her all the time.
What I felt was bad at being in two minds; but only for a
    while, because
perched in my skull above this conflict there was a referee
saying, 'Neither of you can win so shut up
and get on with doing whatever comes next.'

Her collapsed body eased, she was disconcerting to be with
because so alive.
On the edge of ceasing to exist
there she was, herself, tired but perfectly ordinary,
telling me what to do with her dog and where to find her will.
When my cousin protested 'But you'll soon be back home' she
    was cross.
'Don't be absurd,' she said, 'I could go any minute.'

Then, after a long sleep, she turned her head a little and said,
'Did I tell you that last week Jack drove me
to the nursery garden, to buy that eucalyptus?'
I too loved that garden and the drive through country
we had both known all our lives.
'You told me he was going to,' I said. 'Was it fun?'

She answered dreamily – her last words before sleeping again
out of which sleep she didn't wake:
'It was absolutely divine.'

6

Now that I am only seven years younger than my mother when she died, to what extent am I either supported by what I have learnt about dying, or made apprehensive about it? I have received a good deal of reassurance of a slightly wobbly kind, and also a cause for worry.

The reassurance concerns the actual process of dying. There cannot be many families in which so many people have been lucky in this respect as mine has been. Even the least lucky were spared the worst horrors of it (which can, of course and alas, be very bad). My maternal grandmother had to endure several months of distressing bedridden feebleness owing to prolonged heart failure, but she had a daughter to help her through it at home and that daughter was able to report that the attack which finally killed her was a good deal less disagreeable than some of those that she survived. My father had to endure one week that was certainly horrible, though no one could be sure how aware he was of its horribleness: he had a cerebral haemorrhage which deprived him of speech and left him obviously extremely confused. Once settled in hospital he could respond normally when offered a basin to wash in or a meal to eat, and when you came into his room he looked pleased to see you and attempted to speak; but he could find no words and an expression of distress followed by hope-lessness appeared on his face. I got the impression that he knew something was dreadfully wrong, was miserable about it, then thought, 'Oh well, it seems I can't do anything about it so I'd better stop trying.' The doctor saw no possibility of repair to the damage, but found him physically strong, which was alarming: my mother and I couldn't bring ourselves to speak about the possibility of his living for a long time in this condition. But a second haemorrhage struck, killing him instantly, and whatever he was aware of suffering during the intervening days, there were only six of them.

About the deaths of my paternal grandparents, my father's siblings and my mother's father I know little, but nothing was ever said to suggest that they were particularly harrowing, while on my mother's side one sister had a stroke when she was eighty-three from which she died almost at once without recovering consciousness; another aged ninety-four was distressed for less than an hour, then died in a daughter's arms just after saying that she was now feeling much better; another went quietly after becoming increasingly weak and dozy for about three weeks; and their brother, a lucky man whose luck held to the very end, was on his horse at a meet of the Norwich Stag-hounds at the age of eighty-two, talking with friends, when flop! and he fell off his horse stone dead in the middle of a laugh. The eldest of my cousins had similar luck, falling down dead as she was making a cup of tea.

My brother, who died last year, was less lucky, but not because he was painfully ill for a long time, or afraid of death. His trouble was that he resented it because he loved his life so passionately. He was eighty-five. He knew death was coming because, having stubbornly refused to pay attention to various ailments of old age which were obvious to his anxious wife and other people, he was finally forced to recognize that his appetite had gone and that he was feeling dreadfully cold. But he still longed to be out messing about with his boats – he lived on the Norfolk coast in a place he adored and to have to leave that place and its occupations seemed to him the worst possible fate.

One afternoon not long before he died he took me out for a sail. His house is just inland from Blakeney Point, a long spit of sand dunes that runs parallel to the shore, partially enclosing a stretch of water which at low tide becomes a river snaking its way out to sea through exposed mud, but at high tide is a wide, sheltered expanse busy with small sailing boats and easily navigated by larger ones provided they are careful to observe the markers showing where the deeper channels run. On that day there was hardly a breath of wind. Sky and water were mother-of-pearl and the breasts of doves, a blend of soft blues and pinks so delicate that I had never seen its like. A small group of sailing dinghies was lying becalmed, hoping to be able to start a race (we, who were motoring, gave one of them which had no outboard engine a tow to join the group). None of the people lounging at the tiller of these little boats looked impatient or bored, because no one could mind being becalmed in the middle of so much loveliness. When we were some way past them, near the end of the Point, almost in the open sea, a tiny popple began under our hull and and a cat's paw of breeze – a kitten's paw, more like it – just ruffled the water's surface enough for sunlight to start twinkling off the edges of each ripple; I was once told that fishermen at Aldeburgh used to call that effect of light 'tinkling cymbals'. I shall always think of it as that, and no tinkling cymbals I ever saw were better than those we moved through when Andrew was at last able to hoist canvas and very, very gently we started to sail. We didn't talk much. Although we didn't often see each other and differed widely in many of our opinions, he and I had never lost touch with the closeness we had enjoyed in early childhood and there was much that we could understand about each other without words. That afternoon was brimming with a loveliness peculiar to that particular place; he knew that I was appreciating it, and I knew without any doubt how profoundly he was penetrated by it. He was a man who, with the help of the right wife, had finally found himself the place and the life that fulfilled him, and lived it with a completeness and intensity more often seen in an artist than in someone who should have been a farmer, had to become an army officer, and ended by teaching people sailing, and growing oysters, on the edge of the North Sea. What filled him as death approached was not fear of whatever physical battering he would have to endure (in fact there was not, at the end, any of that), but grief at having to say goodbye to what he could never have enough of.

Such a grief, it seems to me, is proof of a good, or at least an agreeable, life, and ought therefore to be something for which one is grateful – provided, of course, that one has not been cut off untimely, and I know that my brother agreed with me that once past eighty one has no right to complain about dying, because he said so. I guess that if I am given the time for it, I too shall feel at least a little of it, and hope to remember that it is simply what one has to pay for what one has enjoyed.

So: I have inherited a good chance of going fairly easily, and I have found it easy to think myself into a reasonable attitude towards death. It is not surprising, therefore, that I spend no time worrying about it. When I worry, it is about living with the body's failures, because experience has shown me that when that ordeal is less hard than it might have been, it is usually because of the presence of a daughter. And I have no daughter. Barry, the person closest to me – we became lovers sixty-three years ago and started sharing this flat eight years later – has beaten me to physical collapse, so that I have to look after him. And I haven't got the money to pay for care of any kind. If I don't have the luck to fall down dead while still able-bodied, as my uncle and my cousin did (and that luck certainly can only be hoped for, not counted on), it is going to be the geriatric ward for me.

Fortunately, if a prospect is bleak enough the mind jibs at dwelling on it. It's not a matter of *choosing* not to think about it, more of *not being able* to do so. Whatever happens, I will get through it somehow, so why fuss? Now that I have attempted to assess my own attitude, that seems to be it. Those last miserable weeks or months (may it not be years!) when you are unable to look after yourself are so disagreeable anyway that it hardly matters how they are spent. My oldest friend died this year, my age, daughterless like me but with enough money first for carers visiting her home, then for a nursing home reckoned to be an exceptionally good one, which given what it cost it damn well should have been. From time to time, in emergencies, she also had to spend a week or so in hospital, in wards full of other ancient people, and she didn't seem to be any unhappier there than she was in the expensive 'home'. The one real drawback to a ward, I felt, was that the nursing was better there so they were more likely to haul you back from the brink to suffer further misery than they were at the 'home'. She, on the other hand, was always glad when hauled back. Perhaps when one comes to it one always is? By the time I've learnt whether that is true for me I shall be past handing on the news.

That is all I have to say about the event of death and what I feel about it in advance, so now I shall move on – or perhaps 'over' is more exact – to the experience of living during one's last years.

7

WHAT HAPPENS TODAY is, of course, closely interwoven with what happened yesterday, being simply a continuation of the same process: only those old people afflicted with senile dementia move on to another plane. For the rest of us, as we have sown, so do we reap. And one of the best parts of my harvest comes from a lucky piece of sowing a long time ago.

Soon after the event described on page 568, when I first had to accept the fact that I was on the wane sexually, Barry Reckord, my lover-turned-just-friend, decided to take a play of his, *White Witch*, to Jamaica. All but one of the people in the play are Jamaicans, so those parts could be cast when he got there, but the 'witch' herself is English, so her interpreter had to be found here and taken with him. He couldn't afford an established actor, so it had to be someone young and inexperienced who was going to be offered the thrill of this big and juicy part, and who would probably be excited enough by it to take off happily for several months in the Caribbean on very little money.

Almost the first he auditioned was a farmer's daughter from Somerset, Sally Cary, who read the part well and was pretty enough for it, although to my mind her looks ought to have been a touch more extreme and eccentric. Barry liked them, however, and judged (rightly) that she would be capable of expressing the part's character once on stage. So off they went, and the production was successful. I was not surprised when it became apparent from Barry's letters that he and Sally had slipped into an affair.

When they got back to England I was, however, slightly surprised to see how serious it was – certainly very far from being a passing flutter. But that was explained almost at once. Barry and I are similar in our responses to intelligence, honesty and generosity, so when it turned out that Sally was one of the nicest young women – one of the nicest people – I had ever met, I had no trouble understanding why he loved her. Certainly if I had still been in a physical relationship with him it would have pained me to see them together, but because by then I had fully acknowledged within myself that sex between us was gone for good, it didn't worry me. It was a great piece of luck that this important shift in our relationship had happened before Sally came into our lives.

She found herself a bedsitter not far from us, and returned to the nerve-racking routine of auditions, getting work so rarely that paying for her room was not easy. Her parents, though both from farming families as well as being farmers themselves, had apparently begun to resent the rigours of their life enough to want to rescue their three daughters from it. The two elder girls had married Americans, and Sally, with her good contralto voice and gift for acting, had been firmly pointed towards a career on the stage. She said that her father positively discouraged her from taking an interest in the farm, and she really seemed to know little about it: I used to tease her for not knowing the difference between wheat and barley. From school she went on to an acting school, and she was still taking singing lessons.

Quite soon it occurred to me that, since she was spending almost every night in Barry's bed, keeping on her bedsitter was a waste of money, so I suggested that she should move in with us. It seemed to me that I would enjoy having her with us, and so I did. I know people thought our *ménage à trois* odd, though whether I acquired undeserved merit for generosity, or disapproval for loose morals, I could never tell because no one was ever impolite enough to comment. I suspect there was more of the former than the latter, given that no one could live through the 1960s without at least hearing possessiveness condemned, even if they didn't condemn it themselves. It is true that many people are so neurotically possessive that they can't bear seeing someone enjoying something even if they don't want it for themselves, but I was not, and still am not, possessive like that, not because I had trained myself out of it but simply because I wasn't made that way – luck, not virtue, for which I am grateful, having often witnessed the miseries of jealousy. When Sally joined us what I felt was that now I had a lovely new friend in the house, as well as a darling old one, and the next two years or so were some of the happiest I can remember.

That stage came to an end when Sally's father's health deteriorated. She had already given up singing lessons (her teacher had said she ought to write I WANT TO BE THE BEST CONTRALTO IN THE WORLD and stick it up above her mirror, and she had thought, 'How bloody silly! I don't in the least want to be the best contralto in the world'); and although she enjoyed acting she was not obsessed by it and detested the often humiliating ordeal of auditions. She therefore came to the conclusion that she ought to go home and help her father, to which end she signed up for a course on farm management at Cirencester. I think I missed her almost as much as Barry did, but by that time friendship had consolidated into a sense of belonging together like family, so that there was no question of 'losing' her, not even when at Cirencester she met Henry Bagenal and they decided to get married. Henry, being a warm-hearted and wise young man very much liked by both Barry and me, simply joined the family, so to speak. On Mr Cary's death the two of them took over the farm, and when Jessamy and Beauchamp were born it was almost as though Barry had acquired two grandchildren, and me too to a slightly lesser degree.

So now, in my old age, although I have not in fact got a daughter and grandchildren, I *have* got people who are near to filling those roles. One of the most impressive things about Sally has been that although she didn't seem to be unusually drawn to children before she married, once she had them she opened out into motherhood with astonishing completeness, yet without losing herself. She was, for instance, determined to breastfeed her babies and to go on doing so until they chose to give it up. Jessamy, her first child, continued to return to the breast when she needed to be comforted well into her third year, by which time she could understand and agree that it must be passed on to her little brother because he couldn't do without it while she could. All the usual arguments had been brought to bear on Sally – it was unnecessary, it was indecent, it would tie her down, it would wear her out, and above all it would make the child neurotically dependent on her – and she had disregarded them. What in fact happened was that conveniently portable Jess was absorbed into adult life instead of imprisoning her mother in the nursery, then developed into a child so secure that her self-confidence and independence were remarkable, and has now become a young adult who leaves us all gaping with admiration and envy as she sails triumphantly into her career as a doctor, living – to our great good luck – in a flat five minutes' walk from us. And her brother Beachy, in his very different way, is equally beautiful and successful, while their mother, who has never for a moment failed either of them and is as much loved as she is loving, simultaneously built herself a full-time career in the organic food movement. Her two children are far from being the only remarkably attractive young people of my close acquaintance – I have nephews, nieces, great-nephews and great-nieces, all of whom make nonsense of gloomy forebodings about modern youth – but they are the two I see most often, so it is they who seem to symbolize my good fortune in this respect.

What is so good about it is not just the affection young people inspire and how interesting their lives are to watch. They also, just by being there, provide a useful counteraction to a disagreeable element in an old person's life. We tend to become convinced that everything is getting worse simply because within our own boundaries things *are* doing so. We are becoming less able to do things we would like to do, can hear less, see less, eat less, hurt more, our friends die, we know that we ourselves will soon be dead . . . It's not surprising, perhaps, that we easily slide into a general pessimism about life, but it is very boring and it makes dreary last years even drearier. Whereas if, flitting in and out of our awareness, there are people who are *beginning,* to whom the years ahead are long and full of who knows what, it is a reminder – indeed it enables us actually to feel again – that we are not just dots at the end of thin black lines projecting into nothingness, but are parts of the broad, many-coloured river teeming with beginnings, ripenings, decayings, new beginnings – are still parts of it, and our dying will be part of it just as these children's being young is, so while we still have the equipment to see this, let us not waste our time grizzling.

And if we are lucky enough, as I am, to be from time to time in quite close contact with young people, they can sometimes make it easier to hang on to this notion when they function, as every person does vis-à-vis every other person they come up against, as a mirror.

Always we are being reflected in the eyes of others. Are we silly or sensible, stupid or clever, bad or good, unattractive or sexy . . . ? We never stop being at least slightly aware of, if not actively searching for, answers to such questions, and are either deflated or elated, in extreme cases ruined or saved, by what we get. So if when you are old a beloved child happens to look at you as if he or she thinks (even if mistakenly!) that you are wise and kind: what a blessing! It's not that such a fleeting glimpse of yourself can convert you into wiseness and kindness in any enduring way; more like a good session of reflexology which, although it can cure nothing, does make you feel like a better person while it's going on and for an hour or two afterwards, and even that is well worth having.

The more frequent such shots of self-esteem are, the more valuable they become, so there is a risk – remote, but possible – of their becoming addictive. An old person who doesn't enjoy having young people in her life must be a curmudgeon, but it is extremely important that she should remember that risk and watch her step. Or he, his. Not long ago I sat at dinner next to a lively man in his late sixties or early seventies who announced blithely that he got on very well with young people, he didn't know why but they seemed to feel as though he were the same age as they were. And as he spoke his intelligent face slid into a fatuous smile. Oh, you poor dear! is what I felt. Then – it was unkind of me, and almost certainly useless – I told a little story from my own experience.

When I was eighteen or nineteen we were all surprised to learn that a man who lived near us had got married. It had been assumed that he was a confirmed bachelor because he had reached the age of (I think) forty-nine as an apparently contented single man, a condition attributed to his dimness, not to any suspicion of his being gay. People were pleased for him when they learnt that he had found a wife, a suitable woman in her mid-forties, but there was a touch of amusement in the way they discussed it. There had been enough talk about it for me to be interested when I went to a dance and saw them there, just back from their honeymoon. I watched them take to the floor together, two small, sandy-haired, plain but cheerful-looking *old people* – no, more than cheerful-looking, rapturously happy. They were glowing. They were gazing into each other's eyes. They had shut their eyes and were dancing cheek pressed to cheek. *And it was disgusting.* 'I suppose,' I thought, 'that old people must still make love [in those days it didn't occur to us to say fuck], but they ought to have the decency not to show it.' And I was a kind, well brought-up girl who would not have dreamt of betraying that response if I had been face to face with them.

It does seem to me that the young nowadays are often more sophisticated than I used to be, and that many of them – certainly my own darlings – relate to their elders more easily than we did; but I am convinced that one should never, never *expect* them to want one's company, or make the kind of claims on them that one makes on a friend of one's own age. Enjoy whatever they are generous enough to offer, and leave it at that.

8

As well as relationships there are, of course, activities, which are almost as important. There was a time, about twenty years ago, when if you lived in London it was possible to take, almost for free, evening classes in a vast number of subjects. For years I had felt snobbishly that such activities were not for me, but when I became too fat to find ready-made clothes I liked in any shop I could afford, it occurred to me that I might learn dressmaking, so I made enquiries and my eyes were opened. I was awestruck, when I went to the local primary school in order to enrol in a dressmaking class, to discover how many subjects were offered: painting, several kinds of dancing, plumbing, languages including Chinese, Russian and Latin, motor mechanics, antique collecting – you named it and you could learn it. So soon a group of us were crouched like gnomes at tiny desks in the infants' library every Wednesday evening, stitching merrily away. We were probably uncommonly lucky in having dear Biddy Maxwell for our tutor, who not only taught us very well, but also became the central figure in a cluster of friendships that endures to this day, but it seemed obvious that we were not the only class having a good time.

About six years later this abundance of almost-free classes began to shrivel. It had started to be under threat a bit earlier: if fewer than ten people turned up at any class it was closed down, so from time to time we had to hijack an obliging husband, give him a scrap of material and tell him to look as though he were making himself a tie. But finally the whole of that particular system ended; though there still, of course, continued to be institutions running evening classes for those willing to pay, and as far as I was concerned classes for adults had become a welcome part of life.

It was my mother who first caused me to associate the idea of them with painting, because in her mid-seventies she had taken up Painting for Pleasure classes. Some of her fellow students were content with making careful copies of postcards, but some, among whom she was one of the bravest, were more adventurous. She produced many bold still lives and one quite startling self-portrait, and she enjoyed it very much, so when I reached my mid-seventies, and after dressmaking had been closed down, it seemed natural to follow her example. I had always loved painting lessons at school, had once enjoyed a short fling as a Sunday painter before realizing that my job simply didn't allow me time for it, and was still aware that if I wanted to draw something I was able to make some kind of stab at it. I was still at work when I joined my first life class (I didn't retire until I was seventy-five), and soon realized that the necessary concentration called for more energy than, in those circumstances, I could command. But after I had retired I found an agreeable and well-equipped life class just round the corner from where I live, and that I continued for some time.

I think I was almost the only student in that class whose aim was to reproduce the appearance of the model. What most of the others seemed to aim for was marks on paper that gave what they hoped was the effect of modern art. To them my attempts must have seemed boring and fogeyish; to me theirs appeared an absurd waste of time, and I still think I was right. This may be because I am old, but being old doesn't necessarily make one wrong. I am pretty sure that it is not only the old who are unable to regard as art anything that does not involve the mastery of a skill.

Given a lot of money I would collect art, both drawings and paintings. There are many ways in which a painting can be exciting, but a drawing that thrills me is always one that has caught a moment of life. Drawings are what artists, great or small, do when they are working their way towards understanding something, or catching something they want to preserve: they communicate with such immediacy that they can abolish time. I possess a drawing by a Victorian artist of his wife teaching their little girl to read by candlelight; in a book about Pisanello, who lived in the fourteen-hundreds, I have four quick sketches he made of men who had been hung. Each, in its different way, makes one catch one's breath: one might be there, looking through the eyes of the men who did those drawings. (Perhaps oddly, drawings presented as works of art are less likely to have this hallucinatory effect than private notes or studies.)

Many people will never have hands and eyes that can collaborate in a way that allows them to draw. A few specially gifted people have them from the start. In some of us they don't work effectively to begin with, but might possibly be trained by practice – and surely the purpose of a life class is to do just that? It is to teach you how to look, and then how to make your hand reproduce what you are looking at, eventually with such confidence that the lines it draws are in themselves pleasing (or perhaps exhilarating, or scary, or whatever) as well as explanatory of the object drawn. Once that degree of skill has been achieved, off you can go and take as many liberties with appearances as you like; what you produce will never be inert.

It was only when I tried to draw a naked body that I began to see how difficult it is, and how important. When you have a naked person in front of you, calmly exposed to your concentrated study, you see how accurate the term 'life class' is. What you are looking at is precisely life, that inexplicable and astounding cause of our being, to which everything possible in the way of attention and respect is due. That is why most people find it more interesting to draw other people, or animals, or plants and trees, rather than man-made objects such as architecture or machinery. (There are, of course, fine draughtsmen who specialize in those – and no doubt it's a foolish quirk of mine that makes me suspect they will be bores.)

Since I first tried to draw a nude figure it has seemed to me that what determines the quality of a drawing is the attention and respect, rather than the ingenuity, that an artist has devoted to what he is looking at. One should become as skilful as possible in order to probe the true nature of the object one is studying.

An object, of course, is needed for such probing, or sometimes a subject embodied in objects – think of Goya's *Disasters of War* or his bullfighting sequence. To make a flat surface interesting to look at simply for its own sake – turn it into an artefact that will hold the attention, move and/or give pleasure to others as well as yourself, does naturally require gifts – you must understand colour and be inventive about pattern, which are not common abilities. But quite often what it chiefly seems to need is taking yourself very seriously. Only a person with a gigantic sense of self-importance could, for example, produce a large number of canvases painted in a single flat colour, or even in two or three flat colours, without being bored to death. That is the kind of non-representational art that strikes me as absurd. Other kinds can be very pleasing in the same kind of way as a good piece of interior decoration, but to me they do not grip, as works that probe, question, celebrate or attack a subject can grip.

Much as I enjoyed that second life class, I gave it up when I saw that only if I worked at it every day could I hope to draw better, and that even then, being a word person rather than an image person, I would never amount to more than an illustrator. I fear that it was a kind of vanity that caused me to lose interest once I was convinced that my best could never be better than second rate. I do still sometimes amuse myself by trying to draw, and wish I had the energy to do so more often because it remains an absorbing occupation. And however far from being an artist my feeble attempts have left me, I am grateful to those classes for one positive result: I am now much better at seeing things than I used to be. That is something often said by people who have tried to draw, and it is a good reason for making the attempt, even in old age, because it adds such a generous pinch of pleasure to one's days.

9

No LESS INTENSELY than drawing, but much more consistently, gardening has been an activity which has given me, and still gives me, great pleasure. In my early youth it was something done for you by employees: a head gardener with two men under him in my maternal grandparents' household, and one man in ours – a full-time man to start with, becoming increasingly part-time as money dwindled. But even my grandmother, who certainly did no digging with her own hands, knew exactly what was happening in her garden and how and why it should be done. Certain things she always did herself: cut back the lavender, for instance, and spread it to dry on sheets so that the flowers could be rubbed off for lavender bags, which were kept with her linen; and spray her roses against greenfly with a big brass syringe which lived in the flower room (a little room with a sink where she arranged flowers for the house, and where the dogs slept). Her spray was nothing more lethal than a bucketful of soft soap dissolved in warm water, and the roses were always pristine. As children we loved the roses, watched eagerly for the first snowdrops, stroked the velvet of pansy petals, had our other favourite flowers, but the garden was not simply a place to be looked at. We *inhabited* it: climbed its trees, hid in its bushes, fished tadpoles and newts from its stream, stole its peaches and grapes (which was a sin and therefore more exciting that eating its plums and apples from the branch, which was allowed). And we were given regular tasks such as picking the sweet-peas for Gran and the strawberries and raspberries which were to come to the table that day. Towards the end of each season such tasks became a bit of a chore, but they were never disagreeable, and because they always involved delicious tastes and smells and pleasant leafy sensations, a garden was naturally accepted as a source of sensuous pleasure as well as a place full of beauty.

That was also true for my mother and her sisters before me (it was a family in which the women were more concerned with gardening than the men). All four of them became enthusiastic and knowledgeable gardeners, and they did more gardening work than their mother had done because none of them married a man as rich as their father. As I grew up, however, I moved away from my childhood and their continuing involvement. I went away, first to Oxford, then to London, and although on my visits home I appreciated the several gardens my mother made over the years, I looked at them rather than inhabited them, and I never worked in them. I never so much as pulled a weed or sowed a seed, and I became ignorant. Once, when I was staying with a friend who had just moved into a new house, she showed me a clump of leaves in a neglected flower bed which she wanted to restore, and asked what I thought they were. 'Pansies, I think,' said I; so we separated the clump and planted bits of it all along the front of the bed. And what those pansies turned out to be was Michaelmas daisies.

The London house, the top flat of which I moved into early in the 1960s and where I am still lucky enough to live, has a small front garden and a back one slightly larger than a tennis court. When my cousin Barbara bought the house the back garden consisted of a lawn with a fairly wide border the length of one side of it, an ivy-swamped raised border across the end, and a scramble of weeds that had once been a border next to the steps leading up to the lawn. The long border was full of still floriferous but very old and gnarled roses, which my cousin kept weeded and from time to time was nudged by her mother into pruning, but otherwise, apart from keeping the grass cut, she let the garden look after itself, which meant that the laurel bush and the fiercely thorny pyracanthus which grew against the wall opposite the rose bed grew almost to house height and plunged most of the space in shade. The lawn served a useful purpose, however, as a playground for her young children and a home for their guinea pigs, and that was what she minded about.

Twenty-six years ago her job took her to Washington, where she was to live for six or seven years, and it was agreed that I should find tenants for the bottom part of the house while the middle flat should be the preserve of her son, who was then at Oxford. Just before she left she asked me if I could 'sort of keep an eye' on the garden so that 'nature didn't quite take over'. And the next morning, leaning out of my bedroom window and surveying what had now become my territory, I suddenly and absolutely unexpectedly became my mother. 'There's only one thing for it,' I heard myself saying. 'I must take the whole thing out and start from scratch.' And that is what I did. I paid someone to do the heavy digging and cutting back, and for new brickwork in the front garden, but all the planting I did myself, and as soon as the first plant I put in with my own hands actually *grew and flowered*, I was hooked.

For a long time I spent most of my evenings and weekends working in that garden, which became quite adventurous and colourful, but gradually digging and mowing became too much for me, and about five years ago I reshaped it into something more sober which could be controlled by a gardening firm coming in once a fortnight – dull, but soothing to sit in on a summer evening – and lost interest in it, although I am still proud of the huge white rambling rose that submerges the crab-apple tree, the magnolia and the three other roses. But by then I had half an acre of garden in Norfolk to think about, *real* garden, rich in possibilities, belonging to the little house my cousin inherited from her mother in which she has generously granted me a share. She loves to sit in it, but is happy to let me run it, and building on my aunt's original creation is a continuing joy.

For some time now most of the work has to be done by other hands, so my cousin employs a young man who mows the lawn and keeps the hedges trimmed, while I have employed a sequence of three serious gardeners, all women, all much more knowledgeable than I am, and each in her different way a wonder-worker. I can afford help only one day a week, but what they have achieved! The first two did a tremendous amount of structural work, and my present treasure is a sophisticated plantswoman with whom I have a delightful time choosing what to plant where: to me the part of gardening that is the most fulfilling. And still, each time I'm there, I manage to do at least a little bit of work myself: tie something back, trim something off, clear some corner of weeds, plant three or four small plants, and however my bones may ache when I've done it, I am always deeply refreshed by it. Getting one's hands into the earth, spreading roots, making a plant comfortable – it is a totally absorbing occupation, like painting or writing, so that you become what you are doing and are given a wonderful release from consciousness of self. And so, for that matter, is simply sitting in your garden, taking it in. The following is from a short-lived diary I kept at a time when Barry was ill. I had not been able to get to Norfolk for two months, but now his brother had come to stay so I could snatch a weekend.

'Back here at last, and in exquisite spring weather, the narcissi full out with later ones still to come, the Japanese cherry by the gate a mass of pale lacy pinkness, the primroses exuberant, the magnolia opening, everything coming alive – intoxicating. However good this garden can be in summer, it's never better than now, thanks to nothing done by me but to the clever way Aunt Doro planted her bulbs in drifts years ago now expanded by their naturalization. This afternoon I sat for a long time by the pond, in the thick of them, trying to tell myself "Beauty is in the eye of the beholder, these starry green and gold creatures are just vegetable organisms shaped and coloured according to natural laws for reasons of survival. They don't exist for the sake of beauty any more than a nettle does" . . . but it was impossible to believe it. It might be true, but so what! I choose it to be untrue because the daffodils don't allow me to do otherwise.'

And still I can see those flowers in my mind's eye, serene beings, quietly living their own mysterious lives, and know that in a few months' time they will be back and with any luck I will be there again to see them . . . Yes, I am much the richer since Barbara asked me to keep an eye on her garden.

10

'WHEN I AM eighty-two I must start thinking about giving up the car.' That resolution, made in my early seventies, was the result of a visit made to my mother by her local policeman (we still had them then) when I happened to be staying with her. I opened the door to him, and he almost embraced me, so glad was he to find an intermediary for his embarrassing message. Could I please try to persuade my mother that the time had come for her to stop driving? No one had liked to say anything to her face, but three people in the village had told him that they had witnessed, or almost been the victim of, her driving, which had recently become . . . well, he didn't want to offend, but it *had* become a little bit erratic. I passed the message on, she dismissed it huffily as nonsense, and about six weeks later, much to my relief, announced, 'Oh, by the way – I have decided to get rid of the car.'

I now understand her reluctance only too well. While pottering about in the car hardly qualifies as an 'activity', it is – for those whose physical mobility is limited – a part of life and a source of pleasure. At a time when strictly speaking I ought to have followed her example by overcoming reluctance, I didn't do so. It was during my seventies when I should have stopped driving, because cataracts in both eyes developed to the point at which I could no longer read the number plate of a car three car-lengths ahead – indeed could hardly read one on a car immediately in front of me. But the licensing authority errs (quite rightly!) on the side of caution, because being unable to distinguish details within an object doesn't mean you can't see the object itself, and since I never suffered any uncertainty as to where or what any object, large or small, near or far, might be, I felt no serious guilt at continuing to drive up to the time of my operations.

André Deutsch, who believed firmly that the more something costs the better it must be, took it on himself to try to organize these operations and bullied me into seeing 'my wonderful man in Harley Street'. I saw him, and when he passed me on to his secretary so that I could make the appointment for the operation, thought to ask her how much it was going to cost. It would be done at the London Clinic, she said, where I would have to stay for two nights, 'so we will be looking at something like £3000'. So what in fact I looked at was the splendid if rather Dickensian-seeming Moorfields Eye Hospital, where the operations were done for free with exquisite precision, the first of them at about lunchtime so that I was home in time for supper, the second early in the morning so I was home in time for lunch. And the whole thing seemed like a glorious miracle because they assumed that I knew the nature of the modern operation, so didn't tell me in advance that they would not be simply removing the cataracts, but would also be giving me new eyes by inserting tiny permanent lenses designed to correct such faults as there had been in my sight before the cataracts began. I had been short-sighted all my life, and suddenly I could see like a hawk and no longer needed glasses, except for the readers that the 'long sight' of old age necessitates. Since then I have heard two or three sad stories of cataract operations which went wrong, but I remember my own with heartfelt gratitude.

When I turned eighty-two I remembered the resolution I had made and I did start thinking about whether or not I should give up my car, but all I could see was that while walking more than a quarter of a mile had become impossible, my driving showed no sign of being any different from what it always had been. Therefore I decided, 'No, not quite yet.' By now, six years on, I probably ought to think again. My legs have almost given out and I am hard put to it to walk a hundred yards. It started with painful feet –

painful for the simple but incurable reason that the flesh padding their soles gradually becomes thinner and thinner until at last your poor old bones are grinding into the ground with every step. This leads to incorrect walking so that soon your knees are affected, and then your hips, until there comes a time when it dawns on you that your legs as a whole have become so useless that if you tried to depend on them for more than a few steps without some sort of prop such as sticks, or god help you a Zimmer, you would simply *fall down*. And at that point your car begins to represent life. You hobble towards it, you ease your unwieldy body laboriously into the driver's seat – and lo! you are back to normal. Off you whizz just like everyone else, restored to freedom, restored (almost) to youth. I always liked my car. Now I love it. But of course this increased love and dependence coincides with the deterioration of other things besides your legs, so the postponed 'thinking about it' *does* need to be done. At the time of writing this, which is precisely a month before my eighty-ninth birthday, I have to admit that my car does carry three scars acquired within the last year, after never having any to show apart from those inflicted on it by others because it lives on the street.

Scar one: a very slight dent on its backside made when I was parking in a space next to a skip and failed to allow for the fact that the top rim of the skip stuck out. Scar two: not really a scar at all because easily straightened out by hand, but my passenger-side mirror did hit something hard enough to be almost flattened against the car's side when, in a narrow street full of oncoming traffic, I failed to judge correctly how much room I had on that side. Scar three, and this one is bad: a scrape, slightly dented, far back on the driver's side, of which I am much ashamed. At the end of a long, traffic-choked drive, when it had become dark, I forgot that the gate into Hyde Park just past the Hyde Park Hotel in the direction of Hyde Park Corner has long been permanently closed, and turned into its entrance, thus trapping myself in a little stub of roadway ending at a shut gate, with cars parked on both its sides and a row of bollards down its middle. The space between the bollards was not wide and was ill-lit, so a U-turn was not going to be easy, but the unbroken stream of headlights roaring past behind me made the prospect of reversing out into it unthinkable, so the U-turn it would have to be. I had nearly completed it when I felt the pressure of a bollard against the car's side. And what did I do? Instead of stopping at once, reversing and starting again at a wider angle, I thought 'If I go on it will make a nasty scrape – oh, what the hell, who cares!' and on I went. Which was wholly the result of being an overtired *old person* flustered by her own silliness in landing herself in an awkward situation.

But oddly enough I was not responsible for the worst accident I ever had – so bad that I still marvel at being alive – which happened earlier in this same year. The M11, where it bypasses Newmarket, has three lanes, and as with most three-lane motorways, the slow lane is so full of heavy vehicles travelling on the slow side of 70 m.p.h. that few cars use it, so in the other two lanes there is nothing to check the traffic from moving rather faster than it ought to, nearer to 80 m.p.h. than 70. I, on my familiar journey between London and Norfolk, was cheerfully buzzing along in the middle lane, not trying to overtake anything but simply going faster in the faster stream, and thus passing the heavy vehicles on my left. Just as my nose came level with the tail-end of one of them (not, thank god, one of the monsters), without having indicated its intention, it started to swing into the middle lane. Either I had to hit it, or I had to swerve into the fast lane. I can't say I made a decision, I didn't have time, I simply followed instinct and swerved. Whereupon crash! A car coming on fast in the fast lane hit me. For what seemed minutes but must have been only seconds I was sandwiched between the two vehicles, ricochetting from one to the other, then I suppose the lorry braked and the other vehicle pulled ahead. I had a flash of 'That's better!' then blank horror: my car had gone out of control and what I did with my steering wheel had become utterly irrelevant, I was spinning across the width of the motorway, zig, zag, whoosh, a complete pirouette, the shoulder coming towards me, grass, thank god it's grass, and there I was on it, facing the wrong way, and the traffic roared on. Not a single other vehicle had been touched.

The lorry didn't stop. The car that hit me did, and its driver's husband walked back – they had to go on some distance before being able to cross the traffic and park – to exchange addresses and insurance companies, and he was concerned and kind. By the time he reached me my greatest piece of luck (after surviving and not having caused a god-awful pile-up) had brought me an ambulance driver and his mate, who had been coming on behind and had seen the whole thing. They not only stopped, but called the police for me and then stayed with me until they came, a long half-hour. 'Someone up there is watching out for you,' said the driver in an awestruck voice. He also said I'd handled it well, but really all I'd done was hung on grimly and refrained from braking. It was a baking hot day, the roar and stink of the traffic was hideous, and I can't think how, in my state of shock, I would have got through that half-hour on that narrow shoulder without the presence of those two kind men. I am still miserable at the fact that because I was in shock it never occurred to me to ask for their names and addresses.

After the first policeman arrived I slowly became able to see in a distant kind of way that it was becoming funny. He took a statement from the ambulance driver, which spared me from having to attempt a description, then said that he must get the traffic stopped so that my car could be turned round. (Because there had been no head-on impact its chassis was undamaged and it was still movable, though it was badly bashed on both sides and its near front wheel was askew. It was to emerge from being repaired as good as new.) He then tried to use his radio, and it didn't work. Never mind, he said, here comes a colleague, and another police car drew up – and his radio didn't work either, greatly embarrassing both of them. But when a third policeman arrived, this one on a motorbike, and his proved just as useless, it dawned on all of us that we must be in a blank spot where there was no reception. From then on, at every stage of the drama – stopping the traffic, starting it up again, summoning the AA (in vain – they deal only with breakdowns, not accidents), finding a firm in Newmarket to tow in and repair the car – the unfortunate bike man had over and over again to speed to the nearest roundabout ahead, turn to speed to the nearest roundabout astern, then turn to speed back to us, all in order to make radio calls, because it seemed that they all relied on their radio equipment so trustingly that they carried no mobiles. I was there on that shoulder for over an hour and a half before a breakdown van arrived to convey me to the repair works in Newmarket.

Once there, I realized that I was feeling distinctly unwell: shock had turned into a general physical malaise. Offered a courtesy car, I accepted it because I was still fifty-odd miles from my destination, but I was not at all sure that I would be able to drive it. There was something quite unreal about standing in that quiet office where people addressed me as though I were a normal customer, while in fact I was someone who ought to be a dead body trapped in a tangle of metal probably surrounded by a number of other dead or damaged bodies in similar tangles. I felt apologetic for being so oddly unreal, although no one seemed to be noticing.

Then, suddenly, Mrs Mattocks and her first-aid classes over sixty years ago, at the beginning of the war, loomed into my mind: our district nurse, very stout (my brother and I referred to her, alas, as Mrs Buttocks), whose task it was to prepare the village for invasion. Mrs Mattocks always said that in cases of shock by far the best thing was Hot Sweet Tea . . . and what was that in the corner of the office where I was stranded? A tea-making machine, with little envelopes of sugar in a paper cup beside it. Of course they allowed me to make myself a cup of tea, into which I put four envelopes of sugar – and Mrs Mattocks had been perfectly right! Halfway through that cup, click, and I came together. By the time it was finished I felt normal. Once in my courtesy car, I drove carefully and slowly but without a qualm. And from then on that horrible accident had so little effect on my nerves that now I say to myself, 'With nerves as strong as that you can go on driving for at least another year. After all, the scars so far have been only on my car, not on people.'

11

WHEN YOU BEGIN discussing old age you come up against reluctance to depress either others or yourself, so you tend to focus on the more agreeable aspects of it: coming to terms with death, the continuing presence of young people, the discovery of new pursuits and so on. But I have to say that a considerable part of my own old time is taken up by doing things or (worse) failing to do things for people older, or if not older, less resistant to age, than myself. Because not everyone ages at the same rate, it is probable that eventually most people will either have to do some caring, or be cared for, and although the former must be preferable to the latter, I don't think I am unusual in having failed to understand in advance that even the preferable alternative is far from enjoyable. Or perhaps that is just my reaction to it. There certainly are unselfish people with a bent for caring to whom it seems to come more naturally. But I can speak only for those like myself, to whom it doesn't.

It is with Barry that this has become apparent – also, to a certain extent, with my oldest friend, Nan Taylor, who died recently, but with her I was one of a team of friends who rallied round, so although it lasted for two years or so it was never full-time. With Barry, it is, or ought to be.

He and I met in 1960, when he was still married and wishing he wasn't. This was not because he didn't love his wife, but because he had become sure of something he had always suspected and had foolishly attempted to ignore: he is temperamentally unfitted for marriage. He detests possessing and being possessed, not just in theory but with every atom of his being. Convinced that he didn't love his wife less because of liking, or even loving, other women, he was unable to feel that she was reasonable when she disagreed with him, thus forcing him to deceive her, which he disliked doing. A typical unfaithful husband, in fact, though with a stronger than usual conviction of being in the right, so sure was he that an over-riding need to be someone's One and Only is neurotic, unwholesome and the cause of many ills.

And I, at the age of forty-three (eight years older than he) felt much the same. I had turned my back with a good deal of relief on romantic love, and I had become so used to not being married that only with difficulty, and without enthusiasm, could I imagine the alternative. We came together, therefore, with no thought of marriage, simply because we liked and were physically attracted to each other, and agreed with each other about what made good writing and acting (Barry wrote plays), both of us valuing clarity and naturalness above all. We had a lot to talk about together in those days, and when he said to me that if he and his wife ever did break up, the one thing he was sure of was that he would never marry again, I remember feeling relieved: I needn't feel guilt! It was even a comfort to know that for now, anyway, there was someone else there to wash his shirts and feed him – I could enjoy all the plums of love without having to wade through the pudding. I marvelled at having gone through so much of the froth and flurry of romantic loving in my youth, when it had now become apparent that being the Other Woman suited me so very well. Our relationship gradually became firmer and firmer, more and more obviously likely to endure, but it never changed from being more like a loving friendship than an obsession.

Finally the marriage did break up (not because of me, though for reasons of convenience I agreed to being cited as the cause) and Barry set about living on his own, at which he was very bad. I can no longer remember exactly how and why he moved in to share my flat – it made little difference to the amount we were seeing of each other – but I think it was after we had stopped being lovers. Yes: piecing together scraps of memory in a way that would be tedious to go into, I am sure it was. But because there was such a gradual move from love affair into settled companionship, it is no longer possible for me to date this.

What I can date, however, is the much later beginning of Barry's illness. It was in January 2002. In fact he had begun to be diabetic some time earlier, with the less acute form of diabetes which strikes in old age, but at first he was unaware of it and then the doctor he happened to consult made light of it, telling him not to worry because it could easily be controlled by medication and a sensible diet. The only parts of that advice he heeded were 'not to worry' and 'medication'. He assured himself and me that all he need do was take his pill and forget about it, that was what Doctor X had said. Doctor X. Given what happened later, it is lucky for her, my publisher and me that I have genuinely forgotten her name. Barry had got himself onto her books before we were living together, when his health was fine, and had decided he liked her. And I, knowing nothing about diabetes except that in its acute form the patient is dependent on insulin injections so what a relief that this was not going to be necessary for Barry, was happy to let him potter along in what I didn't realize was his folly.

Why I failed to recognize his folly was because, except for one emergency which had been dealt with by his wife, I had never known him in anything but excellent health. Not so much as a cold, or a headache, or an attack of indigestion, had he ever had in my experience of him. It is true that his attitude to illness in others was simplistic: 'Is it cancer?', 'Is he going to die?', 'Is he in pain?' were his inevitable questions, and reassured on those points he would dismiss the matter. But it took me quite a while to see that when he himself had to consult a doctor all he paid attention to was the question of pain, which he was less able to tolerate than anyone else I have ever known. If he is hurting, then he becomes frantic for the doctor to stop it. 'Give me morphine!' he insists, and considers the withholding of it an outrage. This, it turned out, was because the one, wife-attended emergency, a twisted gut, had caused him agony, which was eased only when a friend from his days as an undergraduate at Cambridge, who had become a doctor, smuggled him some morphine which not only plunged him into blissful comfort, but also cured him – or so it seemed. So now, if something hurts, he will demand morphine, but any other kind of problem he can't bring himself to think about. As soon as a doctor, or nurse, or anyone else starts giving him advice about diet, or explaining any kind of treatment other than the simply analgesic, he *visibly* switches off. Something inside him decides: 'This is going to be boring, even disagreeable advice, so I shan't listen.' And that's that.

He didn't keep up the pottering for long. Early in January 2002 Doctor X sent him up to the Royal Free Hospital for some kind of minor intervention on his penis, and two days later his waterworks seized up. This process I shall not describe, for which you should be grateful. It is an excruciating business, which involved us in a midnight run by ambulance to Accident and Emergency, where we had a four-hour wait, Barry in increasing agony, before a doctor appeared to put him on a catheter . . . on which, for a complexity of reasons, he was to remain *for three months* before the simple operation on his prostate gland which would end that particular trouble (which was not cancer) was performed. It doesn't take long for anyone on a catheter to learn that the basic discomfort and humiliation is the least of it, because painful infections become frequent. We were soon miserably accustomed to those emergency ambulance runs and those grim hours in Accident and Emergency, but nothing was more appalling than when, having at last called him in for his operation, they then cancelled it at the last minute on the grounds that his heart was not up to it (grounds which luckily, but mysteriously, vanished later), and sent him home without a word as to what was to happen next. Unable to get any information from the hospital, I called Dr X in desperation, asking, 'But is he going to have to continue on a catheter for the rest of his life?' To which she replied: 'Poor Barry. It does sometimes happen, I'm afraid.'

Weeks later, we learnt that a letter from the hospital about Barry's treatment was lying unopened on her desk. What was going on there we never discovered, but from our point of view she, our only hope, was simply fading away. For some time, when I went to her surgery to collect his diabetes pills, they were forthcoming – there was even a short time when I thought what a nice surgery it was compared to my own doctor's, never any wait, without asking myself why there was hardly ever anyone there but me! Then, if one needed to see her, the answer would be: 'Doctor's not in today, perhaps if you tried tomorrow afternoon.' If you asked could you see her partner instead: 'I'm afraid he is out on a call.' And so on and so on, until the day when the answer came as an hysterical-sounding shriek: '*There is no doctor at this surgery.*' At which point I was able to persuade Barry that he would be better off under my own doctor. Not that it got him any nearer his operation.

Given three months of the National Health at its groggiest plus Dr X, both Barry and I were eventually reduced to the condition of zombies – and we were reasonably alert and well-informed old people. What it would have done to less privileged oldies, heaven knows. We ceased to believe that anything we did or said could do any good; no one was ever going to tell us anything, and if they did we would be fools to believe them; so we sank into doing nothing, just sitting there miserably waiting for who knew what. It was our beloved Sally who rescued us. It was she who came up to London, called the consultant's Harley Street number and made an appointment for Barry as a private patient. And my word, the difference £225 can make! The mysterious figure protected by a flock of white coats, vanishing round distant corners of corridors, became a pleasant and reassuring man ready to answer all our questions with lucid explanations. No no no, of course Barry was not going to remain on a catheter for ever, that hardly ever happened and he was sure it wouldn't do so in this case. The delay was simply because he was not going to operate without further consultation with the cardiac specialist so that he could decide between using a normal anaesthetic or an epidural, and the cardiac specialist happened to be away on his holiday and would not be back for another three weeks. Only when we got home after that meeting did it occur to me that this was an amazingly long holiday. Sitting face to face with the consultant our gratitude for having questions answered as though we were rational adults was so extreme that we ceased to be anything of the sort. The humiliations of illness go deep: we didn't cease to be zombies, we just became, for the moment, happy zombies.

The three weeks became nearer five, and very long weeks they were – long enough to include fretful telephone calls (when the consultant announced that he was going to operate tomorrow, he added pettishly 'I was going to operate tomorrow *anyway*, it's nothing to do with those telephone calls', which instantly made me suppose that it was). And it was successful, though the wound took several weeks to heal and a few more infections had to be fought off. But Barry has never recovered his health.

While all this was going on I did something I had never done before. I kept a diary. It was written in fat chunks with long gaps in between, not day by day, so it is more retrospective than diaries usually are, and it gives a better picture of what happened to our relationship than anything I could write now.

I can't remember whether, at the beginning of Barry and me, I felt a passing scruple at taking up so quickly and enthusiastically with yet another married man. I suppose I may have done. But I *can* remember quite clearly thinking what a *comfort* it was that he had a nice, competent wife to look after him, so I needn't ever worry on his behalf. And when, after Mary kicked him out, he ended up living with me, the 'not-having-to-take-care' didn't change much. By then we'd gone off the boil sexually and he was even less keen than I was about 'marriedness', so it was more like friends deciding to share a flat than the setting-up of a ménage. There was never, for instance, any question of my doing his washing, and he was always ready to share the cooking. In recent years, when his eccentricities began to take over to the extent of sometimes being a bit of a bore, and mine the same no doubt, all we had to do was drift gently into going even more our own ways, so it has never been claustrophobic. I think it must be quite rare for a relationship to be as enjoyable as ours was for the first eight years or so, and simultaneously so undemanding. And then for the undemandingness to continue contentedly for the next forty-odd years!

And then – this prostate trouble. Although the habit of not looking after him was ingrained – well, you *just can't* disregard the seizing up of someone's urinary system. That dreadful night when we had to dial 999 for the emergency ambulance plunged us into a situation where looking after just had to be done.

It was interesting to learn that while I was dismayed at having to spend so much time doing things for him or worrying about him, nothing in me questioned for a moment that so it must be. The dismay, though real enough, was on the surface, while something underneath and not even thought about took it for granted that what was necessary had to be done.

I was most forcibly struck by the extent of my acceptance of the situation when, during one of his spells in hospital, he became constipated, largely because the catheter he was on then was a bad one which caused him to suffer spasms at the slight-est provocation. This frightened him so that he was reluctant to move – froze him up. Eventually they gave him a laxative, and when I arrived that afternoon a nurse said, 'I've been trying to get him to the toilet, but he refused to go till you came.' And as soon as I reached his bedside he said, 'Thank god you're here, now I can go to the loo.' [Here I shall spare you several lines of over-detailed description, returning to the scene near its end.] Luckily there were lots of substantial paper towels in the loo, and a large covered bin into which to dispose of them, and plenty of hot water: it was not difficult to clean him, the pan and the floor up. What astonished me was that I didn't mind doing it. There was no recoil, no feeling of disgust – I seemed to *watch myself* doing it in a businesslike way, without making any effort, like a professional nurse. But at the same time I was surprised at this. And indeed, I still feel surprised. Not so much at having done it, but at not having to make an effort to do it. (When Barry was back in bed he remarked that it was lucky that I had been there.

I answered rather tartly that he could perfectly well have gone to the loo with the nurse, to which he replied, 'Yes, but it would have been less pleasant' !!!) After that, I realized that I had moved, after all those years, into a state of Wifehood. Having recognized that, and thought that after such a long time of happy exemption it was perhaps only fair that I should have a taste of munching the pudding, I stopped minding the loss of 'my own way' quite so much. But my word, what bliss any escape into it always is!

It was just as well that this automatic shift into wifehood came about, because I have had to remain in it ever since. Barry's prostate trouble was over, but his diabetes became worse, so that quite soon he had to add insulin injections to his treatment. These, to my relief, he was willing to administer himself, but they have never made him feel any better. Most diabetics seem to be able to live normal lives once their treatment has been decided on and they have learnt how to manage their diet, but Barry, perhaps because he refuses to make any effort to eat right, feels permanently exhausted and hardly ever able to leave his bed. And I – this causes pangs of guilt, but not strong enough pangs to produce much action – have found it impossible to take control of his diet with an iron hand, which would involve not only a great deal of cooking, but also compelling him to eat things he doesn't like, which no one has ever been able to do. While as for preventing him from eating what he does like . . . Naturally I avoid buying cakes, sweet biscuits and so on, whereupon this bedridden man, who has to be driven to the library three or four times a week in order to keep him in reading matter, will, as soon as I am out, get himself to the shops in order to buy a coffee cake or doughnuts without a moment's hesitation, and will stop this idiocy only when his blood-sugar readings go through the ceiling and he feels really terrible. He will then be sensible until the readings become not too bad (they are never very good), at which point he will start all over again, while to wean him from fats and from huge dollops of double cream in his coffee is simply impossible. It is some consolation to me that both Sally and her daughter Jess, who know him as well as I do, are equally unable to control him and assure me that there is nothing I can do about it, but still I can't help feeling that the sort of 'wife' I have shrunk into being is a very bad one.

Our main trouble is that what he calls his 'weakness' – the dreadful draining-away of energy from which he suffers – goes so deep that he has lost interest in almost everything. This intelligent man will now read nothing but crime fiction, and never a whole book of that. At the library he will pick at random five or six such books from the shelves, and the next day will want to take them back because (surprise surprise!) they are 'unreadable', but if you give him something else he will say he 'can't be bothered'. Neither can he be 'bothered' with anything on television except sport, and less and less of that: quite often nowadays I will go into his room while the television is on and find him lying facing away from it. He no longer ever volunteers conversation, and responds to other people's attempts with monosyllables. Days and days go by without his saying anything to me but 'What are we having for supper?' and 'Will you take me to the library?' This means that almost the only pleasure left to him is food, so that depriving him of foods he enjoys seems like cruelty, and I am unable to prevent myself feeling from time to time that if a life so severely diminished is shortened by eating doughnuts, what will it matter?*

He had a flash of return to himself in the summer of 2006, when the Royal Court did a season of readings in their Theatre Upstairs of the plays which made them famous during the 1960s, which included *Skivers*, one of his. This reading was directed by Pam Brighton, who had directed its first performance, and the Royal Court's casting director had got together a wonderful cast of young actors (most of the characters in the play are schoolboys). Although excited at the prospect of it, we had no idea what to expect, so it was a glorious surprise when it turned out to be so well done that within minutes the full house forgot that it was

---

* It has turned out, since this was written, that he has serious heart trouble on top of his diabetes.

watching a reading and felt that it was watching an excellent full performance of the play. The audience was as responsive as any playwright could wish, and when at the end Barry had to go on stage to thank everyone concerned, and said in a choked voice (looking so small and old), 'I never, ever, expected to see that play again,' they rose to him. Sally and I were crying, and Jess and Beachy, who had never seen a play of his, were ecstatic ('But it's the best play I've ever seen!' Jess kept saying), and the post-play party in the bar was a lovely hugger-mugger of old friends and happiness. But when I said in the taxi on the way home 'Do you think it may have started you up again?' he answered calmly, 'Oh no, it won't do that.' And it didn't.

Our life went back to being, in about equal parts, both sad and boring. What, I sometimes ask myself, keeps me and, I am sure, innumerable other old spouses or spouselike people in similar situations, going through the motions of care? The only answer I can produce appears in the shape of a metaphor: in a plant there is no apparent similarity between its roots and whatever flower or fruit appears at the top of its stem, but they are both part of the same thing, and it seems to me that obligations which have grown out of love, however little they resemble what they grew out of, are also part of the same thing. How, if that were not so, could they be so effortlessly binding in spite of being so unwelcome? One doesn't, in these situations, make a choice between alternatives because there doesn't seem to *be* an alternative. Perhaps a wonderfully unselfish person (and they do exist) gets satisfaction from making a good a job of it. If you are a selfish one, you manage by contriving as many escapes and compensations as you can while still staying on the job. It is not an admirable solution, but I don't suppose I am the only old person to resort to it.

12

My escapes have been into gardening, drawing, pottering and – the one I use most often – into books: reading them, reviewing them or (a new use of this particular occupation) writing them. I say 'a new use', but it is new only as far as I am concerned. I have just been reading Jenny Uglow's life of Mrs Gaskell, and if ever someone perfected employment of this method, she did, having had the luck to be born with enough energy for at least ten people. The obligations she accepted willingly, even happily, and survived by dodging, were those of marriage and motherhood, and neither her husband nor her daughters ever had cause to complain; but somehow she managed to clear spaces in her intensely busy life in which to be purely herself, and write her books. Or perhaps it was less a matter of clearing spaces than of having the ability to concentrate her attention fully on what she wanted to do in whatever space, however limited, became available. It is odd that she is so often considered a rather humdrum figure, when she was in fact one of dazzling vitality, a quality much to be envied. Dwindling energy is one of the most boring things about being old. From time to time you get a day when it seems to be restored, and you can't help feeling that you are 'back to normal', but it never lasts. You just have to resign yourself to doing less – or rather, to taking more breaks than you used to in whatever you are doing. In my case I fear that what I most often do less of is my duty towards my companion rather than the indulgence of my private inclinations.

Reviewing books, which I do most often for the *Literary Review*, doesn't go far towards paying the household bills, but is enjoyable because as Rebecca West once said in a *Paris Review* interview, 'it makes you really open your mind towards the book'. It also pushes me towards books I might not otherwise read. Frederick Brown's very stout life of Flaubert, for instance: if I had seen it on one of my visits to our local bookshop (which happily shows no sign of 'struggling' to survive, as people say such businesses are now doing), I would probably have thought 'interesting – but so *fat* and I've no room left on my shelves even for thin books, and anyway I know a fair amount about Flaubert already', and veered off towards the new paperbacks, thus depriving myself of a real feast of enjoyment. And Gertrude Bell – why had I never wanted to read anything by or about her, in spite of loving Freya Stark and taking it for granted that T. E. Lawrence was worth reading even though I didn't much like him? I believe the shaming reason is simply her name. Gertrude: those two syllables, which seem to me ugly, have always evoked the image of a grimly dowdy and disagreeable woman, and I'm sure I would never have picked up Georgina Howell's biography of Bell if the *Literary Review* hadn't asked me to review it – and there, suddenly, was that truly extraordinary woman, to be followed deep into one of the world's most fascinating regions and a hair-raising passage of recent history. It was ridiculous to have known nothing about her until now, but what a wonderful discovery to be pushed, or led, into in one's eighty-ninth year!

(If I may be forgiven a lapse into senile rambling, I'm unable to explain why that name conjured disagreeable dowdiness, because the only Gertrude I ever actually knew was my great-aunt Gertie, whose aura was one not of dowdiness but of tragedy spiced with comedy, poor woman. She was one of the four handsome daughters of Dr Bright, Master of University College, Oxford, a widower who raised his children with the help of his wife's sister and made, on the whole, a good job of picking out suitable husbands for them from among the undergraduates who passed through his care. But with Gertie . . . well, she fell in love with and was either engaged to, or on the verge of being engaged to, not an undergraduate but a junior fellow of his college. And one morning the parlour maid knocked on the door of the Master's study to announce that there was a lady downstairs, with a little boy, who was asking to see him. 'Show her up,' said the Master, and she did, and no sooner was the lady through the door than she whipped out of her muff a pistol and shot him. 'L-l-l-luckily she shot me in p-p-p-profile,' he was to tell a colleague (he had a famous stammer), so his portliness was only grazed, not punctured. The lady, it turned out, was the junior fellow's wife, or perhaps only felt she ought to be. It was a long time before this story was told in a hushed voice to the oldest of my cousins, and another long time before she passed it on to the rest of us, so its details were slightly blurred, but I have since learnt that it was a well-known incident in the college's history. Gertie recovered from what must have been a dreadful shock in time to marry a bishop, but while my grandmother and her other two sisters gave the impression of comfortable assurance, she always seemed to me to be a little frail and querulous.)

Back to books. I am puzzled by something which I believe I share with a good many other oldies: I have gone off novels. When I was young I read almost nothing else, and all through fifty years of working as a publisher fiction was my principal interest, so that nothing thrilled me more than the first work of a gifted novelist. Of course there are many novels which I remember with gratitude – and some with awe – and there are still some which I admire and enjoy; but over and over again, these days, even when I acknowledge that something is well written, or amusing, or clever, I start asking myself before I have gone very far into it, 'Do I want to go on with this?', and the answer is 'No'.

The novel has several ways of hooking a reader: offering escape into thrills and/or the exotic, offering puzzles to be solved, offering daydream material; offering a reflection of your own life; offering revelation of other kinds of life; offering an alternative to recognizable life in the shape of fantasy. It can set out to make you laugh, make you cry, make you gasp with amazement. Or, at its best, it can take you into a completely real-seeming world in which you can experience all those sensations. I well remember my feelings as I approached the end of my first reading of *Middlemarch*: 'Oh no – I'm going to have to leave this world, and I don't want to!'

I never responded with enthusiasm to thrills, puzzles or fantasies, but in my teens I gulped daydream material for quite a while before moving on to 'complete worlds', which is what I prefer to this day when I can find them. But in the 1950s and '60s I veered off towards novels that reflected, more or less, my own life. If they depended on that kind of recognition from people who were not quite like me, then I had no time for them – Angela Thirkell's books, for example, which were catnip to a kind of middle-class Englishwoman not respected by me. But Margaret Drabble's – how cross I was when Weidenfeld captured Margaret Drabble, who hit off the kind of people and situations familiar to me so exactly that I longed to publish her as well as read her. The 'NW1 novel' seemed new at the time, and for several years it was the kind I turned to most eagerly, thoroughly enjoying each moment in a love affair or other kind of relationship which was observed with special accuracy. But eventually novels of that kind seemed to develop a slow puncture, so that gradually they went flat on me; or rather, that happened to my reception of them. I became bored with what they had to tell me: I knew it too well. And because a great many of today's novels still focus mainly on the love lives of the kind of women I see around me all the time, that means that I am bored by a large proportion of available fiction.

Happily that is not true of the fiction that takes one into the lives of people completely different from oneself, V. S. Naipaul's, for example, or Philip Roth's. And it could never apply to the giants: Tolstoy, Eliot, Dickens, Proust, Flaubert, Trollope (yes, I put him up there, I think he has been severely underestimated). They are so rare because they are a different kind of person, just as a musical genius is: they have an imaginative energy of a kind so extraordinary that it is hardly too much to describe it as uncanny. Just occasionally a present-day novelist breaks through into their territory. I would say that David Foster Wallace does in *Infinite Jest*, exhausting though he can be; that Margaret Atwood often gets a foothold there, and Pat Barker with her series of novels about the First World War; and that Hilary Mantel definitely did with *A Place of Greater Safety* (the nerve of it – to take on the French Revolution in the shoes of Robespierre, Camille Desmoulins and Danton!).

And then, of course, there are the fiction writers whose minds one falls in love with regardless of the kind of book they are writing – for me, Chekhov, W. G. Sebald and Alice Munro, but I am not going to attempt an analysis of the attraction of those three very different writers because it would take three separate chapters of a different kind of book, and anyway I am a reader not a critic, so probably couldn't do it even if I wanted to. So 'going off' novels doesn't mean that I don't think being able to write them is a wonderful and enviable gift, only that old age has made me pernickety, like someone whose appetite has dwindled so that she can only be tempted by rare delicacies. The pernicketiness does not extend to non-fiction because the attractiveness of non-fiction depends more on its subject than it does on its author's imagination.

I no longer feel the need to ponder human relationships – particularly not love affairs – but I do still want to be fed facts, to be given material which extends the region in which my mind can wander; and probably the best example of the kind of thing I am grateful for is the way my understanding of the early stages of the industrial revolution has been enlarged by three – no, four – books.

The first of them is *Pandaemonium*, that marvellous compendium of material collected over many years by Humphrey Jennings, published long after his death as a result of devoted work by his daughter Mary-Lou with the help of Charles Madge, and subtitled 'The Coming of the Machine as Seen by Contemporary Observers, 1660–1886'. Because of the astonishing variety and high quality of the texts and the way they are put together, this book generates an addictive excitement of the mind. I couldn't possibly have stopped reading it halfway through, and it left me with an acute awareness of how the delights of discovery and achievement led to tragic consequences as they became more and more orientated towards profit – how idealism capsized into greed and squalor. (We published this book in 1985, but didn't manage to sell many copies of it, so it will be hard to find nowadays. If you can get hold of a copy, I strongly advise you to do so.) The second and third books are a biography, Brian Dolan's life of Josiah Wedgwood, and letters, those of Charles Darwin. Wedgwood's life exemplifies so vividly that moment in history when men suddenly sensed that in science and technology they had found an 'open sesame' to great things . . . To great and *good* things, so Wedgwood and his friends Thomas Bentley, Joseph Priestley and Erasmus Darwin firmly believed, because enlightenment was surely going to be moral as well as intellectual. Wedgwood, within a comparatively short lifetime, turned the simple trade of potter into a dazzling industry, first by discovering the scientist in himself, then (and this is what is so moving about him) by believing that what mattered was doing things as well as you possibly could, which would inevitably lead to success, and that nothing but good could come for the working man from technological advance as a result. It is true that shortly before his death omens did begin to blur the innocence of this vision, but still it is impossible not to envy the climate of hope in which he lived. And Charles Darwin's letters, particularly those of his youth, illustrate not only his own developing genius, but the way in which the most ordinary lives – those of country doctors, clergymen, squires, tradesmen – were also being stirred by ripples of science: how everywhere people were tapping rocks, collecting shells, dissecting plants, observing birds. It was this eagerness to learn by scientific observation that provided the atmosphere in which Thomas Bewick flourished, and it is his life story, told to what I can only call perfection by Jenny Uglow, which is my fourth book.

Bewick himself did not embrace what was 'modern' in his day with much enthusiasm. He adhered to the traditional techniques of wood-engraving, he abhorred enclosure, and he much preferred the tremendously long walks he undertook as a young and middle-aged man to the train journeys which had become possible when he was old. But his innate gifts as a naturalist and his brilliance as an artist brought him fame because they answered what was then a 'modern' need, and in his private life his keen discussion of new developments in science and politics with his fellow tradesmen – the creativity and intellectual liveliness that blossomed among these men of little education, who often gathered together in clubs or debating societies such as Newcastle's 'Lit.and Phil.', the Literary and Philosophical Society to which Bewick belonged and which is still in existence – was typical of this fecund time. It is evoked with such sensitivity, and in such rich detail, by Uglow as she brings to life the passionate, vulnerable, eccentric, reliable, wholly lovable man she clearly hates to leave behind at the end of her book.

I have gained much from many non-fiction books, but will let those four stand for them all. What refreshment, to be able to take a holiday from oneself in such good company.

Another kind of reading which is common among old people, and which I indulge in quite often, is returning to old favourites. Often this is pure pleasure, but sometimes it makes me see that even the run-of-the-mill novel of today is much more sophisticated and interesting than that of my early youth, not to mention those popular just before the First World War, books bought by my parents when they were young which were still on our shelves when I began to move on from children's books, so that I read them too, and enjoyed them. Everyone in my family was familiar with, and loved, the classics, but naturally what they mostly read was the equivalent of what is reviewed on the literary pages of today, ranging from the seriously good to the cosy Aga-saga or Bridget Jones type of entertainment, and some of these still lurk in the little Norfolk house where I spend many weekends. From time to time I pull one out, just to remind myself, and end up unsure whether I am more dismayed or amused. The best of them seem ponderous and verbose, over-given to description (what a lot about cutting from here to there we have learnt from the cinema!), while as for the rest! Infantile tosh: that is what they so often are.

At the end of the 1800s and during the pre-war years of the twentieth century there was an extraordinary fashion for 'historical' romances. A few of them, books by Dumas and Rider Haggard, for example, are saved by imaginative vigour and a gift for story-telling – though perhaps I like Haggard just because he was 'ours', the Haggards being neighbours of my grandparents, so that we went to parties with his grandchildren and on most Sundays listened to Sir Rider reading the lessons in church (very dramatically – his rendering of Shadrach, Meshach and Abednego in the burning fiery furnace was long remembered). But there was a teeming undergrowth of books such as those of Jeffery Farnol, who favoured chapter headings like 'How and Why I Fought With One Gabbing Dick, a Pedlar' or 'In Which I Begin to Appreciate the Virtues of the Chaste Goddess', or Agnes and Egerton Castle, of whose *If Youth But Knew* the following is a typical paragraph:

'What things,' said the fiddler, addressing his violin as the court fool of old his bauble (after the singular fashion which led people to call him crazy) – 'what things, beloved, could we not converse upon tonight, were we not constrained by sinners? What a song of the call of the spring to last year's fawn – of the dream which comes to the dreamer but once in his life's day, and that before the dawn? Chaste and still as the night, and yet tremulous; shadows, mere shadows, yet afire; voiceless, formless, impalpable, yet something more lovely than all the sunshine can show, than all the beauty arms can hold hereafter, than all the music ears shall hear . . . O youth! O love!' sighed the fiddler, and drew from his fiddle a long echo to the sigh.

In these novels young women were called maidens and were wilful but chaste, sometimes defiant, but if so, absolutely certain to end by yielding tremulously to a young man who may have been wrong-headed to start with but proved stunningly honourable when it came to the crunch, and this pair was more than likely to encounter a picturesque tinker or itinerant musician, or suchlike, possessed of endless funds of wry wisdom. Heroes and heroines were of noble, or at least extremely gentle, birth, although because their breeding was *true* they would mingle happily with peasants or with those tinkers (a fairly frequent device was to have them disguised as humbler beings, thus allowing for misunderstandings and revelations). The reverence for class in these books was blatant. The novel in Britain is still a middle-class phenomenon, but no longer so fatuously as it was then. And these ridiculous books were cheerfully enjoyed by intelligent adults – and by me, in my early teens. So who knows what will be made a hundred years or so from now of the perfectly acceptable fiction of which I, and many other old people, have had enough? Perhaps we shall be proved right.

I depend so much on reading because I never developed the habit of watching television. I have never even bought a set. In 1968 I was given one by the woman who used to clean for me, because it had started to go into snaky waves at crucial moments and she was replacing it with one less tiresome, and for a few weeks I watched it all of every evening, always hoping that the next thing to appear on the screen would be wonderful, and it wasn't. So then I put it in my lodger's room, and in that room, now Barry's, it still is (or rather, its successor is – he has replaced it several times), watched by me only for Wimbledon and the Derby, or when Tiger Woods is playing. I used to watch the Grand National too, but can no longer bear to do so because of horses being killed. (Though quite tough when young, now I find any sort of cruelty unwatchable and, if vivid, unreadable: I couldn't read all of even my much admired William Dalrymple's *The Last Mughal*, which describes the destruction of Delhi in 1857, a brilliant and important book, because of the horrors he was having to report. The routine horrors in the daily news are different, in that one *has* to be aware of those, though I dwell on details as little as possible.) I am always embarrassingly at a loss when people discuss television programmes, as they so often do, and the many columns of newsprint devoted to television are meaningless babble to me, but although I realize this ignorance is truly nothing to be proud of, I have to suppose that some foolish part of my mind is attached to it, because I have never been able to remedy it. It is easier to imagine returning to radio than buying a television set. I once listened to Radio Three a lot, being hungry for music, but now that deafness has distorted most musical sounds to the point of ugliness, I have given that up. If, however, I become unable to read, which god forbid, I expect Radio Four will become welcome. I have dear friends in New York who are almost ready to move to London for the sake of Radio Four.

13

THE ACTIVITIES I escape into are mostly ordinary things which have become more valuable because I am old, enjoyed with increasing intensity because of the knowledge that I shan't be able to enjoy them for much longer; but easily the best part of my old age has been, and still is, a little less ordinary. It is entirely to do with having had the luck to discover that I can write. I don't suppose that I shall carry it as far as my friend Rose Hacker, who at the age of a hundred is the oldest newspaper columnist in Britain (she writes for the *Camden News*), but it looks as though it will still be with me when (if!) I reach my ninetieth birthday, and it is impossible adequately to describe how grateful I am for that.

It took me by surprise, and has done so twice, which appears to be unusual, because the majority of writers seem to know quite early in their lives that writing is what they want to do. I knew from early childhood that I loved books, and from my early teens that I enjoyed writing letters and was considered by my friends to write good ones, but I didn't aspire to writing books, probably because when I was young 'books' meant 'novels', and I lack the kind of imagination a novelist must have: the ability to create characters and events and even (in cases of genius) whole worlds. And probably the fact that my love of other people's writing led me into a career as an editor meant that much of whatever creative energy I possessed found an outlet in my daily work, so that it took many years to build up perceptible pressure.

But pressure did build, making its first appearance in the form of little outbreaks like those small hot springs that bubble up here and there in volcanic territory: nine short stories, none of them planned. There would be an agreeable sort of itchy feeling, a first sentence would appear from nowhere, and blip, out would come a story. One of them won the *Observer*'s short-story competition, an intoxicating thrill in that it showed I had been putting down words in the right way, but it didn't make any more stories come after a tenth had fizzled out after two pages. That was followed by a lull of almost a year. Then, looking for something in a rarely opened drawer, I happened on those two pages, and read them. Perhaps, I thought, something could be made of them after all, so the next day I put paper in my typewriter and this time it wasn't blip, it was whoosh! – and *Instead of a Letter*, my first book, began. Those stories had been no more than hints of what was accumulating in the unconscious part of my mind, and the purpose of that accumulation, which I hadn't known I needed, was healing.

Twenty years earlier I'd had my heart broken, after which I had gradually learnt to live quite comfortably by accepting – so I thought – that as a woman I was a failure. Now, when this book turned out to be an account of that event which was as nearly accurate as I could make it, I was cured. It was an extraordinary experience. The actual writing was extraordinary because, although I was longing all day to get back from the office and sit down to it, I never knew (and this is literally true) what the next paragraph I was going to write would be. I would quickly read the last two or three pages from the day before, and on it would instantly go; and yet, in spite of this absolute lack of method, the finished book appeared to be a carefully structured work. (It struck me then, and I am sure this is true, that a great deal of that sort of work must go on in one's sleep.) And the final result was extraordinary too, in that once the book was done the sense of failure had vanished for good and I was happier than I had ever been in my life. I was also sure that writing was what I liked doing best, and hoped that more of it would come to me.

More did come, twice in the shape of traumatic events – one the suicide of a man I had been trying to help, the other the murder of a young woman. I plunged straight into 'writing them out', as what seemed to me the natural and certain way of ridding my mind of distress, and in both cases the events in themselves made 'stories', so the experience of writing them was a good deal less mysterious than that of writing *Instead of a Letter*. 'Enjoyable' seems the wrong word for the writing of them, but absorbing – indeed consuming – it was. And of course both books 'got me over' something painful: so much so that as soon as they were finished I put them away, and away they would have stayed had friends not urged me to get them published (the second of them was in a drawer for sixteen years).

Neither of those books meant a great deal to me after they had served their purpose, though naturally I was very pleased if people spoke well of them, and the same was true of the novel which I wrote in the 1960s because my publisher nagged me. (One can't help being very pleased if told convincingly that one writes well: it's like a shot of essential vitamins to one's self-esteem.) In those days anyone who wrote anything at all good that was not a novel was constantly badgered with 'And now when are you going to give us your novel?' (I never did this myself when I was a publisher because I couldn't see any sense in it. There were plenty of people around who were damn well going to give us their novel come hell or high water, anyway.) I capitulated, against my better judgement, and although I was proud of it in the end because it turned out quite a neat little book, and I still take pleasure in remembering writing parts of it, as a whole it was such appallingly hard work that I swore *never again*. What it proved was that while anyone who can write at all can squeeze out one novel at a pinch, this particular person was right in knowing herself not to be a novelist. I felt detached from that book because I had not really wanted to write it. The other two – perhaps I followed their fortunes with less interest than those of *Instead of a Letter* simply because I had become slightly embarrassed at making public things usually considered private, and for a private reason. I believed, and still believe, that there is no point in describing experience unless one tries to get it as near to being what it really was as you can make it, but that belief does come into conflict with a central teaching in my upbringing: Do Not Think Yourself Important.

Much as I wanted to continue to write, I found it impossible unless something was itching to come out. I could cover paper easily in ordinary ways such as letters, blurbs, reviews of books and so on, but if I tried to tell a story or examine a subject because that was what, intellectually, I wanted to do, not because there was pressure inside me to do it, the writing would be inert. With persistence, I could go on covering paper, but plod plod plod it would go until I was bored out of my mind. It is hard to explain, probably because I have never been able to force myself to examine it, but it seems to be something to do with hitting on a rhythm – perhaps getting down to a level at which that rhythm exists. Without it, my sentences are dead. With it, and I can always tell when I have hit it, don't ask me how, the sentences start to flow as though on their own. Real writers, I am sure, are more disciplined than this and must be able to keep themselves at it, as well as being, no doubt, gifted with readier access to that mysterious rhythm. My own dependence on a specific kind of stimulus has always seemed to me proof that I am an amateur – though that is not to take back the statement that 'writing is what I like doing best'.

Anyway, by the time I retired from my job, at the age of seventy-five, I hadn't written anything for a long time because it was a long time since anything had happened to me that needed curing. I was sorry about that, because I did so greatly enjoy the act of writing, but it had become so firmly attached in my mind to the *need* to write for therapeutic reasons that I couldn't envisage myself doing it for any other reason. People started saying to me 'You had fifty years in publishing, you worked with all those interesting people – you ought to write about it, you know, you really ought!' and a cloud of boredom would descend on me, out of which I would answer: 'But I don't work like that.' And that was true for at least the first two years of my retirement.

Then I began to catch myself remembering incidents from, or aspects of, the past with enough pleasure to want to dwell on them, so every now and then I would scribble a few pages about whatever it was that had floated to the surface in that way. Mostly it was about our firm's early days, because starting up a firm with almost no money and no experience at all really was great fun. (I am speaking for myself when I say 'no experience at all': André Deutsch, the moving spirit of the adventure, had only about a year's experience but had sucked out of that year more than many people gain from a lifetime.) Looking back at it I could see what an unusual and interesting time it had been and how lucky I was to have been involved in it. Once my memories reached the point at which we moved into our offices in Great Russell Street and were able confidently to consider ourselves proper publishers, the fizz went out of them. Indeed, at the thought that there were *still thirty years ahead* the cloud of boredom would reappear, because how on earth could I plod my way through thirty years without sending everyone else to sleep as well as myself? So I would push aside whatever I had just written and forget about it, until another odd or amusing memory floated up.

The two 'bits' that had become the most solid during the writing were two portraits, one of V. S. Naipaul, the other of Jean Rhys. Those I had enjoyed very much, because it pleased me to discover that I could be intensely involved in a piece of writing that had absolutely nothing to do with my own emotional development. There were, of course, feelings involved, but not at any deep level – nothing demanding 'cure'! – and to be enjoying writing simply because I was interested in the subject was a new experience. It was the Jean Rhys piece that steered the whole thing bookwards.

Jean Rhys is a writer who either irritates readers a great deal, or fascinates them. No one questions that her actual writing – the way she uses words – is wonderful, but some people can't be bothered with her ruthlessly incompetent heroines, or rather 'heroine' in the singular because the 'Jean Rhys woman' is always the same. Others find this woman profoundly touching, and guessing that she is in fact Jean Rhys herself, those of them who learn that I knew Jean well during the last fifteen years of her life always want to question me about her. Xandra Bingley, my neighbour across the street (a writer almost as good as Jean and a person so unlike her that they might belong to different species) has a friend, Lucretia Stewart, who is a fan of Jean's, and Lucretia asked Xandra to help her meet me, so Xandra asked us to lunch together. In the course of this lunch I told them that I had recently written quite a long piece about Jean, and Lucretia suggested that I send it to Ian Jack, editor of *Granta*, with which magazine she had a connection.

I knew *Granta*, of course, but I had forgotten that Ian had taken over as its editor from the American Bill Buford; and during Buford's reign, although I had admired it I had found it slightly forbidding, the natural habitat of writers like Martin Amis, for example, whose world seemed so unlike my own that I felt myself going 'square' whenever I glimpsed it. Ian was less alarming. It was not that I thought he, too, was 'square', but I did think he probably took a broader view of writing than Buford did. I had always liked his own writing and I knew that he had liked *Instead of a Letter*. Supposing I submitted something to Ian and he turned it down, I would feel that there was a sensible reason for his doing so, not just that he thought me a boring old trout: I would be disappointed, not hurt. For this rather wimpish reason, I decided to follow Lucretia's advice.

He did turn it down, explaining that it was not right for the magazine, and I had been right in thinking that it would not be a painful moment. Instead, it was an interesting one, because he added that if this piece turned out to be part of a book, then he would like to see the book. Another thing I had forgotten was that *Granta* the magazine was part of an organization which also published Granta Books. So now there was a publisher who had actually expressed an interest in a book about my life in publishing, supposing that those bits and pieces I had been playing with could be persuaded into such a form . . . They suddenly took on a new appearance in my eyes. They became worth fishing out of a drawer and being looked at seriously.

Having done that, I saw to my surprise that not a great deal more work was necessary to convert the material into a two-part book, the first part being about the building of our firm, the second part about some of the writers we published. It was not necessary to plod through all the years of the firm's existence, and it would really be about being an editor rather than a publisher, because an editor was what I had always chiefly been. It would be short, but that wouldn't matter, because to my mind erring on the side of brevity is always preferable to its opposite. The arranging, polishing and filling out (which included following an excellent suggestion of Ian's as to how it should end) turned out to be thoroughly enjoyable, so that I felt sorry when it was finished – or would have done if I had not been so pleased at having a last-minute inspiration about its title. Titles can be a headache if they don't come naturally – the hours I've spent with authors in the past, going through lists of suggestions and getting gloomier and gloomier! So this time, coming up effortlessly with the *mot juste* was most satisfying: *Stet*, that was it, hurrah! And what was more, I had brought this thing off although I was eighty.

And it *was* more, too: very much so. It may even have been the best part of the whole experience. To finish writing a book, to have it accepted at once by a publisher you respect and to see it being well-received: that, at any time of one's life, is gratifying, and to repeat the process within the next two years (as I did with *Yesterday Morning*) is even more so. But to do it when one is old . . . there are, I think, three reasons why being old makes it not just gratifying, but also *absolutely delicious*.

The first is the unexpectedness. If anyone had told me when I was in my early seventies that I was going to write another book I would have thought them mad: the odd bit of scribble for my own amusement, yes – perhaps. But never a book, because there was no book there to be written. How could there be, when I was so long past the stage when the kind of thing which caused me to write could possibly happen to me? To which I would probably have added 'Thank god!', given how painful those things had been to live through. And then, when in fact it had turned out that I was capable of covering a sufficient number of pages simply because I was enjoying remembering first my time in publishing, then my childhood, there naturally came the thought 'This stuff is interesting to me, but why should it interest anyone else?' I could see that the publishing material might amuse people in the book trade, but they are only a tiny part of the reading public, so if I myself were a publisher to whom someone submitted *Stet*, would I risk it? Probably not. And *Yesterday Morning*? All so long ago, so out of fashion! It would not have surprised me in the least if either the publisher or the public had said 'No' to either of those books.

So it was truly amazing when both said 'Yes'. What it felt like was an unexpected and tremendous TREAT.

That was the first gain from being old. The second was that none of it mattered at the deepest level, so that all of it could be taken lightly. When you are young a great deal of what you are is created by how you are seen by others, and this often continues to be true even into middle age. It is most obvious in the realm of sex. I remember a school-fellow of mine, a plump, rather plain girl, pleasant but boring, whom I ran into by chance on a station platform about a year after our schooldays ended and failed, for a moment, to recognize because she had become beautiful. What had happened was that a dashing man known to both of us had fallen in love with her and asked her to marry him: he had seen her as lovely, so lovely in her happiness she now was, and an assured and attractive woman she was to remain. Such transformations can occur in connection with many other aspects of self-esteem, with results either benign or damaging, and there were a good many years in the early part of my grown-up life when my self-esteem was diminished by this fact. But once you are old you are beyond all that, unless you are very unlucky. Being seen as someone who had written and published a book when I was in my forties changed me (for the better, as it happened, but it could have gone the other way and been for the worse). In my eighties that couldn't happen, no event could be crucial to my self-esteem in quite that way any more, and that was strangely liberating. It meant some sort of loss, I suppose, such as the end of thrilling possibilities; but it allowed experiences to be enjoyable in an uncomplicated way – to be simply *fun*. At no other time in my life did I enjoy myself so comfortably, for so long, as I did around the time of *Stet*'s publication, and the pleasure would have been as great in connection with *Yesterday*

Morning if its publication hadn't coincided with the worry of Barry's operation.

The third gain was related to the second: I no longer suffered from shyness. In the past my job had occasionally involved me in having to address an audience, and I was always so afraid of drying up that I typed the whole thing out and read from it. Once I had to go to Blackpool to talk about cookery books in a vast and glittery hotel full of vast and glittery ladies who, it transpired, were the wives of men who made cutlery and were having a convention. My offering was to be made in one of the smaller, darker 'function rooms' which smelt strongly and not unsuitably of gravy, and not a single person turned up for it. The relief was great, but was oddly mingled with shame so that I couldn't fully enjoy it, particularly not when, on creeping away to my room, I found that I had forgotten to pack a book to read in bed.

Because it had always been something of an ordeal I felt nervous about my first exposure by Granta at a literary festival, not understanding how lucky I was in its being at Hay, which is the warmest and most welcoming of all such shindigs. I couldn't write anything in advance because I was to be part of a trio, three people who had written memoirs discussing their reasons for doing so, and that added to the nervousness. But one of my fellow performers was Andrea Ashworth, whose *Once in a House on Fire* I had admired so much that I had written her a fan letter, which had crossed with a fan letter she had written me about *Stet*, a comically gratifying coincidence which made our meeting at the hotel where we were both staying a happy event. Being embraced by this dazzling young woman and bumbling into our tent with her on a wave of amusing and intimate talk, changed the nature of the whole experience, so that when I looked out over that crowded audience it didn't seem surprising that they were all beaming in an apparent expectation of a good time, and I found myself actually *wanting* to communicate with them. Indeed, that evening a closet exhibitionist was released: I could make them laugh! I loved making them laugh! It was all I could do to prevent myself from trying to hog more than my allotted time for talking. And from then on standing up in front of an audience has been enjoyable, while being on *Desert Island Discs* (*much* more impressive to relations, friends and indeed many strangers than any good review had ever been) was an orgy of pleasure. And of admiration, too, because gossiping away with Sue Lawley had seemed so completely natural and spontaneous that I expected to find it considerably cut and modified when it was actually broadcast, and was astonished that not a syllable had been changed: what a pro she was, establishing such an easy atmosphere while remaining in such tight control of timing.

It is not hard to see that writers who have often been through the process of promoting their books come to find it a tedious chore, but to me, for whom it was part treat, part joke and completely unexpected, it turned out to be an agreeable part of an experience which has made my life as a whole a good deal more pleasing to contemplate. I had seen it for so long as a life of failure, but now, when I look back – who would believe it, it was nothing of the sort!

14

IT SEEMS TO me that anyone looking back over eighty-nine years *ought* to see a landscape pockmarked with regrets. One knows so well, after all, one's own lacks and lazinesses, omissions, oversights, the innumerable ways in which one falls short of one's own ideals, to say nothing of standards set by other and better people. All this must have thrown up – indeed it certainly did throw up – a large number of regrettable events, yet they have vanished from my sight. Regrets? I say to myself. What regrets? This invisibility may be partly the result of a preponderance of common sense over imagination: regrets are useless, so forget them. But it does suggest that if a person is consistently lucky beyond her expectations she ends by becoming smug. A disagreeable thought, which I suppose I ought to investigate.

The absence of regret that surprises me most is connected with childlessness, because I know that for a short time I passionately wanted a child, and then lost one. Such a loss I would expect to weigh heavily on a woman, but it never has on me. The explanation seems to be that in spite of that one incident, I have uncommonly little maternal instinct, a deficiency I think I was born with. As a child I was not just indifferent to dolls, I despised them. My very first toy, the one which had eventually to be smuggled out of my cot because of how dirty it became, was a white rabbit, and later I was fond of an elephant, but representations of children – never. And I can remember being left alone for a few minutes with a month-old baby when I was nineteen, leaning over it and studying it earnestly in an attempt to feel moved by it, and coming to the conclusion that this unattractive little creature meant nothing to me – I'd rather pick up a puppy, any day. This reaction worried me, but not deeply, because I told myself at once that when I had a child of my own I would love it. That, obviously, was how it worked, because look how inevitably women did love their own children – the instinct must come with the birth. I went on reassuring myself in that way, particularly when Paul talked happily about the children we were going to have, which he enjoyed doing: choosing names for them and so on, games I would never have played if left to myself, though I disguised that. Never once in my twenties and thirties did I hope for a child, or feel more than a vague goodwill towards anyone else's child. When other women yearned towards babies I kept silent to hide my own feelings, and as for toddlers, I didn't go so far as to blame them for being what they were, but I did feel that they were tedious to have around except in very small doses.

Nevertheless I was probably right in supposing that I would love a child if I ever had one. This became apparent when I was forty-three, when my body took over from my mind and pushed me into pregnancy. It had happened before, whereupon I had terminated the pregnancy without hesitation or subsequent unhappiness, but this time something buried deep inside me woke up and decided to say: 'If you don't have a child now you never will so I'm going to get you one like it or not.' Only after I realized what had happened did it occur to me that my feckless carelessness about contraceptive measures must have been, at an unconscious level, deliberate, and even then I took it for granted that I was dismayed and must set about arranging for a termination. But when I caught myself making excuse after excuse not to take the necessary steps *just yet*, I hit on the truth: I wasn't going to take them at all; and at that point I suddenly became happy with a happiness so astonishingly complete that I still remember it with gratitude: my life would have been the poorer if I hadn't tasted it, and any child to emerge from that experience could only have been loved.

But it didn't emerge, or rather it did so in the form of a miscarriage early in the fourth of what were the happiest months of my life, during all of which I had felt dazzlingly healthy. That miscarriage very nearly killed me. I was rushed to hospital only just in time. I knew how near death I was because although by then consciousness had shrunk to within the limits of the stretcher on which I was lying in a pool of blood, I could still hear the voices of those leaning over that stretcher. They had just sent someone to fetch more blood for the transfusion they were administering, and a man said, 'Call them and tell them *to tell him to run,*' and then, to someone else, 'She's very near collapse.' Not only could I hear, but I could understand. I even thought, 'What a bloody silly euphemism,' because what was the state I was in already if it wasn't collapse? He meant death. So oughtn't I to try to think some sensible Last Thought? I made a dim attempt at it but the effort was beyond me; the best I could do was, 'Oh well, if I die I die.'

The man who had to run ran fast enough, they got me down to the theatre, they performed the curettage, and the next thing I was aware of was hands manipulating my body from stretcher to bed. For a moment I was unsure whether this was after the operation or before it, then I began to vomit from the chloroform, and simultaneously became aware that in my belly peace had been restored: I was no longer bleeding. And as though it came from down there, a great wave of the most perfect joy welled up and swept through me: I AM STILL ALIVE! It filled the whole of me, nothing else mattered. It was the most intense sensation I have ever experienced.

It swept away grief at the loss of the child. Of course I went on to feel unhappy, but it was a subdued and dreary little unhappiness, quite out of proportion with the happiness of the pregnancy. I had only one dream as a result of it, and that was a subdued and dreary little dream: I was getting off an underground train, and as the doors slid shut suddenly realized to my horror that I'd left a child on the train – running anxiously along the platform – how was I going to get to the next station before the train did, so that I could recover her (in the dream it was a little girl, though I had always thought of the child as a boy)? The feeling was one of painful anxiety rather than of loss. And after that life went back gradually, but not very slowly, to being what it had been before.

It seems very odd that what had unquestionably been an important development in my life – tremendously important – should have been diminished, almost cancelled, in that way. I think the whole thing was chemical: the body responding to the approach of menopause by pumping out more of something or other which I don't usually have much of, and after the shock ceasing to pump so that my normal condition was re-established. I don't think not feeling the loss means that I would have been a bad mother. Without the shock, if that child had been born, I would probably have been a perfectly adequate one very much like my own, who loved her children once they had reached a reasonable age better than she did when they were very young (she had nannies to bear the brunt of our infancy, so had no problem seeming to us to be all that she should be, but she was never able to disguise the slight impatience she felt with very young un-nannied grandchildren). But I can't, however hard I try, *mind* having lost the chance to prove it. Now, in my old age, I am much more interested in babies and little children than I used to be: actually delighted by them, so that the recent arrival of a baby in our house is an event which gives me great pleasure, although I'm glad that I don't have to *do* anything about that child beyond observing his progress with interest and admiration. But asking myself 'Are you really not sorry that you have no children or grandchildren of your own?' I get the answer 'Yes, really.' It is precisely because I don't and *can't* have the hassle of close involvement with the infants I encounter nowadays that I have become free to understand their loveliness and promise.

Selfishness: not, I hope, a selfishness that involves all of me, but a stubborn nub of selfishness somewhere in the middle which made me wary of anything to which one has to give one's whole self, as a mother has to give herself to an infant and a toddler. It was that which prevented me from wanting a child for so long, and then made it so easy to get over losing one. So I do have at least one major regret after all: not my childlessness, but that central selfishness in me, so clearly betrayed by the fact childlessness is not what I regret. And now I remember how my inadequacy regarding small children (I always loved them quite easily when they grew older) caused me to let down my cousin Barbara, whose house I live in, in spite of thinking her then as I think of her now as my best friend, when some forty-odd years ago she started a family. No sooner had she got three children than she and her husband separated, so that she had to raise them single-handed, working at a very demanding full-time job in order to keep them. How she struggled through those years I don't know, and I think she herself marvels at it in retrospect. But at the time what did I do to help her? Nothing. I shut my eyes to her problems, even saw very little of her, feeling sadly that she had disappeared into this tiresome world of small children – or world of tiresome small children – and she has said since then that she never dreamt of asking me for help, so aware was she of my coldness towards her brood. About that it is not just regret that I feel. It is shame.

One regret brings up another, though it is, thank goodness, less shameful. It's at never having had the guts to escape the narrowness of my life. I have a niece, a beautiful woman who I shall not name because she wouldn't like it, who is the mother of three sons, the youngest of whom will soon be following his brothers to university, and who has continued throughout her marriage to work as a restorer of paintings. Not long ago she sat at dinner beside a surgeon, and happened to say to him that if she had her time over again she would choose to train in some branch of medicine. He asked her how old she was. Forty-nine, she told him. Well, he said, she still had time to train as a midwife if she wanted to, they accepted trainees up to the age of fifty; whereupon she went home and signed up. The last time I saw her she could proudly report that she had now been in charge of six births all on her own. There had been moments, she said, when she felt 'What on earth am I doing here?', but she still couldn't imagine anything more thrilling than being present at – helping at – the beginning of new life. The most moving thing of all, she said, was when the father cried (there had been fathers present at all six births). When that happened she had to go out of the room to hide the fact that she was crying too.

She is a person of the most delicate reserve, so watching her face light up when she spoke about being present at a birth filled me with envy. Having had the courage and initiative suddenly to step out of a familiar and exceptionally agreeable life into something quite different, she has clearly gained something of inestimable value. And I have never done anything similar.

It is not as though I was never impatient at having only one life at my disposal. A great deal of my reading has been done for the pleasure of feeling my way into other lives, and quite a number of my love affairs were undertaken for the same reason (I remember once comparing a sexual relationship with going out in a glass-bottomed boat). But to turn such idle fancies into action demands courage and energy, and those I lacked. Even if I had been able to summon up such qualities, I am sure I would never have moved over into anything as useful as midwifery, but think of the places to which I might have travelled, the languages I might have learnt! Greek, for example: I have quite often thought of how much I would like to speak modern Greek so that I could spend time earning a living there and getting to know the country in a serious way, but I never so much as took an evening class in it. And when I went to Oxford, I indolently chose to read English literature, which I knew I was going to read anyway, for pleasure, instead of widening my range by embarking on a scientific subject, such as biology. And never at any time did I seriously try to use my hands (except at embroidery, which I am good at). Think how useful and probably enjoyable it would be to build a bookcase! I really am sorry about that.

So there are two major regrets, after all: that nub of coldness at the centre, and laziness (I think laziness played a greater part than cowardice in my lack of initiative, though some cowardice there was). They are real, but I can't claim that they torment me, or even that I shall often think about them. And at those two I shall stop, because to turn up something even worse would be a great bore. I am not sure that digging out past guilts is a useful occupation for the very old, given that one can do so little about them. I have reached a stage at which one hopes to be forgiven for concentrating on how to get through the present.

15

How successfully one manages to get through the present depends a good deal more on luck than it does on one's own efforts. If one has no money, ill health, a mind never sharpened by an interesting education or absorbing work, a childhood warped by cruel or inept parents, a sex life that betrayed one into disastrous relationships ... If one has any one, or some, or all of those disadvantages, or any one, or some, or all of others that I can't bear to envisage, then whatever is said about old age by a luckier person such as I am is likely to be meaningless, or even offensive. I can speak only for, and to, the lucky. But there are more of them than one at first supposes, because the kind of fortune one enjoys, or suffers, does not come *only* from outside oneself. Of course much of it can be inflicted or bestowed on one by others, or by things such as a virus, or climate, or war, or economic recession; but much of it is built into one genetically, and the greatest good luck of all is built-in resilience.

By chance, just as I was beginning to consider this matter, I read in the *Guardian* an interview conducted by Alan Rusbridger with Alice Herz-Sommer, who is 103 years old, and who provides an amazing example of the importance of that quality.

Born in Prague to Jewish parents who were not religious and who knew Mahler and Kafka, she grew up to be a brilliant pianist who studied with a pupil of Liszt's, and married another very gifted musician. When Hitler invaded Czechoslovakia in 1939 she was

living a happy, busy, creative life, which was of course instantly
crushed. With her husband and son she was sent to Theresienstadt,
the 'show case' camp in which more people survived than in other
camps because the Nazis used it to prove their 'humanity' to Red
Cross inspectors, although many did die there, and many many
thousands more, including Alice's husband, were dispatched from
there to die elsewhere. When she and her son got back home after
the war she found it wasn't home any more: all of her husband's
family, most of her own, and all her friends had disappeared. She
moved to Israel, where she brought up her son, who became a
cellist, and it was at his instigation that she came to England twenty
years ago. In 2001 she had to endure his sudden death at the age
of sixty-five. She now lives alone in a one-room flat in north
London, and might well be expected to be a grimly forlorn old
woman.

Instead, the interview was illustrated with three photographs of
Alice: a radiant bride in 1931, a radiant young mother just before
the war – and a radiant old woman of 103 today. The joyful
expression has hardly changed. And when it comes to words, she
remembers that the only person who was kind on the day they were
taken to the camp was a Nazi neighbour, how thrilled she was by
the freedom in Israel, how much she loves England and English
people. Even more important to her is how much she still loves
playing the piano for three hours every day ('Work is the best
invention . . . it makes you happy to do something.' Just as strikingly
as Marie-Louise Motesiczky she illustrates the luck of being born
creative). And she is enchanted by the beauty of life. It is not
religion that inspires her. 'It begins with this: that we are born half-
good and half-bad – everybody, *everybody*. And there are situations
where the good comes out and situations where the bad comes out.
This is the reason why people invented religion, I believe.' So she
respects the hope invested in religion although she herself has felt
no need for its support. She is carried along by her extraordinary
good luck in being born with a nature so firmly tilted towards
optimism that in spite of all that she has endured she can still say:
'Life is beautiful, extremely beautiful. And when you are old you

appreciate it more. When you are older you think, you remember, you care and you appreciate. You are thankful for everything. For everything.' She also says: 'I know about the bad, but I look only for the good.'

Although others must be awestruck by her courage, I doubt whether Alice Herz-Sommer herself would claim this positive attitude as a virtue. She compares it with that of her sister, a born pessimist – and 'born' is the key word. They were given their dispositions in the same way that one is given the colour of one's hair. But while a painful sensitivity to evil may be useful during a person's active years, providing as it sometimes does energy for the necessary, if endless, struggle against mankind's 'bad half', in old age, when one's chief concern must be how to get oneself through time with the minimum discomfort to self and inconvenience to others, it can only be a burden. Unfortunately examples such as Alice's of how an active mind and a positive outlook are what one needs in old age are not likely to be useful as 'lessons', because those able to draw on such qualities will be doing so already, and those who can't, can't. Perhaps there are some of us in between those extremes who can be inspired by her to put up a better show than we would otherwise have done.

16

ONE DOESN'T NECESSARILY have to end a book about being old with a whimper, but it is impossible to end it with a bang. There are no lessons to be learnt, no discoveries to be made, no solutions to offer. I find myself left with nothing but a few random thoughts. One of them is that from up here I can look back and see that although a human life is less than the blink of an eyelid in terms of the universe, within its own framework it is amazingly capacious so that it can contain many opposites. One life can contain serenity and tumult, heartbreak and happiness, coldness and warmth, grabbing and giving – and also more particular opposites such as a neurotic conviction that one is a flop and a consciousness of success amounting to smugness. Misfortune can mean, of course, that these swings go from better to bad and stay there, so that an individual's happy security ends in wreckage; but most lives are a matter of ups and downs rather than of a conclusive plunge into an extreme, whether fortunate or unfortunate, and quite a lot of them seem to come to rest not far from where they started, as though the starting point provided a norm, always there to be returned to. Alice's life swung in arcs far more extreme that most, but still I feel it may have followed this pattern. I suppose I think it because I have seen other lives do that, and I know that my own has done so.

Not long ago a friend said to me that I ought to be careful not to sound complacent, 'because' he added kindly, 'you are not.' I believe he was wrong there, and that I am, because complacent (not to say smug) I certainly started out during a happy childhood wrapped warmly in my family's belief that we were the best kind of people possible short of saintliness: a belief common in the upper levels of the English middle class and confirmed by pride in being English, which I remember deriving from an early introduction to a map of the world. All those pink bits were *ours*! How lucky I was not to have been born French, for example, with their miserable little patches of mauve.

This tribal smugness was not, of course, a licence to rampage. Like all such groups, ours had its regulations which one had to observe in order to earn one's place among the Best. Apart from all the silly little ones about language and dress, there were three which went deeper: one was supposed not to be a coward, not to tell lies, and above all not to be vain and boastful. I say 'above all' because that was the rule against which infantile rumbustiousness most often stubbed a toe: YOU ARE NOT THE ONLY PEBBLE ON THE BEACH might have been inscribed above the nursery door, and I know several people, some of them dear to me, who still feel its truth so acutely that only with difficulty (if at all) can they forgive a book written in the first person about that person's life.

I soon came to see our tribal complacency as ridiculous, and can claim that I never slipped back into it, but the mood it engendered is another matter: it was based on nonsense – on wicked nonsense – but it was sustaining, it made one feel sure of oneself. I was robbed of that mood (by being rejected, more than by seeing through class smugness and imperialism, though that must have modified it a good deal), and such a deprivation – the smashing of self-confidence – whatever its cause, makes a person feel horribly chilly. Now, however, having become pleased with myself in other ways, I recognize the return of the comfortable warmth I knew in early youth. If this is smugness, and I can't help feeling that it is, then I have to report that I have learnt through experience that, though repulsive to witness, it is a far more comfortable state *to be in* than its opposite. And comfort one does need, because there's no denying that moving through advanced old age is a downhill journey. You start with what is good about it, or at least less disagreeable than you expected, and if you have been, or are being, exceptionally lucky you naturally make the most of that, but 'at my back I always hear / Time's wingèd chariot hurrying near', and that is sobering, to say the least of it. For one thing, it's a constant reminder of matters much larger than oneself.

There is, for example, the thought quite common among us who are old: 'Well, thank god I shan't be here to see *that*.' Try as you may not to brood about global warming, *there it is*, and it doesn't go away because I shan't see much of it, or because, having no children, I don't have to worry about their experience of it . . . All that happens when I try to use that for comfort is the looming up of other people's children. I suppose there is a slight relief in the knowledge that you, personally, will not have to bear it, but it is unaccompanied by the pleasure usually expected from relief.

And that capaciousness of life, the variety within it which at first seems so impressive – what does that do after a while but remind you of its opposite, the tininess of a life even when seen against the scale of nothing bigger than human existence? Thought of in that light the unimportance of the individual is dizzying, so what have I been doing, thinking and tapping away at 'I this' and 'I that'? I too, as well as my dear disapprovers, ask that question – though with a built-in expectation, I must admit, of justification.

Because after all, minuscule though every individual, every 'self', is, he/she/it is an object through which life is being expressed, and leaves some sort of contribution to the world. The majority of human beings leave their genes embodied in other human beings, others things they have made, everyone things they have done: they have taught or tortured, built or bombed, dug a garden or chopped down trees, so that our whole environment, cities, farmland, deserts – the lot! – is built up of contributions, useful or detrimental, from the innumerable swarm of selfs preceding us, to which we ourselves are adding our grains of sand. To think our existence pointless, as atheists are supposed by some religious people to do, would therefore be absurd; instead, we should remember that it does make its almost invisible but real contribution, either to usefulness or harm, which is why we should try to conduct it properly. So an individual life *is* interesting enough to merit examination, and my own is the only one I really know (as Jean Rhys, faced with this same worry, always used to say), and if it is to be examined, it should be examined as honestly as is possible within the examiner's inevitable limitations. To do it otherwise is pointless – and also makes very boring reading, as witness many autobiographies by celebrities of one sort or another.

What dies is not a life's value, but the worn-out (or damaged) container of the self, together with the self's awareness of itself: away that goes into nothingness, with everyone else's. That is what is so disconcerting to an onlooker, because unless someone slips away while unconscious, a person who is just about to die is still fully alive and fully her or himself – I remember thinking as I sat beside my mother 'But she *can't* be dying, because she's still so entirely here' (the wonderful words which turned out to be her last, 'It was absolutely divine', were not intended as such but were just part of something she was telling me). The difference between being and non-being is both so abrupt and so vast that it remains shocking even though it happens to every living thing that is, was, or ever will be. (What Henry James was thinking of when he called death 'distinguished', when it is the commonest thing in life, I can't imagine – though the poor old man was at his last gasp when he said it, so one ought not to carp.)

No doubt one likes the idea of 'last words' because they soften the shock. Given the physical nature of the act of dying, one has to suppose that most of the pithy ones are apocryphal, but still one likes to imagine oneself signing off in a memorable way, and a reason why I have sometimes been sorry that I don't believe in God is that I shan't, in fairness, be able to quote 'Dieu me pardonnera, c'est son métier', words which have always made me laugh and which, besides, are wonderfully sensible. As it is, what I would like to say is: 'It's all right. Don't mind not knowing.' And foolish though it may be, I have to confess that I still hope the occasion on which I have to say it does not come very soon.

POSTSCRIPT

The tree fern: it now has nine fronds each measuring about twelve inches long, and within a few days of each frond unfurling to its full length, a little nub of green appears in the fuzzy top of the 'trunk' (out of which all fronds sprout and into which you have to pour water). This little nub is the start of a new frond, which grows very slowly to begin with but faster towards the end – so much faster that you can almost see it moving. I was right in thinking that I will never see it being a tree, but I underestimated the pleasure of watching it being a fern. It was worth buying.